A History of East Asia

Charles Holcombe begins his extraordinarily ambitious book by asking the question: What is East Asia? In the modern age, many of the features that made the region – now defined as including China, Japan, and Korea – distinct have been submerged by the effects of revolution, politics, or globalization. Yet as an ancient civilization, the region had both a historical and a cultural coherence. It shared, for example, a Confucian heritage, some common approaches to Buddhism, a writing system that is deeply imbued with ideas and meaning, and many political and institutional traditions. This shared past and the interconnections among three distinct yet related societies are at the heart of this book, which traces the story of East Asia from the dawn of history to the early twenty-first century. Charles Holcombe is an experienced and sure-footed guide who encapsulates, in a fast-moving and colorful narrative, the vicissitudes and glories of one of the greatest civilizations on earth.

Charles Holcombe is Professor of History at the University of Northern Iowa. His publications include *The Genesis of East Asia, 221 B.C.–A.D. 907* (2001) and *In the Shadow of the Han: Literati Thought and Society at the Start of the Southern Dynasties* (1994).

A History of East Asia

From the Origins of Civilization to the Twenty-First Century

CHARLES HOLCOMBE

University of Northern Iowa

CAMBRIDGE
UNIVERSITY PRESS

CAMBRIDGE UNIVERSITY PRESS
Cambridge, New York, Melbourne, Madrid, Cape Town, Singapore,
São Paulo, Delhi, Dubai, Tokyo, Mexico City

Cambridge University Press
32 Avenue of the Americas, New York, NY 10013-2473, USA

www.cambridge.org
Information on this title: www.cambridge.org/9780521731645

First published 2011

Printed in the United States of America

A catalog record for this publication is available from the British Library.

Library of Congress Cataloging in Publication data

Holcombe, Charles, 1956–
A history of East Asia : from the origins of civilization to the twenty-first century / Charles
Holcombe.
    p.   cm.
Includes bibliographical references and index.
ISBN 978-0-521-51595-5 (hardback) – ISBN 978-0-521-73164-5 (pbk.)
1. East Asia – History.   2. East Asia – Civilization.   I. Title.
DS511.H65   2010
950 – dc22   2010024844

ISBN 978-0-521-51595-5 Hardback
ISBN 978-0-521-73164-5 Paperback

Contents

List of Illustrations

List of Maps

Pronunciation Guide

(Where not indicated otherwise, pronunciations are approximately as might be expected by American English speakers.)

Chinese

East Asians normally do not use the Roman alphabet, but for the purpose of transcribing the sounds of East Asian words in our alphabet, a number of different spelling systems have been devised. For Mandarin Chinese, a spelling system called *pinyin* is increasingly standard. In pinyin, the vowels and diphthongs (two vowels that combine to form a single syllable) of Mandarin are pronounced approximately as follows:

a as in **ah**

ai like the **igh** in s**igh** or h**igh**

ao like the **ow** in h**ow** n**ow** br**ow**n c**ow**

e like the **u** in b**u**t

ei like the **ay** in M**ay** d**ay**

i as in pol**i**ce or like the **ee** in f**ee**t – except in the combinations *chi* (where it sounds more like the **chi** in **chi**rp), *ci* (where it sounds more like the **si** in pop**si**cle), *ri* (where it sounds more like the **ur** in **ur**ban), *shi* (where it sounds more like the **shou** in **shou**ld), *si* (where it sounds more like the **si** in **si**bling), *zhi* (where it sounds more like the **Ge** in **Ge**rman), and *zi* (where it sounds more like the **zi** in **zi**ggurat)

o like the **ou** in **ou**ght

ou like **oh**, or the **o** in **O**klah**o**ma

u like the **o** in wh**o** or the **oo** in h**oo**t

Some exceptional combinations follow:

ui sounds more like **oo-eigh** rather than **oo-ee**

yan sounds like **yen** (rhymes with **Z**en) rather than **yahn**

-ian (in such words as *bian, lian, nian*, etc.) sounds like -**ee-en** (as in **Z**en) rather than -**ee-ahn**

yi sounds no different from a solitary *i* (as in po**li**ce) – in other words, the *i* sound in isolation, or at the beginning of a word, is by convention spelled *yi*

A few unusual consonants in pinyin follow:

c sounds like the **ts** in the Russian title **Ts**ar (the word *cui* therefore sounds like **ts-oo-eigh**, pronounced together quickly)

q sounds like the **ch** in **ch**ance (*Qin* therefore sounds like **cheen**)

x sounds like **hs** or the **s** in **s**ee (*Xia* therefore sounds like **hs-ee-ah**, pronounced together quickly)

zh sounds like the **j** in **j**ay (*zhou* therefore sounds just like the familiar English name **Joe**)

Each Chinese syllable also always has a distinct tone, which is not, however, normally indicated in writing and therefore cannot be guessed from the spelling.

There are also a number of alternate Chinese spelling systems still in circulation (although they are not used in this book) and several old, irregular spellings (and associated pronunciations) that have become conventionally established in English usage such as Peking for Beijing, Canton for Guangzhou, Sun Yat-sen for the man more commonly known in Mandarin as Sun Zhongshan, and Chiang Kai-shek for Jiang Jieshi.

Japanese

The vowels and diphthongs in Japanese are pronounced approximately as follows:

a as in **ah**

ai like the **igh** in s**igh** or h**igh**

e as in t**e**n

ei like the **ay** in **May** day

i as in po**li**ce

o as in **oh**, or the **o** in **O**klah**o**ma

ō (with a macron) is pronounced just like *o* but is sustained for twice the duration

u is like the **o** in wh**o** or the **oo** in h**oo**t

ū (with a macron) is pronounced just like *u* but is sustained for twice the duration

When other vowels appear next to each other in Japanese, they are each pronounced separately rather than combined into a single-syllable diphthong. For example, *ii* is pronounced **ee-ee**.

After an initial *s*, the *u* in Japanese is often also nearly silent. *Sukiyaki*, for example, sounds more like s'kiyaki.

Korean

The vowels and diphthongs in Korean are pronounced approximately as follows:

a as in **ah**

ae like the **a** in h**a**t

e as in t**e**n

i as in pol**i**ce

o like the **o** in **o**rbit

ŏ like the **au** in c**au**ght

u like the **o** in wh**o** or the **oo** in h**oo**t

ŭ like the **u** in p**u**t

ŭi like **we**

Note also that in Korean pronunciation, the consonant pairs *ch/j, k/g, p/b, r/l, s/sh,* and *t/d* are not necessarily clearly distinguished (technically, in one widely used spelling system, they are distinguished with the aid of an apostrophe, e.g., **ch'** represents the English **ch** sound and **ch** the English **j** sound, with *tch, kk, pp, ss,* and *tt* indicating further subtle shades of difference). Chosŏn, for example, therefore sometimes appears spelled as Joseon (with the *ŏ* sound being represented by *eo*), Koguryŏ as Goguryeo, Paekche as Baekje, and Silla as Shilla.

Timeline: Dynasties and Major Historical Periods

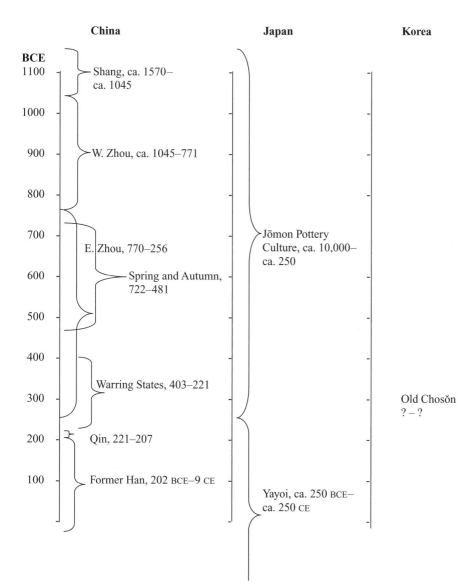

China **Japan** **Korea**

BCE

1100 — Shang, ca. 1570– ca. 1045

1000

900 — W. Zhou, ca. 1045–771

800

700 — E. Zhou, 770–256

Jōmon Pottery Culture, ca. 10,000– ca. 250

600 — Spring and Autumn, 722–481

500

400

300 — Warring States, 403–221

Old Chosŏn ? – ?

200 — Qin, 221–207

100 — Former Han, 202 BCE–9 CE

Yayoi, ca. 250 BCE– ca. 250 CE

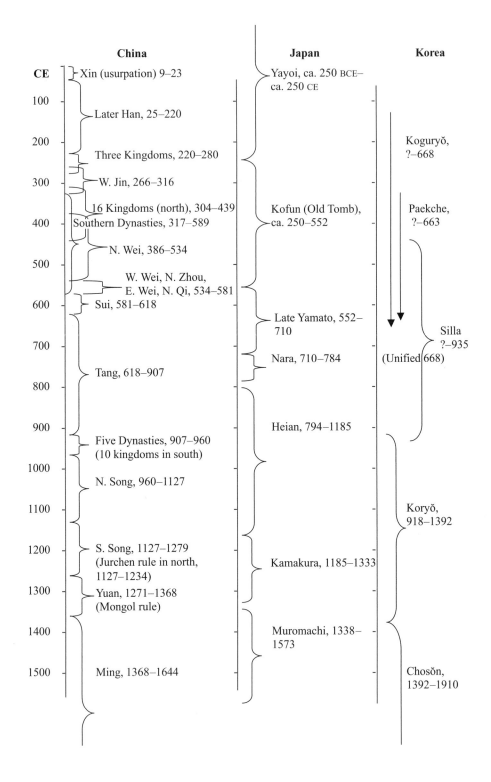

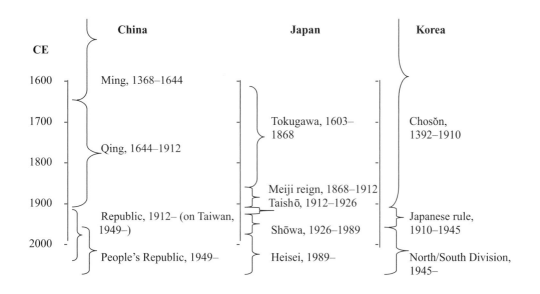

CE

China   Japan   Korea

1600   Ming, 1368–1644

1700   Tokugawa, 1603–   Chosŏn,
                             1868   1392–1910
     Qing, 1644–1912

1800

                   Meiji reign, 1868–1912
1900   Taishō, 1912–1926
     Republic, 1912– (on Taiwan,
     1949–)   Shōwa, 1926–1989   Japanese rule,
                                          1910–1945
2000
     People's Republic, 1949–   Heisei, 1989–   North/South Division,
                                              1945–

Glossary

Altaic	A major, somewhat hypothetical north Eurasian language family, possibly including the Turkic, Mongolic, Manchu, Japanese, Korean, and other languages
Amaterasu	The Japanese sun goddess
Annam	A premodern name for Vietnam
Bakufu	The military "tent government" of the Japanese shōguns
Bodhisattva	An altruistic enlightened Buddhist being (Sanskrit)
Bushi	A Japanese "military gentleman," or samurai
Chaebŏl	A post–World War II South Korean conglomerate (written with the same two Chinese characters as the pre–World War II Japanese word *zaibatsu*)
Chanoyu	The Japanese tea ceremony
Chosŏn	Korea
Comintern	The Communist International, an organization based in Moscow from 1919 to 1943 (English abbreviation)
Daimyō	"Great name": the lord of a regional domain in late premodern Japan
Dao Tong	The Neo-Confucian "Transmission of the Way" (in Chinese)
Dhāraṇī	A Buddhist magical formula (Sanskrit)
Enka	A popular sentimental modern Japanese musical style
Falun Gong	A new "traditional" Chinese religion, founded in 1992 and currently banned in the People's Republic of China
Guandong	Chinese for "East of the Passes," with reference to early-twentieth-century Japanese military activity, usually referring to Manchuria (and frequently spelled "Kwantung" in older publications)
Guanzhong	The region "Within the Passes": a Chinese geographical area roughly corresponding to the modern Shaanxi Province
Guomindang	The Chinese Nationalist Party, alternatively spelled "Kuo-Min-Tang" in the older Wade-Giles spelling system (and abbreviated either GMD or KMT)

Guoyu	The Chinese National Language, or Mandarin
Hakka	"Guest Families" (Mandarin: *Kejia*): a Chinese subethnic group
Han'guk	"The Country of the Han": Korea
Han'gŭl	The Korean alphabet
Hanzi	Chinese characters or written symbols
Hiragana	A Japanese syllabary or set of phonetic written symbols representing complete syllables
Hu	A generic Chinese name for northern non-Chinese peoples, used especially during the Age of Division
Huangdi	The Chinese term for *emperor*
Huaxia	China
Hwarang	"Flower Youths": aristocratic young warriors in Silla (Korea)
Jinshi	"Presented Scholar": the highest degree in the late imperial Chinese examination system
Juche	The modern North Korean ideology of self-reliance
Junzi	Literally the "son of a Lord" but used by Confucius to refer to anyone who behaved as a proper gentleman (in Chinese)
Kami	Japanese gods or spirits
Kantō	Japanese for "East of the Passes," referring to the largest Japanese agricultural plain in the vicinity of modern Tōkyō
Katakana	A Japanese syllabary or set of phonetic written symbols representing complete syllables – now chiefly used to write Western loanwords
Keigo	The Japanese "respect language"
Keiretsu	Post–World War II Japanese enterprise groups
Kokutai	Pre–World War II Japan's "national polity"
Kolp'um	Aristocratic "bone rank" in Silla (Korea)
Kuo-Min-Tang	The Chinese Nationalist Party, alternatively spelled "Guomindang" in pinyin (and abbreviated either GMD or KMT)
Kwantung	Chinese for "East of the Passes," with reference to early-twentieth-century Japanese military activity, usually referring to Manchuria (and now spelled "Guandong" in pinyin)
Li	"Courtesy," "propriety," "rites," or "ceremony" (in Chinese)
Li	The organizing "principle" or "principles" for *qi*, or "matter," in Neo-Confucian philosophy (in Chinese) (note: this word *li* is written with an entirely different character from the preceding *li*, meaning "courtesy")
Logograph	A nonphonetic written symbol, such as a Chinese character, used to represent a word in a particular language (a newly coined English term)
Maripkan	Early native Korean royal title
Minzu	The modern Chinese word for "nation," in the sense of "a people"

MITI	The Ministry of International Trade and Industry in post–World War II Japan (English abbreviation)
Nihon	Japan
Nirvāṇa	"Extinction," or Buddhist enlightenment (Sanskrit)
Pinyin	Literally, "to spell the sound": the modern phonetic system for spelling Chinese using the Roman alphabet that was developed in the People's Republic of China
Qaghan	A supreme Mongol and Turkic title, meaning roughly Khan of Khans, or Great Khan
Qi	The basic matter or substance of the universe according to Neo-Confucian philosophy (in Chinese)
Qipao	"Banner gown," a Chinese female fashion that derived from Manchu clothing styles (in Chinese)
Qiren	"Banner People," an alternate name for the Manchus (in the Chinese language)
Ren	The Confucian virtue of humanity (in Chinese)
Rōnin	Japanese masterless samurai
Rujiao	The "Teachings of the Ru," or Confucian scholars (in Chinese)
Saṃsāra	The cycle of existence: birth and death (Sanskrit)
Sankin kōtai	The alternate attendance system for daimyō in Tokugawa Japan
SCAP	Supreme Commander for the Allied Powers during the postwar occupation of Japan (English abbreviation)
Shangdi	"The Lord on High": the supreme ancient Chinese deity (and a term sometimes also used as a Chinese translation for the Christian God)
Shintō	"The Way of the Spirits": the indigenous Japanese religion
Shōgun	"General": the premodern Japanese military overlord
Śramaṇa	A Buddhist monk (Sanskrit)
Sūtra	A sermon attributed to the Buddha (Sanskrit)
Taigi-meibun	The moral obligation of fulfilling the role proper to one's title or status (in Japanese)
Taiji	The "supreme ultimate" in Neo-Confucian philosophy (in Chinese)
Taotie	A common design on ancient Chinese bronze vessels
Tatami	The floor matting in late premodern Japanese buildings
Tennō	"Heavenly Sovereign": the standard Japanese imperial title
Tianming	The Chinese Mandate of Heaven
Tianxia	Chinese for "Under Heaven," referring to the royal or imperial realm
Tianzi	Chinese for "Son of Heaven," referring to the supreme ruler
Topolect	A proposed alternate term for the Chinese dialects (in English)
Tripiṭaka	The "Three Baskets," or the complete set of Buddhist Scriptures (Sanskrit)
Uji	A Japanese lineage or descent group
Wuwei	The Daoist principle of nonaction (in Chinese)
Xiao	The Confucian virtue of filial piety (in Chinese)

Yangban	The "two orders" of premodern Korean civil and military aristocracy
Yuan	The modern Chinese currency (also known in the People's Republic of China as *renminbi*)
Zaibatsu	The great business conglomerates of pre–World War II Japan
Zhong	The Confucian virtue of loyalty (in Chinese)
Zhongguo	The "Central Country" or "Middle Kingdom," that is, China

Introduction: What Is East Asia?

At the dawn of the twenty-first century, three of the world's five largest national economies were in Asia, and the second and third largest, China and Japan, were both specifically East Asian.[1] This represents an astonishing reversal of the situation that had prevailed a century earlier, when a handful of Western European powers, together with the United States and Russia (and with Japan already as an emerging junior partner), dominated much of the planet economically, militarily, and politically. As late as the mid-twentieth century, East Asia still remained largely preindustrial, often bitterly impoverished, and desperately war ravaged. Even Japan, which had succeeded in asserting itself as a regionally significant modern power by the early 1900s, was left crushed and in ruins by the end of the Second World War in 1945. A fresh start was required in Japan, which gained momentum beginning in the 1960s. Since that time, South Korea, Taiwan, Hong Kong, Singapore, and eventually even the People's Republic of China have all joined Japan – though each in characteristically different ways – in achieving dramatic levels of modern economic takeoff. Beyond any doubt, the economic rise of East Asia has been one of the most important stories of recent world history.

A persuasive argument can be made, moreover, that rather than representing some fundamentally unprecedented departure from past experience, the recent economic rise of East Asia is really more of a return to normal. For much of human history, China – the largest single component of East Asia – enjoyed one of the most developed economies on earth. Especially after the disintegration of the western Roman Empire, for a thousand years beginning around 500, China was probably the wealthiest country in the world, not merely in aggregate total but also in per capita terms. Even as late as 1800, as the Industrial Revolution was beginning in Great Britain, China is still estimated to have accounted for a larger share (33.3%) of total world production than all of Europe, including Russia, combined (28.1%).[2]

It is well known that such crucial technologies as gunpowder, paper, and printing were all invented in China. Less well known is that paper and printing actually had a significant impact on China long before those technologies transformed Europe.

Paper and printing helped to make books, and therefore also knowledge, relatively widely available in premodern China. It has been seriously suggested that China may have even produced more books than all the rest of the world combined prior to about 1500.[3]

Although, when compared to China, the other countries of premodern East Asia were each relatively quite small in size – in 1800, China's population may have been roughly 300 million, Japan's perhaps 30 million, and Korea's 8 million – each made its own notable contributions and produced unique variants of East Asian civilization. Korea, for example, pioneered the development of metal moveable-type printing by at least 1234 (although moveable type made of baked clay rather than metal had been experimented with in China as early as the 1040s). Japan, remarkably enough, became perhaps the first non-Western society in the world to successfully modernize. Despite its relatively small size, in the modern era, Japan in many ways eclipsed China to become regionally dominant in East Asia, and for much of the late twentieth century Japan was the second most important economic power in the entire world, after only the United States.

Even when East Asia was at its relative poorest and weakest in the early 1900s, it continued to be globally significant. World War II, for example, began in East Asia, at a bridge near Beijing in 1937. Today there should no longer be any doubt of the region's importance. China is a major rising world power, and although it remains poor and underdeveloped in per capita terms, parts of what is sometimes called Greater China already compare favorably with almost anywhere else on the planet. Hong Kong, for example, which is now a semiautonomous region of the People's Republic of China, today enjoys a per capita income above that of such highly developed countries as Australia, Canada, France, Germany, Great Britain, Japan, Switzerland, or indeed all but a handful of the world's most prosperous lands. Taiwan and Singapore are both predominantly ethnic Chinese places that have also achieved notable economic success. Singapore now even has a higher per capita income than the United States.[4] Japan, although it may have recently already been surpassed by China in terms of the total real size of its economy (measured in terms of purchasing power parity), probably still remains the world's second most fully mature industrialized economy. South Korea is a spectacular example of a modern Pacific Rim success story, and North Korea, while decidedly less prosperous than the south, as an unpredictable and sometimes belligerent nuclear power nonetheless compels global attention.

East Asia is therefore a critically important region of the world; but what is East Asia? What makes it East Asian? Asia as a whole is actually not a very coherent cultural geographic entity. The concept of Asia is one that we have inherited from the ancient Greeks, who divided the world broadly into two parts: Europe and Asia. For the Greeks, however, this original Asia was primarily just the Persian Empire. As the scope of Asia expanded beyond Persia and what we now call Asia Minor, it came to include so many different cultures and peoples that the label was drained of most of its significance. By the late 1700s, for example, two-thirds of the world's total population and 80 percent of the world's production were all located in Asia. This Asia was nothing less than the entire Old World minus Europe. If

Asia in its entirety is not a very meaningful term, however, the word can still serve a useful purpose as a terminological anchor for certain geographic subregions, such as South Asia and East Asia, which do have more historical coherence.[5]

Even these subregions, of course, must still be somewhat arbitrarily defined. Premodern East Asians certainly did not think of themselves as either Asians or East Asians. Today the U.S. State Department lumps Southeast Asia and even Oceania together with East Asia under its Bureau of East Asian and Pacific Affairs. Geographic regions can be defined in many ways, and a variety of labels applied to them to suit different purposes. In historical terms, however, and especially in consideration of shared premodern culture, East Asia is most usefully defined as that region of the world that came to extensively use the Chinese writing system, and absorbed through those written words many of the ideas and values of what we call Confucianism, much of the associated legal and political structure of government, and certain specifically East Asian forms of Buddhism. It is a fundamental premise of this book that East Asia really is a culturally and historically coherent region, deserving of serious attention as a whole, and not just as a random group of individual countries or some arbitrary lines on a map.

At the same time, East Asia is also part of a universally shared human experience. In the current age of globalization, of course, the planet today is especially closely interconnected – but global human ties actually go back to the very beginning of human existence. Such interconnections always remained reasonably active, particularly within the Eurasian Old World. At the opposite extreme of focus from this global perspective, East Asia itself (like Western Europe) is also composed of several independent countries, each of which in turn contains various internal levels and types of subdivision.

Specifically, East Asia today includes what is sometimes called Greater China (the People's Republic of China, Hong Kong, Taiwan, and somewhat more peripherally, Singapore), Japan, and Korea. In addition, Vietnam presents a marginal case, because it occupies a transitional zone that straddles both East and Southeast Asia. Vietnam did have significant historical ties with China. One book about Vietnam published in the mid-twentieth century was actually even titled *Little China*.[6] At that time, however, Vietnam was perhaps most commonly referred to as Indochina, a composite designation (reflecting both Indian and Chinese influences over a mosaic of indigenous cultures) that appropriately conveys something of Vietnam's true hyphenated cultural complexity. Because Vietnam is typically included in surveys of Southeast Asia, it will not be comprehensively covered in this book.

East Asia has an historical coherence as a civilization that is roughly equivalent to what we think of as Western civilization, with the Bronze Age prototype that first emerged in high antiquity in the region we now call China providing approximately the same sort of core historical legacy for the modern countries of China, Japan, and Korea that ancient Greece and Rome left for modern Italy, France, Britain, Germany, and what we think of somewhat vaguely and imperfectly as "the West." This volume, while paying due attention to both the larger global interconnections and to local differences, will attempt to present a relatively integrated history of

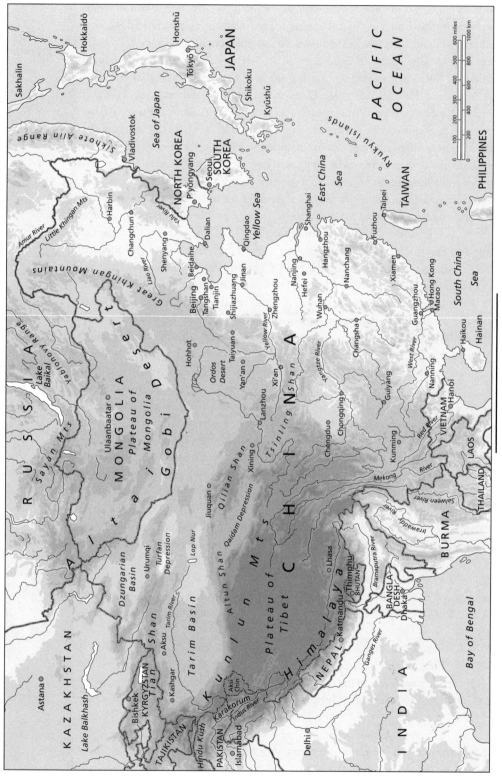

Map 1. East Asia Physical

4

East Asia as a whole. It will also, somewhat unusually, focus relatively closely on that period in Middle Antiquity (beginning roughly in the third century CE) when a coherent East Asian cultural region that included China, Japan, and Korea first emerged.

It should be emphasized, however, that no such "civilization" is a permanently fixed and isolated concrete reality. What we call civilizations are merely abstractions that people imagine around certain historical continuities and connections that someone has decided are significant – they have no hard reality. Borders are always permeable, all cultures interact and exchange both artifacts and ideas, and multiple nested layers of distinction can be discerned everywhere within what is ultimately a single global human community.

In the present age of globalization, moreover, all such regional civilizational distinctions are to some extent blurring. Since the twentieth century, many of the features that made East Asia East Asian, such as the unique writing system, Confucianism, and traditional-style monarchies, have been sometimes quite self-consciously challenged, rejected, or abandoned in the name of either (or both) universal modernization or local nationalism. The various nations of modern East Asia are today, in some ways, both more different from each other and, at the same time, paradoxically, more like every other successful modern country on the planet than may have been the case (at the level of the educated elite anyway) in premodern times. Yet the legacy of the old vocabulary does live on. South Korea, for example, is simultaneously a thoroughly modern, Westernized country with especially close ties to the United States, which is also sometimes called the "most Confucian" country in Asia! The very fact of dynamic modern economic success being so disproportionately concentrated in the East Asian region by itself suggests also that there may still be something distinctive about East Asia.

If East Asia remains a moderately coherent cultural region even today, on the other hand, East Asia has also always been internally diverse. Not only are the major nations of East Asia often sharply different from each other but each nation also contains within itself cascading layers of internal differences. And East Asia has changed greatly over time, too, most obviously and abruptly in the modern period but also throughout history. There was no timeless, traditional continuity in premodern East Asia.

As an illustration of this ongoing process of change, we might ask ourselves a surprising question: how old is China? It is often supposed that Chinese civilization is the oldest continuously existing civilization in the world, having emerged out of the late Stone Age (the Neolithic), flowered into the full glory of Bronze Age civilization beginning as early as 2000 BCE, and survived thereafter without interruption to the present day. In fact, there is some truth to this popular story. Though it may be difficult to pinpoint many aspects of late Stone Age culture that can still be observed today (although silk, a preference for pork among meats, and the cultivation of rice could be cited as conspicuously long-standing cultural markers), it is highly significant that the very first writing samples to be found in the area of China, dating to approximately 1200 BCE, were already written in an archaic version of the same Chinese language, and the same Chinese writing system, that is still used today. In this sense, China is very old indeed.

The earliest books written in that Chinese language, produced over the course of the last thousand years BCE, formed the nucleus of a deeply cherished literary canon that remained continuously fundamental to what we call Chinese civilization, at least until the start of the twentieth century. During the course of that same formative last millennium BCE, a discernable consciousness of being Chinese (called *Huaxia*), in opposition to neighboring alien peoples such as the *Rong, Di, Man,* and *Yi,* may also be said to have emerged. Thus the Warring States of the late Zhou era (403–221 BCE), though each were independent sovereign countries, could also all be described as being different Chinese kingdoms surrounded by various non-Chinese peoples.

After the Qin unification of these Warring States into the first empire in 221 BCE, an enduring ideal of unity under a single centralized imperial government was also firmly planted. Although China's subsequent remarkable record of enduring political unity is sometimes explained in terms of presumed ethnic and cultural homogeneity (it is too easy to assume that the Chinese are naturally unified because, after all, "they are all Chinese"), it may well really have been more the other way around: China's present-day relative ethnic and cultural homogeneity is the end product of millennia of political unity. Certainly the early Chinese Empire's population was quite mixed.

Even after that first imperial unification in 221 BCE, however, China continued to change. There have been roughly eighty historically recognized premodern dynasties in the place we call China (although only about a dozen are considered to have been truly major dynasties). Each dynasty was in some sense a separate state. Many had identifiably non-Chinese rulers. In addition, China has also undergone repeated periods of division since that first imperial unification, and even during periods of great unity, fashions still changed. As Guo Maoqian (fl. 1264–1269) observed in the thirteenth century, "folk songs and national customs also have a new sound each generation."[7] Premodern China was far from static.

If China can be called an ancient civilization, at the other extreme, it is also possible to argue that the very concept of a Chinese "nation" did not even exist until about 1900. It is generally believed that the nation-state is an invention of the modern West, and certainly the word *nation* (*minzu*, designating "a people" rather than a country or state) was imported into the Chinese language only at the end of the nineteenth century.[8] China first attempted to reconfigure itself as a modern Western-style nation-state only with the overthrow of the empire and establishment of the Republic of China in 1912. Moreover, the specific country that most of us think of today simply as "China," which is more formally known as the People's Republic of China (PRC), dates only from 1949. Nor was this merely a new name for an old reality: in the entire history of the planet, there can have been few revolutionary ruptures that were intended to be as total and sweeping as that of the New China following its 1949 "liberation." In hindsight, of course, many of the revolutionary changes imposed after 1949 did not prove to be very durable, and in recent years, there has even been some revival of older traditions; yet the PRC still does mark a sharp break in the continuity of history.

Even the word *China* is itself, literally, not Chinese. The English word *China* probably derives from the Sanskrit (Indian) *Cīna*, which in turn may have derived from the name of the important northwestern frontier Chinese kingdom and first imperial dynasty, Qin. Not only did the Chinese people not call themselves Chinese, it could be argued that there was no precise native-language equivalent term at all, at least before modern times. One distinguished scholar has even gone so far as to claim that the concept and word *China* simply "did not exist, except as an alien fiction."[9]

To be sure, the ancient Chinese did already have some reasonably coherent self-conceptions. The names by which early Chinese people identified themselves were frequently those of specific kingdoms or imperial dynasties, such as Qin, Chu, or Han, but there were also a few more all-encompassing ancient Chinese-language words that we might reasonably translate into English as "China" or "Chinese," such as *Huaxia* 華夏, which has already been mentioned, and *Zhongguo* 中國. Even these, however, were not perfectly synonymous with the English word *China*. Initially, *Huaxia* seems to have been a somewhat elastic cultural marker, referring neither to race nor ethnicity nor any particular country but rather to "civilized," settled, literate, agricultural populations adhering to common ritual standards, in contrast to "barbarians."[10]

Zhongguo – "the central country" (or "countries," since the Chinese language does not make a grammatical distinction between singular and plural), which is often more quaintly rendered as the "Middle Kingdom" – in a somewhat similar manner also contrasts the civilized countries in the center against an outer fringe of barbarians. Initially this term *Zhongguo* may have really referred only to the royal capital city. Later, during the Warring States period, *Zhongguo* definitely had to be understood as plural because there were multiple "central" countries then. This term *Zhongguo* long remained more of a geographic description rather than a proper name, referring simply to the countries in what was imagined to be the center of the world: the Central Plain area of north China. Even as late as the third and fourth centuries CE, some five hundred years after the first imperial unification in 221 BCE, the entire southern half of what we would think of today as China proper could still be explicitly excluded from the *Zhongguo*. After the northern conquest of the southern (Chinese) state of Wu in 280, for example, a children's verse predicted that someday "*Zhongguo* [the north] will be defeated and Wu [in the south] shall rise again."[11]

Today *Zhongguo* is probably the closest Chinese-language equivalent to the English word *China*. Even so, both the modern People's Republic, on the mainland, and the Republic of China (confined to the island of Taiwan since 1949) are still officially known, instead, by a hybrid combination of the two ancient terms *Zhongguo* and *Huaxia*: *Zhong-hua* 中華.

Many Westerners today find the implicit conceit that China is the Middle Kingdom alternately either offensively arrogant or simply ridiculous. Such ethnocentricity was hardly unique to China, however. Nearly all early civilizations, in fact, viewed themselves as occupying the center of the world. While China may be a little unusual in having this ancient conceit preserved in a name that is still used today, our own name for the Mediterranean Sea also comes originally from a Latin expression meaning "middle of the earth." We have merely become accustomed to the name, no longer understand much Latin, and have forgotten what it means.

Furthermore, it was Westerners who more literally referred to foreigners as barbarians. *Barbarian* is an English word that derives from an ancient Greek expression for those unintelligible "bar-bar" noises emitted by strangers who were so uncivilized as not to speak Greek. Not only did the ancient Chinese naturally not use this Greek word, there really was no word in classical Chinese that was exactly equivalent to it. There are, indeed, several Chinese terms that are commonly loosely translated into English as "barbarian," but this (as is often the case with translations) is a little misleading. More precisely, they are all generic Chinese names for various non-Chinese peoples. The word *Yi*, for example, was used for non-Chinese peoples in the east. Such names were often no more accurate or authentic than the name Indian that was mistakenly applied by early modern Europeans to the natives of the Americas, yet like the term *American Indian*, they remain fundamentally names rather than words meaning "barbarian."

If China is not a Chinese name, then, what about our familiar names for the other East Asian countries? The English word *Japan* is actually a distorted version, via Malay, of the Chinese pronunciation (*Riben* in current standard Mandarin, which can also be spelled *Jih-pen* in an older spelling system) of the two-character name 日本 that in Japanese is pronounced *Nihon* (or *Nippon*). This name *Nihon* – the "Origin of the Sun" – is, however, a genuine early native Japanese name for Japan, although one that could probably only have been conceived from a vantage point outside of Japan, further west, and that may have been first used by immigrants to Japan from the continent. The name was apparently consciously adopted by the Japanese court in the late seventh century for the favorable meaning of its written characters.[12]

In some ways, it could be argued that Japan has been less chimerical as a country and has displayed more historical continuity since antiquity than China. Since the dawn of reliably recorded history, Japan has had, quite uniquely in the entire world, only one ruling family. There has been only one Japanese dynasty, in contrast to China's roughly eighty dynasties and two postdynastic republics. Yet on the other hand, Japanese emperors have rarely wielded much real power, court and emperor have often been quite irrelevant to the overall history of the Japanese islands, and Japan, too, has been divided. Much Japanese "tradition" is, moreover, not really so very ancient, and important parts of it ultimately can be traced to foreign origins. Japanese Zen Buddhism, for example, is an especially Chinese form of what was originally an Indian religion. The quintessentially Japanese art of the tea ceremony (*chanoyu*) was born only in the late fifteenth century, although the Japanese had learned to drink tea (from China) centuries earlier. *Sushi*, as we know it, "began as a street snack in nineteenth-century Edo-era Tokyo." The Japanese national sport of *Jūdō* was invented, as such, only toward the end of the nineteenth century – by the same man who would also serve as Japan's first member of the International Olympic Committee. Even the Japanese nation-state itself arguably only took its final shape during the nineteenth century.[13]

As for Korea, the English name derives from that of the Koryŏ Dynasty (918–1392), which in turn was an abbreviation of the name of an even older northern kingdom called Koguryŏ (roughly first-century to 668 CE). In this respect, our English name Korea somewhat resembles the probable derivation of our name for China from the early dynastic name Qin. Just as Qin is not quite really entirely synonymous with China, neither is Koryŏ exactly the same thing as Korea. Today, North Koreans prefer to invoke the memory of the oldest legendary Korean kingdom, Chosŏn, while South Koreans are inclined to use the name Han'guk, the "Country of the Han," the name of the peoples who were the inhabitants of the southern parts of the Korean peninsula in the early historical period. (The Chinese today are also called the Han people, but this is an entirely different Han, written 漢, which just happens to sound like the Korean Han 韓.) Although Korea is today an exceptionally good example of an ethnically homogeneous modern nation-state (marred by political and ideological division, north vs. south, since 1945), it can be argued that Korea, as such, never really existed prior to the first unification of the peninsula under native rule in 668.

Vietnam will not be exhaustively surveyed in this volume, but the story of how Vietnam got its name is nonetheless relevant and fascinating. The name Vietnam was first proposed, incredibly enough, from Beijing in 1803. Prior to that time, what we think of as Vietnam had most commonly been called Annam. (Still later, as a French colony, it was widely known in the West as Indochina, as previously mentioned.) The new nineteenth-century name Vietnam was consciously intended to evoke the memory of an ancient (208–110 BCE) kingdom called Southern Viet (pronounced *Nam Việt* in Vietnamese). Because the capital of that ancient Southern Viet kingdom had been located at the site of the modern city of Guangzhou (in English, Canton), in China, however, nineteenth-century Vietnam was obviously somewhat farther south. When the old name was revived, it was therefore slightly altered by changing it from Southern Viet to South of Viet. This adjustment was achieved in Vietnamese (and in Chinese) simply by transposing the word order: from *Nam Việt* to *Việt Nam*.[14] The reason, then, why the capital of the ancient kingdom of Southern Viet was, somewhat surprisingly, located north of modern Vietnam in what is now China, was because the very earliest Bronze Age kingdom called Viet (in Chinese, *Yue* 越), from which all of these names presumably ultimately derived, had been located even farther north, in the vicinity of the modern Chinese Province of Zhejiang, almost halfway up the coast of what is today China! Early Chinese texts, in fact, referred to most of what is now southeast China as the land of the "Hundred Viets."

This story helps illustrate just how far from being static and unchanging traditional East Asia actually was. Not only was Vietnam a new name in 1803, but the total assemblage of territory and ethnic groups that now make up Vietnam was also rather new and unprecedented at the time. Independent Vietnam had originated (in the tenth century) only in the Red River valley area of what is now the north. After centuries of southward expansion (and sometimes division), when a new emperor finally unified all of Vietnam at the beginning of the nineteenth century, it was in some ways "a kingdom . . . that had never before existed."[15]

To say that Vietnam did not exist before the nineteenth century is, of course, at some levels as absurd as trying to claim that China did not exist until modern times either. Yet in fact, neither China nor Vietnam had really existed previously under precisely their present names and current configurations, despite their genuinely ancient pedigrees. No country, people, or civilization exists unchanged forever. These are dynamic ancient streams that have continually been renewed. History is all about change, and East Asia has experienced as much change as almost any comparable region. This is the story of East Asian history.

For Further Reading

Different ways of defining "East Asia" are discussed in the introduction to John H. Miller, *Modern East Asia: An Introductory History* (Armonk, NY: M. E. Sharpe, 2008). A particularly valuable collection of essays addressing East Asia as a coherent cultural area is Gilbert Rozman, ed., *The East Asian Region: Confucian Heritage and Its Modern Adaptation* (Princeton University Press, 1991). For a fascinating although now somewhat dated exploration of how China and Asia have been geographically conceived by Western minds, see Andrew L. March, *The Idea of China: Myth and Theory in Geographical Thought* (New York: Praeger, 1974).

Standard surveys of East Asian history include Warren I. Cohen, *East Asia at the Center: Four Thousand Years of Engagement with the World* (New York: Columbia University Press, 2001); Patricia Buckley Ebrey, Anne Walthall, and James B. Palais, *East Asia: A Cultural, Social, and Political History* (Boston: Houghton Mifflin, 2006); John K. Fairbank, Edwin O. Reischauer, and Albert M. Craig, *East Asia: Tradition and Transformation*, rev. ed. (Boston: Houghton Mifflin, 1989); and Conrad Schirokauer, Miranda Brown, David Lurie, and Suzanne Gay, *A Brief History of Chinese and Japanese Civilization*, 3rd ed. (United States: Wadsworth, 2006).

1 The Origins of Civilization in East Asia

"Out of Africa": The First East Asians

According to a now lost *Old Record* cited in the thirteenth-century Korean history *Memorabilia of the Three Kingdoms* (*Samguk yusa*), the divinity Hwanung descended from heaven to Mount T'aebaek, a sacred peak at the source of the Yalu and Tumen rivers on the border between present-day Korea and China, where he mated with a she-bear he had helped transfigure into human shape. From their union was born the great Lord Tan'gun, supposedly in the year 2333 BCE, who founded the country known as Old Chosŏn and who is widely celebrated today as the father of the Korean nation.

Meanwhile, according to a quite different *Record of Ancient Matters* (the Japanese *Kojiki*, compiled in 712 CE), the grandson of the sun goddess Amaterasu was sent down to earth from heaven, bearing the three sacred Japanese imperial regalia – the curved *magatama* bead, bronze mirror, and sword – to become the founder of the Japanese imperial line (the same line that still occupies the Chrysanthemum throne in Tōkyō today) and the origin of the Japanese nation.

Much earlier, in China, various ancient royal houses also typically claimed divine or miraculous origins, although Western scholars have generally been more impressed by the relative absence of important creation myths from the dawn of Chinese history. The traditional version of China's story begins, instead, with a more apparently human age of (legendary) cultural heroes, starting with Fuxi (supposedly dating from 2852 BCE), who first domesticated animals; Shennong (from 2737 BCE), who invented farming; and the Yellow Emperor (ruling from 2697 BCE), who is popularly viewed as the ancestor of the Chinese people.

Though the Japanese emperor officially renounced his divinity after World War II, in 1946, and few people today are likely to believe literally the story of Japanese imperial descent from the sun goddess, some of these myths and legends are still quite charming.[1] It is doubtful, however, that many non-natives, coming from different religious and cultural traditions, ever gave much literal credence to any such stories of divine descent. Early modern Europeans, for example, brought their own quite different sets of expectations about possible East Asian origins. Not untypically, in a book published in Amsterdam in 1667, Athanasius Kircher speculated that the Chinese must have descended from the biblical Noah's son Ham via Egypt, which would have also explained the apparent (but very superficial) similarity between Chinese writing and Egyptian hieroglyphics.[2]

Even after Europeans became better informed about East Asia, the theory that civilization must have diffused to China (and everywhere else) from a common universal point of origin somewhere in the Middle East long continued to be widely accepted. The implication that all civilization originated in the West (even though this was a "West" whose history began, strangely enough, in the Fertile Crescent that is now Iraq and Egypt) and that all non-Western native peoples must therefore have been incapable of achieving civilization on their own was understandably rather offensive to many non-Westerners. As new archeological evidence mounted steadily over the course of the twentieth century that Bronze Age civilization in China was actually very ancient and showed little evidence of direct importation from the West, an opposing theory of almost completely independent indigenous origin came to be preferred by many scholars. A classic 1975 study by Ping-ti Ho, for example, famously labeled China the "Cradle of the East," in conscious parallel to the so-called Cradle of (Western) Civilization in the Fertile Crescent of Egypt and Mesopotamia.[3]

It was probably always a mistake, though, to assume that the only option was a binary choice between diffusion from a single common source and entirely independent local development. In fact, these are not necessarily mutually exclusive alternatives. People have always traveled and communicated across sometimes vast distances, yet it is also true that movement was usually extremely slow and difficult in antiquity, and local communities, especially if they are relatively distant and isolated, naturally do develop independently. The most likely explanation for all the different historical civilizations of the world is a combination of common ultimate human origins and multiple ongoing processes of local diversification and exchange, in a process of interaction that has been described as "not so much diffusion as dialectic."[4]

New breakthroughs in the science of genetics, especially the study of mitochondrial DNA, make it seem increasingly likely that all modern human beings everywhere throughout the world share relatively recent common ancestors and are closely related. A currently influential theory is that modern humans spread across the planet from a shared ancestral homeland in Africa only within the last one hundred thousand years. From carbon 14 dating, we know that modern humans had reached eastern Eurasia by at least 25,000 BCE and possibly as early as fifty to sixty thousand years ago. Even leading scientific skeptics of this *out of Africa theory* acknowledge that entirely independent origins for different human populations are improbable and suggest instead merely that local human variations developed over a much longer period of time within a loose network of genetic exchanges sufficient to maintain the overall commonality of the human species.

Globally, then, there were three major centers of late Stone Age (Neolithic) cultural development based on the critical breakthrough to agriculture: one in western Eurasia, involving wheat and barley; one in eastern Eurasia, involving rice and millet; and one in the Americas, based on maize (corn). Within eastern Eurasia, in turn, there were also multiple local late Stone Age cultures. These cultures, furthermore, did not necessarily align with any modern national borders. It is misleadingly anachronistic to think of these Stone Age peoples as already being Chinese or Korean or Japanese, for example.

Merely within the territory that we think of now as China proper, there was much local variation, and also a very significant broad division between north and south. The peoples of the south cultivated rice – by at least 8000 BCE in the lower Yangzi River valley – were fond of boats, tended to elevate their houses above ground level on posts, produced pottery with impressed geometric designs, and probably spoke languages more closely related to those now spoken in Southeast Asia than to modern Chinese.

The peoples in the north, meanwhile, centering especially around the Yellow River valley and what is commonly called the Central Plain, grew millet and often lived in houses dug partially below ground level, perhaps for insulation purposes. At least some of these northern peoples must have spoken an early form of the Chinese language. The most famous of these northern cultural complexes (dating from about 5000 BCE) is called Yangshao by modern archeologists and is known for its vividly decorated "painted pottery."

Along the northernmost fringe, roughly in the region now called Inner Mongolia, the climate apparently became somewhat colder and drier beginning around 1500 BCE, and the peoples living there gradually turned away from agriculture toward the raising of livestock. Animals that can graze, feeding themselves by eating wild grass, such as sheep and cattle, began to predominate over the pigs that have traditionally provided the staple meat in the Chinese diet but that cannot graze and require the support of an agricultural society. As mastery of the technique of horseback riding – apparently first achieved in the western reaches of that great belt of grassland called the steppe, which stretches from the Hungarian Plain in Europe eastward to Mongolia – finally spread to the vicinity of China, perhaps by roughly 500 BCE, these northern peoples became true pastoral nomads.

These livestock-raising nomads then became the great cultural "other," and frequent military opponent, of the Chinese people for most of premodern history. Many of these nomads actually lived within the borders of what is now China, however, in Inner Mongolia, and sometimes even farther south in China proper. These nomads interacted in a dynamic fashion with the agriculturally based Chinese civilization, forming what could alternatively even be conceived of as a single system with two opposing poles. Nomads, or at least seminomadic ranchers, provided not a few of the ruling families of Chinese imperial dynasties. Clearly, despite their sharp differences, the pastoral nomads of Inner Mongolia and the farmers of northern China were historically bound together.

On the Korean peninsula, meanwhile, there were also multiple prehistoric cultures – some overlapping with Manchuria, in what is now China. By the end of Korean prehistory, there are also some tantalizing hints of connections with the Japanese islands. What appears today to be the striking homogeneity of Korean national identity was probably originally "forged from diverse elements."[5] This present-day Korean cultural uniformity, furthermore, did not really coalesce until relatively late. Although rice cultivation was known on the Korean peninsula by at least 1000 BCE, and bronze metalworking appeared perhaps a few centuries later, the details of Korean history remain largely a mystery until the peninsula began to be mentioned in Chinese documents of the early imperial era.

Some time before those first documentary references, people from the Korean peninsula had probably begun crossing the straits south into the Japanese islands. Much earlier still, Japan may have once been connected to the mainland of Asia by a land bridge, and there may have also been some ancient maritime connections between Japan and Southeast Asia. Certainly there were humans on the Japanese islands from very early times. Japan is notable, in fact, for having produced perhaps the earliest known pottery on earth, from around 11,000 BCE. Yet the population of Japan in the late Stone Age always remained sparse – probably never numbering more than roughly a quarter million people throughout the islands – and extensive farming and metalworking did not appear in the Japanese islands until as late as about 300 BCE. The relatively sudden surge of major new developments after that time is associated with new arrivals from the Korean peninsula. As is the case with Korea, moreover, the earliest written description of Japan appears in a Chinese text, this one dating from the third century CE.

If all modern human beings share common ancestors, and if there has always been more contact and exchange between different population groups than is sometimes imagined, it is also the case that in antiquity, mobility was commonly limited, especially for agricultural peoples bound to farmland. Everywhere there was much local independent cultural development. Some communities were relatively more isolated than others, and within the Eurasian Old World, East Asia may have been especially something of a world apart. One particularly visible emblem of East Asian cultural uniqueness was the use throughout East Asia in premodern times of a writing system (a script) that is strikingly different from the Middle Eastern–derived alphabets and phonetic spelling systems that eventually came to be used everywhere else in the world.

East Asian Languages and Writing Systems

"Far more than princes, states or economies, it is language-communities who are the real players in world history," writes Nicholas Ostler.[6] It has been observed that the same Old English word that meant "people" or "nation" could also indicate "language."[7] Languages are frequently central to the self-identification of human communities (and the primary barrier to communication with others), and they constitute a vital piece of the story of East Asian civilization. Indeed, the most Chinese thing about China may very well be the language. Some basic understanding of the languages of East Asia is therefore fundamental at the outset, even though these languages are by definition foreign to native speakers of English, and any discussion of language runs the risk of quickly becoming dauntingly technical. I will try to keep it simple.

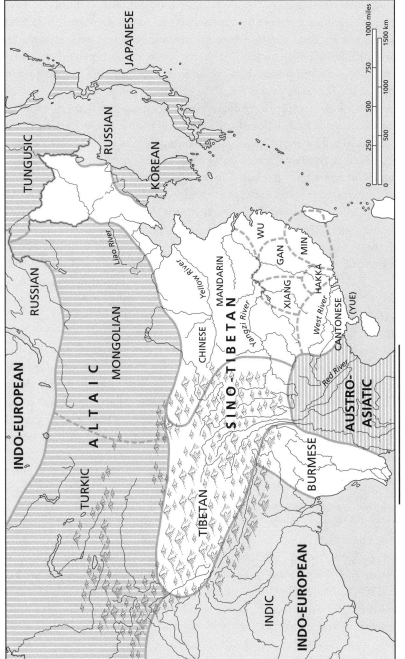

Map 2. Language Families, Languages, and Major Dialects of Chinese

15

The languages of East Asia break into separate national traditions: Chinese, Japanese, and Korean. Far from being unified by its languages, East Asia is divided into three major national language systems, which are further torn between at least two wholly different language families. Each of these language families, furthermore, extends well beyond the borders of East Asia. It is not the languages as spoken, but the language as written – the shared use of a common premodern writing system and, to a surprising degree, even a common written language – that gives East Asia much of its cultural coherence and distinctiveness as a region.

The Chinese and Japanese languages, for example, could hardly be more different. Japanese is polysyllabic, with words compounded out of simple basic syllables piled up in an agglutinative manner to make sophisticated grammatical distinctions, such as the distinction between currently doing something and having done it in the past. Perhaps its most distinctive feature is that Japanese is a *respect language* (*keigo*), meaning that word endings and honorific particles are used to indicate the relative status of speaker and listener, and also the degree of formality or informality. For example, *benkyō-shite-imasu* is a formal way of saying "I am studying," while *benkyō-shite-iru* is a more informal way of saying the same thing. Grammatical particles are also used to mark the different parts of a sentence. A typical sentence pattern takes the form subject-*wa*/ object-*o*/ verb (e.g., "I *wa*/ book *o*/ read"), with the verb invariably coming at the end.

Chinese is almost the opposite. The word order is closer to English, with the verb coming before the object (e.g., "I read [a] book"). The Chinese language is also completely uninflected, having no tenses or plurals or any grammatical modification of word endings whatsoever. Honorifics, for the most part, are absent: Chinese is not a respect language. Chinese is also monosyllabic, at least to the extent that every Chinese character (written symbol), without exception, is pronounced as a single syllable and is a discrete unit of meaning.

In practice, however, Modern Chinese usually then constructs longer compound words from combinations of two or three characters. For example, the familiar Chinese place name Tiananmen is written with three characters: *tian* (heaven), *an* (peace), and *men* (gate), or the "Gate of Heavenly Peace." (*Tiananmen Square* adds two more characters: *guang*, meaning "broad" or "spacious," and *chang*, meaning "an area of level ground.") Although, conceptually, we may regard *Tiananmen* as one word (and *Tiananmen Square* as two), written Chinese characters are never clustered into word groupings separated by spaces: each individual character always occupies a roughly equal square or rectangular space on the page. Traditionally, Chinese was written in vertical columns from top to bottom and then moving from right to left. Since the twentieth century, the Western direction of writing, moving horizontally from left to right, has become increasingly common, but not uniformly so.

Spoken Chinese is also notably different from Japanese (and English) in being a *tonal language*; that is, in speech (but not in writing), the pitch or tone with which a particular syllable is pronounced determines the word. Modern Mandarin, the standard dialect, has four tones and an additional neutral tone. Some dialects have more.

There are multiple regional dialects of Chinese. Some of these dialects are, furthermore, not mutually intelligible. They can sometimes be as different from each other as English and German – which we generally regard as being entirely separate languages rather than dialects of some common Germanic tongue. Partly for this reason, some specialists reject the label "dialects" altogether as a misleading designation for the regional varieties of Chinese speech, preferring instead something more neutral such as *regionalects* or *topolects* (from the Greek *topos*, meaning "place").[8]

As just one example of the possibilities for linguistic complexity, a solid majority (roughly 69%) of the inhabitants of the island of Taiwan today speak as their mother tongue a dialect (or topolect, if you prefer) that is technically called Southern Min and that originated in Fujian Province (on the mainland directly across the straits) but that is now popularly simply called Taiwanese. This Taiwanese dialect is incomprehensible to speakers of the Mandarin that has officially been promoted on Taiwan since 1945 as the (literally so-called) National Language (*guoyu*). Perhaps another 15 percent of the current inhabitants of Taiwan are native speakers of yet another significantly different dialect called Hakka. (In addition, there are also still a few speakers of entirely non-Chinese aboriginal languages on the island.)

Meanwhile, Hakka is also spoken in other places on the Chinese mainland, and Taiwanese remains at least similar to the language spoken directly across the straits in its place of origin in Fujian Province on the mainland. Fujian dialects are also widespread among the overseas Chinese communities living scattered throughout Southeast Asia, while Fujian Province itself is home to some of the most extreme dialectical variety in all China. In general, the major variant dialects of Chinese are concentrated in the southeastern coastal region.

This all makes the linguistic situation in China seem more confusing than it really is, however. Passably standard Mandarin is now spoken almost everywhere throughout the Chinese world, and despite the sometimes bewildering diversity of local dialects (or topolects), the most remarkable feature of the Chinese spoken language overall may actually be its surprising uniformity. It has been said that nowhere else in the entire premodern world "has there ever been a linguistic unity like that of North China."[9] Some three-quarters of all Chinese people, especially in the north and west, are native speakers of a relatively uniform version of the language that we call Mandarin (in English; the Chinese themselves generally refer to it either as *putonghua*, "the common speech," or *guoyu*, "National Language"). The Mandarin dialect of Chinese is, in fact, by far the most commonly spoken native tongue in the entire world today, with approximately nine hundred million speakers. In contrast to this Chinese uniformity, consider the still highly varied linguistic map of Europe.

All the various local versions of Chinese are then, more broadly, sometimes said to belong to a larger Sino-Tibetan language family, which distantly links the Chinese languages to Tibetan, Burmese, and certain other languages extending beyond East Asia. Within East Asia, the major contrast with this Sino-Tibetan language family is presented by Japanese and Korean, which are both sometimes said to belong to yet another, somewhat hypothetical Altaic (or Ural-Altaic) language family that extends in a belt across the north, stretching as far west as Europe, and that notably includes Manchu, Mongolic, Turkic, and possibly even Finnish.

Japanese is certainly closer to Korean than it is to any other living language. It is possible that the two may have split from a common original ancestral tongue, although, if so, they had already become mutually distinct by the dawn of the historical period, and their similarities today should not be exaggerated. Japanese, in turn, even today still includes some distinctive local dialects. The *Ōsaka-ben*, or Ōsaka dialect, sometimes heard on the streets of Japan's second largest city, located in the west of the main island, for example, remains different from the standard Japanese that is based on the dialect of Tōkyō, in the east. Of all modern East Asian nations, Korea today may be the most homogeneous, but even in Korea, one third-century Chinese description specified that at that time, the people living in the southeastern corner of the Korean peninsula spoke a language that was not the same as what was spoken in the southwest of the peninsula.[10]

If Japanese and Korean belong to the Altaic language family, and Chinese belongs to the Sino-Tibetan, much of what is now southeast China may have originally been inhabited by speakers of yet a third entirely different language family, one that may have been ancestral to languages spoken today in Southeast Asia and beyond. These languages must have gradually been displaced from southeast China by the spread of Chinese, leaving behind as a residue only perhaps a contribution to the dialectical complexity of southeast China and a substratum of vocabulary items such as the word commonly used for "river" in south China, *jiang* (as in the *Yangzi jiang*, or "Yangtze River"), which contrasts with the standard northern Chinese word for river, *he* (as in the *Huang he*, or "Yellow River").[11]

East Asia is therefore split between at least two radically different major languages families as well as three modern national languages and multiple regional dialects (not to mention some completely different other languages spoken by ethnic minorities). One linguistic feature that all premodern East Asia shared exclusively in common, however, and that served as a powerful unifying bond, was extensive use of the Chinese writing system.

Globally, the use of written symbols to represent spoken words probably first began in Mesopotamia around 3400 BCE. The idea seems to have been independently reinvented in nearby Egypt not long thereafter. (Ancient Egypt and Mesopotamia, despite close proximity, remained strikingly different civilizations.) In China, writing did not first appear until much later, around 1200 BCE, about the time of the siege of Troy immortalized by Homer. Despite its relatively late date, however, the Chinese script seems to have been another case of independent invention.

All of the world's pristinely invented earliest writing systems – Mesopotamian cuneiform, Egyptian hieroglyphics, Chinese, and Mayan – can technically be described as *logographic* in the sense that they were not primarily phonetic systems but represented instead the meaning of words as much as their sound. Chinese characters (called *hanzi* in Chinese, which simply means "Chinese characters") may have begun with greatly simplified, highly abstract pictures of the things they represented. The limitations of a pictographic writing system must have very soon become apparent, however, and the overwhelming majority of Chinese characters quickly came to have both a component vaguely indicating pronunciation and another component suggesting approximate meaning, such as having something to do with a hand, a mouth, water, fire, fish, and so on.

The most complete Chinese dictionaries today list nearly fifty thousand different characters, but standard desktop dictionaries commonly include only around seven thousand. Many of the characters in even these shorter dictionaries are rarely used, and functional literacy can be achieved with mastery of only a few thousand. In Japan in 1946, the government issued an official list of 1,850 approved characters (known as the *Tōyō Kanji* list) that were intended to be sufficient for all uses. Compared to the much smaller number of symbols used in an alphabet, however, even the shortest feasible list of Chinese characters clearly poses a daunting task to memorize. The undeniable difficulty of learning the system has not prevented users of the Chinese script from achieving relatively high literacy rates in both premodern and modern eras, however, nor has it posed an insuperable obstacle to producing some of the world's finest works of literature. And it can be argued that the system does have certain inherent strengths.

There is a natural tendency to assume that the early logographic writing systems, such as Chinese, cuneiform, or hieroglyphics, represent an early stage in some universal linear progression toward the evolution of an alphabet. A glaring problem with this assumption, however, is that none of these early logographic scripts apparently ever actually did evolve directly into a purely phonetic writing system. In both the Middle East and East Asia, instead, the development of phonetic writing systems seems to have occurred only when the existing logographic scripts had to be adapted by other peoples to write languages other than the ones for which they were originally developed.[12]

In the classic instance, the original alphabet was probably invented sometime before 1500 BCE by scribes in Canaan or Byblos, along the eastern shore of the Mediterranean Sea, who were familiar with Egyptian (and possibly also cuneiform) and were attempting to devise a system more suitable than Egyptian for writing their own language. From this original Canaanite alphabet, the better-known Phoenician alphabet was soon derived (by 1000 BCE) and eventually also the Greek and Roman, Arabic, and Indian scripts, and most of the other phonetic scripts that are still used in the world today.[13] In East Asia, phonetic writing systems were similarly also spun off from logographic Chinese, as both the Japanese and the Koreans eventually devised new scripts to write their own radically different languages.

Most of the world's other original ancient logographic writing systems – cuneiform, hieroglyphics, and Mayan – have since fallen out of circulation altogether, along with their associated languages. The ancient Egyptian language, for example, while it may still tenuously survive in the form of Coptic, has long since been replaced by Arabic as the national language of Egypt. But the Chinese language is not only still widely spoken, it is actually the most commonly spoken language in the world today. There has been, accordingly, little need for the Chinese to abandon their own original writing system, which is well suited to their language.

In China, during the centuries before the first imperial unification in 221 BCE, somewhat variant regional forms of the written characters did emerge, but imperial unification thereafter standardized the writing system, and the civil service examination system that became a defining institution of late imperial China solidified and stabilized the educational curriculum to a remarkable degree, at least at the elite level. The written word, in Chinese characters, came to hold immense prestige.

In the early twentieth century, as China's status as the preeminent regional power was dramatically challenged by the industrialized modern West, China was plunged into a period of profound cultural crisis, and various Western models sometimes appeared irresistible. Many would-be modernizers, including even the Communist leader Mao Zedong, at times came to the conclusion that alphabetization of Chinese writing must be an inevitable part of modernization. In the end, however, although a standardized system of spelling Chinese using our Roman alphabet (called pinyin) was officially approved for educational and other limited applications, all that was actually accomplished after the establishment of the People's Republic in 1949 was the simplification, to reduce the total number of strokes necessary to write them, of over two thousand characters in the 1950s and 1960s. For example, *Hanyu* (the "Chinese language") was simplified from 漢語 to 汉语.

In hindsight, even so-called simplification may not have really made the system very much simpler because it created a need for well-educated persons to learn both the old forms (which are still used in Taiwan, Hong Kong, by many overseas Chinese, and, of course, in old books) and the new forms, and because a reduction in the number of pen strokes has become somewhat irrelevant in the more recent age of computer-generated word processing. In any event, the logographic writing system still survives today in twenty-first-century China and seems to be, if anything, less seriously threatened now than it was a half-century ago.

In view of how completely different the other East Asian languages are from Chinese, it may be more remarkable not that they eventually moved away from the Chinese writing system but how tenaciously long they clung to it. One modern scholar even jokes, for example, that "although no one would wish for it, it would have been far easier to write English, which is structurally similar to Chinese, with Chinese characters than to adapt this system to Japanese."[14]

The early Japanese were faced with three basic options in adapting the Chinese writing system to write Japanese: (1) they could take a Chinese character exclusively for its meaning, forgetting its Chinese pronunciation, and use it to stand for an approximately equivalent preexisting word in the spoken Japanese language; or (2) they could borrow both the meaning and the Chinese pronunciation of the Chinese character, thus importing a wholly new Chinese loanword into the Japanese language. In either of these cases, furthermore, there remained the problem of how to represent Japanese grammatical distinctions that simply do not exist in Chinese. (3) A third option was to borrow the Chinese character exclusively for its pronunciation, forgetting its meaning, and use such characters to then painstakingly "spell out" the sound of native Japanese words. Finally, of course, the Japanese could also learn to read and write directly in the foreign Chinese language itself. In practice, from the time writing first began to appear in Japan around the fifth century, the Japanese did all of the above.

Much early writing in Japan was in the Chinese language, but already in 712, Japan's oldest surviving history, the *Kojiki* (*A Record of Ancient Matters*), was composed in Japanese using Chinese characters. Early efforts to transcribe the Japanese language in this manner made for extremely cumbersome reading, however. One lasting consequence of the multiple different approaches taken to using Chinese characters in Japan is that the characters still used in Japanese today nearly all have at least two completely different pronunciations, one reflecting the borrowed approximation of the Chinese sound, and one representing a roughly equivalent (but originally unrelated) native Japanese word. For example, the Chinese character *dao* 道, meaning "way" (as in Daoism) or "road," can be pronounced in Japanese either (approximately) Chinese style, as *dō* (as in the martial art *jūdō* 柔道, "Way of Suppleness") or *tō* (as in the Japanese religion *Shintō* 神道, "Way of the Spirits"), or native Japanese style, as *michi* 道, a common word for "road."

Over time, in a process that was completed by about the ninth or tenth century, the Chinese characters used to phonetically spell out Japanese were standardized, reduced in number, and simplified. The character 伊, for example, which is pronounced *i* in Japanese (and sounds more like the English letter *e* in "return" than the usual letter *i* in English), was simplified to イ; the character 久, which is pronounced *ku*, became ク; and the character 奈, which is pronounced *na*, became ナ. The eventual result was the creation of two separate sets of some fifty-one symbols each: the angular and "masculine" Katakana and the curved and "feminine" Hiragana (both collectively called *kana*). These *kana* symbols could then be used to fluently write the sounds of all the syllables of the Japanese language. Although these *kana* were derived from Chinese characters, they have been stripped of all meaning, and they also no longer resemble the original Chinese characters very much. It was now possible to write the Japanese language using a native Japanese phonetic script.

Japanese authors soon put these *kana* to use in producing some of the world's truly outstanding early literary masterpieces. Perhaps most famous is *The Tale of Genji* (*Genji monogatari*), written at the beginning of the eleventh century by Lady Murasaki Shikibu (978–1016). *The Tale of Genji* is often called the world's first great true novel, or extended work of prose fiction. It relates the romantic affairs of an imaginary prince at the Japanese imperial court, Prince Genji, and is infused throughout with the characteristic Japanese sentiment of the age: *mono-no-aware*, the "sadness of things," a Buddhist-inspired awareness of the impermanence and transience of all existence. The word *aware*, "sadness," in fact appears no fewer than 1,018 times in this book.[15]

Despite helping make possible the creation of several early works of striking genius and universal appeal, such as *The Tale of Genji*, the phonetic Japanese Hiragana script was at the time often condescendingly referred to as "woman's hand." In practice, the gender distinction between supposedly masculine Chinese characters and feminine Hiragana was often transgressed: men wrote phonetically in *kana*, and a number of memorable Japanese ladies were certainly literate in

Chinese. But the Chinese script, and even the Chinese language itself, long remained the most prestigious vehicle for serious writing in Japan. One distinguished twelfth-century aristocrat, Fujiwara Michinori (1106–1159), for example, did not include even a single text written in the Japanese script in his library. The intellectual primacy of Chinese writing in Japan would not be fatally challenged until modern times. Even the last catalog compiled for the shōgun's library in 1864–1866 still contained 65 percent Chinese or Chinese-style material. When Japan went to war with China in 1894 – a war that would first spectacularly demonstrate Japan's success at transforming itself into a modern, Western-style power, as well as China's corresponding failure to do so – the majority of Japanese war poetry was still being written in the classical Chinese language! The movement toward writing in a standardized vernacular Japanese "national language" (*kokugo*) really only began at that surprisingly late date.[16]

Today, of course, the Japanese language is universally written everywhere throughout the Japanese islands. But Chinese characters are still quite normally used in Japan for the roots of words, with Hiragana added for grammatical matters and certain common basic words. Katakana, meanwhile, is today reserved almost exclusively for Western loanwords, of which there are now a great many. One study conducted in the 1970s estimated that Western loanwords, especially from English, made up as much as 10 percent of the daily Japanese vocabulary. In the process of being absorbed into Japanese, however, these English words have frequently also been domesticated beyond easy recognition. Among the most common English loanwords, for example, are *biiru* (beer), *terebi* (television), *nyūsu* (news), *karā* (color), and *supōtsu* (sports).[17]

Compared to Japan, Korea is geographically closer to China, and the Chinese influence tended to be proportionately greater in premodern times. Beginning perhaps as early as the fifth century, however, Koreans had already started experimenting with adapting Chinese characters to write the native Korean language, in part phonetically, in a form known as *Idu*. Despite this modest breakthrough, only a total of about fifty poems written in vernacular Korean survive today from the entire period prior to the fifteenth century, compared to thousands of Korean documents written in Chinese.[18] Even the proudly nationalistic Korean priest-historian Iryŏn (1206–1289) compiled his invaluable early history of Korea, the *Samguk yusa* (*Memorabilia of the Three Kingdoms*), in 1281, mostly in the Chinese language, although he did include some native-language poetry.

In 1446 the great Korean King Sejong is credited with introducing a unique new twenty-eight-letter Korean alphabet, known as *han'gŭl*. In contrast to the Japanese *kana*, which represented the sounds of entire syllables, the Korean *han'gŭl* is a true alphabet, representing the smallest possible units of sound. *Han'gŭl* can be used very effectively to easily write anything in Korean, without reference to Chinese characters. After its inception, a large and growing Korean-language literature did begin to emerge, but even then, members of the educated Korean elite still tended to view Chinese-language writing as more prestigious, and it was only in the twentieth century that the use of Chinese characters has largely been abandoned in Korea. Since that time, however, the rejection of Chinese characters has been much more comprehensive in Korea than in Japan.

Throughout East Asia, therefore, the Chinese writing system, and to a lesser extent the classical Chinese written language itself, continued to be widely used until modern times. The astonishing durability of this apparently cumbersome Chinese logographic script owes much, of course, to its cultural prestige and the heavy weight of tradition. That the Chinese writing system had relatively few serious regional rivals until the nineteenth century surely also was a factor. But it may also be argued that the system does have some inherent strengths. Though an alphabet is certainly easier to learn, and more flexible in its applicability to a multitude of different languages, an alphabet also merely reproduces phonetically in writing the babel of those different spoken tongues – the cacophony of sound. Chinese characters, by contrast, though difficult to learn and far from providing any magic universal ideographic means of communicating ideas without the need for passing through language first, once learned, do tend always to mean approximately the same thing in every language or dialect and across all time.

This universality should not be exaggerated: for example, the character *shu* 書 that in classical Chinese once meant either "to write" or "something that is written" in modern Chinese has come nearly always to mean specifically "book," whereas in Japan, it is usually used for the verb (pronounced *kaku*) "to write." With late-twentieth-century script simplification in the People's Republic of China, but not in Taiwan or other parts of the greater Chinese world, even Chinese Mandarin speakers no longer all use exactly the same script. Despite these caveats, however, the use of the Chinese script can make written communication across dialects, languages, and centuries of time easier. For anyone who has learned the system, moreover, it can be a thing of beauty and power.

Since new words can also be freely and easily coined by combining existing characters, Chinese characters – far from being stuck with a vocabulary dating from the Bronze Age – are actually extremely flexible in adapting new ideas. *Computer*, for example, is "electricity + brain" (*diannao* 電腦), *democracy* is "people + master" (*minzhu* 民主), and *stock exchange* is "proof + certificate + meet + exchange + place" (*zhengquan jiaoyisuo* 證券交易所). Another modern (or at least nineteenth-century) European concept without much precedent in traditional East Asia, *Communism*, is rendered as "collective + production + ism" (*gongchan-zhuyi* 共産主義, with "-ism" in turn being "master + meaning").

Although printing was invented in East Asia, the Chinese script, with its enormous number of different characters, was never very suitable for moveable type printing, and a convenient Chinese typewriter was effectively impossible. In the post-typewriter age of digital computers, however, the Chinese script now poses considerably fewer disadvantages. Indeed, it has been predicted that Chinese may eventually pass English to become the world's most commonly used computer language, and by some estimates, there are already more people online in China than in any other country in the world.

Despite the strengths of this system, in the twentieth century, under the impact of modern Western influences, Chinese characters were largely abandoned in Korea, while in Japan they have been so thoroughly domesticated as to seem part of traditional Japanese culture. Even within China, sweeping language reforms were implemented, including the abandonment of the classical written language in favor of a modern vernacular in the early twentieth century and script simplification in the People's Republic. It is still the case, however, that over one-third of the vocabulary items in each of the modern Japanese and Korean languages derive from Chinese, so the ghost of this once-shared premodern written language still hovers over East Asia.[19]

This should be less surprising (and less offensive to nationalist sensibilities) if we remember the equally large number of words in modern English that derive ultimately from either Greek or Latin. The prestige that Latin long enjoyed in Western Europe compares roughly to that of classical Chinese in East Asia. As late as the year 1500, some three-quarters of all books in Western Europe were still being published in Latin.[20] To the extent that Western civilization enjoys a common core of Greco-Roman heritage, in a similar way, East Asian civilization is also marked by a shared legacy of writing in classical Chinese, and the reading of a core group of common books written in that language.

Bronze Age China

Northern China, particularly the lower Yellow River area known as the Central Plain, was the location of one of the world's major early *primary civilizations*. This term refers to the indigenous development of a civilization under only limited outside influence. By contrast, Korea, Japan, Western Europe, the United States, and most of the other societies with which we are familiar today are *secondary states* or civilizations, meaning that they emerged chronologically somewhat later, under the influence of older neighbors or predecessors.

Because the major primary civilizations of the world developed in sometimes significantly different ecological environments – the Mayans, for example, amid the tropical forests of Central America, the Egyptians in the arid river valley of the Nile, and the Chinese in the temperate rain-watered Central Plain of north China – it is not entirely obvious why the Central Plain area should have been favored for this breakthrough. There is no evidence that large-scale irrigation was employed in early Bronze Age China, for example, so theories about how the organized mass mobilization of labor for irrigation purposes caused the rise of early civilizations do not seem to be supported in the case of China. The Central Plain is, however, a large and relatively level area suitable for dry-field agriculture (millet, and later wheat, were the principal crops of the Central Plain; wet-field rice cultivation, although equally ancient, was mostly limited to the originally semiforeign south), centering on a major river. The Central Plain is also relatively accessible overland from western Eurasia, which may (or may not) have been a contributing factor. Compared to Mesopotamia, where what is technically defined as "civilization" is said to have emerged as early as 3500 BCE, and Egypt, which was unified circa 3100 BCE, the emergence of Bronze Age civilization in China around 2000 BCE came relatively late. By almost any other measure, however, China's civilization was indisputably ancient.

As we have seen, traditional Chinese histories begin with an age of celebrated culture heroes, including Fuxi, Shennong, the Yellow Emperor, and a series of later Sage Rulers, culminating in Great Yu (ruling from 2205 BCE), who, according to the traditional story, tamed a catastrophic flood and founded the first dynasty, called Xia. Xia then became the first of the so-called Three Dynasties, Xia (traditionally dated 2205–1766 BCE), Shang (ca. 1766–1045 BCE), and Zhou (1045–256 BCE), that form the classical age of Chinese antiquity. The problem is that all the stories concerning these great ancient cultural heroes were recorded only very long after the events they purport to describe – and necessarily had to be because writing did not appear in China until roughly 1200 BCE.

The legends concerning high antiquity were deeply revered by traditional Chinese scholars and usually accepted without question, but the enormous rupture triggered by the end of the Chinese Empire in 1912 and sweeping early-twentieth-century modernization led to calls for a more scientific history, and a movement to "doubt antiquity" began in the 1920s. Everything traditional was now regarded with some skepticism. Certainly all the stories purporting to deal with events dating from before the Zhou Dynasty were legend in the literal sense of the Chinese word for *legend*, *chuanshuo*: "passed-on sayings." Such orally passed-on legends could easily also be legendary in the other sense of being mythical and possibly untrue. In 1899, however, a pair of Chinese scholars happened to notice some particularly archaic-looking Chinese writing on old turtle shells and bones that were being marketed for medicine as so-called "dragon bones." These bones were eventually traced to a source near the modern city of Anyang, in the northern province of Henan. The site was finally excavated by scientifically trained archeologists beginning in 1928, and it proved to be the ruins of an ancient Shang Dynasty capital. The dragon bones turned out actually to be shells and bones that were used for divination by Shang Dynasty rulers, and they are therefore now generally called oracle bones. The inscriptions found on some of these oracle bones are the earliest known examples of Chinese-language writing.[21]

This dramatic archeological rediscovery of the last Shang capital, together with the oracle bone inscriptions that provided unquestionable new documentary evidence for it, spectacularly verified much of the later part of the traditional Chinese story. In general, modern archeology has tended to support traditional Chinese accounts, and there is today much less of a skeptical inclination to doubt antiquity than there was in the early twentieth century. Even so, the very earliest portions of the traditional narrative should still be read with caution. They are at best unverified, and much is rather clearly mythical in flavor. The idea that the Yellow Emperor is somehow the ancestor of all Chinese people, for example, is not only scientifically rather dubious but also racist.

The current academic fashion is to emphasize that Chinese civilization actually had multiple origins, in contrast to the prevailing earlier assumption that Chinese civilization must have spread from a single point of origin in the north. Beyond any doubt, there were numerous local prehistoric cultures scattered throughout the area of what we call China during the late Stone Age, with a particularly broad division between the wet-field, rice-based cultivation of the southern Yangzi River basin and the dry-field, millet-based agriculture of the northern Yellow River region. All these different cultures contributed to the brewing Chinese civilization. A degree of regional diversity, furthermore, has remained a fixture throughout history, even to the present day. However, the late Stone Age peoples of southern China appear to have spoken languages unrelated to Chinese, and it still does seem fairest to say that the northern Central Plains Neolithic cultures, based on millet, sorghum, pig, dog, and silkworm raising, and some of whom must have spoken ancestral forms of the modern Chinese language, probably provided the core for what eventually became China.

Sarah Allan has recently suggested that a standard for what became Chinese civilization may have first been set by the elite culture of what archeologists label "Erlitou" (named after an archeological-type site in modern Henan Province).[22] Erlitou is the closest archeological equivalent to what traditional sources call the Xia Dynasty, and it is radiocarbon dated to approximately 2100–1600 BCE. Erlitou is the first archeologically identified culture to show evidence of the construction of royal palaces and the first to use bronze for casting ritual vessels, which were apparently used for making offerings to the spirits of dead ancestors. Such bronze ritual vessels subsequently spread through the entire region of China. Although these bronzes were produced in enormous quantities, they were always cast in a relatively limited number of fixed standard shapes and with common decorative themes, such as the abstract and somewhat mysterious *Taotie* design (see Figure 1.1). Sarah Allan compares the spread of this elite bronze ritual culture to the dispersal of McDonald's fast-food restaurants around the world today, extending everywhere from Chicago to Cairo, Tōkyō, and Beijing, in that it did not necessarily imply either a single homogenous ethnicity or centralized political control, but rather the widespread acceptance of the artifacts of a prestigious cultural model by independent local communities.

Allan claims that the strikingly different collection of ancient bronzes found at Sanxingdui in Sichuan, in southwest China, in 1986 are all the more amazing because they are the only group of bronzes in all China that seem to spring from an entirely different cultural style (and even they are found mixed together with more standard Erlitou-derived types). The ritual behavior associated with these Erlitou bronzes eventually became the standard of Chinese decorum, known as *li* 禮, a term which has been translated variously as "courtesy," "propriety," "rites," or "ceremony" and that unfortunately lacks any precise English equivalent. At least until the revolutionary changes of the twentieth century, *li* set an ideal standard for cultivated behavior in China and eventually throughout all East Asia, becoming a cornerstone for the cultural coherence of the region. For example, in 707 CE, one Japanese empress proclaimed that "all the ways of government take the *li* [pronounced *rei* in Japanese] as foremost."[23]

The Shang Dynasty (ca. 1766–1045 BCE), which represented a more mature development of this Erlitou culture, is commonly understood to have been an early example of a relatively large territorial state, in contrast to the alternative model of small, independent city-states familiar from ancient Mesopotamia. The Shang

Figure 1.1. A Shang Dynasty bronze bell featuring the characteristic *Taotie* design, ca. twelfth to eleventh centuries BCE, southern China. Arthur M. Sackler Gallery, Smithsonian Institution, Washington, D.C.: Gift of Arthur M. Sackler, S1987.10.

ruler does appear to have been the only leader in the whole area of China at that time to claim the supreme sovereign title "king" (*wang* 王). Even so, however, the Shang probably did not employ an extensively centralized bureaucratic government but rather delegated authority to largely autonomous local leaders based in a far-flung network of walled towns. These local leaders may have often been either directly or indirectly (through marriage) related to the Shang king. Sarah Allan points out, for example, that the names of sixty-four known wives of one particular late Shang king are recorded in oracle bone inscriptions and that most of their names include a component that is also a place name. She speculates that these probably signified royal marriage ties between the Shang king and those places and suggests that Shang may have been at the center of a vast network of marriage affiliations.

Shang families were organized by patrilineal descent and seniority. A group tracing descent from a common (presumably often legendary) male ancestor, called *zu* 族, ideally lived together in a community and performed ancestral cult rituals. (Significantly, in the nineteenth century, when a new Chinese-character translation for the Western word *nation* was coined, it was done by combining the character for "the people," *min*, with this same ancient character for descent group, *zu*, creating the new combination *minzu* 民族.) The oldest member of the senior line headed the entire group. Married sons remained subject to their fathers' authority, and women joined their husbands' families after marriage.

Despite this obvious patriarchal male bias, Shang queens nonetheless appear to have assisted in administration, performed ancestral rituals, and even mobilized armies on occasion. There is at least some evidence to suggest that the status of women in traditional China tended to decline over time, perhaps under the growing influence of Confucian moral ideals, and possibly reaching its lowest point only in early modern times. For example, the ideal of the chaste widow (who would rather die than remarry) may have not been especially influential prior to the Tang Dynasty (618–907 CE) and may have been most strenuously promoted only during the last imperial dynasty, Qing (1644–1912). Female foot binding does not seem to have begun before the Song (960–1279 CE).

It was the exclusive prerogative of the Shang kings to sponsor oracle bone divination, the vehicle through which questions could be asked of the spirits. In this divination, heat would be applied to the chest pieces of tortoise shells and other animal bones, causing them to crack, and the shape of the crack was interpreted as an answer from the spirits. Eventually the questions, and occasionally even the answers, came to be inscribed directly on the bones, creating the famous oracle bone inscriptions that are the earliest known examples of Chinese writing.

This role of the king as a crucial intermediary between the human and the spirit worlds was hardly unique, among early civilizations, to the Shang Chinese. Mayan kings communicated with their ancestors and cosmic spirits through sometimes drug-induced trances, while ancient Egyptian pharaohs claimed a royal monopoly over religious offerings.[24] The Shang monarchy thus had a theocratic dimension in common with many other ancient societies – and one that also sets it apart, to some extent, from subsequent Chinese history.

Bronze Age civilization reached mature form in northern China under the Shang, but the Shang Dynasty that has been reconstructed by archeology is in some ways rather strange and unfamiliar by later Chinese standards. The relatively large scale human sacrifice, for example, that the Shang kings practiced as well as the very existence of those oracle bone inscriptions that have so strikingly confirmed the historical existence of the Shang had been almost completely forgotten in China until they were rediscovered by archeologists in the twentieth century. Around 1045 BCE, moreover, the Shang state was decisively conquered by a foreign people, called the Zhou. The Zhou then founded a new dynasty, and it was this Zhou Dynasty that ushered in the great formative age of classical Chinese civilization.

For Further Reading

On the origins of Bronze Age civilization in China, see Sarah Allan (ed.), *The Formation of Chinese Civilization: An Archaeological Perspective* (New Haven: Yale University Press, 2005); Kwang-chih Chang, *The Archaeology of Ancient China* (4th ed.; New Haven: Yale University Press, 1986); and Kwang-chih Chang, *Shang Civilization* (New Haven: Yale University Press, 1980). An excellent comparative view of some of the world's earliest civilizations is provided by Bruce G. Trigger, in *Understanding Early Civilizations: A Comparative Study* (Cambridge University Press, 2003).

On East Asian languages and writing systems, see John DeFrancis, *The Chinese Language: Fact and Fantasy* (Honolulu: University of Hawai'i Press, 1984); Wm. C. Hannas, *Asia's Orthographic Dilemma* (Honolulu: University of Hawai'i Press, 1997); Bruno Lewin, "Japanese and Korean: the Problems and History of a Linguistic Comparison," *The Journal of Japanese Studies*, 2.2 (1976); Roy Andrew Miller, *The Japanese Language* (University of Chicago Press, 1967); and S. Robert Ramsey, *The Languages of China* (Princeton University Press, 1987).

2 The Formative Era

The Age of the Classics

Zhou Dynasty China (1045–256 BCE)

The Zhou people who conquered the Shang Dynasty around the year 1045 BCE were originally distinct from the Shang people. The Zhou homeland lay farther to the west of the core Shang territory, and they were once politically independent. For a while before their conquest, however, Zhou leaders did acknowledge themselves to be subordinate vassals of the Shang, and much of Zhou high culture, including oracle bone divination and the production and style of bronze vessels (inscribed with a shared written language), was derived from Shang. The outcome of their conquest was a new synthesis or fusion. After their 1045 BCE conquest, the newly established Zhou Dynasty absorbed the preexisting Shang population and even allowed the former Shang royal family to maintain its identity, under the reduced title of dukes (of Song) rather than as sovereign kings, to continue their essential ancestral sacrifices. This illustrates once again the extent to which Chinese civilization was, from the beginning, a hybrid mixture, blending together multiple local cultural traditions. The technology of the horse-drawn chariot, which may have been introduced from western Eurasia in late Shang times, also demonstrates the extent to which, although Chinese civilization did develop largely indigenously, it was never entirely a closed and isolated system.

According to legend, the first ancestor of the Zhou people was conceived when a woman named Jiangyuan stepped into the footprint of the supreme god Shangdi (the "Lord on High") and thereby became pregnant. Jiangyuan's name literally means "Progenitress of the Jiang" – the Jiang being yet another different early people, sometimes said to be ancestral to modern Tibetans, with whom the Zhou apparently intermarried. Jiangyuan's miraculous pregnancy, then, resulted in the birth of a son known as Hou Ji, the "Lord of Millet."

Believing that Shangdi disapproved of her pregnancy, however, Jiangyuan abandoned her son in the countryside, only to have his life be saved by cattle and sheep that lay down beside him to keep him warm. She next tried to abandon him in a forest, where he was rescued by woodcutters, and then once more abandoned him on some ice, where birds warmed him with their wings. After his divine conception and repeated supernatural protection in childhood, the adult Hou Ji discovered agricultural techniques that he passed down to his descendents, who became the Zhou people.

The legend continues that these descendants lived a seminomadic existence for some years, and even temporarily gave up agriculture altogether, before finally settling in a region known as the Plain of Zhou, located some eighty miles west of the modern Chinese city of Xi'an. It was from this plain that they supposedly took their name. The Plain of Zhou, in turn, is situated in a much larger basin that has traditionally been known as the region "Within the Passes" (*Guanzhong*). This is a large, reasonably fertile agricultural area almost completely surrounded by mountains, forming a kind of vast natural fortress, which has repeatedly throughout Chinese history served as a base for the military conquest and unification of China.

The prehistoric Zhou people were themselves, from the start, apparently also the product of cultural mixing and were obviously caught up in the interplay between farming and seminomadic livestock-raising lifestyles on the northwestern fringes of the Bronze Age Chinese world. The Zhou presumably emerged from a fusion of several local prehistoric cultures, under the influence of the nearby Shang civilization, as an early example of what is called *secondary state formation*. Early Zhou bronze ritual vessels were, for example, apparently copied from Shang models, although over time, somewhat unique Zhou styles did develop. The Zhou people were also literally armed by Shang technologies: Zhou chariots and composite reflex bows were identical to Shang weapons, although it has been speculated that Zhou bronze armor may have represented an improvement over Shang leather armor.

No identifiable archeological trace of Zhou culture has been found in the region "Within the Passes" until about a century before the Zhou conquest of the Shang, which supports the legend of their migration there from somewhere else. It is uncertain where that somewhere else was located, but it may have been from slightly farther northeast. On their arrival "Within the Passes," the Zhou people may have mixed with other populations already in the area. After settling "Within the Passes," the Zhou chief was invested by the Shang king as a vassal duke. Not content with that subordinate status, however, the Zhou dukes soon usurped the supreme Shang title of sovereignty, promoting themselves to kings.

According to legend, the second Zhou king was killed by the Shang, and the third Zhou king was held captive by the Shang for seven years, until he was ransomed. After generations of such repeated provocation, the fourth Zhou king, known as King Wu – a posthumous designation that means the "Martial King" – finally declared war on the Shang, accusing the last Shang king of a lengthy list of abuses, including failure to perform the proper ceremonies to the spirits of his own ancestors. King Wu mobilized a huge coalition of other disaffected peoples and decisively defeated the Shang in battle at a place called Muye ("Shepherd's Wilderness"), south of the last Shang capital (near modern Anyang, in Henan Province). The government of the present-day People's Republic of China, regarding this as an important national heritage, has funded a special chronology project to determine the exact dates of events at the dawn of Chinese history. As best as can be determined, the date of this Zhou conquest is now placed in the year 1045 BCE. It is one of the most important dates in all Chinese history.

After the great battle and the Shang defeat, the story continues that the last Shang king withdrew into Deer Terrace Pavilion and burned himself to death. Eight days later, King Wu of the Zhou reported his victory to Heaven and announced his intention to assume residence in the Middle Kingdom. This term, *Middle Kingdom (Zhongguo)*, as previously described, has today become the closest Chinese-language equivalent to our English word *China*. An inscription discovered in 1963 on a bronze ritual vessel cast by the Zhou to commemorate their victory over the Shang is believed to be the earliest known surviving example of the use of this key term.

Although the Zhou and Shang were different peoples, both were in a sense Chinese. More precisely, both fed into a Chinese identity that was still in the process of formation. Over the course of the eight centuries of the Zhou Dynasty, a conscious sense of identity as *Huaxia* (Chinese) apparently did coalesce, especially in contrast to the clearly foreign seminomadic cultures to the north. However, many of the peoples living in what we think of today as China, including virtually the entire south, still lay outside this *Huaxia* world in Zhou times. At the same time, until surprisingly recently, some people in both Korea and Vietnam also claimed descent from the same legendary ancestors and to be part of the same great civilization as these Chinese. As one ninth-century Chinese text explained, "when Confucius composed the *Spring and Autumn Annals*, he treated the various lords who used foreign ritual as foreign, and those who approached the Chinese as Chinese."[1] This early Chinese *Huaxia* identity was obviously rather open and inclusive and defined in terms of civilization (as well as myths of common descent). It was not exactly a modern-style national identity.

King Wu of Zhou died a mere two years after his victory over Shang, and he was succeeded on the throne by his oldest son. Since the new king was still very young, and the Zhou Dynasty still somewhat insecure, the late king's brother, who is known as the Duke of Zhou, assumed power as regent on behalf of the new boy king. Other members of the royal family were suspicious of the duke's motives, however, and soon three of the duke's own brothers rebelled. In renewed military campaigns, the Duke of Zhou crushed this rebellion, killing one older brother and driving another into exile in the process.

According to a particularly treasured story preserved in the *Book of Documents* (one of the five core Confucian Classics), Heaven then sent down a great wind that flattened the crops. In search of a ritual response to this disaster, the young king was inspired to open a certain metal-bound box that had been sealed by the Duke of Zhou. In this box, the king discovered the record of an earlier ritual in which the Duke of Zhou had offered his own life in prayer as a substitute for the ailing, but then not yet dead, King Wu. This previously undisclosed document revealed unexpectedly dramatic proof of the Duke of Zhou's selfless sincerity. After successfully putting the dynasty on a more stable basis, the story continues that the

Duke of Zhou voluntarily relinquished his authority as regent. At least according to the traditional story, therefore, the Duke of Zhou had acted decisively and effectively on behalf of the dynasty, without any thought of personal advantage.

Such stories about the Duke of Zhou became foundational to the Chinese political tradition. They established the overriding Confucian principle of rule by virtue, and also the important corollary that if a dynasty's administration was not virtuous, it might lose its legitimacy and thus its continued right to rule. The figure of the Duke of Zhou is intimately associated with the elaboration of a particularly important Chinese political concept known as the Mandate of Heaven (*Tianming*). Heaven was the supreme Zhou deity (displacing the earlier Shangdi), and Zhou kings claimed to be "Sons of Heaven" (*Tianzi*), with a "Mandate from Heaven" to rule the earth "Under Heaven" (*Tianxia*).

It should be emphasized that if the claim to be a Son of Heaven was ever taken literally, it soon ceased to be. Monarchs in premodern China were not normally seriously portrayed as divine, however much a penumbra of ritual and sacralized authority might surround them. While some in the Zhou royal family might have preferred to understand the Mandate of Heaven as a permanent hereditary right, the Duke of Zhou had already given his interpretation a much more revolutionary twist: the Mandate of Heaven was revocable. Dynastic survival depended on continued good government. The same Heaven looks down on all people, everywhere, and enforces universal principles. The Shang had once enjoyed Heaven's Mandate (and before the Shang, supposedly also the Xia), but because the Shang kings had become corrupt, the Mandate passed to Zhou. Zhou kings would retain the Mandate only for so long as they continued to deserve it.

Because "Heaven sees as my people see," according to the *Book of Documents*, popular discontent itself might be taken as evidence of the loss of the Mandate of Heaven. By the fourth century BCE, the great Confucian thinker Mencius (Mengzi, ca. 385–ca. 312 BCE) was so bold as to say explicitly that the overthrow of a bad ruler was no crime but as fully justifiable as the punishment of any ordinary thief or robber. The concept of the Mandate of Heaven therefore legitimated repeated changes of dynasty throughout premodern Chinese history and imposed an ideal standard obligation of meritorious rule on each. At the same time, the concept of a solitary Son of Heaven holding Heaven's Mandate may have also helped buttress the notion that at any given time there could only be one legitimate dynasty "Under Heaven" holding that Mandate.[2] The concept of the Mandate of Heaven remains not entirely irrelevant even today: "Change of Mandate" (*geming*) is the literal Chinese-language translation of our modern Western word *revolution*, a term that was much invoked in twentieth-century China.

The Zhou Dynasty lasted for some eight centuries, but, although the Zhou ruling house may indeed have brought the previously loose Shang network of regional affiliations into a somewhat more systematic basis, and Zhou claims to sole legitimate sovereignty "Under Heaven" may have helped establish a lasting ideal of political unity in China, the Zhou probably never enjoyed direct centralized administration over a very large area. Especially after the early Zhou capital in the west was sacked by foreign forces in 771 BCE, and the capital was relocated

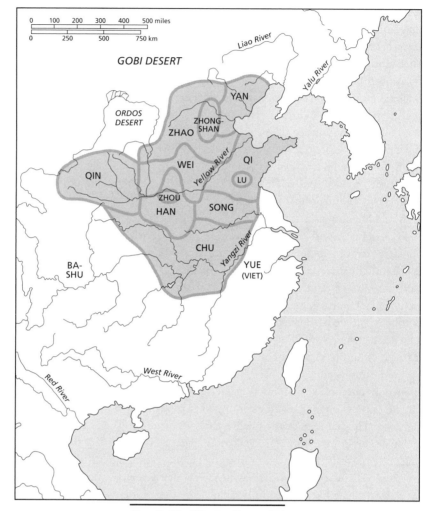

Map 3. The Warring States, 350 BCE

east to Luoyang, inaugurating the so-called Eastern Zhou period (770–256 BCE), the real power of the Zhou kings was increasingly overshadowed by the rise of regional territorial states, which eventually, during the Warring States period (479–221 BCE), became fully independent countries (*guo*) with their own sovereign kings.

The Hundred Schools of Thought

The Zhou Dynasty is regarded as the formative era of Chinese civilization. Nearly all the classic works of Chinese literature, and major schools of indigenous thought, took shape during the Zhou. This reference to schools of thought is a little misleading, though, because one of the most characteristic features of Chinese thought has always been its open eclecticism – a willingness to borrow and incorporate whatever ideas might seem useful or good. Few premodern Chinese people ever fit neatly and exclusively into any particular school of thought. Still, there are certain broad lines of intellectual tradition that can be usefully, if somewhat artificially, distinguished from each other. These most notably include Confucianism, Daoism (also spelled Taoism), and Legalism. As an example of the range of Zhou era thought, which was by no means limited to these three major schools, we may also mention the tradition of military specialists.

Confucianism

Confucianism is commonly considered to be the mainstream of Chinese, and East Asian, tradition. Surprisingly, however, a plausible argument can be made that Confucianism is really "a Western invention."[3] In fact, there is no Chinese word or concept that precisely corresponds with our English word *Confucianism*. The closest Chinese-language approximation, *Ru* (or the "Teachings of the Ru" – *Rujiao*), refers more specifically to scholars who study the ancient classics. It was those classic texts, in particular, that were fundamental to the premodern Chinese cultural tradition.

Although the classics include what may be the oldest books in the Chinese literary tradition (not counting the slightly older inscriptions on oracle bones as "books"), the classics did not assume their final form until relatively late and did not attain venerated canonical status until the late second century BCE. There are five core Confucian Classics:

1. The *Book of Documents* (also called the *Book of History*, *Shujing*, or *Shangshu*). This is a collection of speeches, announcements, and other documents attributed to great figures of antiquity, from the legendary Sage Kings into early Zhou. Much of the Zhou material is believed to be genuine, although the authenticity of the pre-Zhou texts is more dubious.
2. The *Book of Odes* (*Shijing*), a collection of roughly three hundred early Zhou songs or poems, some of which are still of considerable literary value.
3. The *Book of Changes* (*Yijing*; sometimes spelled *I-Ching*). This is a handbook for divination, based on a set of sixty-four hexagrams (variant combinations of six broken and unbroken lines) accessed through the casting of milfoil stalks.
4. The *Rites* (*Li*), which is actually a collective name for three separate books, covering a wide range of matters. These ritual texts appear to have been compiled relatively late, despite the conventional attribution of a portion of them to high antiquity.
5. The *Spring and Autumn Annals* (*Chunqiu*). This is an extremely terse history of Confucius's home state of Lu, covering the years 722–481 BCE. Because it was traditionally believed that Confucius himself had compiled this history, its entries were carefully scrutinized for presumably profound moral judgments conveyed by subtle distinctions in the choice of language.

This list of five core classics was eventually expanded to include a total of thirteen. Much of the importance that was attached to the classics was due to their presumed antiquity, as portraits of an idealized golden age in the early Zhou and the even earlier Sage Kings. From the time they first achieved canonical status in the late second century BCE until the early twentieth century CE, these texts remained at the heart of formal education in China (and to a large extent all of East Asia). Though the study of the classics often took the form of tediously dry memorization and detailed chapter and verse textual commentary, Confucius himself had personally emphasized the need for both study and critical thinking. "To learn without thinking is unavailing; to think without learning is dangerous," Confucius said.[4]

The Confucian Classics spread, together with literacy itself, to both Korea and Japan, where they gained increasing influence over time. In Japan, the heyday of Confucianism is often said to have not come until the early modern Tokugawa period (1603–1868). In Korea, the peak period of Confucian influence also coincided with the last premodern dynasty, Chosŏn (1392–1910). As late as the mid-nineteenth century, one Korean official could still proudly inform a Japanese visitor that the Korean ceremonial code was "based on the precedents" of the Zhou.[5]

East Asia can, to a large extent, even be defined in terms of this shared Confucianism, which coincided also with a shared use of the Chinese writing system and classical language. This common literary language enabled educated premodern Koreans and Japanese to read the Confucian Classics in their original words rather than in translation. It should be emphasized, however, that the appeal of Confucianism in Korea and Japan (and Vietnam as well) was not primarily because it was Chinese. Although the prestige of a powerful and apparently successful Chinese imperial model undoubtedly did play a critical early role in encouraging emulation, many Koreans, for example, ultimately came to see themselves as even better Confucians than the Chinese. In general, the classics were regarded as being no more uniquely Chinese than the Old Testament of the Bible is uniquely Jewish, the Koran uniquely Arab, or the Buddhist scriptures uniquely Indian. The appeal was, instead, to supposedly universal truth.

Except for the *Spring and Autumn Annals*, certain portions of the ritual texts, and the appendices, or *wings*, of the *Book of Changes*, these Confucian Classics were not usually ascribed to Confucius himself. Most were believed to be much older than Confucius, although Confucius was conventionally credited with playing some role in the editing or transmission of each. But if the study of the classics – the special activity of the *Ru* – was central to the actual practice of Confucianism in premodern East Asia, what we call Confucianism is nonetheless named after the man Confucius (551–479 BCE).

"Confucius" is the Latinized (i.e., European) version of the Chinese title *Kong Fuzi* (or more simply, *Kongzi*), which means "Master Kong." His proper name was Kong Qiu, and he was born in the northeastern state of Lu, in what is now Shandong Province. In his own lifetime, Confucius remained a somewhat obscure teacher. Most of what we know reliably about both the man and his ideas derives from a single collection of his conversations that was compiled by his followers some time after his death, called the *Analects* (in Chinese, *Lunyu*).

Confucius's central message was one of leadership by moral example. He believed that any attempt to govern through regulations and punishments would only encourage people to find clever ways to evade the law but that if you led through proper ritual (*li*) and moral force (*de*), the people would spontaneously correct themselves. Confucius, for example, once explicitly rejected capital punishment, saying, "Sir, in conducting your government, why use killing? . . . The virtue of the noble person is like the wind, and the virtue of small people is like grass. When the wind blows over the grass, the grass must bend."

The key to a good society was individual self-cultivation of moral principles by a gentleman (*junzi*), who might then hope to influence other people nearby and eventually even bring peace on earth. As Confucius said, the gentleman "cultivates himself so as to give peace to all the people." Confucius once charmingly described how this process of self-cultivation and internalization of virtue had worked in his own life: "At fifteen, my heart was set upon learning; at thirty, I had become established; at forty, I was no longer perplexed; . . . at seventy, I could follow my heart's desires without crossing the line."

Important specific virtues (among others) that a Confucian gentleman was expected to cultivate were proper observance of ritual (*li*), "humaneness" or "humanity" (*ren*), and filial piety (*xiao*). Ritual was a legacy from the dawn of Chinese civilization, when bronze ritual vessels were cast for offerings to the spirits. For Confucius himself, however, the religious beliefs underlying this ancient ritual were no longer the crucial point; ritual had become merely a standard of proper behavior and a tool for self-discipline. "Through mastering oneself and returning to ritual one becomes humane," said Confucius.

Humanity, then, was most especially the ability to empathize with other people. "As for humaneness – you want to establish yourself; then help others to establish themselves. You want to develop yourself; then help others to develop themselves. Being able to recognize oneself in others, one is on the way to being humane." Or, as Confucius put it most succinctly, "what you do not want for yourself, do not do to others."

Filial piety refers to showing proper respect to parents and ancestors. It is perhaps the most difficult Confucian value for modern Western individualists to feel much sympathy for, but Confucians traditionally viewed filial piety as the absolute bedrock of a good society. As one passage in the *Analects* put it, "Among those who are filial toward their parents and fraternal towards their brothers, those who are inclined to offend against their superiors are few indeed. . . . Being filial and fraternal – is this not the root of humaneness?" In Japan, in 757 CE, one empress decreed:

> The ancients, in governing the people and pacifying the country, had to use the principle of filial piety. As a source of all action, nothing takes priority over this. We should command [each] family in the [Japanese] empire to possess and diligently memorize a copy of the *Classic of Filial Piety*.[6]

The *Classic of Filial Piety* (*Xiaojing*) was one of the later additions to the Confucian canon. It is actually quite inconceivable that all, or even very many, Japanese really read this book in the eighth century. One plausible estimate of the total number of Japanese people who were engaged with Chinese-language written documents at that time is no more than twenty thousand.[7] Yet the imperial Confucian pose in Japan, and the centrality of filial piety to that interpretation of Confucianism, is still significant.

The expectation of hierarchy inherent in this ideal of serving parents filially and not offending superiors also highlights one of the key contradictions in Confucian thought. On one hand, Confucians idealized the memory of a highly aristocratic ancient Zhou social order and conservatively sought to perpetuate it. "I transmit but do not create" is one of Confucius's more famous sayings. Some of the most important Confucian virtues, moreover, such as filial piety and loyalty (*zhong*), can only be expressed through hierarchical relationships. This is one side of the Confucian equation. The other side of the equation, however, was a pointedly egalitarian and meritocratic strand of Confucian thought. Anyone, it was assumed, could potentially perfect himself or herself through self-cultivation and then lead the world by his or her example. As Confucius said, "in education there should be no class distinctions." China had ceased to have a truly hereditary aristocracy already by the third century BCE, and the meritocratic line in Confucian thinking would eventually find realization under the empire in the remarkable Chinese civil service examination system, under which government officials were selected on the basis of anonymously graded performances on written tests.

This contradiction in Confucianism is partially resolved with the realization that merit is necessarily unequal. Anyone can potentially perfect himself or herself (and seniority accrues naturally to everyone equally over time), but not everyone actually does perfect himself or herself. In addition, it may be that internal inconsistencies and variant tendencies within Confucianism allowed it a flexible vitality of interpretation and application. Whereas late imperial China may have become an exceptionally meritocratic society (by premodern standards), for example, in early modern Japan, the same Confucian ideals helped justify a rigidly hereditary social hierarchy under such slogans as *Taigi-meibun*, or the moral obligation of fulfilling the role proper to one's title.

About a century after Confucius's time, a second great Confucian teacher appeared, known as Mencius (mentioned already in our discussion of the Mandate of Heaven). Mencius is most famous for insisting that people are naturally good, just as water, although it can be forced in any direction, naturally inclines to flow downward. Mencius explained the undeniable fact of human misbehavior in practice with a wonderful story:

> The trees on Ox Mountain were once beautiful. But being situated on the outskirts of a large state, the trees were hewn down by axes. . . . [Even so] they do not fail to put forth new buds and shoots, but then cattle and sheep also come to graze. This accounts for the barren appearance of the mountain. Seeing this barrenness, people suppose that the mountain was never wooded.

In a similar way, the innate goodness of people can too often be "fettered and destroyed by what one does during the day," to the point that some might even suppose that people "never had the capacity for goodness." Like the barrenness of Ox Mountain, however, this is not really humanity's natural state. Aside from persuasively making a rhetorical point, this story also reveals a notably early awareness of the process of environmental degradation due to human economic activity.

The third and final major classical era Confucian thinker was Xunzi (ca. 310–ca. 219 BCE). Xunzi lived at the end of the Warring States period and held an understandably darker opinion of human nature than Mencius. Xunzi viewed natural human desires as evil impulses that could only be tamed through conscious training and effort. Xunzi also had a notably rationalistic, nonreligious understanding of the regular order of nature:

> The processes of Heaven are constant.... Respond to them with order, and good fortune will result; respond to them with chaos, and misfortune will result. If you strengthen what is basic and are frugal in your expenditures, then Heaven cannot make you poor.

Heaven, in other words, helps those who help themselves. Although the book that bears Xunzi's name is a superb collection of deliberately crafted essays – in contrast to the scraps of remembered conversation that constitute both the *Analects* of Confucius and the *Mencius* – unlike the other two, the *Xunzi* never achieved recognition as one of the canonical expanded set of thirteen Confucian Classics.

Daoism

After Confucianism, the next most influential school of classical Chinese thought was Daoism. Compared to Confucianism, Daoism had much less influence on parts of East Asia outside China, though it was not unknown in Korea and arguably actually contributed to the founding ideology of the Japanese Empire – even providing the name of the ostensibly "native" Japanese religion *Shintō* (the "Dao of the Spirits").[8] Even by the normally eclectic Chinese standards, Daoism is also remarkably diffuse and difficult to pin down. The word *Dao* itself means "path" or "road." In a philosophical sense, it came to mean "The Way." The word *Dao* is widely used throughout East Asia, however, in many contexts that are not particularly "Daoist." Examples include the Japanese martial art known as *kendō*, or the "Way [Dao] of the Sword," and Chinese *Daoxue*, the "Study of the Way [Dao]," which in English is often called Neo-Confucianism!

Even the things that are actively considered to be "Daoist" can be surprisingly nebulous and varied. The famous yin-yang dualism, for example, is often called Daoist and even imagined as central to Daoism, though it might more usefully be regarded simply as a separate, independent strand of traditional Chinese thought. In addition, a distinctive Daoist religion eventually emerged, beginning in the second century CE, that became a fairly well-defined and discrete religious tradition, with its own canonical body of scripture, liturgy, priests, and institutions. Even this institutionalized Daoist religion was internally complex: the set of Daoist religious scriptures known as the *Daozang* includes over a thousand separate texts. For the classical Zhou era, however, Daoist thought may effectively be defined in terms of just two relatively short and not overtly religious books: *Laozi* (*Lao Tzu*) and *Zhuangzi* (*Chuang Tzu*). Though short, these are two of the greatest and most profound works of world literature.

According to one tradition, the man known as Laozi (from whom the book by the same name derived its title) was an older contemporary of Confucius who served as an archivist at the Zhou capital, and who once allegedly even instructed Confucius himself. Laozi merely means "Old Master," however, and both the identity of the author of the book *Laozi* and its date of composition – which may, or may not, have been as late as the third century BCE – are uncertain. The language of the *Laozi* is simple, poetic, and enigmatic in the extreme.

Zhuangzi (Master Zhuang, whose full name was Zhuang Zhou, ca. 369– ca. 286 BCE), by contrast, is thought to have been a real historical figure. The book that bears his name is a delightful, though often linguistically and conceptually challenging, collection of parables and tall tales. A fine example of Zhuangzi's style is his story concerning Cook Ding. Cook Ding was a master butcher who, in carving, had learned to follow the natural patterns of joints, tendons, and ligaments so that "Flop! The whole thing comes apart like a clod of earth crumbling." After years of practice, he no longer even saw the entire carcass itself but wielded his blade with his spirit. "A good cook changes his knife once a year – because he cuts. A mediocre cook changes his knife once a month – because he hacks. I've had this knife of mine for nineteen years and I've cut up thousands of oxen with it, and yet the blade is as good as though it had just come from the grindstone." Such a cook truly understood the Way.

The Way, or Dao, is obviously the most important central concept in Daoism, but this Dao is inexpressible in words. As the famous opening line of *Laozi* puts it, "The Way that can be spoken of is not the constant Way." The Dao is nonetheless inescapable, pervading and shaping all things. Unlike the Confucian Dao, which was specifically moral and human centered, the Daoist Dao was beyond petty, artificial human considerations. "Heaven and Earth are not humane, regarding all things as straw dogs" (expendable sacrificial tokens), says *Laozi*. In the vastness of nature, humans and human concerns are inconsequential. Daoists, appropriately, were among the first people in the world to develop a fine appreciation of the natural beauty of untamed wilderness.

It was not merely that human morality was artificial: it could even be counterproductive. It is precisely because society honors the worthy that there is competition; it is because gold, jade, and other rare precious goods are treasured that there is theft. "When everyone in the world knows beauty as beauty, ugliness appears. When everyone knows good as good, not-good arrives," cautions *Laozi*. Wisdom, therefore, lies in not pursuing such "goods":

> The sage does not hoard,
> The more he uses on behalf of others,
> The more he has himself.
> And the more he gives to others,
> The more comes back to him.
> The Way of Heaven is to bring benefit and not to harm.
> The Way of the sage is to do things without contending.

Often the best course of action is nonaction (*wuwei*). The Daoists were early advocates of what could be described as laissez-faire policies. In fact, it has seriously been suggested that the French expression *laissez-faire* may have originally been coined in the eighteenth century by certain pioneering French economists (known as the Physiocrats) who admired what they imagined to be the "minimum of government intervention in the Chinese economy."[9] Although Chinese imperial government in practice was actually quite inconsistent on this point, both the Daoist and the Confucian theoretical traditions did tend to consciously advocate an ideal minimalist approach toward rulership. Confucians favored leadership by moral example over regulations and punishments and stereotypically made continual calls for reducing taxes and "giving rest" to the people. Daoists, from their different perspective, believed that active intervention would only make things worse. "The Way is constant: by doing nothing, nothing is left undone. If lords and kings can hold to it, all things will, of themselves, be transformed," advised *Laozi*.

Legalism

A striking contrast to the ideal of minimalist government advocated by both Confucians and Daoists is provided by the third great school of classical Chinese thought: Legalism (*Fajia*). As the name implies, Legalism emphasized techniques of government based on written law – clearly codified and strictly enforced. Legalism was even less of a formal academic philosophical "school" than Confucianism. Although there are a few important Legalist texts, notably *The Book of Lord Shang* (*Shangjun shu*, attributed to Shang Yang, d. 338 BCE) and, most especially, the *Han Feizi* ("Master Han Fei," written by a student of the Confucian Xunzi named Han Fei, d. 233 BCE), Legalism developed less out of teaching and theory than through certain tendencies in administrative practice that emerged over the course of the Warring States period.

Against Confucian morality and idealism, the Legalists are sometimes said to have offered realism. Though the virtuous example of a Sage King may, or may not, impel a few people to correct themselves, as the Confucians hoped, genuine Sage Kings are in practice rare. All people, however, are naturally driven by their pursuit of self-interest, and their behavior can therefore be modified, as desired, by drafting clear laws, backed by the powerful incentives of fixed rewards and punishments.

As *The Book of Lord Shang* explained,

> The way to administer a state well is for the laws regulating officials to be clear; one does not rely on men to be intelligent and thoughtful. The ruler makes the people single-minded so they will not scheme for selfish profit. Then the strength of the state will be consolidated, and a state whose strength has been consolidated is powerful, but a country that loves talking is dismembered.

This single-minded commitment to the state goals of building a "rich country and a strong army," as the slogan had it, helped transform the Qin Kingdom, where Lord Shang served as prime minister in the fourth century BCE, into the most powerful of the Warring States, and eventually enabled it to unite all the other kingdoms into the first Chinese Empire. The ancient Chinese Legalist slogan "rich country, strong army" was also, incidentally, consciously reinvoked in modern Japan to serve as the "formal ideological foundation of industrial and technological development" in the late nineteenth century.[10] In modern China, too, the memory of ancient Legalism was somewhat rehabilitated in the twentieth century, when it came to be viewed as a progressive movement that, more than two thousand years earlier, had already argued against blindly following conservative traditions and had insisted on changing with the times. People had once lived in caves, as the ancient Legalists pointed out, but it would be foolish to continue living in caves now just because that was the ancient way.

The compilation of legal codes in China may have begun as early as the ninth century BCE, and the seminal *Classic of Law* (*Fajing*) was composed in the late fifth century BCE. Legalism became the ideological foundation of the first Chinese Empire, and though explicit Legalism was soon thereafter somewhat discredited because of its alleged harshness and rigidity, the Chinese Empire long remained shaped very much around the idea of government by law. This was so much the case that in the formative stage of early Japanese history, in the eighth century CE, when a new Japanese imperial government was self-consciously establishing itself on what was perceived to be the continental Chinese model, the Japanese took codes of law to be the very essence of that model. Japanese historians today routinely label this period the "Age of Penal and Administrative Law" (*ritsuryō jidai*). In Japan, however, Chinese-style legal codes would soon lapse, to be replaced by more indigenous developments. In premodern China, too, although government by law was never entirely abandoned, over the centuries it was the more humanistic Confucianism, instead, that was increasingly ascendant.

The Art of War

Confucianism, Daoism, and Legalism were the three major schools of thought in late Zhou China, but there were also many other strains of thought. One important early group were the followers of Mozi (fifth century BCE), who advocated universal love, and trained a band of followers in the techniques of defensive warfare to help protect small countries from foreign aggression. No fewer than nine chapters of the book called *Mozi* deal with issues of military defense, including such items as scaling ladders and techniques of siege warfare. Not surprisingly, the aptly named Warring States era produced a number of specialists in military affairs. The first military text, said to be the oldest military treatise in the world, was *Sunzi's Art of War* (*Sunzi bingfa*). This book is still studied today at military academies around the world and has also inspired certain modern politicians and businesspersons. In late imperial times in China, six ancient Zhou Dynasty military treatises were combined with one later text to form what are known as the *Seven Military Classics* (*Wujing qi shu*).[11]

As is true of many early Chinese texts, the date and authorship of the *Sunzi* are hotly debated. Suggested dates range from the late sixth century (when the alleged author, Master Sun, or Sunzi, is supposed to have lived) to the late fourth century BCE. In general, the date of composition of these early texts is a matter of interest only for specialist scholars, but in the case of *Sunzi*, it may make a considerable difference because of the rapidly changing nature of warfare in the late Zhou period.

In early Zhou, armies had typically been small, campaigns brief, and combat focused on chariot-riding aristocrats adhering to chivalric ritual ideals. If the early histories can be believed, fighting with honor was regarded as more important even than winning. As China entered the Warring States era, however, large countries increasingly organized for total war. The right to bear arms, which had once been an aristocratic monopoly and privilege, was now a universal male obligation. Military conscription – a draft army, based on compulsory household registration lists – made possible huge new armies of peasant infantrymen, numbering up to hundreds of thousands of men, armed now with deadly crossbows and sometimes mobilized for quite lengthy wars. No fewer than 590 separate wars, moreover, were recorded during the two and a half centuries of the Warring States period – an average of more than two wars every year. War had become a grim familiarity.

One consequence of the changing nature of war was a much greater ruthlessness. Winning, not honor, was now everything. *Sunzi*, notoriously, declared the military "a way (*dao*) of deception," which would seem to reflect this new Warring States ruthlessness. Surprise is essential: "Attack where he is unprepared. Emerge where he does not expect." At the same time, mask your own dispositions so that to the enemy, it appears that your forces are without form or pattern. At the point of attack, then, apply overwhelming force. The objective is not glory or heroics; it is victory.

An easy victory is better than a bloody one, and a decisive triumph is best achieved by making sure of preconditions before ever striking the first blow. "Therefore, the victorious military is first victorious and after that does battle." Intelligence is critical. For *Sunzi*, a key word was *shi* 勢. Although the standard dictionary definition of *shi* is simply "power" or "force," for *Sunzi*, it meant, more precisely, the latent disposition of potential force, like an avalanche poised to fall or a crossbow cocked and ready to be fired with a slight pull on the trigger. "Thus the *shi* of one skilled at setting people to battle is like rolling round rocks from a mountain," explained *Sunzi*.

The idea is to win with as little fighting and destruction as possible, based on intelligence rather than brute force. If you know yourself and know your enemy, *Sunzi* advises, there will be no danger "in one hundred battles." Such an emphasis on intelligence (if not always on avoiding bloodshed) was also in keeping with the new Warring States approach. The huge new peasant conscript armies required massive and sophisticated logistical support, including the large-scale manufacture of arms and armor and supplies of food and clothing. Training and organization became critical, and the military treatises of the era typically emphasized the importance of discipline and planning. The commander was no longer a chariot-riding aristocrat or a warrior who heroically personally leads the charge into battle but rather a grand strategist operating behind the lines. *Sunzi*, famously, put attacking the enemy's strategies ahead of striking at his cities. Cerebral warfare took precedence over physical combat.

Sunzi suggested the intriguing ideal of possibly even winning a war without the need for any actual fighting. This is sometimes said to represent a uniquely Chinese approach to warfare, and Chinese civilization is also sometimes described as particularly unmilitaristic. It is in fact true that under the later empire, a military career was not nearly as honored as a literary one, and that even in military affairs, brains were typically valued over brawn. One of the more notable contrasts that can be drawn between the Chinese Confucian ethos and the familiar Western (and Japanese) traditions may indeed be a consistent tendency to prefer the civilian and literary (*wen*) over the martial (*wu*). According to the *Analects*, when asked about tactics, "Confucius replied, 'I have heard about sacrificial vessels but have learned nothing about the deployment of troops.' The next day he made his departure." But Confucianism was never the only strand of thought in China. One modern scholar who has carefully studied the *Seven Military Classics* and their application in late imperial warfare concludes that the central paradigm of Chinese strategic culture was actually not so very different from the Western realist's epigram: "If you want peace, prepare for war."[12] Certainly there have been many wars throughout China's long history. The first imperial unification of China, in particular, was forged in bloody war.

First Empire

"The Faults of Qin" (221–207 BCE)

The ancient Greek world of multiple small city-states was transformed into the Hellenistic age of large autocratic empires by the conquests of Alexander the Great (356–323 BCE). Roughly a century later, in eastern Eurasia, China went through a similar process. In China's case, the many small, semi-independent domains that had made up the early Zhou realm had already long since been consolidated into a handful of relatively large territorial kingdoms. These kingdoms were all unified into a single empire for the first time in 221 BCE.

The man who would become the first emperor of China, Ying Zheng (260–210 BCE), was thirty-nine years old, by Chinese reckoning, when he unified what seemed to be the entire civilized world – a triumph so complete that he boasted, "Wherever there are traces of people, there are none who are not my subjects."[13] Despite such obvious exaggeration, and continued use of the ancient expression "[All] Under Heaven" (*Tianxia*) as a designation for the realm, it was approximately what we think of today as China that was now, for the first time, seriously unified into a single country. As natural as this unification may seem to us now, it was probably not altogether inevitable. The early Zhou had established an ideal of a universal Son of Heaven, under Heaven's universal moral order, but had not attempted a single central government. The classical world of the ancient Chinese philosophers had been one of multiple independent countries and considerable local diversity. Even a century after the first unification in 221 BCE, there were

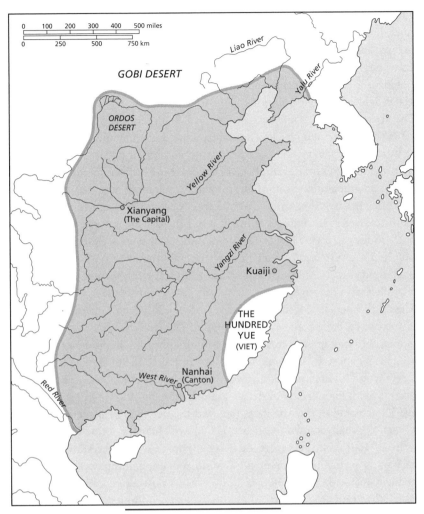

Map 4. The Qin Empire, ca. 210 BCE

still several different languages spoken within the empire, descended from the languages of the former Warring States.

Ironically, the kingdom that conquered all the others and founded the first version of the Chinese Empire, Qin, had begun as only a peripheral, semi-Chinese, frontier state on the edges of the Chinese world. The Qin state was officially founded (after having been a minor Zhou vassal for some time) in 770 BCE in that same region "Within the Passes" that had been the original Zhou heartland. Among the earliest distinctively Qin-style archeological artifacts, which were at first confined to an area west of the region "Within the Passes," there is clear evidence of a blending of Zhou-style Chinese and Rong- and Qiang-style non-Chinese influences.

Until the Warring States period, Qin remained less developed than the other states on the Central Plain to its east. The Qin location on the northwestern frontier of the Zhou world may have encouraged warlike inclinations, however, and its relatively weak commitment to traditional Confucian values may have also made it more open to experimentation with the radical new ideas of Legalism. Qin may therefore represent an early example of what is sometimes today called the "advantages of backwardness." Qin was in a position to make a selective borrowing of useful ideas from the more advanced kingdoms in the east without being burdened by the weight of all their traditions.

The arrival in Qin, from the east, of Lord Shang in 361 BCE marks a turning point in the history of both Qin and China. One of the notable features of the Qin state was a remarkable degree of openness to immigrant talent. A scurrilous (and probably untrue) rumor even alleged that the First Emperor himself, a century later, was the illegitimate son of an immigrant merchant who had become chancellor. After his arrival in Qin, Lord Shang was given a chance to experiment with Legalist reforms in the Qin government. Over the course of the next decade, Lord Shang promulgated new law codes, unified the systems of weights and measures, established a centralized bureaucratic system of administration, and created new nonhereditary titles. Although Lord Shang himself was executed in 338 because of a conflict with the royal family, he set the Qin war machine in motion.

A century later, in 247 BCE, the man who would become the first emperor of China assumed the throne as the last king of Qin. Surviving several assassination attempts, this king grew increasingly fearful of appearing in public or even of disclosing his location. In 221 BCE, his armies conquered the final remaining Warring State (Qi), and his first recorded act following this unprecedented achievement was to consult with his officials to devise a more majestic title for himself than mere "king." The result of their deliberations was the new title *huangdi*, or "emperor." This man is usually known to history as Qin Shi Huangdi, a title (after ascending the throne, East Asian emperors are never supposed to be referred to by their personal names – while they remain alive, a range of euphemisms are employed, and after their death, they are referred to by various posthumous titles) that literally means "First Emperor of Qin." The title *huangdi* continued to be used in China until 1912, and it inspired related imperial terminology in Japan and Vietnam as well (while in premodern Korea, the humbler and older title "king" continued in use).

The First Emperor of Qin famously standardized the writing systems, legal codes, coins, and weights and measures of all the conquered kingdoms in an effort to promote a single unified imperial culture. He erected fortifications across the northern borders, which are popularly thought of as the first version of the Great Wall of China; established forty-four new administrative units north of the Ordos desert; and relocated hundreds of thousands of people from the interior to settle the northern frontier. The First Emperor's southern conquests, which extended into what is now northern Vietnam, also brought much of what is now southeast China into the Chinese world for the first time. Altogether, according to one estimate, no fewer than 3.17 million people were relocated to both the northern and southern frontiers by the First Emperor, in the process helping to dissolve old local identities and establish new empirewide allegiances.[14]

Traditional Chinese histories portray the Qin regime as incredibly systematic and intrusive, and skeptical modern scholars have sometimes been inclined to doubt that any premodern government could have ever really exercised that degree of effective control over such a large area. In 1975, however, archeologists discovered roughly a thousand strips of wood – the principal writing material in China before the invention of paper – containing Qin era documents at a place called Yunmeng, in central China. These and other discoveries have tended to reconfirm the traditional picture of relatively efficient Legalist bureaucratic machinery. At the same time, if the Qin "reputation for Draconian punishments is not exactly controverted" by these new discoveries, "neither is it strikingly confirmed."[15] Revisionists now argue that the Qin government may not have been quite as tyrannical as later Chinese Confucians traditionally remembered it. These archeologically rediscovered Qin texts also reveal a greater diversity of thought, and evidence of a less docile subject population, than might have previously been imagined.

The First Emperor justified his conquests in the name of providing peace and uniform justice to the people, after a long period of incessant warfare. Two thousand years before Thomas Hobbes was born, a book compiled at the Qin court around 239 BCE already prefigured Hobbes's famous notion that it may be necessary for people to submit to the authority of a powerful state in the sheer interest of self-preservation: "there is no greater disorder than the absence of a Son of Heaven. Without a Son of Heaven the strong subdue the weak, the many abuse the few, and mutual destruction through the deployment of troops cannot cease." As the First Emperor himself put it, "that the whole world is tormented by warfare without cease is because there are Lords and Princes."[16]

The First Emperor initially made a display of promoting traditional values by appointing seventy scholars as advisors to the throne. Continued dissent, especially criticism of the new Qin regime by comparing it unfavorably to the idealized memory of antiquity, proved intolerable, however. In 213 BCE, the First Emperor notoriously ordered the burning of all books, except for histories of the Qin state and a few useful technical treatises. In 212 BCE, he reportedly went further and ordered the execution, for subversion, of 460 scholars. In Confucian memory, these two horrifying acts became indelible emblems of Qin tyranny.

The First Emperor was also deeply interested in arcane techniques for prolonging life and may have even envisioned himself as a god figure (*di*), wielding cosmic power to align the universe.[17] Perhaps the ultimate example of his self-aggrandizement may be the enormous tomb that he had constructed for himself. The tomb, which is twenty miles in circumference, contains, as just one small part, an entire terra-cotta army consisting of thousands of life-sized clay soldiers, which was buried and only recently rediscovered by accident. Thus, though the First Emperor's reputation may have been darkened by Confucian biases under subsequent dynasties, the staggering scale of his ambition was real enough.

According to traditional histories, the very harshness and inflexibility of the Qin Legalist regulations soon provoked revolt. Within a year of the First Emperor's death in 210 BCE, the land was writhing with rebellion. At the same time, a power struggle at court was simultaneously also tearing it apart from within. It is said that when Qin Shi Huangdi died, a certain eunuch (eunuchs were castrated imperial household servants) conspired to briefly keep news of the emperor's death secret and forged an edict ordering the emperor's capable eldest son to commit suicide. The throne therefore passed to an incompetent younger son, who was soon reduced to a puppet. With the eunuch's encouragement, this Second Emperor began to suspect other members of his own family and ordered twelve of his own brothers and ten of his sisters executed. After three years, the Second Emperor's position had become so pathetic that he killed himself. By this time, rebels were already at the gates.

The Qin fell in 207 BCE, after only fifteen years as an imperial dynasty. The reasons for Qin's meteoric rise and fall were eloquently summarized by a man born just nine years after the First Emperor's death, Jia Yi (201–169 BCE), in a classic essay titled "The Faults of Qin." Jia Yi wrote that Qin had succeeded in "rolling up the empire like a mat, enveloping the entire universe, pocketing all within the Four Seas, and swallowing up everything in all Eight Directions." Yet Qin was then brought down abruptly by some rustic rebels. "Why? Because the ruler lacked humaneness and rightness; because preserving power differs fundamentally from seizing power."[18] The Qin suppression of dissent only compounded these errors by making it impossible for wise men to show their true loyalty by warning of the impending dangers.

Despite being a perceptive critic of the Qin Dynasty, Jia Yi ascribed the dynasty's fall to its abuses and excesses and the incompetence of the First Emperor's successors rather than to the imperial system itself. After a relatively brief civil war, a new imperial dynasty was established on the ruins of the Qin. Explicit Legalism may have been discredited by the Qin failure, but the imperial system was not, and in a more moderate form, the Qin institutional model (and the imperial title *huangdi*) would survive for two thousand years, until 1912. The Qin model of China as a single, unified country survives still today, and appropriately enough, it is likely that our English word *China* derives (through Sanskrit) from the name Qin.

The Han Empire (202 BCE–220 CE)

The Qin Dynasty had unified the Warring States but only lasted fifteen years. At the time Qin fell, therefore, for many people, the old independent kingdoms were still a living memory, and a return to some version of the old Warring States multinational order might have been a not unreasonable expectation. Despite the fleeting revival of some of those kingdoms as participants in the anti-Qin rebellion, however, it was the unified imperial model that was soon restored instead.

In the long run, the most important rebel leader proved to be a man named Liu Bang (d. 195 BCE). Liu was a man of humble birth – he began his career by passing a test and becoming a local Qin Dynasty police chief – but by 207 BCE, a rebel army under his command had penetrated the region "Within the Passes" and captured the Qin capital, putting an end to the Qin Dynasty. There had been a prior agreement among the rebel leaders that whoever took the region "Within the

Figure 2.1. A bronze model horse and carriage, with driver and attendant, from the Eastern Han Dynasty (second century CE). Excavated in 1969 at Wuwei, Gansu. Gansu Provincial Museum, Lanzhou, China. Erich Lessing/Art Resource, New York.

Passes" first would become its next king, but Liu Bang nonetheless sealed up the Qin treasuries and awaited the arrival of the supreme rebel coalition commander.

In the aftermath, Liu Bang was not after all awarded the historically and strategically significant region "Within the Passes" but was instead made king of Han in the Han River valley area somewhat farther south. An enduring consequence of this assignment was that Han would become not only the name of the imperial dynasty Liu Bang soon founded but, by extension from that, eventually also the standard name for all ethnic Chinese people. Today the Han people are the Chinese people.

When the king of Chu was treacherously assassinated by another commander in 206 BCE, that act gave Liu Bang a pretext to reopen the civil war. Liu's first move was to strike north and retake the region "Within the Passes." This put Liu Bang in possession of the very same base area from which both the Zhou and the Qin had previously conquered China. After several more years of seesaw conflict, by 202 BCE, Liu Bang had defeated all his rivals and made himself the founding emperor of a new dynasty, the Han. By this time, however, the land had reportedly been so devastated by years of civil war that the new emperor was unable even to assemble a team of four horses of matching color for his own carriage. (For a bronze model of a carriage from the late Han Dynasty, see Figure 2.1.)

As emperor, Liu Bang is known to history by his posthumous temple name Han Gaozu (the "High Ancestor of the Han"). Emperor Gaozu rewarded his leading lieutenants and relatives with appointments as kings (or princes) over what were initially semiautonomous principalities. Such refeudalization may have been necessary at first, but subsequent Han emperors quickly reversed the policy. Within about a half-century, semi-independent principalities had effectively been eliminated, and Qin-style centralized administration had been restored throughout the empire.

Once Han Gaozu (the former Liu Bang) achieved control of the Central Plain, he then led a huge military force, reportedly consisting of 320,000 infantrymen, against the nomadic tribes to the north. The Qin Dynasty had done much the same thing a decade or two earlier, but this time Han Gaozu encountered a rude surprise: organized opposition. The nomadic tribes to the north of China had unified into their first imperial confederation, the Xiongnu.

Despite the apparent clarity provided by the line of the Great Wall, China's northern frontier is actually more of an uneven transitional zone from Chinese-style farming to ranching and, eventually, true steppe nomadism. The Great Wall may have originally even been constructed more as a projection of Chinese imperial power onto the nomads than to keep the nomads out. In fact, the Qin walls brought some of the best Xiongnu archaeological sites inside the Qin Empire. Although the region is generally called Mongolia today, the word *Mongol* did not yet exist in Qin and Han times. Chinese sources themselves commonly make an important distinction between regions north and south of the Gobi Desert, roughly corresponding to modern Outer and Inner Mongolia. Areas south of the Gobi have frequently been included inside Chinese imperial borders, even though much of the terrain is better suited to grazing than to farming.

The rise of the first nomadic imperial confederation to the north of China may actually have been a direct military response to the challenge posed by the creation of the first Chinese empire – a new form of political organization capable of mobilizing the military potential of the scattered steppe tribes. The Xiongnu were not a homogeneous people but a confederation of tribes, including different ethnic and linguistic groups. The Xiongnu language, if there was one, remains a mystery.

This should not be surprising. Most steppe nomadic empires were actually just such mixtures. A Roman visitor to the camp of Attila the Hun (ca. 406–453 CE) in western Eurasia, for example, reported that the Huns were a mixed group, speaking the Hunnic, Gothic, and Latin languages. Attila's own name was actually Gothic. There has been a persistent theory that these Huns who so famously terrorized the Roman Empire may have been a splinter group of the very same Xiongnu who had earlier confronted Han Dynasty China and who had migrated westward. Since both the Xiongnu and the Huns are known to have been internally mixed groupings, however, such speculation may ultimately be rather meaningless. Nonetheless, the steppe grasslands, which stretch from north of Beijing to the Hungarian Plain in Europe, did form a single reasonably coherent cultural zone.

The early Han Dynasty, like the Qin before it, had a conscript or draft army. All adult males were required to perform two years of military service – typically one year of training and one year of active duty. This enabled the Han Dynasty to muster a truly enormous army, but also one that essentially consisted of amateur peasant infantry. Han Gaozu's forces on this occasion, as they marched north, to their surprise found themselves no match for Xiongnu mounted archers, who were accustomed to life in the saddle as warriors. The first Han emperor, Gaozu, was surrounded and trapped on a mountaintop near modern Datong, just east of the northernmost bend of the Yellow River, for a whole week in 200 BCE.

Humbled by this first encounter with Xiongnu nomadic military power, for the next half century, the Han Dynasty pursued policies of peace with the Xiongnu, appeasing them with lavish gifts and sending Han imperial daughters to become brides for Xiongnu chieftains. This appeasement policy ended only after Wudi (Emperor Wu, the "Martial Emperor") took the throne in 141 BCE as the sixth Han emperor. Wudi would rule for fifty-four years (141–87 BCE), longer than any emperor of China prior to the eighteenth century, and his reign would be marked by both great success and controversy.

Soon after taking the throne, Wudi held formal court debates over the wisdom of the appeasement policy toward the Xiongnu. Appeasement was now rejected, if only because it had not actually prevented continued Xiongnu raiding. Moreover, the Han Dynasty had by this time developed the military resources to successfully confront the Xiongnu. At the start of the dynasty, the Han army had been conspicuously lacking in cavalry, but by the time Wudi assumed the throne, several horse-breeding stations had been established, and the Han army now had access to some three hundred thousand horses. Infantry equipped with crossbows fitted with precision triggers and fired from wagon trains had also proved effective against nomadic warriors. Even so, however, the Han still faced enormous logistical difficulties in trying to mount sustained warfare on the vast open reaches of the steppe, where the nomads could always simply pull back their tents and wait until supplies ran out for the Chinese armies.

Wudi therefore developed a new grand strategy for outflanking the Xiongnu. To the northeast, this involved the conquest and incorporation into the Han Empire of southern Manchuria and northern Korea. In the northwest, Emperor Wu began by dispatching an embassy, with a Xiongnu defector as a guide, to seek allies in the western regions. Some members of this party may have penetrated as far west as Persia, but they were twice captured by the Xiongnu, and of a hundred men, only two finally managed to return to China thirteen years later. Although this embassy forged no military alliances, it gained strategically valuable information and established more formal diplomatic and commercial exchanges with the western regions. Over the next several decades, Han military campaigns brought what are now Gansu and Xinjiang (Eastern Turkestan) provinces into the empire as part of the western extension of the Han imperial offensive against the Xiongnu. On one occasion, crossing the Pamir Mountains into Central Asia in 101 BCE, Han armies even captured the area of Samarkand, in what is now Uzbekistan.

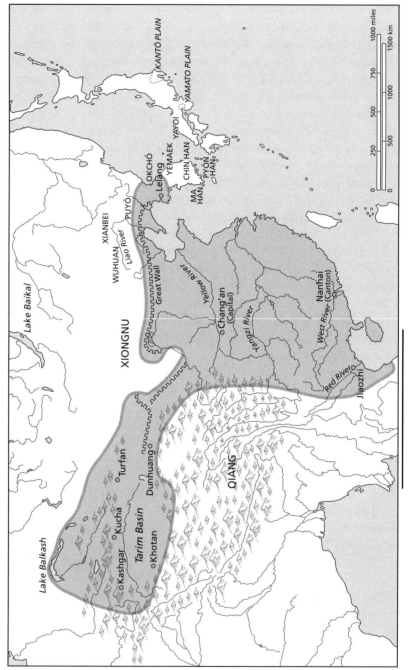

Map 5. The Han Dynasty under Emperor Wu (r. 141–87 BCE)

The Han established a chain of garrisons and fortifications in the northwest, which disrupted the oasis sources of tribute for the Xiongnu and led ultimately to the disintegration of the Xiongnu Empire (by about 73 BCE). The financial cost of this strategy also almost bankrupted the Han Dynasty, however. One recent estimate puts the total expense of Han Wudi's military operations in the northwest at 1.89 trillion cash over forty years.[19] Although the expansion of the Han Empire to the northwest helped promote what later came to be called the silk roads, across which camel caravans brought grapes from Persia and glass from the Mediterranean in exchange for Chinese silk, Emperor Wu's aggressive military campaigns put a severe strain on the Han economy. It also prompted intrusive new state economic interventions, including such measures as taxes on merchant inventories and government monopolies on mines and the manufacture and distribution of iron, salt, alcohol, and coins. A fascinating record of a court debate in 81 BCE over the wisdom of continuing these economic policies survives, known as the *Discourses on Salt and Iron.*

Despite Han Wudi's economic interventionism and aggressive military expansionism, which might seem reminiscent of Qin Dynasty Legalism, Wudi was also ironically the emperor who first established Confucianism as imperial orthodoxy. The original Han founders had been rough military men. One famous story tells of a scholar presenting the first Han emperor with copies of the classics. Patting his mount, the emperor said that he had won his empire from horseback and had no need for books. The scholar's swift reply was, You may have conquered the empire on horseback, but can you rule it that way? With Legalism discredited by the fall of Qin, the Han Dynasty needed a new theoretical basis for its legitimization. Although Wudi himself was not exactly a Confucian, he found his source of imperial justification in that school.

The Confucian canon was first officially defined by Han Wudi in 136 BCE, when he assigned a master to teach each of the Five Classics.[20] In 124 BCE, Wudi also established an imperial academy for the study of the classics. This academy initially had only a few students, but by the end of the Han Dynasty, there were reportedly thirty thousand students in 1,850 rooms. Systems of testing, and regional recommendations of students, began to be elaborated. Local officials were encouraged to recommend men with a reputation for Confucian virtue for government office. The expectation was increasingly planted, over the centuries of the Han Dynasty, that officials should be scholarly gentlemen. Ambitious families encouraged their children to study for the purpose of career advancement. Over time, schools began to be promoted even in rural communities. In late Han times, tablets were placed marking the doors of villagers who conspicuously exhibited Confucian virtues, and Confucian expectations even came to be enforced by law. For example, in the last century BCE, people who were in mourning for deceased parents, or whose parents were aged, were exempted from compulsory labor service. In 116 CE, high officials were required to observe three years of mourning following the death of their fathers. A final consummation of Confucianism as Han Dynasty imperial orthodoxy was achieved in 175 CE, when it was decreed that correct texts of the Five Classics literally be carved on stone outside the imperial academy.

Han Dynasty Confucianism was rooted in the meticulous study of the classics. There were, however, certain aspects of Confucian thought peculiar to the Han Dynasty that are best exemplified by a man named Dong Zhongshu (179–104 BCE). Central to Dong's interpretation of Confucianism was the idea that "Heaven and man are mutually connected." The special function of the ruler, therefore, is to harmonize relations between Heaven, earth, and man. It was believed that humane behavior could reverberate sympathetically throughout the natural order so that if only the monarch corrected his own heart, even the seasons might follow in proper order. This created an ideology that legitimized the Han Empire by linking it to the very cosmological structure of the universe, yet simultaneously also restricted autocratic conduct with threats of dire supernatural sanctions.

The dynastic *History of the Former Han*, for example, tells the story of one high government official who rode past a brawl without intervening but stopped to inquire about the panting of an ox. The official explained his seemingly bizarre behavior by saying that brawls were routine minor affairs that should be handled by subordinates, but an ox panting due to unseasonable heat was the responsibility of top officials, who "are charged with the task of harmonizing the yin and yang."[21] Thus Confucianism promoted a kind of autocratic imperial minimalism.

The Han Dynasty lasted for some four hundred years (interrupted briefly by the usurpation of Wang Mang in 9–23 CE), and its legacy remains so important that the Chinese are still today called the Han people. Nonetheless, the Han eventually fell. One growing problem was economic polarization. By the late Warring States period, the practice of private ownership of land had already been well established, but the Warring States and early imperial governments were founded on a tax and conscript base that consisted of many roughly equal small farmers. Over the course of the Han Dynasty, however, some wealthy families were able to acquire large estates. In the process, many smallholders were dispossessed and often reduced to tenants, servants, or even vagrants and bandits. This in turn reduced the central government's tax base and put an even heavier burden on the dwindling number of small farmers remaining on the tax rolls.

Court politics generated other problems, especially the allegedly undue influence exercised by eunuchs and the families of imperial consorts. Dissident critics of eunuch power were punished in a series of purges, stretching over some two decades beginning in 166 CE. During these purges, more that a hundred distinguished gentlemen died in prison, and some six or seven hundred others were banned from office for life. Paradoxically, this gave the pose of lofty withdrawal and disengagement from government a degree of fashionable moral cachet.

In 184 CE, a religiously inspired rebellion, known as the revolt of the Yellow Turbans, erupted. Although the Yellow Turbans themselves were soon suppressed, in the process, power passed into the hands of independent military commanders. In 191, one of these generals carried away the heir to the throne and destroyed the late Han capital (Luoyang), looting and burning, among other things, the great imperial libraries. "The fine silks of charts and books were used by military men as curtains and sacks."[22] As warlord armies tramped across China, "beside their horses they hang the heads of men; behind their horses they carry the [captive] women."[23] The lady poet who wrote these last lines was herself captured and lived with a Xiongnu prince for twelve years before being ransomed. After her ransom, she reported that the private library of four thousand rolls of books that her father had left her was all lost.

The *Romance of the Three Kingdoms* (220–280 CE)

By the year 196, there were thirteen major independent warlord regimes within the ruins of the Han Empire. Reportedly, some of their armies lacked plans even to see themselves through the year, plundering when they were hungry and throwing away the leftovers when they were full. One warlord, however, Cao Cao (155–220), whose father had been an adopted son of the Han Dynasty chief eunuch, gained custody over the person of the puppet Han emperor and leveraged this control over the emperor into domination of all north China. By 207, he may have controlled half the total population of China. It was not until after Cao Cao's own death in 220 that Cao's son finally had the audacity to formally depose the last Han monarch and proclaim himself the founding emperor of a new imperial dynasty, called the Wei (or Cao-Wei, to distinguish it from various other states called Wei).[24]

Before long, the situation stabilized somewhat, as the various warlord enclaves resolved themselves into three relatively substantial empires, popularly known as the Three Kingdoms. Cao Cao's family ruled the Wei Dynasty in the north (220–265); another empire called Wu (222–280) was established in the southeast, in the lower Yangzi River region, with its capital at Nanjing (Nanking); and a third dynasty called Shu-Han (221–263) was formed in the southwest, in the area of modern Sichuan. The name Shu-Han is obviously a compound. Shu was an old place name for the area, and Han referred to the Han Dynasty, since the Shu-Han emperors claimed special legitimacy through descent from the old Han imperial family.

The Three Kingdoms era has been richly immortalized in Chinese fiction (and more recently in movies and video games) as the great age of Chinese military strategy and heroic warfare. One of the most beloved and widely read premodern Chinese novels was called the *Romance of the Three Kingdoms* (*Sanguo zhi tongsu yanyi*). Although it was not written until much later – the earliest surviving edition of the novel dates from 1522 – the book is a fictionalized retelling of the history of this period, with Cao Cao cast in the role of leading villain. The clever stratagems, battles, and dramatic political rivalries of the era have been much glorified on stage and in fiction. Although this warfare is what has captured the popular imagination, the Three Kingdoms period was also an age of notable awakening in thought and literature, of individualism, and of some remarkably colorful eccentrics.

The fall of the Han Dynasty brought down with it much of the ideological underpinnings of Han Confucianism. Seemingly arid classical chapter and verse scholarship became less fashionable now than elegant discussions of lofty meta-physical principles, known as Mysterious Learning (*Xuanxue*), often especially involving references to the *Laozi*, *Zhuangzi*, and the *Book of Changes*. Such profound questions as what existed before the universe began or what lies beyond the borders of heaven and earth were asked, and answered, *Laozi* fashion, paradoxically, with, "nothing." Nothing, therefore, it came to be argued, was the origin of all things.

A vogue emerged for retreat into libertinism, hedonism, wine, and drugs, sometimes with the cynical observation that both the Sage and the Tyrant "wind up equally dead" anyway. One amusing character was said to go out riding in a wheelbarrow with a jug of wine in his hand, and a servant following with a shovel, instructed to bury him wherever he died. For some of the more memorable figures of this era, however – such as Ruan Ji (210–263), one of the celebrated "Seven Sages of the Bamboo Grove" – the pose of habitual drunkenness and remote philosophical abstraction was chiefly a vehicle for escape from murderous political intrigue, and the deliberate flouting of the staid conventions of Confucian decorum (*li*) was in the name of a more sincere morality. In the late Han Dynasty, the need to win a local reputation for Confucian virtue in order to be recommended for office had created a powerful incentive for hypocritical pretense, and such third-century figures as Ruan Ji represent an appealing counterreaction to hypocrisy.

In 265, the Three Kingdoms Wei throne was usurped by one of its own generals, who founded a new dynasty called the Western Jin (265–316). In 280, the Western Jin then successfully completed the unification of the other Three Kingdoms, with the final subjugation of Wu in the southeast. The Chinese empire was thus reunified, but this reunification proved to be ephemeral, effectively lasting little more than a decade before it began to fragment again. Drawing a lesson from the ease with which he himself had seized the throne through a palace coup, the first Western Jin emperor tried to strengthen the position of his family by appointing twenty-seven (eventually fifty) of his close relatives as princes. Rather than solidifying the dynasty, however, this instead created the conditions for a vicious power struggle within the imperial family itself, after the founding Western Jin emperor died in 290. Imperial power soon tore itself apart completely in the resulting Disturbances of the Eight Princes.

These warring princes typically relied on cavalry forces drawn from semi-nomadic tribal auxiliaries. Over the course of the Han Dynasty, the practice of military conscription had lapsed, and the draft-based citizen army was replaced by more professional forces, many of whom were ethnic minorities. Much of the burden of northern frontier defense, meanwhile, had also been assumed by nomadic allies, who had settled within the borders of the Han Empire in a belt stretching from Manchuria in the east to the northern loop of the Yellow River in the west. Now, as Chinese imperial government imploded amid protracted and devastatingly self-destructive civil wars, non-Chinese warriors often found themselves in control of the battlefields. In 304, one Xiongnu chieftain proclaimed himself ruler of an independent state in north China. In 311, the Western Jin capital at Luoyang fell, and in 316, the alternate Western Jin imperial capital at Chang'an (modern Xi'an) was also captured. By this time, as a contemporary lamented, "marauding nomads watered their horses in the Yangzi."[25]

Far to the west, dramatic parallel events were also occurring. In 376, bands of Goths, fleeing the depredations of the Huns, crossed the Danube and delivered the first of several military shocks that eventually brought down the western Roman Empire. In China's case, although there were no literal invasions from beyond the borders, there were certainly similar roaming bands of "barbarian" warriors. Chinese imperial unity was shattered. Between the third century and the seventh, there would be thirty-seven historically recognized dynasties in China, twenty-two of which, moreover, had identifiably non-Chinese rulers. The greatest Age of Division in two thousand years of Chinese imperial history had begun.

For Further Reading

Comprehensive coverage of China's formative age is provided by Michael Loewe and Edward L. Shaughnessy, eds., *The Cambridge History of Ancient China: From the Origins of Civilization to 221 B.C.* (Cambridge University Press, 1999). On the Zhou Dynasty, see Cho-yun Hsu (Zhuoyun Xu), *Ancient China in Transition: An Analysis of Social Mobility, 722–222 B.C.* (Stanford University Press, [1965] 1977); and Cho-yun Hsu and Katheryn M. Linduff, *Western Chou Civilization* (New Haven, CT: Yale University Press, 1988).

An important study of the classic textual canon that became so central to Chinese and East Asian civilization is Mark Edward Lewis, *Writing and Authority in Early China* (Albany: State University of New York Press, 1999). On the Chinese classics, see also Burton Watson, *Early Chinese Literature* (New York: Columbia University Press, 1962). For the military treatises, see Ralph D. Sawyer and Mei-chün Sawyer, trans., *The Seven Military Classics of Ancient China* (New York: Basic Books, [1993] 2007).

On classical Chinese thought, see A. C. Graham, *Disputers of the Tao: Philosophical Argument in Ancient China* (La Salle, IL: Open Court, 1989), and Benjamin I. Schwartz, *The World of Thought in Ancient China* (Cambridge, MA: Harvard University Press, 1985). A somewhat dated but still valuable comprehensive survey is Yu-lan Fung, *A Short History of Chinese Philosophy*, ed. Derk Bodde (New York: Free Press, 1948).

For the early imperial Qin and Han dynasties, see Denis Twitchett and Michael Loewe, eds., *The Cambridge History of China*, vol. 1. *The Ch'in and Han Empires, 221 B.C.–A.D. 220* (Cambridge University Press, 1986). See also Chun-shu Chang, *The Rise of the Chinese Empire*, 2 vols. (Ann Arbor: University of Michigan Press, 2007); Mark Edward Lewis, *The Early Chinese Empires: Qin and Han* (Cambridge, MA: Harvard University Press, 2007); and Michael Loewe, *Everyday Life in Early Imperial China during the Han Period 202 B.C.–A.D. 220* (Indianapolis, IN: Hackett, [1968] 2005). Early imperial relations with the steppe world are expertly explored in Nicola Di Cosmo, *Ancient China and Its Enemies: The Rise of Nomadic Power in East Asian History* (Cambridge University Press, 2002).

On the Three Kingdoms period, see Rafe de Crespigny, *Generals of the South: The Foundation and Early History of the Three Kingdoms State of Wu*, Faculty of Asian Studies Monograph 16 (Canberra: Australian National University, 1990); Howard L. Goodman, *Ts'ao P'i Transcendent: The Political Culture of Dynasty-Founding in China at the End of the Han* (Seattle: Scripta Serica, 1998); and – concerning Ruan Ji and the "Seven Sages of the Bamboo Grove" – Donald Holzman, *Poetry and Politics: The Life and Works of Juan Chi, A.D. 210–263* (Cambridge University Press, 1976).

3 The Age of Cosmopolitanism

The Five Hu and Sixteen Kingdoms (North China, 304–439 CE)

In the early fourth century, centralized imperial government disintegrated almost completely in north China. For over a hundred years, the ancient Chinese cultural heartland in the north was shredded among what are conventionally known as the Sixteen Kingdoms.[1] More precisely, historians actually recognize twenty-one distinct dynasties in north China between the years 304 and 439 (not to mention other independent, small, local communities that never aspired to become full-blown empires). Despite the conventional English label "Sixteen Kingdoms," moreover, these dynasties were also usually really still empires in the sense of being relatively large, multiethnic, military-conquest regimes ruled by men claiming the Chinese title "emperor" (*huangdi*). Unlike previous Chinese dynasties, however, these were now typically organized around identifiably non-Chinese tribal armies. They were also, obviously, all quite ephemeral. Except for one minor Chinese-ruled regime in the far northwest that lasted sixty-three years, none survived longer than half a century.

As north China plunged into chaos during the fourth century, perhaps an eighth of the entire northern Chinese population may have fled to the relative shelter and stability of the south. Many of these refugees settled in the general region of the lower Yangzi River valley, where members of the Western Jin imperial family reestablished a court in exile, known to history as the Eastern Jin Dynasty (317–420). The Eastern Jin capital was the city that is today called Nanjing (in English, Nanking). This became the nucleus for a series of five (Eastern Jin, Song, Qi, Liang, and Chen) culturally and economically flourishing, but politically and militarily weak, Southern dynasties. Including the earlier third-century southern state of Three Kingdoms Wu, these Southern dynasties are sometimes also alternatively referred to as the Six Dynasties. Those people who remained in the north, and who survived, meanwhile huddled behind thousands of improvised local fortifications.

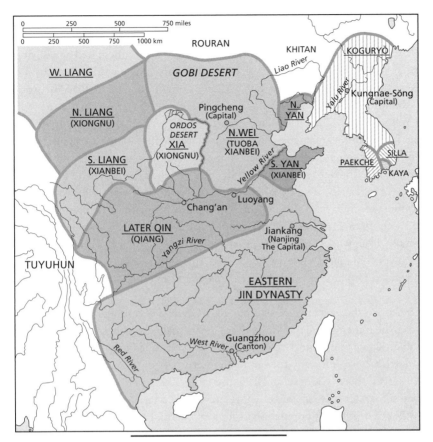

Map 6. States and Peoples in 410 CE

Trade and commerce ground to a virtual halt in the north during this period. No new coins were issued in north China for almost two hundred years. Much farmland was given over to pasture (or stood vacant), and a ranching or herding economy spread deeply into north China. The raising of livestock was a fundamental part of the lifestyle of the non-Chinese peoples, collectively known as the Five Hu, who now came to dominate the northern landscape politically and militarily.[2] Some scholars believe there may have even been millions of these non-Chinese Hu in fourth-century north China.

The Hu were typically ranchers (though not necessarily actual nomads) rather than Chinese-style farmers, and they consumed much animal flesh, such as mutton, as well as quantities of the dairy products that Chinese cuisine has otherwise traditionally abhorred. They spoke languages that were not merely different from but completely unrelated to Chinese. Most of their languages were probably affiliated with either Turkic or Mongolic, but it has been speculated that one group may have even originally been speakers of an Indo-European language. At least some of these people were, furthermore, said to have a distinctive physical appearance, featuring deep-set eyes, high (i.e., protuberant) noses, and full beards. There are even a few scattered references in surviving Chinese sources to "yellow" hair or beards. Most critically, they were also still conscious of having identities that were different from the people who were already beginning to be called Han Chinese.

Nevertheless, there is also no clear evidence that any of them had actually come from anywhere outside of the modern borders of China anytime recently. There were no actual "barbarian invasions." Many Xiongnu (one of the Five Hu groups), for example, had long been living in the vicinity of the great northward loop of the Yellow River. The particular group who are suspected of possibly originally being Indo-European language speakers, wherever their ultimate origins may have been, had for some time made their home in central Shanxi Province, well inside China proper and very near what might even be called the heartland of traditional Chinese civilization. The tribal cluster that is said to have arrived from farthest away most recently (and also the one that became historically the most important), the Tuoba branch of the Xianbei people, according to their own legends, came originally from what is today northeastern Inner Mongolia, inside today's People's Republic of China. By the fourth century, moreover, even these Tuoba Xianbei had resided for some time in the area adjacent to the northern loop of the Yellow River.

To explain the existence of so many non-Chinese peoples deep inside China, it needs to be remembered that throughout the formative ancient Zhou Dynasty, various identifiably non-Chinese communities had continued to live scattered throughout north China. Virtually the entire southern part of China proper, meanwhile, had scarcely been Chinese at all in the early Zhou period. The Qin and Han empires, then, greatly expanded Chinese-controlled territory, in the process bringing still other different population groups inside the empire. In addition, the Han Dynasty also consciously allowed certain nomadic groups to settle along its northern borders, forming a kind of defensive buffer zone. The Qin and Han dynasties were both therefore significantly multicultural and multiethnic empires, albeit with a single overarching written language and a relatively uniform elite culture. The non-Chinese groups who appeared so suddenly on the historical scene in the fourth century had therefore, in reality, already long been there. Many of them, furthermore, were at least nominally Chinese imperial subjects. Many had learned to speak the Chinese language, and their elites not infrequently had some acquaintance with the Chinese classics.

The collapse of imperial government in north China in the early 300s provided unprecedented opportunity for warriors to display their military prowess. Since the Five Hu peoples were typically ranchers, they were naturally splendid horsemen. When, in the fourth century, the stirrup and complete armor for both horse and man was added to their equipment, such mounted Hu warriors became truly formidable.[3] From the fourth century until the sixth, Hu cavalry (including people of Chinese descent who had adopted Hu culture) would remain militarily dominant in north China.

At the same time, political legitimacy still tended to be most convincingly defined in Chinese terms. Several of the armed bands that arose in the early 300s, whether they were ethnic Chinese or not, did so in the name of saving the throne – that is, at least nominally rallying to the defense of the legitimate but disintegrating

Western Jin Dynasty. Significantly, also, the first major Hu leader to rebel against Western Jin and form an impendent kingdom, in 304, was a Xiongnu man who claimed descent, on the maternal side, from the Chinese Han Dynasty founder Liu Bang (Emperor Han Gaozu)! Since the early Han Dynasty had provided imperial brides for Xiongnu leaders, the Xiongnu elite had literally intermarried with Chinese royalty. This particular Xiongnu chieftain's ancestors had earlier taken for themselves the Han Dynasty Chinese imperial surname Liu, he had personally lived for years in the Chinese imperial capital, and he initially even called his new state Han.

In another illustration of the elasticity of premodern Chinese identity, this Xiongnu leader is even quoted as claiming that both Great Yu, the legendary founder of China's first Xia Dynasty, and the revered King Wen of ancient Zhou had also been born among non-Chinese peoples. "What is of concern" in founding legitimate dynasties worthy of the Mandate of Heaven, he concluded, "is only who has been conferred with virtue."[4] Whether such words were really uttered by this Xiongnu ruler, or merely put into his mouth later by a Chinese historian, the argument very clearly was that the Mandate of Heaven did not belong to any one particular people. As the Zhou had conquered the Shang, and the Shang had supposedly conquered the Xia before that, so, too, the legitimate Mandate could always pass again to some other group. Why not to the Xiongnu?

Perhaps even more significantly, these words, though placed by the historian in the mouth of a Xiongnu leader, were recorded in the Chinese language. Despite the multiethnic and multilingual character of the era, and the fact that identifiably non-Chinese people were frequently the political and military rulers, Chinese remained (with minor exceptions) almost the only written language. Even a particularly notorious "barbarian" tribal ruler of northeast China in the mid-fourth century, Shi Hu (d. 349), felt compelled to dispatch a scholar to copy the stone inscriptions of the Confucian Classics in the former Chinese capital at Luoyang. Although fourth-century Hu kingdoms often had at their core a non-Chinese tribe, with conscious bonds of tribal solidarity, and often administered their Hu and Han (Chinese) populations separately, by the late fourth century, some of those ethnic divisions were already beginning to be deliberately erased.

The Southern Dynasties (South China, 317–589 CE)

As the Western Jin Dynasty tore itself apart amid vicious civil wars in the early fourth century, one imperial prince established a new headquarters for himself in 307, just south of the Yangzi River, in the city we now call Nanjing. After the final collapse of the Western Jin, this prince assumed the throne in 317 to become the founding emperor of an Eastern Jin Dynasty in exile, the first in a series of five Southern dynasties that claimed to represent the sole legitimate line of Chinese imperial succession. Despite a reasonably plausible claim to superior legitimacy, however, their immediate situation was precarious.

The watery terrain – with many rivers, canals, lakes, and flooded rice paddies – of the south provided a degree of natural protection against northern Hu cavalry, but the south was thrown into confusion by a flood of refugees from the north. These recent émigrés from the north may have amounted to as much as 17 percent of the total southern population. Because refugee members of former northern Great Families carved out large new estates for themselves in the south and tended to dominate the Southern dynasty governments, there was a serious potential for resentment and conflict with the older southern Chinese natives – who themselves, meanwhile, remained distinct from the pre-Chinese aboriginal population of the south, which was also still quite large.

In the third century, Three Kingdoms Wu had experienced much conflict with so-called Mountain Viet (in Chinese, *Shan Yue*) peoples in the lower Yangzi River area. These were presumably, at least in part, descendants of the Hundred Viets who had inhabited much of southeast China in antiquity. As recently as the Han Dynasty, this southland had still been something of a frontier region. In one three-year campaign beginning in 234, Three Kingdoms Wu reportedly forced the surrender of a hundred thousand Mountain Viet people in modern Anhui Province, converting the more vigorous among them into soldiers for the Wu Dynasty and the less vigorous into ordinary tax-paying farmers. After the Three Kingdoms period, the label "Mountain Viet" ceased to be heard much, but large numbers of aborigines continued to exist, under other names, throughout the Southern dynasties.

Despite the potential for conflict between northern refugees and older native southerners, between ethnic Chinese and aborigines, and with Hu invaders from the north, and despite the serious weakness of its government, the Eastern Jin Dynasty enjoyed a surprisingly lengthy period of stability and prosperity. The secret of the Eastern Jin's somewhat unexpected success was compromise, conciliation, and a relatively robust balance of power, in which the threatened rise of any one Great Family to supreme power (at a time when the emperors themselves were particularly weak) stimulated all the others to rally against that family to restore stability. Much credit should also go to the adroit leadership provided by a number of outstanding statesmen such as Wang Dao (276–339). Wang Dao, although a northern émigré himself, immediately began to practice the local southern dialect to win southern support. According to one contemporary description, "there were few who could resist Wang Dao's welcome," and everyone felt that Wang Dao "met them like an old friend."[5]

The Eastern Jin Dynasty produced an astonishing cultural efflorescence in the arts, which included China's first truly famous painter, Gu Kaizhi (341–402), and arguably the most admired calligraphic genius of all time, Wang Xizhi (303–379). In a much celebrated story, Wang Xizhi once, in 353, hosted an elegant literary gathering at an orchid pavilion in Zhejiang, during which wine cups were floated down a gently winding stream. Wherever the cup touched the bank, each of forty-one guests in succession had to compose a poem or be forced to drink a penalty. The preface to the record of this gathering that Wang Xizhi personally brushed was so treasured for its calligraphy that a later emperor (Tang Taizong, 600–649) supposedly took the original copy of it with him to his grave.

The brilliant poet Tao Qian (Tao Yuanming, 365–427) also belongs to the Eastern Jin period. Tao is considered one of China's first great landscape poets and an extoller of the joys of a simple life of contentment in rural reclusion. He is famous also as the author of a brief pioneering work of utopian prose fiction known as "Peach Blossom Spring." This short story tells the tale of a fisherman who once followed a stream into a grove of flowering peach trees, where he found a cave. Entering and passing through this cave, he discovered an entire community filled with happy people, who had been entirely cut off from the outside world for centuries. Although the residents asked the fisherman to keep their existence a secret, on his return home, he reported directly to the government. Despite much searching, however, no one was ever able to find this marvelous land again.

Another Eastern Jin artistic genius was the painter and musician Dai Kui (d. 396). Dai was known for his performances on a delicate horizontal stringed instrument called the *qin*. According to one story, around the year 345, when a certain prime minister and prince of the imperial family summoned Dai to play for him, Dai smashed his *qin* in front of the messenger instead, remarking that he was not an entertainer for princely houses. Although the prince was reportedly furious, he was unable do anything about Dai's defiance. This story illustrates the remarkable degree of independence from imperial power that gentlemen of this era enjoyed.

The amazing cultural splendor of the Southern dynasties owed much to the fact that scholarship and literary ability had become essential requirements for high social status and officeholding since the late Han Dynasty. After the fall of the Han, and with the weakening of imperial government, the focus of learning and education shifted to individual private families. Literary cultivation became one of the most important criteria that separated the Great Families, who were the dominant figures throughout the age of division, from ordinary commoners.

Another contributing factor to the cultural richness of the Southern dynasties was the growing availability, and variety, of books, both in imperial and private collections. In the mid-sixth century, one imperial library is said to have contained as many as 140,000 rolls of books and charts. The possession of some thirty thousand rolls helped one early-sixth-century prince to compile an influential literary anthology, the *Selections of Refined Literature (Wen xuan)*, which "became the text from which most educated men obtained their literary education" for centuries thereafter and which was also widely read by early Korean and Japanese elites.[6] This proliferation of books was partly due, in turn, to a revolution in writing materials that had finally replaced wood, silk, and bamboo with true paper by Eastern Jin times. The vibrant marketization of the southern economy also helped make books more widely available.

Not only did agriculture expand considerably in south China during the Age of Division but the Southern dynasty economy was also increasingly privatized and commercialized. By the fifth and sixth centuries, the circulation of money and commerce had penetrated nearly every level of society. Commercialization of the economy was further stimulated by a growing volume of international maritime trade, which had already linked southern Chinese ports with markets as far away as the Mediterranean by late Han times. From the Han Dynasty through the Age of Division, China's most important port was probably located, surprisingly enough, in the vicinity of modern Hanoi, in the Red River valley area of what is now northern Vietnam. Thanks to this commercial vitality, it is likely that the Southern dynasty capital (modern Nanjing) had become the largest city in the world by the early 500s, with a population of perhaps 1.4 million.[7]

The remarkable cultural and economic dynamism of Southern dynasty China stands in obvious contrast to what was happening in western Europe at about the same time, where – although the trauma associated with the fall of the Roman Empire may sometimes be exaggerated – there does seem to have been a "startling decline in western standards of living during the fifth to seventh centuries."[8] This Southern dynasty Chinese economic and cultural efflorescence also makes a striking contrast to simultaneous developments in the original heartland of Chinese civilization in the north. One sixth-century Buddhist author even marveled at how the Central Plain in the north had once been "China" but had since become a "barbarian waste," while the south had once been "barbaric" yet had now become a "Chinese" land.[9] It almost seemed as if north and south had exchanged places!

Yet the Southern dynasties also had serious weaknesses. Wealth and learning were sharply concentrated in a few hands. The exuberant process of monetization and commercialization, while greatly benefiting some, apparently also reduced many independent small farmers to abject dependency. Economic polarization seems to have become extreme. And although the first Southern dynasty, the Eastern Jin, enjoyed a degree of stability and legitimacy, it was overthrown in 420 by a military usurper. No subsequent Southern dynasty survived long, and every one was founded by an ambitious general. These upstart military houses then frequently tore themselves apart through internal rivalries and suspicions. Of twenty-eight sons of Emperor Xiaowu of the Song (r. 454–465), for example, not one died a natural death – all were killed by other members of their own family. A ditty popular around the year 454 captured something of the viciousness of the internal conflict: "First see son slaughter father, later see younger brother slaughter older brother."[10]

Not surprisingly, there may have been little popular sense of identification with these brief and less than thoroughly admirable Southern dynasties (little sense of what we might call national identity). Despite the cultural brilliance of the Southern dynasties – in the mid-sixth century, for example, one southern writer could sweepingly dismiss all but a few northern literary efforts as little more than "the braying of assess and barking of dogs" – ironically, in some ways, a conservative version of traditional Confucianism may have been better preserved by the non-Chinese regimes of the north.[11] After a devastating rebellion in 548–552, the Southern dynasties never fully recovered. In the end, reunification came from the north.

Northern Wei (North China, 386–534 CE)

In north China, as a degree of stability began to return following the chaos of the fourth century, the most important of the Five Hu peoples turned out to be a subgroup of the wide-ranging Xianbei people called the Tuoba. The Xianbei, in general, are thought to have originated roughly in the northeastern area of modern Manchuria. The legends of the Tuoba tribe located their own particular homeland just west of Manchuria in what is now northeastern Inner Mongolia. The early history of the Tuoba Xianbei remains unclear, however, and their native language (which is now extinct) cannot be identified any more precisely than as Ural-Altaic, somewhere between Turkic and Mongolic. By the late second century, the Tuoba Xianbei had established their grazing area in the belt of hilly grassland that stretches from the northernmost loop of the Yellow River in the west to just north of modern Beijing in the east. Emperor Wu of the Han Dynasty had made an effort to incorporate this area into the Han Empire, constructing fortifications and establishing agricultural colonies, but by the third century, Chinese administration had largely been evacuated. The historical Tuoba Xianbei emerged out of the mixture of populations, and cultures, in this area at this time.

In 261, a Tuoba chieftain sent his son to attend the Chinese imperial court, and as Chinese government began disintegrating amid disastrous civil war, the seminomadic Tuoba were enlisted by one faction (and courted by others) of the Western Jin ruling family as military auxiliaries. As a reward for their service, the Tuoba chieftain was invested by Western Jin as first duke, and by 315, as king of Dai (the name of a Chinese administrative unit in the vicinity of their grazing area). After the fall of the Western Jin Dynasty, the Tuoba Xianbei were themselves briefly conquered and incorporated into one of the many non-Chinese kingdoms of the fourth century north, but Tuoba independence was restored in 386 at a meeting of the tribes near modern Hohhot in Inner Mongolia. The Tuoba ruler then quickly elevated his title from king to emperor, and the name of his state was changed from Dai to Wei. Thus began what is known to history as the Northern Wei Dynasty (386–534).

In 398, the until-then still seminomadic Northern Wei emperor established a new permanent capital near the site of modern Datong, in northern Shanxi Province, and began to develop an agricultural base in the region. In the process, Northern Wei made much use of captive labor, resettled on a truly massive scale around their capital. There are records of over a million persons being forcibly relocated there in the first half of the fifth century, including Chinese people, other subgroups of Xianbei, Xiongnu, persons from what is now northern Korea, and others. By extensively reshuffling and relocating population groups in this fashion, the Northern Wei helped dissolve older identities and began to forge a new and more cohesive Northern Wei identity.

By about 439, the Northern Wei had completed the conquest and reunification of north China. Even so, Northern Wei long remained a distinctly Xianbei dynasty. The grazing of livestock remained fundamental to the Northern Wei economy, and historical records mention literally millions of head of cattle, sheep, horses, and camels. Well into the fifth century, the hunting of wild game – often with hawks or falcons – appears to have retained an actual economic significance as well as being a favorite leisure activity for the Northern Wei elite. In 415, a year when there was a poor harvest, someone proposed moving the capital farther south into the Chinese heartland. A counterargument prevailed, however, that as long as the Tuoba Xianbei remained in the north, the Chinese would imagine them as having

Figure 3.1. Northern Wei Dynasty terra-cotta funerary statuette of a horseman (fifth–sixth centuries). Musee des Artes Asiatiques, Guimet, Paris. Erich Lessing/Art Resource, New York.

vast hordes of warriors. Relocating the capital south would expose their small true numbers. Better to remain in the north, from where they could strike south swiftly when necessary, and the Chinese would tremble and submit at the sight of the dust kicked up by their horses' hooves (see Figure 3.1).

In 443, the Northern Wei sent an emissary to offer sacrifices at what they believed to be the newly rediscovered "original" Tuoba Xianbei ancestral temple, in a cave in remote northeastern Inner Mongolia. Whether or not this really was the ancestral home of the Tuoba Xianbei, a commemorative inscription was then etched into the cavern wall, and the text of that inscription was recorded in the dynastic history. Amazingly, in 1980, archeologists rediscovered this same cave, complete with its fifth-century inscription. This archeological discovery strikingly confirms the traditional historical account, but with some qualifications. There are minor but interesting variations between the actual text of the rediscovered inscription and what was recorded in the dynastic history. In particular, the original inscription used the title "khan" for early Tuoba Xianbei rulers (perhaps the earliest known use of that now familiar nomadic title), whereas the dynastic history omitted that term. Khan is not a Chinese title, and this discrepancy is a reminder that the Northern Wei Dynasty may have been less thoroughly Chinese than the standard histories, which were written in the Chinese language by Chinese authors, suggest. On the other hand, though, even the non-Chinese word *khan* in this original inscription is still written in Chinese characters.

Until the mid-fifth century, Northern Wei emperors ruled north China essentially as Xianbei-style overlords, did not apparently envision themselves as sole legitimate successors to the Chinese Mandate of Heaven, and did not display much evidence of any driving ambition to conquer the still independent Southern dynasties and reunify China. A majority of high-ranking Northern Wei officials, moreover, were still identifiably non-Chinese.[12] Eventually, however, in 494, Northern Wei actually did relocate its capital farther south to the hallowed early Chinese imperial site at Luoyang. Even before then, led first by a powerful empress dowager and then by Emperor Xiaowen (r. 471–500), the court began promulgating measures to convert Northern Wei into more of a Chinese-style regime. These included the construction of a Confucian temple with seasonal sacrifices to the spirit of Confucius, the adoption of Chinese names (for example, the non-Chinese imperial surname Tuoba was changed at this time to the Chinese name Yuan), and mandatory court use of the Chinese language. The underlying motive for these actions was probably less due to any obvious superiority or attractiveness of Chinese culture than it was to lay the groundwork for a Northern Wei conquest of the south and reunification of China.

One of the new measures implemented at this time was a remarkable system of per capita state farmland allocation known as the Equitable Fields (*juntian*) system. This Equitable Fields system would continue in operation in China from roughly 485 to 780 and would exert an important influence on early Japanese institutions. It is also a fascinating example of an intrusive early government attempt at management of the economy. Despite drawing on ancient Chinese Confucian egalitarian ideals, however, the Northern Wei per capita assignment of farmland emerged more directly out of the non-Chinese Xianbei practice of putting captive labor to work tilling the fields. From the seminomadic Xianbei perspective, farming remained very much a base, servile occupation. Even the imperfect implementation of such an Equitable Fields system was only possible because of the massive dislocation of population and extensive vacant lands that characterized war-ravaged fourth- to fifth-century north China. Despite its historical interest, the Equitable Fields system was therefore actually something of an anomaly in the overall pattern of Chinese economic history, and the private commercial development that characterized the contemporary Southern dynasties was more representative of long-term Chinese trends.

Even after the relocation of the Northern Wei capital to Luoyang in 494, there were apparently still enough Xianbei people who were not yet proficient in the Chinese language that it was felt necessary to have the gist of the Confucian *Classic of Filial Piety* translated into Xianbei. A number of books are reported to have been written in the Xianbei language around this time (although today, nothing survives of the language except a handful of words in Chinese transcription). The Northern Wei imperial command to dress in Chinese fashion was also apparently ineffective. To the contrary, it was the Chinese who adopted Xianbei-style shirts and trousers as the new Chinese national costume.

However, the Tuoba Xianbei people did come to imagine themselves as descendents of the same mythical Yellow Emperor, and other early legendary figures, as the Chinese. The Northern Wei became enough of an authentically Chinese dynasty that the original version of the classic Chinese story *Mulan* (familiar from the recent Disney animated movie) may have actually been composed under Northern Wei. The dynasty came to be considered not merely a legitimate Chinese dynasty but even (although contemporary Southern dynasties would have disputed this at the time) as the sole legitimate possessor of the Chinese Mandate of Heaven. After the reunification of China in 589, one seventh-century historian even wrote that the reason "the Dao of China did not fall" during the centuries of division was because of the efforts of Emperor Xiaowen of the Northern Wei.[13] In 601, a seventh-generation descendant of a Tuoba Xianbei chieftain actually helped compile a rhyming dictionary, called *Qieyun*, that set an influential standard for "correct" Chinese language pronunciation! Interestingly enough, the name of the Tuoba tribe, through the Turkic variant of its pronunciation as "Tabgatch," later even became a generic Central Asian name for China.

If the Xianbei who moved south into China proper eventually simply became Chinese people, however, those Xianbei who remained in the far north (and others who joined them) did not. Northern Wei military power remained based largely on Xianbei-style cavalry, especially those stationed in the Six Garrisons at the top of the Yellow River's northern loop. These garrisons commanded the strategic grasslands south of the Gobi Desert, where potential nomadic invaders from the steppes might launch an attack on China. The warriors in these frontier garrisons felt increasingly neglected by the China-oriented Northern Wei court in Luoyang, however, and in 524, a rebellion erupted out of the Six Garrisons that ultimately resulted in splitting the Northern Wei Dynasty in half, east and west, by 534. Both these so-called Eastern and Western Wei dynasties themselves soon suffered further usurpations and changes of dynasty.

A counterreaction against the pro-Chinese cultural policies of the late Northern Wei government followed, together with a considerable revival of Xianbei culture and identity. Xianbei names were restored, and some ambitious Chinese people even took Xianbei names themselves and learned to speak the Xianbei language in the mid-sixth century. At the same time, however, the regime in the northwest, partly because of the extremely small number of Xianbei warriors at its disposal, also began making unprecedented efforts to incorporate ethnic Chinese into its military. Perhaps because its base area also happened to be the very same region "Within the Passes" that had been the ancient Zhou (and Qin) homeland, this regime also began to consciously evoke the memory of ancient Zhou ideals and standards. In 589, after yet another usurpation and change of dynastic houses, this regime (now called the Sui Dynasty) based in the northwestern region "Within the Passes" finally reunified China.

Cosmopolitan Elite International Culture

"The most striking feature of sixth-century China was its cultural diversity."[14] In north China, as late as the 570s, the rulers, much of the army, and the language of military command were all still identifiably non-Chinese Xianbei. These non-Chinese warriors sometimes shockingly disparaged ethnic Chinese farmers and civilian officials, calling them such offensive things as "Han dogs."[15] At the same time, however, many of the Xianbei had also already absorbed a great deal of Chinese culture. One powerful mid-sixth-century northeastern warlord (Gao Huan, 496–547) – who is famous for urging his Xianbei warriors to regard the Chinese as useful servants who should therefore not be mistreated, while simultaneously telling the Chinese that the Xianbei were their defenders who should therefore be fed and clothed without resentment – is particularly interesting because it is actually difficult to say with any certainty whether he himself was Chinese or Xianbei.

According to the historical record, he was the grandson of a Chinese attendant censor from the eastern Central Plain who had been exiled to a northwestern frontier garrison in the region of the Ordos Desert. Two generations later, however, this man himself was now clearly culturally Xianbei (although apparently fluent in both the Chinese and Xianbei languages). Some modern scholars have accordingly argued that his claim to Chinese descent must have been a fabrication. Such genealogical fabrication might indeed have been both convenient and possible, but it is also conceivable that he really was of Chinese descent (although perhaps not from such a distinguished family as he claimed). His claim to Chinese descent, at any rate, must have seemed plausible at the time. In the end, there is really no certain proof either way, and the very ambiguity of his identity illuminates something important about this era.

The culture of this age was something of a hybrid mixture. As early as the third century, it had already become fashionable among wealthy Chinese to adopt such foreign things as so-called Hu beds (an early type of folding chair) and cooking techniques. Foreign influences sometimes even came from surprising distances. A silver pitcher found in the grave of a garrison commander who died in northwest China (modern Ningxia) in 569 was apparently made in what is now Afghanistan, in Persian style, and decorated with scenes from the Trojan wars![16]

In the south, ethnic Chinese rule was maintained throughout the Age of Division, but the southern population was also mixed, and the south, too, was open to wide-ranging contacts. According to historical records, for example, the sixth-century Southern dynasty court was continually visited by embassies, not just from the nearby Korean peninsula but also from Southeast Asia, India, Persia, and Central Asia. Some scholars even believe that stone pillars at certain southern imperial tombs show evidence of Greek influence.

If China was extraordinarily open to outside influences during this Age of Division, and if some of those influences emanated from surprisingly distant sources, on the other hand, this was also exactly the time when certain key cultural features that make East Asia East Asian were planted. A relatively common elite culture spread throughout East Asia in this period, extending to modern China, Korea, Japan, and northern Vietnam. The various local East Asian elites of this period in some ways even had more in common with each other than with the peasants in their own nearby villages. This was the age when East Asia was born. One of the key features of this new East Asian cultural community – and one that simultaneously also linked it, at another level, to a much larger world – was Buddhism.

Buddhism Comes to East Asia

Indian Origins

Buddhism was the world's first great missionary religion. During precisely those same centuries when China was most divided politically, a vast swath of the planet, including much of South Asia, Central Asia, East Asia, and portions of Southeast Asia, came to be united by a shared religious faith in Buddhism. Buddhism had originated, of course, in South Asia. The historical Buddha (the "Enlightened One"), Siddhārtha Gautama, who is also called the "Sage of the Śākya tribe" (Śākyamuni), was born in the vicinity of present-day Nepal around the sixth century BCE. His breakthrough realization is said to have been that, although the realm of material existence continues endlessly (the cycle of birth and death and rebirth that the Indians called *saṃsāra*), nothing within it is permanent, and it is devoid of any higher purpose; that is, to the classic religious question, What is the meaning of life?, the Buddha's answer was that life really has no meaning. After you die, there is no permanent personal identity that is passed on to future incarnations. The various components of your identity instead scatter and recombine in new ways. Nothing is permanent, nor is there any purposeful direction to this endless change. All things are merely the consequences of prior causes, which themselves are the cause of other effects, and so on forever. Existence is therefore ultimately empty, and meaningless, and the truly enlightened goal can only be to escape this endless cycle of misery.

This realization moved the Buddha to preach his first sermon, in which he formulated the Four Noble Truths. The first Noble Truth is that life is suffering. The second is that the cause of our suffering is our attachment to the things of this world. The third Noble Truth then follows with remorseless logic: the way to end our suffering is to break those attachments and desires. The way to do this is explained by the fourth and final Truth, which is to follow the Eightfold Path of proper living. If one succeeds in breaking all attachments, one may ultimately attain an end to reincarnation, or *nirvāṇa*.

Although the Four Noble Truths are said to represent the core of Buddhist doctrine, they have not generally been much emphasized in Chinese Buddhism. The essential Chinese approach to Buddhism may best be captured by the popular saying "the bitter sea [of existence] has no end; [but just] turn your head, and there is the shore" (*Ku hai wu bian; hui tou shi an*); that is, though there is no end to the miseries of life, release can be achieved through a simple realization of the truth.

For many Chinese and other East Asian Buddhists, furthermore, the most realistic hope for salvation seemed to lie not in any rigorous path of spiritual detachment from desires or sudden burst of enlightenment, but rather simple faith that appeals to the compassionate intervention of a Bodhisattva – an enlightened being who deliberately chose to remain in the realm of existence to help save others – might bring rebirth in paradise. The most important of these Bodhisattvas was Amitābha, the Bodhisattva of Infinite Life and Infinite Light, who had taken a vow to cause anyone who invoked his name in genuine sincerity to be reborn in the western Pure Land. East Asian Buddhism is predominantly what is called Mahayana (Greater Vehicle) Buddhism, a tradition that promises universal salvation, in which the Buddha and Bodhisattvas have come to be worshipped as deities and rebirth in paradise is often seen as a more immediate goal than an end to reincarnation in *nirvāṇa*.

If this version of Buddhism seems strikingly different from what has been described earlier as the Buddha's own original realization, it must be emphasized that it is difficult to speak with any certainty about the original Buddhism because there are no reliable records for the earliest period and because multiple different versions of Buddhism quickly sprang up. Buddhism soon became enormously complex and sophisticated, defying easy generalization. The standard modern edition of the Chinese Buddhist canon, for example, includes some 2,184 different complete texts, and this is only one of three different major collections of Buddhist scriptures that have survived (the other two being the Tibetan and the Southeast Asian, or Pali, canons). A great many texts, furthermore, have not survived.

The earliest Buddhist community may have emerged in the Ganges River valley of northeastern India, but by the third century BCE, there were Buddhists all across South Asia, from Sri Lanka in the south to Gandhāra in the northwest (in what is now Pakistan and Afghanistan). Meanwhile, the conquests of Alexander the Great (356–323 BCE) had brought actual Greeks into that very same area of modern Pakistan and Afghanistan. Around the year 160 BCE, one Greek king in that region, Menander, supposedly converted to Buddhism. The result was something of a fertile fusion of Hellenistic, Persian, and Indian cultural influences. Because the main silk road trade routes also passed through this same region, some of these cultural and artistic influences began extending eastward into China.

Stone grotto temples began to appear in India by as early as the second century BCE, as places for Indian holy men to practice their austerities. In the first century CE, images of the Buddha began to be created in the Gandhāra region. Both Buddhist images and cave temples spread from there to China and East Asia. Over 120 cave temples are known in northern China, the oldest dating from the fifth century. This cave temple style extended as far east as southeastern Korea. The result was a visible expression of Buddhist cultural commonality linking together the entire region from modern Afghanistan to Korea. The world's largest Buddhist statues (until they were destroyed by the Taliban in 2001) were created at Bamiyan, Afghanistan, around the sixth century. Among the finest examples in China is the complex of Buddhist grottoes at Yun'gang, near the Northern Wei Dynasty capital at modern Datong, which was largely constructed between 460 and 494

Figure 3.2. Colossal stone Buddha at Yun'gang, cave 20, Northern Wei Dynasty, 460–494 CE, near Datong, China. Werner Forman/Art Resource, New York.

(see Figure 3.2). The Yun'gang complex contains altogether some fifty-one thousand Buddhist images, the largest statue being roughly fifty-five feet tall.

At the same time that Buddhism united vast stretches of Asia into a single religious community, there remained important regional differences, even in specific matters of Buddhist practice. The fashion for constructing cave temples did not extend to Japan, for example, and was also rare in south China. The pagoda, a symbolic Buddhist structure that merged together older Han Dynasty Chinese-style tower architecture with imported Indian religious elements, and that matured in China by the fifth century, is uniquely East Asian.[17] Within East Asia, furthermore, Chinese pagodas were characteristically made of masonry and Japanese pagodas of wood, while Korea is most famous for its stone pagodas.

In China, the spread of Buddhism was also paralleled by the simultaneous emergence of a new indigenous Chinese Daoist religion that interacted with Buddhism in complicated ways. Although this Daoist religion drew on more ancient Chinese beliefs in the possibility of physical immortality, divinely revealed texts, an underworld bureaucracy, and both the classical text and deified figure of *Laozi*, the temples, clergy, and scriptural canon of a specifically Daoist religion developed only belatedly around this time. By the fifth century, many new Daoist scriptures were being conspicuously modeled after Buddhist *sūtras*, although such originally alien Buddhist ideas as rebirth were also modified to suit the somewhat different Daoist purposes.[18] At the same time, Buddhism itself was also being transformed in China.

Buddhism's Spread to China

Buddhism spread to China along the caravan trade routes that led through Central Asia, as well as, somewhat later, the maritime trade routes through Southeast Asia. The pre-Buddhist Indian Brahmanical teachings had forbidden sea travel, but the Buddhist Bodhisattva of compassion Avalokiteśvara became a patron saint for travelers, providing merchants with the courage to face the real and imagined dangers of distant voyages in ancient times. Perhaps for that reason, many early Indian merchants were Buddhists, and Buddhist monks not infrequently accompanied them on their journeys.

In a charming example of Buddhism's ability to adapt and transform itself locally, in China, this Indian deity Avalokiteśvara eventually came to frequently (but not always) be portrayed in female form, as the beloved goddess of mercy Guanyin (Kannon in Japanese, Kwanŭm in Korean). Chinese women frequently prayed to Guanyin in the hope that she would help them give birth to a male child. In Tibet, much later, the revered Buddhist leaders known as the Dalai Lamas (a title that dates from 1578) also came to be viewed as incarnations of Avalokiteśvara, known locally as Chenrezig.

Buddhism had unquestionably reached China by the early first century, but it did not initially have much appeal there. Although the preexisting native Chinese religious beliefs, which recognized a wide variety of different spirits, did not necessary exclude the introduction of new foreign gods, the early Buddhist missionary monks appeared quite outlandish, begging for their existence with bare feet, shaved heads, saffron robes, and bare right shoulders. Most fundamentally, the Buddhist message of withdrawal from a world filled with misery was contrary to the characteristically optimistic Chinese tradition of active worldly participation. Confucian ideals of service to family, community, and state conflicted directly with the Buddhist goal of leaving the family and society to become a celibate monk. As a consequence, Buddhism took root only very slowly in China, and it was not until the third century that the first known Chinese person was ordained as a Buddhist monk. For roughly the first three hundred years of its existence in China, Buddhism was largely confined to the foreign community there.

It was only after the collapse of imperial government in north China in the fourth century and the beginning of a period of large-scale ethnocultural flux that Buddhism found a more receptive audience. Much of Buddhism's appeal then was because of its alleged ability to work miracles. For example, one Indian missionary in early-fourth-century south China reportedly enthralled crowds by cutting his tongue off with a knife and then putting it back, and placing paper in a fire only to pull it intact from the ashes. The great missionary monk Buddhacinga (in Chinese, Fotucheng; d. 348) – who arrived from the western regions in the Chinese imperial capital Luoyang in 310, just in time to see the city fall to Hu conquerors – was "skilled at reciting supernatural incantations and able to marshal demons. He would smear sesame oil mixed with rouge in the palm of his hand, and affairs from a thousand *li* beyond could all be observed in his palm, as though right before your face."[19] Buddhacinga presented himself to one important Hu commander and, filling his begging bowl with water, burning incense, and saying a prayer, caused a blue lotus flower to bloom miraculously from the bowl. As the wielder of such awesome supernatural powers, Buddhacinga was then welcomed as a trusted advisor to the throne of this Hu kingdom in north China for some thirty years.

It is sometimes alleged that the non-Chinese rulers of the Northern dynasties were especially receptive to Buddhism precisely because it was foreign, like themselves. In fact, textual sources do place just exactly such a claim in the mouth of at least one Hu ruler in the fourth-century north. Nevertheless, of the four most notorious purges of Buddhism in all of Chinese history, two were conducted by such non-Chinese Northern dynasties in the fifth and sixth centuries, and none by the so-called native Chinese Southern dynasties of this era. At least one motive for these northern purges of Buddhism, moreover, may have been exactly the desire to demonstrate their credentials as legitimate Chinese-style empires. In addition, government supervision and regulation of the Buddhist church began in the north, in the late fourth and early fifth centuries, and the Northern dynasties were generally more rigorous in exerting control over Buddhism than the Southern dynasties. In the south, meanwhile, the philosophical sophistication and ability to engage in elegant conversation of certain distinguished fourth-century monks had helped make Buddhism respectable. Buddhism flourished in both south and north, and among both Chinese and non-Chinese.

Unlike in medieval Europe, governments in China did early claim the authority to regulate religion and successfully asserted the principle of the superiority of state over church. Nevertheless, with rare exceptions, there was no official state church to which everyone was expected to belong in premodern China. The government's concern was chiefly to limit the number of religious tax exemptions and to suppress potential religiously inspired rebellions. Beyond that, the government was generally tolerant of differing faiths. Premodern Chinese people enjoyed a surprising degree of individual religious freedom. For this reason, despite the great popularity of Buddhism in China at its peak, China was never an exclusively Buddhist civilization.

If Indian Buddhists supposedly viewed the endless round of existence as a curse, and *nirvāṇa* as release from the cycle of reincarnation, in China, ironically, the previously unfamiliar Indian idea of reincarnation – of rebirth – seemed to imply a promise of eternal life, which, for many Chinese people, was not unappealing. The idea of reincarnation also solved the classic moral conundrum of why bad things seem to happen to good people: their good deeds, it turns out, will be repaid in the next life. In China, Buddhists came to believe that after death, one could either go to hell for a period of punishment (where Yama, the God of the Dead, judges evildoers), be doomed to haunt the land as a hungry ghost, be reborn as an animal, be reborn as a human, be reborn in a paradise (such as the Pure Land in the west), or be reborn as a kind of demon called an *asura*.

Buddhism was transformed as it traveled from India to China, but this should not be surprising. Not only were the cultural backgrounds very different but an enormous linguistic gulf existed between the languages of India, in which the concepts of Buddhism were first articulated, and Chinese. For centuries, the first priority of Buddhists in China was translation. In the early period, the region in far northwest China that is today called Xinjiang played a critical role in the transmission process. Most early Buddhist translators were not actually Indians but Central Asians, many of them from Xinjiang.

Xinjiang has, for good reason, been called the crossroads of Eurasia.[20] The principal silk road trade routes lay both north and south of the Tarim basin desert that occupies the heart of Xinjiang. Although Xinjiang was first brought into the Chinese Empire as early as the second century BCE, it was only sporadically included inside Chinese borders thereafter, and it long remained largely un-Chinese in culture and population. For example, in parts of Xinjiang such as Kuchā, an oasis community on the northern branch of the silk roads, an Indo-European language called Tocharian continued to be spoken until as late as the ninth century.

It was from Kuchā that the greatest of the early Buddhist translators came: Kumārajīva (344–413). Kumārajīva was born in Kuchā, reportedly to an Indian father and a local mother, and as a boy, he traveled with his mother to Kashmir, in India, learning the languages of various lands. In 384, Kuchā, and together with it Kumārajīva, was captured by one of the Hu regimes in north China. It is said that on his return from Kuchā, the victorious general needed twenty thousand camels to carry all his loot. Along with this loot came the Buddhist master Kumārajīva. Eventually Kumārajīva settled in the old Han Dynasty capital at Chang'an, in the historic region "Within the Passes." There Kumārajīva assembled a team of eight hundred scholars and embarked on a major translation project. Even the vastly talented Kumārajīva nevertheless still lamented that much was lost in translation.

Eventually a number of Chinese pilgrims went to India itself to study Buddhism at its source. The most famous early Chinese pilgrim was Faxian, who traveled throughout South Asia in 399–412 and left an important record of his journeys. Even going to India did not lessen the language barrier, however. There was no way to avoid using Chinese words to translate (or at least explain) Indian concepts – in the process, inevitably implicating preexisting Chinese ideas. As Mouzi (late second century), an early Chinese apologist for Buddhism, when asked why he responded to questions about Buddhism with answers drawn from the Confucian Classics, replied, "If I were to speak the words of the Buddhist sūtras . . . it would be like speaking of the five colors to a blind person, or playing the five sounds to a deaf person."[21]

Buddhism simply had to be filtered through the lenses of existing Chinese words and ideas. Although Mouzi drew on Confucian principles, and most Chinese Buddhists were at pains to emphasize the fundamental compatibility of Buddhism with Confucianism, in the long run, it was Daoist terminology that was most influential in translating the Indian Buddhist ideas and shaping Chinese interpretation of Buddhism. For example, *nirvāṇa* was sometimes translated into Chinese using Laozi's favorite expression *wuwei* (nonaction). It has been suggested that the title of an important Chinese Pure Land Buddhist text, *The Great Sūtra of Longevity without Measure (Da wu liang shou jing)*, betrays a Daoist-inspired quest for immortality that is quite at odds with the Indian notion of the goal of *nirvāṇa* as extinction.

Interestingly, one Chinese monk who has been credited with laying some of the theoretical foundations of what became Pure Land Buddhism, Tan Luan (476–542), was a northerner who sought out the immortality techniques of a famous Daoist alchemist at Mao Mountain in the south. There he received a Daoist *Classic of Immortality*, but on returning to the northern capital, he supposedly then encountered an Indian monk, who conferred on him the allegedly superior Buddhist *Sūtra Contemplating Longevity without Measure* (*Guan wu liang shou jing*). "Longevity without measure," or "infinite life," was another name for the Bodhisattva Amitābha. This story nicely illustrates the complex swirling patterns of interaction between north and south, Chinese and non-Chinese, and Buddhism and Daoism that characterized this age of cosmopolitanism.

A milestone in the Chinese domestication of Buddhism was the claim, which began to be heard in the fifth century, that all beings already contain within themselves the Buddha Nature (*Fo xing*). The key to salvation is therefore already inherent in all things. A particularly important text for Chinese Buddhists was the *Sūtra of the Lotus of the Wonderful Law* (*Miao fa lianhua jing*), or more simply, the *Lotus Sūtra*. The actual Indian origins of this *sūtra* are obscure, but it was claimed that this *Lotus Sūtra* contained the final sermon that the Buddha had preached on Vulture Peak before he attained *nirvāṇa*. In it, the Buddha explains that what he had said previously about *nirvāṇa* was not exactly the whole truth but merely an expedient intended to elevate the consciousness of his listeners. The ultimate truth is that *nirvāṇa* is not real extinction. Because the Buddha nature is already present in all things, you need only awaken to it to be saved.

By the sixth century, a number of distinctively Chinese schools of Buddhism began to emerge, which were largely without precedent in India. In addition, approximately one-third of all the scriptures in the Chinese Buddhist canon are thought to be apocryphal, meaning that they are original Chinese compositions rather than translations from Indian texts.[22] Buddhism, in other words, was being domesticated, and becoming Chinese.

Most of the ordinary faithful, of course, were little concerned with fine scripture-based scholastic distinctions. The promise of rebirth in paradise, the threat of hell, and stories of karmic retribution – good and bad deeds being justly rewarded – excited more popular enthusiasm. Buddhism came eventually to be popularized in China through public sermons, consisting of excerpts from the *sūtras* followed by prose and poetic explanations. To enhance the appeal of the Buddhist message, the entertainment value of the stories was often highlighted. For a sermon by a famous master, an audience would be summoned by the sound of a bell, each arrival making a small cash donation to pay for incense. The priest would ascend his dais holding a *ruyi*, a Chinese-style scepter, amid clouds of incense, and the sermon would begin.

China changed Buddhism, but Buddhism also greatly changed China. The religion exercised a profound influence on Chinese art, especially statuary, as it developed during this period. Buddhist temples and pagodas became characteristic features of the Chinese, and East Asian, landscape. Buddhism enriched the scope of Chinese literary forms, introducing such things as fables, parables, and Indian-style hymns. The knowledge of Indian phonetic writing systems that was introduced with Buddhism may have contributed to the invention of a new Chinese system for indicating pronunciation (using combinations of two characters) and also for the first time to the conscious recognition and analysis of the tones of spoken Chinese. Chinese people moved from kneeling to (sometimes) sitting cross-legged during the Age of Division, apparently under Buddhist influence, and the chair was also introduced from the northwest in these centuries. The ancient practice of sacrificing live animals in religious ceremonies was ended because of the deep Buddhist abhorrence of killing. For a time, during the Age of Division, it even became quite fashionable for Chinese people to take Sanskrit or other Buddhist names. A Chinese emperor who ascended the throne in 307, for example, went by the childhood name Śramaṇa (Sanskrit for "monk"), one sixth-century man styled himself Bodhisattva, another styled himself Arhat (Sanskrit for "holy man"), and the founding emperor of one sixth-century dynasty in northwest China styled himself Dhāraṇī (Sanskrit for "magical verses"). A great many people included the Chinese character for "monk" (*seng*) in their personal names.

By the end of the Age of Division, there were thousands of Buddhist temples throughout China, and by some reports even millions of monks and nuns. One devout sixth-century southern emperor donated his person to the Buddhist church four times, obliging his government to lavishly ransom him back on each occasion. A contemporary complained, perhaps with some exaggeration, that the empire had "lost almost half" its population to the Buddhist monasteries.[23] By the late sixth century, copies of the Buddhist scriptures were said to have been more numerous in China even than the Confucian Classics. As a final example of the pervasiveness of Buddhism in sixth-century China, the great emperor who would finally reunify China in 589 (Yang Jian, 541–604) was born in a Buddhist monastery and raised as a child by a Buddhist nun, who gave him a Sanskrit baby name.

Buddhism and the Birth of East Asia

It was from China that Buddhism spread to the rest of East Asia – but from a China that was itself also both divided and part of a much larger Buddhist world. For example, Buddhism was first introduced to the northernmost Korean kingdom of Koguryŏ in 372 by an apparently Chinese monk (known as Sundo in Korean and Shundao in Chinese) who was sent by one of the non-Chinese Hu regimes of fourth-century north China, whereas Buddhism was separately introduced to the southwestern Korean kingdom of Paekche in 384 by a non-Chinese monk (Mālānanda) sent by a so-called native Chinese Southern dynasty. Despite the international flavor of early East Asian Buddhism, the transmission of the religion was also intermixed, at the same time, with more specifically Chinese cultural influences. In 541, for example, the Korean kingdom of Paekche requested and received from Southern dynasty China not only copies of the Buddhist *sūtras* but also physicians, craftsmen, painters, and specialists in the Confucian Classic

The Book of Odes. Most critically, it was in Chinese language translation that the scriptures of Buddhism spread to both Korea and Japan, in conjunction with the introduction of writing itself.

In Korea, it apparently took some time for Buddhism to diffuse from the level of the elite to ordinary people. The known sites of Buddhist temples within the Paekche kingdom, for example, are concentrated in a limited area around its successive capitals and not in outlying regions of the realm. Meanwhile, it was from Korea, especially Paekche, that Buddhism was introduced into Japan.

The earliest Japanese Buddhist temples were constructed in Korean style, and actual Korean monks played a leading role in early Japanese Buddhism. The Hōkōji (a temple also known as Asukadera), for example, was completed in 596 by craftsmen and with priests from Paekche. The first official head (*Sōjō*) of the Japanese Buddhist church, in 623, was an immigrant priest from Korea. Although it is impossible to say with any certainty when the first person with knowledge of Buddhism actually landed in the Japanese islands, the dates conventionally given for the introduction of Buddhism are either 552 or 538. Interestingly, one of the earliest native Japanese histories presents the court debate that supposedly ensued in 552 over whether to accept Buddhism precisely in terms of foreign versus native, one minister arguing that because "all the Western frontier lands without exception" worship the Buddha, Japan should not alone refuse to join them, while others replied that if the Japanese began now to worship "foreign Deities, it may be feared that we should incur the wrath of our National Gods."[24]

Because this book of history was not actually compiled until 720, long after the events it describes, and because the account may be colored by special interests, it should be read with caution. There can be little doubt, however, that Buddhism was the cutting edge of a powerful wave of continental influences that swept across Japan in these centuries. These influences came most immediately from Korea, but ultimately, they were more broadly East Asian. Beyond East Asia, some degree of Indian, Persian, and even Mediterranean influences have also been claimed for Japanese art of the seventh and eighth centuries. An actual person from India supposedly officiated at the ceremony "opening the eyes" of an enormous bronze statue of the Buddha that was cast in Japan in 752.

At the same time, early Japanese Buddhism also retained aspects of local native culture. For example, many of the first Buddhist professionals in sixth-century Japan were unmarried young ladies, reflecting the indigenous tradition of shrine maidens (*miko*) in pre-Buddhist Japanese religion. Many early Japanese temples were also clan temples (*ujidera*), reflecting the importance of the clan in pre-Buddhist Japanese society and religion. And many local pre-Buddhist spirits (*kami*) were absorbed into Japanese Buddhism – a phenomenon that may also be observed everywhere the Buddhist religion spread, beginning in India itself.

By 623, there were reportedly forty-six Buddhist temples in Japan, all clustered in the vicinity of the capital. With the turn into the eighth century, a newly systematized Japanese imperial government began vigorously promoting Buddhism throughout the islands. In 741, for example, the central government ordered the construction of a Buddhist monastery and a nunnery in every province. Japan became a quite thoroughly Buddhist land – in some ways arguably eventually even more so than either China or Korea. Yet despite this important early transplantation and flourishing of Buddhism in Japan, it has been suggested that it was not until as late as the fifteenth century that Buddhism was finally domesticated to the level of the ordinary daily life of commoners, as Buddhism came to monopolize funeral services and ancestral sacrifice in Japan.

The Emergence of Korean Kingdoms

Early Korea (ca. 2000 BCE–313 CE)

By the seventh century, as Buddhism was taking firm root in Japan, the great Age of Division had finally ended in China. This Chinese Age of Division coincides with the dawn of recorded history for both Korea and Japan, and the first stirrings of a culturally coherent East Asian region. Long before this time, however, for many thousands of years human beings had already inhabited both the Korean peninsula and the Japanese islands. Both Korea and Japan enjoyed lengthy and culturally rich prehistoric eras. Pottery, for example, was being made on the Korean peninsula as early as 10,000 BCE.

In Korea, an age of megalithic (large stone) monuments, reminiscent of the dolmens of prehistoric Europe, began around 2000 BCE. Northern-style dolmens in Korea were typically formed by four upright stone slabs capped by an over-hanging horizontal lid, roughly in the shape of a stone table. Some of these are very large. Though dolmens in the southern style, which did not have the large, uplifting vertical side pieces, are associated with burials, the purpose for the table-shaped dolmens is less clear. Estimates of the total number of prehistoric stone monuments in Korea range as high as an astonishing one hundred thousand.[25] While dolmens can also be found in adjacent regions beyond the Korean peninsula, they are concentrated in Korea and were evidently an indigenous development.

By the last millennium BCE, rice farming and bronze metalworking had been added to the prehistoric cultural complex in Korea. Rice cultivation probably originated in what is now southern China, but rice was little grown in the Chinese cultural heartland in the north, where the staple grain was millet (and later wheat). Bronze, meanwhile, may have been an influence from north China, but there is a notable lack of the characteristic Chinese-style bronze ritual vessels in Korea, where bronze was commonly used, instead, for daggers and mirrors. In a number of ways, therefore, late prehistoric culture in Korea was distinct from that of the Central Plain in China.

The first written accounts of what we now call Korea, however, come from Chinese sources. Little was recorded until the wars surrounding the collapse of the Qin Empire and the founding of the Han Dynasty, when a refugee named Wiman fled to northern Korea and established a small kingdom there called Chosŏn in 195 BCE, ruling over a mixed population of natives and refugees. Over three generations, friction developed between this Chosŏn kingdom and the Han Dynasty, and in 108 BCE, Emperor Wu of the Han Dynasty invaded and conquered Chosŏn. At

Figure 3.3. A bird-shaped earthenware vessel from Korea, ca. late second–third centuries. Purchase, Lila Acheson Wallace Gifts, 1997 (1997.34.1). The Metropolitan Museum of Art, New York. © The Metropolitan Museum of Art/Art Resource, New York.

its peak, thereafter, roughly the northern half of the Korean peninsula was directly incorporated into the Han Chinese Empire.

At least a portion of northern Korea would remain under Chinese rule for some four centuries, until 313 CE. The principal seat of Chinese rule was called Lelang (in Korean, Nangnang), an administrative city located near modern P'yŏngyang. Archeological evidence makes it clear that local cultures in the area of Korea remained distinct from the standards of the Chinese Central Plain (see Figure 3.3), but Han Dynasty Chinese administration in Korea was not necessarily any more (though also certainly no less) a matter of foreign imperial colonial rule than it was in a number of other parts of the still quite multiethnic Han Empire. Under the early Chinese Empire, it was not uncommon for local culture to vary from metropolitan imperial standards. As late as the Han Dynasty, it has even been suggested that the language spoken near what is now Beijing may have been "still foreign to the Chinese ear and rather close to the languages spoken in the northern part of the Korean peninsula."[26]

If the native populations under Han Dynasty rule in Korea remained culturally distinct from the Chinese imperial metropolitan elite, however, they also did not yet constitute a single unified and homogeneous Korean people either. Internally, there remained a surprising variety of different ethnic groups, and externally, the borders of anything that might be called "Korea" had yet even to be imagined. Although, as a peninsula, the geographic map of Korea might appear to have been drawn by the very hand of nature itself, the modern land border in the north, which now follows the line of the Yalu and Tumen rivers, was not actually fixed until as late as the fifteenth century CE. An influential Korean book written in 1784 could still claim that the peninsula was really only the southern part of a Korean identity that more properly extended well north into Manchuria.[27] In the south, even the water's edge was not necessarily an inevitable end point. On a clear day, the Japanese island of Tsushima can be seen from the coast of Korea, and in the third century, this appears to have been "an area connected by water" rather than separated by it, across which "one of the most common scenes must have been people going back and forth in their boats."[28]

A third-century Chinese history (the *Sanguo zhi*, or *Chronicles of the Three King-doms*) describes several different peoples occupying the general area that we now call Korea. The Puyŏ lived well north of the peninsula, in central Manchuria, and might not seem relevant, except that according to Korean legend, the Puyŏ were directly ancestral to other more obviously Korean peoples such as Koguryŏ. To the south of the Puyŏ, in southern Manchuria and in the Chinese Han Dynasty–administered area of northern Korea, the kingdom of Koguryŏ was emerging. Koguryŏ had completely replaced Chinese government in northern Korea by 313. Koguryŏ was said to be a splinter group of the Puyŏ and resembled the Puyŏ in language and culture. East of Koguryŏ, bordering on the ocean, were the Okchŏ people, whose language was said to be slightly different from that of Koguryŏ. South of the Okchŏ were the Yemaek (or Ye) people, living along the eastern seaboard of the Korean peninsula. In the southern half of the peninsula, beyond the maximum zone of Han Dynasty Chinese administration, were the Three (Korean) Han peoples. (Despite the similarity of pronunciation, the Korean name Han is written with an entirely different character from the name of the Chinese Han Dynasty.)

These Three Han (*Samhan*) peoples were probably linguistically and culturally most directly ancestral to modern Koreans, since the eventual unification of the Korean peninsula was achieved by a kingdom that emerged from one of them, in the southeast. In the third century, however, they were themselves still far from unified. The three were called Mahan in the southwest, Pyŏnhan in the center, and Chinhan in the southeast. According to the Chinese account, Chinhan and Mahan did not even speak the same language. Mahan, by itself, was described as a collection of over fifty so-called countries (*guo*) in the third century. These countries were apparently small agricultural communities, scattered between the mountains and the sea, without walled cities. The largest reportedly contained over ten thousand households and the smallest only a few thousand. Pyŏnhan and Chinhan were both less populous, each having only a dozen somewhat smaller countries. In Pyŏnhan and Chinhan especially, people tattooed their bodies and used stones to compress the heads of newborn babies into an artificially narrow shape. Pyŏnhan was also notable as a major producer of iron for the entire region.

The people of Koguryŏ, in the north, were highlanders who occupied rugged mountainous terrain and lacked any very satisfactory agricultural base. In the third century, their population was reported at thirty thousand households. They were allegedly warlike and rode small ponies that were adept at clambering over the mountains. In striking contrast to the most typical Chinese marriage practice, in which the bride moves in with her husband's parents, in Koguryŏ, it was said that the husband moved into a smaller son-in-law's house constructed behind the bride's parents' home, and the newly married couple continued to live there until their own children were adults.

Three Kingdoms Korea (313–668 CE)

Koguryŏ was the first of the communities in Korea to form a politically organized territorial kingdom. In the year 32 CE, the Koguryŏ leader for the first time supposedly took the Chinese title "king" (*wang*). With the gradual weakening of the Chinese Han Dynasty, Koguryŏ began raiding its borders in the early second century. After the total collapse of the Han Dynasty by 220, southern Manchuria was left as a political vacuum that was filled by the rise of various Xianbei, non-Chinese states. By around the year 300, these Xianbei states had effectively severed communication between China and northern Korea, and in 313, the last Chinese administration in Korea fell to Koguryŏ.

By the fifth century, the chaos of the fourth-century age of the Five Hu and Sixteen Kingdoms (304–439) had stabilized considerably into two large and powerful states in northern East Asia: the Tuoba Xianbei–ruled Northern Wei Dynasty in north China and Koguryŏ in southern Manchuria and northern Korea. Both states had non-Chinese rulers (although Northern Wei presumably had a Chinese majority subject population), but both Northern Wei and Koguryŏ had also, by this time, absorbed a substantial amount of Chinese culture, helping to convert the Tuoba Xianbei Northern Wei into a reasonable facsimile of a legitimate Chinese dynasty and touching off a process of East Asian secondary state formation that would eventually extend the length of the Korean peninsula and across the sea to Japan. In 372, Koguryŏ had established an academy for the study of the Chinese classics, and in 373, Koguryŏ promulgated its first Chinese-style law codes. In 427, Koguryŏ moved its capital from what is today the Chinese side of the Yalu River in Manchuria to the vicinity of modern P'yŏngyang in northern Korea. The focus of Koguryŏ's attention by this time was increasingly directed toward domination of the Korean peninsula.

The second of the Korean Three Kingdoms, Paekche, was founded, according to Korean legend, by a son of the founder of Koguryŏ. Like Koguryŏ, therefore, the Paekche royal line claimed Puyŏ descent. Paekche was initially only one of

Figure 3.4. Silla period Korean silver crown, sixth century. Asian Art Museum of San Francisco. Werner Forman/Art Resource, New York.

the more than fifty small countries in the Mahan region of southwestern Korea, and it took shape out of the gradual consolidation of those Mahan communities, with a presumably predominantly Mahan population (whether or not its rulers really were of Puyŏ descent). Contact between Paekche and a Chinese dynasty was first recorded in 372, and by 386, the Paekche ruler had been invested with such Chinese titles as "General Garrisoning the East" and "King of Paekche." The keeping of written records also reportedly first began in Paekche around the mid-fourth century. In the fifth and sixth centuries, Paekche would enjoy particularly close relations with Southern dynasty China, becoming a highly sophisticated Chinese-style kingdom. At the same time, Paekche also had important ties with the newly emerging state in Japan.

The third Korean kingdom, Silla, developed out of a community called Saro in the Chinhan region of southeastern Korea. This was the most remote, and the slowest to develop, of all the Korean Three Kingdoms. It was not until 503 that Sillan leaders finally abandoned native titles such as Maripkan and took the Chinese title "king" (see Figure 3.4). It was also in 503 that "Silla" was first standardized as the name of the country. In 520, Silla promulgated its first Chinese-style law codes. By around 535, opposition to Buddhism was overcome, and Buddhism was officially endorsed in Silla. In 545, by royal command, Silla began the compilation of a written history of the kingdom.

What the Koreans were learning from China in these centuries were the institutions and techniques of state building. Despite the spread of Chinese influences, it should be emphasized that the Korean Three Kingdoms were all characterized by warrior aristocracies quite distinct from the Chinese literati elite, and many aspects of traditional native culture survived. Most people in Koguryŏ continued to live in simple thatched huts, with only royal palaces, government offices, and Buddhist temples adopting heavy Chinese-style tiled roofs. Yet one Chinese account nonetheless insists that by the seventh century, even the poorest villages and humblest families in Koguryŏ encouraged study of the written word and built imposing structures where unmarried young men gathered to recite the Confucian Classics and practice archery.

Aside from their obvious distinctions from the Chinese, these three early Korean kingdoms were also apparently somewhat different from each other in both language and custom. Each had, for example, their own distinctive ceramic traditions.[29] The monumental tumuli called old tombs (*kobun*) that appeared in each of the Three Kingdoms between the fourth and seventh centuries had somewhat different regional styles: stone burial chambers with painted murals in Koguryŏ, arched brick chambers in Paekche, and wooden coffins piled over with stone in Silla. The Three Kingdoms were also more or less constantly at war with each other. At the same time, though, they were also continuously exchanging influences.[30] In the seventh century, they would finally be unified for the first time in what could even be called the birth of Korea.

Yamato Japan (ca. 300–645 CE)

Some of the earliest known pottery in the world has been found in the Japanese islands. These early ceramics mark the beginning, around 11,000 BCE, of what archeologists call the Jōmon period of Japanese prehistory. The word *Jōmon* literally means "cord pattern" in Japanese. It refers to a characteristic decorative pattern produced by making impressions in the wet clay with cords. Despite Japan's remarkably early breakthrough to ceramic culture, however, the prehistoric inhabitants of Japan long remained primarily hunter-gatherers. The total population also remained quite sparse, probably never exceeding roughly a quarter million. Nevertheless, despite the fact that agriculture was little developed, Jōmon period people did eventually settle into permanent villages of perhaps thirty to fifty persons, who caught their food with bows and traps and by riding dugout canoes to fish with harpoons, hooks, and nets. They consumed so much seafood that the sites of their villages are often still marked by piles of discarded shellfish.

Certain tantalizing hints of southern cultural influences on Japan – resemblances to prehistoric southeast China and later Southeast Asia – have been observed. These include such things as the custom of building homes of wood elevated above the ground on posts. Some of these southern traits, such as rice cultivation, did not appear in Japan until the very end of the Jōmon period, and others cannot be

verified until relatively late, such as the practice of tattooing the body. Some, however, can be detected already in Jōmon times. These include ritual tooth extraction
(of canines or incisors), perhaps to celebrate rites of passage to puberty or marriage; a fascination with comma-shaped decorative beads (called *magatama*); and
a fondness for boats and seamanship.

Japan's prehistoric culture then underwent some fairly dramatic changes beginning around 300 BCE, when the predominant direction of influence also shifted to
the north – coming especially now from the Korean peninsula. These influences
included significant new genetic contributions to the population of the islands,
sufficient to indicate either very large numbers of new immigrants (some estimates
reach as high as a million) or a relatively small group that succeeded in reproducing itself disproportionately after arrival. Other influences included wet-field rice
cultivation and metallurgy. Among the new introductions at this time may have
even been the Japanese language itself, which is thought to be distantly related to
Korean. This new phase of prehistoric culture is called *Yayoi* (roughly third century
BCE–third century CE).

It was at the end of the *Yayoi* period that the oldest written description of Japan
finally appears. As with the case of Korea, this is found in a Chinese source. The
Chinese *Chronicles of the Three Kingdoms* (*Sanguo zhi*), which was compiled in the
late third century, includes a fascinating account of Japan based on diplomatic
contact. It describes a land called Yamatai, formed from a coalition of some thirty
smaller entities and ruled by a princess named Himiko who excelled at magic and
lived in a fortified palace with a thousand female attendants, but who was rarely
seen. A younger brother assisted in her rule.

In modern Japan, there has been intense historical controversy over whether
Himiko's realm of Yamatai was located in northern Kyūshū, the southwestern-
most of Japan's four largest islands and the point of nearest approach to the Korean
peninsula, or on the large plain at the eastern end of the Inland Sea on the main
island. This plain has traditionally been known as the Yamato plain, and it was
home to the imperial capital for most of recorded Japanese history. The obvious
similarity between the names Yamatai and Yamato is tantalizingly suggestive.[31] So,
too, is mention of a great earthen tomb raised for Princess Himiko after her death,
since just such tumuli began to appear roughly at this time, concentrated in the area
of the Yamato Plain. The exact location of Himiko's kingdom of Yamatai remains
uncertain, however. It is clear, moreover, that as of the third century, Japan was
still divided among multiple small communities, although the Himiko story also
indicates that some consolidation of authority was already being attempted. It may
also be observed that the Yamatai described in this third-century Chinese account
is in some ways already recognizably Japanese in culture.

Archeologists speak of an old tomb (*kofun*) period in Japan, covering roughly
the years 250–552 CE (see Figure 3.5). The largest of these massive, earthen old
tombs is a hundred feet high and covers eighty acres. It is interesting that the exact
same term, *old tomb*, is also used for the tumuli of roughly contemporary Three
Kingdoms Korea. Though the word is pronounced *kofun* in Japanese and *kobun* in
Korean, both are written with the same two Chinese characters. To some extent,

Figure 3.5. Female *Haniwa* earthenware figurine, fifth–sixth centuries, Kofun (Tumulus) period, Japan. Arthur M. Sackler Gallery, Smithsonian Institution, Washington, D.C.: Gift of Joseph H. Hirshhorn to the Smithsonian Institution, S1986.518.

of course, the creation of tumuli for deceased great leaders may have merely been a general phenomenon. The first emperor of China (Qin Shi Huangdi) and other Chinese emperors also had large earthen mounds heaped over their graves. Many of the Japanese tombs, furthermore, are in a highly unique keyhole shape – round at one end and square at the other – which distinguishes them from the Korean old tombs. Still, fourteen of these distinctively Japanese-style keyhole-shaped tombs have also been found in extreme southwestern Korea, and fairly frequent contact between the islands and the peninsula in these centuries is beyond doubt.[32]

Fierce modern nationalistic debates over whether Japan conquered Korea or Korea conquered Japan in this period are largely misguided and anachronistic, if only because neither Japan nor Korea really existed yet as a coherent identity. However, people from the Japanese islands apparently did have some presence on the Korean peninsula in these early centuries, and the Japanese islands clearly did absorb a number of highly critical influences from the peninsula, including such technologies as stirrups and armor as well as a significant number of actual immigrant persons. In early historical Japan, this was still openly acknowledged. In a record of 1,059 prominent families living in the capital region that was compiled in 815, for example, some 30 percent were explicitly said to be of foreign descent.[33]

In these critical centuries, at the dawn of Japanese history, immigrants played a vital role in shaping the emerging Japanese state.

Japan's mountainous terrain tends to naturally divide the islands into separate local communities, but the main island of Honshū is also blessed with two significantly large plains. The largest of these, the Kantō Plain in the east, around modern Tōkyō, was too remote from continental influences to figure significantly in early state formation, but the Yamato Plain in the west (at the eastern end of the Inland Sea) was well situated to become the heart of a major agricultural civilization. By contrast, Korea's relative lack of comparably large, flat land areas may have constrained Korea's premodern development somewhat.[34] Because of the critical importance of imported continental technologies, such as ironworking and wet-field rice cultivation, on early Japan, the regions closest to and most accessible from the continent (northern Kyūshū and the Inland Sea area, including the Yamato Plain) quickly became the most developed areas. Archeological evidence suggests that by the 400s, the Yamato Plain had already to some degree been brought under consolidated rule.

Newly emergent East Asian rulers in Manchuria, Korea, and Japan all, at various times, tried to buttress their positions against possible rivals by offering tribute to Chinese dynasties and being invested in return with prestigious Chinese titles. Himiko had already been proclaimed "Queen of Wa" (the earliest written name for Japan) in 238 by the Three Kingdoms Chinese state of Wei. Between the years 413 and 502, no fewer than thirteen Japanese tribute missions are mentioned in Chinese dynastic histories. One of the titles the Chinese Southern dynasties bestowed on fifth-century Japanese rulers was "Great General Pacifying the East." This originally Chinese title "general" (*jiangjun*) is pronounced *shōgun* in Japanese, and it is a word that would have a prominent future in Japan.

The rise of centralized royal authority in Yamato Japan, especially in the period from the fifth through the early seventh centuries, owed much to the court's ability to control and monopolize the distribution of imported foreign prestige goods such as iron – which was imported from Korea in the earliest period – bronze mirrors, and swords. This included also control over groups of immigrant people who possessed useful specialized skills such as writing. By the fifth century, record keeping was beginning at the Japanese court, with immigrants forming the nucleus of a literate scribal class. Immigrant artisans were often organized into special hereditary production units called *Be*. Besides writing, other key crafts that tended to be dominated by immigrants in the fifth and sixth centuries included silk weaving, metalworking, and architecture.

The Yamato court also attempted to gain leverage over the major native Japanese descent groups, called *uji*, which were the primary organizational units of early Japanese society, by conferring new titles as surnames on their leaders and converting these leaders into orientations of dependency on the Yamato court. These *uji* often claimed descent from deities (called *kami* in Japanese) and cohered around shared worship of those deities. What became the Japanese imperial line, in particular, claimed descent from the sun goddess Amaterasu. Over time, the ascent of this sun goddess to the top of the religious hierarchy was successfully engineered.

To a degree that is relatively unique in East Asia, politics and religion were closely interrelated in early Japan. One Japanese word for government, *matsuri-goto*, actually derives from a word meaning "matters of religious ritual."[35]

Throughout this entire early phase, not only did the Yamato ruler not style himself (or herself – there were a striking number of female rulers in early Japan) "emperor," but even the posthumous names by which the early Japanese rulers are known today had not been invented yet. Contemporaries apparently simply referred to the earliest Japanese rulers by the name of the palace where they lived. By the sixth century, however, the Yamato leaders had begun proclaiming themselves "true sovereigns" (*sumera-mikoto*).

In 587, one Yamato ruler supposedly indicated a willingness to accept the foreign, continental religious doctrines of Buddhism. Political opposition stiffened, and when the ruler died later that same year, a coalition of five royal princes, together with the head of the powerful Soga family, marched against the leaders of the opposition and annihilated them. The Soga family had been early supporters of Buddhism and had risen to great power through attaching themselves closely to the service of the throne, eventually attaining the title of "senior minister." After their victory in this swift civil war of 587, the Soga family head emerged as the dominant personality in Japan.

In 592, the Soga leader even audaciously arranged the assassination of the reigning monarch and the installation of his own niece, who is known to history as Empress Suiko (r. 592–628), on the throne – now located in a new palace in the heart of the Soga family stronghold near Asuka, in the Yamato region. Empress Suiko, together with her renowned regent Prince Shōtoku (Shōtoku Taishi, 574–622), then became associated with a range of extremely important innovations that helped transform Yamato into a more continental-style centralized state. These new developments may have included the adoption, for the first time, of such Chinese titles as "emperor" (written with two characters that are pronounced *kōtei* in Japanese and *huangdi* in Chinese), although what would become the distinctively Japanese variant of this East Asian imperial title, "Heavenly Sovereign" (*tennō*), was not definitely first used until the end of the seventh century.[36] In 604, Prince Shōtoku also supposedly issued a landmark Seventeen-Article Constitution that outlined a new vision of an ethical and political order based on a combination of Confucian and Buddhist ideals and asserted an unprecedented royal monopoly on ultimate authority throughout Japan, stating flatly that "in a country there are not two lords; the people have not two masters."[37]

Although Japan's two earliest native histories, the *Record of Ancient Matters* (*Kojiki*, completed in 712) and the *Chronicles of Japan* (*Nihon shoki*, also known as the *Nihongi*, completed in 720) purport to describe Japanese history from the primordial creation of the islands, and date the beginning of the alleged first emperor's reign to 660 BCE, much of this early material is clearly legendary. It is only now, roughly around the time of Empress Suiko, that we can begin to read these accounts as reasonably reliable history. Even at this time, much of the northern part of the main island of Honshū, southern Kyūshū, and other outlying islands were still largely outside the pale of Japanese civilization. In important senses, however, it may be said that in this era, Japan was born.

For Further Reading

China during the Age of Division is well covered by Mark Edward Lewis, *China between Empires: The Northern and Southern Dynasties* (Cambridge, MA: Harvard University Press, 2009). For material culture, see Albert E. Dien, *Six Dynasties Civilization* (New Haven, CT: Yale University Press, 2007). A fine collection of essays on the period is Scott Pearce, Audrey Spiro, and Patricia Ebrey, eds., *Culture and Power in the Reconstitution of the Chinese Realm, 200–600* (Cambridge, MA: Harvard University Press, 2001).

For aspects of literary culture and non-Buddhist religion in China during the Age of Division, see Stephen R. Bokenkamp, *Ancestors and Anxiety: Daoism and the Birth of Rebirth in China* (Berkeley: University of California Press, 2007); Robert Ford Campany, *Making Transcendents: Ascetics and Social Memory in Early Medieval China* (Honolulu: University of Hawai'i Press, 2009); Isabelle Robinet, *Taoism: Growth of a Religion*, trans. Phyllis Brooks (Stanford University Press, [1992] 1997); and Xiaofei Tian, *Beacon Fire and Shooting Star: The Literary Culture of the Liang (502–557)* (Cambridge, MA: Harvard University Asia Center, 2007).

The classic study of the arrival of Buddhism in East Asia is Erik Zürcher, *The Buddhist Conquest of China: The Spread and Adaptation of Buddhism in Early Medieval China*, 3rd ed. (Leiden, Netherlands: Brill, 2006). For a short overview, see Arthur F. Wright, *Buddhism in Chinese History* (Stanford University Press, 1959). Robert H. Sharf, *Coming to Terms with Chinese Buddhism: A Reading of the Treasure Store Treatise* (Honolulu: University of Hawai'i Press, 2002), offers a penetrating analysis of the interaction of Buddhism with Chinese culture. For early Korean Buddhism, see Peter H. Lee, trans., *Lives of Eminent Korean Monks: The Haedong Kosŭng Chŏn* (Cambridge, MA: Harvard University Press, 1969). For Japan, see Kōyū Sonoda, "Early Buddha Worship," in *The Cambridge History of Japan*, vol. 1. *Ancient Japan*, ed. Delmer M. Brown (Cambridge University Press, 1993).

For a general, overall introduction to East Asian religion, see Joseph M. Kitagawa, ed., *The Religious Traditions of Asia* (New York: Macmillan, 1987). See also H. Byron Earhart, *Religions of Japan: Many Traditions within One Sacred Way* (San Francisco: Harper and Row, 1984); Joseph M. Kitagawa, *On Understanding Japanese Religion* (Princeton University Press, [1979] 1987); Toshio Kuroda, "Shinto in the History of Japanese Religion," *Journal of Japanese Studies* 7, no. 1 (1981); Daniel Overmyer, *Religions of China: The World as a Living System* (Prospect Heights, IL: Waveland Press, [1986] 1998); and Laurence G. Thompson, *Chinese Religion: An Introduction*, 5th ed. (Belmont, NY: Wadsworth, 1996).

On the origins of an East Asian cultural community, see Gina L. Barnes, *China, Korea and Japan: The Rise of Civilization in East Asia* (London: Thames and Hudson, 1993), and Charles Holcombe, *The Genesis of East Asia, 221 B.C.–A.D. 907* (Honolulu: University of Hawai'i Press, 2001).

Concerning pre-seventh-century Korea, see Jonathan W. Best, *A History of the Early Korean Kingdom of Paekche: Together with an Annotated Translation of the Paekche Annals of the Samguk sagi* (Cambridge, MA: Harvard University Asia Center, 2006); Kenneth H. J. Gardiner, *The Early History of Korea: The Historical Development of the Peninsula up to the Introduction of Buddhism in the Fourth Century A.D.* (Honolulu: University of Hawai'i Press, 1969); Sarah Milledge Nelson, *The Archaeology of Korea* (Cambridge University Press, 1993); and Hyung Il Pai, *Constructing "Korean" Origins: A Critical Review of Archaeology, Historiography, and Racial Myth in Korean State-Formation Theories* (Cambridge, MA: Harvard University Asia Center, 2000).

On Japan before the seventh century, see Gina L. Barnes, *State Formation in Japan: Emergence of a 4th-Century Ruling Elite* (London: Routledge, 2007); Mark J. Hudson, *Ruins of Identity: Ethnogenesis in the Japanese Islands* (Honolulu: University of Hawai'i Press, 1999); Keiji Imamura, *Prehistoric Japan: New Perspectives on Insular East Asia* (Honolulu: University of Hawai'i Press, 1996); and Joan R. Piggott, *The Emergence of Japanese Kingship* (Stanford University Press, 1997).

4 The Creation of a Community: China, Korea, and Japan (Seventh–Tenth Centuries)

Chinese Imperial Restoration: The Sui (581–618) and Tang (618–907) Dynasties

The Sui Reunification (589) and the Founding of the Tang

In 581, a palace coup brought a new dynasty, called Sui, to power in the history-haunted region "Within the Passes" in northwest China. The founder of this dynasty was a man named Yang Jian (541–604). As emperor, he is known as Sui Wendi (the "Cultured Emperor of the Sui"). His father had been a high official, ennobled as the Duke of Sui, under the last Xianbei-ruled regime in northwest China (the Northern Zhou Dynasty). Yang Jian inherited his father's title as Duke of Sui, and his daughter was selected to be a consort for the imperial crown prince. When this crown prince, in due course, inherited the throne in 578, it made Yang Jian the father-in-law of the reigning emperor – always a potentially influential position. Because this emperor only lived two more years and was succeeded by a young boy, Yang Jian was then well placed to step in and grab supreme power for himself. After eliminating all potential legitimate heirs to the throne, and quelling a certain amount of armed opposition, Yang Jian usurped the throne outright, founding the Sui Dynasty.

A few years earlier, in 577, the last independent Xianbei-ruled dynasty in northeast China (the Northern Qi) had already been conquered by the one in the northwest (Northern Zhou), accomplishing the reunification of north China. The new Sui Dynasty now aspired to conquer the south, too, and complete the reunification of an entire Chinese world that had been divided (with one brief exception) ever since the disintegration of the Han Dynasty that began in 184. The south, meanwhile, had never recovered from a devastating mid-century rebellion (548–552), which had severely diminished Southern dynasty imperial resources. In particular, control over the upper (western) reaches of the Yangzi River had now passed from the south to the north. During the centuries of division, the north had frequently been able to field superior cavalry-based armies, but the south had always been protected, when all else failed, by the natural barrier of the Yangzi River. Now the

---

Some time ranges listed in the subheads in this chapter include additional dates in brackets. These dates indicate either the beginning or the ending of a dynasty (or other conventional historical period) that extends beyond the period covered in that section.

south was vulnerable to attack down the line of the river from the west. The final southern military defense also appears to have been ineptly commanded. Although the Sui Dynasty spent eight years preparing for its invasion of the south, a relatively small Sui expeditionary force was able to capture the southern capital (modern Nanjing) in less than one month of combat operations in 589.

The southern capital, which may have been the largest city in the world in the early sixth century, was ordered to be completely destroyed. The city that we know today as Nanjing had to be rebuilt again later, almost from scratch. Nearly four centuries of southern independence also ended forever (with only fleeting temporary exceptions). Chinese dynasties would continue to rise and fall, punctuated by occasional brief periods of division, but China had now effectively been permanently reunified. The Sui completion of the Grand Canal in 611, a manmade waterway linking the Yangzi River in the south to the Yellow River in the north, can be said to have capped the Sui Dynasty's economic and cultural unification of the entire Chinese world.

This spectacular Sui Dynasty success story soon unraveled, however, due to a classic example of what historian Paul Kennedy calls "imperial overstretch."[1] The second Sui emperor (Yangdi, r. 604–618), who gained the throne under a cloud of suspicion of having murdered his own father, attempted to continue the Sui imperial expansion. Most of south China had fallen quickly to Sui armies in 589, but the Red River valley area in the extreme south (in what is now northern Vietnam) was not reconquered by Sui until 602. From there, under its second emperor, the Sui launched an even more ambitious invasion farther south into the wholly foreign kingdom of Champa, in what is now central Vietnam, in 605. Despite some military victories, the expedition suffered heavy losses because of tropical diseases. The Sui also launched an invasion of an island that may have been Taiwan. In the north, by 612, the Sui had subdued the Eastern Türks (in the mid-sixth century, the Türks had emerged from obscurity to forge a powerful nomadic empire in the region we now call Mongolia) as well as other nomadic groups in the northeast and west and extended Sui authority in the northwest as far as Turfan and Hami in Xinjiang. Even successful Sui military campaigns placed heavy burdens on the resources of the empire, however, and in 612, Sui began an attack on the kingdom of Koguryŏ (in northern Korea and southern Manchuria) that proved to be a fatal failure.

In 607, the second Sui emperor had discovered that Koguryŏ was making secret diplomatic contacts with the Türks. Because he felt this was improper behavior for what he haughtily regarded as a vassal state, the Sui emperor threatened that if Koguryŏ did not promptly dispatch an appropriately submissive embassy, he would personally lead an armed "inspection" into Koguryŏ. More than imperial vanity and diplomatic protocol was at stake: a military alliance between Koguryŏ and the Türks might seriously threaten China. Koguryŏ had already launched an attack into Sui territory in 598, so the Koguryŏ threat was not purely imaginary. Furthermore, much of the territory of Koguryŏ had once fallen inside the Han Dynasty Chinese frontiers, and a desire to match the glories of the Han may well have fired Sui imperial ambition.

A massive Sui army, reportedly involving over a million combat troops, was assembled, and Koguryŏ was invaded in 612. Although one Sui naval contingent actually penetrated the outer walls of the Koguryŏ capital, it was quickly expelled. The Sui armies operating in northern Korea could not obtain adequate provisions and eventually were forced to retreat – or starve. Much of the Sui force was annihilated during this retreat. Undeterred by this first fiasco, however, the Sui emperor called for a second attack on Koguryŏ in 613. This time, the Sui forces were obliged to turn back quickly to deal with a domestic rebellion. Yet a third invasion was ordered in 614, which achieved some limited success, but by this time, the Sui Dynasty was rapidly disintegrating from within.

The massive conscription and mobilization of resources that made possible these monstrous invasions put a severe strain on the common people, especially in northeast China. In 611, one rebel, based in the Long White Mountains of modern Shandong Province, attracted draft evaders to his camp with a song about not "rashly dying" in northeastern military campaigns. Further rebellions quickly spiraled out of control. Soon some of these rebellions were being led by high-ranking former Sui Dynasty officials rather than by desperate peasants. Clearly even well-placed men within the dynastic establishment were turning against it. Eventually, as many as two hundred separate identifiable rebel groups arose.

Meanwhile, in 615, the Sui emperor had been encircled and trapped by Türks at a place called Wild Goose Gate (Yanmen) in northern Shanxi, near the great northward loop of the Yellow River. He was rescued from this trap by troops led by his maternal cousin Li Yuan (566–635), the Duke of Tang. On the strength of Li Yuan's proven combat effectiveness against the Türks, Li was made garrison commander of the frontline northern city today known as Taiyuan, in Shanxi, while the emperor himself retreated to the comfort of his favorite refuge in the south. The Sui emperor was suspicious of his cousin Li Yuan, however, and delegated two officers to keep their eyes on him. When these men conspired with the Türks against him, Li Yuan was tipped off and trapped them instead, rising in open rebellion against the Sui emperor in 617. In 126 days, his army marched south to occupy the Sui capital in the region "Within the Passes." In 618, the second (and last) Sui emperor was strangled to death at his southern refuge by some of his own courtiers, and Li Yuan ascended the throne as the founding emperor of a new Tang Dynasty.

The Consolidation of Tang Rule

After proclaiming the establishment of this new Tang Dynasty, the name of its capital city (modern Xi'an) was restored to what it had been in the glorious days of old, when it had served as the capital of the Former Han Dynasty (i.e., Chang'an), to invoke the memory of China's first great age of imperial unity.[2] (The actual layout of the Sui and Tang dynasty city, however, more closely followed the recent example of the Tuoba Xianbei Northern Wei capital at Luoyang.) A claim was also publicized that the spirit of the ancient Daoist Sage Laozi had supernaturally revealed himself to be Li Yuan's ancestor (since the "Old Master" Laozi's surname was also believed to have been Li) and divinely predicted that Li Yuan was destined to win the empire. Despite such brave assertions, however, at the time Li Yuan seized the throne, he actually controlled little more than the region "Within the Passes," and years of further warfare would be necessary before all the many other rebel bands were eliminated and all China reunified again. Significantly, early Tang population figures (as of 639) show serious population decline from the heights of the Sui Dynasty just a few decades earlier. Whether or not there were actually fewer people, fewer people were being counted by the government. The years of transition from Sui to Tang witnessed much upheaval.

The second Tang emperor (Tang Taizong, r. 626–649), then, came to the throne in an especially horrifying manner. In the final stages of a desperate power struggle with his own elder brother (during which, at one point, Taizong supposedly survived an attempted poisoning), in 626, Taizong bribed the commander of a palace gate (the Xuanwu gate) to set up an ambush. As his older brother, accompanied by a younger brother, rode in, they discovered the trap and spurred their horses in an attempt to escape. Taizong chased them, firing arrows, and his older brother was shot and killed. Taizong himself was then knocked from his horse by some branches, but before his younger brother could take advantage of this sudden vulnerability, Taizong's men arrived and put the younger brother to death also. When the heads of the two assassinated princes were displayed, resistance ended. Taizong then dispatched a man to "safeguard" his father, the reigning emperor, who was boating on a palace lake at the time. Whether out of shock and horror, or perhaps because he had all along coldly calculated that the succession would have to be determined by such ruthless competition,[3] the father soon vacated the throne, elevating himself to the ceremonial position of Retired Emperor, and Taizong became emperor of Tang.

Despite the bloody way in which he gained the throne, and the fact that just days after becoming emperor, a massive Türk army penetrated to within a few miles of the capital and had to be humiliatingly appeased before withdrawing, Tang Taizong is remembered as one of the most capable and outstanding emperors in all Chinese history. The reign of Taizong became a time of peak Chinese political and military power, and Taizong also presided over an age of exceptionally glorious cosmopolitanism. This cosmopolitanism extended even to the Tang imperial family itself, which was of culturally mixed descent. It has even been suggested that the fratricidal power struggle that brought Taizong to the throne may have been a lingering influence of Xianbei nomadic cultural traditions.

Until the establishment of the Sui Dynasty in 581, the rulers of north China had mostly still been clearly identifiably Xianbei non-Chinese. In the mid-sixth century, there had even been a revival of Xianbei names and language. Although the new Sui imperial family are usually said to have been Chinese (tracing descent through the paternal line), and they did restore the use of Chinese names after 581, they had also lived for generations in what we now call Inner Mongolia and had extensively intermarried with the Xianbei elite. Their cousins, the Tang imperial family, sprang from identical origins. Li Yuan, the Tang founder, was said to have been a great archer and hunter who "never missed his shots."[4] Elements of nomadic culture long remained noticeable at the Tang court, and during the Sui and Tang dynasties, Xianbei-style clothing even became a new standard Chinese costume.

Actual Türks gave valuable assistance to Li Yuan in establishing his Tang Dynasty, and although relations between the Tang and Türk empires then turned hostile for a generation, in 630, the Eastern Türks were decisively defeated, and Tang Taizong assumed for himself the title of "Heavenly Qaghan" as a Türkic-style supreme ruler of the steppe (as well as Chinese-style emperor of China).[5] By the mid-seventh century, Tang military and political influence had penetrated deeply into Central Asia, although direct Tang administration probably never extended any farther west than Hami and Turfan in Xinjiang. The renowned Chinese pilgrim Xuanzang (ca. 596–664), who traveled to India in 629–645 to study Buddhism at its source, reported encountering an "orphan city" near the Talas River, in what is now Kazakhstan or Kyrgyzstan, where more than three hundred households of formerly Chinese inhabitants lived. By the time Xuanzang arrived, they had become acculturated to Türkic standards of dress and activity, but they still preserved the Chinese language and certain Chinese customs.[6]

Traveling in the other direction, the game of Polo, which appears to have originated in Persia, became popular in Tang China. Nestorian Christianity also reached China during Taizong's reign, and a Christian church was established in the Tang capital by imperial decree in 638. A number of Nestorian Christian churches apparently existed in Tang China, although the religion never sank deep roots into Chinese society. Other exotic Western religions, such as Zoroastrianism and Manichaeism, also enjoyed official toleration and may have been more widespread.

If the Tang began as a militarily expansive, culturally mixed, and "self-consciously multi-ethnic empire," however, it ended three hundred years later, in 907, as a much more "self-consciously mono-ethnic empire united by significantly more homogenous Chinese culture." The Tang Dynasty was "perhaps *the* crucial period in the formation" of a Chinese ethnic, and even proto-national, identity.[7] The aborigines who had lived scattered throughout south China, and who had made up a substantial portion of the total population of the Southern dynasties, largely disappeared during the Tang – absorbed into the general Chinese population (although a considerable number can still be found even today, especially near the frontiers). Many descendants of the Xianbei and of the other Five Hu who had ruled north China from the fourth century until 581 also lost their separate identities and simply became Chinese during the Tang era.

At least forty-three persons of traceable Hu descent are known to have reached the highest government office (grand councilor) during the Tang Dynasty. The general who captured Tashkent in remote Central Asia for the Tang in 750 was a second- or third-generation descendant of an émigré from Korea. Several of the most renowned Tang Dynasty Chinese-language poets, such as Li Bai (also spelled "Li Po," 701–762), Liu Yuxi (772–842), Bai Juyi (also spelled "Po Chü-I," 772–846), and Yuan Zhen (779–831), were all of known, or suspected, Hu descent. Whatever their ancestry, however, by this time, they had all effectively become Chinese, and unparalleled masters of the Chinese language. As already mentioned, a rhyming dictionary (the *Qieyun*), which set an influential standard for "correct"

Chinese-language pronunciation, was compiled in 601 in part by a man of known Xianbei descent. And, even as persons of Xianbei descent became native speakers of Chinese, the Xianbei language itself became extinct. Of the many Xianbei-language songs that had frequently been performed at Northern dynasty courts, by 801, although fifty-three were still in existence, only six titles could still be understood.[8] Despite the fact that some degree of multilingualism was probably only normal throughout much of the premodern world, this was not the case in Tang Dynasty China. Within the geographic place we call China, the Chinese language had prevailed.

The Harmonization of Diversity

An obscure mid-sixth-century religious figure named Lu Fahe (dates unknown) may help illustrate how the cultural diversity of the Age of Division came to merge into the relative uniformity of the late Tang. Lu first attracted notice while living in reclusion as an ascetic *Śramaṇa* (Buddhist monk) on Thirty Mile Island, in the middle reaches of the Yangzi River. His place of origin was unknown, but some said he came from the centermost of the five sacred peaks in the ancient Chinese cultural heartland in the north. He spoke, however, with a southern aboriginal accent, and he initially appears frequently in close association with aborigines. Lu developed a reputation for being able to predict the future and was much sought after in helping people design houses and lay out graves in such a way as to avert disaster and bring good fortune (what is called *fengshui*, or geomancy). He also gathered medicines to cure the many diseases of the lush southern climate and cast imprecations that allegedly prevented venomous insects and wild animals from biting or stinging. Once, when someone tested a new blade on an ox, severing its head with one blow, Lu warned the man that he must perform meritorious services for the spirit of the ox or be struck by karmic retribution. The man scoffed, but died a few days later.

At the time of a major southern rebellion in 548, Lu joined loyalist imperial forces in counterattacking the rebels. He summoned eight hundred aboriginal disciples to a river ferry and set sail aboard a warship with some regular imperial troops. At a place called Red Sands Lake, they encountered the enemy. Because the wind was wrong for releasing fireships to drift down on the rebel fleet, Lu (according to the story) magically changed the direction of the wind by waving a white feather. After the defeat of the rebel forces, Lu became an imperial official, but when the southern empire split, and the southern emperor he served was killed by an invasion from the Xianbei-ruled dynasty in the northwest, Lu Fahe defected in 555 to the rival Xianbei regime in the northeast. As Lu Fahe approached the northeastern capital (Ye, near modern Anyang in Henan), the northeastern emperor, who had heard of Lu's uncanny arts, went out from his city several miles to respectfully meet him. When Lu caught sight of the distant city, he dismounted and performed the Pace of Yu. In the city, later, Lu would again rise to high office.[9]

The Pace of Yu refers to the legendary founder of the first Chinese dynasty, Great Yu. According to the legend, Great Yu traipsed the length and breadth of

China taming floods that were ravaging the land and, in the process, supposedly became lame, developing a peculiar gait or pace. By the Age of Division, something called the Pace of Yu had become a potent performance in the ritual arsenal of religious Daoism.

Lu Fahe is an extremely obscure and unimportant figure, but his career is of some interest nonetheless. Aside from illustrating the role of religion in China in living practice (as opposed to scripture-based sectarian doctrine), it also nicely demonstrates the inextricable mingling of Indian Buddhism with assorted native Chinese religious ideas, and the merging of north and south, aborigines, Xianbei nomads, and Chinese, and the possibility of melding them all together through the invocation of the grand Chinese cultural tradition, symbolized by the legend of Great Yu. The stage was set for reunification.

The Age of Division had been marked by sweeping population movements, which not only brought the Five Hu to power in north China but also dispersed large numbers of Chinese refugees from the ancient heartland in the Central Plain to new locations in the far northeast, northwest, and, above all, south of the Yangzi River. The result was to promote cultural exchange, ethnic blending, and a general expansion of Chinese civilization. For example, the manuscript of a set of civil service examination answers written in 408 has recently been discovered near Turfan, Xinjiang. Although the test itself had probably actually been administered in Gansu, in the somewhat less extremely remote northwest, and the literary quality of the writing is hardly outstanding, it is nonetheless noteworthy that Chinese-language civil service examinations were being conducted at such a time and place.[10]

The last Xianbei-ruled dynasty in the northwest, based in the region "Within the Passes," initially had only a small number of Xianbei warriors at its disposal – perhaps fewer than ten thousand. After a military defeat by its northeastern rival in 543, it began recruiting ethnic Chinese into the army out of necessity and, in the process, erasing the long-standing occupational division between Xianbei (or Five Hu) warriors and Chinese (Han) farmers. When its successor Chinese dynasty, the Sui, forced many soldiers to return to civilian status and farming in 590, following its reunification of China, the division between non-Chinese warriors and Chinese farmers effectively ended.

Meanwhile, despite a revival of Xianbei names, language, clothing, and culture in the mid-sixth century, that same final northwestern Xianbei Dynasty had also, paradoxically, simultaneously revived an idealized memory of ancient Chinese Zhou Dynasty institutions. This may have been in part simply because the regime happened to be based in the ancient Zhou homeland "Within the Passes," and also because it needed some unifying ideology to rally an otherwise decidedly mixed population. The Sui Dynasty emerged directly out of this regime in 581, and reunified China in 589.

The reunified Sui and Tang dynasties then transformed the empire into a single, highly centralized country. The Tang, for example, established a network of 1,639 post stations along the main roads leading to the capital to facilitate communications. Beyond mere administrative centralization, moreover, Tang also began promoting a more uniform Chinese culture. Near the beginning of his reign, in 619, the Tang founder established temples to the Duke of Zhou and Confucius at the Imperial Academy, with seasonal sacrifices to their spirits. In 628, Confucius was elevated to a position of superiority over the Duke of Zhou, and in 630, every province and county in the empire was ordered to establish such Confucian temples. Although the practice of offering sacrifices to the spirit of Confucius at his own home state of Lu (in modern Shandong) dates back to at least the beginning of the Han Dynasty, and a Confucian temple may have first been erected at the Imperial Academy in the capital in 386, these seasonal rites at Confucian temples, which became a hallmark of traditional Chinese civilization, reached mature form only in the Tang Dynasty.

The early Tang also established empirewide standard editions of the Confucian Classics and went to unprecedented efforts to construct a continuous narrative history of the Chinese past. In 593, the Sui Dynasty had imposed a ban on the private composition of state histories, which did not begin to be relaxed until the middle of the Tang. History writing was therefore concentrated at the imperial court, as a great affair of state. The Tang Dynasty then sponsored major imperial history-writing projects. Of the unparalleled sequence of "Twenty-four Dynastic Histories" that provide the standard version of the story of China from the time of the legendary Sage Kings to the end of the premodern era, eight, exactly one-third of the total (including two that were somewhat unofficial), were compiled within roughly a twenty-year period at Tang Taizong's court.

Education is a particularly powerful tool for promoting a common cultural identity. Emperor Wu of the Han Dynasty had, to a large extent, first defined the Confucian canon and established Confucianism as state orthodoxy when he appointed teachers and established an Imperial Academy in the second century BCE. Now, in 624, the Tang founder ordered every province and county in the empire to establish schools. By 738, at least on paper, there should have been nineteen thousand official schools in Tang China.[11]

Before long, official state-run schools came to be eclipsed by private education. Such late-Tang literary giants as Li Bai, Du Fu (712–770), and Han Yu (768–824) all received their educations privately. The result of this privatization may have only been to further universalize education in late Tang, however, and the educational content remained a common core of Chinese studies. Many people undoubtedly were still illiterate or poorly educated, but in 824, it was nonetheless claimed that the latest fashionable poetry was in the mouths of every "prince, duke, concubine and wife, child tending cattle, and passerby on horseback."[12] What had once been exclusively elite cultural standards were increasingly diffused to become universal Chinese norms, and in the process, the old divisions between Great Families and commoners, and between Chinese and non-Chinese, were collapsing into a more universal Chinese civilization. For example, in a cache of old texts preserved by the arid climate of remote northwestern Dunhuang, over a thousand anonymous popular lyrics from the Tang period have been found, many of which may have been written by fairly ordinary folk.

The new technology of woodblock printing was also already beginning to play a role in this process of diffusing a common Chinese culture by the end of the

Tang Dynasty. The origins of printing are obscure, and the oldest known surviving printed text is a Buddhist charm discovered in Korea dating from sometime before 751. By the early ninth century, however, a complaint was already heard in Tang China that printed calendars were on sale in the markets throughout the empire even before the Bureau of Astronomy issued its official calendar each year.[13] Although a genuine explosion in the availability of books due to printing would have to wait until the next dynasty, such humble printed items as calendars were already becoming available for use by ordinary people in late Tang, and were helping to promote a common Chinese culture in the process.

Even private education in Tang times was, furthermore, directed toward specifically imperial goals by the civil service examination system. Tests had been used in the selection of Chinese officials since at least the beginning of the empire, but only as part of a selection process that was driven mostly by recommendation. During the Age of Division, beginning in 220, a so-called Nine Ranks system had been introduced, under which specially designated regional administrators evaluated potential candidates for office and ranked them – in practice, largely based on family background. The result was to deeply entrench the status of a few Great Families, who acquired something even of an aristocratic aura. In the early sixth century, however, one Southern dynasty emperor asserted the radical idea that officials should be selected purely based on ability demonstrated through examination, without regard to family background. In 587, the Sui Dynasty terminated the evaluating authority of the Nine Ranks administrators and began to move toward a system based more on examinations.

Several different academic degrees came to be offered. For the Understanding the Classics (*Ming jing*) degree, all but one line of a selected passage from one of the Confucian Classics would be covered up, and several characters of the remaining line would also be concealed. The candidate was then expected to be able to supply the missing characters from memory. After this, there would also be an oral examination and answers to test questions. During the reign of the second Sui emperor, another new degree, called *Jinshi* (Presented Scholar), was introduced, which put more emphasis on questions of current relevance as well as poetry and literature and less on memorization of the classics. The *Jinshi* quickly became by far the most esteemed degree, and in later dynasties, it would eventually come to be the highest of a standard sequence of three successive degrees. During the late Tang Dynasty, an annual average of about thirty *Jinshi* degrees were awarded, and the degree's prestige was incomparable.

Obtaining a degree such as the *Jinshi* conferred status and qualified a man to potentially hold government office, but to actually be appointed to office, it was still necessary to be further examined by the Ministry of Personnel. In the Tang, this examination paid special regard to physical appearance and deportment, speaking ability, calligraphy, and ability to pronounce judgments. Under the growing authority of Empress Wu Zetian (ca. 625–705) in the late seventh century, anyone who believed they had talent – even commoners – were encouraged to recommend themselves for advancement, and the practice of testing candidates anonymously may have already first been introduced.

The civil service examination system, which reached full maturity only after the Tang, became perhaps *the* defining institution of late imperial China (until it was abolished in the name of modernization in 1905). Although the system always had its critics, it may be said that it did promote a relatively fluid and apparently meritocratic social and political order, and it was certainly a powerful force for cultural homogenization. Several grandsons of one eighth-century Türk from the remote northwest, who had himself attained distinction through military service to the Tang, for example, "all became known for Confucianism" and achieved their own success through the civil service examination system.[14]

Commercial exchange also contributed to Tang Dynasty cultural integration, as will be examined in more detail later. One new product circulated by the Tang commercial markets was tea. During the Age of Division, tea drinking had become popular in the south. In the north, meanwhile, the prevalence of ranching had made dairy products the beverage of choice (for perhaps the only time in Chinese history). Under the reunified Tang Dynasty, the passion for drinking tea spread from the tea-producing regions in the southeast to the entire country. One explanation for tea's sudden popularity was that it was promoted as an aid to staying awake during Buddhist meditation.

Domesticating Chinese Buddhism

Although the reunified Sui and Tang dynasties depicted themselves as restorations of the earlier Han Dynasty imperial unity, in many ways, China was now a substantially different place. The spread of tea, and chairs, during Tang times are but two examples of such innovations. The most glaring difference was probably Buddhism. Buddhism had been unknown in China at the start of the Han Dynasty, and even at the end of the Han, it was still very much a religion for foreigners. By the time of the Sui reunification in 589, however, there were reportedly more copies of the Buddhist *sūtras* in China than of the Confucian Classics. China had become a thoroughly Buddhist land.

In Sui and Tang, monks from the major capital monasteries took turns contemplating the Buddha in a place of worship within the imperial palace, day and night without cease. Once under the Sui, and four times under the Tang, empirewide networks of Buddhist temples were ordered constructed, with obligations to perform services for the imperial family and recite *sūtras* for the religious protection of the state. Public preaching reached a large popular audience by late Tang, and ordinary people sometimes bankrupted themselves making religious donations. By late Tang times, even criticism of Buddhism was frequently couched in Buddhist terms. For example, if all earthly activity is an illusory dream – the mere "shadow of a bubble," as the Buddhists liked to say – then a counterargument could be offered that expenditure and labor on behalf of Buddhist temples is also in vain and that such efforts might more appropriately be diverted to the relief of the poor and the service of the state. Although there never was a time when all Chinese people universally were Buddhist – there were always other religious traditions, and personal belief remained largely a matter of individual choice – by Tang times,

China had become deeply Buddhist. At the same time, though, Buddhism had also become thoroughly Chinese.

Buddhist monks in China frequently resided in permanent, sometimes magnificent, monasteries. By Sui and Tang times, some of these monasteries had grown into complex tax-exempt economic institutions, with their own estates, slaves, pawnshops, and sometimes even floating high-interest loans. Following the secular Chinese family model, the Chinese Buddhist abbot handed monastic property down to a chosen successor, establishing patriarchal lines of succession. This, combined with certain doctrinal variations, helped generate what are often called the sects of Chinese Buddhism. It should be emphasized that while these sects did become formally distinct in Japanese Buddhism, in China, especially through Tang times, the situation remained more fluid.[15] Nonetheless, there were certain subdivisions in Chinese Buddhism that can loosely be considered as sects. In particular, through long resonance with native Daoist language and ideas, the Chinese domestication of Buddhism reached a kind of culmination in something called Chan (in Japanese, Zen; in Korean, Sŏn). ,

From the early Chinese conviction that there was a Buddha Nature in every person, it began to be supposed that this Buddha Nature was everywhere and that salvation could be attained in this life merely through realization of this truth. In Chan Buddhism, enlightenment is sought not by escaping from the world but by awakening to the reality of the world around you. The word *Chan* literally means "meditation" (from the Sanskrit *dhyāna*), and meditation was central to Chan: not merely as a way to enlightenment but as enlightenment itself in practice. Chan meditation – the stripping away of thoughts and sensations and the elimination of superficial distinctions to realize the fundamental unity of all things – was aided by characteristically enigmatic riddles intended to stimulate awakening. The study of scripture, on the other hand, was said to be useless because ultimate truth simply cannot be reduced to words. Chan Buddhism famously has been described as "a special transmission outside the scriptures, not founded upon words and letters" but rather "pointing directly to [one's] mind."[16] Appropriately enough, the particularly renowned Sixth Chan Patriarch Huineng (638–713) began life as an illiterate firewood seller and apparently never learned to read.

By the end of the Tang Dynasty, and especially under the next dynasty (Song, 960–1279), Chan had become perhaps the mainstream of Chinese Buddhism. Chan, by this time, was quite thoroughly Chinese, and most of its actual development can be traced back to the Chinese Sixth Patriarch Huineng. Even with Chan, however, a legendary Indian origin was still obligatory. According to tradition, the Chan transmission had passed through twenty-eight generations in India, starting from Śākyamuni Buddha himself, until a south Indian Brahman known as Bodhidharma brought it to China sometime around the year 500. Bodhidharma was certainly a real historical figure, but most of the legend associated with him developed only later, together with the maturation of the Chan school itself. He is best known for supposedly introducing the meditative technique of "wall watching" as a method of calming the mind. Bodhidharma, then, is regarded to have been the First (Chinese) Chan Patriarch.

Despite the Chinese domestication of Buddhism, genuine Indian connections still existed. The great Chinese pilgrim Xuanzang went on a seventeen-year journey to India and the western regions in early Tang. He returned in 645 and presided over the translation into Chinese of more than thirteen hundred rolls of Indian scriptures he had brought back. In the middle of the Tang Dynasty, three prominent South Asian missionary monks, Śubhakarasiṃha (637–735), Vajrabodhi (671–741), and Amoghavajra (705–774), introduced Esoteric (Tantric) Buddhism to the Tang court. Amoghavajra was especially influential, enjoying the support of three Tang emperors. In 765, when the Tang capital was threatened by an invading enemy army, the emperor, instead of organizing military resistance, sent copies of Amoghavajra's new version of the *Sūtra for Benevolent Kings* to two temples, where priests recited the scripture and officials burnt incense for the protection of the state. When the invasion failed, Amoghavajra was credited with the victory.

Among Amoghavajra's Chinese disciples was the monk Huiguo (d. 805), who in turn instructed the visiting Japanese monk Kūkai (774–835) as well as at least one monk from Korea and another from what may have been the island of Java. Kūkai was then responsible for introducing Esoteric Buddhism to Japan, where it is called Shingon. In Japan, this Esoteric Buddhism became much more important than it was in China, largely as a result of Kūkai's own incomparable talents. As Kūkai described it, a direct sequence of transmission from Vairocana (the first of the five celestial Buddhas) linked Esoteric Buddhism directly to Amoghavajra, then Huiguo, and finally Kūkai himself. Despite such claims, however, Kūkai actually studied under the Chinese master Huiguo a mere six months. Any real transmission of learning must have been somewhat tenuous.

Chinese contacts with India continued during the Tang and afterward, and the volume of maritime trade with Indian ports actually accelerated. But the center of gravity for Chinese (and East Asian) Buddhism had shifted now to China, and Chinese Buddhism developed thereafter almost exclusively in the Chinese language. A number of late Tang monks, such as Huaisu (b. 737), are best known for their achievements in calligraphy, which is not only a quintessentially Chinese art form but is also necessarily in the Chinese language (see Figure 4.1). Other late Tang monks are famous for their Chinese-language poetry, including Jiaoran (ca. 734–ca. 792), who once playfully wrote, "I don't like foreign languages; I won't study them; And I've never translated barbarian words."[17] Given the extreme importance placed on translating Indian scriptures in the early phase of Chinese Buddhism, this represents a remarkable loss of interest in anything foreign. Such self-absorption, however, is entirely consistent with the general monolingual self-confidence that Chinese civilization was beginning to display.

Watershed: The Mid-Tang Crisis

Tang Taizong was succeeded on the throne in 649 by a weaker son, who was (inappropriately) attracted to one of his father's former concubines, Wu Zetian (ca. 625–705). This Lady Wu soon became the real power behind the throne, and after the emperor's death, she placed two of her own sons on the throne in

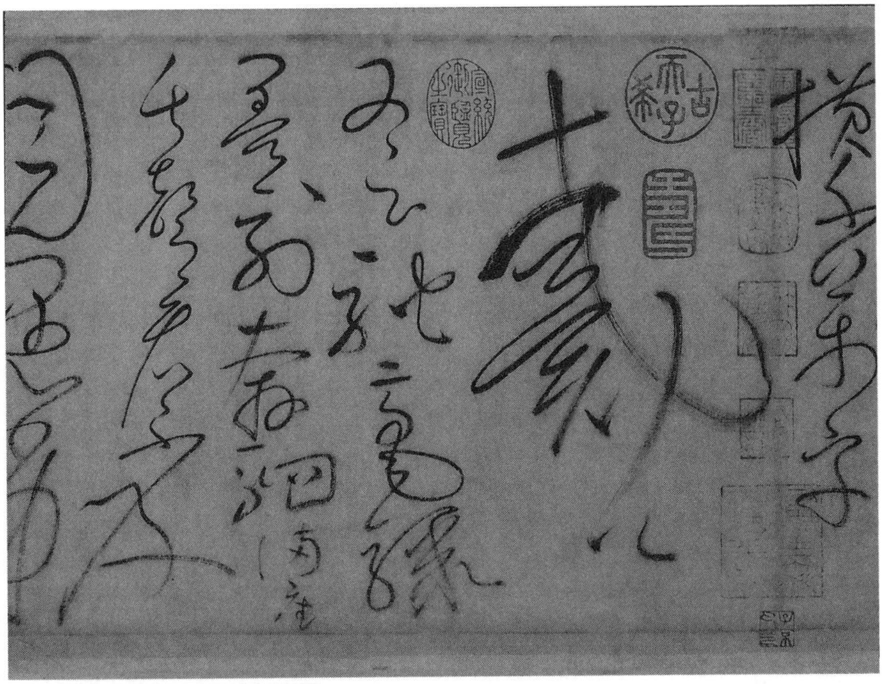

Figure 4.1. "Autobiography," calligraphy by the Tang Dynasty Chinese Buddhist monk Huai-su (Huaisu; 737–ca. 770s). National Palace Museum, Taiwan, Republic of China.

quick succession. In 690, drawing on the support of the Buddhist *Great Cloud Sūtra*, which predicted that the Future Buddha Maitreya would one day be reincarnated as a female ruler, she broke completely with precedent and proclaimed herself the founding emperor of a new Zhou Dynasty. Although there have been several women in Chinese history who exercised actual supreme power, typically from the position of empress dowager, Wu Zetian is the only woman to ever officially hold the title "emperor." Wu Zetian was ruthless (and undeniably a usurper), but she was also a dynamic individual and a capable monarch, and she has understandably been the subject of considerable fascination ever since.

In her old age, however, when Empress Wu was about eighty, power finally slipped from her hands. She was compelled to restore the Tang Dynasty in 705 and allow her son to resume the throne. After several more years of palace intrigue, in 713, another great Tang emperor, Xuanzong (r. 713–756), ascended the throne. The reign of Emperor Xuanzong is commonly regarded as the golden age of the Tang – the most glorious period of a generally glorious dynasty – and is especially celebrated for the outstanding poets it produced. Xuanzong's reign ended, nonetheless, in disaster.

For roughly a century, the Tang Empire had remained militarily dominant. In 647, a Tang army had been able to intervene as far away as India to suppress a rebellion. In 659, the Tang defeated the Western Türks (having already defeated those in the east). In 668, in alliance with Silla, Tang crushed the northern Korean kingdom of Koguryŏ. The ultimate Tang military high water mark did not come until as late as 750, when Tang armies captured Tashkent in Central Asia. Long before that time, however, the military tide had already begun to turn. Korea, under unified Sillan rule, proved stubbornly independent. Around 679, the Eastern Türks restored their independence in what is sometimes called the second Türk Qaghanate. By the end of the seventh century, there were also the first stirrings of Khitan power in the northeast. Most dangerous, however, was the rising new Tibetan Empire.

The various tribes of Tibet were first unified under King Songtsen Gampo (Srong-btsan sgam-po, r. ca. 618–641). The royal seat was initially in the southeast, at Yarlung, and then later at Lhasa. Songtsen Gampo's reign also coincides with the introduction of Buddhism into Tibet, from both Tang China in the east and India in the south. The king accepted a royal Chinese bride, who supposedly discouraged the Tibetan practice of smearing their faces with red ochre, but the king also married a princess from Nepal and adopted an Indian, rather than the Chinese, writing system, laying the foundations for the emergence of a distinctive Tibetan civilization. Beginning around 665, this new Tibetan Empire overran Khotan, Kuchā, Karashar, and Kashgar in previously Tang-dominated Xinjiang and, shortly before that time, also captured the area of modern Qinghai. Although Tang counteroffensives recaptured some of these outposts, the Tang now confronted a highly formidable imperial rival in the west.

In 747, a Tang general of Korean descent named Gao Xianzhi (Ko Sŏnji in Korean) won a victory in the vicinity of Gilgit, Kashmir. Growing overconfident, he began offensive operations against the small kingdoms in the western regions, and in 750, he took Tashkent. The captive king of Tashkent was sent to the Chinese capital, where he was executed, but the king's son fled west, where he gained the assistance of an Arab army. In 751, these Arabs defeated Tang forces at the Talas River in what was one of the great pivotal battles of world history. This Arab victory marked the beginning of the rise of the new religion of Islam in Central Asia and a permanent end to Chinese influence west of the Pamir Mountains.

Meanwhile, the Tang emperor Xuanzong had become besotted by the beautiful Yang Guifei ("Precious Consort Yang"). Yang Guifei extended patronage to her own favorites at court, among whom was a certain military general of mixed Central Asian (Sogdian) and Türkic parentage named An Lushan (ca. 703–757). An Lushan was supposedly so fat that he caused more than one horse to collapse and die under him. Thanks to Yang Guifei's support, An Lushan came to control the major Tang frontier armies in the northeast, in the vicinity of modern Beijing. After a dispute with Yang Guifei's brother, however, An Lushan rebelled in 755.[18] The Tang capital quickly fell to the rebels. Emperor Xuanzong fled, and was forced to execute his beloved Yang Guifei along the road.

Emperor Xuanzong's heir reorganized the loyalist imperial forces and proclaimed himself the new emperor, and in 757, both Tang capitals (Chang'an and Luoyang) were retaken with the aid of Uighur Türk and Arab allies. Although An Lushan was killed in 757 by his own son, the warfare touched off by his rebellion was not finally quelled until 762. To hasten the peace, rebel generals were confirmed in positions

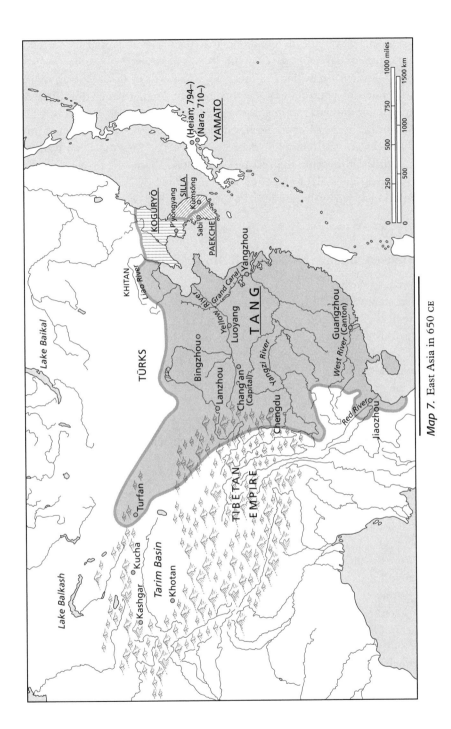

Map 7. East Asia in 650 CE

of independent power on the condition that they at least nominally surrender. Effective centralized Tang imperial authority was never entirely restored.

After An Lushan's rebellion, as much as 80 percent of the country's military force fell under the control of largely independent frontier commands. The central imperial government was unable to collect taxes from large swathes of China. Even within the imperial court itself, eunuchs (a eunuch was a castrated imperial household servant), through their control of the Imperial Guard and the Palace Secretariat, became the real power holders. From 821 to the end of the dynasty, seven out of eight emperors were enthroned by eunuchs, and two may have even been killed by the eunuchs. Politically, the Tang Dynasty had been greatly weakened.

The "Transmission of the Way" and Growing Commercialization

An Lushan's rebellion in 755 is commonly thought to mark an important watershed, not merely in the history of the Tang Dynasty but also for the entire course of Chinese history. Conventional wisdom has it that the exotic foreign origins of the rebel An Lushan provoked increased suspicion of foreigners thereafter. Although Uighur Türks and other non-Chinese forces helped Tang loyalists suppress the rebellion, they also unleashed much looting and slaughter of the Chinese population in the process. Despite these developments, however, the volume of foreign trade actually continued to increase after the rebellion, bringing with it, among other things, increasing numbers of Arabs and Persians to Chinese coastal ports. China definitely did not retreat into economic isolationism after An Lushan. But the great age of Chinese cultural cosmopolitanism really was over, whether or not An Lushan was to blame.

Part of the reason for the decline of the old cosmopolitanism may have been because, for the first time in history, China was coming to be surrounded by comparably organized foreign states or countries. China could no longer very credibly pretend to be a universal civilization surrounded merely by barbarian tribes. Some of these new foreign countries, moreover, were militarily threatening. During An Lushan's rebellion, for example, the Tibetan Empire took advantage of the distraction to resume its offensive, briefly even capturing the Tang capital in 763. From 780 to 848, the Tibetans controlled the important northwestern silk road oasis of Dunhuang, in Gansu.

After 842, the Tibetan Empire began to split apart due to internal disputes. Tibet would not be reunified again until the era of Mongol domination in the thirteenth century, and would never again be a major military power. But the Tibetan imperial presence in the northwest was replaced by the new forces of the Uighurs and Tanguts. A Uighur Türkic Empire (744–840) had succeeded the second Türk Qaghanate on the steppe directly to the north of China (in what is today called Mongolia), but in 840, the Uighurs were scattered by yet another steppe tribe, the Kirghiz, and the center of Uighur power relocated west to Xinjiang.[19] This brought Uighur Türkic-language speakers in substantial numbers to Xinjiang for the first time and is the origin of Xinjiang's modern alternative designation as

Eastern Turkestan. Much of the population of Xinjiang today is still Uighur. The Tanguts, for their part, did not establish a formal empire, called Xia (or "Western Xia," Xi Xia), in the Ordos region of northwestern China until 1038 (–1227), but they were already mentioned in Chinese sources from early Tang times.

In the northeast, in eastern Inner Mongolia, Manchuria, and extending into parts of China proper, a people called the Khitan had formed a powerful imperial state by 907 (–1125), which formally adopted the Chinese-style dynastic name Liao in 947. Also in Manchuria, an independent kingdom called Parhae (which had both Chinese and Korean influences) lasted from 698 until it fell to Khitan forces in 926. Korea, meanwhile, had been unified under independent native rule since 668.

In the southwest, in modern China's Yunnan Province, a regionally powerful kingdom called Nanzhao flourished from about 738 to 937, and was succeeded by another independent kingdom called Dali (937–1253). In the southeast, Vietnam (then called Annam) gained permanent independence in 939, becoming a foreign country. By late Tang times, China was increasingly, therefore, becoming just one country among other roughly equivalent countries. Some of these foreign countries were organized in fashions similar to the Chinese empire, and some posed serious military threats. The result was a multistate international system, fostering some of the preconditions for what might even be called proto-national identity formation. Two short Tang Dynasty essays written in the late ninth century explicitly considered the issue of what was Chinese identity, and both concluded that political loyalty and adherence to Confucian ideals were the main criteria for being Chinese.[20]

Another reason for the demise of the great age of cultural cosmopolitanism in China may have been because, as described earlier, Chinese culture was by this time becoming increasingly standardized. The extension of formal Chinese-language education and the spread of common cultural expectations during the Tang Dynasty may have been more responsible for a growing consciousness of difference between Chinese and foreigners than any fear inspired by An Lushan's rebellion. Central to this more unified culture of late Tang were the first stirrings of a great Confucian revival, which would color all the remainder of premodern Chinese and East Asian history. This Confucian revival began with a call to reject the ornate literary parallelism of recent prose writing and return to the so-called ancient writing of the classics. A new emphasis was placed on fundamental philosophical principles, such as human nature and "principle" itself (*li*), and on understanding the broad meaning of the Confucian Classics rather than narrow textual study.

Two authors in particular prefigure what has come to be known as Neo-Confucianism: Han Yu (768–824) and Li Ao (d. ca. 844). In their writings, they fabricated a new vision of an "orthodox transmission" of the Confucian Way, or *Dao*, that began with the legendary Sage Kings Yao, Shun, and Yu and was passed to the founders of the Shang and Zhou dynasties, the Duke of Zhou, and finally to Confucius and Mencius. As Han Yu wrote in a letter in 820, this Orthodox Dao then went into decline after the time of Confucius and never completely recovered from the First Emperor of Qin's notorious book-burning campaign, hanging at times by only a thread.[21] The implicit claim was that this Confucian Dao had now been rediscovered and revitalized in a kind of Chinese Renaissance. The explicit claim, unambiguously, was that there is only a single line of correct succession and a unitary Confucian truth. Under the next dynasty (the Song), this would begin to be called the *Dao Tong*: the "Transmission of the Way."

Despite the claim to origins in remote antiquity, this was actually a rather new idea that may furthermore have even been influenced by contemporary Buddhist concepts of patriarchal lines of transmission. Neo-Confucianism, in fact, was deeply shaped by Buddhist and Daoist influences. However innovative it may have been, however, this idea of the *Dao Tong* helped cement in place a powerful vision of a unitary China that had supposedly existed since the dawn of time.

The circulation of material goods through trade, even as it brought China into more extensive contact with foreigners, also helped create a more uniform Chinese market and provided expanded opportunities for both physical and social mobility throughout the empire. Late Tang China was becoming highly commercialized. Following An Lushan's rebellion, the Equitable Fields land allocation system, first put into operation by the Northern Wei, collapsed, together with many of the other old government economic regulations. Agriculture came increasingly to be performed by tenant farmers, based on written contracts. Trade and commerce boomed. Even the government turned toward sources of commercial profit to sustain its finances, and state monopolies on such products as salt and alcohol relied increasingly on the operations of expert merchants and market forces.

The story of Dou Yi (d. ca. 840) may help illustrate the new entrepreneurial energy of late Tang China, as well as some of its limitations. As a youth, Dou Yi had some female relatives in the imperial palace and an uncle who was a high official, with a family temple in the capital. When Dou was a teenager, he received a pair of fine silk shoes as a gift, which he promptly sold in the market for 500 cash, beginning a small accumulation of capital. In spring, when there were many winged elm seeds floating in the city air, Dou collected some and planted them in his uncle's family temple. The trees that grew from these he cultivated and sold in various forms, beginning to amass real wealth. After various other clever initiatives, Dou purchased some inexpensive, apparently worthless, low-lying swampland in the city's western market. He set up stalls around the edges of the depression, where he sold fried pastries and dumplings, and he encouraged children to throw bits of rubble at a flag he planted in the middle of the mire, rewarding those who hit the flag with pastry treats. The rubble they threw into the muck quickly filled it in, and Dou then built a handsome shop with twenty rooms on the newly reclaimed land. Dou went on to cultivate good relations with officials and become a broker in government offices and an investor, dying a wealthy man.[22]

This story of Dou Yi does not come from an orthodox history and may even be more what we would today consider fiction than an accurate record of actual events. The story was recorded already in the ninth century, however, so the type of entrepreneurial behavior it describes must at least have not seemed entirely implausible to a late Tang audience. Clearly Dou Yi's brand of enterprise is not modern-style industrial capitalism, but the tale is nonetheless colorful testimony to the kind of urban business energy and acumen that was fueling unprecedented economic development by late Tang times. The market-based commercial development that began in late Tang and culminated in the subsequent Song Dynasty was "so remarkable that some scholars . . . view it as an early stage of protocapitalism."[23]

By the end of the Tang Dynasty in 907, although modern nationalism and the nation-state were still far in the future, something like an emergent Chinese national identity may have already been prefigured. The economy was highly commercialized and largely market based. The social order was becoming surprisingly fluid, with a nonhereditary meritocratic elite increasingly determined by anonymously graded performance on written tests. Even the technology of woodblock printing was beginning to have an impact. The obvious contrast is with what was happening in Western Europe, where, although Charlemagne was anointed "Emperor of the Romans" in 800 and promoted a justly famous "Carolingian renaissance," Charlemagne himself was scarcely literate, the former unity of the Roman Empire throughout the Mediterranean was never restored, status was becoming rigidly hereditary, and there had been a long-term decline in the production and commercial exchange of material goods. This was a time in human history when Western Europe became a relative backwater, and China, which may have contained one-third of the world's total population by the tenth century, strode to global center stage.

The Birth of Korea: Unified Silla (668–935)

Unification of the Korean Peninsula (668)

Among the new countries that emerged along the borders of the Tang Empire was the one we call Korea. The early histories of both Korea and Japan would be incomprehensible except as parts of a larger East Asian community. During the centuries of division in China following the collapse of the Han Dynasty, and continuing on through the reunified Sui and Tang dynasties, a degree of shared international aristocratic culture had developed throughout East Asia. This was a time when elites in China, Korea, and Japan (as well as northern Vietnam, which remained directly part of the Chinese Empire until 939) in some ways had more in common with each other than they did with their own peasants living in nearby villages. In particular, educated East Asians shared a common written language and literary canon. The glories of Tang poetry were as much admired by contemporary elites in Korea and Japan as they were in China. In fact, Bai Juyi was arguably even more highly regarded in Japan than he was at home in China – a healthy reminder that even direct cultural influences can take different local forms, based on local variances in taste and experience and the almost universal human desire for self-assertion.

Particularly vital to the formation of a shared East Asian cultural community were the connections provided by Buddhism. When the Sui Dynasty in China ordered the establishment of a network of Buddhist reliquary pagodas in every province, for example, ambassadors from the Three Korean Kingdoms all requested relics from the Sui court and erected similar pagodas in their own states. A monk from

Koguryŏ called Hyegwan (fl. 625–672) studied in China under the master who is credited with founding the Three Treatise school of Buddhist doctrine. After returning to Koguryŏ, he traveled to Japan in 625, where he is considered to have formally introduced the Three Treatise school (although he may not really have been the first to bring its ideas to Japan), and eventually even became official head (*Sōjō*) of the Japanese Buddhist church.

The sacred scriptures of East Asian Buddhism came to Korea and Japan in Chinese-language translation. Almost imperceptibly, this Buddhist transmission was a lubricant bringing with it other Chinese influences as well. For example, the Sillan monk Chajang went to Tang China in 636 to study Buddhism. In 643, he was summoned home by the king of Silla. It was at his suggestion, then, that in 649, Silla officially adopted Tang-style clothing and, in 650, the Tang calendar and reign periods for dating purposes.

Another Sillan monk, Wŏn'gwang (d. 640), studied for eleven years in Tang and was subsequently honored at the Sillan court, lecturing frequently on the scriptures. Wŏn'gwang is credited with formulating, in 602, a highly influential Sillan secular code of conduct in five precepts: (1) serve one's lord with loyalty, (2) serve one's parents with filial piety, (3) interact with friends in good faith, (4) do not retreat from battle, and (5) exercise discretion in the killing of living things. The first two of these precepts are explicitly Confucian, even using the standard Chinese characters for *loyalty* and *filial piety*. Only the last precept can be called Buddhist, and even it appears somewhat modified, since, presumably, a proper Buddhist should refrain from killing altogether. The fourth precept, enjoining fearlessness in battle, may represent native Korean tradition. Altogether, these five precepts constitute a classic example of cultural interaction. Wŏn'gwang is also credited with drafting a successful Chinese-language written request on behalf of the Sillan king for Chinese military assistance against the rival Korean kingdom of Koguryŏ.[24]

In the early seventh century, each of the Three Korean Kingdoms sent envoys requesting Chinese military assistance against their Korean neighbors. Somewhat surprisingly, it was Silla that proved successful. There had been little contact between Silla and China until the end of the sixth century. According to one sixth-century Chinese report, Silla was still preliterate, and all communication had to go through Paekche. Over the course of the sixth century, however, Silla was reorganized along more familiar East Asian lines. Sillan Buddhist monks began to make the journey west to China in search of the dharma. In 631, the new Chinese Tang Dynasty constructed expanded school facilities in its capital, and thousands of foreign students were reportedly attracted there from the Three Korean Kingdoms, Tibet, Turfan, and elsewhere. Beginning in 640, members of the Sillan royal family itself went to study at the Tang capital.

There had been repeated conflicts between China and Koguryŏ throughout the Sui and early Tang dynasties. The first Sui clash with Koguryŏ had come in 598. The massive series of disastrous Sui invasions of Koguryŏ that began in 612 are conventionally blamed for the rapid disintegration and fall of the Sui

Dynasty. In 618, Tang replaced Sui, and after Tang rule was stabilized, conflicts with Koguryŏ reignited. Between 644 and 658, Tang conducted five substantial campaigns against Koguryŏ. The repeated Chinese inability to defeat Koguryŏ by direct invasion, and the stiffness of Koguryŏ resistance, may have finally persuaded Tang to adopt a new strategy: outflanking Koguryŏ with an attack from the south, in alliance with Silla.

This shifted the immediate point of attack to the southwestern Korean kingdom of Paekche. In 650, a Sillan emissary (the future King Muyŏl, r. 654–661) was sent on a mission to personally ask the Tang emperor for military assistance against Paekche. In 651, a member of the Sillan royal family named Kim In-mun (d. 694) began service in the Tang imperial bodyguard. Kim In-mun was then able to use his position as an intermediary with a foot in both the Tang and Sillan courts to help coordinate a successful military alliance between Tang and Silla. Kim finally died at the Tang capital in 694, after helping to smooth over later ruptures between the two allies.

With guidance from Kim In-mun, and a hundred Sillan warships to convey Tang troops to the battlefield, a combined Tang and Sillan attack on Paekche in 660 successfully captured its capital. The Paekche royal family was brought back to China as prisoners, but a Paekche prince who had been away in attendance at the court in Japan was proclaimed by the Japanese as the new king, and with Japanese support, an expedition was launched to restore Paekche. At a great river battle fought in 663, the combined Tang and Sillan navies reportedly sank four hundred Japanese warships, sealing the fate of Paekche and ending Japanese influence on the continent for almost a millennium.

Meanwhile, Koguryŏ had been weakened by internal conflict. In 642, the Koguryŏ aristocrat Yŏn Kaesomun killed the king and, appointing a figurehead monarch, assumed the role of strongman himself. When he died in 666, his sons quarreled among themselves. One of these sons, Chŏn Namsaeng, eventually defected to Tang, bringing with him a powerful force. This last strongman of Koguryŏ then contributed to the final Tang and Sillan conquest of his own former kingdom in 668, for which he was rewarded with an appointment as a Tang general.

After the fall of Koguryŏ in 668, the Tang Dynasty is reported to have relocated as much as 5 percent of its total population to sparsely inhabited areas of China.[25] A surprising number of persons from both Koguryŏ and Paekche are known to have subsequently served with distinction in the Tang military – the most famous being the second- or third-generation descendant of a Koguryŏ émigré who captured Tashkent for the Tang in 750. In Korea, the victorious Tang Dynasty apparently expected to incorporate the peninsula directly into the Chinese Empire. Tang governors were appointed, but the Tang did not station sufficient occupation forces on the peninsula to maintain control against determined resistance. By 676, Silla had expelled the Tang presence, and the Korean peninsula (up to a line somewhere north of modern P'yŏngyang) was now unified, for the first time ever, under native rule.

Silla

Silla may have originated as a cluster of six tribes governed by a council of tribal elders. Although Silla gradually became a more centralized (and larger) state, acquiring a single hereditary ruler, known as the *Maripkan*, by the fourth century, and reportedly adopting the Chinese title "king" (*Wang*) in 503, a degree of collective decision making by the top aristocracy always remained a distinctive feature of Sillan society. A Council of Nobles (*Hwabaek*) decided such crucial issues as the royal succession. Sillan society also remained highly aristocratic, graded in terms of something called bone rank (*kolp'um*). The framework of a Chinese-style bureaucratic government had been proclaimed in 520 with new legal codes that established seventeen official titles, but these titles were awarded strictly according to hereditary bone rank. Bone rank determined the highest possible title to which a man could aspire, the maximum size of his home, and even what clothing he could wear.

There is some evidence to suggest that the status of women in Sillan society may have been somewhat higher than it was in contemporary China (or later Korean history). There were, for example, three reigning Sillan female kings (*Yŏwang*), as distinct from queens, who were merely consorts of male rulers. In general, descent continued to be traced through both paternal and maternal lines throughout the Sillan era, which naturally also made the inheritance of family names awkward. The Sillan royal Kim and royal consort Pak families may have been among the first in Korea to adopt hereditary surnames, by perhaps the sixth century, but the use of patrilineal surnames remained inconsistent even among royalty until as late as the tenth century – a clear indication that Silla was still a very different society from neighboring China. China, by contrast, may have been the first place on earth where hereditary family names were universal.

Also unlike nearby China, Silla had a warrior culture. Particularly renowned were the young aristocratic warriors called *Hwarang*, or Flower Youths. The *Hwarang* cultivated military skills and a heroic image. They also traveled to sacred mountains and rivers to perform ceremonial songs and dances and appear to have had multiple dimensions beyond mere fighting ability. In addition, in 583, a new oath banner system was implemented, organizing some of Silla's military forces around flags with differently colored borders (an intriguing organizational forerunner of the much later seventeenth-century Manchu banner system). Since top aristocrats of True Bone status sometimes still controlled their own private armies, this oath banner system may have helped bring military force more closely under centralized royal control.

After a Sillan king died in 632 without leaving any direct heir, and following two subsequent female kings, the exclusively royal bone rank of *sŏnggol*, or Hallowed Bone, became extinct, and Sillan kings thereafter shared the next lower True Bone rank (*chin'gol*) with the top aristocracy. This may be one reason why later Korean kings never claimed the pretensions to divinity that Japanese emperors did and why Korean kings also never (except briefly in the tenth century, and again in 1897) assumed the supreme East Asian title of "emperor" (unlike Japanese and

Vietnamese as well as Chinese monarchs). This may also help explain why Korean kings, despite their determined and ultimately successful struggle for independence from Tang China, remained more willing than Japanese rulers, for example, to accept the nominal status of tributaries to the Chinese emperor, since that delegation of status from a Chinese sovereign gave Korean kings some leverage against the otherwise powerful domestic Korean aristocracy.

In a phenomenon that has been observed in many other monarchies throughout world history, Sillan kings also aligned themselves domestically with persons of relatively humble rank against the independent power of the top nobility. In the case of Silla, that meant especially persons of Head Rank Six, which was the next highest rank below True Bone. Here, again, the Chinese bureaucratic model, with its ideal of possible upward mobility based on demonstrated merit (and service to the throne) rather than heredity, may have been useful in supporting the interests of the Korean kings.

After the unification of the Korean peninsula and the expulsion of Tang forces, Sillan contact with Tang China, ironically, seems to have actually increased. Much of this contact was commercial. In late Tang times, Sillans came to dominate the maritime trade of all northern East Asia, despite the fact that Silla produced no coins of its own and used Chinese money instead. With a favorable breeze, it was a two- or three-day voyage by boat from the west coast of Korea to China, and there seems to have been a large Korean presence in late Tang China. Several Tang cities had "Sillan wards," or "Sillan villages" in the suburbs.

There was also a "Sillan Office" in the Tang capital, designated to house Korean embassies. Sillans remained probably the most numerous group of foreign students studying in late Tang Chinese schools. Some eighty-eight Sillans are known to have passed the civil service examinations in China during roughly the last century of the Tang Dynasty. Several of them served in Tang government office before returning to Korea, where they became voices for the promotion of Confucian ideals.

Confucianism in Korea was still only in its infancy, however. In 682, Silla established a National Academy, where a small number of young Koreans were instructed in a Chinese-style curriculum that included the Confucian Classics, Chinese history, and Chinese literature. In 788, Silla inaugurated its first Chinese-style civil service examinations. The examination model had obvious attraction for both strong monarchs and ambitious men born into anything less than the highest ranks of the nobility. The role of examinations remained quite limited in Sillan times, but the introduction of Chinese-language education had profound implications for Korea (as well as Japan). The use of the Chinese writing system brought Korea into a distinctive East Asian cultural sphere to which some of Tang China's other neighbors – such as Tibet, with its Indian-derived script – did not equally belong.

At the same time, although the Chinese written language prevailed in Korea (only twenty-five native Korean-language poems survive from the tenth century or earlier, and even they had to be written using Chinese characters), the spoken language was overwhelmingly Korean. The modern Korean language, which is spoken today fairly uniformly throughout the peninsula, probably derives from

Sillan. Before Silla unified the peninsula in 668, there had certainly been at least some regional linguistic diversity. After the Sillan unification, however, everyone on the peninsula gradually came to speak the same language. This Korean language is, furthermore, entirely unrelated to Chinese and quite unlike even its probable closest relative, Japanese. Despite significant Chinese influences, therefore, the people of the peninsula became very distinctively Korean.

After about 780, the rising power of local warlords caused Sillan central government to enter a period of decline. Between 800 and 890, Silla experienced no fewer than fourteen revolts or coups by members of the royal family. Few Sillan kings died natural deaths in those years. Perhaps the most colorful figure from this age of warlordism was Chang Po-go (d. 846). Chang was an apparently Sillan-born swashbuckler of obscure origin who had traveled to Tang China, where he had served as a minor officer in the Tang army. Later, returning to Silla, he reported to the king that he had observed Sillans serving as slaves everywhere in China. Chang Po-go proposed establishing a garrison on what is now called Wando (Wan Island), off the southwestern tip the Korean coast, from where he could dominate the sea lanes and prevent further slave raids. The island base was duly established in 828, and Chang Po-go became a powerful sea lord, dominating the entire Yellow Sea region. When Chang Po-go tried to arrange a wedding between his daughter and the Sillan king, however, he was murdered by an outraged member of the aristocracy in 846.

As the Sillan state weakened, between 901 and 935, the Korean peninsula was temporarily divided once more into three kingdoms, which briefly even revived the old names Paekche and Koguryŏ. This division did not last, however, and in 935, the peninsula was again reunified under a new kingdom called Koryŏ. This name was an abbreviation of Koguryŏ (written with two characters instead of three) and is the origin for our English word *Korea*. The dynasty's founder was a man named Wang Kŏn (King T'aejo, r. 918–943). The subtlety of his position as the ruler of a fiercely independent country with a uniquely Korean culture that was nonetheless also simultaneously firmly part of a larger East Asian cultural sphere is nicely expressed by his injunction to his heirs in 943:

> We in the east have long admired the Tang style. Our literary matters, ritual, and music all follow their institutions. Yet, in strange regions and different lands, peoples' natures are each different. They need not improperly be made the same.[26]

Imperial Japan: Nara (710–784) and Early Heian (794–ca. Tenth Century [–1185])

The Taika Coup (645)

The reunification of the Chinese Empire under the Sui Dynasty in 589 dramatically altered the strategic balance in East Asia. For the first time in centuries, a resurgent, unified China was asserting its traditional nominal claim to authority over all "Under Heaven" and aggressively expanding its empire beyond the nuclear area of the Chinese heartland. This had serious implications for China's neighbors, and when the Sui Dynasty began to threaten offensive operations against the Korean peninsula, the Yamato court in Japan felt compelled to open direct contact with the Sui at the start of the seventh century. Within a period of just fourteen years after 607, Yamato dispatched no fewer than five embassies to first Sui and then Tang China. By this time, however, the Japanese court was no longer interested in buttressing its domestic authority with delegated Chinese titles, nor was it willing to play the humble Chinese-allotted role of tributary. Instead, the Yamato court was now claiming rival – if not actually superior – imperial status. The credentials of the embassy that was sent to Sui in 607 were notoriously addressed from the "Son of Heaven in the place where the sun rises to the Son of Heaven in the place where the sun sets."[27]

Japanese rivalry was inseparable from a certain degree of imperial imitation, however. Leading figures at the Japanese court were now consciously trying to build a powerful centralized state, somewhat like the model provided by Sui and Tang China. Japanese monks who had been sent to study in China with the early embassies began returning home in the 630s, bringing with them firsthand knowledge of conditions in the Tang Dynasty. A coalition developed involving some of these returned masters of Chinese learning, centering around the royal figure of Prince Naka no Ōe (who ruled later as Emperor Tenji, r. 662–671) and led by a man named Nakatomi Kamatari (614–669). According to tradition, Nakatomi Kamatari carefully weighed the ability of all the royal princes and judged Naka no Ōe the most promising for the purpose of promoting his cherished project of government centralization. Kamatari still lacked a personal relationship with Prince Naka no Ōe, but one day (the story goes), when the prince was playing kickball, he accidentally threw off a shoe, and Kamatari, respectfully retrieving the shoe, was finally able to establish the necessary connection. Only one thing now stood in the way of continental-style imperial centralization: the power of the Soga family.

After the death of the great Prince Regent Shōtoku in 622, the Soga, who had already been the most powerful court family for more than thirty years, began casting a lengthening shadow over the Yamato court. The Soga were even suspected of harboring ambitions to usurp the throne. Then, at a state ceremony in 645, in the presence of the empress herself, Prince Naka no Ōe and his co-conspirators struck suddenly, assassinating the leaders of the Soga family. A new Chinese-style imperial reign period was proclaimed, Taika (645–650), which literally means "Great Change" (although it is quite possible that this highly symbolic reign period name may have actually been chosen only retroactively, a few years later), and a momentous program of reforms was initiated. As a reward for his crucial service in this Taika coup d'état, a new family name was bestowed on Nakatomi Kamatari: Fujiwara. The name Fujiwara literally means "Wisteria Plain," and it supposedly commemorates the place where the conspirators first met to plot the removal of the Soga. This Fujiwara family would later become the leading family in Japan.

Traditional Japanese accounts probably paint a somewhat idealized portrait of the Taika reforms that were implemented after 645, but there is little doubt that a radical new centralization of power began to be rapidly asserted in the middle to late seventh century. As of the early 600s, it is likely that many local Japanese chieftains had still been really little more than "autonomous allies of the king," and the reach of the Yamato court may not have extended very far beyond the palace itself, except for some direct royal estates and certain groups of workers.[28] After the Taika coup d'état, the process of centralized state development in Japan accelerated and intensified. Part of the urgency behind this drive may have been fear of invasion from Tang China.

The Taika coup in Japan in 645 happened to coincide with the beginning of a new series of Tang Dynasty attacks on Koguryŏ, in Korea. When the Tang strategy shifted from direct frontal assault from the north to an alliance with Silla and an attack on Koguryŏ from the south, through Paekche, Yamato sent an expeditionary force to assist Paekche. The Japanese expeditionary force was annihilated in 663, however, with the reported loss of four hundred boats and ten thousand men. Paekche ceased to exist, and in 668, Koguryŏ was obliterated also. For a few years after 668, it even appeared as though the entire Korean peninsula might be brought under Tang control, which would have put Japan within easy reach as the next potential target of Tang conquest. Efforts to strengthen the Japanese state in this moment of crisis took the form of an accelerated adoption of Chinese-style imperial institutions, which was simply the most impressive administrative model then available, and which was also probably mostly introduced at this time only indirectly, through the intermediary of Silla in Korea rather than directly from Tang China.[29]

These late-seventh-century innovations included a new name for Japan. In speech, the old name Yamato probably long continued to be used, but Yamato was not a written word. The oldest written name for Japan was Wa. But though the origins of this name are obscure, and it did not become flagrantly offensive until much later, by the late 600s the Japanese court had already apparently become dissatisfied with Wa and favored a new written name, chosen for the meaning of its Chinese characters: Nihon ("Origin of the Sun," sometimes also pronounced *Nippon*). Nihon is still the standard Japanese name for Japan today. It was also about this time that the rulers of Japan definitely began using what has since become the standard Japanese title for "emperor," *Tennō* (literally, "Heavenly Sovereign"). This is a variant of the Chinese imperial title *Huangdi* (pronounced *Kōtei* in Japanese), but the complete set of standard Chinese imperial titles were also officially adopted in Japan.

These Chinese titles were originally used only in writing, however. The commentary to an eighth-century Japanese law code specified that in speech, Japanese monarchs should continue to be referred to by native-language titles such as *sumera mikoto*.[30] Oral pronouncements, in Japanese, remained central to the self-representation of the Japanese monarchy. The uniquely Japanese cult of imperial descent from the sun goddess Amaterasu, and imperial worship at the shrine in Ise, may have also only really crystallized at the end of the seventh century, and in the seventh and eighth centuries, the role of Japanese emperors as manifest deities (*akitsumikami*) was also clarified. In these centuries, Japan was refashioning itself as a Chinese-style centralized empire, but in a manner very much of its own choosing.

Nara (710–784)

The administration of this newly organized Japanese Empire received its clearest expression in a series of Chinese-style penal and administrative law codes. The earliest of these Japanese legal codes may have been issued in 668, but the system reached maturity with the Taihō Code of 701. Eight or nine of the nineteen persons who drafted this Taihō Code came from immigrant families, and some had participated in embassies to the continent, so its authors must have been reasonably familiar with continental precedents. The Japanese imperial bureaucracy that was structured by these codes included a state council, eight ministries, and forty-six bureaus. A comprehensive administrative hierarchy of provinces, districts, and villages was established throughout the empire. Household registration began in 670 as the basis for government-directed farmland allocation, tax collection, and military conscription. A new census was intended to be conducted every six years, and rice paddies were to be reallocated after each census, roughly along the lines of the Equitable Fields system that was then still in effect in China. Mandatory military service for all adult males was instituted, coins began to be minted, and the preparation of Japan's first written national histories began (resulting in the *Kojiki* and the *Nihongi*). Japan had now become a unified empire, even though some of the outlying islands still remained beyond imperial reach, and the far northeastern tip of the main island also remained largely independent until the twelfth century or even later.

At the heart of this newly centralized Japanese Empire was a great new capital city, Nara, which was planned and built between 708 and 712. Early Japanese capitals had changed with each ruler and often consisted of little more than a thatch-roofed wooden palace, not much different from the halls of other local Japanese chieftains. By the early seventh century, more impressive structures were being constructed, however, and Japan's first true Chinese-style capital city was at Fujiwara, just south of Nara, which was occupied from 694 to 710. Nara was not exactly, therefore, Japan's first capital, nor did it serve as capital very long. But Nara was a permanent city that still exists today. Notably, Nara's eighth-century Tōdai-ji (Eastern Great Temple) is still operational in its current reconstruction. In typical Chinese fashion, Nara was laid out in a regular grid design, orientated north to south, although Nara differed from most traditional Chinese cities in not being surrounded by a wall. The significance of this city is so great that it has given its name to what is conventionally called the Nara period of Japanese history.

Standard textbook descriptions of the Nara period emphasize the functional administrative aspects of the law codes and also Buddhism. Confucianism, however, was inseparable from the contemporary Chinese model, and written Japanese sources (at least) also do contain much Confucian-style rhetoric about rule by virtuous example. In 757, for example, Empress Kōken (r. 749–758) proclaimed, "To secure the rulers and govern the people, nothing is better than the [Confucian] Rites."[31] In the same year, she also ordered every household to maintain and study a copy of the *Classic of Filial Piety*, in imitation of an earlier Tang decree. Because it is inconceivable that many eighth-century Japanese households could have actually satisfied this command, this may also illustrate the extent to which continental influences were often a rather thin façade.

An Academy was established in Nara, near the palace gate, where instruction was provided in the Confucian Classics, calligraphy, law, mathematics, and Chinese-language pronunciation (necessary for reciting books written in Chinese). A network of schools, extending to every province, was also ordered opened. Twice-annual sacrifices to the spirit of Confucius were mandated at the academy, by law, beginning in 701. In ninth-century Japan, after participating in a spring sacrifice to Confucius and attending a lecture on the *Classic of Filial Piety*, Sugawara Michizane (845–903) exclaimed that the spirit of "the Sage [Confucius] was never far away."[32]

Ironically, however, this same Sugawara Michizane is more famous for recommending the abandonment of the last official Japanese embassy to Tang China in 894. Unlike in Korea, a Chinese-style examination-based meritocracy never matured in Japan, and growing frustration at the poor chances for bureaucratic promotion through the academy caused Miyoshi Kiyotsura (847–918) to lament in 914 that the academy had become "a pit of disappointment," to the extent that "parents warned each other not to let their children mention school."[33] In the eighth century, out of a total Japanese population of perhaps six million, it has been estimated that only about twenty thousand participated in elite literate culture, and the academy had only four hundred students. Provincial schools had difficulty finding qualified instructors, and even in the capital, teaching positions gradually became hereditary. In the twelfth century, the academy burned down and was not replaced.

Chinese influences had always been limited, and they were often wielded, moreover, in a conscious spirit of rivalry. Japan became, not part of the Chinese imperial order, but the center of its own independent Chinese-style imperial order. Highlighting this is the fact that, although the Nara period is conventionally considered to have been the peak period of continental influence on Japanese institutions and culture, paradoxically, compared to both earlier and later periods, "the country was in fact relatively closed."[34] Following the defeat of the Japanese expeditionary force to Korea in 663, an office was established on the southern island of Kyūshū, at the point of closest approach from Korea, which was intended to regulate all international contact, for the first time ever effectively sealing Japan's borders.

Rather than a regional superpower (in this case, Tang China) simply "influencing" its neighbors, what actually happened was that elements of the powerful Chinese model were selectively borrowed by China's East Asian neighbors and domesticated, often becoming ingredients of the "native" culture, with dynamics of their own. Some continental influences also had no affiliation with any particular country and might be quite inadvertent. A disastrous epidemic of smallpox introduced from the continent, for example, spread from Kyūshū to all the major population centers of Japan in 735–737 and may have killed a quarter or more of the entire Japanese population.[35] Buddhism, although it came to Japan from the continent in Chinese-language translation, and often in the form of specifically Chinese sects, nonetheless functioned as an independent variable. Buddhism had,

Figure 4.2. The Great Buddha (*Daibutsu*) at Tōdai-ji in Nara, Japan, bronze statue, 748–751? CE. Vanni/Art Resource, New York.

of course, originally been a foreign influence in China, too, and it stimulated complex patterns of interaction. For one thing, Buddhism arguably became a more powerful presence in Nara Japan than it did in Tang China.

After 746, the Buddhist Tōdai-ji (Eastern Great Temple) Construction Office in Nara became the largest Japanese government office. Tōdai-ji served as the headquarters for an empirewide system of state-sponsored Buddhism, with a branch temple in every province. For this there was Sui and Tang Chinese precedent, but no temple in the Tang capital overshadowed the city in quite the way Tōdai-ji did in Nara. The temple's awesome influence was symbolized by the completion of the sixty-four-foot-tall bronze Great Buddha at Tōdai-ji in 752 (see Figure 4.2). This Great Buddha also illustrates the international range of Buddhist connections. The grandson of a Korean who had fled to Japan after the fall of Paekche in 663, Kuninaka Kimimaro (d. 774), played a role in the casting of the Great Buddha, and the ceremonial opening of its eyes in 752 is said to have been performed by an actual Brahman from India named Bodhisena.

Chinese may have been the language of the Buddhist scriptures throughout East Asia, but the Indian Sanskrit language retained an aura of at least potentially superior sanctity. Around 770, one Japanese empress had a million copies of a *Dhāraṇī* charm, written in Sanskrit using Chinese characters, printed and placed in miniature wooden pagodas.[36] Shortly after the end of the Nara period, the renowned Japanese monk Kūkai was motivated to pursue Buddhist studies in China in part because he could not obtain a satisfactory explanation of the Sanskrit mantras and other esoteric symbolism in Japan, and he carefully brought forty-four rolls of Sanskrit texts back to Japan as evidence of his interest in Sanskrit. We may doubt that Kūkai really learned much Sanskrit, but as far as that is concerned, it is unlikely that he became very fluent in spoken Chinese either. After only one year in the Tang capital, Kūkai petitioned to be allowed to return to Japan with the embassy of 806. In Japan, Kūkai then played a decisive role in shaping the Japanese Shingon (Esoteric) sect and put his religion to the service of the Japanese state.

Early Heian (794–ca. Tenth Century [–1185])

In 764, a Buddhist nun and retired (female) emperor resumed the throne again, and in 766, she elevated a Buddhist monk to a position of virtual coruler, awarding him the title "dharma king." In 769, an oracle was even presented to the court suggesting that it might be auspicious if this monk himself were to become emperor – threatening to turn Japan into an outright Buddhist theocracy (and simultaneously also entailing a change of dynasty, and of ruling family). This must have alarmed many people at court, however, and the interpretation of this oracle was quickly reversed. The nun emperor promptly died in 770, and a greater distance was soon introduced between the sources of imperial legitimacy (rooted especially in the claim to descent from the native sun goddess Amaterasu) and Buddhism.

It may have been in part to escape the influence of the powerful Nara Buddhist temples that the imperial capital was permanently moved away from Nara in 784, although at the time, frequent shifts of capital were also still simply customary. After an abortive effort to build a capital somewhere else, a small village was chosen as the location for the new capital in 794, and the site was renamed Heian. This new city of Heian, known today as Kyōto (which simply means "capital"), would serve as the imperial capital of Japan for over a thousand years, until 1869. After 1185, however, real political power shifted for many years away from the imperial court, and historians therefore refer to the years between 794 and 1185, when Heian was the functioning center of Japan, as the Heian period.

Over the course of these four Heian centuries, the pattern of Japanese history profoundly shifted, and it also diverged fairly pointedly from the continental East Asian trajectory. The early Heian period can be viewed simply as a continuation of the Nara period from a different location. In some ways, Chinese influences were still only increasing in early Heian times, especially in matters of aristocratic high culture. The era when male and female monarchs occupied the throne for roughly equal lengths of time (which was decidedly unlike the Chinese imperial model) came to a rather abrupt end, for example, after 770. In all of Japanese history, there would only be one more reigning female emperor (Meishō, r. 1630–1643). In the early Nara period, some of the palace buildings had still been constructed in the native Japanese style – which typically featured cedar bark roofs; plain, untreated wood; and elevation above the ground on posts – but in the mid-eighth century, the Nara palace and administrative center was entirely rebuilt in the Chinese style, with heavy tiled roofs. Although the Nara period produced one magnificent collection of native Japanese-language poems, the *Manyōshū* (*Collection of Ten Thousand Leaves*, ca. 760), much of the literary energy in early Heian times was directed toward writing poetry in Chinese. By late Heian, however, the balance was reversing itself, and more uniquely Japanese styles and themes began to emerge.

In general, the tipping point between two quite different eras in Japanese history fell in mid-Heian, roughly around the tenth century, although most changes occurred only gradually and almost imperceptibly. Two particularly critical Heian era developments were the long-term weakening – to the point of virtual irrelevance – of centralized imperial government, and the rise of a new class of provincial warriors, who would come to be known as *bushi* or samurai. Both developments were largely without parallel in China. Another notable divergence was the almost complete triumph in Japan of a Buddhist-centered worldview (or episteme), even as China was experiencing its great Neo-Confucian renaissance and the beginning of a relative decline in the pervasiveness of Chinese Buddhism.[37] The roots of all these uniquely Japanese developments, which came to full fruition in late Heian, can be traced as far back as Nara times.

After the anticipated invasion from Tang China never materialized in the seventh century, for example, Japan no longer faced any serious foreign military threats, and the conscript army was allowed to lapse by as early as 792. Eventually, even the business of policing the Japanese countryside was abandoned by the central government and was delegated (or fell by default) to local warriors – the embryonic samurai. Meanwhile, the Nara system of direct imperial farmland allocation also began to fray in as little as half a century. The minting of copper coins, which had begun in 708, ended in 958. Japan had largely reverted to direct commodity exchange by the ninth century, due to inflation and other problems with the use of money, and many government-imposed market regulations also lapsed around that time. This did not mean that commerce necessarily declined – in fact, there is some evidence that commerce may have actually been increasing – but it did coincide with a weakening of the central government. Diminishing government revenue also encouraged powerful nobles to find other, private sources of income beyond their official stipends. These especially took the form of private landed estates, which, over time, characteristically became exempt from taxation and even entry by government officials.

Already in the Nara period, great noble families typically employed large private household staffs, and increasingly, these private aristocratic family administrations came to be the real bases of power. Even the imperial family itself eventually came to exercise its greatest authority privately, through the offices of so-called "Retired Emperors," by the end of the Heian period in the twelfth century. Among the small group of court nobles who came to dominate Heian politics and society, the Fujiwara family that had been founded by Nakatomi Kamatari at the time of the seventh-century Taika coup emerged as absolutely preeminent.

The formal basis of Fujiwara power was appointment as regent over either minor or adult emperors (two different titles in Japanese), but the real secret of Fujiwara success was intermarriage with the imperial family. Especially in a society such as Heian Japan, where children were commonly raised in the homes of their mother's (not their father's) families, the father-in-law or maternal grandfather of an emperor could wield great authority. The most renowned member of the Fujiwara family, Fujiwara Michinaga (966–1028), for example, actually held the title of regent for only one year, but four of his daughters married emperors, who gave birth to three more emperors, and at one point, Michinaga was simultaneously both grandfather and father-in-law to the same emperor![38]

While these political and economic structural changes were occurring, there were also important new developments in Japanese culture. As direct centralized imperial administration of the provinces was increasingly abandoned to custodial governors, who collected taxes and forwarded them to the court, the perspective of the great Heian aristocrats increasingly shrank, until it was effectively confined to the capital city alone. The lives of aristocratic women were especially sedentary and secluded. This was not because the status of Heian women was unusually low – Heian women, for example, retained their family name after marriage and had the right to initiate divorce – but they were expected to stay at home, secluded from prying eyes behind screens. If they ventured out, they traveled in covered oxcarts and generally did not go far. Though the mansions of leading Heian aristocrats could be very large, including multiple buildings and gardens with artificial hills and lakes, this was still a very circumscribed existence. For entertainment, some women turned to literature and developed it into a fine art.

By the tenth and eleventh centuries, self-consciously literary diaries began to be compiled, which were sometimes deliberately intended for others to read. In one famous case, Sei Shōnagon (b. ca. 965) claimed that her so-called *Pillow Book* began as private jottings that were accidentally discovered by a visitor and passed around at court.[39] Fictional tales were also composed to entertain the household and circulated in manuscript form. This newly developing Heian women's literature was written in the Japanese language, using the new Japanese syllabic writing system.

The Japanese Hiragana script, which had come into use by the start of the tenth century, was largely reserved for informal documents, frivolous entertainments, and women's writing. Serious texts were still expected to be written in Chinese. Hiragana was, in fact, commonly known as women's hand (*onnade*). This was so much the case that, although the first great literary diary in Japanese, Ki no Tsurayuki's (d. 946) *Tosa Diary*, was actually written by a man (around 936), he apparently felt obliged to adopt the pose in writing it of being a woman. The *Tosa Diary* is an account of a fifty-five-day return journey by the governor of Tosa, on the southern island of Shikoku, to the capital. The diary is introspective and self-consciously artistic, with a generous admixture of poetry, and it ends with the governor returning to his old home in Heian to find his garden in ruins – evoking the artistic melancholy and sensitivity to the mutability of all things that was the favorite sentiment of Heian Japan.

The full-length fictional prose novel also emerged from this Heian women's literature. The titles of some eighty tales survive from the ninth and tenth centuries, but the renowned *Tale of Genji* overshadows all other Heian productions and puts its stamp on the age. Lady Murasaki's (978–1016) lengthy fictional narration of the life and loves of the Shining Prince Genji is the consummate example of the exquisitely refined aesthetic taste perfected by the Heian court at its eleventh-century peak. This Heian period women's literature, moreover, although not without references to China, was uniquely and thoroughly Japanese. From the late ninth century, a distinctively Japanese high culture had emerged that was not so much a return to ancient pre-Taika native traditions as a dynamic new creation, revealing itself in cooking, clothing, and painting styles as well as the new Japanese-language literature.

Between 607 and 894, the Japanese government commissioned twenty official embassies to China. Of these, three never left Japan, and four got no farther than Korea. Perhaps three thousand people altogether participated in these embassies, but by one estimate, only about 130 Japanese pursued longer-term study in China during these centuries. China remained a very remote place for even the best-educated Heian aristocrats. It took, for example, three years for news of An Lushan's rebellion to reach the Japanese court. In 839, three people who had been assigned to accompany an embassy to China as students ran away and hid rather than obey the terrifying order.[40] In 894, the last embassy was simply cancelled.

The six great Chinese-style Japanese national histories (*Rikkoku shi*) that were compiled, beginning with the *Nihongi* in 720, came to an end in 887. Under the reign of Emperor Murakami (r. 946–967), one more official national history was commissioned but never finished, and the last Chinese-style legal code was begun but was also never completed.[41] The last Japanese coins were minted in 958. Meanwhile, after a lengthy period when Chinese-language poetry had been favored, the first imperial collection of Japanese-language poems, the *Kokinshū* (*Collection of Ancient and Modern* [*Poetry*]) was compiled in 905. Clearly the early tenth century, which witnessed the fall of the Tang Dynasty in China and of Silla in Korea, was also an important watershed for Japan.

The cancellation of the last Japanese embassy to China in 894 did not mean an end to all contact with the continent. Trade would actually continue to grow, continental cultural influences remained strong, and China may have even gradually come to seem somewhat less remote. Zen Buddhism (in Chinese, Chan), for example, had made only a limited impact on Japan before the tenth century, and it did not really flourish until the late twelfth and thirteenth centuries. The first recognized Chinese Zen master arrived in Japan in 1246, and during the thirteenth century, the full array of Chinese-style Zen practices was eagerly embraced by the new Japanese warrior elite.[42] But this warrior elite itself, which had no real counterpart on the continent, and even the growing dominance of Zen culture in medieval Japan – despite its self-proclaimed Chinese sources – was eloquent testimony that the broad course of Japanese history had begun to follow a distinctly independent trajectory.

For Further Reading

Authoritative coverage of China during this period is provided by Denis Twitchett, ed., *The Cambridge History of China*, vol. 3. *Sui and T'ang China, 589–906, Part 1* (London: Cambridge University Press, 1979). On the Sui Dynasty specifically, see Arthur F. Wright, *The Sui Dynasty* (New York: Alfred A. Knopf, 1978), and Victor Cunrui Xiong, *Emperor Yang of the Sui Dynasty: His Life, Times, and Legacy* (Albany: State University of New York Press, 2006). On the Tang, see Marc S. Abramson, *Ethnic Identity in Tang China* (Philadelphia: University of Pennsylvania Press, 2008); S. A. M. Adshead, *T'ang China: The Rise of the East in World History* (New York: Palgrave Macmillan, 2004); and Arthur F. Wright and Denis Twitchett, eds., *Perspectives on the T'ang* (New Haven, CT: Yale University Press, 1973). For Tang Dynasty religion, see Stanley Weinstein, *Buddhism under the T'ang* (Cambridge University Press, 1987).

On the controversial figure of Empress Wu Zetian, see Jo-shui Chen, "Empress Wu and Proto-Feminist Sentiments in T'ang China," in *Imperial Rulership and Cultural Change in Traditional China*, ed. Frederick P. Brandauer and Chun-chieh Huang (Seattle: University of Washington Press, 1994), and R. W. L. Guisso, *Wu Tse-t'ien and the Politics of Legitimation in T'ang China* (Bellingham: Western Washington University, 1978). On Empress Wu and the invention of printing, see also Timothy H. Barrett, *The Woman Who Discovered Printing* (New Haven, CT: Yale University Press, 2008).

The Tang Dynasty is considered to have been the golden age of Chinese poetry. The glories of Tang poetry may perhaps best be encountered through a series of books by Stephen Owen: *The Poetry of the Early T'ang* (New Haven, CT: Yale University Press, 1977), *The Great Age of Chinese Poetry: The High T'ang* (New Haven, CT: Yale University Press, 1981), and *The Late Tang: Chinese Poetry of the Mid-Ninth Century (827–860)* (Cambridge, MA: Harvard University Asia Center, 2006).

An excellent general introduction to Korean history is Ki-baik Lee, *A New History of Korea*, trans. Edward W. Wagner (Cambridge, MA: Harvard University Press, 1984). For premodern Korea, see also the more recent volume by Michael J. Seth, *A Concise History of Korea: From the Neolithic Period through the Nineteenth Century* (Lanham, MD: Rowman and Littlefield, 2006).

On Japan's relations with China in this era, see Zhenping Wang, *Ambassadors from the Islands of Immortals: China-Japan Relations in the Han-Tang Period* (Honolulu: University of Hawai'i Press, 2005).

Valuable studies of pre-Heian Japan include Herman Ooms, *Imperial Politics and Symbolics in Ancient Japan: The Tenmu Dynasty, 650–800* (Honolulu: University of Hawai'i Press, 2009), and Joan R. Piggott, *The Emergence of Japanese Kingship* (Stanford University Press, 1997). See also Bruce L. Batten, "Foreign Threat and Domestic Reform: The Emergence of the *Ritsuryō* State," *Monumenta Nipponica* 41, no. 2 (1986). On pre-Heian Japanese Buddhism, see also Kyoko Motomochi Nakamura, trans., *Miraculous Stories from the Japanese Buddhist Tradition: The Nihon Ryoiki of the Monk Kyōkai* (Cambridge, MA: Harvard University Press, 1973).

For Heian Japan, Donald H. Shively and William H. McCullough, eds., *The Cambridge History of Japan*, vol. 2. *Heian Japan* (Cambridge University Press, 1999), is authoritative. See also Mikael Adolphson, Edward Kamens, and Stacie Matsumoto, eds., *Heian Japan, Centers and Peripheries* (Honolulu: University of Hawai'i Press, 2007); Robert Borgen, *Sugawara no Michizane and the Early Heian Court* (Cambridge, MA: Harvard University Press, 1986); Paul Groner, *Saichō: The Establishment of the Japanese Tendai School* (Seoul: Berkeley Buddhist Studies Series, 1984); and Ivan Morris, *The World of the Shining Prince: Court Life in Ancient Japan* (Harmondsworth, UK: Penguin Books, [1964] 1985).

5 Mature Independent Trajectories (Tenth–Sixteenth Centuries)

Late Imperial China: The Song (960–1279), Yuan (1271–1368), and Early Ming Dynasties (1368–ca. Sixteenth Century [–1644])

The Song Dynasty Situation

In 907, an upstart military commander dethroned the last Tang emperor and proclaimed himself the founder of a (brief, as it turned out) new dynasty. Once again, China was plunged into a period of division. In north China, Five Dynasties followed each other in rapid succession – three of them founded by Shatuo Türks rather than ethnic Chinese – while southern China was simultaneously partitioned into ten separate regimes. This time, however, the division was only temporary. In 960, the mother of the seven-year-old boy emperor of the last of the northern Five Dynasties, acting in the capacity of a regent, ordered the commander of the Palace Guard, Zhao Kuangyin (927–976), to lead an army north against a rumored Khitan invasion. On the second morning of their march, some of Zhao's officers entered his residence with swords drawn and hailed him as emperor.

The result was a bloodless coup that brought a major new dynasty, the Song, onto the stage. Zhao Kuangyin is known to history as Emperor Taizu of the Song (r. 960–976). Because this Emperor Taizu was acutely aware of the fragmentation that had been caused by warlordism since the middle of the Tang Dynasty, and of the frequency of military coups like the one that had brought him to power, as emperor, he was determined to clearly separate military command from civilian administration. Emperor Taizu hosted a legendary palace banquet for his senior generals at which, with a toast, he relieved them of their military commands and retired them to lives of civilian comfort in the capital.

Emperor Taizu's policies would be successful enough that dynastic change would thereafter be very much less frequent and would never again be the result of an internal military coup. Although there were roughly eighty dynasties in premodern Chinese history, only three of them came after the Song (not counting peripheral alien regimes that sometimes extended into Chinese territory). Each of the

---

Some time ranges listed in the subheads in this chapter include additional dates in brackets. These dates indicate either the beginning or the ending of a dynasty (or other conventional historical period) that extends beyond the period covered in that section.

relatively few remaining changes of dynasty, furthermore, can be attributed to foreign invasion. The premodern Chinese sociopolitical order became rather remarkably stable in the thousand years remaining after the Song Dynasty began in 960 – but the flip side of this same coin was also a long-term decline in the prestige of military service and relative military weakness. China would thereafter repeatedly be threatened with foreign conquest.

The paradox of the Song Dynasty is that, although it was a time when China led the world in technology, commercial prosperity, and sophisticated culture and the arts – and a time when China may have held a third of the world's total population – yet even after the Song reunification was complete (by about 978), it was still a somewhat diminished, militarily more vulnerable China. Most formidably among the Song Dynasty's neighbors, a nomadic people called the Khitan had organized a semi-Chinese-style Liao Dynasty stretching across the northern steppes, which included sixteen prefectures of northeastern China proper. After a treaty that was concluded in 1005, the Song Dynasty was even compelled to make annual payments to the Liao of two hundred thousand bolts of silk and one hundred thousand ounces of silver and to treat the Khitan Liao Dynasty as an equal.

A dynasty formed by the Tangut people called Western Xia (Xi Xia, 1038–1227) controlled substantial territory in what is now northwest China.[1] In addition, the area that is now northern Vietnam had become independent during the post-Tang period of division and was never successfully brought back inside the Chinese Empire. The Red River valley area of northern Vietnam had first been conquered by the Qin Dynasty in the third century BCE. Under the Han Dynasty, it had actually been the location of the leading southern Chinese port and a major center of Chinese population in the southeast.[2] Although the region then enjoyed sporadic autonomy during the centuries of division between the Han and Tang dynasties, and it had been surpassed by Guangzhou (Canton) as a hub for China's maritime trade by the early Tang, northern Vietnam had nonetheless been part of the Chinese Empire for more than a thousand years by Song times. Yet the second Song emperor was persuaded to let it go. Reconquest, he was told, would not be cost-effective because northern Vietnam "is burning hot and pestilential, and twenty to thirty percent of our troops will die before seeing combat. Even if we get it, we will be unable to hold it."[3] Perhaps it was simply beyond the capacity of the Song Dynasty to reconquer Vietnam.

Independent Vietnam at least played along with the (quite nominal) role of being a Chinese tributary, but other Song neighbors were less compliant. Notably the Khitan Liao Dynasty and the Tangut Western Xia developed their own writing systems (as the Tibetans in the west had also already done) rather than use Chinese. Their use of non-Chinese scripts placed these societies largely outside the sphere of shared East Asian civilization. At the same time, however, the Khitan Liao Dynasty did, to some extent, adopt the Chinese political model. The Khitan dynastic founder – the same man who ordered the adoption of the first version of the distinctive Khitan writing system in 920 – could also speak the Chinese language, and had himself enthroned twice: once as a native Khitan-style leader in 907, and again later as a Chinese-style emperor in 915.[4] In fact, ironically

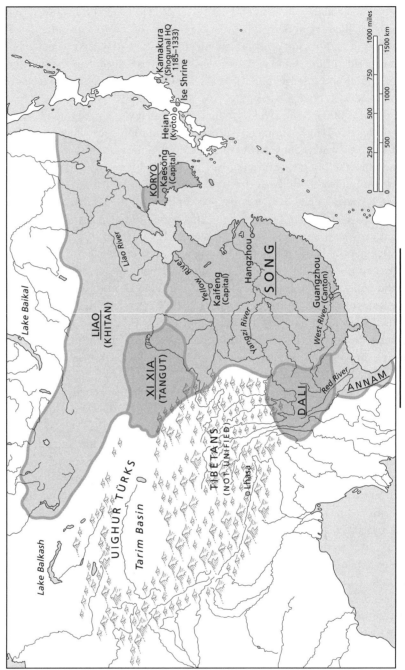

Map 8. East Asia in 1050 CE

enough, *Khitan* is actually the ultimate source of our word *Cathay*, which is today a somewhat poetic alternate English name for China. It has been perceptively observed that an "increasing emphasis on differences between" the Khitan north and the Chinese south "coincided with a growing political similarity between the two," suggesting that international rivalry may even be intensified by a degree of comparability in political form.[5]

The Khitan Liao Dynasty, meanwhile, ruled over a variety of different tribes and peoples, including several Jurchen tribes in the area of modern Manchuria. Beyond the Jurchen who submitted to the Liao Dynasty were still other so-called wild Jurchen living farther east, in the area of the Amur, Ussuri, and Sungari rivers in Manchuria. These Jurchen tribes were speakers of Tungusic languages, ancestral to what we now call Manchu. Although the Jurchen were forest-dwelling semi-agricultural villagers, not nomads, they learned from the Khitan the techniques of nomadic cavalry warfare and became skilled horsemen.

In 1114, Jurchen warriors, under a dynamic tribal leader named Aguda (1068–1123), rebelled and attacked the Khitan Liao Dynasty, soon taking the Chinese-language dynastic title Jin ("Gold") for themselves. By 1122, this new Jurchen-ruled Jin Dynasty had effectively destroyed the Khitan Liao regime, at which point they came into conflict with Song Dynasty China farther south. These Jurchen proved to be even more deadly foes for the Song than the Khitan had ever been. By 1127, a Song emperor had been captured and the Jurchen Jin Dynasty had overrun all of north China. A younger brother of the captive Song emperor then took the Chinese throne, and the Song Dynasty continued, withdrawing south to a temporary capital at Hangzhou and beginning what is known to history as the Southern Song (1127–1279). After some further military action, the border between the Jurchen Jin Dynasty and the Southern Song stabilized along the line of the Huai River, about a hundred miles north of the Yangzi.

Following their lightning conquest of north China, many of the Jurchen people moved down from Manchuria into China proper. In 1153, the Jurchen Jin capital was also relocated from Manchuria to what is now Beijing. The Jurchen people remained a minority, however, perhaps 10 percent of the total Jin Dynasty population: two or three million Jurchen ruled over some thirty million Chinese. Initially, the ethnic Jurchen and the Chinese populations of the Jin Dynasty were organized separately, and there was even some conscious revival of Jurchen cultural practices later in the dynasty, following a bout of Chinese-style imperial centralization. From their new homes scattered across north China, however, the Jurchen soon began intermarrying with the Chinese and speaking the Chinese language. Leading Chinese Confucian scholars living under the dynasty fully accepted its legitimacy.[6] In some senses, this Jin Dynasty even became what could legitimately be called a Chinese dynasty. Yet the Jurchen-ruled Jin Dynasty's rivalry with the Southern Song did not diminish. Some scholars have even seen in Song Dynasty Chinese hostility to the Jurchen an early stage in the development of a spirit of Chinese nationalism.[7] Then, in 1234, the Jurchen Jin Dynasty was inundated by an even greater new menace from the north: the Mongols.

Economic and Social Change

Compounding the paradox of a militarily weak Song Dynasty that nonetheless managed to flourish culturally and economically, after the loss of the north in 1127, the geographically much diminished Southern Song in some respects may have actually even begun the most flourishing phase of the whole dynasty. Although the land area controlled by the Song had shrunk dramatically, the Southern Song was the period when what has been called the Chinese "medieval economic revolution" reached its climax.[8]

Archeologists have uncovered large quantities of Chinese porcelain and other artifacts on the islands of Java and Sumatra (in what is now Indonesia), in what is now Malaysia, in the Philippines, in India, in East Africa, in the suburbs of Cairo in Egypt, and in the Persian Gulf, dating from late Tang times and swelling in volume during the Song. Song China enjoyed a flourishing maritime trade with the entire Islamic world, reaching as far west as Moorish Spain and almost everywhere in between. In the earliest phase of China's international maritime trade, much of the shipping that arrived in Chinese ports had been foreign – at first mostly Southeast Asian and then later Arab and Persian – but by Song times, China's own ships were the largest and finest in the world. With watertight compartments, sternpost rudders, and guided by magnetic compasses since at least the twelfth century, Song Dynasty Chinese ships became regular visitors to Indian ports and sometimes even appeared in the Persian Gulf and the Red Sea. The fourteenth-century Arab traveler Ibn Baṭṭūṭa, observing large Chinese ships with four decks and up to a dozen sails on the southwestern coast of India, concluded, "There is no people in the world wealthier than the Chinese."[9]

By Song times, the high-value, low-bulk luxury goods that had traditionally been the staple of long-distance world trade were yielding to more bulky and inexpensive commodities such as textiles, porcelain, pepper, rice, sugar, and even lumber, which could now be economically transported great distances in quantity for a profit. A number of Song ports were active in international trade, but the most important was Quanzhou (located on the mainland across from Taiwan). Although much of the Old World was incorporated into these trade routes, the largest importer of Chinese porcelains and coins in these centuries was probably Japan.[10] One fourteenth-century shipwreck off the Korean coast, explored by modern archeologists, sank while carrying 18,600 pieces of ceramics, sandalwood, and several tons of Chinese coins en route from China to Japan and had an apparently mixed crew of Chinese, Koreans, and Japanese, with a Japanese captain.[11]

Song Dynasty Chinese society was commercialized, technologically sophisticated, and urban. The city-dwelling population of Song China may have even been equal to the entire urban population of the whole rest of the world at the time.[12] It was not uncommon for wealthy merchants to combine their capital for fixed periods of investment, credit was available on commission from local brokers, and even futures contracts with commissioned agents were already being signed. Commercialization had become so pervasive that market forces determined even such less than obviously economic activities as the sale of concubines (secondary wives) and religious behavior. For example, it was now normal to hire different types of religious professionals to perform different specific religious services, as a kind of market transaction, and to abandon any god who did not appear able deliver tangible blessings. Coal-fired blast furnaces were producing iron in quantities that may have peaked in the eleventh century at levels nearly equal to that of all Europe combined as late as 1700.[13] Gunpowder was put to at least limited military application, for example, as an igniter for naphtha-based flame throwers. Paper money – which had first appeared in late Tang – was in wide circulation, and the technology of woodblock printing was promoting a revolution in the availability of books.

The first imperially printed edition of the Confucian Classics was completed in 953. The first complete printing of the standard East Asian Buddhist scriptures (the *Tripiṭaka*) was completed in 983, in 5,048 chapters. Soon after the establishment of the Song Dynasty, the Song law code was also ordered printed and distributed throughout the empire in 963, using the new technology of printing to help legitimize the new dynasty.[14] Not just central and local governments but also private academies, individuals, and professional bookshops all contributed to a (relative) explosion of printed books.

Among other literary achievements, the Song Dynasty is notable for the compilation of a number of still-valuable encyclopedias such as the *Taiping yulan* ([Encyclopedia Assembled for] Imperial Inspection during the Taiping Era [976–984]), which was completed in 983 in a thousand chapters. This encyclopedia arranges quotations from some two thousand different pre-Song texts, many of which are now lost, according to topic. Although the very earliest Chinese encyclopedias had appeared at the end of the Han Dynasty and in the Age of Division, and some still survive from the Tang, the Song represents a major step forward in this useful form of assembled and ordered human knowledge.

The increased availability of books may have also contributed to a major social transformation. In late imperial China, beginning with the Song, although there certainly were other ways of becoming wealthy, there was to a very large extent only one true elite career path: that of the scholar-official, or mandarin. The word *mandarin* is English, not Chinese. It is derived from Portuguese (and ultimately Sanskrit), but it is nonetheless used to describe a very uniquely Chinese sociopolitical class. In China, of course, there was nothing new about an association between elite status and a career in government, but the late imperial mandarins now – unlike their ancient predecessors – held office overwhelmingly on the strength of academic degrees obtained through anonymously graded written tests. The Chinese imperial civil service examination system finally came of age in the Song Dynasty.

If an annual average of only thirty *Jinshi* degrees were awarded in late Tang, by the Southern Song Dynasty, the average was four or five hundred. Roughly 95 percent of all men (i.e., virtually all) were eligible to participate in what was now an empirewide series of examinations that began with qualifying tests in every county. Although the examination route never became the only way to become a government official in imperial China, it had, by Song times, become both the

Figure 5.1. Examination compound, Guangzhou (Canton), China, showing a few of the twelve thousand examination cells (photographed in 1900, but characteristic of late imperial China). Library of Congress, LC-USZ62-54326.

normal and the most prestigious path.[15] And, although the number of government offices always remained strikingly few – in 1800, under the last dynasty, there were only about twenty thousand posts in the entire regular civilian bureaucracy – merely participating in the examination system marked one as a member of the elite, even if one never actually passed any tests. By the final two dynasties, Ming and Qing, about a million men at any given time were actively engaged in taking examinations, and the holders of the lowest-level academic degrees made up perhaps 1 or 2 percent of the total population (see Figure 5.1).

For better or for worse, the examination system helped shape the kind of society late imperial China became. To a remarkable degree, it was a society focused on education and book learning. The elite were scholars. According to Confucian notions of rule by moral example, government itself is essentially an act of educating people to improve themselves. Confucius is regarded as China's first teacher.

On balance, it may be concluded that the examination system never really permitted as much upward social mobility as is sometimes imagined by enthusiasts. True rags-to-riches cases were rare, and a larger stratum of relatively wealthy families produced most degree holders. The system also did not reward technological or scientific innovation. But by any premodern standard, this was a relatively fluid social order, with elite status not directly hereditary and opportunities for advancement through ability and effort clearly visible (if not always actually attainable). The examination system provided at least the appearance of fairness of opportunity and at the same time ensured that the elite were extremely well educated and steeped in common Confucian values. This, too, helps explain why late imperial Chinese society was exceptionally stable.

The ethical values that were spread by this pervasive education were not always necessarily ones of which we might approve today. For example, the renewed emphasis on the study of the Confucian Classics is sometimes blamed for a perceptible deterioration in the status of women. It would actually be a little unfair to blame Neo-Confucian moralists for the foot-binding fashion that just happened to begin spreading in Song times, and if any Neo-Confucian scholars wrote about infanticide, it was only to condemn it. But Neo-Confucianism did reaffirm patrilineal principles and such patriarchal ideals as the chaste widow and gender separation. In general, the Neo-Confucian revival may have contributed to a hardening of patriarchal attitudes.[16]

Neo-Confucianism

The economic prosperity of the Song Dynasty coincided, unsurprisingly, with a period of great cultural vitality, both in the realm of popular street culture and in the fine arts. Chinese landscape painting, for example, reached a level of exquisite perfection in the Song Dynasty that has never been surpassed, though it may sometimes have been equaled (see Figure 5.2). The most important intellectual development during the Song Dynasty was undoubtedly the great Confucian revival we call Neo-Confucianism.

The Neo-Confucian movement grew out of the late Tang, matured in the Song, and continued to dominate East Asian higher culture until the early twentieth century. Though "Neo-Confucianism" is a convenient English label for this broad movement, there was actually no single Chinese name for it, and the Chinese tended to perceive it instead in terms of multiple schools associated with individual scholars or groups of scholars. By far the most influential single figure was Zhu Xi (1130–1200), whose approach was sometimes called *Daoxue*, or the "Learning of the [Confucian] Dao." Zhu Xi's writings became so widely influential that they "served as the common denominator of education in premodern East Asia" after this time.[17]

This Neo-Confucianism is notable for transcending the meticulous textual commentary that had dominated earlier Confucian studies to ask more grand philosophical questions and for a new interest in metaphysics and cosmology. As is so often the case, broad generalization is likely to be misleading, but it may be said

Figure 5.2. Xia Gui (Hsia Kuei, fl. 1180–1230), *Remote View of Streams and Hills*, a Song Dynasty landscape painting. National Palace Museum, Taiwan, Republic of China.

that the underlying vision of much Neo-Confucianism was a kind of organic holistic understanding of the universe, on the grounds that all things in the universe are supposedly composed of the same basic substance, *qi*, which is given unique specific shape according to principle(s), called *li*. A further elaboration was the idea, derived from the classic *Book of Changes*, that all of the endless transformations of the material stuff in this universe are ultimately driven by a single common "supreme ultimate" (*taiji* – sometimes spelled *T'ai-chi*, as in "supreme ultimate boxing," the well-known therapeutic martial arts exercise). These ideas resulted in the famous "diagram of the supreme ultimate," a schematic representation of how this *taiji*, as the pivotal point of alternation between yin and yang, ultimately produces all things in the universe.

This new Confucian interest in cosmology reflects the continuing influence of Buddhism and Daoism. The private Confucian academies that began to be built in the countryside during the Song Dynasty "closely resembled Buddhist monasteries in their architecture and physical layout."[18] Their regulations for community life, style of lecturing, and practice of venerating portraits of former patriarchs were also all similar to those of Buddhist monasteries. Yet if some early Song Buddhists did try to make the argument that Buddhism was now simply part of Chinese civilization, the Neo-Confucian mainstream nonetheless rejected Buddhism explicitly.[19]

The fundamental Confucian objection to Buddhism was the idea that personal pursuit of individual religious salvation was inherently selfish – the abandonment of essential social responsibilities. Confucians continued to insist on an obligation to work for the larger public good. The Neo-Confucian reconciliation of this secular imperative with Buddhist-inspired influences was deftly achieved with a new emphasis on a short text drawn from one of the ancient classics, now often published and studied separately, called the *Great Learning* (*Daxue*). This text made individual self-cultivation (which, in the particular form of the Neo-Confucian practice called quiet sitting, might not differ all that much from Buddhist meditation) the first step toward world peace:

> The ancients who wished to illustrate illustrious virtue throughout the kingdom, first ordered well their own states. Wishing to order well their states, they first regulated their families. Wishing to regulate their families, they first cultivated their persons. . . . From the Son of Heaven down to the mass of the people, all must consider the cultivation of the person the root of *everything*.[20]

Despite this great Neo-Confucian revival, the standard textbook tendency to depict the triumph of a Neo-Confucian "dominant ideology" over previously dominant Buddhism and Daoism during the Song Dynasty is an exaggerated caricature. All three remained influential, and the Buddhist and Daoist religious establishments were themselves part of Song Dynasty elite society, below which were other levels of religious orientation extending down to humble village spirit mediums. A huge Song Dynasty collection titled the *Record of Hearsay* (*Yijian zhi*), compiled by Hong Mai (1123–1202), for example, contains roughly two hundred accounts of spirit possession.[21] China was a big place, and late imperial Chinese society remained richly complicated.

Mongol Tempest: Chinggis Khan (ca. 1162–1227)

Mongols were unheard of before the twelfth century. Though there are some obscure references in Tang period sources to a tribe whose name, although written differently, might have been pronounced something like "Mongol," it is uncertain whether this was really the same tribe.[22] In any case, as of the mid-twelfth century, the Mongols were still only one obscure steppe nomadic tribe living among others. The legendary story of their rise to earth-shaking prominence begins with the fatal poisoning of a Mongol leader at what was expected to be a friendly meal with the neighboring Tatar tribe around 1167. After this murder, the Mongol tribe temporarily scattered. The dead chieftain's son, Temüjin, fled with his mother to the mountains, where they survived by hunting and fishing. Gradually, after many exploits, Temüjin built up a personal following of sworn companions, who supposedly pricked their fingers and mixed their blood to become blood brothers. Eventually, Temüjin won recognition as khan, or leader, of the Mongol tribe and took the title Chinggis ("Boundless") Khan (also spelled Genghis Khan).

Meanwhile, Tatar power had been growing in the area of the eastern Gobi Desert. To oppose these Tatars, Chinggis Khan sought an alliance with another nomadic tribal confederation, the Kereyids, many of whom happened to be Nestorian Christians. Around the year 1198, this Mongol-Kereyid alliance went to war with the Tatars, and Chinggis Khan was finally able to avenge his father's murder. In the process, Chinggis Khan also emerged as a remarkably successful warrior leader. By 1206, Chinggis Khan's army numbered around ninety-five thousand men, and at an assembly of tribal notables known as a *khuriltai*, in that year, he received recognition as Great Khan over "all those who live in felt tents." Many of the warriors who fought for Chinggis Khan were actually speakers of Türkic languages rather than Mongolic, and they were certainly not all members of the original Mongol tribe, but as Chinggis Khan's star rose dramatically, the Mongol identity also began to spread.

Throughout imperial Chinese history, since the beginning of the Han Dynasty in the second century BCE, the military superiority of nomadic cavalry had posed a recurring threat. As we have seen, seminomadic emperors ruled many of the Northern dynasties during China's great Age of Division, and the reunified Sui and Tang dynasties sprang from culturally mixed origins. It has even been claimed that seminomads or nomadized persons actually ruled a majority of all the dynasties in imperial Chinese history. But these various ruling groups had nearly all begun as frontiersmen in China's immediate border areas. They were commonly already thoroughly exposed to Chinese civilization and in some senses often could be considered Chinese. The Mongols were different.

In general, the nomadic lifestyle, which is based on the mobile raising of goats, sheep, cattle, horses, and camels, is fundamentally different from the stereotypical Chinese lifestyle based on intensive sedentary farming. The ecological boundary between steppe grassland and fertile farmland is, furthermore, especially sharp along the frontier between Mongolia and China. In other parts of Eurasia bordering on the steppe the ecological division may be less pronounced, and especially where both nomads and farmers were Muslim, the sources of conflict may have been reduced. Confrontations between nomads and farmers on the frontier of China may have therefore been especially acute. But not all Chinese are really necessarily farmers. There have always been ranchers and seminomadic tribes living inside the Chinese Empire, which frequently extended northward to include at least Inner Mongolia. Frontier warriors often played a useful role in the service of the Chinese Empire, and a degree of occupational specialization for different groups always existed inside China.

Chinggis Khan's Mongols were the exception. They came more truly from outside the Chinese world and remained more permanently outsiders. Their conquests were also unparalleled. The explanation for their sudden eruption from the steppe at this particular moment has always been something of an historical puzzle. Some scholars have attempted to explain the Mongol invasions as a result of climate change, arguing that there was a decrease in average temperature in the years 1180–1220, leading to shorter growing seasons and driving the nomads off the steppe in search of other resources. In this case, however, the much maligned "great-man" approach to history may also explain a great deal. The dynamic personality of Chinggis Khan himself, a vigorous commander who believed that the sky god Tenggeri had given him a mission to bring the entire world under one sword, may have been much of the reason for the explosive Mongol conquests. Although the entire population of the Mongolian steppes in the twelfth century may have been only about one million, the hardiness of the nomads and their skill with horse and bow made them an almost unstoppable force.

After consolidating his command over the tribes of the Mongolian steppe, in 1210, Chinggis Khan struck south at the Jurchen-ruled Jin Dynasty in northern China. Between this first assault and about 1260, however, the Mongols made little serious attempt to occupy and rule the territory they overran in north China, resulting in widespread and lasting devastation. Chinggis Khan next turned west, leading an attack on Central Asia. In 1220, he captured the Central Asian city of Bukhara. Legend has it that on entering the great mosque in Bukhara, Chinggis Khan proclaimed himself the "scourge of God."

Chinggis Khan died in 1227, before the Mongols had completed their destruction of the Jurchen Jin Dynasty in north China in 1234, and before the Mongol attack on Southern Song had even begun in 1235. But the Mongol onslaught continued after Chinggis Khan's death. Previous nomadic cavalry armies had always been stopped by the barrier of the Yangzi River and the rice paddies and generally wet terrain of south China. To conquer the Southern Song, the Mongols had to learn the techniques of naval and siege warfare and such novel Chinese technologies as the use of gunpowder. They also made good use of the classic strategy for conquering the lower Yangzi River valley by outflanking it and attacking down the line of the river from the west. By 1279, the last pretender to the Song throne had drowned off the southeast coast, and the Mongols had completed their conquest of China.

The Mongols conquered the largest land empire in the history of the world. In the west, they overran parts of Poland and Hungary and pushed as far as the Adriatic Sea. In the south, they raided into India, although they did not then attempt to occupy it. In the northeast, the Mongols won the submission of Korea. Two huge amphibious invasions of the Japanese islands were both scattered by typhoons, with disastrous results, however, and a strike southeast into the region of Vietnam became mired in tropical jungles and fierce resistance. Even the Mongol Empire eventually reached its limits. While the Mongol conquests were still accumulating, meanwhile, Chinggis Khan's grandson, Khubilai Khan (1215–1294), was acclaimed as Qaghan – that is, Khan of Khans, or Great Khan – in 1260 and began to consolidate a semi-Chinese-style Yuan Dynasty based at Beijing, in the east.[23]

The Yuan Dynasty (1271–1368)

Although Khubilai Khan styled himself Great Khan, his position as supreme leader of the Mongols was contested by a younger brother and later by a cousin. Cracks were already beginning to appear in the vast Mongol world empire. These fissures can be traced all the way back to the time of Chinggis Khan's death, when each of his four principal lines of descent received their own separate territorial bases. These evolved into what became four effectively independent Mongol khanates: the Golden Horde in the area of Russia, the Il-khanate in the area of Persia, the Chaghadai Khanate in Central Asia, and the Yuan Dynasty in East Asia. The conversion of the Mongol khans in the west to Islam in 1295 – just sixteen years after the Mongols had finished conquering Southern Song Dynasty China – can be said to mark the effective end of any unified Mongol world empire.

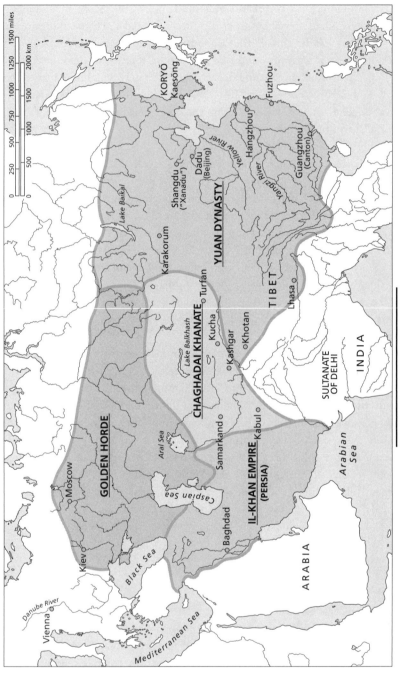

Map 9. The Mongol World Empire, ca. 1300

Chinggis Khan had not been Chinese, had not spent much time in China, and did not speak the Chinese language. His grandson Khubilai Khan, on the other hand, lived most of his life in, and ruled primarily over, China. Although he probably never learned to read Chinese, and relied on Chinese interpreters, he did learn to speak enough Chinese that he sometimes pointedly corrected those interpreters. Khubilai Khan frequently dressed in Chinese-style clothing, and in 1266, he built a magnificent new Chinese-style capital at Beijing (then known as Dadu, the "Great Capital"). Khubilai Khan attempted to conciliate his Chinese subjects by forbidding nomads from grazing their herds on Chinese farmland. In 1271, he also took the Chinese-language dynastic title "Yuan" (which means, roughly, "Beginning"). To some extent, Khubilai Khan did rule China in Chinese style.

But the Mongol Yuan Dynasty was more than just China. The Mongols had, for example, subdued Tibet in 1252, for the first time establishing a patron-priest relationship between an empire based in China and Tibetan lamas. The implications of this relationship, first established in the Yuan Dynasty, remain controversial today. Khubilai Khan also divided the entire population of his empire into four hierarchical ethnic categories, with the Mongols on top, western and central Asians in the next position, then northern Chinese and Jurchens, and finally, the southern Chinese on the bottom. Most high-level positions in the Yuan Empire were held by non-Chinese, and in 1289, Khubilai Khan even felt obliged to prohibit southern Chinese from possessing bows and arrows out of fear they might rebel.

By the time he had completed his conquest of the Southern Song in 1279, Khubilai Khan was already in his late sixties. He was old by the standards of the day, and his final years were dogged by failures. Khubilai Khan, for example, attempted to impose a new universal writing system, based on Tibetan, which simply failed to win acceptance. His two invasions of Japan were disasters. In 1294, he died. Within a few years after his death, the Mongol empire in China began to tear itself apart amid succession disputes. Such struggles over succession were a frequent feature of steppe history. Although the steppe tradition was that leadership should be broadly hereditary within a single family, there were no fixed rules for selection, and descent could just as easily pass from older brother to younger brother or from father to younger son, as from father to eldest son. The result was that when a khan died, it was normal for there to be a power struggle.

In addition, and catastrophically, the bubonic plague also made its appearance in the Mongol-ruled Yuan Empire sometime around the 1320s. From there, the plague spread along the newly established transcontinental Mongol trade routes to the Mediterranean and Europe, where the resulting Black Death had a major impact on medieval European history. In China, it has been estimated that as much as a third of the entire population may have died of the plague. For many, it seemed as if the end of the world was at hand.

The chaos was interpreted by some people as foretelling the apocalyptic arrival of the Future Buddha Maitreya. When Mongol authorities reacted fearfully by trying to suppress this apocalyptic religion, the faithful began to arm themselves and go into rebellion. Meanwhile, a certain teenage boy named Zhu Yuanzhang

(1328–1398) had been orphaned and taken into a Buddhist monastery, where he prepared to become a monk. When the monastery where he had lived was destroyed by Mongol troops, he joined a religiously inspired rebel band called the Red Turbans. As a rebel, Zhu Yuanzhang demonstrated considerable military talent, and he quickly rose through the ranks, eventually becoming a king with his own independent forces. In 1368, at the age of forty, Zhu's armies succeeded in capturing Beijing and reunifying China. Zhu Yuanzhang now proclaimed himself the founding emperor of a new dynasty, which he called Ming.

The word *ming* means "bright," and the title was chosen to signify the supposed victory of the forces of light. Despite the natural tendency of modern Chinese nationalists to see the Ming as a restoration of native Chinese rule following a dark interlude of foreign conquest, however, people did not necessarily see it in quite those terms at the time. Many Chinese families who had served the Mongol Yuan Dynasty had come to see it as the legitimate object of Confucian loyalty. It took years before everyone in China entirely accepted the legitimacy of this new "native Chinese" Ming Dynasty. In his accession decree, even the Ming founder himself acknowledged the century-long legitimacy of the Mongol Yuan Dynasty, though he insisted it had now come to end.[24]

Bubonic plague aside, the years of Mongol rule in China had not been altogether terrible. They were, for example, something of a golden age for Chinese painting and theater. And the Mongols did promote trade and cultural exchange. These were the years when the Arab traveler Ibn Baṭṭūṭa and the Italian Marco Polo both visited China, and Nestorian Christians from China had audiences with the pope and the kings of England and France. The century of the Mongol Peace (ca. 1250–1350) saw increased global connections and helped inspire a later age of European world exploration. Marco Polo's account of his twenty-four years traveling in the Far East revolutionized European knowledge of world geography. Whether or not Christopher Columbus had actually read Polo before setting sail on his epochal voyage of discovery, Columbus was certainly familiar with the Polo story.[25]

In China, the Ming Dynasty reaction to the memory of Mongol rule may have been somewhat the opposite of the Western European reaction: to retreat into defensive isolationism. Of perhaps greater significance for world history, however, was that both China and Western Europe recovered from the crisis of Mongol conquest and bubonic plague more successfully than the Islamic world. After the Mongol capture of Baghdad in 1258, the Middle East, which had until then arguably always been the leading world center of human civilization, entered a phase of long-term relative economic decline, and Europe, India, and China emerged as the world's principal new economic leaders.[26]

The Early Ming (1368–ca. Sixteenth Century [–1644])

Both out of reaction to the memory of Mongol rule, and perhaps also due to sensitivity about his own extremely humble origins, the Ming founder Zhu Yuanzhang (known as emperor by the posthumous temple name Ming Taizu, r. 1368–1398) was notoriously paranoid and despotic. Paradoxically, however, he also upheld as never before a Confucian ideal of puritanical austerity and of limited government by means of moral example. Of peasant origin himself, his vision of the empire was one of a vast collection of semiautonomous peasant villages. Taxes were deliberately held low and paid in kind (i.e., in rice or some other commodity rather than with money). The total civilian government bureaucracy was initially kept to only about eight thousand. Physical movement was also restricted. Under the Ming founder, an official certificate was required for anyone to travel more than thirty miles from home, and travel beyond the Ming borders without official permission was punishable by death.

Despite the stereotype of Ming isolationism, however, throughout the dynasty, the Ming was actively engaged in foreign wars. The Ming waged a total of 308 external wars, or an average of more than one war every year.[27] Most of these wars were against the Mongols. At first, the Ming took the offensive against the Mongols, but by the mid-1400s, Mongol power had revived considerably under the leadership of the great Oirat Mongol Esen (d. 1455).[28] In 1449, Esen even captured a Ming emperor and penetrated to the walls of Beijing. This Mongol resurgence led to a Ming strategic shift from the offensive to the defensive and resulted in the Ming reconstruction of the Great Wall of China in its now familiar form. A more brooding symbol of Ming defensive isolationism could hardly be imagined.

Yet the late Ming Dynasty would also paradoxically become conspicuous for its growing commercial prosperity and participation in international trade, and even the early Ming sponsored China's single most famous episode of world exploration. The Ming founder's fourth son (born of a Mongol consort) seized the throne by force from his own nephew in 1402, becoming the third Ming emperor, who is known to history as the Yongle Emperor (r. 1403–1425). This Yongle Emperor had some astoundingly grandiose ambitions. Most notably, he commissioned a series of naval expeditions under the command of a Chinese Muslim eunuch named Zheng He (1371–1433). For the first expedition in 1405, a fleet of sixty-two large ships – some as large as approximately four hundred feet in length – was assembled, carrying some 27,800 persons. By 1433, seven major voyages had been launched, which sailed up the eastern seaboard of Africa, cruised past Hormuz into the Persian Gulf, and ventured into the Red Sea. A small party apparently even made it to Mecca. These voyages brought back tribute from Hormuz, Mogadishu, Bengal, and other places; a king from Ceylon was taken to China; and also such exotic beasts for the imperial menagerie as giraffes from Africa.[29]

The scale of these immense naval expeditions, which dwarfed anything European monarchs could have put to sea at that time, is breathtaking. Nonetheless, they were not actually voyages of exploration, since they followed trade routes that had already been well known since Roman times. Zheng He's father, a Muslim, had apparently already even made the pilgrimage to Mecca! The voyages did not make any significant new discoveries, nor were they intended to promote trade because the Ming government was not much interested in trade (and private commerce was developing on its own initiative, anyway). The voyages were expensive and put a considerable strain on imperial resources. Confucian officials, always concerned with reducing taxes and "giving rest to the people," were convinced that such expeditions were not worth the cost. After 1433, the expeditions stopped entirely.

In the early fifteenth century, the Ming Dynasty had the most powerful navy in the world, but over the next hundred years, this mighty fleet shriveled away. In 1525, there was even an imperial edict ordering the destruction of all oceangoing ships. Ironically, however, even as the Ming government was apparently retreating into conservative isolationism, private Chinese commerce was entering a new age of dynamic growth by the sixteenth century. China was approaching the threshold of its early modern era.

These were also times of exciting new intellectual developments. A particularly important Ming Dynasty departure from the Neo-Confucian orthodoxy of Zhu Xi emerged, for example, in the teachings of Wang Yangming (1472–1529). Wang Yangming was a man of considerable practical accomplishment in government and military service, who also insisted that knowledge must be realized through action – that "filial piety cannot be learned by mere talk," for example, but must be achieved through actual practice. Yet the core of his philosophy was a Buddhist-style sudden enlightenment (in the middle of the night in 1508) that all principles are inherent already in one's own mind and that understanding could therefore be achieved simply through introspection, requiring no external authority for validation. In contrast to Zhu Xi, who had believed it was necessary to first studiously acquire the knowledge to distinguish between right and wrong, Wang Yangming believed in the preexistence within everyone of intuitive knowledge, or innate conscience (*liang zhi*, a term that Wang borrowed from Mencius), of right and wrong.[30] In extreme form, this faith in instinctive knowledge foreshadowed the development of what came to be known as "wild Chan" (or "wild Zen") in late Ming, a freethinking movement that contributed much to the intellectual open-mindedness, and sometimes eccentric individualism, of China's early modern seventeenth century.

Confucian Korea: Koryŏ (918–1392) and Early Chosŏn (1392–ca. Sixteenth Century [–1910])

Koryŏ (918–1392)

The Koryŏ Dynasty was founded in 918 with a rebellion led by Wang Kŏn, a man from a locally powerful northwestern Korean mercantile and naval family. As ruler of Koryŏ, Wang Kŏn is known to history as King T'aejo (r. 918–943). Although he founded the dynasty in 918, it was not until 935 that the last king of Silla abdicated in his favor, and a period of rivalry between the so-called Later Three Kingdoms ended with the reunification of the Korean peninsula under Koryŏ.

The Koryŏ Dynasty, as its choice of names implies, to some extent presented itself as heir to the old Koguryŏ kingdom that had once straddled both sides of what is today the Korean border with Manchuria. Whatever ambitions Koryŏ may have cherished for Manchuria, however, were thwarted by the rise of Khitan nomadic military power (and later, Jurchen and Mongol). After the Khitan conquest of the partially Korean-influenced independent state of Parhae in Manchuria in 926,

Koryŏ found itself locked into the peninsula, and the geographic shape of what we think of today as Korea was confirmed. The very real threat posed by Khitan and later Jurchen military power may have also been an incentive to Korean political and cultural consolidation.

Wang Kŏn's (King T'aejo's) rebellion, which established the Koryŏ Dynasty, was explicitly justified with reference to Chinese Mandate of Heaven theory and the revered Chinese historical example of the eleventh-century BCE Zhou conquest of the Shang. Political, legal, and economic institutions in Koryŏ also continued to be structured after the now vanished Tang Chinese imperial model. But, at the same time, Korea also achieved greater distance from China during this period and, in a sense, became more Korean. After the fall of the Tang Dynasty in China in 907, and with the rise of intervening powers such as the Khitan Liao Dynasty and the Jurchen Jin, contact between Korea and China was interrupted. The early Koryŏ period "vibrates with Korean tremors of independence and assertiveness," and the founder Wang Kŏn's "instructions emphasize Korea's unique culture and values."[31]

The Koryŏ approach to rule reflected the continuing hold of native traditions. Wang Kŏn, for example, sought marriage alliances with local lords to strengthen his position. Altogether, he took twenty-nine queens. Of the nine daughters to whom they gave birth, Wang Kŏn married two to the last Sillan king, and others were married to their own half brothers. In China, where there was an ancient and total taboo on any marriage between people having the same family name (whether or not they were actually related), this would have been shocking. But the earliest Koreans did not have family names at all, and marriage between cousins and even half brothers and sisters was not unusual in antiquity, at least among the Korean aristocracy. Although family names had already been introduced by Koryŏ times, some of theses older native marriage practices continued. For example, a young married man quite commonly lived with his wife's family, and if a man had several wives, they were all regular wives, rather than Chinese-style secondary wives or concubines. Koryŏ women were also still commonly entitled to an equal share with their brothers of the family inheritance.

As the elder statesman Ch'oe Sŭng-no (927–989) summarized the balance at the end of the tenth century, "although Chinese systems are good to follow, as the customs of each area have their own characteristics, it would be difficult to change every custom. . . . We need not be like China in everything."[32] Even direct Chinese influences were adapted in uniquely Korean ways. For example, connoisseurs regard Koryŏ "china" (i.e., celadon porcelain) as even finer than the Chinese! Printing may have been invented in China, and most documents in Korea may have long continued to be written in the Chinese language, but the world's first use of metal moveable-type printing was in Korea, by at least 1234. And, if Buddhism was transmitted to Korea from China, often in specifically Chinese forms, the Koreans consistently took a more interdenominational, syncretistic approach. This culminated with the great monk Chinul (1158–1210), one of the few leading Korean Buddhist masters who never studied in China, who synthesized the divergent scriptural and meditative wings of Korean Buddhism with his formula of sudden enlightenment followed by gradual cultivation. In this way, Chinul reconciled the seemingly irreconcilable differences between the careful doctrinal study of the *sūtras* and Chan (in Korean, Sŏn; in Japanese, Zen) views on the inexpressible nature of ultimate truth.[33] Koreans, despite immersion in a shared general East Asian pattern of civilization, consistently displayed unique streaks of innovation.

Rather than a highly centralized Chinese-style imperial bureaucracy, local administration under Koryŏ was initially left largely in the hands of local lords. These lords often controlled their own private armies, and the central government merely recognized the fact of their preexisting local authority by conferring official titles on them. The old bone rank system of the Silla period gave way, however, to a new system in which aristocratic families were closely identified with the particular place where their lineage was based. Accompanying this change, the use of family names also spread.

In tension with this native Korean aristocratic system, however, in 958, Koryŏ also implemented Chinese-style civil service examinations, with the assistance of an advisor who had come from the last of the northern Five Dynasties in post-Tang China. Although the examinations began on a small scale, in the long run, most Korean officials came to be selected through such testing. Even this did not eliminate aristocratic dominance in Korea, but it did give the Korean aristocracy a more bureaucratic and Confucian orientation. The examination system may have also encouraged greater prestige for the civil aristocracy over the military. By Koryŏ times, the Korean aristocracy was coming to be known collectively as *Yangban*, which refers to the "two orders" of civil and military officials.

Military dissatisfaction with this civilian preference may have contributed to a coup in 1170. In that year, a commander of the Royal Guard massacred many of the court officials and exiled the king, later executing him. After this, real power was long held by generals and their private household retainers. This rise of a military dictatorship in Korea intriguingly parallels the almost simultaneous establishment of the Shogunate, and warrior domination, in Japan. Centralized, civilian, bureaucratic institutions remained more vigorous in Korea than in Japan, however, and the period of military domination in Korea was, in any case, soon terminated by the Mongol conquest.[34]

The Era of Mongol Domination (1270–1356)

Mongol attacks on the Jurchen-ruled Jin Dynasty in north China had begun in 1210, and Mongol strikes at Korea began in 1231. Although the assaults were sporadic, Mongol armies overran and laid waste to almost the entire peninsula. Amid the general destruction, for example, the first edition of the Korean Buddhist *Tripiṭaka* was burned. The Koryŏ government nonetheless stubbornly continued to resist the Mongols from a base on a small island off the western coast, and fighting continued off and on until 1270, when a pro-Mongol government was finally established in Korea.

The Mongols did not directly incorporate Korea into their Yuan Dynasty. Instead they allowed the Koryŏ kings to retain the form of having their own Korean dynasty. But, although Korean kings continued to rule the peninsula, from 1270 to 1356 they did so in subordination to Mongol overlords, at first under the watchful eyes of resident Mongol commissioners known as *darughachi*, and, after 1280, overseen by a Mongol institution known as the Eastern Expedition Field Headquarters. During these years, the Mongols dethroned Koryŏ kings no fewer than seven times. The Mongols, however, also attempted to maintain good relations with their Koryŏ vassals. The Korean king's son married a daughter of Khubilai Khan, and Koryŏ princes soon became regular travelers between the Koryŏ capital at Kaesŏng and the Mongol capital at Beijing. During the period of Mongol domination in the thirteenth and fourteenth centuries, the heirs to the Koryŏ throne nearly all had Mongol mothers and grew up in Beijing. Koryŏ became what has been colorfully described as a "son-in-law" state to the Mongol Yuan Dynasty, and Koryŏ kings took Mongol names and often wore Mongol dress and hairstyles.

Under the Yuan Dynasty, the city that is today called Beijing was the capital of a vast, transcontinental Mongol Empire. It was more than just a Chinese city. At the same time, nonetheless, it was also still a largely Chinese city. In Beijing, visiting Koreans encountered Neo-Confucianism. In 1313, one Korean king even retired to Beijing, where he founded a Sino-Korean-Mongol Neo-Confucian salon called the "Hall of Ten Thousand Volumes." Meanwhile, the Korean Academy was rebuilt and the Korean national shrine to Confucius restored. Leading Confucian scholars were appointed as teachers in the academy, and they gathered dedicated followings, spurning the old-style textual studies for more stimulating discussions of the true meaning of the classics. Paradoxically, Mongol overlordship in Korea did much to promote a Neo-Confucian revival in Korea.

As Mongol rule began disintegrating in China, in 1356, King Kongmin (r. 1351–1374) broke with the pro-Mongol faction in Korea and regained Korean independence. After the Chinese rebel leader Zhu Yuanzhang defeated the Mongols and founded his new Ming Dynasty in China in 1368, King Kongmin stopped using the Mongol reign period (traditional calendars in East Asia did not date from any fixed benchmark in the past and instead used imperial reign periods, the acceptance of which implied submission) and adopted pro-Ming policies. Though King Kongmin successfully asserted Korean independence from the Mongols, he also, less successfully, tried to extend royal authority over the powerful Korean families. In 1374, he was assassinated by a Korean aristocrat.

Early Chosŏn (1392–ca. Sixteenth Century [–1910])

With the weakening of Mongol power, Koryŏ regained independence, but the dynasty still confronted many challenges. A military hero named Yi Sŏng-gye, who had risen to prominence fighting Japanese pirates, was dispatched in 1388 at the head of a Koryŏ army to resist Ming Dynasty Chinese claims to disputed territory in the north. After reaching the Yalu River, however, Yi Sŏng-gye turned his army around and marched back, overthrowing the Koryŏ king instead. In 1390, he dramatically burned all the land registries and enacted land reforms, which may have helped weaken the established power of the Koryŏ Great Families. With the enthusiastic support of Neo-Confucian scholars, in 1392, he then established his own new dynasty.

At the suggestion of the Ming emperor, the name of the legendary ancient Korean state of Chosŏn was resurrected for the title of this new Korean dynasty. The Chosŏn Dynasty is also sometimes referred to as the Yi Dynasty, after the name of its ruling family. Exactly like the founder of the previous Koryŏ Dynasty, as ruler, Yi Sŏng-gye is also known to history as King T'aejo (r. 1392–1398). The explanation for this repetition is because T'aejo means "Great Founder" or "Grand Progenitor" and is a common posthumous title for founders of East Asian dynasties. In fact, the contemporary founder of the Chinese Ming Dynasty, Zhu Yuanzhang, is also known by exactly the same posthumous title (pronounced "Taizu" in Chinese). This new Korean Chosŏn Dynasty would endure a remarkable 518 years, until 1910, although we will only discuss the early Chosŏn period in this chapter.

At the start of the fifteenth century, the Chosŏn capital was moved from Kaesŏng to what is today called Seoul. Under the new dynasty, private military forces were finally eliminated, and armed might was brought under central command. During the reign of the especially renowned King Sejong (r. 1418–1450), the northern border was finally permanently stabilized at the line of the Yalu and Tumen rivers. The native Korean alphabet, commonly called *han'gŭl*, was also officially promulgated by King Sejong in 1446. Unlike the Japanese *kana* syllabaries, this is a true alphabet, with twenty-eight symbols, and it is furthermore an entirely independent invention, not derived from Chinese characters like the Japanese *kana*. Among other accomplishments during the reign of King Sejong, a system of rain gauges was established in the kingdom in 1442, providing Korea with "the longest records of measured rainfall in the world."[35] In the sixteenth century, Korean inventiveness would reveal itself again in the world's first use of ironclad warships.

Chosŏn officials were selected through Chinese-style civil service examinations conducted in written Chinese. Because, in Korea, ancestry was scrutinized before men were allowed to take the examinations, however, and because the Korean *Yangban* – the "two orders" of civil and military officials – married only other *Yangban*, unlike in late imperial China the Korean elite remained a closed hereditary group, perhaps 10 percent of the total population, despite the meritocratic aspect of the Chinese-style examination system. Beneath the *Yangban* elite were the majority of commoners, most of whom were poor peasants, and beneath these commoners was yet another relatively large group of hereditary slaves. Slaves may have even made up as much as 30 percent of the total population. They did not work in teams on large plantations but often farmed small plots without much direct supervision, not altogether unlike ordinary peasants.

Through their study of the Chinese Classics, zealous Korean Neo-Confucians came to adopt ancient China as an idealized model. Chosŏn Korea went further than anywhere else in East Asia, including China, in actually attempting to recreate the golden age of Chinese antiquity, as they understood it from the classics. The Chosŏn reforms, which were literally written into a series of legal codes, included an attempt to legislate a restructuring of the Korean family according to the supposedly universal Confucian moral order of patrilineal descent, ancestor veneration, and fixed mourning obligations. A 1390 law, for example, required Korean officials to perform ancestral sacrifices in each season.[36]

As late as Koryŏ times, family descent in Korea had still been traced through both male and female lines, but in the fifteenth century, mourning requirements for matrilineal relatives were downgraded. Women gradually lost their inheritance rights, and after 1402, women were legally forbidden to ride horses. The principle of primogeniture was increasingly promoted, tracing inheritance from eldest son to eldest son by the sole legal wife, and reducing the status of secondary sons and of all daughters. Sons born to secondary wives (concubines) eventually became ineligible to take the civil service examinations. Intermarriage between persons with the same family name was banned. Although the implementation and enforcement of all these measures was gradual, at least among the *Yangban* elite Chinese-style marriage and family patterns eventually became pervasive.

In the early Chosŏn Dynasty, the pressure to conform to Confucian family ideals came largely from the government, but by the seventeenth century, Confucian values were being privately promoted through popular literature and the private academies that had begun to emerge in the countryside. The first Neo-Confucian private academy (*sŏwŏn*) in Korea was founded in 1543. By the end of the eighteenth century, 823 had been established.[37] The result was what is now often regarded as "traditional" Korean society: patrilineal families sharing surnames and ancestral seats, claiming descent from and venerating a common male ancestor, and with the main line of descent carried through the first-born son of the primary wife. By about the eighteenth century, Korea had become a thoroughly Confucian society. These Confucian ideals were understood as universal truths, however, rather than necessarily as Chinese influences. In fact, late Chosŏn Koreans even came to feel that they were better custodians of proper Confucian civilization than the degenerate Chinese, who had fallen under foreign Manchu rule.[38]

Confucianization was not the whole story, however. There continued to be flickers of Korean innovation, as we have seen. Female shamans, known as *Mudang*, testify to the lingering strength of older native traditions. Even Confucian influences were domesticated in uniquely Korean ways. And Buddhism remained influential, despite Neo-Confucian disdain. Under the Chosŏn Dynasty, Buddhist temples were excluded from the capital and lost their official support and tax exemptions. In 1395, Buddhist-style cremation of the dead was prohibited in favor of Confucian-style burial. Over the course of the Chosŏn Dynasty, Buddhist funeral practices were gradually displaced even at the lowest levels of society. Yet when government forces were driven back by a great invasion from Japan (led by the warlord Hideyoshi) in 1592–1598, bands of Korean Buddhist monks still played a prominent role in waging fierce guerilla resistance.

Warrior Japan: Late Heian ([794–] Tenth Century–1185), Kamakura (1185–1333), and Muromachi (1333–1568)

The Rise of the Warriors

From Japanese literature of the Heian period (794–1185), it is easy to get the impression that the aesthetically refined aristocrats of the capital, Heian (modern Kyōto), were scarcely even aware of life beyond the outskirts of the city. The aristocracy lived off taxes collected in the provinces, but was otherwise not much interested in them. Parallel to this elite inattention, the central government's ability to exercise actual administrative control over the countryside also progressively diminished. In the beginning, the performances of provincial governors had been carefully audited by their successors. By the eleventh century, however, it was rare for governors even to visit their assigned provinces at all – local administrative responsibilities were instead passed to deputies.

In the meantime, out in the provinces, new types of local strongmen were emerging. A major intention of the sweeping reorganization of the Japanese state that had followed the Taika coup d'état in the late seventh and eighth centuries had been to create a Chinese-style centralized empire, not the least of whose enhanced capabilities would be to mobilize a large army – like the huge massed continental armies that had fought the seventh-century wars for the unification of the Korean peninsula. Military conscription was introduced in Japan, and an army of peasant foot soldiers was created, armed with crossbows and organized into provincial units under the command of governors. But the threat of an invasion from the continent quickly receded. Military conscription put a heavy burden on ordinary farm families, and the draft was abandoned by as early as 792.

Japan would not face another serious foreign enemy for many years, but external peace did not eliminate the need for internal, domestic armed forces. For one thing, non-Japanese people called the Emishi still lived in the extreme northeast of the main island. These Emishi raided Japanese settlements, and significant conflict with the Emishi did not end until 811. In addition, local security – law and order – was always a concern. Even at its height in the eighth century, the conscript peasant infantry had already been supplemented by mounted warriors drawn from elite rural families. The art of mounted archery had been practiced in Japan since about the fifth century, and especially in eastern Japan, there was a long tradition among the local elite of hunting from horseback and of bearing arms.

The Japanese warriors who began to emerge at this time were not yet quite the familiar samurai. The word *samurai* originally only meant "attendant," and in the eighth century, it typically referred literally to household servants. By the early Heian period, the word had begun to be applied to armed household guards in attendance on court nobles. Such private guards had become necessary because of the deteriorating security situation even in the capital. Another relatively familiar term for the warriors, *bushi*, or "military gentleman," did not come into use until about the twelfth century. In the early period, Japanese warriors were most commonly called *tsuwamono*. The evolution of these relatively rustic warrior farmers into the familiar hereditary elite samurai class was not completed until as late as the sixteenth century.[39]

Early Japanese warriors were most especially mounted archers. The Way of the Warrior was "the way of the bow and horse." The cult of the sword was a later development. In the eighth century, Japanese peasant infantry armies had made the crossbow their principal weapon. But, though a crossbow is relatively easy to point and shoot, it is difficult to manufacture. By the ninth century, the crossbow had largely been abandoned in Japan. The longbow, by contrast, is easier to make but requires very much more skill to use effectively, especially from horseback.[40] At least if we can believe the Japanese warrior tales, single mounted combat became the preferred style of fighting. Combat would begin with a ritualized exchange in which the names, age, rank, and genealogy of the combatants were announced to establish suitable adversaries. A warrior's reward was then calculated by his taking of enemy heads.

Initially, Japanese warriors were only part-time warriors and part-time farmers who joined into relatively unstable rural armed bands. Warriors in the east began fortifying their homes with ditches and palisades, and in the late eleventh century, these eastern warriors also began forming groups aligned, notably, with either the Taira or Minamoto families. The Taira and Minamoto families were junior branches of the imperial line. The Japanese imperial family was quite large: in the early tenth century, there were roughly seven hundred members who were entitled to public support.[41] To help reduce the strain on diminishing central government resources, in the ninth century, junior descendants of emperors began being reduced from imperial to merely noble status and given new family names such as Minamoto or Taira. (The Japanese imperial family, to this day, still does not have a family name.) Although no longer royalty, these new houses still enjoyed immense prestige, especially in rural areas outside the capital.

At roughly the same time that warrior bands began to form around the Taira and Minamoto families in the countryside, the domination of the imperial court by the Fujiwara family, which had endured for nearly two centuries, was also challenged by the institution of the Retired Emperor; that is, the hold that had been exerted over emperors by their Fujiwara mother's father or brother was now replaced by that of their own fathers. In 1068, the first emperor in 170 years whose mother was not a Fujiwara took the throne. For roughly a century thereafter, a succession of three emperors each abdicated early and then established administrative offices out of their households as Retired Emperors, from which they exercised effectively supreme power. Emperor Shirakawa (1053–1129), for example, abdicated the throne in 1086 but did not die until 1129. These Retired Emperors took Buddhist orders, and are also therefore sometimes referred to as Cloistered Emperors. Between 1068 and 1180, there were ten reigning emperors, but a mere three Retired Emperors were the truly dominant figures for most of that period. This institution of the Retired Emperor proved to be an effective device for enhancing the economic and political position of the imperial family, but it naturally also created a potential for tension between the officially reigning emperor and the Retired Emperor.

Figure 5.3. Detail from one of the *Heiji Scrolls*, illustrating a Japanese warrior tale narrating the story of the Heiji conflict, 1159–1160. Kamakura period, 1185–1333. Museum of Fine Arts, Boston. Werner Forman/Art Resource, New York.

In the early twelfth century, one branch of the Taira family demonstrated its military capability by quelling piracy on the Inland Sea, and became attached to the Retired Emperor as his personal armed escort. In 1156, for the first time in centuries, military force was called in to settle a dispute within the imperial family. A Taira family leader named Kiyomori (1118–1181) backed the reigning emperor Go-Shirakawa (1127–1192) against a Retired Emperor, whose own armed forces were largely drawn from the Minamoto family. Although in practice battle lines were never precisely drawn into separate family camps – it was quite normal for some family members to fight against other members of their own family – a great rivalry between the Taira and Minamoto clans began, which was destined to change forever the course of Japanese history.

The Gempei War (1180–1185)

In the conflict of 1156, the Taira-backed Emperor Go-Shirakawa prevailed. He then abdicated in 1158, becoming Retired Emperor himself. Following yet another armed dispute in 1159–1160 (see Figure 5.3), the principal remaining Minamoto family leader was treacherously murdered in his bath. The lives of two of his sons were unexpectedly spared, however. One was spared, the story goes, because Taira Kiyomori was captivated by his mother's beauty, while the other, the older brother, Minamoto Yoritomo, was spared because Taira Kiyomori's stepmother was sentimentally reminded by him of her own lost son. Although Minamoto Yoritomo's life was spared, he was banished to a peninsula in the distant east, where he spent the next two decades in exile. The east – the great Kantō plain surrounding what is now Tōkyō – would become his permanent new home.

Taira Kiyomori now commanded an almost unchallengeable military force at the Heian capital. Although he long remained a client attached to the authority of the Retired Emperor, by 1167, Kiyomori had risen to the top court office. In 1171, Kiyomori engineered the marriage of his daughter to the emperor, and after this daughter bore the emperor a son, in 1180, that grandson of Taira Kiyomori himself became the reigning emperor (Antoku, r. 1180–1183). At the peak of Taira Kiyomori's power, his family seemed to exercise a stranglehold over the entire court. "Altogether more than sixty governors of provinces, military zones, and districts, as well as sixteen nobles and more than thirty courtiers, derived from his clan. It seemed that the whole world was ruled by his kinsmen alone."[42]

The one remaining restraint on Taira Kiyomori's power had been eliminated by a coup in 1179, during which the Retired Emperor Go-Shirakawa was dismissed and placed under house arrest. This proved to be one coup too many, however, because it aroused opposition within the imperial family. In 1180, Go-Shirakawa's son issued a call to arms against the Taira. This imperial prince had been deprived of his own chance to become emperor because of Kiyomori's maneuvering to put a Taira grandson on the throne. Although the rebellious prince was soon killed, his call was answered by a now adult Minamoto Yoritomo from the remote eastern Kantō region.

Yoritomo declared the Kantō independent, and local warriors eagerly stepped in to replace officials appointed from the imperial capital. By rewarding his warrior followers with land confiscated from the enemy or confirming their existing land titles, Minamoto Yoritomo was able to raise a huge army. He soon established his headquarters at a place called Kamakura, at the base of a peninsula in the Kantō. The war that was now unleashed between the Minamoto warriors of the east and the court-based Taira forces in the west is known as the Gempei War (1180–1185). (The name Gempei derives, confusingly enough, from alternate Japanese pronunciations of the Chinese characters with which Minamoto and Taira are written.) The story of this war unfolds in what may be the greatest of all the Japanese warrior tales, the *Tale of the Heike*, a book that developed out of a tradition of oral storytelling by blind itinerant monks in the thirteenth century.

Almost immediately, the Taira launched an expeditionary probe into the Kantō to suppress the Minamoto-led rebellion. The Taira troops were spooked by the noise made by some birds at night, however, which they mistakenly thought indicated an imminent surprise attack, and the Taira forces fled without even joining battle. For the next three years, then, there was something of a phony war, as Minamoto Yoritomo preoccupied himself with consolidating his hold over the Kantō. For a time, it even seemed possible that Japan might be divided between east and west. In the twelfth century, the Kantō plain in the east and Japan's other great plain in the west near the capital, between them, together held about 40 percent of the total population of the Japanese islands.

In 1183, the war finally resumed in earnest as Minamoto Yoritomo now took the offensive, although Yoritomo personally remained behind in Kamakura and allowed others to assume tactical command on the battlefield. Taira Kiyomori had meanwhile died of a fever at the outset of the war in 1181. The Taira were quickly dislodged from the capital and retreated slowly west to the farthest tip of the main island, where, in a climactic naval battle from a multitude of small craft in 1185 at a place called Dan no Ura, the last remnants of the Taira were wiped out and the boy emperor drowned. The winner, Minamoto Yoritomo, then did a remarkable thing: he stayed in Kamakura and did not move to the imperial capital.[43]

The Kamakura Shogunate (1185–1333)

The Gempei War proved to be a great turning point in Japanese history. The victor, Minamoto Yoritomo, remained in his eastern headquarters at Kamakura, which came to be known as a *Bakufu*, or military "tent government." The imperial court remained far away to the west, in the old capital Kyōto (Heian). Yet Japan was not divided between them – at least, not into two separate parts, although the erosion of central government power continued. Yoritomo claimed direct authority only over his own network of vassal warriors, or "housemen." He solidified his hold over these warriors by also claiming the right to reward them with appointments as estate stewards throughout Japan. But the emperor, in Kyōto, remained the font of legitimate government.

In 1192, Yoritomo received from the emperor the title *Sei-i tai-shōgun*, or "Great General Pacifying the Barbarians." This is commonly shortened simply to shogun (*shōgun*). Yoritomo was Japan's first shogun. It is clear that in the last decades of the twelfth century, Japan had crossed some important threshold, moving from the Heian age of centralized, civilian, aristocratic rule to a time of increasingly decentralized military rule in the age of the shoguns. As a sign of the radically changed times, between 1200 and 1840, no Japanese emperor appears to have actually held what we think of now as the standard imperial title, *Tennō*.[44]

These changes were not necessarily perceived at the time as what we might call "progress." Quite the contrary: there was a pervasive feeling of decline. It became common for Buddhists to speak of having entered the "last age of the law," when the Buddha's teachings had reached a final stage of human decay. The melancholy theme of the *Tale of the Heike* was of the victory of rough eastern warriors over the culturally sophisticated Taira of the imperial court. Japanese warriors still had no special monopoly over the carrying of arms or the riding of horses, and were often still quite rustic fellows. Court nobles still epitomized cultural polish and social prestige. Minamoto Yoritomo owed his own towering stature more to his imperial descent than to any particular abilities as a warrior.

Perceptions are not necessarily realities, though. There were also signs of more positive developments in the Kamakura period, including a narrowing of the gap between elite high culture and that of ordinary commoners through the medium of popular Buddhist preaching and the new, often oral literature of the warrior tales. An especially attractive Japanese custom – regular bathing – also first manifested itself now with the appearance of public baths in monasteries beginning in the thirteenth century. Local markets began to spread in the thirteenth century, and a new agricultural surplus accumulated and began to be sold in what was an increasingly monetized cash economy.[45]

The cash came in the form of Chinese copper coins, imported from the continent in large quantities. It would not be until the sixteenth century that coins would again be minted in Japan. Despite the unique trajectory taken by developments in Japanese history during the age of the shoguns and the samurai, contact with other parts of East Asia remained important. Japanese warrior society was, in fact, arguably more deeply Confucian in its ethical values than the old Heian aristocracy had been. The war tales, for example, emphasized warrior relations with their lords in terms of the Confucian ideal of loyalty. Even the Buddhist idea of the "last age of the law" had been developed first in China.

Important developments in Japanese Buddhism in this period were often extensions of Chinese influences. For example, Hōnen (1133–1212) was a Japanese monk from the great Tendai sect temple complex on Mt. Hiei, the tallest mountain overlooking Kyōto in the northeast. Living at the time of the Gempei War, he found it very easy to believe that the "last age of the law" was at hand, a time when salvation was no longer possible except through faith in the compassion of the Bodhisattvas. Hōnen began to preach an inspired message of universal salvation through the intervention of the Bodhisattva Amitābha, with his promise of rebirth for the faithful in the Pure Land. All that was necessary was to sincerely recite, "I put my faith in Amitābha Buddha" (in Japanese, *Namu Amida Butsu*). Although Hōnen was expelled from Mt. Hiei because of controversy in 1207, his exile only served to further spread his message of faith as he traveled and preached beyond the capital. After his death, although belief in Amitābha and the Pure Land had long been widespread throughout East Asia, Hōnen's followers established a distinctive Pure Land sect (*Jōdo*), which eventually acquired the largest Buddhist following in Japan.

Zen Buddhism (in Chinese, Chan) was especially welcomed by the Shogunate in Kamakura as a way of transforming the rough warriors of the eastern Kantō into trendsetters in sophisticated new fashions, both secular and sacred, imported from the continent. At the end of the Kamakura period, there were more than two hundred Chinese monks living in Japan, and hundreds of Japanese monks had made the trip to China.[46] This Zen Buddhism did much to establish what we think of today as characteristically "Japanese" tastes for poetry, rock gardens, tea, monochromatic painting, and architecture.

Despite these ongoing continental contacts, though, it should be emphasized that all this occurred in the context of a still quite uniquely Japanese culture that was, furthermore, currently evolving along independent lines that curiously, in some ways, might even be said to better echo developments in contemporary medieval Western Europe than in China. The Japanese islands remained detached from the mainland of East Asia. Yet the Mongol invasions of 1274 and 1281, though they were successfully repulsed, were also reminders that the islands did not really exist in isolation. In the aftermath, the Japanese began to become somewhat more active again overseas.

Initially, much of this activity took the form of piracy, directed first especially against the Korean peninsula. In 1350, a fleet of one hundred Japanese pirate ships descended on the Korean coast, and Japanese pirates returned to Korea five more times that same year. As we have already seen, Japanese piracy played a role in the establishment of the new Korean Chosŏn Dynasty in 1392. The legacy of the Mongol invasions also left much domestic dissatisfaction in Japan because there were very few spoils of victory with which to reward the warriors who had beaten the Mongols. Driving away Mongol invaders, after all, did not produce any new land to give away.

Minamoto Yoritomo died in 1199, and his widow lived on for another quarter century. She became the real power – sometimes called the "Nun Shogun." She was ruthless, and is even suspected of engineering the end of Minamoto Yoritomo's direct line of descent with the murder of her own younger son in 1219. The end of Yoritomo's line left her own family, the Hōjō, in a position from which to control the Kamakura Shogunate as regents. Naturally, however, other leading Kamakura vassals were inclined to resent such Hōjō family domination.

Muromachi (1333–1568)

Circumstances must be unusual for an emperor to rebel, but that is what happened next. A succession dispute had emerged between two branches of the imperial family, which had been resolved with an agreement to alternate the throne between the two lines after 1290. Rather than abdicate to that other branch of his own family, however, in 1331, Emperor Go-Daigo (r. 1318–1339) rebelled. The Kamakura Shogunate might have had the military resources to contain this rebel emperor, but too many warriors rallied to the imperial cause instead. Even some of Kamakura's own leading vassals defected, including a man named Ashikaga Takauji (1305–1358). Takauji's mother was from the Hōjō family of Kamakura regents, and he claimed descent from a branch of the Minamoto family. With such leading vassals turning against it, in 1333, the city of Kamakura was burned, the Hōjō family and its remaining faithful retainers committed mass suicide, and the Kamakura Shogunate came to an end.

Emperor Go-Daigo's aspiration was not merely to keep the throne but to achieve a genuine imperial restoration: a return of real power from the military headquarters of the shoguns to the central imperial government. Emperor Go-Daigo therefore made his own son shogun, and combined the previously separate offices of civilian and military provincial governor into a single new office that was to be appointed by the emperor rather than by the shogun. Leading warriors were naturally unsatisfied with being excluded by this imperial arrangement, however, and rivalries between great warriors also created fissures at the court. In 1336, Ashikaga Takauji forcefully expelled the emperor from Kyōto, enthroned a new emperor of his own choosing, and had himself appointed shogun in 1338. Takauji thus became the first in a new line of Ashikaga shoguns. This Ashikaga Shogunate is also called the Muromachi period, after the name of the section of Kyōto where the Ashikaga shoguns established their headquarters.

But Emperor Go-Daigo did not relent. After being driven from the capital, he took refuge at a location south of Kyōto called Yoshino. There were now two rival imperial courts, and sporadic warfare between these "Northern and Southern dynasties" would continue for more than half a century, until 1392. Questions of imperial legitimacy were now subsidiary to personal ambition, however, as warriors used the pretext of loyalty to one or the other emperor to raid their neighbors and acquire land. In 1351, Ashikaga Takauji himself even changed sides, after his brother had temporarily gained the upper hand in Kyōto. Once Takauji had defeated and killed his brother, he changed sides again. It has been observed that Takauji's rise was accomplished through three betrayals: first of Kamakura, then of Emperor Go-Daigo, and finally of his own brother. Japan was entering an age of instability, when it became commonplace for vassals to treacherously overthrow their lords.

Ashikaga Takauji returned the seat of power to the imperial capital Kyōto, though he made sure that real power remained in the shogun's hands rather than the emperor's. Kyōto flourished once again, and the Ashikaga shoguns were now able to tap into a growing urban commercial economy. By the time the Northern and Southern dynasty courts were reunified in 1392, under the third Ashikaga Shogun Yoshimitsu (1358–1408), most of the Shogunate's revenue actually came from trade: from taxes on shipping, at barrier gates and markets, and on wealthy money lenders and sake brewers. Yoshimitsu also sponsored trade with China, approaching the Ming Dynasty with a request for a resumption of friendly relations in 1401. The Ming Dynasty interpreted his lavish gifts as tribute, and in 1403, the Ming even conferred on Yoshimitsu the title "king of Japan" (the memory of which has outraged modern Japanese nationalists because it disregards the legitimate Japanese emperor). It was this commercial prosperity that made possible Yoshimitsu's construction of his fabled Golden Pavilion (*Kinkaku-ji*) in 1397, a literally gilded retreat in the northwestern suburbs of Kyōto (see Figure 5.4).

Even at its peak, however, the Ashikaga Shogunate's control over the countryside beyond Kyōto had been limited. Ashikaga Takauji had worked to appoint many of his own relatives as provincial governors (or "constables"), but this was an age when even family loyalty could not be depended on, and the provincial governors – or their deputies – tended to become independent regional lords. After the assassination of the sixth Ashikaga Shogun in 1441, the power of the shoguns effectively ended. As the Shogun Yoshimasa (d. 1490) explained in 1482, "the daimyo do as they please and do not follow orders. This means there can be no government."[47]

This word, *daimyō*, was a relatively new term that would continue to be important in Japan until the late nineteenth century. Literally, it means "great name," and it refers to the holders of many rice fields. Unlike the old aristocratic estates of the Heian and Kamakura periods, which had been scattered across many locations and

Figure 5.4. Temple of the Golden Pavilion (*Kinkaku-ji*), originally built in 1397 but burned and reconstructed in the twentieth century. Kyōto, Japan. Werner Forman/Art Resource, New York.

involved a complicated hierarchy of production rights culminating in great court nobles or temples, the lands of these new *daimyō* were now compactly consolidated territories dominated by on-the-spot warlords from heavily fortified castles. These *daimyō* exercised largely independent authority over domains that even came to be referred to as "countries" (*kokka*).

A dispute between the Hosokawa and Yamana families over who should succeed Yoshimasa as shogun resulted in the outbreak of the so-called Ōnin War (1467–1477) in 1467. This war lasted for a decade and involved hundreds of thousands of warriors, yet it was fought mostly in the streets of Kyōto, and neither the shogun nor the emperor involved himself in its conduct. Amid the battles, Kyōto was reduced to two separate walled and moated camps about a half mile apart. Much of the rest of the city was destroyed by fire. As one contemporary recorded, "across our charred land, all human traces have been extinguished. For blocks on end, birds are the sole sign of life."[48]

Having been notably ineffectual in handling the warrior squabbles that devastated his capital, in the wake of the Ōnin War the Shogun Yoshimasa retired to his villa in the Eastern Mountains (Higashiyama) section of northeastern Kyōto. There he cultivated the arts, and constructed an intentionally rustic Silver Pavilion (*Ginkaku-ji*), into which he moved in 1483. Although it is called the Silver Pavilion, it was never in fact coated with silver leaf – an omission that only intensifies the contrast with the garishness of Yoshimitsu's older and more ostentatious Golden Pavilion on the other side of town.

If Yoshimasa was a failure as a warrior leader, he was an outstanding patron of the arts. Yoshimasa actually helped establish many of the cultural styles that we have come to think of as "traditionally Japanese." These included a conscious aesthetic of rustic simplicity. Yoshimasa's Silver Pavilion became something of a model for the "traditional" Japanese house, including such characteristic touches as tatami matting on the floors (which became widespread only in the fifteenth century), sliding internal papered partitions called *shōji*, a special alcove for the display of artwork (the *tokonoma*), and staggered wall shelves. Other features of traditional Japanese culture that were particularly cultivated, if not actually invented, in this period include Nō theater (developed in the late fourteenth and early fifteenth centuries out of older entertainments), the art of flower arranging (*ikebana*), raked-sand gardens, and linked-verse poetry (*renga*). Although tea drinking had been introduced from China centuries earlier, the first known use of the Japanese word for the tea ceremony, *chanoyu*, appears in 1469, and the characteristically Japanese art of tea matured in the time, and in the company, of the Shogun Yoshimasa.[49] (Still other aspects of "traditional" Japanese culture are even more recent, such as Kabuki theater, the geisha girl, the "Way of the Warrior," or *bushidō*, and such cooking styles as tempura and sushi.)

Kyōto was ravaged by the Ōnin War, and in the war's aftermath, the great lords and their warriors returned to the provinces, leaving behind a now powerless shogun and emperor. Although the last Ashikaga shogun would not be driven from Kyōto until 1573, after 1467 there simply was no effective central government in Japan. The century following the Ōnin War is often called the Warring States period. It was a century of conflict and of almost total decentralization. In the provinces, governors found themselves unable to control their own subordinates, who were often themselves confronted with similar insubordination from below. As one European observer reported in 1580, Japan was "continually torn by civil wars and treasons, nor is there any lord who is secure in his domain. This is why Japan is never a firm whole, but is always revolving like a wheel; for he who today is a great lord, may be a penniless nobody tomorrow."[50]

Rural society, meanwhile, reorganized itself from scattered farm residences into more compact villages, often initially with a defensive orientation. Although the samurai had originally been household attendants of top court nobles, now many wealthy peasants who happened to possess swords, a little land, and ties of vassalage to some lord began to call themselves samurai. At least in places, samurai may have made up as much as 20 percent of the rural population.

Even as decentralization reached an extreme, however, some of the more successful and energetic of the two or three hundred *daimyō* who divided the Japanese islands between themselves at the start of the sixteenth century began reversing the process and consolidating their control over surrounding land and warriors. Some *daimyō* began conducting systematic land surveys to convert their domains into more closely integrated economic units. The income of vassals gradually began to be assessed in regular standardized units (called *koku*), and this was eventually translated into an actual paid salary, as *daimyō* began to pull their samurai off the land and into permanent residence as garrisons in the *daimyō*'s castle. In the sixteenth century, some *daimyō* even began to issue their own money, and the increasing monetization of the economy enabled the mobilization of still larger armed forces and the construction of even greater fortifications. In 1568, one *daimyō* named Oda Nobunaga (1534–1582) marched into Kyōto, and the great age of Japanese reunification began.

For Further Reading

An excellent comprehensive survey of the entire late imperial period in China is Frederick W. Mote, *Imperial China: 900–1800* (Cambridge, MA: Harvard University Press, 1999).

On Song Dynasty China and the major late imperial cultural, social, economic, and intellectual transformations, see Peter K. Bol, *"This Culture of Ours": Intellectual Transitions in T'ang and Sung China* (Stanford University Press, 1992); John W. Chaffee, *The Thorny Gates of Learning in Sung China: A Social History of the Examinations*, new ed. (Binghamton: State University of New York Press, 1995); Edward L. Davis, *Society and the Supernatural in Song China* (Honolulu: University of Hawai'i Press, 2001); Dieter Kuhn, *The Age of Confucian Rule: The Song Transformation of China* (Cambridge, MA: Harvard University Press, 2009); and Linda A. Walton, *Academies and Society in Southern Sung China* (Honolulu: University of Hawai'i Press, 1999). For women in late imperial China, see in particular Patricia Buckley Ebrey, *The Inner Quarters: Marriage and the Lives of Chinese Women in the Sung Period* (Berkeley: University of California Press, 1993). For a popular introduction to Song Dynasty China, see Jacques Gernet, *Daily Life in China on the Eve of the Mongol Invasion, 1250–1276*, trans. H. M. Wright (Stanford University Press, [1959] 1970).

On painting and the fine arts, which reached a high state of perfection in the Song Dynasty, see James Cahill, *Chinese Painting* (New York: Rizzoli, [1960] 1985), and Sherman E. Lee, *A History of Far Eastern Art*, 5th ed. (New York: Prentice Hall, 1994).

On the Mongol period, see Herbert Franke and Denis Twitchett, eds., *The Cambridge History of China, vol. 6: Alien Regimes and Border States, 907–1368* (Cambridge University Press, 1994). See also John W. Dardess, *Conquerors and Confucians: Aspects of Political Change in Late Yüan China* (New York: Columbia University Press, 1973), and Morris Rossabi, *Khubilai Khan: His Life and Times* (Berkeley: University of California Press, 1988).

For the early Ming Dynasty, see Edward L. Farmer, *Early Ming Government: The Evolution of Dual Capitals* (Cambridge, MA: East Asian Research Center, Harvard University, 1976), and Louise Levathes, *When China Ruled the Seas: The Treasure Fleet of the Dragon Throne, 1405–1433* (New York: Oxford University Press, 1994).

Concerning Korea in the tenth–sixteenth centuries, see Robert E. Buswell Jr., trans., *The Korean Approach to Zen: The Collected Works of Chinul* (Honolulu: University of Hawai'i Press, 1983); Martina Deuchler, *The Confucian Transformation of Korea: A Study of Society and Ideology* (Cambridge, MA: Harvard University Press, 1992); Kichung Kim, *An Introduction to Classical Korean Literature: From Hyangga to P'ansori* (Armonk, NY: M. E. Sharpe, 1996); and Michael C. Rogers, "National Consciousness in Medieval Korea: The Impact of Liao and Chin on Koryŏ," in *China among Equals: The Middle Kingdom and Its Neighbors, 10th–14th Centuries*, ed. Morris Rossabi (Berkeley: University of California Press, 1983).

A splendid general overview of Japan in this period is Pierre François Souyri, *The World Turned Upside Down: Medieval Japanese Society*, trans. Käthe Roth (New York: Columbia University Press, [1998] 2001). For a much narrower but fascinating case study, see Mimi Hall Yiengpruksawan, *Hiraizumi: Buddhist Art and Regional Politics in Twelfth-century Japan* (Cambridge, MA: Harvard University Asia Center, 1998).

Studies focusing on the rise of the Japanese warrior class include William Wayne Farris, *Heavenly Warriors: The Evolution of Japan's Military, 500–1300* (Cambridge, MA: Harvard

University Press, 1992); Karl F. Friday, *Hired Swords: The Rise of Private Warrior Power in Early Japan* (Stanford University Press, 1992); Rizō Takeuchi, "The Rise of the Warriors," in *The Cambridge History of Japan; vol. 2, Heian Japan*, ed. Donald H. Shively and William H. McCullough (Cambridge University Press, 1999); and H. Paul Varley, *Warriors of Japan as Portrayed in the War Tales* (Honolulu: University of Hawai'i Press, 1994).

The leading English-speaking authority on Kamakura period Japan is Jeffrey P. Mass. See his *Yoritomo and the Founding of the First Bakufu: The Origins of Dual Government in Japan* (Stanford University Press, 1999). For the Muromachi period, see Mary Elizabeth Berry, *The Culture of Civil War in Kyoto* (Berkeley: University of California Press, 1994); Kenneth A. Grossberg, *Japan's Renaissance: The Politics of the Muromachi Bakufu* (Ithaca, NY: Cornell University Press, [1981] 2000); and John Whitney Hall and Toyoda Takeshi, eds., *Japan in the Muromachi Age* (Berkeley: University of California Press, 1977).

For Japanese institutional history, see Martin Collcutt, *Five Mountains: The Rinzai Zen Monastic Institution in Medieval Japan* (Cambridge, MA: Council on East Asian Studies, Harvard University, 1981), and John W. Hall and Jeffrey P. Mass, eds., *Medieval Japan: Essays in Institutional History* (Stanford University Press, 1974).

For Japanese culture during this period, the following books are highly recommended: Donald Keene, *Yoshimasa and the Silver Pavilion: The Creation of the Soul of Japan* (New York: Columbia University Press, 2003), and William R. LaFleur, *The Karma of Words: Buddhism and the Literary Arts in Medieval Japan* (Berkeley: University of California Press, 1983).

6 Early Modern East Asia (Sixteenth–Eighteenth Centuries)

Late Ming ([1368–] Sixteenth Century–1644) and Qing (1644–Eighteenth Century [–1912]) Dynasty China

Late Ming Consumer Culture

Even to suggest that East Asia had an early modern period remains somewhat controversial. The word *modern* comes from Late Latin, and the entire concept of modernity emerged originally in the specific context of European history.[1] There is, furthermore, no denying the driving role that was played by the West in giving shape to what we think of as the modern world. With regard to non-Western civilizations, there is a natural tendency to prefer imagining them as societies that had always been changelessly traditional, from some primordial beginning until relatively recently, when the process of modernization (often understood as being synonymous with Westernization) finally started, as a direct consequence of contact with the modern West. East Asian history is still commonly divided into only two major parts, premodern and modern, with the point of transition placed somewhere in the nineteenth century. Yet paradoxically, the use of paper money, printing, gunpowder, urbanization, market-based commercialization, complex bureaucratic administration, and a relatively fluid meritocratic sociopolitical order based on the examination system all make Song Dynasty China (960–1279) seem curiously modern already a thousand years ago! The idea of a changelessly static East Asia, at any rate, is a fantasy, sustained only by lack of historical knowledge.

If long-term historical change is acknowledged for the non-Western world, another common approach has been to assume that it must naturally have followed the familiar three-stage European historical sequence of ancient, medieval, and modern. This sequence is often presumed to be universal and is applied rather mechanically, for example, to East Asian history. As it happens, in East Asia, the case of Japan actually does provide one of the closest parallels to this European developmental curve that can be found anywhere in world history. Between Japan's age of classical antiquity and modern times, Japan did experience a feudal middle phase that was uncannily (though imperfectly) reminiscent of the European Middle

---

Some time ranges listed in the subheads in this chapter include additional dates in brackets. These dates indicate either the beginning or the ending of a dynasty (or other conventional historical period) that extends beyond the period covered in that section.

Ages.[2] Neither China nor Korea, however, fits this three-stage European formula nearly as well. While there have indeed been many commonalities in global human history – especially in the Eurasian Old World, where some degree of exchange was always continuous – it is probably a mistake to assume that a universal model can be constructed based exclusively on the details of any one particular case. Each local society is to some degree unique, and it may be presumptuous to think that any one represents a universal norm.

Still, perhaps because of that continuous (if often slow and limited) ongoing process of cross-cultural interaction, there do appear to have been some overarching common trajectories in the history of the Eurasian Old World. Beginning in the sixteenth century, in particular, there are a few tantalizing similarities between Western Europe and both China and Japan that make an argument that they were all part of some more general Eurasian early modern age seem at least plausible. These parallels include points of both apparent convergence and actual contact. In China, the signs of such early modernity include the appearance of a commercialized consumer culture in the late Ming and the forging of a vast new "gunpowder empire" under the subsequent Qing Dynasty.

The conventional verdict on the early Ming Dynasty is that it was hopelessly isolationistic. Under the first Ming emperor, a special document was required to travel more than thirty miles from home, and travel abroad without official permission was punishable by death. Confucian moralists, moreover, were inclined to decry the growing commercialization of the dynasty as a decline from the ideal order established by the dynastic founder. Whether the government and Confucian moralists approved or not, however, private commerce still blossomed in the late Ming. Precisely because the government neither understood nor approved, much of this commerce took place outside the sphere of government surveillance. Ming commercialization therefore could be described as laissez-faire in approach partly by accident or default. In some cases, however, the Ming government's attitude may have even been deliberately laissez-faire: one late Ming official, writing in the 1580s, boasted, for example, of how a reduction in commercial tax rates in Nanjing not only resulted in increased trade but also caused a net increase in tax receipts![3]

Given China's huge size, most of China's trade has always been domestic. The Ming government inadvertently helped facilitate internal trade by reopening and maintaining the Grand Canal. Some twelve thousand government barges plied this canal to bring tax grain from the south to the capital at Beijing in the north, and the private vessels that also took advantage of this manmade waterway as well as of the many other rivers and canals of south China were beyond count. Increasing economic specialization further stimulated interregional domestic trade. For example, concentration on the cultivation of cotton for textile production in the lower Yangzi River area created a local demand for imported food grain that was satisfied by shipments of rice from farther upriver. By the 1730s such shipments had reached a volume in excess of a billion pounds a year.[4] The invention, by at least Ming times, of that invaluable tool of trade, the abacus, is another indication of growing commercialization. The mobility made possible by ease of transportation also encouraged increasingly large-scale recreational tourism. By late Ming, it had become common to complain that "crowds of tourists" and souvenir vendors were spoiling the tourist attractions.[5]

At sea off the Ming coast, in any single day, there might be as many as 1,200 ships.[6] Although much coastal shipping was for domestic purposes, the volume of foreign trade was also substantial. Since the Ming government viewed foreign trade with suspicion, however, a large portion of this traffic operated outside the law, including both smuggling and piracy. The contradiction between growing trade and government restriction of it reached its climax in a period of so-called Japanese pirate raiding (in Japanese, *Wakō*; in Chinese, *Wokou*) along the Ming coast, especially in the 1540s–1550s. Although actual Japanese people were certainly among these pirates, many of the seaborne marauders were really Chinese or Korean.

Officially authorized trade between the Ming Dynasty and Japan was initiated by the Shogun Yoshimitsu in 1401, but this authorized trade was very limited in scale, and merchants who did not have the necessary official seals were probably always much more numerous. They developed a flourishing contraband trade with the Ming. Imported luxury goods from Japan, especially lacquerware and metalwork, became notably fashionable items of late Ming consumption. In addition to the Japanese imports, there were also other even more exotic items such as edible sea slugs from eastern Indonesia and Australia and even turkeys from America.[7]

The turkey has always remained a somewhat exotic creature in China, but another product native to the Americas, tobacco, was beginning to become genuinely popular in China by as early as the seventeenth century. For the first 142 years of the Ming Dynasty, the only legally acknowledged foreign trade had been that which was conducted under the rubric of formal diplomatic tribute missions (though these were sometimes merely fictitious pretexts for trade, and there was much extralegal activity), but in 1509, Guangzhou (in English, Canton) was legally opened to private merchants from tributary countries, and in 1567, a port in Fujian Province was opened to private Chinese traders.[8] By that date, there was also already a permanent Portuguese presence on the southeast coast of China. Conditions were significantly changing, and China was being swept up into the now, for the first time, truly global trade routes that had been opened by the great early modern European Age of Exploration.

The first Portuguese landfall in south China was probably made in 1513 (although the earliest Portuguese apparently came as passengers aboard Asian vessels, and the first actual European ship may not have arrived until 1517). Because of mutual misunderstandings, Portuguese relations with Ming China got off to a poor start, but by 1557, the Portuguese had a permanent base on Chinese soil at Macao, a small peninsula near the mouth of the river leading up to Guangzhou, across from what would later become the British colony of Hong Kong (see map 15 in chapter 12). Macao would remain under Portuguese jurisdiction until the end of the twentieth century. By the 1560s, official Ming restrictions on overseas trade were beginning to relax, and the Portuguese were soon joined by the Spanish, who had established a base at Manila in the Philippines in 1571.

In the sixteenth century, most Portuguese profits from their Asian trade came from handling shipping between destinations within Asia rather than from trade between Asia and Europe. With their seafaring and navigation skills (and heavy seaborne firepower), the Europeans had carved an important niche for themselves among ancient Asian maritime trade routes, alongside Southeast Asians, Indians, Arabs, and Chinese, but at this point, the Europeans were still far from dominant, at least as far as volume was concerned. When Portuguese firearms were first introduced to Japan in 1543, for example, it was by three Portuguese merchants who just happened to be aboard a Chinese ship that was blown off course to a Japanese island (Tanegashima). It is not even certain if the guns they introduced were of European or Middle Eastern manufacture. The pioneering Christian missionary to Japan, Saint Francis Xavier (1506–1552), also arrived in Japan aboard a Chinese rather than a European ship.[9] Chinese merchants, who had fanned out across Southeast Asia in substantial numbers beginning especially after about 1500, still dominated much of the retail trade throughout the region. In Spanish Manila, for example, between 1571 and 1600, there were an annual average of seven thousand Chinese visitors, in comparison to a resident ruling Spanish and Mexican population of fewer than one thousand.[10]

Andre Gunder Frank has recently argued that Europe, in its early modern Age of Exploration, did not really pull the rest of the world into a European-centered economic system – at least, not initially. "Instead, Europe belatedly joined . . . an already exiting world economy," in which, if any location could truly be called "central" prior to about 1800, "it was China." Early modern Europeans, moreover, still had no product that would sell consistently in China, except for money itself. But in the matter of cash, the Europeans were fortunate. Between 1492 and 1800, some 85 percent of the world's total silver supply, and 70 percent of its gold, came from the new European colonies in the Americas.[11] In Ming China, raw silver literally was money, and early modern Europeans used a substantial portion of their New World silver to pay for imported Chinese luxury products such as porcelain, silk, lacquerware, and (later) tea.

The Dutch became the most dynamic European power in Pacific waters in the seventeenth century, and though the focus of their attention came to be directed at what is now called Indonesia, the Dutch also attempted to trade with China. In the first half of the seventeenth century, the Dutch imported some three million pieces of Chinese porcelain (which is often simply called "china," or chinaware) into Europe and established a successful outpost on the island of Taiwan. On Taiwan the Dutch erected their second-largest fortress in Asia, and there they purchased silk from Chinese merchants to exchange for silver in Japan.[12] This Dutch base on Taiwan survived for four decades (1624–1662) and was, ironically enough, responsible for encouraging the ancestors of the people we now call "Taiwanese" (as distinct from the aborigines, who were there already) to begin settling the island. The Dutch were forcibly driven off Taiwan in 1662, however, by a colorful Chinese freebooter named Zheng Chenggong (known in Europe as Koxinga, 1624–1662), the son of a Chinese Christian and a Japanese mother, who became the first Chinese ruler of Taiwan.[13] After about 1690, the Dutch generally stopped even trying to trade directly with China, finding it easier simply to allow Chinese and Portuguese merchants to come to the Dutch base on Java (in Indonesia) to conduct trade themselves.

Europeans were therefore among the participants in China's overseas trade by the seventeenth century, but they were hardly a dominant presence. Even so, Europe had already begun to make an impact on China. The telescope, for example, was introduced to China by 1618, within thirty years of its European invention around 1590.[14] A European-style world map, with captions written in Chinese, was prepared by the Italian Catholic missionary Matteo Ricci (1552–1610) in 1584. This was quickly copied and printed by the Chinese. A copy of a revised version of this map was eventually even hung in large panels on the wall of the emperor's palace in Beijing. In addition to his mapmaking contributions, Ricci also worked with the Chinese scholar Xu Guangqi (1562–1633) to produce the first good Chinese translation of Euclid in 1607.[15] This same Chinese scholar, Xu Guangqi, later rose to the highest office in the Ming government and became a baptized Christian, taking the Christian name Paul.

Matteo Ricci was a Jesuit. The Jesuits were a Roman Catholic counterreformation order that produced some of the best-educated minds in seventeenth-century Europe. Jesuits were expected to undergo a nine-year course of study that included mathematics and astronomy, classical philosophy, art, and the humanities as well as Christian theology. The first Jesuit missionary came to China – from Japan, as it happens – in 1552, when the Spanish (Basque) missionary Saint Francis Xavier arrived on an island off the southeast coast. He died later that same year without ever making it to the mainland, but other Jesuits followed. In 1601, Matteo Ricci became the first European Christian missionary (since Mongol times) to be allowed to reside in Beijing. Ricci may have also been the first European ever to learn to speak the Chinese language proficiently. With his profound erudition, scientific knowledge, and accommodating approach, Matteo Ricci made a favorable impression on many Chinese. The Jesuit mission to China enjoyed a measure of real success, and by the end of the seventeenth century, there may have been two hundred thousand Chinese Christian converts.

Arguably, however, the Jesuit reports from China had as much impact on Europe as their missionary activity had on the Chinese. Matteo Ricci drew on Chinese as well as European sources for his famous world map, and native Chinese and Japanese maps were of great interest to contemporary Europeans.[16] Curious early modern Europeans were amazed to learn of China's reported antiquity – which supposedly, and very perplexingly, extended back even before the widely accepted date of the biblical flood. Europeans were also impressed by China's enormous size and apparent good government. Ideas about China and Confucius had explicit influences on such important European Enlightenment figures as Leibniz (1646–1716), Voltaire (1694–1778), and the eighteenth-century French school of pioneering economists known as the Physiocrats. There was, in addition, a long-standing vogue in Europe for Chinese-style art objects, called chinoiserie, which, among other things, had a significant impact on English gardening styles.[17]

In China, the seventeenth century was a time of remarkable tolerance, individualism, and open-minded intellectual inquiry. Li Yu (1611–1680), for example, has been called "China's first professional writer," who intentionally made "writing a profit-making business venture." Li was best known as a writer of fiction – short stories and plays – but he was also an authority on gardening and interior design, a theater manager, critic, publisher (with his own publishing firm), and the inventor of a heated chair for use in winter. In his writing, he expressed some curiously modern-sounding opinions such as protofeminist views about the equality of women, and in his fiction, he portrayed thieves, beggars, prostitutes, and homosexuals sympathetically, as characters to be judged by their behavior as human beings rather than as stereotypical moral categories automatically to be condemned.[18]

The new age of commercial wealth, which began roughly in the mid-1500s, supported an affluent consumer lifestyle of conspicuous consumption. As one Ming author observed in the 1570s, "long skirts and wide collars, broad belts and narrow pleats – they change without warning. It's what they call fashion."[19] Word of the latest fashions was spread throughout China by books on connoisseurship and etiquette guides, which described even such things as the most tasteful way to display fruit on a plate, and which circulated widely, even to persons of relatively modest means in rural villages. (The male literacy rate in seventeenth-century China has been estimated at between 40 and 50 percent.[20]) Anxiety to follow constantly changing fashions also produced a large market for cheap imitations and outright fakes. For fashion-conscious shoppers who feared they might not be discriminating enough to judge product quality on their own, the maker's marks of well-regarded craftsmen and workshops began to function as an early form of reliable "brand names."

All this seems strangely modern and reminiscent of Western developments. Because newly wealthy merchants in China wished to be seen as men of good taste, however, many of their favored collectors' items were drawn from the scholar's study, including the paraphernalia of writing itself: brushes, ink, and ink stones (necessary for grinding the solid cakes of ink). Such fashions reflected a uniquely Chinese sociopolitical order, in which academic degree holders were the admired elite. Wealthy merchants emulated the lifestyle of scholars. Other fashionable collector's items included paintings and calligraphy, musical instruments, antique bronzes, and curios of every description. Perhaps the finest coordinated displays of late Ming taste and commercial wealth were the exquisite garden homes that began to be landscaped in extravagant numbers, most famously in Suzhou (see Figure 6.1).

If late Ming China seems in some ways surprisingly modern, therefore, it was a modernity that took characteristically Chinese forms. European cultural influences were a minor undercurrent, and European cash (in the form of silver) served a still predominantly Chinese economy. Despite the appearance of prosperity, moreover, the Ming government itself was bankrupt and disintegrating by mid-century. The Manchu conquest of China that began in 1644 would usher in a more conservative reaction, and the open-minded tolerance that gave Li Yu's seventeenth-century fiction such a surprisingly modern flavor would be bluntly banned as immoral in

Figure 6.1. Covered walkway at the Humble Administrator's Garden (Zhuozheng yuan), Suzhou, China. Originally built in 1509–1513 and restored in the seventeenth–eighteenth centuries, this is an example of the style of magnificent garden houses that became characteristic of late Ming Dynasty China. Vanni/Art Resource, New York.

the eighteenth century. These Manchu conquerors took China in other directions after 1644.

The Manchu, Qing, "Gunpowder Empire" (1644–Eighteenth Century [–1912])

Some of the greatest empires in the early modern world were not Western European. Examples include the Ottoman Empire (1300–1919), which captured Constantinople in 1453 and besieged Vienna in 1529, and yet again in 1683; the Safavid Empire in Persia (1501–1722); the Mughal Empire in India (which flourished ca. 1556–1707); and the Russian Empire. Moscow fully escaped from Mongol domination only in the 1460s and then embarked on a course of explosive expansion that eventually made Russia the largest country in the world. These early modern empires were typically distinguished by heavy reliance on the new artillery technology and have sometimes therefore been described as "gunpowder empires." While the early modern empires of Western Europe were characteristically seafaring adventures, these others were mostly continental land empires. Either directly or indirectly, they also often claimed some connection to the memory of Chinggis Khan. Among the greatest of all these early modern empires was the one forged by the Manchus, based in China.

Before the seventeenth century, there literally were no Manchus. The first known use of the word *Manchu* was in 1613, and the name was not officially adopted until

1635.[21] Nor was Manchu just a new name for an older reality; the Manchus were a significantly new group, with a new corporate identity. The core around which this new Manchu identity coalesced did consist, however, of much older Jurchen tribes. The Jurchen had inhabited the region we now call Manchuria for centuries, and what became the Manchu language was indeed essentially another name for Jurchen. Jurchen was a Tungusic language, related to others spoken in eastern Siberia and, more distantly, perhaps also to that northern belt of so-called Altaic languages that includes Turkic, Mongolic, and possibly even Korean and Japanese.

In the late sixteenth and early seventeenth centuries, the land we call Manchuria was still sparsely inhabited, with a total population of less than half a million. This thin scattering of people was divided among various tribes – some of whom did not submit to the new Manchu Empire until long after most Chinese people had. Parts of southern Manchuria had been included, off and on, inside Chinese imperial dynasties since the first one, but Manchuria was also separated from China proper by the line of the Great Wall. Manchuria's northern border, on the other hand, would remain open and ill defined until the end of the seventeenth century. It was a rough frontier land, with every residence surrounded by some sort of defensive stockade. Among the local strongmen at the turn of the seventeenth century was one named Nurgaci (1559–1626). Nurgaci founded what was to become the Manchu imperial lineage (the Aisin Gioro) and began the process of empire building. He started with only a few hundred men, however, and for many years, he accepted the role of Ming tributary.

Nurgaci introduced the device of different colored banners as an organizational tool to cut across the old tribal allegiances and assemble larger armed forces. In Chinese, the Manchus were in fact commonly referred to simply as the Banner People (*qiren*). This banner system was a form of military and political mobilization, and over the course of the seventeenth century, it brought together people of surprisingly diverse origin, including persons of Chinese, Korean, Mongolic, Turkic, Tibetan, and even some of Russian descent as well as the core group of Jurchen. Once established, however, banner status became hereditary and closed. A degree of uniformity in such matters as hairstyle and clothing was imposed upon the Banner People, and all were expected to learn to speak the Manchu language. These Manchus therefore gradually acquired an unmistakable ethnic identity.[22]

In 1635, Nurgaci's successor officially adopted the name Manchu for his following. At the same time, he also took the Chinese-language dynastic name Qing (which means "pure" or "clear") and the Chinese title "emperor" (*Huangdi*). As several frontier peoples had before in the past, the Manchus thus began constructing a native Manchu dynasty roughly along Chinese imperial lines.

The Manchus were not steppe nomads, but from the beginning they interacted closely with the eastern Mongols. Nurgaci's family intermarried extensively with Mongol nobility, the Mongol language was frequently spoken at the early Manchu court, and the Manchu writing system, which was developed in the sixteenth and seventeenth centuries, was adapted from Mongol. The capture of the Mongol Great Seal in 1635 also allowed the Manchu emperors to make the potent claim that they were the legitimate successors to Chinggis Khan.

Meanwhile, in the 1640s, the western Mongols – through marriage alliances between different tribes, a shared adherence to Tibetan Buddhism, and a new universal Mongol law code – were once again constructing a mighty Mongol empire, this time called the Zunghar Empire. The Zunghar Mongols were based in the grasslands of the Yili River region of northern Xinjiang, in the remote northwest of what is now China. Their rise was an obvious challenge to the Manchu Qing Dynasty that was also rising at that very same time in the northeast. One common thread linking them all was Tibetan Buddhism. In 1578, an eastern Mongol khan had bestowed a new title on a leader of the reformed sect of Tibetan Buddhism: "Dalai Lama." (*Dalai* is actually a Mongol rather than a Tibetan word, meaning "ocean," and translating the Tibetan word *gyatso*.) The Dalai Lamas and Mongol khans were therefore linked from the beginning, and important priest-patron relationships were cultivated between them. Thanks in part to spiritual support provided by the Dalai Lama, by 1680, the Zunghar Mongols in the northwest had expanded their empire to gain control over all Xinjiang.

The Manchu emperors in the northeast, meanwhile, also presented themselves as patrons of Tibetan lamas (see Figure 6.2). As an indication of the importance of Tibetan Buddhism in the overall Manchu empire-building project, there would eventually be no fewer than thirty-five separate buildings in the Manchu imperial palace in Beijing dedicated specifically to Tibetan Buddhism and ten more Tibetan shrines elsewhere in the palace complex.[23] In a dispute over the Dalai Lama's succession, the Manchus, before long, managed to outmaneuver the Zunghar Mongols and bring Tibet into the orbit of the Qing Dynasty as a Manchu protectorate. A Qing garrison was installed in the Tibetan capital at Lhasa in 1720, although it was soon reduced to a mere one hundred troops and two officials. With its leverage over Tibet relatively secure, the Qing unleashed a series of major military campaigns against the western Mongols and completely obliterated the Zunghar Mongol Empire by 1759.

More Zunghar Mongols may have died from smallpox – a disease to which Mongols were shockingly vulnerable – than from Qing military action. Others fled to the Russians and Kazakhs. The Zungharian steppes were depopulated and the few remaining survivors reduced to Qing servitude.[24] For the first time in imperial Chinese history, the closing of the northern steppes that was caused by the meeting of the borders of the rapidly expanding Russian and Qing empires had finally made it possible to completely eliminate the nomadic threat to China. The Zunghar Mongols were gone, and elsewhere in Mongolia, nomadic military ferocity may have also been tamed somewhat by the fact that about one-third of all Mongol men were now peaceful Buddhist monks. Mongol nobles were given Qing imperial titles, and Mongol tribes were assigned fixed, separate pasturelands to limit their mobility. Mongolia, including Outer Mongolia, was incorporated into the Qing Dynasty.

Xinjiang was also incorporated and, in the late eighteenth century, finally began actually being called Xinjiang (New Frontier) for the first time. The Manchus initiated a major project to map and record the details of Xinjiang history and ethnography. Qing rule in Xinjiang remained fairly indirect, however, conducted through native Turkic officials called *Begs* (a Uighur Türk word for "noble"), under

Figure 6.2. Portrait of the Manchu, Qing Dynasty, Qianlong Emperor of China (r. 1735–1796) as the Buddhist Bodhisattva Mañjuśrī, in the style of a Tibetan *thangka* but with the face painted by the Italian Giuseppe Castiglione (1688–1766). Freer Gallery of Art, Smithsonian Institution, Washington, D.C.: Purchase – anonymous donor and museum funds, F2000.4.

the loose supervision of Manchu officials known as *Ambans*. The Manchus ruled Xinjiang and Mongolia largely as inner-Asian-style khans of the steppe, and their patronage of Tibetan Buddhism was something of an extension of the previous Mongol role.

The Manchu population of the Qing Dynasty continued to be administered by its separate banner system, and Mongols, Uighurs, and Tibetans were supervised by a Court of Colonial Affairs rather than the regular central imperial bureaucracy.

Most of the population of the empire was still governed by that regular bureaucracy, however, because by this time the Qing Empire also included, and was largely based in, China proper. Even as the Manchus were beginning their imperial expansion, the Ming Dynasty in China was collapsing. The fabulous commercial wealth of the late Ming period was enjoyed mainly by a fortunate few, and there was simultaneously also much economic distress. Spanish trade with Ming China declined after 1620, as Spain's supply of silver from the Americas took a sharp downturn. The expulsion of the Portuguese from Japan after 1639 also ended their profitable role as middlemen in the trade between China and Japan. For these and other reasons, by the mid-seventeenth century the Ming government was bankrupt. Communications were disrupted, government offices went unfilled, and troops went unpaid. Unrest erupted into rebellion, and in 1644, one Chinese rebel (Li Zicheng, ca. 1605–1645) captured the Ming capital at Beijing.

A loyal Ming general commanding the strategic pass in the northeast where the Great Wall comes down to meet the sea refused to submit to these rebels, however, and sent a letter requesting military assistance from the Manchus. A young boy sat on the Manchu throne at this decisive moment, but the fourteenth son of Nurgaci (Dorgon, 1612–1650), acting on the emperor's behalf as regent, accepted the invitation and attacked, routing the Chinese rebel army. On June 5, 1644, Manchu forces entered Beijing. There they took immediate measures to win Chinese popular support by announcing tax cuts, burying the last Ming emperor with full ceremonial protocol, and making the claim that the traditional Chinese Mandate of Heaven had legitimately passed to them.

After having rather swiftly subdued north China and occupied Beijing, the Manchu expansion of their conquest to south China proved much more difficult. Resistance was, at times, stiff. A shocking total of over eight hundred thousand bodies reportedly were cremated after the fall of a single southern city (Yangzhou). Manchu rule over China proper was not fully consolidated and stabilized until after the Qing conquest of Taiwan in 1683. Even then, the slogan "overthrow the Qing and restore the Ming" long remained popular among secret societies such as the Triads. Manchu rule in China was never entirely secure, and the Qing emperors were always suspicious and fearful of rebellion. Partly for this reason, there were more literary inquisitions and books banned by the Qing Dynasty than by any other dynasty in Chinese history.

On the other hand, though, throughout the premodern world, it has never been all that unusual for the king or the ruling elite to be strangers to their subject population. In England, for example, a French-speaking Norman aristocracy ruled the land after 1066, and a House of Hanover from Germany occupied the British throne after 1714. Global examples could easily be multiplied. In China, furthermore, Chinese civilization had always been a multiethnic fusion from the beginning. Since the time of the Zhou conquest of the Shang three thousand years ago, a number of different peoples have been viewed as perfectly legitimate holders of the Mandate of Heaven. It is only in the modern age of nation-states and representative self-government that "foreign rule" became objectionable by definition. Manchu rule over China, from 1644 to 1912, was therefore not altogether an aberration, either by world or by traditional Chinese standards; in fact, it came to be fairly widely accepted.

The Manchu Banner People did impose themselves on China as a consciously separate ruling elite, however. Banner soldiers were stationed throughout the empire in over ninety walled garrisons. The largest Manchu concentration was in Beijing, where ethnic Chinese residents were supposed to be confined only to the southern suburbs. Banner men were initially only permitted to serve as soldiers or officials and were paid a regular government stipend. A disproportionate share of top government offices were also always held by Manchus. The Banner People were distinguished from their subject populations by their "national language" (which was Manchu, not Chinese) and by their practice of the art of mounted archery. Mounted archery, in fact, became so central to the Manchu identity that when the mounted archery requirement for banner men was finally lifted in 1905 – by which time it had already long lost any real military value – one British observer reported that the decree was still greeted with much indignation by Beijing banner men.[25] Manchus were also distinguished by their polysyllabic non-Chinese names and by the fact that Manchu women did not practice foot binding. Manchus and ethnic Chinese were also kept separate by a number of prohibitions. They were forbidden to intermarry, and ethnic Chinese were forbidden to move to Manchuria.

The Qing Dynasty was a vast, multiethnic conquest empire that, by the eighteenth century, may have ruled over as much as 40 percent of the world's total population. It had three official languages, Manchu, Mongol, and Chinese, with Tibetan also enjoying considerable prominence. The eighteenth-century Qianlong Emperor (r. 1736–1796) reportedly was able to speak Manchu, Mongol, Chinese, Tibetan, Uighur, and Tangut. During the seventeenth century, the Manchu language remained dominant in government, and even in the eighteenth century, Manchu was still commonly spoken at meetings of the Grand Council. But the Banner People made up only about 1 percent of the total population of their empire, and it became a struggle for many of them to maintain competence in their own language. The Chinese language tended to prevail, and today, Manchu is nearly extinct as a living language.

Nonetheless, the Manchus retained their position as a distinctly separate ruling group until the very end of the dynasty in 1912. Manchu culture also had some impact in setting standards for the entire empire. The Manchu hairstyle – the queue – was strictly imposed on all male subjects by law, and the Manchu banner gown (*Qipao*) ironically enough became what many people think of today as traditional Chinese women's clothing. At least at the start of the dynasty, the Qing was also surprisingly cosmopolitan.

The great Kangxi Emperor (r. 1661–1722) was personally of mixed Manchu, Chinese, and Mongol ancestry because of intermarriage. His avid interest in hunting and military exploits reflects his Manchu heritage, but he also promoted Chinese literary culture, and it was he who first established a special clientage relationship with the Dalai Lama in Tibet. At the same time, the Kangxi Emperor also studied Latin from Jesuit missionaries and collected European clocks. Unlike the Tokugawa Shogunate in Japan (1603–1868), with its relatively strict exclusion policy after 1639, the Qing Dynasty in China after 1644 did not try to shut off European contact.

Quite the opposite: the Qing Dynasty made early use of the most advanced European mapmaking experts (who had recently developed methods to accurately chart both latitude and longitude) in an imperial mapping project very similar to those sponsored by early modern European governments. The Qing actually completed its early modern mapmaking project before either France or Russia.[26] Less than two months after Manchu forces first entered Beijing in 1644, the German Jesuit missionary Johann Adam Schall von Bell (1591–1666) offered to submit to a public test of the accuracy of his prediction of a solar eclipse anticipated for that September. Schall's calculations proved more accurate than the traditional Chinese methods, and Schall was rewarded with appointment as director of the Qing Bureau of Astronomy. Schall even became a respected senior intimate of one young Manchu emperor. In 1664, his fortunes abruptly fell when he was accused of spying, after which he lived under house arrest until his death in 1666. However, the Belgian missionary Ferdinand Verbiest (1623–1688) posthumously vindicated Schall with yet another dramatic astronomical challenge, and Verbiest, too, was made director of the Qing Astronomical Bureau.[27] Into the eighteenth century, Europeans were still designing buildings for the Qing summer palace on the outskirts of Beijing and painting Qing court portraits (see Figure 6.2).

The total number of Jesuit missionaries who came to China remained small, however, and they were reluctant to increase their numbers by ordaining native Chinese priests, making it difficult to adequately serve a large Chinese Christian population. By the eighteenth century, moreover, the Jesuit order was under assault in Europe itself. In East Asia, the Jesuits had made a conscious decision to adopt local manners and culture, in a policy known as cultural accommodation, to make themselves more acceptable to East Asians (see Figure 6.3). In China, the Jesuits also chose to treat Confucianism as a secular philosophy rather than a religion and therefore viewed it as compatible with Christianity. The argument was that reading Confucius should be no more objectionable for a good Christian than studying other great pagan philosophers such as Plato or Aristotle. Even the traditional Chinese offerings of food at household ancestral tablets, and some of the rituals conducted for the spirit of Confucius, might be tolerated as purely social obligations rather than heathen religion.

Other Catholic orders, however, particularly the Dominicans and Franciscans, were outraged by this Jesuit tolerance of Confucian rites. Serious criticism of the Jesuit approach began as early as the 1640s, and altogether, no fewer than eight popes became involved in deciding the so-called rites controversy. In 1704, a Vatican decree banned Christian participation in Confucian rites, and a papal bull (*Ex illa die*) in 1715 further reinforced this decision. In 1773, the Jesuit order was even (temporarily) suppressed altogether by the Roman Catholic Church. In 1724, meanwhile, a Qing emperor had condemned Christianity. The unraveling of the once promising Jesuit mission to China is symptomatic of an apparently

Figure 6.3. Portrait of the Belgian Jesuit missionary to China Nicholas Trigault (1577–1628), in Chinese costume, by Peter Paul Rubens (1577–1640). Purchase, Carl Selden Trust, several members of the Chairman's Council, Gail and Parker Gilbert, and Lila Acheson Wallace Gifts, 1999 (1999.222). The Metropolitan Museum of Art, New York. © The Metropolitan Museum of Art/Art Resource, New York.

widening gap in mutual appreciation between China and Europe in the eighteenth and nineteenth centuries.

After the establishment of the Qing Dynasty in 1644, meanwhile, although a scattering of embassies came to China from the Netherlands, Portugal, Russia, and the Vatican, there was little formal diplomatic contact between China and the major Western European countries. Substantial private trade, however, resumed after the consolidation of Manchu authority. The leading European traders were now the British, who, according to one story, in 1664 first imported two pounds of a curious Chinese leaf thought to have medicinal properties. In a local southeastern Chinese dialect, this substance was called something that sounded like "tea" to British ears. The British tea trade would soon grow to enormous importance. In the meantime, however, a new restriction had been placed on European trade with

China. Beginning in 1760, the Qing Dynasty limited all Western maritime trade to one port: Guangzhou (Canton).

Despite this new restriction on European trade, the Qing Dynasty was still not really all that especially closed and isolationistic – nor was it obviously in decline in the eighteenth century. In forging their vast gunpowder empire, the Manchus may have directed attention from the southeast coast to the northwest continental interior, in the process becoming more interested in Mongols and Tibetans than in Europeans. In promoting stability and traditional Chinese culture, they may have also reaffirmed conservative values, putting, for example, unprecedented emphasis on the Confucian ideal of widow chastity. But the Qing Empire was still an active major participant in world trade, and in terms of such things as demographic structure, average life expectancy, level of commercial development, legal property rights, and overall standard of living, Qing China still compared favorably with Western Europe until as late as 1800, when the industrial revolution finally began to accelerate in Great Britain. Even in 1800, China may still have produced a larger share of total world manufacturing output than all Europe, including Russia, combined.[28]

The Hermit Kingdom: Late Chosŏn Korea ([1392–] Sixteenth–Nineteenth Centuries [–1910])

Ironically, Korea was still only just settling into what we normally think of as "traditional" cultural patterns when the early modern age began.[29] The process of creating "traditional" Korea had, to a large extent, only begun with institutional reforms in the early Chosŏn period, after 1392, and took a couple of centuries to fully mature. Any overarching shared Eurasian early modern tendencies remained relatively muted in Korea during this period. Instead, Korean history followed its own unique trajectory, in which the participation of Europeans, world trade, and commercialization figured less prominently than in either contemporary China or Japan. If it is relatively difficult to convincingly see late Chosŏn Korea as in any sense being early modern, however, that is a healthy reminder of both the diversity of local experience and the arbitrariness of our historical labels.

Since the history of the late Chosŏn Dynasty is commonly treated separately from the early Chosŏn, it is not merely for the purpose of (approximately) synchronizing our presentation of Korean history with Chinese and Japanese history that a brief summary of the late Chosŏn is presented here, even though the late Chosŏn may not really seem very "early modern." An especially convenient dividing point in the lengthy history – more than five hundred years – of the Chosŏn Dynasty is provided by the Japanese invasions that began in 1592.

Following an age of extreme decentralization, as will be explained further later, Japan was reunified in the late sixteenth century by a series of three great warlords, including, in particular, one named Hideyoshi (1536–1598). Having completed his conquest of the Japanese islands, Hideyoshi boasted that he would conquer China, too. Invading China involved going through Korea first, and in 1592, Hideyoshi landed a massive force of over 158,000 men on the southeastern tip of the Korean

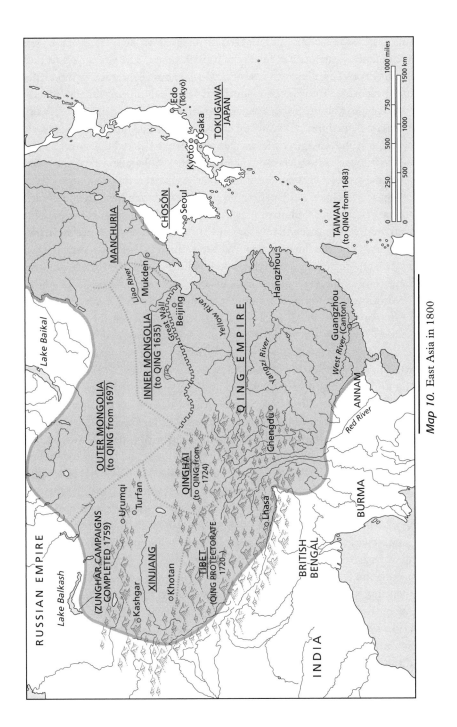

Map 10. East Asia in 1800

peninsula. The Koreans were unprepared for the assault, and within three weeks, the fierce Japanese warriors had taken the capital, Seoul. The Korean court fled to the Yalu River on their northern frontier, and Japanese samurai overran virtually the entire peninsula. However, a resourceful Korean admiral named Yi Sun-sin (1545–1598) was able to disrupt Japanese shipping, making use of the world's first iron-plated warships (called turtle ships), and win a stunning series of naval victories. The Ming Chinese, meanwhile, somewhat belatedly also sent a relief force of fifty thousand men to assist Chosŏn, and anti-Japanese guerrilla warfare erupted in many places throughout the Korean countryside.

Under these pressures, the Japanese invaders were driven back to a foothold on the southeast coast, and diplomatic negotiations began. When diplomacy stalled, Hideyoshi ordered yet a second invasion in 1597, but this time, the defenders were better prepared, and the Japanese enjoyed little success. Hideyoshi then promptly died in 1598, and the Japanese warriors soon withdrew from the Korean peninsula. But seven years of bloody warfare had, in the meantime, laid waste to much of Korea. Notoriously, between one and two hundred thousand severed Korean and Chinese human noses (which were more easily portable across the water than the enemy heads that samurai traditionally collected) had been sent back to Japan as tokens of Japanese martial achievement. Many of these were heaped into a (somewhat mistakenly so-called) Mound of Ears (Mimizuka) in Kyōto.[30] Despite emerging as the winner, therefore, Korea had been devastated by these invasions, and the seeds of lasting bitter antagonism were planted between Korea and Japan.

It was presumably also in partial reaction to these Japanese invasions that late Chosŏn Korea became the most genuinely isolationistic country in East Asia. Westerners would later come to picturesquely describe it as the "hermit" kingdom.[31] Although Chosŏn continued its regular tributary relations with China, private trade with China across the Yalu River was forbidden. Trade with Japan, through the lords of Satsuma Island, did resume, but it was limited to some twenty-one ships annually during the years between 1609 and the 1870s. Japanese merchants in Korea, moreover, were confined to a single walled compound at Pusan. Contact with the wider world was relatively nonexistent.

Even relations with China were soon significantly altered. In the early seventeenth century, a new Manchu empire had begun to organize itself – beginning precisely in the Yalu River border area adjacent to Korea. Early Manchu demands for Chosŏn support put the Koreans in an awkward position because of Korea's long-standing tributary relationship with the Ming Dynasty (not to mention sincere Korean gratitude for the recent Ming assistance in defeating Hideyoshi's invasions). The Manchus responded by invading Korea in 1627 and again in 1637, taking the Korean crown prince hostage for eight years and reducing Chosŏn Korea to a tributary of the Manchu Qing Dynasty. This was even before the Manchus took Beijing and assumed the Mandate of Heaven in China in 1644. Although Korea remained thereafter a tributary of the Qing Dynasty, many Koreans looked down on the Manchu rulers of the Qing with considerable disdain as barbarians.

With the long-acknowledged center of the civilized world in China trampled now under Manchu barbarian hooves, many Koreans came to perceive their own land as the sole remaining, isolated outpost of proper (Confucian) civilization. As King Yŏngjo (r. 1724–1776) explained, "the Central Plains [China] exude the stenches of barbarians and our Green Hills [Korea] are alone."[32] Despite remaining formal tributaries of the Qing Dynasty, Chosŏn Koreans continued to use the Ming rather than the Qing calendar and to wear Ming-style clothing and hairstyles (even as Chinese men were forced to adopt the Manchu queue). Even while the Ming Dynasty had still stood, some Koreans had already disapproved of certain Ming Chinese departures from Zhu Xi's Neo-Confucian orthodoxy (such as the thought of Wang Yangming). After the Ming had fallen, Chosŏn Korea envisioned itself as the last bastion of proper Neo-Confucianism. Paradoxically, this also helped promote a new sense of pride in, and awareness of, Korean identity.

In addition to the sophisticated elaboration of Neo-Confucian metaphysics, which continued to be written in the classical Chinese language, the seventeenth and eighteenth centuries also saw a large increase in the amount of literature written in the native Korean language, in the new *han'gŭl* script. This included, notably, much fiction. The arts also continued to be richly cultivated in late Chosŏn Korea (see Figure 6.4), and there does appear to have been at least some economic development in this period. In the seventeenth century, agricultural production increased because of improved irrigation and the spread of the technique of transplanting rice seedlings. By planting rice in a small seedbed first, and later transplanting the seedlings, a prior crop of barley was able to ripen earlier in the same fields. Farming also became somewhat less for subsistence and more for commercial markets. Coins came into wider circulation. In 1801, most official slaves were freed, although slavery in Korea was not completely abolished until as late as 1894. Despite these developments, however, Korea remained much less commercially developed than either China or Japan. Seoul remained Korea's only major city, with a population of about two hundred thousand in the early nineteenth century.

Part of the reason for the low level of commercialization was the lack of convenient water transportation. There was nothing comparable in Korea to the dense network of rivers and canals in southern China or the Inland Sea in Japan. Aristocratic and Confucian elite disdain for commerce, and official policies of seclusion, surely also played a role. Yet even the hermit kingdom of Korea was not really completely isolated from developments in the outside world. One of the major new Chosŏn commercial crops, for example, was tobacco – introduced from the Americas in the seventeenth century! Chili peppers, which were also introduced from the Americas, completely transformed Korean cuisine. Today, the characteristic and outstandingly delicious Korean cooking style would be almost unimaginable without hot peppers. A European telescope and clock were also brought to Korea (from China) as early as 1631.

In 1784, one Korean returned from an embassy to Beijing as a baptized Catholic Christian. Even in the absence of European missionaries, a number of Koreans converted themselves to Catholicism through reading Christian texts written in the Chinese language. Amazingly, only Italy, France, and Spain have produced more canonized Catholic saints than Korea! But though Confucianism was generally

Figure 6.4. Wrestling, from an *Album of Scenes from Daily Life* after Kim Hong-do (ca. 1745–ca. 1806), late Chosŏn Dynasty Korea (nineteenth century). British Museum, London. © The Trustees of the British Museum/Art Resource, New York.

tolerant of differing religious beliefs, such toleration did not extend to religious practices that contradicted what were believed to be fundamental secular moral obligations. Once it became clear in Korea, after 1790, that the Catholic Church had forbidden the performance of Confucian ancestral rites, one Korean Christian responded by burning all of his family's ancestral tablets. He was arrested for violation of the mourning laws and executed.[33] Especially after the turn into the nineteenth century, there were serious, if sporadic, persecutions of Christians in Korea.

In 1866, a U.S. merchant schooner called the *General Sherman* sailed up the Taedong River toward P'yŏngyang with the intention of forcing trade. Grounded by low tide, the ship was mobbed and burned and all of its crew killed. That same year, a punitive expedition consisting of seven French warships was dispatched in reaction to the earlier execution of nine French missionaries, and a detachment of French soldiers was put ashore on Kanghwa Island. When large Korean forces were mobilized against the French, the French withdrew, and the Koreans interpreted this as a victory. In 1871, a squadron of five U.S. warships arrived in belated response to the burning of the *General Sherman*. When the Koreans refused to negotiate, the Americans bombarded the city of Kanghwa and destroyed Korean fortifications. When the Americas eventually withdrew, however, the Koreans were again convinced that they had militarily prevailed. Long after British naval power had compelled Qing China to open new ports for Western trade (in 1842), and the U.S. Navy, under Commodore Perry, had opened Japan (in 1854), Chosŏn Korea still had serious hopes of being able to forcibly keep unwelcome foreigners out.

The Reunification of Japan (1568–1600) and the Tokugawa Shogunate (1603–1868)

Three Reunifiers

If the Qing Dynasty in China was a classic example of an early modern gunpowder empire, the term might also be applied to contemporary Japan, although in some ways Japan was certainly an exceptional case. After the accidental introduction of firearms to the southern Japanese island of Tanegashima by stranded Portuguese in 1543, the Japanese immediately appreciated the usefulness of the deadly new technology, and skilled Japanese artisans quickly began reproducing these new weapons. Gunfire proved to be decisive in combat, and matchlocks became a vital tool in the military reunification of the Japanese islands. Attempts to extend this wave of military conquests beyond the zone of Japanese culture and forge a genuinely multiethnic empire, such as Hideyoshi's invasions of Korea, were not successful, however. Japan's emperors also remained quite powerless under the surveillance of shogunal military authority, and the island empire soon closed its borders and imposed relatively strict policies of isolation. So Japan was a somewhat unusual example of an early modern empire. Yet Japan did experience significant early modern economic development, and at the beginning of this period, centralized political control was rapidly extended across a large area, thanks in no small part to the availability of guns. Not entirely coincidentally, Europeans also figured prominently in the early phases of this story.

Sixteenth-century Europeans introduced more than just firearms into Japan. They also, for example, introduced tobacco, which soon began to be cultivated domestically. The habit of smoking became fairly widespread in early modern Japan. Another European influence may have been the cooking style known as tempura: batter-fried seafood and vegetables. The Japanese word *tempura* is thought to derive from Portuguese *temporada*, or "season," referring to periods when Catholics were expected to abstain from eating meat. Christianity, too, was a sixteenth-century European introduction, which briefly was quite influential.

The Jesuit missionary Saint Francis Xavier landed in Japan in 1549, on the southwestern island of Kyūshū. Perhaps because there were some striking similarities between sixteenth-century Europe and Japan – including such features as a hereditary military elite, castles, and widespread faith in a religion of salvation (Christianity was initially even sometimes mistaken by the Japanese for a variant sect of Buddhism!) – Japanese and Europeans greeted each other with a fair measure of initial mutual respect. The Japanese port at Nagasaki was developed after

1568 specifically for European trade, and the city was actually founded in 1571 by Jesuit missionaries, who continued to administer it for some years thereafter. For a time, it was fashionable in Japan to wear a cross and rosary. At its peak in the early seventeenth century, there may have been as many as three hundred thousand Japanese Christian converts.

The arrival of the Portuguese also brought increased foreign trade. Japanese mines just happened to be producing unprecedented quantities of silver in the sixteenth century, and because the Portuguese had a base in China at Macao, where raw silver was literally money, a flourishing trade developed between China and Japan, with the Portuguese serving as middlemen. This contributed to the ostentatious ornamentation of what was something of a literally gilded age in Japanese art history. The new wealth also helped great *daimyō* construct ever more massive fortifications and field ever larger armies. Guns, moreover, meant that the days of single combat between gallant mounted warriors, as portrayed in the old war tales, were over, and simple mountaintop castles were no longer secure. Massed ranks of infantry carrying guns, and huge fortifications with moats and earthen ramparts, were necessary. Amid the intense competition to survive a quintessentially Darwinian struggle for survival of the fittest, the process of political decentralization began to reverse itself.

In the middle of the sixteenth century, Japan was divided into roughly 120 *daimyō* domains, each of which was virtually an independent state. One relatively minor domain at Owari, in central Japan, belonged to Oda Nobunaga (1534–1582). The Oda family had emerged from obscurity while serving as deputies for the military governors of the province, and following the Ōnin War (1467–1477), they seized outright control of the domain for themselves. Oda Nobunaga then catapulted into greater prominence in 1560, when he surprised the vastly superior forces of a neighbor in a pouring rain and soundly defeated them. In 1568, an Ashikaga shogun requested Oda's assistance in regaining shogunal control in Kyōto, and Oda's march into the imperial capital in that year is sometimes said to mark the beginning of the reunification of Japan.

Oda had no intention of merely providing military support for Ashikaga shoguns, however. He assumed personal decision-making authority and, in 1573, drove the last Ashikaga shogun into exile. Thereafter, Oda simply left the position of shogun vacant. Oda scorned the trappings of formal legitimization and was content to rule by military force alone. As one European observer described Oda in 1569, he "treats all the Kings and Princes of Iapan with scorn, & speaks to them over his shoulder as though to inferiors."[34]

Oda Nobunaga's most intractable opponents in his rise to power were the Buddhists of the True Pure Land League (*Ikkō ikki*), based at the league's temple-fortress Ishiyama Honganji in Ōsaka, at the eastern end of the Inland Sea. Such leagues had emerged during the Japanese Warring States period as collective defense organizations, in an alternative to the form of a domain ruled by a single *daimyō*. Participants typically took an oath signed in blood, with their names written in a circle so that no one name came first. Most of these leagues dissolved fairly quickly, however, or transformed themselves into more conventional *daimyō* domains. By this time, the True Pure Land League itself was also no longer really very greatly different from a typical *daimyō* domain, except that it was specifically religious. Oda Nobunaga's conflict with this Buddhist sect raged for ten years before its great fortress at Ōsaka finally fell in 1580.

Since Buddhist religious institutions were particularly resistant to accepting subordination to his command, Oda Nobunaga could be especially ruthless in his assaults on them. In one shocking incident in 1571, for example, Oda destroyed the Tendai sect's ancient headquarters on Mount Hiei, overlooking Kyōto. Thousands of monastic buildings were burned and their inhabitants put to the sword.

As his headquarters, Oda built a great new castle for himself at Azuchi, on the shores of Japan's largest lake, Lake Biwa, just east of Kyōto, in 1576. Although moats and ramparts formed the most useful fortifications in this age of gunpowder, Japanese castles of the period also typically contained soaring central towers. When completed, the tower at Azuchi was 138 feet high, gilded at the top and whitewashed below, and decorated inside by screen paintings from the hands of master artists. By 1582, Oda Nobunaga controlled about one-third of all Japan. In that year, however, he was surprised after taking tea in a Kyōto monastery and murdered by a treacherous vassal, and his great castle at Azuchi was demolished.

Little survived of Oda's castle, but his accumulated conquests remained as a base on which others could build. At the time of Oda's death, his top lieutenant had been Hideyoshi. Hideyoshi sprang from such humble ancestry that he originally did not even have a family name (although the surname Toyotomi would eventually be bestowed on him by the emperor). He rose from the ranks of warrior farmers, at a time when the samurai class was still poorly defined, on the strength of his ability. When Hideyoshi learned of Oda Nobunaga's treacherous murder, he moved quickly to punish the assassin, putting him to death within eleven days. Hideyoshi was then well poised to assume command over Oda's forces and continue the process of reunification. Within eight more years, the reunification of Japan was complete.

Hideyoshi not only completed the military reunification of Japan but also lived to die of old age. Part of the explanation for his striking success was that some of the most difficult fighting had already been accomplished by Oda Nobunaga, but Hideyoshi was also more willing than Oda had been to compromise.[35] Many of Hideyoshi's most powerful rivals simply were converted into his vassals. The price Hideyoshi paid for this successful approach, however, was that not only did many of the old *daimyō* continue to exist but some of the strongest were made even stronger because the most generous rewards often had to be given to the lords who were already most powerful.

For example, Hideyoshi's foremost ally, Tokugawa Ieyasu (1542–1616), was ultimately assigned control over the lands of Hideyoshi's greatest defeated enemy, the Hōjō family of Odawara, in the eastern Kantō region, after they were crushed in 1590. Tokugawa Ieyasu then became the largest landholder in Japan, with holdings rated at 2,402,000 *koku* – greater even than Hideyoshi's own total. Inevitably, this made Ieyasu a serious possible threat to Hideyoshi, but at least in the short run, it also moved Ieyasu far away from the vital western region near the imperial capital and confronted Tokugawa Ieyasu with tremendous initial administrative challenges in bringing his new, and still potentially hostile, eastern domain under control. Tokugawa Ieyasu moved to the Kantō and established his headquarters at a small castle town called Edo (modern Tōkyō).

Because of Hideyoshi's humble birth, he was unqualified to receive the title "shogun," which still required a plausible claim to Minamoto descent. Instead, Hideyoshi engineered his adoption into the ancient aristocratic Fujiwara family and revived the traditional Fujiwara position of regent. Hideyoshi went on to publish regulations for *daimyō* conduct, survey the rice land of all Japan, and, through so-called sword hunts beginning in 1588, to disarm the peasantry. For the first time, a clear line began to be drawn between peasants and samurai. An edict of 1591 was intended to permanently fix Japanese class identity.

Having subdued Japan, Hideyoshi boasted that he would conquer China and twice launched massive invasions of Korea. Hideyoshi not only failed in his invasion of the continent, however, but also failed to establish an enduring dynasty – chiefly because his heir was still too young to take active command at the time of his own death. Hideyoshi's first son had died early. Lacking an heir, Hideyoshi designated a nephew as his successor. In his old age, however, Hideyoshi unexpectedly produced another son, Hideyori (1593–1615). Hideyoshi then ruthlessly eliminated the nephew, but this meant that his son and heir was still only five years old when Hideyoshi died in 1598. From his deathbed, Hideyoshi maneuvered to safeguard the succession. He appointed a board of five elders to act as the boy's guardians until he came of age, with the idea that these five men would at least balance each other so that none of them could become dominant. The plan failed, however, when one of the most reliable of these five elders promptly died himself in 1599, after which the balance of power tilted swiftly in favor of Tokugawa Ieyasu. An anti-Tokugawa coalition was hastily assembled, but it collapsed on the battlefield, largely because of defections. After his victory at the crucial battle of Sekigahara in 1600, the "Old Badger" Tokugawa Ieyasu emerged with unchallengeable military supremacy.

Since he had sworn an oath to protect Hideyoshi's son, despite his military victory Tokugawa Ieyasu still felt obliged to allow Hideyori to continue living comfortably in his castle at Ōsaka. On the strength of a distant claim to Minamoto descent, though, Ieyasu was granted the title "shogun" in 1603, founding what is known as the Tokugawa Shogunate. Finally, in 1614, claiming that a somewhat ambiguous inscription Hideyori had cast on a bronze bell was a veiled insult, and accusing Hideyori of assembling masterless samurai (*rōnin*) in his castle in preparation for a coup, Tokugawa Ieyasu besieged Ōsaka castle. The castle's defenses proved formidable, but it fell eventually in 1615, and Hideyori and his mother were forced to commit suicide. The destruction of Hideyori's castle in Ōsaka in 1615 would be the last major military conflict in Japan for two and a half centuries.

The Tokugawa Shogunate (1603–1868)

The most significant exception to this sustained record of Tokugawa peace came early, in a bloody rebellion by Japanese Christians at Shimabara, near Nagasaki, in 1637–1638. This Christian rebellion undoubtedly helped harden the Tokugawa resolve to strictly limit all sources of possible foreign interference. After a century and a half of incessant warfare, and as a fundamentally military regime, the Tokugawa Shogunate was understandably obsessed with maintaining order. One way of strengthening internal security was to restrict external contact. For that purpose, foreign travel by Japanese people was banned in 1635. Christianity appeared to be a particularly destabilizing source of outside influences, and a mounting series of proscriptions and persecutions were directed against that foreign religion (beginning as early as 1587 under Hideyoshi). In 1624, the Spanish were expelled from Japan altogether, and following the Christian rebellion at Shimabara, the Portuguese were also expelled in 1639. From that time on, all Japanese people were required to register with a Buddhist temple and verify that they were not Christian. After 1639, the Dutch were the only Europeans who were allowed a presence in Japan, and in 1641, even the Dutch were restricted to a small manmade island called Deshima, in Nagasaki harbor.

The Dutch remained, but their walled island at Deshima was guarded at night, and by day a pass was required to venture in or out. Contact between the Dutch and Japanese was therefore limited, and, although as many as twenty-two Dutch ships each year had sailed for Japan and Taiwan in the early seventeenth century, by the early nineteenth century, an average of only one Dutch ship per year visited Japan.[36] This Japanese seclusion policy was therefore relatively extreme, but even so, Japan was not actually totally cut off from world developments in these centuries. For example, Japan did not, popular myth to the contrary, abandon firearms. When a U.S. Navy expedition opened Japan and ended its seclusion in 1854, the fortifications at Nagasaki already included 137 cannon. The sophisticated modern technology of the pocket watch introduced by the Americans in 1854 also sparked surprisingly little interest – because pocket watches were already familiar in Japan.[37]

If some news of Western developments managed to penetrate Tokugawa Japan, contacts with other parts of East Asia were naturally even greater. In fact, it has actually been claimed that Tokugawa Japan was "oriented more than ever before toward the language and classical culture of continental China"[38] (see Figure 6.5). Higher education in Japan was still conceived primarily as mastery of the written Chinese language and the Confucian Classics. Tokugawa Ieyasu himself founded a Confucian academy. Thrust suddenly into an age of peace, Japan's samurai warriors pondered how to justify their continued privileges in an age when there were no more wars to fight. In the seventeenth century, this led some samurai to formulate what is known as *bushidō*: the "Way of the Military Gentleman." Yamaga Sokō (1622–1685), for example, argued that samurai justified their economically nonproductive existence because leisure from work allowed them to cultivate the Confucian values of loyalty, duty, and service and to lead the common people in the classic Confucian fashion by setting a virtuous example.

The Tokugawa period, in fact, became the acknowledged golden age of Confucianism in Japan. Hayashi Razan (1583–1657) reportedly drew crowds with his public lectures on Neo-Confucian interpretations of the *Analects*. In the great western Japanese commercial city of Ōsaka, where 95 percent of the population were not samurai, the Kaitokudō (Hall of Embracing Virtue) academy introduced all

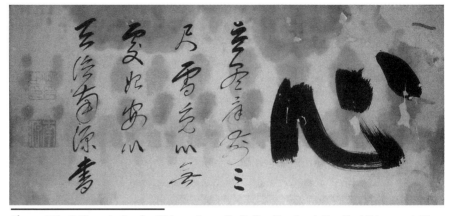

Figure 6.5. Calligraphy by the Chinese-born (in Fujian Province) Zen Buddhist monk Nan-gen (1631–1692), from the predominantly Chinese Mampuku-ji (Mampuku Temple) that was completed in Japan in 1669 near Uji (not far from Kyōto). Until as late as 1740, all of Mampuku-ji's abbots came from China. Private collection. Werner Forman/Art Resource, New York.

classes of Japanese people to Confucian values, but most especially merchants, who were supposed to be concerned with putting their businesses on a Confucian ethical foundation.[39]

Somewhat predictably, though, there were also nativist counterreactions against all this Confucianism. A school of National Learning emerged, eager to emphasize Japan's distinctive native traditions. The greatest of these National Learning schol-ars was Motoori Norinaga (1730–1801), who devoted his life to a careful study of the oldest Japanese history, the *Kojiki*, in search of a more purely Japanese national essence uncontaminated by foreign Chinese influences.

Even more fundamentally essential to the Tokugawa peace than excluding for-eign sources of instability was the formulation of new methods for maintaining domestic order. The Tokugawa Shogunate did not attempt to eliminate the *daimyō* or their independent authority over their own domains. At the end of the Tokugawa period in 1868, there were still 276 *daimyō* of varying degrees of wealth and power. But the Tokugawa shoguns did attempt to subordinate these *daimyō* to themselves, using oaths of allegiance, a claimed right to confirm *daimyō* holdings or transfer them to other domains (which happened quite often in the early years), supervi-sion of marriage alliances, and restrictions over how many armed men and castles they could maintain. Most important, all *daimyō* were required to spend half their time in Edo, in a system of alternate attendance (*sankin kōtai*) between their own domains and the shogun's city. This oriented all the *daimyō* toward the shogun, left crucial family members as hostages beneath the shogun's castle, drained *daimyō* resources in maintaining expensive dual establishments in Edo and in their own domains, and incidentally, helped develop networks of roads and communications centering on Edo, in the process promoting the development of a more integrated national economy. Merchants, too, converged on Edo and the other castle towns to satisfy the needs of the *daimyō* and their samurai attendants.

At the start of the sixteenth century, most samurai had still lived in rural villages, where they collected taxes, administered justice, and served as local authorities. During the wars of reunification in the second half of the sixteenth century, however, the *daimyō* consolidated their resources, built enormous new castles, and pulled samurai off the land to garrison them. No longer able to support themselves from their own lands, the samurai were instead paid stipends by their lords. Merchants, artisans, and craftsmen were also drawn in to serve the large military establishments, creating whole new castle towns. Many of Japan's modern cities began this way, as castle towns, in a great spurt between about 1580 and 1610, including, especially, Edo (modern Tōkyō).

In the early eighteenth century, the largest city in Europe was Paris, with a population of over half a million. At that time, Edo held over a million.[40] Ōsaka, in western Japan, had also become a notably large city, but Ōsaka was a merchant's town and prospered as a commercial center. Edo was the shogun's city. Half the population of Edo were samurai. All *daimyō* were required to spend half their time in Edo, and direct retainers of the shogun were not permitted to travel more than ten miles from the shogun's castle without official permission. There was, therefore, a large captive warrior audience that needed to be fed, housed, clothed, and entertained. While the shogun, *daimyō*, and samurai continued to cultivate the older traditional elite culture, the other half of the city – the townspeople (*chōnin*) – patronized a newly emerging popular culture. This was Japan's first true pop culture, a mass-production culture of the marketplace.

The relatively flashy Kabuki theater, for example, catered to the tastes of townspeople and dates almost precisely from the beginning of the Tokugawa period.[41] Because of its somewhat disreputable moral tone, the Shogunate soon banned women from the stage (much as in Shakespeare's England), and female roles came to be performed by male specialists known as *onnagata*, who mimicked the movements of women. Like most occupations in Tokugawa Japan, acting became a hereditary profession, with performers often carrying on lengthy family acting traditions, playing the same roles their ancestors had first made famous. Kabuki sets, costumes, and makeup were lavish, and a revolving stage was introduced to provide quick scene changes.

Surprisingly enough, some of the finest Tokugawa playwrights preferred to write for the puppet theater (*bunraku* or *jōruri*), which, for a time, seriously rivaled live theater. Puppets sometimes became huge, as large as three or four feet tall and requiring three manipulators to operate. These puppets were obviously capable of stunts and special effects no human actor could perform live on stage. Perhaps the most renowned Tokugawa playwright was Chikamatsu Monzaemon (1653–1725), who perceptively observed that the art of the puppet theater lay "in the slender margin between the real and the unreal."[42]

The best-loved Tokugawa play, written by a trio of other authors, was called *Chūshingura* ("The Treasury of Loyal Retainers") – popularly known as the story of the "forty-seven *rōnin*." It was first performed in 1748. A complete performance of *Chūshingura* requires about eleven hours, but the outlines of the story are quickly told. It was based on actual events that had taken place in 1701–1703. A certain *daimyō* had been assigned to help receive an imperial emissary in the shogun's castle in Edo, but because he had neglected to present adequate gifts to the man responsible for teaching him the necessary protocol, he did not know how to properly perform his duties. In humiliation and rage, he finally drew his sword and wounded his uncooperative instructor. The punishment for drawing a sword in the shogun's castle was death, and this lord was obliged to commit suicide that same evening. With his death, his retainers became *rōnin*, or masterless samurai. Samurai ideals of loyalty and duty dictated that they should seek vengeance, but to put their enemy off his guard, they first pretended to become dissolute and debauched. Then one night, they assaulted the villain's mansion and killed him. This satisfied the demands of duty and honor, but unfortunately, they had in the process also committed the unpardonable crime of murder. The Shogunate's elegant solution was to allow them all to commit honorable suicide, making the forty-seven *rōnin* tragic heroes.

The Tokugawa Shogunate attempted to strictly legislate a separation between elite and popular culture. Townspeople were forbidden to stage performances of the refined Nō drama, and samurai were not supposed to attend Kabuki. In practice, however, many samurai became avid patrons of Kabuki, even if they had to attend the theater in secret. At the same time, even commercial pop culture to some extent reflected supposedly elite Neo-Confucian values. For example, one of the perennial grand themes of Tokugawa theater was the conflict between duty (*giri*) and human feeling (*ninjo*) – most famously in stories of star-crossed lovers driven by the pressure of events to commit suicide.

Books, many of them now written in the Japanese language rather than in classical Chinese, were suddenly being published in great numbers. These were intended for a relatively wide popular audience and included such things as manuals for household management and bookkeeping guides as well as novels and other entertainments. By 1692, there were some seven thousand titles in print in Kyōto.[43]

The Shogunate apparently regarded entertainment as something of a necessary evil, to be regulated and restricted but nonetheless permitted. The Shogunate therefore designated specially licensed pleasure quarters, often referred to poetically as the "floating world" (*ukiyo*). These were centers of teahouses, theaters, and brothels. After some fires in the 1650s, the theaters in Edo came to be clustered in the area of Nihonbashi (the "Bridge of Japan," from which all distances were supposedly measured), east of the shogun's castle, while other entertainments were moved northeast to the region of the city now called Asakusa. The geisha (literally, "artists"), who were skilled dancers, singers, musicians, conversationalists, and consummate female entertainers, were the heart of this floating world.

From these licensed pleasure quarters, the popular woodblock print art form known as *ukiyo-e* also took its name: "pictures from the floating world." These prints – scarcely viewed as art at the time but much appreciated in the modern West – typically drew their subjects from the entertainment quarters, depicting such themes as geisha, Kabuki actors, and sumo wrestlers. Many of the most superb prints were landscapes, however, such as those by (Andō) Hiroshige (1797–1858) and (Katsushika) Hokusai (1760–1849). Hokusai reportedly produced an astonishing thirty-five thousand different designs during his long life, although he

Figure 6.6. Katsushika Hokusai (1760–1849), "The Great Wave at Kanagawa" (from a series of "Thirty-six Views of Mount Fuji"), Japanese woodblock print, ca. 1830–1832. Bequest of Mrs. H. O. Havemeyer, 1929. The Metropolitan Museum of Art, New York. © The Metropolitan Museum of Art/Art Resource, New York.

is best known for his set of *Thirty-six Views of Mount Fuji*, which includes the famous "The Great Wave at Kanagawa" (see Figure 6.6).

The World Turned Upside Down: Early Modern Economic Development

In the first century of the Tokugawa period, the population of Japan more than doubled, and castle towns swelled in size. Population growth then stopped, however, and from 1721 to 1846 remained constant at roughly twenty-six million. Many castle towns even saw their populations decrease. This long-term population stability seems to have been at least partially the result of deliberate choices by individual families such as restricting marriage to only one son in each generation to preserve the family farm intact. At the same time, however, technology was also gradually improving, education was spreading, and rural trade and production were increasing. Per capita income therefore increased, but the center of activity shifted from the castle towns to the countryside. One reason for this shift, perhaps, was the relative inability of governments based in castle towns to enforce monopoly restrictions, impose taxes, and regulate prices outside those towns. As one late-eighteenth-century Japanese statute complained, "now people from the castle-town go to the country to shop."[44]

By the end of the Tokugawa period, some farm families were earning more than half their income from nonagricultural sidelines. In addition to sideline production of textiles and other activities on the farms themselves, there was also much new rural industry – such things as sake (alcohol) or soy sauce brewing, ceramics, and iron production – worked by part-time or seasonal labor. One result was that

Japanese work habits were already relatively well prepared for the late-nineteenth-century onset of modern mechanized industrialization.

Another result, however, was to gradually undermine the position of the warrior elite. Samurai status was now fixed and hereditary, and marked by such privileges as the exclusive right to wear two swords and to have a family name. The samurai were also paid regular stipends by their lords. But the samurai were a relatively large group, roughly 7 percent of the total population, and in an age of prolonged peace, their employment possibilities as professional warriors were obviously limited. Some samurai served their lords as domain officials, but many samurai did not really have much to do.

The *daimyō*, meanwhile, collected their taxes in rice, which they shipped to Ōsaka or Edo for marketing and conversion into the cash they needed to meet domain expenses. Through servicing this trade, great merchant houses emerged and prospered, and a money-based economy flourished. Since the land tax rates remained relatively flat after 1700, however, while expenses naturally always tended to increase, *daimyō* were sometimes forced to borrow from wealthy merchants. Some lords fell deeply into debt. Merchants and other townspeople were forbidden by law from aspiring to samurai status, but despite their official inferiority, their growing economic clout to some extent reversed what the warrior elite felt should be the proper social order. To economize, many *daimyō* reduced samurai stipends (which would have remained stagnant at best anyway), typically by as much as 30–40 percent, leaving many of the lower samurai seriously impoverished and creating much samurai discontent.

Paradoxically, therefore, while Tokugawa Japan saw significant early modern economic growth, which may have helped prepare Japan for rapid industrialization in the late nineteenth century, the ideal social order had also been substantially undermined. By the nineteenth century, there was widespread evidence of contempt for established authority. As one early-nineteenth-century author observed, "the shogunate's proclamations and ordinances are called 'three-day laws.' No one fears them, and no one pays any attention to them.... They are disregarded after that short period of time."[45] Significantly, among the most discontented and disenfranchised by these long-term developments were lower-ranking members of the samurai elite.

For Further Reading

On the critical conjuncture of cultural, commercial, and political developments in late Ming China, see Timothy Brook, *The Confusions of Pleasure: Commerce and Culture in Ming China* (Berkeley: University of California Press, 1998); Chun-shu Chang and Shelley Hsueh-lun Chang, *Crisis and Transformation in Seventeenth-Century China: Society, Culture, and Modernity in Li Yü's World* (1992; Ann Arbor: The University of Michigan Press, 1998); Craig Clunas, *Empire of Great Brightness: Visual and Material Cultures of Ming China, 1368–1644* (Honolulu: University of Hawai'i Press, 2007); Craig Clunas, *Superfluous Things: Material Culture and Social Status in Early Modern China* (1991; Honolulu: University of Hawai'i Press, 2004); Ray Huang, *1587, a Year of no Significance: The Ming Dynasty in Decline* (New Haven: Yale University Press, 1981); and David Johnson, Andrew J. Nathan, and Evelyn S. Rawski (eds.), *Popular Culture in Late Imperial China* (Berkeley: University of California Press, 1985). Andrew H. Plaks argues that the sixteenth century witnessed the crystallization of full-length serious Chinese prose fiction in *The Four Masterworks of the Ming Novel: Ssu ta ch'i shu* (Princeton University Press, 1987).

Early-modern European encounters with East Asia are described in Chester Ralph Boxer, *The Christian Century in Japan, 1549–1650* (Berkeley: University of California Press, 1967); Reinier H. Hesselink, *Prisoners from Nambu: Reality and Make-Believe in 17th-Century Japanese Diplomacy* (Honolulu: University of Hawai'i Press, 2002); David. E. Mungello, *The Great Encounter of China and the West, 1500–1800* (Lanham: Rowman and Littlefield, 1999); and Jonathan D. Spence, *The Memory Palace of Matteo Ricci* (Harmondsworth: Penguin Books, 1983). On the 1793 British embassy to China that may be said to mark the last major "traditional" encounter, see James Louis Hevia, *Cherishing Men from Afar: Qing Guest Ritual and the Macartney Embassy of 1793* (Durham: Duke University Press, 1995).

For Qing Dynasty China, see Pamela Kyle Crossley, *The Manchus* (Oxford: Blackwell, 1997); Evelyn S. Rawski, *The Last Emperors: A Social History of Qing Imperial Institutions* (Berkeley: University of California Press, 1998); and William T. Rowe, *China's Last Empire: The Great Qing* (Cambridge: Harvard University Press, 2009). A fascinating study of the intersection of art, religion, culture and power under the Qing Dynasty is Patricia Berger, *Empire of Emptiness: Buddhist Art and Political Authority in Qing China* (Honolulu: University of Hawai'i Press, 2003).

On late Chosŏn Korea, see JaHyun Kim Haboush and Martina Deuchler (eds.), *Culture and the State in Late Chosŏn Korea* (Cambridge: Harvard University Asia Center, 1999); James B. Palais, *Confucian Statecraft and Korean Institutions: Yu Hyŏngwŏn and the Late Chosŏn Dynasty* (Seattle: University of Washington Press, 1996); and Michael J. Seth, *A Concise History of Korea: From the Neolithic Period through the Nineteenth Century* (Lanham: Rowman and Littlefield, 2006), chapter 8.

Comprehensive treatment of early-modern Japanese history is provided by Conrad D. Totman, in *Early Modern Japan* (Berkeley: University of California Press, 1993).

For early-modern Japan before the establishment of the Tokugawa Shogunate, see Mary Elizabeth Berry, *Hideyoshi* (Cambridge: Harvard University Press, 1982); and George Elison and Bardwell L. Smith (eds.), *Warlords, Artists, and Commoners: Japan in the Sixteenth Century* (Honolulu: University of Hawai'i Press, 1981).

On Tokugawa era intellectual developments, see Masao Maruyama, *Studies in the Intellectual History of Tokugawa Japan*, trans. by Mikiso Hane (Princeton University Press, 1974); Tetsuo Najita, *Visions of Virtue in Tokugawa Japan: The Kaitokudō Merchant Academy of Osaka* (University of Chicago Press, 1987); and Herman Ooms, *Tokugawa Ideology: Early Constructs, 1570–1680* (Princeton University Press, 1985). For Tokugawa literature, see Donald Keene, *World within Walls: Japanese Literature of the Pre-Modern Era, 1600–1867* (New York: Grove Press, 1976). Mary Elizabeth Berry describes a Tokugawa period revolution in the dissemination of printed knowledge in *Japan in Print: Information and Nation in the Early Modern Period* (Berkeley: University of California Press, 2006). For excellent essays covering a wide range of Tokugawa period topics, see John W. Hall and Marius Jansen (eds.), *Studies in the Institutional History of Early Modern Japan* (Princeton University Press, 1968).

For aspects of Tokugawa culture that may have been conducive to later Japanese modernization and industrialization, see Robert Bellah, *Tokugawa Religion: The Cultural Roots of Modern Japan* (1957; New York: The Free Press, 1985); and Thomas C. Smith, *Native Sources of Japanese Industrialization, 1750–1920* (Berkeley: University of California Press, 1988).

7 The Nineteenth-Century Encounter of Civilizations

The world was fundamentally transformed in the nineteenth century by the Promethean new powers unleashed by the industrial and scientific revolutions. Modern transportation and communications technologies, such as the steamship, the railway, and the telegraph (a telegraphic link between China and Europe was first established in 1871), knit the planet together more tightly than ever before. New military technologies – including ironclad steam warships and machine guns – gave industrialized countries unprecedented military superiority over nonindustrialized peoples. The power and wealth of these industrialized countries also made them widely attractive models, although a perceptible time lag occurred before many peoples outside the early-industrializing core perceived the apparent irresistibility of modernization, and many never welcomed it. "From 1860 to 1914, the web of steel [railways] spread throughout the world, and so did the political, financial, and engineering techniques that had evolved along with it," yet "among non-Western peoples, only the Japanese showed real enthusiasm for railways," and even in Japan, the first eighteen-mile stretch of rail line was not laid until 1872[1] (see Figure 7.1). In China, the first short rail line was built by a British firm in 1876 but purchased by the Chinese government the following year and dismantled.

Despite this delayed start, by the end of the nineteenth century, a virtual tidal wave of Westernization was beginning to sweep the world. Consciously Western-style clothing and hairstyles became widely fashionable, especially among elites. In the 1870s, for example, Japanese samurai cut their topknots and tentatively began adopting Western fashions. By 1900, it is said that most Japanese men owned at least one Western-style suit and hat. Representative democratic government also seemed to be the irresistible trend of the times by the end of the century. By 1890, Japan had a written modern Western-style constitution and an elected legislature (called the Diet). Soon after the turn into the twentieth century, even China adopted a formal constitution and held elections for provincial assemblies, and in 1912–1913, China experimented with its first nationwide democratic elections.

Figure 7.1. Hiroshige III (ca. 1843–1894), "Picture of a Steam Locomotive along the Yoko-hama Waterfront," ca. 1874, Japanese woodblock print. Arthur M. Sackler Gallery, Smith-sonian Institution, Washington, D.C.: Gift of the Daval Foundation, from the Collection of Ambassador and Mrs. William Leonhart, S1991.151a-c.

In many ways, this nineteenth-century wave of Westernization foreshadowed the current phenomenon of globalization in the late twentieth and early twenty-first centuries. Transportation and communications became not only much more rapid but also more standardized. The newly constructed railroads were everywhere quite similar operations, and typically employed common standard gauges of track. An International Telegraph Union was established in 1865 and a Universal Postal Union in 1875. A global modern business culture also emerged, based on shared technology and managerial techniques. By the end of the nineteenth century, there were integrated global capital markets, nearly instantaneous communications via the telegraph, refrigerated shipping of perishable food from farms and ranches in the far-flung corners of the world, and new global markets for such things as coffee, bananas, rubber, copper, and tin. Indeed, as a percentage of gross national product, international capital flows peaked in the early twentieth century (from Britain) and have never been matched again since, while international trade as a percentage of total output did not return to its 1913 (that is, pre–World War I) levels again until as late as the 1980s.[2]

Some predicted that growing international economic integration would make war between developed countries impossible. The outbreak of World War I in 1914 proved this assumption rather spectacularly wrong, and also dealt a blow to the interdependent international financial system, especially in Europe. The onset of the Great Depression and rise of fascism and Communism by the 1930s then brought this earlier age of globalization to a close. But before that happened, much of the world had already been irrevocably changed by modernization. In East Asia, the peak period of Westernization actually did not arrive until the early twentieth century, but the deep forces underlying these changes had intruded much earlier.

Industrialization was the key. Although the early achievements of the European scientific revolution are justly much celebrated, the extent to which pure science contributed to early industrialization remains a matter of debate. Pioneering break-throughs in technological invention, and early examples of relatively large scale production, also did not necessarily automatically lead to an industrial revolution. The premodern porcelain workshops at Jingdezhen in southeast China, for exam-ple, which employed some seventy thousand workers, have been called "the largest industrial complex anywhere in the world prior to the eighteenth century," and in the seventeenth and eighteenth centuries, China exported over a hundred million pieces of porcelain to Europe alone.[3] The Chinese had also learned to burn coal as a fuel at a very early date and developed most of the mechanisms for a steam engine, such as double-acting piston/cylinder arrays and methods for the transfer of rotary to linear motion.[4] Yet the Industrial Revolution did not begin in China. Instead, it was in Great Britain in the early nineteenth century that all the necessary contributing factors were first harnessed into a true industrial revolution.

Early coal-fired steam engines were so inefficient that they were almost useless, except at the sites of coal mines themselves, where coal was relatively cheap and abundant. There steam engines were initially used to pump water out of the mines to enable deeper mining. As the engines became more efficient, they began to be used also to haul the coal aboveground, and eventually, in 1825, in northern England, the world's first railway line was constructed. It just happened that nineteenth-century Britain combined some of Europe's largest coal reserves with a serious firewood shortage, encouraging the switch to coal for fuel. Britain also enjoyed a high level of commercialization and convenient water transportation, as well as, of course, individuals with considerable mechanical ingenuity and entrepreneurial flare.[5]

The conversion to fossil fuel–powered mechanization was the signature moment in the Industrial Revolution, but Britain's earlier development of a global trad-ing network (and empire) was also an important precondition. Colonies and trading partners in America and elsewhere provided both markets for the prod-ucts of British manufacturing and essential supplies of raw materials such as sugar and cotton. The development of worldwide trade also provided the frame-work for experimenting with large-scale business formats such as the joint-stock corporation.

In 1795, David Davies had already remarked on the peculiarity of the English working-class habit of drinking tea sweetened with sugar: "After all, it appears a very strange thing, that the common people of any European nation should be obliged to use, as part of their daily diet, two articles imported from opposite sides of the earth."[6] Remarkably, all of this British tea came from China, and most of the sugar came from the Caribbean. This is striking testimony to the global reach of British commerce.

In the seventeenth century, a new kind of private chartered trading company had emerged to become the leading edge of European business activity in Asia. Espe-cially important initially was the Dutch VOC (Vereenigde Oost-Indische Compag-nie, or East India Company), which was founded in 1602. The Dutch established a base at Batavia (modern Jakarta) on the island of Java in 1619 and soon achieved a near-monopoly of the still vital spice trade among the islands of what is now Indonesia. Thanks to the actions of the Japanese Tokugawa Shogunate, the Dutch also gained a complete monopoly on European trade with Japan after 1639. Meanwhile, the French Compagnie des Indies for a time seriously rivaled British interests in India, but after British military victories in such battles as Plassey, in 1757, and Pondicherry, in 1760, it was the British East India Company (EIC) that emerged as the dominant force in India. From its bases in India, the EIC then began projecting British interests to China.

The British EIC had been founded in 1599, when a group of London merchants acquired a royal charter from Queen Elizabeth I. The EIC enjoyed a monopoly over all British trade east of the Cape of Good Hope and soon became the largest British chartered company doing business outside of England. The "East India" in its title originally referred to the "East Indies" (modern Indonesia), but the British were driven from there by the Dutch, and the focus of EIC activity turned to the Indian subcontinent. As of the start of the nineteenth century, all British imports from the Far East were required to be deposited and sold from EIC warehouses. The EIC docks and warehouses in London employed fifty thousand persons, the company owned some 115 ships, and it had the largest standing army in Asia. In fact, as of the 1830s, the EIC army was more than twice the size of the regular British government army. The Crown granted the EIC the right to coin money and administer justice, and it was actually the EIC rather than the British government that first brought India under British control.

Victory in the Napoleonic wars in the early nineteenth century established overwhelming global British naval superiority and, together with the early British lead in mechanized industry, made Britain the sole global superpower of the century – and the largest empire in the history of the world. British success stimulated imitation, however, and before long, a second wave of late-industrializing countries arose, including the United States, Germany, Russia, and Japan. The United States and Germany, in particular, had seriously eroded Britain's industrial lead by the early twentieth century. These countries (together with France, which, although now in relative decline, was still a major player) became the new great powers, and they soon engaged in a frantic competition for empire. Between 1876 and 1915, a quarter of the world was colonized by these roughly half dozen major modern powers.[7] Many older powers found themselves eclipsed by these developments. China and the Ottoman Empire were especially diminished, becoming the so-called "sick men" of Asia and Europe, respectively.

The Nineteenth-Century Impact on China

In the eighteenth century, China had enjoyed a standard of living roughly equivalent to that of Western Europe. By some estimates, China actually consumed more sugar per person and produced at least comparable volumes of textiles as Europe at that time, and "western European land, labor, and product markets, even as late as 1789, were on the whole probably *further* from perfect competition . . . than those in most of China."[8] In the aggregate, if no longer in per capita terms, China was probably still the richest country in world as late as 1800, with something like one-third of the world's total production. Even well into the nineteenth century, conditions in China did not necessarily appear all that bleak to European observers. Robert Fortune, for example, a botanist sent to China by the EIC, still insisted in 1857 that although, "as their farms are all small," Chinese farmers "are probably less wealthy than our farmers in England," yet those Chinese farmers still "live well, dress plainly, and are industrious, without being in any way oppressed. I doubt if there is a happier race anywhere than the Chinese farmer and peasantry."[9]

By 1900, however, China's share of world production had fallen to only 6 percent. This was probably not the result of any absolute decline but instead was only relative to the explosive new growth of the industrialized economies. Yet, to the considerable bewilderment of many people in China, China was rapidly becoming marginalized, relatively impoverished, and surrounded by dynamically expanding new empires. Neighboring countries that had formerly been viewed as tributaries of the Chinese Empire were, one by one, pulled into new foreign imperial configurations: Burma was ceded to Britain in 1886, and Nepal became a British protectorate in 1815; France acquired Vietnam, Laos, and Cambodia in stages between 1862 and 1885; Japan successfully claimed the Ryūkyū (in Chinese, Liuqiu) island chain in 1878 and, in 1895, pulled Korea into the Japanese orbit and acquired Taiwan as an outright colony. Except for Taiwan, actual Chinese territory was not directly colonized by these modern empires, but many Chinese people did eventually conclude that China was being reduced to at least "semi-colonial" status under the terms of a so-called treaty port system. This treaty port system referred, literally, to ports opened by formal diplomatic treaties, starting with the treaty that ended the first Opium War in 1842.

The Opium Wars

Beginning in 1760, all Western maritime commercial activity in China was officially confined by the Qing Dynasty government to the single port of Guangzhou (in English, Canton). Rather than being some ancient Chinese tradition, this was actually a new application of imperial border control policies that had recently proven rather successful against the nomads of the northwest.[10] The policy also did not apply to the Russians, who could travel overland to Beijing, nor to Chinese merchants themselves, who came and went relatively freely. But Western shipping was limited to Guangzhou, where a number of Chinese firms joined to form a monopolistic association (called the Co-hong by the English) that handled every aspect of contact with the Western merchants.

Most prominent, now, among those Western merchants were the British, who had developed a considerable appetite for a certain Chinese product called tea, which they were beginning to purchase in substantial quantities – by the 1830s, thirty million pounds per year. Even in Guangzhou, Westerners were not allowed inside the city walls but were confined, instead, during the six-month trading season, to a cluster of so-called factories south of the city walls near the

Pearl River. More permanent foreign residences were downriver in Portuguese Macao. Repeated British efforts to renegotiate these restricted terms of trade, most famously with the mission led by Lord George Macartney in 1793, were simply rebuffed by Beijing.

Although Western merchants sold many different products in exchange for Chinese tea, silk, porcelain, and lacquerware, only rarely could they sell enough to balance the exchange. The deficit, or trade imbalance, had to be made up with payments in cash (which, in China, meant silver). One contemporary American, for example, estimated that between 1805 and 1825, a net sixty-two million U.S. dollars in cash was transferred from the United States to China.[11] Western merchants were naturally, therefore, interested in finding a product that they could market successfully in China, and in the late 1700s, they finally did: opium.[12]

Opium is a narcotic drug produced from a flower called the poppy. Opium had long been a familiar substance throughout the Old World and may have even been grown in ancient Egypt. What was new was the technique of smoking opium, which appears to have begun as a spin-off from the practice of smoking New World tobacco. Although opium smoking may have started simply by mixing tobacco and opium together, ultimately, instead of lighting the opium on fire and directly inhaling the smoke, the technique became to apply heat to a bead of opium in a pipe until it vaporized and then inhale the vapor. Such opium smoking became especially widespread in China, but the Chinese government also took a global lead in outlawing the practice, banning nonmedicinal use of opium by as early as 1729. Elsewhere in the world, opium use was far from universally illegal prior to the twentieth century. Indeed, nineteenth-century British mothers not uncommonly dosed their own children with a liquid tincture of opium called laudanum.

Initially, there was not very much opium in China. Only two hundred chests were imported in 1729, and domestic cultivation was minimal. In 1770, however, a famine in Bengal, in northeastern India, caused the EIC to petition Parliament for assistance, resulting in the Tea Act of 1773, which allowed the EIC to sell its products tax-free in the British colonies. This provoked some irate colonists in Boston, Massachusetts, to react angrily by dumping EIC tea into the ocean – the so-called Boston Tea Party – in December 1773. Also in 1773, and as a result of that same Indian famine, the EIC gained a monopoly on the sale and production of opium in Bengal. This opium was shaped into balls bearing the EIC seal and marketed in China. During the decade 1780–1790, imports of Indian opium into China quadrupled, and by the early nineteenth century, opium is said to have become the most valuable commercial crop in the world.

The obvious problem with this lucrative opium trade was that it was illegal in China, although it was not illegal elsewhere. In a concession to Chinese government pressure, therefore, in 1800, the EIC agreed to stop selling opium in China. This made little difference, however, because the EIC continued to grow and manufacture opium in India, where it was perfectly legal, and auction the opium off to private firms, who then shipped it to China. The EIC's British monopoly on trade with the Far East applied only to trade between Asia and Britain and never to trade between different ports within Asia. Opium imports into China continued unabated.

Then, in 1834, the EIC British monopoly expired and was not renewed. Like most other European countries, early modern Britain had favored policies of mercantilism, or protected trade, but in the early nineteenth century, a new ideal of free trade was taking hold. In 1776, Adam Smith, in *The Wealth of Nations*, coined his famous phrase about the "invisible hand," suggesting that the free exchange of goods through market forces was the most efficient means of organizing an economy. In 1817, David Ricardo further developed the idea of comparative advantage, using the example of Portuguese specialization in wine production, which could then be exchanged for English cloth to mutual profit. Nineteenth-century British "classical" economists came to believe that government interference with the operation of market forces was likely to do more harm than good and advocated a laissez-faire approach and free trade. The inherent intellectual persuasiveness of this argument was underwritten by the rapidly increasing productivity of British industry – by 1840, Britain enjoyed about one-third of the world's total international trade – and Britain now moved decisively toward a goal of free trade.

The expiration of the EIC monopoly on British trade with China in 1834 was a step in this direction, and it brought increased British trade – but correspondingly, also increased sales of opium. Between 1830 and 1836, the annual number of chests of (British controlled) Indian opium imported into China increased from 18,956 to 30,302. Since the balance of trade had now shifted against China, and silver was pouring out to pay for opium imports, Beijing perceived a mounting economic as well as criminal and moral crisis. Although a number of proposals were considered, Beijing resolved to crack down and end the illegal drug trade. In 1839, a special imperial commissioner named Lin Zexu (1785–1850) was sent to Guangzhou to eliminate opium smuggling.

Lin arrived in March, and by July, he had arrested some seventeen hundred Chinese involved in the drug trade and confiscated seventy thousand opium pipes. Smugglers found it almost impossible to sell opium at any price. But Lin was not content with this and sealed off the Western factories, demanding that they surrender all their opium supplies. The highest-ranking official in the Western community in Guangzhou, the British superintendant of trade, was placed in an awkward position because his authority over the private businessmen was limited. He also could hardly wait for instructions from London because, at that time, it still would have taken six months before he could expect a reply. On his own initiative, therefore, he promised the merchants that the British government would reimburse them for any opium confiscated by the Chinese. With that encouragement, the foreign merchants turned over twenty-one thousand chests, or two and a half million pounds, of opium to Commissioner Lin, who had it carefully dissolved in specially dug trenches.

Because the British home government proved unwilling, in the end, to pay for the confiscated opium, the huge financial loss involved then became an issue. In addition, Commissioner Lin was not satisfied with merely confiscating the existing opium supplies and also demanded that any foreign merchant wishing to do business in China must sign an oath, on penalty of death, never to bring opium into China again. The British, as a group, refused to sign, arguing that it would subject British citizens to what they viewed as a barbaric Chinese criminal justice system, exposing them to possible extortion and the probability of torture and execution if accused, whether falsely or not. Before long, shots were fired, and in early 1840, a British fleet arrived to enforce British interests. China and Great Britain went to war.

The Qing Dynasty had no real oceangoing navy at all, whereas Britain had the most powerful navy in the world. The British fleet also already included a pioneering iron steam warship called the *Nemesis*. The war at sea was therefore entirely one sided. On land, however, there were not enough British troops to have much impact on the huge Chinese Empire. Eventually, the British fleet managed to sail up the Yangzi River and cut the Grand Canal, which transported vital tax grain from the south to the capital at Beijing in the north. The Qing Dynasty was compelled to agree to terms, signing the Treaty of Nanjing (Nanking) in August 1842. This treaty opened five ports to British trade (including, most importantly, Shanghai) and gave the island of Hong Kong permanently to Great Britain (it was the surrounding New Territories that were merely leased, for a term of ninety-nine years beginning in 1898, and which triggered the return of Hong Kong to Chinese rule in 1997), and the Qing Dynasty also agreed to pay reparations amounting to some twenty-one million dollars.

After the war, opium remained illegal in China, while the volume of legal British sales in China remained disappointing. As Britain industrialized, British manufacturers entertained visions of China as the largest potential market in the world, but such hopes were never fully realized. At the end of the nineteenth century, China was still importing fewer British manufactured goods than the Netherlands.[13] Although the reasons for this are complicated, British "old China hands" were inclined to blame their frustration on continuing unfair Chinese trade restrictions. At least initially, moreover, this was not entirely without reason because the British were still not actually being allowed inside the city of Guangzhou, there were still only five ports open to British trade, and taxes on British imports were collected erratically. British merchants therefore pressured their government to take more vigorous steps to pry open the tantalizingly vast China market.

An opportunity arrived in October 1856, when Chinese authorities at Guangzhou arrested some crewmembers of a ship called the *Arrow*. The owner of the ship was Chinese, the arrested crewmen were also "natives," and her Hong Kong British registration had technically expired eleven days previously, but the ship's master was British, and it was the British flag that was allegedly hauled down. The British governor of Hong Kong used this occasion to press further demands for the opening of China. The result was a second Opium War, in which Britain was this time joined by France – provoked to war by the execution of a French Christian missionary. The prosecution of this second war was delayed by the eruption of the bloody Sepoy Mutiny in India (1857–1858), but eventually, in 1860, a large British and French army landed on the northern coast near Beijing, the

Chinese coastal defenses were stormed, and British and French troops marched into Beijing. The imperial Summer Palace in the northwestern suburbs of Beijing was burned and looted, and the emperor fled to Manchuria, where he died the next year. A five-year-old boy, known as the Tongzhi Emperor (r. 1862–1874), ascended the throne of a dynasty that appeared on the verge of collapse.

Domestic Rebellions

Even as the Qing Dynasty was waging two losing wars against European powers between 1840 and 1860, it was simultaneously also confronted with multiple domestic rebellions, some of which were on a vastly larger scale of destructiveness. The most devastating of all was the Christian Taiping Rebellion (1850–1864). The origins of this Christian rebellion were linked to those same recent foreign activities on the southeastern Chinese coast. The region around Guangzhou had been most affected by the fighting in the first Opium War (1840–1842), and the opening of other ports that resulted from that war not only ended Guangzhou's monopoly on Western trade but Guangzhou soon also found itself absolutely eclipsed by the rise of Shanghai in importance. For these and other reasons, there were regional economic dislocations, distress, and banditry. Banditry led to the formation of local self-defense militias, which then tended to represent local majority populations in confrontations with minorities.

It happened that southernmost China had some especially large minority groups, including such aboriginal peoples as the Miao, Yao, and Zhuang. Among the ethnic Chinese, there were also significant subethnic differences, including occupational groups like the so-called boat people (who spent their entire lives afloat) and, most critically, a division between the Cantonese "natives" (*bendi*) of Guangdong and the Hakka (in Mandarin, *Kejia*) "guest families." While these Hakka are unquestionably Chinese (for a time in the 1980s–1990s, the leaders of the People's Republic of China, Taiwan, and Singapore were all three simultaneously Hakka), they are distinguished by speaking a unique dialect of the Chinese language. They were also relatively late migrants into the far south, often relegated to marginal farmland, and felt much discriminated against by the local Cantonese majority in the nineteenth century.[14]

The founder of the Taiping movement was a Guangdong Hakka named Hong Xiuquan (1814–1864).[15] Hong Xiuquan had made the thirty-mile journey from his native village to Guangzhou city four times between 1827 and 1843 to sit for the imperial civil service examinations, but though he passed the preliminary exams, he never obtained even the lowest degree. During his second visit to Guangzhou in 1836, he was exposed to Christian street preaching and accepted some Christian pamphlets. After his third examination failure, he suffered a nervous breakdown and experienced mysterious visions of, among other things, an old man who gave him a divine sword. After his fourth examination failure in 1843, he finally read those Christian pamphlets and came to the conclusion, based on them, that his visions were of God and Jesus Christ – who, as his father and older brother, had commissioned him to "restore" Christianity to China.

Although Hong did spend two months in 1847 studying at a Southern Baptist mission in Guangzhou under the Reverend Issachar Roberts of Tennessee, and a complete Chinese-language translation of the Bible was available to him, his training in Christian theology was obviously limited, and he developed a somewhat eccentric individual form of the faith, much influenced by his otherwise fairly conventional Chinese upbringing. The very name Taiping (great peace), for example, was drawn from ancient Chinese Daoist religious texts. There is no denying the sincerity of Hong's Christian zeal, however. Evangelizing in the countryside, he won some ten thousand converts by 1849. These were mainly, like Hong himself, Hakka or members of other minorities. They formed a God-Worshippers Society that practiced baptism and congregational worship and strictly enforced the Ten Commandments.

These God-Worshippers clashed with Cantonese self-defense militias, and early military successes inspired Hong Xiuquan to declare open rebellion against the Qing Dynasty in 1851, from a base on Thistle Mountain in the Yao aboriginal area of Guangxi Province. Hong pronounced himself the Heavenly King of a Heavenly Kingdom of Great Peace (*Taiping tianguo*). From this starting point in the far south, Taiping armies smashed their way through encircling imperial forces and marched north, picking up new recruits along the way. The Taiping soldiers maintained impressively taut discipline – they were forbidden to smoke, drink alcohol, loot, or have sexual relations – and the Qing imperial armies seemed unable to resist them. By 1853, the Taipings had captured Nanjing (Nanking) and made it their capital.

Many Westerners were at first excited by the idea of a Christian rebellion in China, especially one that appeared likely to emerge victorious and overthrow the Qing Dynasty. An early British fact-finding mission to the Taiping capital at Nanjing in 1853, however, was bluntly informed that the Taiping Heavenly King, Hong Xiuquan, was "the Lord of the whole world; he is the second son of God and all people in the whole world must obey and follow him.... The True Lord is not merely the Lord of China ... he is your Lord also."[16] Such haughty attitudes understandably tended to alienate Western opinion, not least among Christian missionaries, who were especially displeased by Hong's claim to be the literal younger brother of Jesus Christ. Up through their seizure of Nanjing in 1853, the Taiping rebels appeared unstoppable, but thereafter their offensives stalled, and an internal coup in 1856 led to much mutual Taiping slaughter. After 1856, Taiping cohesion and élan dissipated, and Qing imperial counteroffensives began to gain ground.

The Western powers soon adopted postures of neutrality in this Chinese civil war and, after the Anglo-French victory in the second Opium War in 1860, even openly supported the Qing imperial side. An American mercenary named Frederick Townsend Ward (1831–1862), though he had originally dreamed of becoming a Taiping prince, instead organized an "ever victorious army," trained European-style, on behalf of the Qing Dynasty. When Ward was killed, he was replaced by a regular British army officer, Charles Gordon (1833–1885). Although this Western contribution was colorful, it actually played only a small part in the massive imperial effort to suppress the Taipings. By 1864, Nanjing was recaptured by the Qing Dynasty, and great effort was expended to eradicate every trace that the Taiping movement had ever existed. The Taiping Rebellion was therefore ultimately a complete failure, and it left some twenty million people dead in its wake, together with widespread devastation. But because the imperial armies that eventually suppressed the Taipings were regionally rather than centrally organized, it contributed to the long-term decentralization of the Qing Dynasty, and the Taiping Rebellion also served as a conscious inspiration for more successful twentieth-century Chinese revolutionaries.

This Taiping Rebellion was merely the largest of several mid-century rebellions. To mention only one other, in 1864, Muslims in the far northwestern province of Xinjiang rebelled, echoing earlier Muslim rebellions in Gansu, Ningxia, and Shaanxi. The ruler of a small Islamic state on the opposite side of the Pamir Mountains, Khokand, sent a detachment of sixty-eight men across the mountains to intervene, under the command of Ya'qub Beg (ca. 1820–1877). ("Beg" is a Uighur Türkic title meaning "noble.") Ya'qub Beg soon brought all of the Tarim basin area of southern Xinjiang under his control, and after the fall of Khokand to the expanding Russian Empire, he became an independent force. While managing to remain autonomous, Ya'qub Beg accepted the title of "emir" from the Ottoman Empire and received substantial Ottoman military assistance. The British, who hoped that Ya'qub Beg's emirate might serve as a buffer in the so-called great game of imperial rivalry between Britain and Russia, also granted Ya'qub Beg full diplomatic recognition and allowed him to open an embassy in London.

Ya'qub Beg portrayed himself as a defender of the Islamic faith against the infidel Chinese and strictly enforced Sharia law. Women were required to be veiled, for example, and drinking alcohol and eating pork were banned. Since the core of Ya'qub Beg's forces were outsiders from the other side of the Pamir Mountains, and because of such harshly puritanical regulations as well as the closing off of trade with China, the Muslim population of Xinjiang, which had initially supported Ya'qub Beg, grew disaffected over time. The Qing Dynasty, meanwhile, resolved to make a massive commitment of resources to retake Xinjiang, and after about a decade and a half of independence, the Qing reconquest of Xinjiang (except for a small pocket in the northwest that had been occupied by Russia) was completed by the end of 1877.[17] This was to be the last major successful military campaign ever waged by the Chinese Empire.

The Tongzhi Restoration (1862–1874)

The Qing Dynasty was therefore confronted with multiple serious crises in the mid-nineteenth century. As a foreign conquest dynasty, ruled by a relatively small hereditary ethnic elite, the Manchu position in China was also inherently vulnerable. During the first British diplomatic mission to China in 1793, Lord George Macartney had concluded that Manchu rule was "the tyranny of a handful of Tartars [a word the British sometimes used for Manchus] over more than three hundred millions of Chinese" and predicted the dynasty's inevitable collapse, perhaps even during his own lifetime.[18] Yet the Qing Dynasty not only outlived Lord Macartney, it also survived all the mid-nineteenth-century wars and rebellions and even experienced a burst of renewed vigor. This period of revitalization is known as the Tongzhi Restoration, since it coincided with the Tongzhi reign period (1862–74) of a young new emperor.[19]

For a generation beginning in the 1860s, China experienced relative peace, and the Qing Dynasty also began making some pragmatic adjustments to the dramatically altered circumstances of the late-nineteenth-century world. Although, when compared to the Meiji Restoration in contemporary Japan (1868–1912), the Chinese Tongzhi Restoration was visibly less successful in transforming China into a modern, Western-style nation-state and industrialized power, when compared to almost everywhere else in the non-Western world, "China's Response to the West" was actually relatively effective.[20] To the extent that China's response to the challenge of the modern West was different from Japan's, this may have been partly because the domestic threats to the dynasty in China initially absorbed more attention. Unlike Japan, China also was not forced to emerge abruptly from two centuries of isolation under irresistible foreign pressure, so the changes in China were more gradual and imperceptible. Though their sense of self-assurance may have been seriously misplaced, the Chinese long continued to feel relatively self-confident in their traditions.

Yet, unlike Japan, China's capital city was militarily occupied by hostile foreign forces at the end of the second Opium War. Even as the court in Beijing was still preoccupied with suppressing the massive Taiping Rebellion, it had little choice but to make concessions to the new Western ways. When British and French troops marched into Beijing in 1860, the emperor retreated to Manchuria, leaving the emperor's brother, Prince Gong, to deal with the foreigners. Prince Gong responded pragmatically.

In 1861, China's first ever government agency for handling foreign affairs (the *Zongli Yamen*) was established. After defeat in two Opium Wars, the need for military modernization was particularly obvious. Not content with merely purchasing advanced foreign weapons, under the slogan of "self-strengthening," new Western-style arsenals and shipyards began to be constructed in China. Because some Qing reformers concluded that modern Western military superiority was ultimately rooted in math and science, the study of those subjects – so different from the preparation in the humanities for the traditional Confucian examinations – began to be promoted in the 1860s.

A College of Foreign Languages (the *Tongwen guan*) was opened in 1862 to teach such unfamiliar languages as English, French, Russian, and German. Considerable effort was invested into translating Western books, and in 1872, the first group of 120 Chinese students made the journey to Hartford, Connecticut, for a modern Western education. This project came under conservative criticism, however, and it was abandoned in 1881. As of 1879, there were only 163 students enrolled in the College of Foreign Languages. For a country the size of China, these were not impressive numbers.

This emphasis on education, however, did reflect a glimmering recognition that "superficial imitation in concrete things is not so good as arousing intellectual curiosity. The forges and hammers of the factories cannot be compared with the apparatus of people's minds." Even the modernizing Chinese journalist who wrote these words around 1870 still insisted, however, that "the Way of Confucius is the Way of Man."[21] Even among reformers, many people long remained convinced that modern Western technologies could merely be selectively adopted for their utility (*yong*) in defending the essence (*ti*) of traditional Chinese civilization. Most ordinary Chinese people probably saw even less reason to abandon traditional ways.

The decision to dispatch China's first permanent diplomatic missions abroad was not approved by the court until 1875, and when the first ambassador was appointed to a European country, his boat was mobbed and burned. When rumors spread in the port city of Tianjin in 1870 that nuns in the French Sisters of St. Vincent de Paul orphanage were purchasing dying children for diabolical purposes (in fact, the sisters were taking in children, and even paying for them, to baptize them and save their souls), a mob massacred ten nuns, two priests, the French consul, and his chancellor. Many leading figures in the Tongzhi Restoration era, moreover, were convinced that China's crisis was primarily a spiritual or moral one, for which the best solution was a reinvigoration of traditional values and Confucian education. Most people remained largely ignorant about the wider world beyond China's borders. As late as 1895, one reformer complained that he could not find a decent map of the world for sale in Beijing.[22]

Although modern industrial technologies were slowly introduced into China – China's first steamship company was formed in 1872, for example, and a scattering of cotton mills and other modern facilities were constructed, in addition to the government's arsenals – outside of the Western-dominated treaty ports, these long remained little more than isolated experiments that were not always entirely successful. As late as 1933, the modern manufacturing, mining, transportation, and utilities sectors combined still produced only 7 percent of China's gross domestic product.[23] China did not industrialize to any statistically significant extent.

This was not due to any lack of commercial drive or capitalistic enterprise. As one British official complained in 1865, "nine-tenths of the whole of the foreign trade are under the sole control, ownership, and combination of the Chinese." By the 1890s, it is estimated that Chinese people "owned about 40 percent of the stock of Western firms in shipping, cotton spinning, and banking, and held shares in roughly 60 percent of all foreign firms in China." Even in the British colony of Hong Kong, by 1880, of the eighteen largest property tax payers, all but one were Chinese.[24] Although the vast majority of the Chinese people remained poor farmers, even agriculture was extensively market oriented, and the Chinese business classes were indisputably industrious.

Yet the abundant availability of cheap labor, the tendency of much production to be performed as a sideline activity by individual households for just a little extra cash, and the inherent risks and uncertainties of large-scale modern ventures reduced the private incentive to purchase costly labor-saving machinery or build large and expensive factories. Commercial law was underdeveloped, and all the necessary surrounding infrastructure of a modern economy was still largely nonexistent. The late Chinese Empire may have also carried laissez-faire well beyond the point of diminishing returns, since the central government no longer maintained roads, guaranteed much security, set uniform standards for weights and measures, or even issued a standard national currency beyond small-denomination copper cash (this in the land that had first invented paper money centuries earlier!). The weakness of late imperial government, and decentralization of authority following the Taiping Rebellion, also meant that there was little concerted mobilization of any sense of national purpose or concerned awareness of China's strategic interest in promoting deliberate industrialization, as was the case in Meiji Japan. And finally, there was pure inertia: the forms of modern industry that had been pioneered elsewhere simply took time to develop in China.

The Treaty Ports

The Treaty of Nanking that ended the first Opium War in 1842 opened five Chinese ports to British trade. To these initial five, other ports (and similar treaties with other countries) were soon added, and by the early twentieth century there were ninety-two treaty ports, including both ocean and river ports and inland railway junctions. All that such treaty port status really meant was that citizens of the countries that had signed treaties with China were allowed to reside and do business in those cities. In most of the treaty ports, moreover, the foreign presence remained small. Some of the larger treaty ports did become major centers of Western activity, however. Foremost among these was Shanghai, which quickly became the largest and most modern city in China.

Shanghai's abrupt rise from obscurity was mainly due to its location, midway down the Chinese coast and near the mouth of the Yangzi River, which was the principal premodern commercial artery reaching into the interior of China, and also near the major tea- and silk-producing regions. It was a city built on trade, and the British – or more precisely, Anglo-Indians, because they operated extensively from bases in India and included a fair number of actual Indians – were the dominant presence. One 1881 estimate put Britain's share of China's total foreign trade at 77.5 percent.[25] Shanghai became a thoroughly international city, however, with residents from all around the world. English-, French-, German-, and Russian-language newspapers were published, and special schools were established for the children of the foreigners.

The Shanghai International Settlement was originally intended exclusively for foreign residence, but when the Taiping Rebellion threatened to overrun the area, large numbers of Chinese people sought refuge inside the International Settlement. Thereafter Chinese people always remained the overwhelming majority of its population. By the early twentieth century, more Chinese-language daily newspapers were being printed inside the International Settlement at Shanghai than in all the rest of China combined.[26] Yet the International Settlement remained a foreign concession, a kind of autonomous merchant republic that was inside China

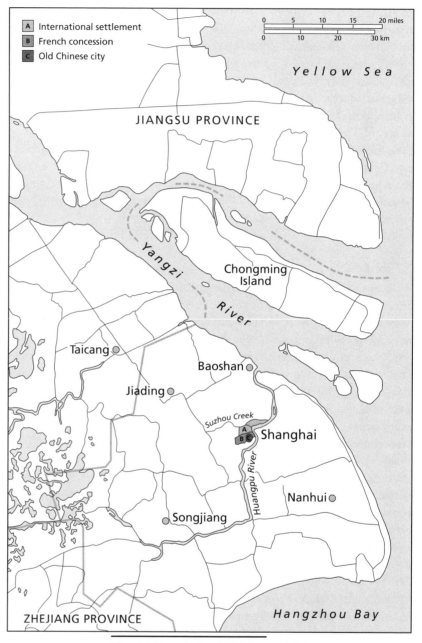

Map 11. Shanghai and Vicinity, ca. 1930

but not under Chinese control. Some twenty-seven hundred of the wealthiest foreign property tax payers annually elected a nine-member municipal council that
governed the International Settlement. In addition, there was a separate French
Concession, under direct French administration. Only the suburbs and the old city
were under Chinese jurisdiction.

Modern Shanghai became one of the great cities of the world. By the end of the nineteenth century, the International Settlement in Shanghai boasted paved roads, streetlights, running water, telephones, and electricity. The mansions of the great foreign taipans (a regional slang expression meaning "big bosses") lined Bubbling Well Road with their tennis courts and gardens. Western entertainments included the club, amateur theater, golf, horse racing, and cricket. If wealthy foreigners lived comfortably in Shanghai, moreover, Shanghai was also a magnet for ambitious Chinese, who were attracted by the promise of security and economic opportunity. By about 1870, some of the Chinese agents of foreign businesses were already beginning to invest in their own modern enterprises, forming the nucleus of an emerging modern Chinese business class.

Yet Shanghai's modern success had an unmistakably dark underside. Shanghai "was literally built on the opium trade," and by the early twentieth century, there were some eighty opium shops and fifteen hundred opium dens inside the city.[27] Shanghai's somewhat shady reputation was notorious. For a time in the early twentieth century, the leading gangster in the French Concession was simultaneously also chief superintendent of the Chinese police squad. Continued foreign administration of the International Settlement and French Concession was also a potentially explosive affront to the growing sense of Chinese nationalism. The first Chinese member of the Shanghai Municipal Council was not seated until 1928.

The Boxer Rebellion (1898–1900)

The Tongzhi emperor died young in 1874, providing his mother, the Empress Dowager Cixi (1835–1908), with an opportunity to place yet another pliable minor, this time her nephew, the Guangxu Emperor (r. 1875–1908), on the throne. As the real power behind the throne, this empress dowager balanced conservative and reformist factions against each other, with her chief concern being simply the preservation of her dynasty (see Figure 7.2). Despite the steps that had been taken toward "self-strengthening" during the Tongzhi Restoration, the Qing Dynasty was militarily humiliated when it became embroiled in a war with Japan, over Korea, in 1894–1895 – even though, on paper, the Chinese army was nearly six times the size of the Japanese army, and the Chinese navy had twice as many ships. The indemnity that China was forced to pay Japan as a result of its defeat was equal to 15 percent of Japan's total gross national product in that year, and this massive transfer of financial spoils then helped underwrite Japan's further industrialization. In China, the defeat came as a great shock.

The war with Japan severed China's ancient tributary relationship with Korea, transferred the island of Taiwan from the Chinese to the Japanese empire, and initially threatened to make further inroads into China's northeastern territories. Although Russia, France, and Germany intervened to prevent that from happening, just three years later, these very same Western great powers themselves began extracting leaseholds from Chinese soil. In 1898, Russia began building a naval base, called Port Arthur, at the tip of Liaodong peninsula in Manchuria. Germany acquired the port of Qingdao on the Shandong peninsula, France leased a harbor

Figure 7.2. The Qing Dynasty Empress Dowager Cixi with foreign envoys' wives, 1903–1905. Freer Gallery of Art and Arthur M. Sackler Gallery Archives, Smithsonian Institution, Washington, D.C.: Negative # SC-GR 249.

in far south China, and Britain leased a port in Shandong (Weihaiwei) and signed a ninety-nine-year lease on the New Territories surrounding Hong Kong. The Russians began constructing railways across Manchuria, and despite Shanghai's undisputed preeminence among the treaty ports, the city in China that soon had both the largest total number and the highest percentage of resident foreigners became Harbin, which was founded in 1898 as a Russian railway town in the very center of Manchuria.[28] At its peak, more than half of Harbin's population was Russian, and it boasted a Russian university, schools, courts, and churches.

Alarmed by these concessions, and also by the extension of even larger, more nebulous foreign "spheres of influence" into the interior of China, the youthful Guangxu Emperor was emboldened to take radical action and embarked on the so-called one hundred days of reform in 1898. As the name implies, however, these reforms quickly proved abortive. Conservatives were horrified, and the empress dowager staged a palace coup, placed the emperor under house arrest in the rebuilt Summer Palace, executed six reformers and drove others into exile, and declared herself regent.

In the next year, 1899, north China began to suffer from a severe drought. A mysterious religious society called the *Yihequan* (Boxers United in Righteousness, or simply Boxers) provided an explanation: the alien religion of Christianity was causing the people to abandon their traditional gods, and in retribution, the gods were withholding the life-giving rain. This Boxer movement emerged from the variety of religious and martial arts self-defense groups that were widespread in the Chinese countryside. Many Boxers apparently were quite young boys. As the senior U.S. diplomat in Beijing explained to the Secretary of State in 1900, "a number of teachers go through the country, gather together the idle young men at the various villages and organize them into companies and pretend if they will, under their direction, go through certain gymnastic movements and repeat certain incantations, that they will become impervious to all weapons and nothing can harm them."[29]

Though the Boxers were anti-Christian and antiforeign, they were at least potentially also anti-Manchu and anti-Qing. Conservatives at the Qing court in Beijing were sympathetic, though, and on June 21, 1900, Empress Dowager Cixi actually issued a sweeping declaration of war against foreigners in China. The Legation Quarter in Beijing was besieged, as was the foreign community in the important northern port city of Tianjin, which at the time contained some nine hundred foreign civilians, including the future American president Herbert Hoover. Cooperation between the Boxers and regular imperial officials was poor, however, and most Qing officials, including those in the entire south of China, simply chose not to participate. Ironically, in view of their antiforeignism, the Boxers were generally less active in areas where the Western presence was strongest. Most of the relatively small number of foreign deaths (a much larger number of Chinese Christian converts were killed) were in remote northwestern Shanxi Province and Inner Mongolia. In response to this Boxer uprising, in August 1900, a multinational army marched into Beijing and rescued the foreign community there (see Figure 7.3). The Boxers were crushed, and a so-called Boxer Protocol was imposed on the Qing Dynasty, which included the payment of an indemnity equal to nearly twice the annual tax revenue of the dynasty. In the aftermath, even the empress dowager belatedly recognized the need for Western-style reforms, and with the turn into the twentieth century, the Qing Dynasty finally embarked on a conscious course of rapid modernization.

The Nineteenth-Century Opening of Korea

At the start of the nineteenth century, Korea's only foreign contacts were with Qing Dynasty China and Tokugawa Japan. Chosŏn Korea was a self-acknowledged tributary of China. This meant that the Korean kings were expected to use the Chinese calendar and seek confirmation of their enthronement from the Chinese emperor, who also issued approximately annual proclamations to Korea. Over the course of the Qing Dynasty, Seoul sent an average of nearly three embassies each year to Beijing. The Koreans called this "serving the great" (sadae). However, the Korean elite also retained deep feelings of loyalty to the previous Chinese Ming Dynasty, which had come to Korea's aid during Hideyoshi's invasions, and felt considerable disdain for the alien Manchu rulers of the Qing. The Qing Dynasty sealed its border with Korea with a palisade, boat traffic between China and Korea was forbidden (Korean fishermen were, in any case, confined to coastal waters), and contact was limited only to official embassies. And although Korea may have

Figure 7.3. The Ninth U.S. Infantry lined up before the imperial palace in Beijing, 1901, following the suppression of the Boxer Rebellion. Library of Congress, LC-USZ62-68813.

been an acknowledged tributary of the Chinese empire, as one Chinese official explained in 1876, this really meant that except for the obligatory ceremonial tribute missions, Korea was entirely autonomous in both its domestic and foreign affairs.[30] The peculiar ambiguity of Korea's relationship with China even became a convenient excuse for rebuffing early Western approaches. When the British attempted to advance trade proposals with Korea in 1845, it was explained that this would be impossible because Korea "could not be opened to trade by China, for it was not a part of China," and it also "could not open itself to trade, for it was not independent."[31]

Korea's relationship with Japan was also somewhat complicated. Following Hideyoshi's invasions and the subsequent establishment of the Tokugawa Shogunate in Japan, contact with Korea was restored by a trade agreement in 1609. The Koreans viewed the Tokugawa shogun as equal in status to their own king, and a small number of Korean embassies were sent to the shogun's castle in Edo, but no Japanese embassies traveled to Korea, and direct Korean contact with the Shogunate ended in 1811. Instead of the shogun (or the Japanese emperor), it was the *daimyō* (lord) of Tsushima, a small Japanese island midway between the

Figure 7.4. Kojong (1852–1919), emperor, and previously king, of Korea, ca. 1904. Library of Congress, LC-USZ62-72798.

main islands and the Korean peninsula, who enjoyed a monopoly of Korean trade. This lord of Tsushima acted simultaneously as a vassal of the Japanese shogun and as a kind of tributary of the Korean king, having been granted official titles by the Korean court. Approximately a thousand persons from Tsushima traveled to Korea each year, but they were confined to a strictly monitored Japan House in the single port of Pusan.

The 1860s were a decade of restorations everywhere in East Asia. China had its Tongzhi Restoration, Japan had its Meiji Restoration, and there was also a sort of royal restoration in Korea, as well. Certain rough parallels between these three restorations may be explained by the fact that the ruling elites in each country were imbued with many of the same Confucian ideas and confronting some of the same challenges. All three countries also had youthful new monarchs in the 1860s. In 1864, King Kojong (r. 1864–1907) came to the throne of Korea at the age of twelve (see Figure 7.4). The king's father, who was known as the Taewŏn'gun (the "Lord of the Great Court"), was still alive (he had not himself ever been king), and this father acted as an informal regent from 1864 to 1873 on his son's behalf.

The Taewŏn'gun attempted to promote reforms that would strengthen the Korean monarchy by reducing corruption, inefficiency, and *yangban* aristocratic privileges. At the same time, he also intensified the crackdown on Christianity and hardened Korea's resolve in fending off the growing number of Western approaches. Korea's apparent successes in driving off a French fleet in 1866, and then a U.S. naval squadron in 1871, encouraged Koreans to believe that this was still militarily possible. If the Tokugawa Shogunate in Japan reacted to news of the Opium War in China by concluding that resistance to modern Western military power would be futile, the Taewŏn'gun in Korea drew the opposite conclusion: the way to avoid humiliation was to stand firm and resolutely reject all foreign demands for trade.

After the Meiji Restoration of imperial rule in Japan in 1868, and the dissolution of the Tokugawa Shogunate, Japan's new Western-style Imperial Foreign Office officially assumed jurisdiction over Korean relations from the *daimyō* of Tsushima in 1871. The Korean government, however, refused to accept these changes. Among other things, the Koreans objected to Japanese officials now dressing in Western-style clothing, but most especially, the Koreans refused to acknowledge the position of the Japanese emperor. This was because the Japanese imperial title was equal in rank to the Chinese, and as a tributary of China, the Koreans could not recognize another emperor. While, at first glance, this may seem absurdly obscurantist, in fact, recognition of the Japanese emperor would have implied Japanese superiority over the lower-ranking Korean king. Indeed, many of Japan's Meiji Restoration leaders actively hoped that the restoration of imperial rule in Japan would also bring a "restoration" of what they believed to have been Korea's ancient (but mythical) subordination to Japan.

Korea's refusal to recognize the imperial government in Japan was regarded as an outrage by many patriotic Japanese and provoked debate over the desirability of immediate war with Korea. Although cooler heads prevailed, in 1875, a Japanese navy warship engaged in surveying off the coast of Korea's Kanghwa Island attempted to put a small boat ashore for fresh water. Korean shore batteries fired some shots, which may have been intended only as warnings, and the Japanese returned fire and landed troops. In 1876, Japan further signaled the firmness of its intentions by dispatching three warships, four transports, and eight hundred soldiers to Korea. King Kojong had, meanwhile, begun to rule in his own name, ending the regency of the Taewŏn'gun in 1873. King Kojong was less resolute in his opposition to all foreign contacts than the Taewŏn'gun had been, and under the looming threat of a Japanese invasion, and acting under Chinese advice, in 1876, Korea signed a modern Western-style treaty (the Treaty of Kanghwa) with Japan. This treaty formally declared Korea to be an independent country (supposedly clarifying its relationship with China) and granted Japan various treaty port-style concessions.

While Korean conservatives looked to China to balance the growing Japanese influence, some Korean modernizers aligned themselves with Meiji Japan. In 1884, a handful of Korean reformers plotted a coup, in consultation with the Japanese minister in Seoul. On December 4, during a banquet celebrating the opening of a modern post office, the conspirators struck. Seven Korean officials were assassinated, and guards from the Japanese legation took the Korean king and queen into "protective" custody. A new Korean government was proclaimed, and modernizing reforms were outlined. Chinese troops counterattacked the palace immediately, however, regaining custody of the king. The result of this failed coup, which only lasted two days, was to tarnish the reputations of both the reform and the pro-Japanese positions.

The Qing Dynasty in China, meanwhile, which supported certain self-strengthening modernizing efforts in Korea and had actually negotiated modern treaties on Korea's behalf with the United States, Great Britain, and Germany in 1882, had by this time broken with its traditional posture of noninterference and was now actively intervening in Korea. In 1885, the Qing appointed a resident commissioner to Korea (a man named Yuan Shikai, who would later become the first official president of the Republic of China). The tensions inevitably resulting from the conflicting Chinese and Japanese ambitions in Korea were temporarily cooled by an agreement in 1885 that both China and Japan would withdraw their troops. This uneasy peace was brought to an abrupt end, however, by a religiously inspired Korean rebellion in 1894.

In the 1850s, a Korean named Ch'oe Che-u (1824–1864), who had been ineligible to take the Korean civil service examinations because his mother had remarried, received what he claimed was a revelation from the Lord of Heaven. This inspired him to formulate a new religion, which was something of an eclectic mixture of traditional East Asian ideas and was called *Tonghak* (Eastern Learning), in conscious opposition to the alien ideas of the West. Although Ch'oe was executed in 1864, *Tonghak* beliefs continued to simmer in the Korean countryside. In 1894, a local *Tonghak* uprising swept across southwest Korea, fueled by popular discontent with heavy taxes and high interest rates. This became the most massive rebellion in recorded Korean history. An anxious Korean king asked China for military assistance, and the Qing Dynasty responded by sending a small detachment of soldiers. Japan countered by deploying a much larger force of its own. Although the Korean authorities, alarmed by the possibilities unleashed by this dual foreign intervention, quickly offered concessions to the *Tonghak* rebels, who agreed to lay down their arms, the Japanese troops remained. On July 23, a Japanese infantry regiment seized the Korean palace. On August 1, war was declared between China and Japan.

Over the following nine months, the Japanese army easily expelled Chinese troops from Korea, captured territory in Manchuria, and even gained a foothold in coastal China proper. Qing Dynasty Chinese forces proved to be badly led, undermined by corruption, and split by faction and regionalism. A substantial portion of the Chinese navy actually refused to participate in a war they considered beyond their concern. Japan won this Sino-Japanese War (1894–1895) with surprising ease. The war was much celebrated in the modern Japanese press but came as a tremendous shock, and a wake-up call, to China. Under the terms of the resulting Treaty of Shimonoseki that ended the hostilities, China was forced to transfer the island of Taiwan to Japan (as well, initially, as a strategic peninsula in southern Manchuria, which intervention by Russia, France, and Germany promptly compelled Japan to return) and to pay Japan an enormous indemnity equal to roughly 15 percent of Japan's total gross national product. In addition, China formally acknowledged the independence of Korea, which in practice meant the ascent of Japanese interests there.

During the Sino-Japanese War, Japan moved quickly to assume a dominant position in Korea, extracting the right to begin constructing railways on the peninsula and to provide advisors for Korean domestic affairs. Even while the war with China was still raging, pro-Japanese Korean officials reorganized the government, introducing sweeping modernizing reforms (known as the Kabo reforms) in 1894–1895. The Chinese calendar was dropped from official Korean documents and a new Korean calendar substituted in its place. The Confucian civil service examination system was abolished, as was the institution of slavery and formal distinctions between the aristocratic *yangban* classes and commoners. Western-style clothing and hairstyles were forcibly promoted. Altogether, there were 208 new laws, culminating in a new constitution in January 1895.

Despite Japanese victory in the war with China, Korea once again temporarily eluded reduction to an outright Japanese protectorate, partly because of the obvious contradiction inherent in the Japanese policy of pursuing domination in Korea while simultaneously proclaiming a goal of promoting Korean "independence" from the archaic Chinese tributary system. The order that all Korean men cut their topknots and adopt Western hairstyles provoked great popular discontent, and when, in October 1895, a Japanese-backed coup assassinated the Korean queen and restored pro-Japanese officials to power, this assassination outraged and horrified Korean opinion. In February 1896, King Kojong, seeking to escape Japanese domination, allowed himself to be smuggled out of the palace by Russian marines in the palanquin of a court lady. The king took refuge in the Russian legation, where he spent the next year.[32]

By playing off Russian interests against the Japanese, as he had previously used the Chinese against the Japanese, King Kojong was able to retain a measure of Korean independence. In 1897, the king returned to his palace and formally assumed the supreme East Asian title of "emperor" (in Korean, *Hwangje*), asserting his sovereign equality with both the Chinese (Manchu) and Japanese monarchs. Over the next few years, modern army units were organized, postage stamps issued, and streetcars and electric lights introduced into the capital (see Figure 7.5), and in 1902, the newly renamed Korean Empire even acquired a Western-style national anthem. The Christian mission to Korea, meanwhile, was on its way to becoming the most successful in East Asia, and modern Western-style education began exerting a profound effect on Korean thought. A newspaper published by the Independence Club beginning in 1897 was the first to be published entirely in the Korean alphabet (*han'gŭl*), without any Chinese characters. A new spirit of modern Korean nationalism began to glimmer, and the hope kindled that Korea might successfully be transformed into an independent, modern, Western-style

Figure 7.5. The West Gate of Seoul, Korea, ca. 1904, showing an American electric tramway. Library of Congress, LC-USZ62-72552.

nation-state.[33] The degree of material modernization remained limited, however (see Figure 7.6), and in the early twentieth century, the dream of Korean independence would prove to be a false hope, as the lengthening shadow of the Japanese Empire stretched across the land.

The Meiji Restoration (1868–1912): Japan "Leaves Asia"

In the early nineteenth century, Western contact with Japan was limited to an annual average of only one Dutch ship. In Japan, the Dutch were confined to the single port of Nagasaki, where they were effectively quarantined on a small island, surrounded by a high fence topped with iron spikes, and linked to shore by one bridge. Yet, even so, Japan's isolation should not be exaggerated. After 1716, official permission resumed for the study of Western books, with a particular interest in books concerning medical and military science. This became a specialized form of learning known as Dutch studies (*Rangaku*). In 1811, the Tokugawa

Figure 7.6. Korean women with a sedan chair, 1919. Library of Congress, LC-USZ62-72675.

Shogunate itself set up an agency to translate selected Dutch works. By the 1840s and 1850s, even before the arrival of Commodore Perry, a few domains were already independently constructing foundries for the casting of modern Western-style munitions.

Commodore Perry and the Opening of Japan (1853–1854)

Because Japan appeared to be a poor country, unlikely to buy significant amounts of any European goods, and having no known local products that were particularly in demand in Europe – and because the Japanese islands were also quite remote and out of the way for European shipping coming from the west – Great Britain and the other major European powers had been relatively content to leave Japan in its self-imposed isolation. Two of the newly emerging modern great powers, however, did have special interests in the Pacific Ocean that made opening relations with Japan seem more crucial: the United States and Russia. In the eighteenth and nineteenth centuries, the Russians had made repeated efforts to establish relations with Japan, without success. The United States, meanwhile, had expanded to the shores of the Pacific with the acquisition of California in 1848. American clipper ships, on the voyage from California to Guangzhou (Canton), often came within sight of the Japanese islands, and American whalers frequently found themselves in Japanese waters by the 1840s. In the age of sail, shipwrecks were an all too common occurrence, and the U.S. government was concerned about the treatment of American sailors shipwrecked in Japan. As steam navigation was increasing in importance, there was also a growing need for widespread and strategically located coaling stations. And, of course, there was always the possibility of trade.

At least twenty-five times before the arrival of Commodore Perry's squadron, U.S. ships, either officially or privately, had attempted to establish contact with Japan. In 1846, an official mission under the command of Commodore Biddle had failed – according to the interpretation prevailing in Washington, because Commodore Biddle had not made a forceful enough impression on the Japanese. When the decision was reached to send another expedition in 1851, therefore, its commander, Commodore Mathew Calbraith Perry (1794–1858), was encouraged to be firm.

Commodore Perry gathered what little information he could find about a Japan that was still largely unknown to the West and approached cautiously. In July 1853, Perry arrived in what is now called Tōkyō Bay with four ominous black warships, including the powerful steam frigates *Mississippi* and *Susquehanna*. Perry's flagship, the *Mississippi*, mounted eight large eight-inch guns and two even larger ten-inch cannons. Precisely because Japanese officials were not entirely ignorant of developments in the outside world and were well aware of China's humiliating defeat in the Opium War in 1842, these big guns left a sobering impression. On arrival, Commodore Perry remained in his cabin and refused to meet with junior Japanese officials, demanding instead that he be allowed to deliver a letter from President Fillmore into the hands of senior officials ashore.

Because the Americans were unclear about the institution of the Japanese military overlord known as the shogun, the president's letter was addressed to the Japanese emperor. In fact, however, a young shogunal chief councilor handled the negotiations. The shogun himself, who was on his deathbed, was not even told of the American arrival, and the emperor was quite powerless. Perry's men went ashore with loaded weapons, while the Japanese concealed armed samurai under the floorboards of the reception room, in mutual anticipation of trouble. An American missionary who had learned a few words of Japanese while living in China had been brought along to serve as interpreter, but most negotiations were actually conducted in the Dutch language. After delivering his letter stating the American demands, Commodore Perry departed, promising to return again next spring with an even larger squadron to receive the Japanese answer.

Armed resistance appeared futile, but yielding to foreign demands would mean a great loss of shogunal prestige, so the shogunal authorities took the unprecedented step of asking for *daimyō* advice. In the mid-nineteenth century, Japan was still divided into some 276 *daimyō* domains, each of which, despite acknowledging Tokugawa overlordship, retained its own independent government, armed forces, and sometimes even currency. Since most *daimyō* now urged the Shogunate not to give in to foreign demands, but also cautioned against war, the act of seeking *daimyō* advice only made the Shogunate's position even more awkward. Financially, the Tokugawa treasury was empty. Shogunal authority had also recently been threatened by the economic revival of some of the more powerful outlying domains. Although most *daimyō*, like the Shogunate itself, were deeply in debt, a few key domains had succeeded in restructuring their economies and putting their finances on relatively sound footing. These included, in particular, the domains of Chōshū, at the western tip of Japan's main island, and Satsuma, in southern Kyūshū.[34] Satsuma, for example, in part because of its southern climate, had achieved something of a monopoly on sugar production in Japan.

In February 1854, Commodore Perry returned with ten warships, and the Tokugawa Shogunate abruptly yielded, signing a treaty (the Treaty of Kanagawa) with the United States. Before long, other countries had also signed treaties, and a treaty port system similar to what had previously been established in China was now extended to Japan as well. Foreign residence in Edo (the Shogun's castle town, modern Tōkyō) was permitted beginning in 1859. Nagasaki, Yokohama, Kobe, and other ports were opened, the standard treaty port privilege of extraterritoriality (foreign exemption from local law) was conferred, and fixed low tax rates on foreign imports were established. In the process, shogunal military power had been exposed as hollow for everyone to see. Since shogunal authority had no real ideological basis for legitimacy apart from its military dominance, the Tokugawa position now became precarious.

The Meiji Restoration (1868)

In the eighteenth century, the school of National Learning, whose most famous representative was Motoori Norinaga (1730–1801), had revived an interest in ancient native Japanese myths and literature, especially the imperial mythology enshrined in the oldest Japanese history, the *Kojiki*. Tokugawa shogunal authority had theoretically been justified from the beginning merely as a delegation of power from the emperor, and with the Shogunate now demonstrating obvious weakness in the face of foreign threats, the slogan "revere the emperor and expel the barbarians" (*sonnō-jōi*; more literally, "revere the king," since this was originally a four-character Chinese expression traceable to commentaries to the preimperial era *Analects* of Confucius) began to rally patriotic opposition both to the foreign concessions and, at least implicitly, to the Tokugawa Shogunate itself, in the name of loyalty to the emperor.

Yoshida Shoin (1830–1859), a samurai from Chōshū, had attempted to stow away aboard one of Commodore Perry's ships to learn more about the mysterious foreigners. He was caught, however, and placed under arrest. After his release, he organized an influential patriotic school. Yoshida blamed the Shogunate for its failure to expel the foreigners and decided that the Tokugawa Shogunate must be overthrown. He plotted to assassinate a shogunal emissary to the imperial capital, Kyōto, in 1858, but was caught once again and this time beheaded. Yoshida became, however, a hero for many Japanese patriots. In 1860, furthermore, the shogunal grand councilor actually was assassinated while entering Edo castle by warriors from the domains of Mito and Satsuma.

The years following the signing of the first foreign treaties were marked by several outbursts of patriotic terrorism, as samurai vented their indignation through individual acts of violence. Two Russian sailors were killed in 1859. The American consul's Dutch interpreter was murdered in 1861. In 1862, the *daimyō* of Satsuma delivered an imperial command to the shogun, demanding that the shogun report to Kyōto in person to explain his concessions to the foreigners. As this *daimyō* was returning from delivering the message, his procession encountered a small group of British people on the road near Yokohama who failed to dismount in token of respect for the *daimyō*. Outraged samurai attendants attacked the foreigners, killing one Englishman and wounding two others. In 1863, the British legation in Edo was burned by arsonists (including Itō Hirobumi, who would later become one of Meiji Japan's leading statesmen).

By 1863, extremists had gained control of the imperial court and compelled the Shogunate to agree to set a date for the expulsion of all foreigners. This was to be June 25, 1863. Although most of Japan failed to take any action on that date, fortifications in the western domain of Chōshū did begin firing on passing ships. In retaliation, in 1864, a combined British, French, Dutch, and American fleet stormed the forts and destroyed them. The previous year, in 1863, a British squadron had also shelled the castle town in Satsuma, in retribution for the earlier attack on Englishmen on the road near Yokohama. Tokugawa Japan's defenselessness against modern firepower was exposed.

Thereafter, attempts to expel the foreigners were swiftly abandoned as obviously futile, and a new patriotic slogan began to replace "revere the Emperor and expel the barbarians": "enrich the country and strengthen the army" (*fukoku kyōhei*, also a four-character expression originally dating from Warring States China). By the late 1860s, the situation had changed from one of conflict between patriotic Japanese and foreigners to one of competition between different groups of Japanese, each often with its own sources of foreign assistance. The Shogunate, for example, was leaning toward France, while the domains of Satsuma and Chōshū were dealing especially with the British.

In the meantime, the requirement of alternate attendance at the shogun's castle in Edo had been effectively lifted in 1862, and *daimyō* families departed Edo for their own domains. In 1864, a radical faction gained control in Chōshū and began promoting its agenda at the imperial court in Kyōto. When fighting in July reduced much of Kyōto to ashes, the imperial court ordered the Shogunate to launch a punitive expedition against Chōshū. This was supported by other domains and initially was moderately successful, but when a second campaign was begun against the recalcitrant Chōshū in 1866, this time, many other domains remained neutral. A secret agreement was arranged for mutual support between Satsuma and Chōshū in March, which brought together the two most powerful "outside" domains, and a Shogunal attack on Chōshū that month was militarily defeated. The Tokugawa Shogunate was crumbling.

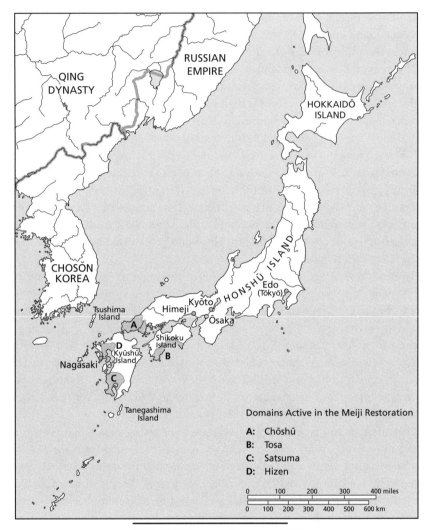

Map 12. Tokugawa Japan, ca. 1860

The death of the Shogun Iemochi in 1866 (at age twenty-one, apparently of beriberi) provided a suitable pretext for the Shogunate to call off its war with Chōshū, but soon thereafter, an order was issued in the name of the emperor calling upon Chōshū and Satsuma to actively assume the military offensive against the Tokugawa Shogunate. At this juncture, samurai from the domain of Tosa (on the smaller southern island of Shikoku) prevailed on the new shogun, who had been personally reluctant to accept the title in the first place, to resign. Amazingly, the shogun did exactly that, petitioning the emperor in November 1867 to accept a reversion of shogunal authority back to the imperial throne. The ex-shogun retained vast landholdings, however, and remained a powerful *daimyō*. Anti-Tokugawa forces were not satisfied, therefore, and on January 3, 1868, samurai, primarily from Satsuma, seized the imperial palace and proclaimed an imperial restoration. This is known to history as the Meiji Restoration, after the name of the Meiji imperial reign period (1868–1912). Although the ex-shogun did resist this coup d'état, his army was defeated by imperial forces in four days of heavy fighting. The ex-shogun soon surrendered and was generously treated by the victors, eventually even receiving the highest rank in a newly created modern peerage. In November, the young Meiji emperor departed the ancient capital, Kyōto, in western Japan and took up residence in the former shogun's castle in Edo, which now became known as Tōkyō (Eastern Capital).

In theory, this was a restoration of the sole legitimate ancient Japanese imperial government after centuries of improper domination by military usurpers (the shoguns), performed in the name of the quintessentially traditional Confucian virtue of loyalty. In the early years of the Meiji Restoration, there was even some actual revival of ancient court titles. The mid-ranking samurai who led this Meiji Restoration, moreover, had for many years been indignant at the incompetence of the few thousand hereditary families who monopolized Tokugawa wealth and power and the correspondingly sweeping lack of career opportunities for the much larger number of, often bitterly impoverished, lower-ranking samurai. In many ways, the meritocratic ideals underlying this revolutionary change were as traditionally Confucian as they were modern and Western.[35]

At the same time, however, this was also a quite revolutionary break from the past. The Meiji Charter Oath that was issued in the name of the emperor in April 1868, which famously urged that "evil customs of the past shall be broken off and . . . Knowledge shall be sought throughout the world so as to strengthen the foundations of imperial rule," provides what one historian has called "a perfect example of this blending of tradition with intended change." New foreign ideas were to be openly considered, but chiefly to buttress an allegedly primordial Japanese imperial throne.[36] Another striking example of this process of blending tradition with novelty is provided by the composition of Japan's modern national anthem in the 1870s: by a German bandmaster, who set verses from the tenth-century *Kokinshū* to music. A modern Japanese nation-state was created that was in many ways new, but popularly imagined as ancient. Into modern Japan's frontiers, also, certain peoples who had formerly often been viewed as foreign, such as the Okinawans of the Ryūkyū Islands in the south and the Ainu of the far north, were reconceived now, not as foreign but as more pristine survivals of the ancient Japanese.[37]

Despite a patina of tradition, the first two decades of the Meiji reign period were a time of considerable enthusiasm for foreign Western ideas, which came to be flatly labeled "civilization and enlightenment" (*bunmei kaika*). Abandoning the use of Chinese characters in writing was seriously debated, and the possibility of moving to a Western-style alphabet was considered. One future minister of education even suggested, in 1872–1873, replacing Japanese with English as the national language. In the end, although neither Chinese characters nor the native Japanese *kana* syllabaries were abandoned (to say nothing of the Japanese language itself), a new standard modern vernacular Japanese written national language did take shape by the end of the nineteenth century.[38]

Among the most ardent popular Westernizers of the age was Fukuzawa Yūkichi (1835–1901), who, in 1885, went so far as to editorialize that Japan should culturally "leave Asia" and distance itself from its more backward neighbors. "It is better for us to leave the ranks of Asian nations and cast our lot with civilized nations of the West," wrote Fukuzawa.[39] Fukuzawa Yūkichi had begun life as a student of Dutch learning. In the 1860s, he visited Europe and the United States and published a best-selling book based on his experiences called *Conditions in the West* in 1866.

Even Fukuzawa could be described as a vigorous Japanese nationalist, however, and in a predictable reaction to some of the more extreme Westernizing initiatives, conservative Japanese became incensed that the Meiji government was outdoing the old Tokugawa Shogunate in making concessions to the foreigners. Meiji Restoration leaders sometimes, therefore, found themselves the targets of patriotic attacks, among them that very same minister of education who had once proposed abolishing the Japanese language and replacing it with English. He was stabbed to death in 1889 because of his allegedly disrespectful behavior at the Imperial Grand Shrine in Ise.[40]

Meiji Modernization

In the immediate aftermath of the Meiji Restoration, institutions were in considerable flux in Japan, shifting uncertainly from American to British, French, or German models. As Fukuzawa Yūkichi described the Japan of the 1870s, "there was a government but no nation." It would not be until the late 1880s that the certainty of a (supposedly primordial) Japanese national, or more grandly, imperial identity firmly gripped the popular consciousness.[41] Indeed, as of 1868, it was not even obvious that the new government would survive. It was so closely associated with the southwestern domains of Chōshū and Satsuma, and to a lesser extent, also Tosa and Hizen, that certain other domains in the northeast rebelled in July. The rebellion was put down, but by what was still essentially a Chōshū and Satsuma rather than a truly national army.

Although the four domains that had led the Meiji Restoration contained only about 7 percent of the total Japanese population, as late as 1890, they still provided some 30 percent of the central government's leaders and filled roughly half of all the top positions.[42] Despite the Meiji slogan of "personal rule by the emperor," real power was wielded in the emperor's name by a handful of senior officials. A narrow circle of some twenty individuals came to be known as the Meiji oligarchy. As elder statesmen (*genrō*), these same Meiji oligarchs continued to dominate Japanese politics well into the twentieth century. This new Meiji government did have the clear-sighted practical objective, however, of transforming Japan into a strong, modern, centralized nation-state.

In July 1869, all the *daimyō* were ordered to transfer their domains to the central imperial government. The former *daimyō* were initially well compensated with substantial revenue and new government titles as local governors. In 1871, however, these same governors were stripped, without advance notice, of those titles and forced to retire to Tōkyō. The underlying regional uniformity that had already emerged during the centuries of the Tokugawa Shogunate, and that had already succeeded in imposing a degree of early modern bureaucratic centralization, made the transition from aristocratic domains to a centralized system of administrative prefectures a relatively smooth process. By 1871, the new imperial government appeared stable enough that half of the leading oligarchs confidently embarked on an extended tour of the West. While they were gone, however, a diplomatic crisis emerged over Korea's refusal to recognize Japanese imperial titles. Several of the Meiji leaders wanted to dispatch a punitive force against Korea immediately. When a more cautious approach against Korea was finally adopted, the oligarchs Saigō Takamori (1827–1877), Itagaki Taisuke (1837–1919), and others resigned in protest in 1873.

Saigō, who had been one of the heroes of the Meiji Restoration, now retuned to his old domain in Satsuma and became a leading figure representing samurai class discontent. After the abolition of the *daimyō* domains in 1871, the central government had assumed the responsibility for paying all samurai stipends. This was an enormous financial obligation, however, which absorbed approximately one-third of all government revenue. It was clearly unsustainable, and the payment of samurai stipends was permanently suspended in 1876: converted into interest-bearing bonds. In that same year, the samurai privilege of wearing two swords was also banned. One by one, all the special samurai privileges were abolished, until none remained. In 1870, commoners had been granted surnames; in 1871, commoners were permitted to ride horses, travel freely, and marry samurai; in 1873, a new conscription law obligated commoners to serve in the army. Whereas commoners had once been actively forbidden to bear arms, they were now required to do so, in the service of the new Japanese nation-state.

The 1876 ban on carrying two swords, the government's failure to avenge the alleged Korean insults, and general unease at the rapid pace of change and Westernization fed samurai discontent, especially in the very domains that had led the Meiji Restoration, where samurai expectations were often most acutely disappointed. In Satsuma, neither the ban on carrying swords nor the elimination of samurai stipends was enforced. Notable samurai rebellions occurred in Saga in 1874, in Chōshū in 1876, and finally in Satsuma in 1877, this one led by Saigō Takamori himself.

A year earlier, the central imperial government, then under the domination of the oligarch Ōkubo Toshimichi (1830–1878) – himself originally a samurai from Satsuma – had sent agents to disarm the arsenal in Satsuma's castle town. Captured by local men, one agent "confessed" under torture that he had been sent to assassinate Saigō. Declaring that he had questions to ask the central government, in February 1877, Saigō led a large force of fifteen thousand samurai on a march toward Tōkyō. Though they never got off the southwestern island of Kyūshū, and their samurai army, with its lingering regional loyalties, ultimately proved no match for the modern conscript army of the central government, it still took six months for the full weight of the imperial army to put this samurai rebellion down. In September, his cause a failure, Saigō Takamori committed ritual suicide (*seppuku*). In a sense, the entire samurai class died with him. Although the Meiji oligarch Ōkubo was himself then assassinated the very next year, in 1878, the old warrior class never again posed a serious threat to the new Meiji order.

The Meiji Constitution

Like Saigō Takamori, the oligarch Itagaki Taisuke had also resigned from the government over the dispute involving Korea, but unlike Saigō, he adopted a dissident approach based not on samurai nostalgia but on modern Western liberal political ideals. Itagaki began to lobby for the creation of a representative government assembly. This was the origin of what is known as the popular rights movement. In the decade of the 1870s, no fewer than 130 petitions were submitted to the emperor, calling for the establishment of representative self-government. Self-government seemed to be one of those irresistible Western trends of the times, and even the Meiji government itself encouraged some degree of modern popular participation. The oligarch Ōkubo Toshimichi took a conservative stance, however. Under his watch, a press law in 1875 imposed advance censorship and restricted political criticism.

After the assassination of Ōkubo in 1878, the Meiji government made some concessions, and it soon publicly pledged to put a written Western-style constitution and an elected national assembly in place by 1890. In anticipation of this, the first Japanese political parties began to form in 1881. Because the trend toward representative government seemed unstoppable, the Meiji oligarchs concluded that their best course of action was to quickly adopt an acceptably conservative version of a modern constitution rather than be outrun by the pace of liberal expectations from outside the government. In 1881, a list of minimally acceptable conditions was drawn up, which included the stipulations that the new constitution be conferred from above as a gift from the emperor and that if the elected assembly refused to pass a proposed budget, the last year's budget would take effect automatically (thereby, if not denying, at least limiting, the power of the purse to the elected legislature).

In 1882, the oligarch Itō Hirobumi (1841–1909) went to Europe to study various modern constitutional models directly (see Figure 7.7). Although Itō did stop in Britain, and an associate went to France, Itō spent seven months in Germany, and the Meiji oligarchs appear to have, from the beginning, favored the German model. This was the newly unified imperial Germany of the kaiser and the Iron Chancellor, Prince Otto von Bismarck (1815–1898), which, although it made significant concessions to representative self-government, also retained firm central imperial control. Returning to Japan, Itō Hirobumi was then placed in charge of drafting the new Meiji constitution.

As a further countermeasure against suspiciously liberal Anglo-American democratic ideas, German influences were now combined with ancient East Asian tradition in the formation of a new Japanese peerage in 1884, which was designed to fill a hereditary Upper House that would balance the popularly elected lower chamber of the future legislature. The legal framework was German, but most of the

Figure 7.7. Itō Hirobumi (1841–1909), the first prime minister of Japan. National Diet Library Web site.

members of this newly created nobility were former Tokugawa *daimyō* or old court nobles, and the titles for this new aristocracy were actually drawn from the ancient Zhou Dynasty Chinese classics.[43] A cabinet, or modern Western-style executive branch, was established in 1885 (before the election of the first legislature), with the idea that it might function as a "transcendent" cabinet, answerable only to the emperor rather than to the legislature. Itō Hirobumi became Japan's first prime minister.

Meanwhile, under tight secrecy, and in consultation with a German legal advisor on the faculty of Tōkyō Imperial University, Itō and his assistants produced a draft constitution. On February 11, 1889, this new Meiji constitution was formally promulgated. On the German model, it was a gift from the emperor to the people, with the emperor remaining "above the clouds." In addition, the army and navy ministers were answerable to the emperor alone and independent of civilian control. The awesome potency of the imperial symbol was, furthermore, deliberately renewed and strengthened. In 1888, an engraving of the Meiji emperor was distributed to all public schools and official buildings, making the emperor's image a ubiquitous presence throughout the new Japanese nation. In 1890, an "Imperial Rescript on

Education" was issued, urging students that "should any emergency arise, offer yourselves courageously to the state; and thus guard and maintain the prosperity of our Imperial throne, coeval with heaven and earth."[44] Japanese schoolchildren were obliged to bow to the imperial portrait and hear the "Rescript on Education" recited regularly. Once again, this was a blending of allegedly ancient Japanese traditions with the forms of modern, Western-style nation building.

The first election for the Lower House of the new national legislature (called the Diet) was held in 1890. Since the franchise was limited to relatively wealthy taxpayers, only a little over 1 percent of the population were actually eligible to vote, and the government continued in practice to be largely directed by the same handful of Meiji oligarchs, in the name of the emperor. Still, Japan had become the first nation east of Suez to have a modern, Western-style constitution and an elected legislature. This was a conservative constitutional order that would soon be put to the service of expansive imperialism, but it was nonetheless an unmistakable emblem of modernity. In addition, Japan was also on its way to becoming the first non-Western society in the world to successfully industrialize.

Industrialization

One of the major reasons for nineteenth-century Japanese modernizing success was the sharp clarity with which the Meiji oligarchs perceived the strategic urgency of the situation and moved swiftly to implement necessary, even if sometimes painful, measures to achieve their overarching goals of national security. Though their most pressing concern was to duplicate modern Western military power, there was also a quick recognition that the secret underlying modern military power was modern economic productivity. The Meiji government managed to put its new national economy on a sound footing, in part by keeping foreign debt minimal and by eliminating the payment of samurai stipends. In 1871–1872, a new standardized currency system, based on the yen, was established, and a modern banking system modeled on the U.S. Federal Reserve was implemented. In 1882, a central Bank of Japan was established.

Initially, some Japanese leaders were under the impression that trade and commerce alone were the source of modern national wealth, but by the 1870s, the Meiji oligarchs had realized that mechanized industrialization was the magic key that unlocked the secrets to exponential increases in productivity. The Meiji elite therefore determined that rapid industrialization would be necessary, not only for strategic military considerations but also to prevent Japan from slipping into poverty and becoming a mere supplier of raw materials for industrialized foreign countries. Early attempts to stimulate private investment in modern industry were not particularly successful, however, in part because of the aversion to risky new business ventures by conservative old merchant houses, and in part because the amount of capital necessary for industrialization was simply too large. The Meiji government was furthermore unable to protect domestic industrial development by placing a wall of high taxes on competing foreign imports because import taxes had been fixed at low rates by treaty. The Meiji government resolved to

Figure 7.8. The model industrial silk-reeling factory that was built in 1872 in Tomioka, Gunma Prefecture, Japan (woodblock print). Snark/Art Resource, New York.

compensate, therefore, by itself deliberately promoting domestic industrialization. The Tomioka silk-reeling factory, for example, was built by the government in 1872, both to provide employment and to encourage private mechanization by demonstrating how (see Figure 7.8). The first modern industries in Japan were mostly built and administered by the government itself.[45]

A substantial focus of this government-led industrialization, moreover, was strategic and military. The modern arms industry was initially owned and operated by the government, and though private light textile manufacturing soon prospered and became more important in foreign trade, generating much critically needed foreign exchange, even some of the technology used in private textile production derived from spinoffs of military applications. In the 1880s, for example, an absolute majority of private cotton textile mills in Japan were powered by steam engines made by a government arsenal. "Virtually every major firm in Japan benefited from the Meiji military industrial program . . . including Toshiba and Nikon, which were created directly by and for the Meiji military."[46]

On the other hand, however, Japan's success in industrialization also owed much to the skills, attitudes, and commercial practices that had already developed indigenously in late Tokugawa times, and the actual takeoff of the industrial economy was led by small-scale private textile manufacturing.[47] And if government initiative was critical for technological borrowing and the early development of large-scale (and initially often unprofitable) heavy industry, the government's resources themselves were also far from infinite. Because taxes on imports were fixed at relatively low rates by treaty, and the Meiji oligarchs were deeply concerned to avoid incurring any debilitating foreign debt, the principal source of government funding was the land tax, which, in the 1870s, contributed some 90 percent of all government revenue.

The serious economic constraints facing the Meiji government led to a program of enforced austerity in the 1880s, which imposed much hardship but also may have strengthened the overall economy. By the mid-1880s, the government was financially solvent. Also in the 1880s, the government deliberately began to transfer its infant industrial plant into private hands. The government-built silk mill at Tomioka, for example, was sold to the private firm Mitsui in 1893.

Since the early Meiji "government could not afford the luxury of a gestation period during which the shipping industry might build a 'model' organization" naturally by itself, after several failed experiments, the government moved toward a policy of official support for a single favored private firm. In the shipping industry, that favored firm was Mitsubishi. Mitsubishi had begun under another name in 1866 as an industrial promotion agency belonging to the domain of Tosa, but it was subsequently reorganized into a private firm and, in 1873, renamed Mitsubishi. After Mitsubishi successfully provided military transport during the government's punitive expedition against the aborigines in Taiwan in 1874, the government gave thirteen large steamships to Mitsubishi and began providing it with an annual government subsidy. Among other things, "the financial reports made necessary by the subsidy led to Mitsubishi's rapid adoption of Western accounting techniques." Mitsubishi developed and prospered, with government backing, to meet the Meiji government's strategic needs in providing transport in war and also in competing with the West, which was perceived as an urgent national concern due to the fact that Western shipping long continued to dominate Japan's foreign trade.[48]

Mitsubishi became one of the distinctively Japanese conglomerates called *zaibatsu*, which dominated the modern sector of the Japanese economy in the years between the Meiji Restoration and World War II. The word *zaibatsu* might loosely be translated as "wealth lord," in an expression parallel to *gunbatsu*, or "warlord." There were perhaps a score of *zaibatsu* in pre–World War II Japan, but by every reckoning, there were four particularly great *zaibatsu*: Mitsubishi, Sumitomo, Yasuda, and Mitsui. Although Mitsui dated from early Tokugawa times, the *zaibatsu* as a whole were a significantly new kind of business enterprise. In part, they merely reflected a general trend toward larger businesses in the industrialized world of the later nineteenth century. Mergers, monopolies, trusts, syndicates, and cartels seemed to be the order of the day: in 1880, for example, Standard Oil controlled some 90 percent of all U.S. oil refining. The Japanese *zaibatsu*, however, rarely monopolized a given market sector, but instead duplicated and competed with each other through extensive diversification into a wide range of endeavors, typically including manufacturing, banking, and trade.

Japan became the first non-Western society to successfully industrialize, but the takeoff of Japan's modern economy was far from instantaneous. In the 1880s, Japan's foreign trade was still only about a quarter of the volume of China's, and much of Japan's foreign trade was still controlled by Western merchants. As late as 1900, an approximately equal percentage of China's population (to say nothing of absolute numbers) was employed in industry as in Japan.[49] Traditional-style enterprises continued to produce most of the commodities for the Japanese domestic market. As late as 1898, 82 percent of the Japanese population was still rural, and Japan remained a largely poor country. Despite the Meiji Restoration, for most people, lifestyles did not change all that dramatically in the second half of the nineteenth century. The rickshaw, a two-wheeled vehicle pulled by human muscle power, far from being an ancient East Asian tradition, was actually not invented until after the Meiji Restoration in Japan, and the emperor did not enjoy his first ride in a horse-drawn carriage until 1871. (Roads had been poorly developed in premodern Japan, and wheeled vehicles were rare.) The first short railway line, linking Tōkyō to nearby Yokohama, did not commence operations until 1872. Electric light service in Tōkyō only began in 1887.[50]

Yet Japan was already becoming militarily strong. By 1880, Japan was producing its first modern rifle of its own design. In 1899, a renegotiated treaty with Great Britain took effect, ending many of the more objectionable features of the treaty port system that had been in effect since the 1850s (although Japan did not regain the right to set its own taxes on imports until 1911). In 1895, Japan defeated China in war. In 1902, Japan officially became a British ally, and in 1905, Japan defeated a recognized modern great power, Russia, in war. By this time, Japan had convincingly demonstrated its claim to the status of a being modern world power.

For Further Reading

On comparative industrialization and economic development in China and Europe, see Lloyd E. Eastman, *Family, Fields, and Ancestors: Constancy and Change in China's Social and Economic History, 1550–1949* (New York: Oxford University Press, 1988), esp. chaps. 6–8; Andre Gunder Frank, *ReOrient: Global Economy in the Asian Age* (Berkeley: University of California Press, 1998); Robert B. Marks, *The Origins of the Modern World: A Global and Ecological Narrative from the Fifteenth to the Twenty-first Century*, 2nd ed. (Lanham, MD: Rowman and Littlefield, 2007); and Kenneth Pomeranz, *The Great Divergence: China, Europe, and the Making of the Modern World Economy* (Princeton University Press, 2000).

On the Opium Wars, see Peter Ward Fay, *The Opium War, 1840–1842: Barbarians in the Celestial Empire in the Early Part of the Nineteenth Century and the War by Which They Forced Her Gates Ajar* (New York: W. W. Norton, 1975), and Harry G. Gelber, *Opium, Soldiers, and Evangelicals: England's 1840–42 War with China, and Its Aftermath* (New York: Palgrave Macmillan, 2004).

For the Taiping and other nineteenth-century Chinese domestic rebellions, see Albert Feuerwerker, *Rebellion in Nineteenth-century China* (Ann Arbor: Center for Chinese Studies, University of Michigan, 1975); Philip A. Kuhn, *Rebellion and Its Enemies in Late Imperial China: Militarization and Social Structure, 1796–1864* (Cambridge, MA: Harvard University Press, 1970); Franz Michael, in collaboration with Chung-li Chang, *The Taiping Rebellion: History and Documents*, 3 vols. (Seattle: University of Washington Press, [1966] 1972); Elizabeth J. Perry, *Rebels and Revolutionaries in North China, 1845–1945* (Stanford University Press, 1980); and Jonathan D. Spence, *God's Chinese Son: The Taiping Heavenly Kingdom of Hong Xiuquan* (New York: W. W. Norton, 1996).

A classic study of the Tongzhi Restoration is Mary Clabaugh Wright, *The Last Stand of Chinese Conservatism: The T'ung-Chih Restoration, 1862–1874* (Stanford University Press, 1957).

The treaty ports and Sino-Western contact are dealt with in John King Fairbank, *Trade and Diplomacy on the China Coast: The Opening of the Treaty Ports, 1842–1854* (1953; Stanford University Press, [1953] 1969); Michael Greenberg, *British Trade and the Opening of China, 1800–42* (Cambridge University Press, 1951); and Rhoads Murphey, *The Outsiders: The Western Experience in India and China* (Ann Arbor: University of Michigan Press, 1977). On the final phase of the mature treaty port system in Shanghai, see Nicholas R. Clifford, *Spoilt Children of Empire: Westerners in Shanghai and the Chinese Revolution of the 1920s* (Hanover, NH: Middlebury College Press, 1991).

Concerning the Boxer Rebellion, see Paul A. Cohen, *History in Three Keys: The Boxers as Event, Experience, and Myth* (New York: Columbia University Press, 1997), and Joseph W. Esherick, *The Origins of the Boxer Uprising* (Berkeley: University of California Press, 1987).

The end of the traditional order in Korea is described in Martina Deuchler, *Confucian Gentlemen and Barbarian Envoys: The Opening of Korea, 1875–1885* (Seattle: University of Washington Press, 1977); Peter Duus, *The Abacus and the Sword: The Japanese Penetration of Korea, 1895–1910* (Berkeley: University of California Press, 1995); and Key-Hiuk Kim, *The Last Phase of the East Asian World Order: Korea, Japan, and the Chinese Empire, 1860–1882* (Berkeley: University of California Press, 1980).

Indispensable sources for the Meiji Restoration in Japan include Marius B. Jansen, *The Making of Modern Japan* (Cambridge, MA: Harvard University Press, 2000), and Marius B. Jansen, *Sakamoto Ryōma and the Meiji Restoration* (New York: Columbia University Press, [1961] 1994). A detailed narrative of events preceding the Meiji Restoration is provided by Conrad D. Totman, *The Collapse of the Tokugawa Bakufu, 1862–1868* (Honolulu: University of Hawai'i Press, 1980). The doomed samurai rebellion of Saigō Takamori is narrated in chapter 9 of Ivan I. Morris, *The Nobility of Failure: Tragic Heroes in the History of Japan* (New York: Holt, Rinehart, and Winston, 1975). For a study of one important Meiji oligarch, see Roger F. Hackett, *Yamagata Aritomo in the Rise of Modern Japan, 1838–1922* (Cambridge, MA: Harvard University Press, 1971).

The changing self-image of the Japanese nation in this period is skillfully surveyed by Carol Gluck, *Japan's Modern Myths: Ideology in the Late Meiji Period* (Princeton University Press, 1985). Changing Chinese perceptions of Japan during the 1870s–1880s, as East Asia's premodern cultural community was seriously shaken by rapid Japanese modernization, are examined in D. R. Howland, *Borders of Chinese Civilization: Geography and History at Empire's End* (Durham, NC: Duke University Press, 1996).

For Meiji Japan's precocious economic modernization, see Johannes Hirschmeier, *The Origins of Entrepreneurship in Meiji Japan* (Cambridge, MA: Harvard University Press, 1964);

Byron K. Marshall, *Capitalism and Nationalism in Prewar Japan: The Ideology of the Business Elite, 1868–1941* (Stanford University Press, 1967); Thomas C. Smith, *Political Change and Industrial Development in Japan: Government Enterprise, 1868–1880* (Stanford University Press, 1955); and Kozo Yamamura, ed., *The Economic Emergence of Modern Japan* (Cambridge University Press, 1997). Mikiso Hane provides a rare glimpse into the impact of modernization on the lives of ordinary Japanese in *Peasants, Rebels, and Outcastes: The Underside of Modern Japan* (New York: Pantheon Books, 1982).

8 The Age of Westernization (1900–1929)

Empire's End: Republican Revolution in China

Defeat at the hands of Japan in the Sino-Japanese War of 1895 irrevocably shattered China's traditional sense of self-assurance, and what remained of the premodern Chinese world order was rapidly undermined thereafter. In 1891 and 1897, the reformer Kang Youwei (1858–1927) published two controversial (and repeatedly banned) books that argued that the existing texts of the Confucian Classics had been distorted by forgeries dating from the first century and that Confucius, far from being a conservative transmitter of ancient traditions, had actually been a reformer in his own day.[1] Despite this attempt to rejuvenate the Sage Confucius in the modernizing guise of a reformer, such scholarship already betrayed a profound loss of faith in tradition.

In 1898, one important official, while apparently arguing conservatively for maintaining "Chinese learning for the fundamental principles," simultaneously also acknowledged that in a time of "drastic transformation," substantial modernizing reforms were appropriate. After 1898, even this relatively moderate approach tended to be abandoned in favor of more radical modernization.[2] The Japanese victory in 1895 had sounded an alarm, and following the Boxer disaster in 1900, even the Qing government recognized the need for rapid reform. China had been exposed as vulnerable – a once mighty empire apparently reduced to being the "sick man of Asia" – and in need of some fairly dramatic measures to pull itself out of the past and adjust to modern world realities (see Figure 8.1). *New (xin)* suddenly became a highly fashionable buzzword in early-twentieth-century China, beginning with the Qing Dynasty's "new policies" and "new schools" in the first decade and reaching its climax with the "new culture" of the May Fourth Movement in the second decade of the century – epitomized by the title of its most famous journal, *New Youth*.[3]

In 1902, the Empress Dowager Cixi authorized an edict ordering the abolition of foot binding (a painful and disabling custom that had been widespread among Chinese women since about the Song Dynasty). Although foot binding

Figure 8.1. The last days of the Chinese Empire. A lone rider at the Ming tombs in north China, 1907. Library of Congress, LC-USZ62-56190.

took decades to thoroughly eradicate everywhere, the abolition of the traditional examination system in 1905 was immediately effective and dealt a fatal blow to the old examination-selected Mandarin elite. Also in 1905, a group of imperial commissioners traveled for eight months in Japan, the United States, and Europe to study models of modern constitutional government. After their return, a nine-year program of constitutional reform was announced in 1908 that included the installation of elected provincial representative assemblies by 1909 and a promise of gradual transition to "self-government."

Yet even these dramatic reforms were no longer enough. The "new schools" were often simply converted temples or former Confucian academies that remained far from universally accessible and that were not necessarily really very different from their premodern predecessors. The electorate for the 1909 provincial elections was no more than half of 1 percent of the population.[4] The Meiji Japanese and imperial German model that was favored for the Qing Dynasty reforms, with its assertive role for centralized authoritarian imperial government, also disappointed would-be local leaders as well as reformers who held more liberal Anglo-American-style aspirations. In addition, breaking with long-standing Qing Dynasty precedent, princes from the imperial family began to play a more active role in government, and the number of ethnic Manchus in high office actually increased. For example, although the Manchu Banner People were only a little over 1 percent of China's population, they held eight of thirteen heads of ministries in 1906 and five of nine governor-general positions in 1907.[5]

This was particularly unfortunate because it coincided with the introduction of modern Western ideas of national self-determination. After some two centuries of widespread acceptance of Manchu rule under the Qing Dynasty, at the turn of the twentieth century, many Chinese people suddenly awoke to the idea that they were the conquered subjects of "foreign" Manchus. Ending Manchu rule became the first priority of the new Chinese nationalism.

Something like the nation, of course, is an ancient phenomenon. But premodern states, in China and elsewhere, were often defined more by their ruling elites than by their peoples. It has been argued that true modern nationalism had its origins in sixteenth-century England, when the people first began to be conceived as the ultimate source of legitimate sovereignty. As the spread of print technology promoted increasingly standardized national languages (High German and Parisian French, for example, gaining prestige over local dialects as national standards), a new sense of participation in a shared national community began to take shape among the reading public.[6]

The first East Asian invocation of this originally European concept of "nation" apparently came during the Meiji era Japanese popular rights movement, when a new two-character Japanese expression *minzoku* (meaning, roughly, the "people clan") was coined to translate the *nationale* in French expressions such as *Assemblée Nationale* – in this case, obviously, still referring to popular sovereignty. By the end of the nineteenth century, however, this Japanese word was coming to be used more commonly in approximation of the German word *Volk*, indicating a community with supposedly shared linguistic, cultural, historical, and other ties.[7] Nations in that sense, as peoples possessing allegedly distinctive characteristics, and ideally independently self-governing, came to be widely viewed as the natural divisions of humanity in nineteenth-century Europe, and Germany itself became a classic example of modern nation-state building, as the Prussian Kingdom expanded between 1866 and 1871 to forge the first-ever unified Germany.

Like many other modern Japanese translations of European terms, this new word for "nation" soon made its way to China, where the same two-character combination (pronounced "minzu" in Chinese) could be imported and easily understood directly in written form.[8] Both in the political sense of popular sovereignty and in the communal sense of *Volk*, this new idea of nationalism demanded an end in China to hereditary rule by non-Chinese Manchu emperors. Because such nationalism was originally a Western idea, in China as elsewhere, the earliest nationalists tended to emerge from the ranks of persons who were deeply exposed to modern Western thought. In China's case, appropriately, the first great nationalist revolutionary was also one of the most thoroughly Westernized major figures in all of Chinese history: Dr. Sun Yat-sen (1866–1925).

Sun Yat-sen (see Figure 8.2) was a Cantonese peasant by birth – born, that is, far from the traditional centers of Chinese culture and power and speaking

Figure 8.2. Dr. and Mrs. Sun Yat-sen. Photograph signed and dated by Mrs. Sun, Canton, January 14, 1926. Hoover Institution Archives. Paul Myron Wentworth Linebarger papers.

an unintelligible local southern dialect – but in 1879, he was sent to join an older brother in Hawai'i. In Hawai'i, Sun was placed in a boarding school, where the language of instruction was English. Sun became fluent in English, and he also became a Christian. He completed his formal education in Hong Kong with training in Western-style medicine. Altogether, Sun spent some thirteen years as a student or protégé of Western Protestant missionaries, and until age forty-six, he lived most of his life outside China.[9] Inspired by his intimate knowledge of the modern West, Sun hoped to create a Western-style nation-state and republic in China, sometimes specifically taking the United States as his model.

The 1911 Revolution

Sun Yat-sen organized his first revolutionary group in Hawai'i in 1894. In 1895, he attempted his first armed revolutionary uprising, in Guangzhou. This came immediately after the Qing defeat in the Sino-Japanese War, which might have presented a timely opportunity to overthrow the Qing, but the uprising was delayed for two days because its preparations were incomplete, and during the interval, the police discovered the plot. Forty-eight conspirators were arrested, and 205 revolvers were confiscated. Sun Yat-sen escaped to British Hong Kong and then traveled on to Japan. From this time until the final success of the Republican Revolution in 1911, Sun spent a total of only one night in China.

Sun Yat-sen spent much of his time abroad in Japan, where he acquired the alias by which he is still most commonly known to Chinese-language speakers: (Sun) Zhongshan, the Mandarin Chinese pronunciation of the Japanese surname Nakayama. But Sun also spent some time in French colonial Vietnam, and he was particularly active with fund-raising in the United States and Britain. In a famous episode in 1896, Sun was kidnapped and held prisoner in the Qing legation in London. Fortunately for Sun, he was able to smuggle a message out to a British friend, who raised a clamor in the English press that forced his release. This incident catapulted Sun to a certain degree of international notoriety, but most Chinese people were probably still largely unaware of Sun and his revolutionary movement as late as the beginning of the twentieth century. However, in Tōkyō, Japan, in 1905, a loose coalition of Chinese revolutionary groups was formed called the Revolutionary Alliance (*Tongmenghui*), with Sun Yat-sen as a central figure.

Over the next few years, this Revolutionary Alliance sponsored several armed uprisings in China, all of which failed dismally. As the litany of defeats lengthened, the revolutionaries turned with growing fascination to the tactics of terrorism, including bombings and assassinations. On October 9, 1911, as some revolutionaries were making bombs in the headquarters of a group called the Forward Together Society, located in the Russian concession in the cluster of three mid-Yangzi River cities collectively known as Wuhan, some ashes from a cigarette they were smoking fell and accidentally detonated one of those bombs. The police came and uncovered a list of members in the rubble and immediately arrested dozens. Three revolutionaries were executed early the very next day, October 10, which precipitated an unplanned mutiny in the local New Army garrison. The mutinous troops seized control of the arsenal, the Manchu governor-general fled, and on October 11, the president of the local provincial assembly met with the rebels and declared his support. This was the beginning of the Republican, or Nationalist, Revolution in China.

Ironically enough, the modern Western-style New Armies that had been created by the Qing to save the dynasty instead provided the military force that overthrew it. The first four provinces that rebelled were all led by New Army uprisings, and New Army support was also critical in most of the other provinces that joined the revolution later.[10] Before long, fifteen provinces, mostly concentrated in the south, had declared independence from the Qing. Although there was some locally fierce combat, within about a month the fighting had reached a stalemate, and negotiations began in Shanghai. Dr. Sun Yat-sen, meanwhile, was in Colorado at the time this unplanned revolution erupted and read about it in the news while traveling by train from Denver to Kansas City. Sun eventually made his way from the United States back to China, where he was appointed provisional president of the new republic. He held that title for only forty-five days, however, because Sun soon joined in offering the presidency to another man: Yuan Shikai (1859–1916).

Yuan Shikai had been a crucial player in the formation of the main modern army in north China, and his ability to control that armed force now made him a pivotal figure. Initially, he was recruited by the imperial court in Beijing to try to rescue the Qing Dynasty, but the republican revolutionaries made him a tempting counteroffer. After some negotiations, Yuan switched sides, and on February 12, 1912 – just four months after the revolution had begun – the last emperor of China abdicated the throne. The five-year-old ex-emperor was given favorable treatment, including a generous government subsidy and permission to continue living in the old imperial palace. Yuan Shikai then became the first official president of the new Republic of China. And three days after the abdication of the last emperor, Sun Yat-sen visited the tomb of the founder of the last ethnically Chinese dynasty (the Ming) to announce the restoration of Chinese rule after three centuries of subjugation under the "alien" Manchus.

The May Fourth Movement: Science and Democracy

It was not merely Manchu rule that abruptly came to an end with the revolution in 1912: an imperial system that had lasted for more than two thousand years also ended forever. With it, in important senses, also died traditional China. Even the classical Chinese written language was now fairly rapidly replaced by a modern vernacular (roughly comparable to switching from Latin to Italian). By 1921, the Ministry of Education required all primary school textbooks to be written in the vernacular. Building a modern Chinese nation-state meant, paradoxically, a rejection of much Chinese tradition. Sun Yat-sen, for example, insisted on switching immediately to the Western solar calendar as "the first important reform of our successful revolution."[11] Most Chinese men immediately cut their Manchu-imposed queues in 1912, and rather than revert to older pre-Manchu Chinese hairstyles, modern Western-influenced hairstyles and clothing were widely adopted.

Contrary to the popular stereotype of a closed and isolationistic and deeply traditional China, China had long been heavily involved in world trade, and in the late nineteenth century, many Chinese people were already surprisingly receptive to new things. Those who could afford it, especially in the big coastal cities, took fairly quickly to new technologies such as electric fans and photography, and even many of the humblest rural peasants also welcomed modern kerosene lamps, machine-manufactured enamel wash basins, and mass-produced inexpensive mirrors – although these modern mirrors might then be placed outside doorways to frighten away "traditional" evil spirits. By 1935, half of all Chinese villagers regularly used imported foreign kerosene. China's continuingly disappointing low volume of manufactured imports from the West was due less to a stubborn refusal to accept new products than to the speed with which locally made substitutes began to compete with foreign goods. Especially after the suppression of the Boxer Rebellion, by 1901, even in a city deep in the interior, such as Changsha, foreign kerosene, clocks, tinned vegetables and fruit from America, and European beer were easily available. The first motion picture to be shown in China was in 1897. The empress dowager received an automobile, a Benz, in 1902 (although she apparently never rode in it), and the first privately Chinese-owned automobile may have been in 1909. In 1911, China acquired its first two airplanes. Typically, one American journalist was disappointed on arrival in 1925 to find that his first glimpse of China was a billboard advertising chewing gum.[12]

For many, the revolution of 1911 brought a sweeping repudiation of the entire old order. The most famous statement of this almost complete reversal of attitudes may be a passage in an experimental short story – one of the first to be published in the new vernacular – called "A Madman's Diary," written in 1918 by modern China's most admired man of letters, Lu Xun (1881–1936). The main character in this story begins reading China's histories, only to find that "my history has no chronology, and scrawled all over each page are the words: 'Virtue and Morality' [i.e., traditional Confucian values]. Since I could not sleep anyway, I read intently half the night, until I began to see words between the lines, the whole book being filled with the two words – 'Eat people.'"[13] That is, unlike the dynamic modern West, China's premodern history had no progress, and all the lofty rhetoric about Confucian virtue merely concealed the hidden reality of cannibalism and exploitation.

What suddenly now appeared to be the "bad customs" of old China were denounced, including such things as foot binding, opium addiction, arranged marriages, the sale of female bondservants, uncleanliness, spitting in public, and "superstition." Superstition (*mixin*, another new word in China) referred to traditional Chinese religions, which many in the educated Chinese elite, whether they were Christian or not, now felt were embarrassing signs of backwardness. Of roughly a million temples in China at the start of the twentieth century, more than half had been closed down by the 1930s.[14] Confucianism itself, moreover, now seemed to be the biggest obstacle to modernization of all. The idea of progress rendered antiquity obsolete, and tradition now seemed sweepingly discredited because it had left China so obviously weak and impoverished. As a result of the Industrial Revolution, by 1913, Europe and the United States together accounted for 88.6 percent of world manufacturing, while China's share had been reduced to only 3.6 percent.[15] The proven wealth and power of the West made Westernization attractive, especially to the young, urban, and educated. Although "the West" is something of an elastic, value-laden concept rather than a concrete, permanent, clearly defined reality, as an idea, it has sometimes been undeniably powerful.

There was a fair amount of conscious Westernization, but even this still had to be on Chinese terms, suiting Chinese tastes (and, for patriots, to be in the service of the Chinese nation). The result was a complicated pattern of hybridization: an often bewildering mix of old and new, Chinese and Western (see Figure 8.3). When the British-American Tobacco Company, for example, transplanted modern American commercial advertisements directly to China in 1902, the Chinese reaction was bewilderment. But when the same company installed advanced printing presses in Shanghai in 1905 and began producing modern advertising designed by Chinese

Figure 8.3. Beijing, ca. 1925, looking toward the Qianmen (gate). Library of Congress, LC-USZ62-137036.

people, and tailored to Chinese sensibilities, this modified advertising campaign soon penetrated every corner of China with remarkable success.[16]

Although genuinely traditional clothing and hairstyles were largely abandoned after 1912, in the 1920s, a major new fashion for Chinese men became the Sun Yat-sen suit (an early form of what later came to be known as the Mao suit). This was adapted from modern student uniforms and represented neither tradition nor a slavish imitation of the West but a distinctly Chinese version of modernity. Although the Western solar calendar was widely accepted, and also the foreign idea of a seven-day week with a regular day of rest on Sunday, the old lunar calendar simultaneously continued to be used for the celebration of holidays such as the New Year.[17] Significantly, under the Republic, dates were (really, in widespread actual practice) calculated not from the birth of Christ but taking the foundation of the Republic of China in 1912 as the year 1.

Also significantly, China's greatest burst of popular enthusiasm for sweeping Westernization takes its name from what began as anti-Western (though most especially anti-Japanese) student protests: the May Fourth Movement. China had participated on the Allied side in World War I, and perhaps as many as two hundred thousand Chinese people had labored abroad as China's contribution to the Allied war effort. Because China had therefore been on the winning side, and especially in view of the American president Woodrow Wilson's stirring evocations of the ideal of national self-determination, Chinese students felt encouraged to hope that former German concessions in China would revert to Chinese rule after the war. Instead, the German base in Shandong was granted to Japan at the Versailles peace conference in 1919. When the news reached Beijing on May 4, 1919, many students felt betrayed, and several thousand gathered at Tiananmen (the old Gate of Heavenly Peace, not the Square, which did not yet exist) to stage protests.

The May Fourth Movement that began with these patriotic student demonstrations in 1919 then gave its name, more broadly, to an entire age of enthusiasm for New Culture. For the "new youth" of the May Fourth generation, "science and democracy" became the most revered mantra. Some young people even hoped for total Westernization. It was a time of youthful excitement and the discovery of new ideas. The American educator John Dewey lectured to eager audiences in China in 1919–1921. The renowned British philosopher Bertrand Russell was invited to Peking University in 1920. Hundreds of new magazines and periodicals began to be published. A modernizing attack on the entire patriarchal Confucian values system was unleashed in the name freedom and equality, and the 1910s–1920s became the great age of Chinese individualism, feminism, and other modern Western ideals.

At the start of the twentieth century, modernizers throughout East Asia had often looked to Japan as a successful model. Japan had, after all, shaken off the treaty port system and defeated Russia in war by 1905. By 1914, Japan was one of only five countries in the entire world that were self-sufficient in railway locomotive production (a key index of early industrialization), together with Britain, France, Germany, and the United States.[18] For this, as well as reasons of convenience, the largest number of Chinese students studying abroad in the early twentieth century went to Japan – by 1906, about thirteen thousand. A truly impressive number of important early Chinese revolutionaries spent time in Japan, including both Sun Yat-sen and the future president of the Republic of China Chiang Kai-shek (in Mandarin, Jiang Jieshi, 1887–1975), who trained at a Japanese military academy in 1908–1911.

By World War I, however, Japan was already beginning to be viewed with suspicion as an imperialist aggressor by many Chinese people, and Japan had always served chiefly, anyway, only as a convenient filter through which modern Western ideas could be communicated. It was "the West" that fired the youthful May Fourth imagination. In particular, "the political thought of the French Revolution had an almost unrivaled vogue among young Chinese revolutionaries and reformers." Chen Duxiu (1879–1942), for example, who may have been in France

Figure 8.4. Deng Xiaoping as a sixteen-year-old student, during his study in France, 1920. New China Pictures. Magnum Photos.

between 1907 and 1910, used French rather than English for the Western-language alternate title of the extremely influential journal he founded, *La Jeunesse Nouvelle* (*New Youth*, or *Xin Qingnian* in Chinese), and for its first issue, he also wrote an article on "The French and Modern Civilization."[19] Chen Duxiu would later become the first leader of the Chinese Communist Party, when it was founded in 1921.

A surprising number of early leaders of the Chinese communist movement went to France, many in connection with a work-study program developed during World War I. The list includes Zhou Enlai (1898–1976), who became a Communist Party member while in France in 1920–1922, and who later served as premier of the People's Republic and was Mao Zedong's single most distinguished associate. Deng Xiaoping (1904–1997), who succeeded Mao as leader of the People's Republic in 1978, was in France from 1920 to 1926 (see Figure 8.4), where he also joined the

Communist Party. Li Lisan (1899–1967), who was the Comintern's (an abbreviation for Communist International, headquartered in Moscow) pick to head the Chinese Communist Party in a time of crisis after 1927, before Mao Zedong's rise to power, was in France between 1919 and 1921. Mao's close friend (before his execution in 1931) Cai Hesen (1895–1931) also was in France in 1919–1921. Chen Yi (1901–1972), a future foreign minister, was in France from 1919 to 1921. In fact, during the first decade after the establishment of the communist People's Republic of China in 1949, nearly a quarter of the top leadership had been in France during this formative moment at the end of World War I.[20]

One exception was Zhu De (1886–1976), who joined the Communist Party in Germany rather than France in 1922. Zhu was the first commander of the Chinese Red Army and was the military genius probably most responsible for developing its successful tactics of guerilla warfare.[21] In fact, among the top early Chinese revolutionaries (both Communist and Nationalist), it may have been Mao Zedong (1893–1976) who was most conspicuous for his lack of cosmopolitan experience. Mao never became proficient in any foreign language, and he never traveled outside China until after he had become head of state, when he finally made a trip to Moscow in 1949. Since Mao eventually rose to become the supreme figure in China's communist revolution, his lack of international experience is telling. Yet even Mao was a graduate of a modern-style provincial teacher's college, read widely in Western books in Chinese translation, and happened to be in Beijing at the height of the May Fourth Movement. By 1920, Mao was calling himself a Marxist.[22]

English-speaking readers may find it incredible that one of the principal outcomes of the first great wave of Westernization in China was the rise of communism. The enthusiasm with which some educated young Chinese embraced Westernization was fired, however, by a confidence that it represented a potentially universal pattern of progress rather than something exclusively European. Nowhere was this universalism articulated more explicitly (or more rigidly) than in the theoretical Marxist sequence of stages, or "modes of production," through which all societies supposedly advanced. Of particular relevance, these included a universal transition from feudalism to capitalism, and then from capitalism to communism in the supposedly inevitable future. Communism was modern, Western (Karl Marx, after all, was a German who did much of his work in England), and ostensibly scientific, and Marxism-Leninism also offered a scathing critique of great power imperialism that could be comforting to those who felt victimized, or at least humiliated, by it. And communist organization provided a tightly disciplined program of action that made it simply more effective than other, initially more appealing Western ideologies such as anarchism (which, by definition, was not well organized).

The Chinese Communists were committed to a goal of industrialized (though socialist) modernity, and this remained true even after Mao Zedong, for reasons of tactical necessity (and very awkwardly for Marxist theory), shifted the base of his revolution from urban industrial workers (the proletariat) to rural peasants. By the time of the final Communist victory in 1949, a large majority of party members were peasants, yet the party never endorsed a so-called peasant mentality. Peasants were regarded as perhaps the most backward segment of a generally backward and feudal old regime from which the revolution was supposed to liberate China, and under the Communist People's Republic, peasants even came to be treated, according to some observers, as second-class citizens.[23]

In any case, interest in communism in China was long confined to relatively narrow intellectual circles, and it was not until after the global descent into the "dark valley" of economic depression, fascism, and war during the 1930s and 1940s that communism threatened to gain control in China. Yet despite much genuine youthful Chinese interest in individualism, democracy, and other Western ideals during the May Fourth era, there was also an overriding sense of concern at China's palpable weakness and vulnerability and a patriotic desire to regenerate national strength. Nationalists as well as Communists tended to see the solution in terms of political centralization and national unity. The Nationalist revolutionary Sun Yat-sen's most famous lament was that the Chinese people were "like loose sand," and his conclusion was that what China needed was discipline more than freedom.[24] Such discipline and unity seemed especially crucial because, after the initial success of the Republican Revolution in 1912, China had dissolved into warlordism.

The Warlord Era, 1916–1928

In the early twentieth century, representative self-government seemed to be an irresistible trend that was sweeping the entire planet and an essential component of modernization. Following the success of the Republican Revolution in 1912, nationwide elections were scheduled almost immediately for a planned constitutional assembly. In this first Chinese experiment with democracy at the national level, some forty million men were eligible to vote – fully a fifth of the entire adult male population.[25] The elections went reasonably smoothly, and a newly organized, modern, Western-style political party known as the Nationalist Party (*Guomindang* in Chinese, alternatively spelled *Kuo-Min-Tang* and abbreviated either GMD or KMT) emerged as the clear winner. The first president of the Republic (Yuan Shikai), who had gained office through a deal rather than through the ballot box, was apparently alarmed by this Nationalist Party success, however, and is suspected of being implicated in the assassination of the party's dynamic young leader in 1913. President Yuan ordered the Nationalist Party dissolved later that same year, and in 1914, he dismissed the elected legislature.

In 1915, then, the president "allowed" himself to be declared emperor. He held the imperial title for only eighty-three days, however, because even some of his own officers took up arms against this attempt to revive the empire, and he was soon compelled to step down. In 1916, this first president died. Unfortunately, by that time, the constitutional process was also thoroughly bankrupt. Effective central government in China virtually ceased to exist for a dozen years after 1916. Purely for diplomatic convenience, foreign governments continued to address whichever warlord regime happened to control Beijing as if it were the government of China, but in practice, local authorities at various levels became independent. Chambers of commerce in some cities, for example, maintained their own armed forces, constructed railways, and sometimes even conducted negotiations with foreign governments.

Shanghai, the largest city in China, remained substantially under foreign administration. Because police in each of the three administrative jurisdictions (the International Settlement, the French Concession, and the Chinese city) had no authority in the other two, Shanghai was particularly ripe for the emergence of modern organized crime, especially after the re-prohibition of opium (which had been legalized in 1860) in 1919 provided opportunities for large illegal profits. Most notorious was the Green Gang, which came to be led by "Big-eared" Du Yue-sheng (1888–1951). Du had been born on the wrong side of the river in a Pudong slum and began life as a fruit vender's helper. After joining a gang as a teenager, he developed a new crime cartel to more efficiently distribute illegal profits, and he eventually even became prominent in legitimate public and charitable activities. Among his other titles, Du became deputy chairman of the Chinese Red Cross, chairman of the Shanghai Chinese Municipal Council, and director of the Shanghai Stock Exchange.[26] Du was perhaps the single best example of those colorfully sinister figures who gave pre–World War II Shanghai its rather shady reputation.

In the countryside, there was also widespread more traditional banditry. In a particularly notorious incident in 1923, bandits in Shandong derailed an express train and took twenty Westerners hostage, including a member of the wealthy American Rockefeller family. This drew international attention, and the incident was resolved by giving the bandits positions in the regular Chinese army, the bandit leader becoming a brigadier general. The line between bandits and soldiers was, in fact, often unclear, and few of China's armies were under effective central control.

As the Qing Dynasty had begun to modernize its military in the late nineteenth century, curiously, it did not attempt to forge a single, unified national army. In the aftermath of the revolution, the armed forces of the early republican era remained essentially separate provincial armies. With the collapse of clearly legitimate civilian central authority after 1916, military commanders stepped into the vacuum and became locally independent forces, or warlords.

Among these various military commanders, perhaps the most successful overall was the warlord of Manchuria, Zhang Zuolin (ca. 1875–1928). Zhang had begun his career as a bandit, and he gained control over Manchuria at the time of the 1911 Republican Revolution as a would-be Qing Dynasty imperial loyalist. After the fall of the Qing, he operated independently, and in 1922, he openly declared the independence of the three Manchurian provinces. Because Manchuria was, at this time, rapidly falling under Japanese domination, Zhang was obliged to coexist with rising Japanese power. By 1928, there may have been as many as fifty Japanese advisors attached to Zhang's Chinese army in Manchuria. But Zhang was also attended by a scattering of English, American, French, and White Russian advisors.[27] In his own way, moreover, Zhang was a Chinese patriot, and he may have even envisioned himself as the great reunifier who would rebuild China. In 1924, he gained control of Beijing and soon made it his headquarters. In 1928, he was assassinated by rogue Japanese army officers.

In the meantime, Sun Yat-sen had been driven back into exile in Japan by the authoritarian behavior of the first president. After President Yuan Shikai's death, in 1917 Sun returned to China and attempted to establish a regional base in Guangzhou. Sun was joined there by 130 members of the dissolved legislature and also the minister of the Navy, who resigned and brought with him fifteen warships. The warlord commanders of the surrounding countryside were intermittently hostile, however, and Sun's effort to revive the republic, and the Nationalist Party, remained fragile. Seeking foreign aid – a recurrent theme throughout Sun Yat-sen's career – Sun now found that the only available source was the Soviet Union.

The apparent success of the Russian October Revolution in 1917, the newly established Soviet Union's public stance of avowed opposition to imperialism, and the fact that China and the Soviet Union shared the longest land border in the world all naturally drew Chinese attention to the north. Although Sun Yat-sen did not embrace communism, in 1923, Sun did reach a formal agreement with the Soviet Union. For its part, Moscow agreed that China was not yet ready for communism and pledged to assist the cause of the Nationalist revolution, while Sun Yat-sen permitted individual members of the Chinese Communist Party (CCP) also to join the Nationalist Party. Young Mao Zedong, for example, served as director of the Nationalist Party Propaganda Bureau.

Because military reunification of a China torn between contending warlord armies now seemed necessary, it was decided to create a separate new Nationalist Party army. In 1924, a Nationalist military academy was established (known as Huangpu or Whampoa). Moscow provided the bulk of the funds, and this new military academy was unique in China at the time for its incorporation of political as well as military instruction. On the model of the Soviet commissar system, Nationalist Party representatives were appointed to the army.[28] The man who was to be the first commandant of this Nationalist military academy was then sent to Moscow for three months of training. His name was Chiang Kai-shek.

In 1925, Sun Yat-sen died and was soon succeeded as leader of the Nationalist Party by Chiang Kai-shek. Acting swiftly, in 1926, Chiang launched a Northern Expedition to reunify China militarily from the Nationalist base in the far south at Guangzhou. Although John Pratt, a brother of the famous Hollywood actor Boris Karloff, predicted in a lecture to the British Imperial Defense College in February 1928 that China still might not have an effective central government "perhaps for a generation or two," by late 1928, Chiang Kai-shek's Northern Expedition had in fact succeeded in reunifying most of China proper, up to about the line of the Great Wall.[29]

After being admitted into the Nationalist Party following the 1923 agreement to cooperate, Chinese Communists had quickly become active in labor and political organization. During the Northern Expedition, a General Labor Union under leftist direction actually gained control of the city of Shanghai before Chiang Kai-shek's troops arrived. Chiang was unhappy with this leftist orientation, however, and in April 1927, while the Northern Expedition was only about half completed, Chiang broke suddenly with the leftists, striking at communist and labor organizations. Perhaps as many as twenty-five thousand Chinese Communists were killed in the first few months after this purge, and Chiang Kai-shek now emerged as a staunchly anti-communist figure.

By the end of 1928, therefore, with the completion of the Northern Expedition, a reunified Republic of China had been restored, led by Chiang Kai-shek and a now firmly anti-communist Nationalist Party, from a new capital at Nanjing (Nanking). But in reality, most of China still remained beyond effective central government control, and the revived republic was also now reconfigured as a single-party state. Sun Yat-sen had originally anticipated a three-stage process, beginning with the military reunification of China, followed by a supposedly brief period of Nationalist Party tutelage preparing the people for representative self-government, and then a transition to democracy. But the formation of opposition parties was banned after 1928, and the republic settled into a protracted period of Nationalist Party rule. Although the ban was initially only supposed to last for six years, the formation of opposition political parties in the Republic of China would not actually be legalized again until 1987 (by that time on the island of Taiwan, where the transition to genuine multiparty democracy was finally achieved). Despite Chiang Kai-shek's purge of the Communists in 1927 and turn to the political Right, however, this did not immediately mark a complete end to the May Fourth spirit. The Nationalist Party was still a self-proclaimed modernizing revolutionary party, and official documents in Chiang Kai-shek's new government were still stamped "the revolution is not yet complete."[30]

Korea under Japanese Rule, 1905–1945

The emperor (and former king) of Korea was able to temporarily maintain Korean independence by playing Russian interests off against Japan, but room for any further maneuver evaporated suddenly after Japan defeated Russia in war in 1905. From the Japanese perspective, the Korean peninsula – which reached to just fifty miles from Japan's shores, like "a dagger pointed at the heart of Japan" in one persuasively threatening image – was understandably perceived as strategically vital. The Chinese had been expelled from Korea after the Sino-Japanese War in 1895, but in the meantime, the Russians had begun building their Trans-Siberian Railway in 1891 and acquired a naval base at Port Arthur on the tip of Liaodong peninsula in southern Manchuria in 1898. To oppose this approaching Russian power, instead of demobilizing after the Sino-Japanese War, the Japanese budget of 1896 actually called for doubling the size of the military.

Russia's primary interests lay in Manchuria, while Japan's lay in Korea, but neither power was willing to renounce its wider ambitions in order to reach an accommodation. In part to counter the Russian threat, Japan signed a formal alliance in 1902 with Russia's foremost global imperial rival, Great Britain. Under the terms of this Anglo-Japanese treaty, both countries pledged to aid the other if it became involved in a war with more than one adversary. This gave the Japanese a freer hand to confront Russia in Korea. Negotiations with Russia broke off on February 6, 1904, and war was declared four days later (see Figure 8.5). Active hostilities began a day before the formal declaration of war with a surprise Japanese

Figure 8.5. "Naval Battle of the Russo-Japanese War at Chinmulpo," 1904, by Migita Toshi-hide (1863–1925), Japanese woodblock print. Arthur M. Sackler Gallery, Smithsonian Institution, Washington, D.C.: Gift of Gregory and Patricia Kruglak, S2001.37a-c.

night attack on the naval base at Port Arthur, in which two Russian battleships and a cruiser were struck by torpedoes.

Russia was a major world power with vastly superior potential resources than newly industrializing little Japan, and although the Japanese scored some early victories on the battlefield, none were decisive. The cost of the war to Japan was staggering, both in the number of lives lost (81,455 Japanese dead) and in the skyrocketing debt necessary to fund it. Russia, on the other hand, was large enough to suffer heavy losses and continue fighting. The Japanese high command therefore grew anxious to negotiate an end to the war quickly, and an opportunity to seek peace on favorable terms came after a smashing Japanese naval victory at Tsushima on May 27, 1905. The Russian Baltic fleet, consisting of eleven battleships, had sailed halfway around the world to reinforce the Russian forces in the Pacific, but it was intercepted toward the end of its long voyage near Tsushima, an island lying midway between Korea and Japan, by a fleet of five Japanese battleships. The Japanese performed the classic naval maneuver known as "crossing the T," in which all of their big guns were able to fire broadsides on the oncoming Russian ships, while the Russians could only bring their forward guns to bear. In just forty-five minutes of action, the Russian fleet was annihilated, while the Japanese suffered only minimal losses.

Japan was now in a position to approach the president of the United States, Theodore Roosevelt, with a request to mediate, and the war was ended by the Treaty of Portsmouth (New Hampshire) in September 1905. As a result of the war, Russia ceded its concessions in southern Manchuria to Japan and renounced Russian interests in Korea, but the Russian bargaining position was still strong enough that Russia could not be compelled to pay war reparations to Japan. Although Japan had won the war, therefore, many Japanese people felt disappointed, and serious rioting broke out, especially in Hibiya Park in Tōkyō. A majority of Tōkyō's police boxes were reportedly destroyed, troops had to be brought in, martial law was declared, and some two thousand Japanese rioters were arrested.

Meanwhile, at the start of the war, the Korean government had attempted to remain neutral, but Japanese troops occupied Seoul, and the Koreans were obliged to accept advisors recommended by the Japanese – with the power even to approve Korean cabinet-level decisions. After the war, in 1905, Korea was reduced to a formal Japanese protectorate. The Meiji oligarch Itō Hirobumi – architect of the Meiji constitution and Japan's first prime minister – was brought in to serve as Japan's first resident-general in Korea. But Emperor Kojong had agreed to the Japanese protectorate only under duress, if at all, and in 1906 and 1907, he publicly appealed for world support against Japan, in particular, with a mission to a peace conference at the Hague, in the Netherlands.

Japanese domination was now irreversible, however, and in 1907, Emperor Kojong abdicated in favor of his son. By now, all laws, important decisions, and appointments of high officials required the Japanese resident-general's approval. The Korean army was disbanded, and many former Korean soldiers joined anti-Japanese guerrillas in the countryside. According to Japanese count, between 1907 and 1910, there were 2,819 armed clashes with Korean guerrillas, and in 1907, in a coordinated attack on the headquarters of the Japanese residency-general, one particularly large guerrilla force penetrated to within eight miles of Seoul.[31] The modern Japanese army was too powerful for disorganized guerrillas to overcome, however, and the overall Japanese presence in Korea was, meanwhile, expanding rapidly, multiplying tenfold between 1900 and 1910. In the southern port city of Pusan, half the population became Japanese, and much of the town was Japanese built.[32]

In the years after the establishment of the protectorate, the Japanese residency-general financed its program for the creation of modern banking facilities and roads in Korea through Japanese loans to the Korean government. This put the Koreans heavily in debt to Japan. Partly on the pretext of these unpaid debts, and after the assassination of Itō Hirobumi by a Korean nationalist in 1909, Japan openly annexed Korea as a formal colony in 1910.

By the early twentieth century, in the heyday of what is called the new imperialism, much of the entire world had been reduced to colonial status. The Japanese colony in Korea was exceptional, even so, because of the extremely large number of resident Japanese colonists and because of its high degree of intrusiveness of the colonial regime. By the 1930s, there was one policeman for roughly every four hundred Koreans, and the number of Japanese colonists in Korea was more than twenty times the number of French colonists in Vietnam.[33] Japanese rule in Korea was, moreover, at first extremely ironfisted. After annexation, all the Japanese governors-general of Korea were active-duty generals in the imperial army, with one exception, who was a retired navy admiral. From 1910 to 1920, no Korean-owned newspapers were permitted, and all Korean political meetings and public assemblies were banned. Colonial economic policy also focused initially on the exploitation of raw materials and agriculture, and little development of modern business was envisioned, especially if it was not Japanese owned.

On March 1, 1919, Korean resentment erupted in mass protest. Inspired by Wilsonian ideals of national self-determination, and coordinated with the upcoming funeral of former Emperor Kojong, demonstrations – ultimately involving as many as one million Koreans – began with the reading of a Korean "Declaration of Independence." Although these demonstrations were brutally suppressed, the Japanese colonial regime did shift to a gentler approach afterward, introducing some reforms that treated Koreans less harshly. New business start-ups no longer required government permission, and the Japanese government even began providing subsidies to certain Korean companies. The military police were replaced by civilians who no longer routinely carried swords. Censorship was relaxed, and Korean-language newspaper and magazine publishing flourished. Yet it has also been observed that even as the external appearance of the police force softened, their numbers also increased.[34]

Paradoxically, Japanese colonization of Korea in some ways did promote modernization, and even Westernization. For example, although Korea's nonagricultural commercial economy had been notably less developed than either China's or Japan's in the nineteenth century, by the end of the colonial period in 1945, Korea was more thoroughly industrialized than any other part of East Asia, except for Japan itself. Modern Western-style consumer culture also arrived in Korea together with Japanese rule. The cinema, phonographic records, radio, commercial advertising, magazines, department stores, and modern Western-style fashions in clothing all made their appearance in Korea's larger cities during the period of Japanese rule. Modernization in Korea thus followed a complicated trajectory, including simultaneous Japanese-ization, Westernization, and also the maturation of a new sense of Korean nationalism.

Since the beginning of the twentieth century, with the aid of a modern Korean-language press (recall that until the end of the nineteenth century, much elite writing in Korea had still been in classical Chinese), Korean national consciousness had been brewing. The same new two-character word for "nation" that was used in both Japan and China (pronounced "minjok" in Korean) was adopted, and Korean history began to be conceived as the history of a Korean *Volk*, or "people." In 1921, the Korean Language Research Society was founded to promote and standardize grammatical and *han'gŭl* spelling rules for the Korean language and compile a pioneering Korean-language dictionary. In an example of the complexity of modernizing impulses, the colonial Japanese government's subsidy of radio broadcasting in Korea also helped substantially to promote the spread of the Seoul dialect as a standard pronunciation for the Korean national language.[35] Despite some early toleration of this pioneering Korean linguistic activity, however, the promotion of the Korean language eventually came to be seen as subversive of the Japanese goal of assimilation, and during World War II, many Korean linguists found themselves under arrest.

From a quite early date, much of the Korean nationalist movement was driven abroad into exile. The future president of the Republic of Korea, Syngman Rhee (Yi Sŭngman, 1875–1965), for example, went into exile after 1904, and a few years later founded the Korean National Association in Hawai'i. Inside Korea, the Japanese colonial regime favored assimilation. As early as 1910, the Japanese language was officially designated Korea's "national language." The Japanese regarded Koreans as racially and culturally akin to themselves and therefore potentially as fellow "imperial peoples." At the same time, however, and with a fatal contradiction, they also stereotypically imagined Koreans as backward and underdeveloped. Koreans were therefore allowed to remain unrepresented in the Japanese legislature, intermarriage between Japanese and Koreans was discouraged, and Koreans continued to be treated with offensive condescension by many Japanese.[36] Despite the official policy of assimilation, Korean ethnicity was also still specified on identification cards.

The attempted integration of Korea into the Japanese Empire began to accelerate after Manchuria was brought into the Japanese-led yen-bloc in 1931, and even more rapidly after the outbreak of World War II in China in 1937. Beginning in 1935, Korean worship at Japanese-style *Shintō* shrines became mandatory – which was particularly objectionable to the relatively large number of monotheistic Korean Christians. In 1939, all Koreans were required to take Japanese-style names. Most officially did so, although it is questionable how many ever came to identify closely with these new Japanese names. Between 1937 and 1939, the use of the Korean language was banned in stages, in government, public schools, and finally in the private press. In spite of all this coerced assimilation, however, it has been estimated that as of 1942, only about 20 percent of the Korean people could actually even understand the Japanese language.[37]

Increased integration into the Japanese Empire brought rapid industrialization and economic modernization. Although some Korean businesses certainly did benefit, however, this industrialization was not only Japanese dominated but also largely state led, for strategic military purposes. After 1937, industrial mobilization even included compulsory conscription of Korean labor. In a negative parallel to this swift industrialization, a fairly drastic decline in per capita Korean consumption of rice has also been observed in this period, since much of Korea's rice crop was now exported to Japan, while Korean agriculture saw relatively few improvements in productivity.[38]

Beginning in 1943, Koreans could be drafted into the wartime Japanese imperial army. Notoriously, more than one hundred thousand Korean women were pressured into becoming so-called comfort women, providing sexual services for the Japanese military. The combination of rapid industrialization and forced mobilization for Japan's war effort in World War II created enormous dislocations in what had previously been a settled agrarian Korean society. By the end of World War II, perhaps 20 percent of the entire Korean population had been uprooted and moved away from their native province or even beyond the borders of Korea itself, many going to Manchuria or the Japanese home islands.[39] In the midst of Japan's rapidly deteriorating military situation in late World War II, all this population

Figure 8.6. Showroom of the Mitsukoshi Dry-Goods Store, Japan, 1911. National Diet Library Web site.

dislocation, hardship, and forced assimilation of a proud people simultaneously faced with continuing discrimination planted bitter seeds of lasting anti-Japanese resentment in Korea.

Japan: Taishō Democracy

Explicitly Western things had begun to be fashionable in Japan from early in the Meiji era. For example, reading and writing in horizontal lines from left to right, Western-style, as opposed to the traditional East Asian vertical columns marching from right to left, was introduced in Meiji times (though the practice remains inconsistent even today); chairs began to be used in government buildings as early as 1871 (although at home, many Japanese still sit – and sleep, quite comfortably – on their tatami-matted floors); and the modern department store, complete with commercial advertising, had appeared in Japan by the early twentieth century (see Figure 8.6). The game of baseball was introduced in early Meiji, and the first international game may have been in 1896, when a Japanese school team beat an American team.[40] Beer was introduced from Europe in 1868 and began to be brewed domestically within a decade. Eventually, after World War II, beer (and whiskey) came to commonly be sold from vending machines on the street. Military service on the continent at the start of the twentieth century introduced large numbers of Japanese soldiers to more Western-style foods, including beef (as in sukiyaki), which had rarely been consumed in premodern Japan. Pseudo Indian-style curry rice was popularized during World War I and eventually became a Japanese staple. The now ubiquitous pork cutlet (*tonkatsu*) made its debut in the Japanese national diet shortly thereafter. Despite the early date of some of these adoptions, though, daily life for most Japanese people did not really significantly begin to alter until the World War I period.[41]

There was, moreover, even something of a nationalistic counterreaction to the early Meiji enthusiasm for Westernization beginning around 1887.[42] Interest in traditional Japanese art, literature, history, and Confucian morality was revived, and the idea of an enduring Japanese "national polity" (*kokutai*), closely identified with an unbroken and supposedly divine ancient imperial line, began to be sometimes stridently promoted. Yet, although there were countercurrents, in Japan, as in China, the first great wave of Westernization in many ways only peaked in the 1910s–1920s.

It was also during roughly this period that the modern Japanese industrial economy finally matured. A huge government steel mill had been opened at Yawata in 1901, but during its first decade of operation, it suffered heavy financial losses, and as late as 1914, Japan was still only producing about a third of its own domestic steel requirements. Up to the outbreak of World War I in 1914, the Japanese government continued to provide 30–40 percent of the total capital investment in the modern sector of the economy.[43] The start of World War I, however, not only brought war-related orders to Japanese factories but also caused the withdrawal of much European and American competition, opening up new Asian and African markets for Japan. Japan's exports tripled in four years, and during the war years (1914–1918), Japan's gross national product increased by 9 percent annually.

The number of Japanese factory workers doubled during the war, but this also led to a labor shortage and rising prices, which strained the resources of those on fixed incomes. Food prices tripled during World War I, and the increased cost provoked major rice riots in 1918. Over a million persons participated, there were twenty-five thousand arrests, and the prime minister was obliged to step down. The end of World War I, then, brought resumed European and American competition and a postwar slump. The Japanese stock market crashed in 1920, and many companies went bankrupt. Plummeting prices for agricultural products led to deep, endemic rural poverty. This contributed to an already "growing chasm between the lifestyles of the 'two Japans,'" urban and rural.[44] Work conditions in many of the new factories were also often grim. The development of the Japanese textile industry, for example, depended heavily on cheap labor, and a large majority of the labor force was female, typically employed only briefly and working twelve-hour shifts under often harsh conditions.

In 1923, the great Kantō earthquake struck in the vicinity of Tōkyō, destroying half a million homes and killing 105,000 people. A bank panic in 1927 led to the withdrawal of some 11 percent of all deposits. Major banking institutions failed, including the imperial household's own bank. Thirty-two banks closed their doors. The 1920s were therefore a decade of repeated economic crises. Yet despite this, Japan's overall real economic growth rate in the period 1913–1938 was more than three times that of the United States. A critical threshold in the industrialization process seems to have been crossed, and certain developments in this era are said to have already foreshadowed the spectacular post–World War II Japanese economic "miracle."[45]

Not only did the industrialized economy mature, but parliamentary democracy also came of age in the aftermath of World War I, as rule by unelected oligarchs was finally replaced by a regular parliamentary-style political party system. The Meiji emperor died in 1912, and the reign period of his successor, the Taishō Emperor (r. 1912–1926), was known as an age of relatively liberal "Taishō democracy." From 1918 to 1932, the prime minister was usually the head of one of the political parties elected to the Diet, and in 1925, all Japanese men aged twenty-five or older were given the vote: universal adult male suffrage.

The old Meiji period ideal of "transcendent" government – that is, an administration that was supposedly above party politics – had broken down in the early twentieth century, as cabinet after cabinet was obliged to seek the support of politicians in the legislature. After 1905, no prime minister was able to govern entirely without party support. Meanwhile, the elder statesman Itō Hirobumi had joined with the leading faction in the Diet to form a political party of his own in 1900 (called the Seiyūkai). The rice riots in 1918, then, were the largest such disturbances in recorded Japanese history and led to the fall of the current administration. In this moment of crisis, the surviving Meiji era oligarchs (acting in the name of the emperor) turned to the then president of the Seiyūkai Party, Hara Kei (also known as Hara Takashi, 1856–1921), to form the first-ever Japanese party government in September 1918. Although Hara's ancestry was samurai, he had renounced his former samurai status and refused a peerage, and he is therefore also considered to be the first commoner ever to serve as prime minister of Japan.

In 1921, Hara was stabbed to death at a Tōkyō train station by a man who was enraged by the naval arms limitations agreed to at the Washington Conference earlier that year. After Hara's death, there followed four brief administrations in quick succession, three of them non-party, but in 1924, another party politician was made prime minister, and this now became the norm (until a new age of militarism began in the 1930s). "Taishō democracy" reached its height at this time. Military expenditures were reduced in 1924, and four divisions were cut from the army. In March 1925, the movement toward democracy culminated in the implementation of universal adult male suffrage. Although the Taishō Emperor died in 1926, technically putting an end to Taishō democracy, his successor, the Shōwa Emperor (former prince regent Hirohito, r. 1926–1989), had personally visited Europe and enjoyed a reputation for Western-style interests such as golf and marine biology.

As in contemporary China, the 1920s were an era of modernity and often consciously Western-style fashions in Japan. Giant multistory department stores, with solid Western-style floors (so that it was no longer necessary to follow the custom of leaving shoes at the door), and featuring such modern goods as Shiseido cosmetics, became places of entertainment as well as commerce. Neon lights lit the streets of major cities at night, and the first Tōkyō subway line began operations in 1927.

Movies had begun to be shown in Japan as early as the 1890s, but cinema especially flourished in the 1920s. Japanese women styled their hair to resemble international movie stars like Gloria Swanson and Greta Garbo. A few experimental radio stations were already broadcasting by 1922, and Tōkyō Broadcasting Station began operations in 1925. Panel-narrative comic strips began to be published in the 1920s – ancestors of today's ubiquitous manga. At the more consciously elevated cultural level, Western-style avant-garde art also found a niche. There was an enormous reading public, for serious books as well as for light entertainment. At the start of World War I, Japan was publishing twice as many different book titles as the United States.[46] Today, Japan may actually provide the largest per capita audience for the quintessentially American-style jazz music in the world, and in the 1920s, Japanese musicians were consciously performing in the style of American jazz legends (although later, during the World War II years, there was an attempt to find a "native" Japanese jazz style).[47] Individualism was fashionable in the Japan of the 1920s, and feminism also took root in this era with the founding of the New Woman's Association in 1920 and the beginnings of a women's suffrage movement. The 1920s were popularly known as an age of "modern boys" and "modern girls."

The sudden swing toward militarism and ultranationalism that emerged in the 1930s might therefore appear surprising. This dramatic change of direction was driven in large part by the onset of the Great Depression and other major world trends and conditions. However, as we have already remarked, there had been an earlier period of nationalistic reaction in the late 1880s and 1890s, much of Japan's rural population had been left out of the heady urban modernization and Westernization of the 1920s, strategic military considerations had always been paramount from the beginning of the Meiji Restoration, and expansionist overseas imperial ambitions had also been a recurrent theme. Even at the peak of Taishō democracy, there were powerful countercurrents. At the very moment that the vote was being extended to all adult males, for example, a new peace preservation law in 1925 also made it illegal to advocate any change in Japan's somewhat mystical, emperor-centered "national polity" (*kokutai*) or the abolition of private property.[48] Midnight raids on March 15, 1928 – provoked by leftist gains in an election the previous month – arrested some sixteen hundred persons suspected of being Communists. In that same year, five professors were dismissed from imperial universities because they were suspected of harboring "dangerous thoughts."

In 1924, just as party government was stabilizing in Japan, the U.S. Congress passed legislation preventing immigration by persons ineligible for U.S. citizenship, which at that time pointedly included all Japanese.[49] This deeply insulted many Japanese people, including some of those who found Western ideals most attractive. Many in the army, especially those from impoverished rural villages, had already, in the 1920s, begun contemplating the need for a military coup to return power and wealth from the allegedly corrupt and self-interested capitalists and party politicians to the emperor, in a so-called Shōwa Restoration. The modern mass media that had matured in the 1920s could, furthermore, perhaps just as easily be turned to mobilize ultranationalist patriotic sentiments as to promote liberal democracy.

The banking crisis of 1927 brought down the cabinet, and a conservative retired army general was made prime minister. Viewing Chiang Kai-shek's Northern Expedition to reunify China as a threat to Japanese interests on the continent, in 1927–1928, his government intervened militarily three times in China to protect Japanese interests and to prevent Manchuria from being included in the reunified Republic of China. To stimulate the economy, this prime minister also increased military expenditures. Yet even this conservative ex-soldier was also the president of a political party and a party politician himself. In 1928, his government signed the Kellogg-Briand Pact that attempted to formally renounce war as an instrument of national policy.

Also in 1928, however, the Chinese warlord of Manchuria, Zhang Zuolin, was blown up and killed in his railway car by Japanese army officers, acting without the knowledge of the home government in Tōkyō, who apparently hoped to create an incident that would provide a pretext for Japanese seizure of Manchuria. The Japanese prime minister was outraged by these actions and resolved to bring the assassins to a court-martial. The army refused to cooperate, however, with the result that the prime minister was forced to resign in 1929.[50]

Ironically, this brought a temporary return to more liberal policies under the next administration in 1929, which became the first in Japan to support women's suffrage. A proposal was actually drafted to let women have the vote in local elections, though it did not become law. But this new prime minister was fatally shot in 1930 by an outraged nationalist because of the government's acceptance of an arms limitation agreement reached at the London Naval Conference. The political climate in Japan was suddenly becoming very chilly. With the onset of the Great Depression, and the successful seizure of southern Manchuria by the Japanese army in 1931 (after yet another staged explosion), and after one more brief and ineffectual liberal cabinet, in 1931, a new, more conservative prime minister (Inukai Tsuyoshi, 1855–1932) took office. He survived in office only five months before he, too, was struck down by assassins – this time Japanese naval and army officers. After his death, there would be no more prime ministers from political parties. Japan had begun its descent into the "dark valley" of militarism and war.

For Further Reading

On China's Nationalist Revolution, see Marie-Claire Bergère, *Sun Yat-sen*, trans. Janet Lloyd (Stanford University Press, [1994] 1998); John Fitzgerald, *Awakening China: Politics, Culture, and Class in the Nationalist Revolution* (Stanford University Press, 1996); Edward J. M. Rhoads, *Manchus and Han: Ethnic Relations and Political Power in Late Qing and Early Republican China, 1861–1928* (Seattle: University of Washington Press, 2000); and Mary Clabaugh Wright, ed., *China in Revolution: The First Phase, 1900–1913* (New Haven, CT: Yale University Press, 1968).

A fine extended essay on the problem of modernization in China is Rana Mitter, *A Bitter Revolution: China's Struggle with the Modern World* (Oxford University Press, 2004). On the early-twentieth-century modern transformation of China, see Sherman Cochran, ed., *Inventing Nanjing Road: Commercial Culture in Shanghai, 1900–1945* (Ithaca, NY: Cornell University East Asia Program, 1999); Frank Dikötter, *Exotic Commodities: Modern Objects and Everyday Life in China* (New York: Columbia University Press, 2006); and Leo

Ou-fan Lee, *Shanghai Modern: The Flowering of a New Urban Culture in China, 1930–1945* (Cambridge, MA: Harvard University Press, 1999). The still-classic study of China's May Fourth movement is Tse-tsung Chow, *The May Fourth Movement: Intellectual Revolution in Modern China* (Stanford University Press, 1960).

On the warlord era in China, see Edward A. McCord, *The Power of the Gun: The Emergence of Modern Chinese Warlordism* (Berkeley: University of California Press, 1993), and Gavan McCormack, *Chang Tso-lin in Northeast China, 1911–1928: China, Japan, and the Manchurian Idea* (Stanford University Press, 1977).

For Korea under Japanese rule, see Ramon H. Myers and Mark R. Peattie, eds., *The Japanese Colonial Empire, 1895–1945* (Princeton University Press, 1984), and Michael Edson Robinson, *Cultural Nationalism in Colonial Korea, 1920–1925* (Seattle: University of Washington Press, 1988).

On early-twentieth-century Japan, see Marius B. Jansen, *The Making of Modern Japan* (Cambridge, MA: Harvard University Press, 2000); Tetsuo Najita, *Hara Kei and the Politics of Compromise, 1905–1915* (Cambridge, MA: Harvard University Press, 1967); and Edward Seidensticker, *Low City, High City: Tokyo from Edo to the Earthquake* (New York: Alfred A. Knopf, 1983). Stephen Vlastos, ed., *Mirror of Modernity: Invented Traditions of Modern Japan* (Berkeley: University of California Press, 1998), provides a fascinating collection of essays on the modern reimagination of Japanese tradition.

9 The Dark Valley (1930–1945)

The Rise of Japanese Ultranationalism

The first great wave of modern globalization (which, because of the industrialized West's initial leading role in defining global modernity, in this early phase sometimes overlapped fairly closely with what might even be described as Westernization) had begun in the late nineteenth century and, in East Asia, culminated in the 1910s–1920s with China's May Fourth Movement and Japan's Taishō democracy. Because Korea was a Japanese colony during these years, developments in Korea took the slightly different form of combined simultaneous modernization, Westernization, and Japanese-ization. The high tide of globalization receded rapidly after the disastrous collapse of the U.S. stock market in 1929, however. By the 1930s, the entire world was descending into what some Japanese historians have appropriately dubbed a "dark valley." As a result of the Great Depression, in the United States, real gross domestic product had declined 35 percent by 1933, a quarter of American workers were out of work, and there were calls for the newly inaugurated president Franklin D. Roosevelt to assume dictatorial powers. Even socialism no longer seemed entirely unthinkable in America. In Germany, the Weimar Republic gave way to Adolph Hitler. In China, the Nationalist Republic became an authoritarian single-party state with an increasingly nationalized economy. In Japan, Taishō democracy was thrust aside by the rise of ultranationalistic militarism.

Surprisingly, the industrial sector of Japan's economy recovered fairly quickly from the depths of the Great Depression, due to a sharp devaluation in the exchange value of the yen (which made the price of Japanese exports globally competitive), low interest rates, and increased government spending on public works and armaments. The volume of Japanese exports actually doubled between 1930 and 1936. But as much of the rest of the world responded to the Great Depression by adopting strict protectionist measures – such as high taxes or outright quotas on imports, which threatened Japan's ability to continue exporting – the argument began to resonate that what Japan really needed was to create an economically self-sufficient

Figure 9.1. The Japanese battleship *Yamato* running trials, 1941. It and its sister ship, *Musashi*, were the largest battleships ever built. National Archives.

yen-bloc that would be independent and under Japan's own control. Manchuria, in particular, came to be viewed as a potential economic "lifeline" for Japan.

The purely economic argument for self-sufficiency was also reinforced by the strategic military lessons of World War I, which seemed to suggest that future wars would be protracted and total, pitting the entire available resources of one adversary against another. To prepare for such a total war, it was thought that Japan needed to build a self-sufficient "National Defense State."[1] To safeguard Japan's vital interests, military expenditures accelerated rapidly. In 1934, Japan departed from the Washington and London naval arms limitation agreements, and in 1937, Japan began construction of what would become the largest battleships (the Yamato class) in the history of the world (see Figure 9.1).

The modern national public school system in Japan promoted ideals of patriotic loyalty to the emperor and military valor.[2] Organized state *Shintō* religion, although it was, as an institution, really only a modern creation of the Meiji era, nonetheless emphasized the ancient mythology of imperial descent from the sun goddess Amaterasu, dating from before the dawn of Japanese history. This supposedly divine imperial line was proclaimed to be the core of Japan's unique national polity (*kokutai*), which invested modern Japanese imperialism with a special sense of sacred mission. Exultation of the imperial majesty reached a crescendo in the late 1930s, when over two million copies of the Ministry of Education's *Cardinal*

Principles of the National Polity were published (beginning in 1937), and it became required reading in Japanese schools.[3]

The sense of a special divine mission also coincided with a romantic idealization of the remembered "traditional" virtues of village life, and much criticism of alleged capitalist greed and the corrupt special interests of party politicians. The idea that Anglo-American-style "selfish" individualism should give way to a more native Japanese spirit of harmony was emotionally appealing to many people. Rather than representing a genuine return to premodern tradition, though, much of this ultranationalist celebration of the "spirit of Japan" was really a new phenomenon. It was also much encouraged by the modern mass media and modern expectations of popular mass mobilization. Combined with considerable real rural economic distress in the early 1930s, these ideas fostered radical plots and conspiracies, and Japan was wracked by a staggering series of high-level assassinations and attempted military coups.

In 1930, Prime Minister Hamaguchi was shot, and later died of his wounds, for his role in agreeing to naval arms limitations. Efforts in 1931 by the civilian government in Tōkyō to bring the conflict in Manchuria to a peaceful resolution proved so unpopular at home that it contributed, together with the onset of the Great Depression, to bringing down the administration. Despite the fact that the next prime minister, Inukai Tsuyoshi, was relatively hawkish, on May 15, 1932, a group of naval officers and army cadets burst into his residence and shot him to death. After the assassination, incredibly enough, the war minister publicly praised the selfless sincerity of the killers, and the chief of military police actually called them patriots, suggesting that they should have coordinated their attack with the military police! Earlier that same year, a former minister of finance and a leading businessman were also assassinated.[4]

The wave of violence and military disobedience climaxed on the morning of February 26, 1936, when the army's First Division, stationed in Tōkyō, mutinied. The rebels seized important government buildings and assassinated former Prime Minster Saitō, Finance Minister Takahashi, and Inspector General of Military Education Watanabe in their homes. The grand chamberlain, Admiral Suzuki, was seriously wounded and left for dead. Prime Minster Okada narrowly escaped only because the mutineers shot his brother-in-law by mistake. An attempted takeover of the imperial palace was blocked, however, by alert palace guards. After the assassinations, the rebels issued a manifesto proclaiming the virtuous motives for their actions and calling for a "Shōwa Restoration" (the name of the current imperial reign period) in a hoped-for echo of the glorious nineteenth-century Meiji Restoration. The mutiny was not universally supported even in the army, however, and encountered direct opposition from the Shōwa Emperor himself (often somewhat disrespectfully referred to outside of Japan by his personal name, Hirohito), who had the mutineers surrounded with loyal troops and ordered the rebels to return to barracks. On February 29, they surrendered. Two rebel leaders committed suicide immediately, and seventeen others were quickly condemned and executed, without being given an opportunity to publicize their message.

This turned out to be the last great act of unauthorized pre–World War II violence by the imperial Japanese army. By now, however, civilian politicians were effectively intimidated, and a turn to less radical military leaders seemed a natural alternative. In the 1937 Japanese cabinet, there would not be a single party politician. Even after the final dissolution of political parties in 1940, elections continued to be held and the forms of parliamentary government maintained, but the era of Taishō democracy had ended, and a new age of ultranationalistic militarism had begun.

Manchukuo

Until the late nineteenth century, much of Manchuria – with the exception of the southern agricultural regions that, although they lay beyond the Great Wall, had long functioned as something of an extension of China proper – remained a sparsely populated frontier. This was at least partially intentional, since the Manchu rulers of the Qing Dynasty had forbidden Chinese migration into Manchuria to preserve the integrity of their homeland. Meanwhile, however, Russian Cossacks in search of furs had begun to appear in the area as early as the seventeenth century. A formal border between the Chinese and Russian empires, along the line of the Amur River, was first fixed by treaty in 1689.

By the nineteenth century, the Russians had become a dynamic presence in the far northeast. Russia obtained a port on the Pacific Ocean at Vladivostok in 1858. In 1896, thanks to Russian intervention (together with France and Germany) to prevent Manchuria's Liaodong peninsula from being ceded to Japan after the Sino-Japanese War, a deal was signed with the Qing Dynasty conceding to Russia the right to build a railway straight across Manchuria – a considerable shortcut in the Trans-Siberian route between Vladivostok and Moscow. In 1898, the Russians also obtained from the Qing Dynasty a leasehold on some territory at the tip of Liaodong peninsula and began constructing a Russian naval base (Port Arthur) and civilian port facilities there, with a rail connection joining the main Russian rail line at Harbin, in central Manchuria. After the Boxer debacle in 1900, for a time, the Russians were the dominant power in Manchuria.

But Russia was defeated by Japan in a war, largely fought on Manchurian soil, in 1905. As a result of this victory, Japan acquired control over Russian installations in southern Manchuria. These included the leasehold at the tip of Liaodong peninsula and that portion of the railway leading north from there as far as Changchun. This line now became known as the South Manchurian Railway (in Japanese, *Mantetsu*), and it became the single largest Japanese corporation of the early twentieth century. The Japanese government provided half of its initial capitalization, and although the balance came from private investors, it was government controlled. In addition to the railway itself, the South Manchurian Railway also handled the administration of policing, taxation, schooling, and other important public functions along the line of the tracks. Its first president (Gotō Shimpei, 1857–1929) had previously served as Japanese colonial governor of Taiwan. He had trained in Germany as a physician, and was a progressive-minded administrator concerned especially with matters of public health. Whatever other criticisms may be leveled at early-twentieth-century

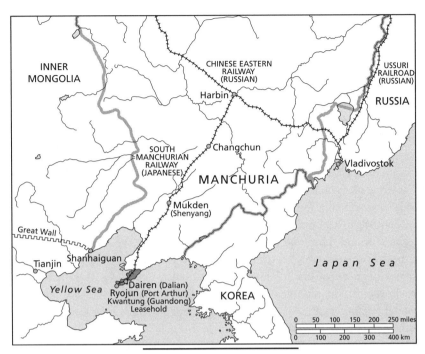

Map 13. Manchuria, ca. 1920

Japanese imperialism, it often did accomplish certain modernizing improvements. Under Japanese colonial rule, for example, the death rate in both Taiwan and Korea declined significantly in the early twentieth century.[5]

Dreams of massive Japanese settlement of the new frontier opening up to them in Manchuria – supposedly thereby relieving population pressure in the crowded Japanese home islands – were never fully realized. Relatively few Japanese people found the idea of becoming peasant farmers in a remote (and foreign) frontier very attractive. The number of Japanese who did migrate to Manchuria, moreover, was eclipsed by a flood of new Chinese arrivals. The Qing Dynasty had only belatedly realized that to cement its claim to the region against the growing Russian presence, Manchuria would have to be more thickly settled and lifted its ban on Chinese migration in the late nineteenth century. Large-scale Chinese in-migration then caused the population of Manchuria to explode.

The Manchurian economy also boomed in the early twentieth century, although in this case, it was chiefly the result of Japanese investment. By 1932, when Manchuria first became a Japanese-controlled puppet state, 64 percent of the total capital invested in Manchurian industry was already Japanese.[6] Thereafter, the pace of Japanese investment only accelerated. In the single decade between 1931 and 1941, Japanese investment in Manchuria multiplied more than fivefold. Although actual production results did not entirely match expectations, Manchuria became the most industrialized region of China by the end of World War II.[7]

The Chinese warlord in Manchuria, Zhang Zuolin, had cooperated with the growing Japanese interests there, but he also moved his headquarters to Beijing in 1926 and exhibited signs of increasingly national Chinese ambitions. When Chiang Kai-shek's Northern Expedition for the military reunification of China approached Beijing from the south in 1928, Zhang Zuolin was informed by his Japanese advisors that he must either withdraw to Manchuria immediately or be disarmed by Japanese guards at the pass separating Manchuria from China proper if he tried to do so later. He accepted the Japanese warning and returned to Mukden (the Manchu name for the capital of Manchuria) immediately, but was blown up and killed in his railway car anyway by the unauthorized action of rogue Japanese army officers. His assassination was presumably intended to provoke an incident that might allow the Japanese Kwantung Army (a now conventional old spelling of the Chinese term *Guandong*, which means "East of the Passes" – in this case referring to the passes separating Manchuria from China proper) to seize control over Manchuria. The attempt backfired, however (this time). Both the emperor and the prime minister of Japan were outraged, and Zhang Zuolin's son, now understandably hostile to Japan, inherited his position. This son reached an agreement with Chiang Kai-shek's Nationalist Chinese government to bring Manchuria into the reunified Chinese Republic, which, in 1931, also announced a goal of regaining Chinese control over the Japanese Liaodong leasehold and the South Manchurian Railway.

The combination of this new Chinese Nationalist threat to Japanese holdings in Manchuria, the global economic crisis created by the Great Depression, and changing conditions in domestic Japanese politics, all made a second attempt in 1931 to provoke a Japanese military takeover in Manchuria by staging an explosion much more successful. Lieutenant Colonel Ishiwara Kanji (1889–1949), who had studied for three years in Germany and was considered by many to be Japan's most brilliant military theoretician, envisioned a future apocalyptic "final war" between Asia, led by Japan, and the West, led by the United States. In preparation for that cataclysmic final showdown, Ishiwara believed that Japan needed access to the vital resources of Manchuria. He, and like-minded other officers, therefore carefully planned a Japanese takeover.[8]

On September 18, 1931, a senior officer from the Japanese general staff arrived in Mukden with orders to restrain the Kwantung Army from taking any unauthorized, rash actions. Forewarned, however, the conspirators decided to strike before they were ordered not to. The distinguished visitor from the Tōkyō general staff was taken immediately on arrival to a restaurant to be entertained. While he was thus diverted, around ten o'clock that evening, a bomb exploded on the tracks of the South Manchurian Railway north of Mukden. The damage was so slight that a train was able to pass over it soon afterward with little difficulty, but the explosion was blamed on Chinese saboteurs, and the Kwantung Army sprang into action, swiftly grabbing control over a growing portion of the northeast.

The Japanese Kwantung Army, which had originally been established to defend the Liaodong leasehold won from Russia in 1905, had a total force of only about ten thousand men. Japanese media now enthusiastically celebrated the ease with which such a relative handful of Japanese troops defeated the much larger force of two hundred thousand Chinese soldiers stationed in Manchuria – conveniently ignoring that the Chinese were under orders not to resist. The modern mass media in Japan, notably the still very new radio, found the eager popular hunger for war news to be a valuable commercial opportunity and helped generate a burst of patriotic war fever in Japan following the Manchurian incident in 1931.[9] For now, at least, the actions of the Kwantung Army on the continent were highly popular back home in Japan.

Elsewhere in the world, however, the Japanese occupation of Manchuria was widely condemned as a violation of the Kellogg-Briand Pact (a 1928 agreement that had attempted to outlaw aggressive warfare and that was ultimately signed by sixty-three countries). The Japanese tried to justify their actions before the League of Nations with the argument that China did not have an organized central government and was therefore not a sovereign nation, and that Manchuria, furthermore, was not necessarily a part of China. The League of Nations was not persuaded, however, and in February 1933, it adopted a resolution, 42–1, condemning Japanese behavior. The Japanese delegation walked out, and in March 1933, Japan officially withdrew from the League of Nations.

In the aftermath, rather than attempt to directly colonize Manchuria, the Japanese reorganized it into a nominally independent new country called Manchukuo ("kuo" being an old spelling of the standard Chinese word *guo*, meaning "country"). The former last emperor of the Manchu-ruled Qing Dynasty in China, Puyi, was brought in to serve as head of state. In 1934, his title was elevated to "emperor of Manchukuo." In reality, however, the Japanese Kwantung Army was the real power now in Manchuria.

In Manchukuo, Japanese planners envisioned building a showcase of modernity, which would, furthermore, intentionally exclude what they considered to be the corrupt special interests of party politicians and big private business and that might become a shining example of state-planned economic development. State-run, or joint state and private, corporations were created to administer different sectors of the economy. Despite the army's suspicions of big business, the Kwantung Army eventually did find it necessary to welcome much private investment in Manchukuo. The army was especially cordial toward so-called new *zaibatsu* such as Nissan. Yet even the private investment went overwhelmingly into state-controlled enterprises because they provided risk-free, guaranteed returns.

The centerpiece of modern state building in Manchukuo was to be the city that was now literally renamed the New Capital (Xinjing, the former Changchun). Xinjing was rapidly transformed, with many magnificent new public buildings, wide tree-lined avenues, numerous parks, and the novelty of universal indoor plumbing.[10] After 1934, Xinjing was linked to the ports of the original Liaodong leasehold by an ultra-high-speed Asia Express, which featured streamlined, futuristic locomotives and air-conditioned coaches.[11]

In Manchukuo, the Japanese sought to portray themselves as saving the common people from brutal and disruptive warlords, as upholders of an ideal Confucian "Kingly Way," and as promoters of a new order of ethnic harmony among the Chinese, Manchu, Mongol, Korean, and Japanese populations of the region. The Japanese Empire differed from most other colonial empires of that era in acknowledging a degree of racial and cultural commonality with its East Asian subjects. "Co-prosperity" became an important slogan in the 1930s, and many individual Japanese people were undoubtedly sincerely inspired by a genuine sense of idealism. The Concordia Association that was established in Manchukuo, for example, was intended to transcend not only the old-style imperialist exploitation of the colonized but also the enforced mass uniformity of modern nationalism by creating a harmonious multicultural new nation composed of many nationalities. Such ideals were fatally undermined, however, by pervasive (and highly contradictory) Japanese assumptions of their own racial superiority. In practice, the Concordia Association merely became another tool of Kwantung Army rule.[12]

Despite enormous Japanese capital investments, moreover, Manchukuo became more of a net drain on the Japanese economy than the hoped-for lifeline. The integrated yen-bloc that was supposed to make the Japanese Empire economically and strategically self-sufficient failed to materialize. Instead, especially after full-scale war erupted with China in 1937 and the economy shifted to an emergency war footing, Japan found itself, ironically, even more critically dependent on imported resources from the United States and elsewhere.

Nationalist China

By 1928, Chiang Kai-shek's Northern Expedition had been successfully completed, and a nominally reunified Republic of China had been restored. Nanjing (Nanking) was chosen for the site of its new capital, as the "Father of the Chinese Republic," Sun Yat-sen, had originally intended at the time of the 1912 Republican Revolution. Unlike Beijing in the far northeast, Nanjing was centrally located and conveniently accessible, it was unburdened by the weight of the supposedly obsolete past and the legacy of "foreign" Manchu rule symbolized by Beijing, yet it also had a glorious ancient Chinese imperial tradition of its own (as capital of the Southern dynasties – when it may have even been the largest city in the world – and of the early Ming). As an added attraction, it also held much vacant land that would be available for new construction, since the city had never entirely recovered after being laid waste by Qing forces during their suppression of the Taiping Rebellion in 1864. Plans were drawn up to rebuild Nanjing as a gleaming, modern, world-class capital, a Chinese Washington, D.C., or Paris. Owing to a chronic shortage of funds – and, as it would transpire, a desperate shortage of time before the outbreak of World War II – most of these dreams were, unfortunately, never realized.[13]

The new government of the Republic of China also had highly ambitious plans for the rapid development of a modern, industrialized, and technologically advanced Chinese nation. Through funding by the National Economic Council, a network of modern motorways, railways, and air transportation links was rapidly expanded. Science and engineering were energetically promoted. But again, the overall actual results fell far short of the hopes. Following the Japanese takeover of Manchuria in 1931–1932, the Chinese government also felt increasingly threatened and responded with militarization. Building a strong national defense economy, under central government control, became the driving goal. By 1942, more than half of all industry in Nationalist China was state run.[14]

In addition to extending state control over the modern sector of the economy, the reconstituted Republic of China after 1928 was from the beginning – unlike the abortive multiparty parliamentary republic that had briefly followed the overthrow of the Qing Dynasty in 1912 – a single-party state. In 1928, opposition political parties (other than the ruling Nationalist Party, or *Guomindang*) were banned. Both free-enterprise capitalism and political democracy faced certain constraints, therefore, in the Nationalist China of the 1930s. But if the Chinese Republic is viewed in the general context of world trends in the 1930s, these developments appear considerably less shocking.

The 1930s were difficult and complicated times, and Nationalist China was confronted by a swirl of various challenges, influences, and pressures. Chiang Kai-shek's wife had gone to college in the United States and spoke impeccable English. Both she and her husband were also Christians. But Chiang, personally, had attended a military academy in Japan and had visited Moscow. One of his sons, Chiang Ching-kuo (Jiang Jingguo, 1910–1988), spent twelve years in the Soviet Union and married a Russian woman. As future president of Taiwan, after his father's death, this man would become a key figure in the transition to genuine multiparty democracy there (see Figure 12.2). Another son, Chiang Wei-kuo (Jiang Weiguo, 1916–1997), graduated from a military academy in Germany and, as an officer candidate there, participated in the 1938 *Anschluss*, or Nazi takeover of Austria.[15]

In fact, after Chiang Kai-shek broke with the Communists in 1927 and sent his Russian advisors packing, for the next decade, Nationalist China had especially close relations with Germany. This was partly because Germany had lost its treaty port privileges in China (a sensitive issue for Chinese nationalists) after Germany's defeat in World War I and partly because of the mutual convergence of interests between Germany's search for markets and sources of industrial raw material and China's search for a successful model for rapid modernization. This friendly relationship with Germany terminated abruptly after the start of full-scale war between China and Japan, however, when Germany opted to align with Japan. German aid and advisors were withdrawn from China in 1938. Thereafter, Nationalist China developed its closest relationship with the United States.[16]

Although this growing American influence probably did play a role in the eventual democratization of the Republic of China on Taiwan in the 1980s–1990s, as of the mid-twentieth century, Nationalist China was an authoritarian single-party state. It was also heavily militarized. Forty-three percent of the central Nationalist Party leaders were military men as of 1935, and twenty-five of thirty-three provincial chairmen were also generals during the decade of feeble peace between the nominal Nationalist reunification of China in 1928 and the outbreak of World War II in 1937.[17]

Yet despite this authoritarianism, in many ways, the Nationalist Republic's most outstanding characteristic was really weakness. "Far from being a dictator," observed U.S. general Albert C. Wedemeyer, Chiang Kai-shek "was in fact only the head of a loose coalition." The Nationalist Party was heavily factionalized, and even more important, its control over the Chinese countryside was extremely limited. At the height of World War II in 1944, the government of Nationalist China was only able to mobilize about 3–5 percent of China's gross national product for the war effort, compared to the 47 percent that was mobilized by the United States.[18] Some Chinese provinces long continued to print their own separate currencies. One province (Shanxi) built its railways on a different gauge than the rest of China. Much of China's military force also remained under local rather than central control. Despite the nominal reunification of China in 1928, many of the former warlords had actually merely declared their allegiance to the republic and continued doing business as usual, as effectively independent powers. We will never be able to know what might eventually have emerged from this unpromising beginning, if only China had been left in peace. Instead, however, the outbreak of full-scale war with Japan in 1937 effectively sealed Nationalist China's fate on the mainland.

The Rise of Mao Zedong

"Science and democracy" had been the great slogan of China's May Fourth Movement, and as late as the end of 1919, the man who would become the first leader of the Chinese Communist Party, Chen Duxiu, was still advocating an Anglo-American model of democracy in China. By 1920, however, he had become a self-proclaimed Marxist.[19] During a period of profound disillusionment among many of the more radical May Fourth intellectuals, in the spring of 1920, a Comintern agent arrived in Beijing from Moscow with details of the Bolshevik model for revolutionary organization. It was the organizational effectiveness of Bolshevik discipline, more immediately than any theoretical appeal of Marxism, that resulted in the creation of the Chinese Communist Party.[20] The first Chinese Marxist cells emerged out of study groups in Beijing in 1920. By 1921, there were roughly fifty Chinese Communists, and the First Congress of the Chinese Communist Party convened in secret that summer, holding its opening session in a girl's school in the French Concession in Shanghai.

In its early years, the Chinese Communist Party remained under the general direction of the Comintern in Moscow, and because the Soviet Union had also reached an agreement with Sun Yat-sen and the Chinese Nationalist Party in 1923, there followed a brief period of cooperation between these two Chinese parties. Chiang Kai-shek's sudden purge of leftists in April 1927, however, dealt the Communists a devastating blow. The disaster was compounded by misguided Communist efforts to stage uprisings in several cities that year, in a desperate effort to maintain some connection with the urban industrial working class – the so-called proletariat – which, according to Marxist theory, the Communist Party was supposed to represent. All these uprisings failed, however. During the last one, the so-called Canton Commune in December 1927, participants wore red scarves or armbands as a kind of uniform. After the uprising was crushed, these were hastily removed, but anyone discovered with telltale red stains on their skin was executed on the spot.[21] In the chaos after Chiang's purge, at one point, even Mao Zedong was caught by Nationalist soldiers and only narrowly managed to escape.[22]

The Chinese Communists were driven underground or out into the countryside. As devastating as this purge was, however, it also gave young Mao Zedong a chance to try a radically unorthodox approach to Marxism: peasant revolution. Mao's faith in the revolutionary potential of peasants stood orthodox Marxism on its head. In theory, the communist revolution was supposed to be driven by objective material conditions at a particular stage of historical development, through class struggle between workers and wealthy industrialists in the most advanced modern capitalist economies. But Mao believed he could adapt the general Marxist-Leninist principles to China's unique circumstances and tap into the explosive desires of the peasantry as a force that might bring Communism to power even before material conditions made it "inevitable." Mao had faith that with the right leadership and indoctrination, a "proletarian consciousness" could then be instilled into the peasantry and advanced socialist goals eventually realized.[23]

Chiang Kai-shek's purge in 1927 gave Mao a chance to put his theories to the test. At Mt. Jinggang, Jiangxi, in southeastern China, Mao led about two thousand followers to begin developing a rural Communist base in late 1927. There they began experimenting with techniques for gaining the support of poorer farmers through a program of forced land redistribution, backed by the guns of the newly created Red Army. They also began developing innovative tactics of guerrilla warfare to compensate for the Red Army's conventional military weakness. Although this style of peasant revolution was criticized by the Chinese Communist Central Committee, Mao was, for a time, beyond their effective reach and free to experiment. Details are murky, but Mao's rural Jiangxi base was successful enough that it eventually expanded to include several million people.

Success brought unwanted attention, however. Chinese Communist Party leaders began drifting into the rural Jiangxi base from their beleaguered urban headquarters in Shanghai around 1932. These newly arriving leaders were still oriented toward Moscow and critical of Mao's peasant deviations from orthodox Marxist theory. Before long, Mao was removed from real decision-making power in the Communist Party, and there are even rumors that at one point he may have been placed under house arrest, although this has been denied.[24]

Chiang Kai-shek's attention had also been caught by Mao's rural experiment, and Chiang's Nationalist armies now launched a series of military campaigns against this agrarian Communist base in the southeast. The first Nationalist attacks were repulsed by Communist guerilla tactics, but in 1934, Nationalist forces finally succeeded in totally destroying the Communist base in Jiangxi. Before it was overrun, however, in October 1934, a core group of about eight-six thousand Communist cadres and Red Army soldiers managed to break out of the Nationalist encirclement and begin what is known to history as the Long March. Initially, this was something of an aimless flight from disaster, but eventually, a preexisting Communist base area in Shaanxi Province, in the arid and poor northwest, was decided on as a destination. Of the large number who had begun the Long

Figure 9.2. Mao Zedong at an airfield in north China – probably Shaanxi – in 1936. Collection J. A. Fox. Magnum Photos.

March, only about seven or eight thousand finally arrived in Shaanxi the next year, in October 1935. Along the way, however, Mao Zedong was able to blame the disastrous collapse of the "Jiangxi Soviet" on mistakes made by others and for the first time establish himself as the dominant figure in Chinese Communism (see Figure 9.2).[25] It was, ironically, Chiang Kai-shek's near-success in exterminating the Chinese Communists at the time of the Long March that helped raise Mao to the top Communist leadership, and it would be the Japanese invasion, and World War II, that would provide the context for a final Communist victory.

World War II in China

In 1936, Mao Zedong's little Communist group settled on the remote Shaanxi market town of Yan'an for its new headquarters. By this time, Chiang Kai-shek felt that he had the Communists cornered and ordered his generals in the area to finish them off. Public opinion in China, however, was now generally much more alarmed by the growing Japanese menace than by the internal Communist threat.

It also happened that one of the principal Nationalist commanders in Shaanxi was none other than the son of the Manchurian warlord Zhang Zuolin, who had been assassinated by the Japanese in 1928 and who had himself been driven out of Manchuria by the Japanese establishment of their puppet state there. The Chinese Communists had, meanwhile, astutely changed their tactics. They were now promoting a truce in the domestic civil war with Chiang Kai-shek's Nationalist Party and the formation of a United Front against Japan. When his generals in Shaanxi did not pursue the war against the Communists as aggressively as Chiang would have liked, Chiang Kai-shek flew in person to the largest city in Shaanxi Province, Xi'an (sometimes spelled either "Sian" or "Hsi-an"), to encourage them to make greater efforts. There, at a hot springs located in the outskirts of the city, in what is known to history as the "Xi'an incident," in December 1936, Chiang Kai-shek was kidnapped by his own troops, forced to negotiate with the Communists, and agree to the formation of a United Front with them against Japan.

This Xi'an incident is important because it led to the start of World War II a few months later. During the night of July 7, 1937, a small detachment of Japanese troops were on maneuvers at Marco Polo Bridge, just a few miles outside of Beijing (which was then being called Beiping, "Northern Peace," rather than Beijing, "Northern Capital," since it was not the capital of the Nationalist Republic), when some shots were fired. This might easily have remained a relatively insignificant incident, except that because of the formation of the United Front and Chiang Kai-shek's new determination to resist further Japanese aggression, Nationalist China responded by reinforcing its troops in the Beijing area. The Japanese also sent reinforcements, and by July 25, full-scale war had erupted.

Based on the ease with which a small number of Japanese soldiers had earlier overrun Manchuria, and widespread Japanese feelings of contempt for warlord China, the Japanese anticipated a quick victory. The war minister assured the Shōwa Emperor that this China incident would be over in a month, and in July 1937, the Japanese cabinet authorized operations for only three divisions for three months. Although Chinese Nationalist armies did put up surprisingly stiff resistance, especially in the Shanghai area (see Figure 9.3), by December 13, the Nationalist capital at Nanjing (Nanking) had in fact fallen to the Japanese. There the Japanese soldiers, who had behaved with notably good discipline during the earlier war with Russia, went on a notorious rampage known as the Rape of Nanking.[26]

Although it took somewhat longer than originally anticipated, the Japanese did swiftly capture most of the major Chinese cities and the principal agricultural plains of eastern China. But the Nationalist Chinese capital merely retreated farther up the line of the Yangzi River, finally settling in the city of Chongqing (in English, Chungking), in Sichuan Province – a vast natural fortress protected by steep encircling mountains. Despite prolonged Japanese aerial bombing of Chongqing, the Chinese Nationalists continued to resist and stubbornly refused to surrender.

Despite their repeated battlefield victories, the Japanese found themselves unable to inflict any decisive defeat on Chiang Kai-shek's Nationalist China. To the end of

Figure 9.3. A terrified baby in Shanghai's South Station following a Japanese bombing at the start of World War II, August 28, 1937. National Archives.

World War II, the Japanese found it necessary to continue to station about half of all their total available forces in China, yet even that was not enough for conclusive success. After the Japanese offensive stalled, however, Chiang Kai-shek's ability to launch a counteroffensive was also seriously limited. Roughly one million Japanese troops held strategic central positions in China, while some four million Chinese troops were spread out in a vast surrounding arc, often in highly mountainous terrain and linked together only by crude roads and inadequate transportation facilities. Much of China's industrial capacity (only modest to begin with) had been overrun by the Japanese, and the Nationalist Chinese government's arsenals were now only able to produce about four bullets per soldier per month. As a result of unresolved residual warlordism, furthermore, at one time half of Chiang Kai-shek's frontline military commanders were men who had previously been in conflict with him. The result was a stalemate. Neither the Chinese nor the Japanese were able to achieve a final victory. This stalemate degenerated into an increasingly cynical phony war, lubricated by pervasive smuggling across enemy lines, and a growing cloud of corruption.[27]

Nationalist China's loss of the developed modern sector of its economy, which had been almost exclusively confined to the large coastal cities, especially Shanghai, and which had been the government's principal source of tax revenue before the war, led the Nationalist government to issue mountains of poorly backed paper money. This resulted in absolutely catastrophic hyperinflation. Between 1937 and 1945, average prices in Nationalist China increased by more than two-thousand-fold. In the end, it has been suggested that "inflation did more than any other single issue to undermine public confidence" in the Nationalist government and cause it to eventually lose control of mainland China.[28]

The Japanese had hoped that Chiang Kai-shek could quickly be brought to terms, but they were disappointed by Chiang's continued stubborn defiance. In exasperation, the Japanese government announced in January 1938 that they would have no further dealings with Chiang Kai-shek. Because they had never seriously contemplated assuming direct Japanese administration over all of China, however, the Japanese were obliged to find other Chinese collaborators. Aside from the nominally independent country of Manchukuo in the northeast, the chief collaborator in central China turned out, ironically, to be a former Chinese nationalist hero: Wang Jingwei (1883–1944).

In 1910, toward the end of the Qing Dynasty, Wang had attempted to assassinate the Manchu prince regent. He failed, was caught, and was sentenced to death. Rather than create a revolutionary martyr, however, the Qing Dynasty commuted his death sentence to life in prison. After the sudden success of the Republican Revolution in 1912, Wang was released to a hero's welcome. When Sun Yat-sen died in 1925, Wang even briefly became Sun's successor as head of the Nationalist Party. But when cadets from the Nationalist military academy, headed by Chiang Kai-shek, moved suddenly in 1926 to end a nine-month-long antiforeign boycott in Guangzhou (Canton) without even consulting Wang, Wang Jingwei resigned in humiliation and went off to Paris. After the Japanese stopped negotiating with Chiang Kai-shek in 1938, they established what they euphemistically called a Reformed Government of the Republic of China at Nanjing. By 1940, they had persuaded Wang to serve as its leader. Although the verdict of history is undoubtedly that Wang Jingwei collaborated with the enemy during wartime, he appears to have been no simple opportunist. Wang seems to have sincerely believed that cooperation with Japan was the best way to protect Chinese interests in a time of extreme vulnerability. At her war crimes trial after the war, Wang's widow (Wang himself having already died) still vigorously defended her husband's record – to the applause of her courtroom audience – arguing that he had not given up an inch of Chinese territory that had not already been lost and that he had done all he could to defend China's sovereignty.[29]

Elsewhere in Asia, in the former European colonies, cooperation with Japan during World War II could actually hold some nationalistic appeal. In the Dutch East Indies (now Indonesia), for example, wartime association with Japan did little to damage Sukarno's credentials as a nationalist hero. In China, though, the focus of nationalist outrage was not Western imperialism but Japanese. Aside from great atrocities like the Rape of Nanking and the mounting horrors of a war that eventually cost China some twenty million dead, there were also routine humiliations like the need to bow to Japanese sentries on the streets of China's occupied coastal cities. These wartime memories planted lasting seeds of bitterness in China.

But for Japan, too, the war was hardly going very well either. Predictions of a quick and easy victory had proved false. Even before the attack on Pearl Harbor added the weight of U.S. and other Allied military power into the balance against Japan, Japan had already lost 185,000 dead in China, and Japan's economy was already under severe strain. It was in growing exasperation with this "quagmire" in China that Japanese strategists began to look south.

World War II in the Pacific

The huge costs of waging war on a continental scale in China, especially when combined with Japan's strategic ambition to simultaneously gear up quickly for military self-sufficiency, drove Japan from a surprisingly robust export-led recovery from the Great Depression in the early 1930s to what would turn out to be a fatal dependency on heavy industrial imports by the end of the decade. Increased military spending after 1936 led to inflation, which raised the cost of Japanese products and made them less competitive as exports. Government controls over imported raw materials favored those with military applications rather than materials, such as cotton, that could be used to manufacture textiles for reexport. Government control also funneled new investments into war industries rather than consumer or export-oriented businesses. As a direct result of her quest for self-sufficiency, ironically, Japan therefore only became more critically dependant on such imported things as machine tools, iron, and oil.[30]

A February 1938 National Mobilization Act put all economic resources in Japan under government control. One of the first effects was the imposition of rationing and other austerity measures. Beginning in 1938, gasoline was strictly rationed in Japan. Rice, matches, sugar, and charcoal had joined the list of rationed items by 1940, and in May 1940, Japanese stores were forbidden to sell any nonessential goods. Not only Western-style clothing but even traditional Japanese kimonos were replaced by khaki "people's uniforms" and peasant pantaloons for women.[31]

Ever since defeating Russia in war in 1905, Japanese army planners had anticipated a future war of revenge with the Russians. The communist revolution in Russia only seemed to make such a war more inevitable. Some Japanese army officers, notably Ishiwara Kanji, the mastermind of the takeover in Manchuria, had even opposed intervention in China south of the Great Wall because it would deplete vital resources and distract Japan from the more important confrontation with Russia (which he expected would precede the final showdown with the United States). In fact, Japan actually did engage the Soviet Union in a little-known but bitter struggle during the summer of 1939, at a place called Nomonhan on the border between Mongolia and Manchuria. Soviet armored forces proved disconcertingly effective in this action, however, and Japan suffered heavy loses. Even as Japan was being mauled by the Soviets at Nomonhan, meanwhile, Germany signed a nonaggression pact with the Soviet Union in August 1939. Japan, which had already signed an anti-Comintern pact (opposing communism without specifically mentioning Russia) with Germany in 1936, and reached a formal alliance with the Axis powers Germany and Italy in 1940, responded by arranging its own neutrality pact with the Soviet Union in 1941. Despite Hitler's betrayal of his pact with Stalin and invasion of Russia soon afterward, the Soviet agreement with Japan held. The Soviet Union would remain neutral in World War II in the Pacific until the very last days.

Meanwhile, Japan hoped that its Axis alliance with Germany and Italy would make other powers (such as the United States) reluctant to intervene against Japanese interests in Asia. Largely in an effort to cut off supplies to Nationalist China, by July 1941, Japanese troops had occupied French colonial Indochina (Vietnam). The French, who by this time had been defeated and forced into cooperation with Hitler's Germany in Europe, did not resist in Vietnam, but the United States, Great Britain, and the Netherlands imposed economic sanctions on Japan, notably including embargoes on oil and scrap metal. These sanctions had real teeth. In 1940, 80 percent of Japan's total oil supply came from the United States.[32] Japan's principal alternative to American oil was Dutch colonial Java (in what is now Indonesia). Japan's predicament, therefore, had become quite daunting.

Going to war against Japan's own largest supplier of vital war materials (the United States) hardly seemed sensible, especially since the United States was also much more populous and more extensively industrialized than Japan as of 1941. But Japan's options were limited. By late 1941, Japan's stockpiles of oil were dwindling alarmingly, while the United States was already beginning a massive military buildup. If Japan was to have any chance of victory in a war with the United States, it would have to begin soon. Some leaders in the Japanese army were, moreover, confident that Japanese fighting spirit would overcome the material disadvantages. At an imperial conference on November 5, 1941, a decision was made to go to war if no settlement had been reached by December. The imperial navy drew up plans to temporarily paralyze U.S. forces by striking at the U.S. Pacific Fleet based in Hawai'i. A Japanese aircraft carrier task force sailed for that purpose on November 26 and struck at Pearl Harbor on December 7.

The attack achieved complete surprise, and most of the American battleships anchored in Pearl Harbor were at least temporarily put out of action. A simultaneous Japanese invasion of British Malaya also began. British Hong Kong fell to the Japanese on Christmas Day, and on December 26, Manila, in the American-controlled Philippines, was declared an open city. On the Malay peninsula, Japanese troops hacked their way through the jungle to attack the British fortress at Singapore from its relatively unguarded rear. Singapore fell to the Japanese on February 8, 1942. On March 9, the most valuable prize of all, the Dutch island of Java, with its rich supplies of oil, rubber, and tin, surrendered. In May 1942, the last American holdouts in the Philippines, on the island of Corregidor, surrendered. By this time, there were even rumors of a possible Japanese invasion of British colonial India and talk of evacuating all of northern Australia.

Japan needed just a few more victories to complete the ring of defensive island fortresses it envisioned in preparation for the eventually expected Allied counteroffensive. These last few victories were denied to Japan, however. All the American aircraft carriers had miraculously escaped the slaughter at Pearl Harbor simply by

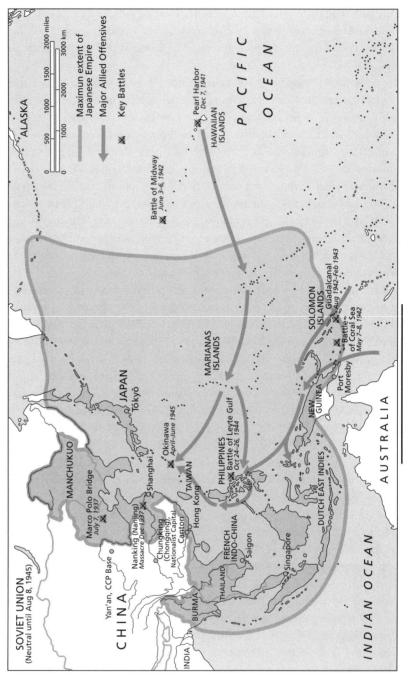

Map 14. World War II in East Asia and the Pacific

being out of port at the time of the attack. On May 8, 1942, an American aircraft carrier task force intercepted a Japanese invasion fleet heading for Port Moresby, New Guinea. In the resulting naval air battle of the Coral Sea, located between Australia and New Guinea, although neither side won a decisive victory, the Japanese were forced to cancel their invasion of Port Moresby. In June 1942, Japanese forces staged successful amphibious landings on actual U.S. soil in the Aleutian Islands, Alaska. This was only intended as a diversion, however, as part of an elaborate plan to lure out and sink the remainder of the U.S. Pacific Fleet. Thanks to some good luck, and the fact that the Americans had broken the Japanese code and were able to decipher Japanese messages, the U.S. fleet surprised the Japanese instead. In the ensuing naval air battle of Midway Island, beginning June 4, 1942, four Japanese aircraft carriers were sunk to the American loss of only one. This battle of Midway became the crucial turning point of the war in the Pacific.

Instead of serving as an impenetrable defensive shield, Japan's island empire in the Pacific proved to be full of holes. U.S. submarines, sailing deep into Japanese waters with relative impunity, almost immediately began to wage an aggressive campaign to cut off the flow of essential raw materials from Java, and elsewhere, to the factories on the Japanese home islands. As a result, Japan's industrial economy ground to a standstill, and Japan was increasingly unable to replace the ships and planes it lost in battle. Japanese-held islands in the Pacific that were especially strongly fortified could furthermore simply be bypassed, or skipped over, in the Allied counteroffensive, in a process called "island hopping."

The Allied counteroffensive began with landings on Guadalcanal, in the Solomon Islands, in August 1942. A fiercely fought battle for supremacy there raged for some six months before the Allies finally drove the Japanese from Guadalcanal in February 1943. From there, the Japanese Pacific island empire was rolled up in a two-pronged counteroffensive, with Allied land forces (under the command of General Douglas MacArthur) driving up from the south through New Guinea to the Philippines and the navy island hopping across the central Pacific from the Marianas to Okinawa.

American industrial productivity, meanwhile, was unleashing a tsunami of steel against the Japanese Empire. Until late 1943, the U.S. Pacific Fleet never had more than four aircraft carriers at any given time, but by the end of 1944, the U.S. Navy had nearly a hundred aircraft carriers in operation in all theaters of the war.[33] By October 1944, General MacArthur had assembled a massive fleet consisting of some seven hundred ships for his long-promised return to the Philippines. Japan committed her last remaining warships to their defense, and in the naval battle of Leyte Gulf – the largest naval battle in world history – the Japanese were decisively defeated. In desperation, Japan even began to resort to suicide (kamikaze, or "Divine Wind," a reference to the typhoons that had scattered the thirteenth-century Mongol invasion fleets) attacks on Allied ships.

In November 1944, air raids on the Japanese home islands began with long-range B-29 bombers based in the Marianas. Altogether, some sixty-six Japanese cities were reduced to charred rubble. Incendiary bombs ignited raging conflagrations among the mostly wooden Japanese houses. Of Japan's major cities, only the

Figure 9.4. Japanese representatives arrive aboard the battleship USS *Missouri* in Tōkyō Bay to participate in surrender ceremonies at the end of World War II, September 2, 1945. National Archives.

ancient imperial capital of Kyōto was spared. Before long, Allied aircraft enjoyed almost complete command of the air above Japan. Yet the unconditional surrender demand that had been adopted by the Allies at the Casablanca conference in 1943 remained unacceptable to Japanese authorities. Some Japanese leaders still hoped that by winning one last major battle, and inflicting unacceptably heavy casualties on the Allies, Japan might be able to obtain better terms. The bottom line for many Japanese authorities was a deeply felt need to preserve the national polity embodied in the imperial institution.

After Germany was defeated in May 1945, Japan found herself fighting alone against almost the entire world. During the summer of 1945, the Japanese made a futile attempt to request Soviet mediation in negotiating an end to the war, not realizing that Stalin had already pledged, at the Yalta Conference in February, that Russia would enter the war against Japan after Germany surrendered. On August 6, an atomic bomb was dropped on Hiroshima. On August 8, the Soviet Union unleashed a massive assault on Japanese forces in Manchuria. On August 9, a second atomic bomb was detonated at Nagasaki. Even then, on August 10, the Japanese government still broadcast a message indicating that Japan would be willing to accept Allied surrender terms only if the preservation of the emperor could be guaranteed. The U.S. response, approved by both Britain and the Soviet Union, was to agree, but with the crucial modification that "the authority of the Emperor . . . shall be subject to the Supreme Commander of the Allied Powers."[34]

This answer was still unsatisfactory to many in the Japanese army. After considerable more debate, however, the emperor himself finally broke the deadlock on August 14 with a decision to surrender. Even then, the night before the emperor's prerecorded surrender speech was scheduled to be broadcast, a group of army officers rebelled and attempted to destroy the recording. They failed, however, and at noon on August 15, 1945, the Japanese people heard the voice of their emperor for the first time, speaking in hard-to-comprehend formal court language. Without ever actually using the word *surrender*, and noting (with considerable understatement) that recent developments in the war "did not turn in Japan's favor," the emperor called on his people to "endure the unendurable."[35]

Formal surrender documents were signed aboard the American battleship *Missouri* on September 2, 1945 (see Figure 9.4). World War II was over. In East Asia, Japan had been catastrophically defeated and lay in smoldering ruins, having suffered some 2.7 million war dead. Korea was to be liberated from Japanese colonial rule but would initially be subject to divided zones of Soviet and American military occupation. China had been on the winning side. But China, where World War II first began in 1937, had also suffered horribly from the war, and the postwar situation in China remained unencouraging. Almost alone in the world, the United States emerged from World War II actively strengthened. In the aftermath of World War II, the U.S. economy accounted for an astonishing 50 percent of all goods and services on earth.[36] Few people could have predicted then that in the following decades, East Asia would reemerge to become (at least in purely economic terms) perhaps the single most successful region of the planet, or that it would be Japan that would lead this spectacular economic "miracle."

For Further Reading

On the rise of ultranationalism in prewar Japan, see Michael A. Barnhart, *Japan Prepares for Total War: The Search for Economic Security, 1919–1941* (Ithaca, NY: Cornell University Press, 1987); W. G. Beasley, *Japanese Imperialism, 1894–1945* (Oxford: Clarendon Press, [1987] 1991); Mark R. Peattie, *Ishiwara Kanji and Japan's Confrontation with the West* (Princeton University Press, 1975); Ben-Ami Shillony, *Revolt in Japan: The Young Officers and the February 26, 1936 Incident* (Princeton University Press, 1973); and George M. Wilson, *Radical Nationalist in Japan: Kita Ikki, 1883–1937* (Cambridge, MA: Harvard University Press, 1969). Concerning Manchukuo, an excellent volume is Louise Young, *Japan's Total Empire: Manchuria and the Culture of Wartime Imperialism* (Berkeley: University of California Press, 1998).

On Nationalist China, see the fine biography of Chiang Kai-shek by Jay Taylor, *The Generalissimo: Chiang Kai-shek and the Struggle for Modern China* (Cambridge, MA: Harvard University Press, 2009). See also Parks M. Coble Jr., *The Shanghai Capitalists and the Nationalist Government, 1927–1937* (Cambridge, MA: Harvard University Press, [1980] 1986); Lloyd E. Eastman, Jerome Ch'en, Suzanne Pepper, and Lyman P. Van Slyke, eds., *The Nationalist Era in China, 1927–1949* (Cambridge University Press, 1991); and James E. Sheridan, *China in Disintegration: The Republican Era in Chinese History, 1912–1949* (New York: Free Press, 1975).

Studies of early Chinese communism and the rise of Mao Zedong include Arif Dirlik, *The Origins of Chinese Communism* (New York: Oxford University Press, 1989); Benjamin I. Schwartz, *Chinese Communism and the Rise of Mao* (Cambridge, MA: Harvard University Press, [1951] 1979); and the short biography by Jonathan D. Spence, *Mao Zedong* (New York: Viking, 1999). Edgar Snow was an American journalist who scooped an early interview with the guerilla leader Mao Zedong and published a still extremely valuable account of Mao's early years as *Red Star over China* (New York: Grove Press, [1938] 1968).

For World War II in China and Japan, see John Hunter Boyle, *China and Japan at War, 1937–1945: The Politics of Collaboration* (Stanford University Press, 1972); Iris Chang, *The Rape of Nanking: The Forgotten Holocaust of World War II* (New York: Penguin Books, 1997); Thomas R. H. Havens, *Valley of Darkness: The Japanese People and World War Two* (Lanham, MD: University Press of America, 1986); Saburō Ienaga, *The Pacific War, 1931–1945* (New York: Pantheon Books, [1968] 1978); and Barbara W. Tuchman, *Stilwell and the American Experience in China, 1911–1945* (New York: Bantam Books, 1972). A still-valuable account by contemporary American journalists reporting from China is Theodore H. White and Annalee Jacoby, *Thunder out of China* (New York: William Sloan Associates, [1946] 1961).

World War II in the Pacific is covered by John W. Dower, *War without Mercy: Race and Power in the Pacific War* (New York: Pantheon Books, 1986); Max Hastings, *Retribution: The Battle for Japan, 1944–45* (New York: Alfred A. Knopf, 2008); and Ronald H. Spector, *Eagle against the Sun: The American War with Japan* (New York: Free Press, 1985).

10 Japan since 1945

The Postwar Allied Occupation

The Shōwa Emperor's surrender speech was broadcast over the radio airwaves on August 15, 1945, and on August 28, a few days before the formal surrender ceremonies were conducted aboard the battleship *Missouri* on September 2, the first small advance party of what would eventually become an Allied occupation force reaching up to a quarter million persons touched down in a C-47 transport plane at an airport outside Tōkyō. These first Allied arrivals were uncertain what sort of reception they might encounter. The Japanese, too, were anxious and uncertain what sort of behavior to expect from the arriving foreign army of occupation, whose soldiers had until recently been such bitter enemies. Many Japanese were relieved that the war was finally over, but many were also, understandably, apprehensive. With relatively few exceptions, however, the arriving Allied forces were treated with respect and even privilege – until 1951, for example, the Japanese government provided occupation authorities with free servants – whereas the occupation authorities, for their part, behaved with marked magnanimity toward their defeated foe. Not a few participants in the occupation discovered a lifelong love and fascination for Japanese culture.[1] In retrospect, the usual verdict is that the postwar Allied occupation of Japan was an overall great success.

Although it is conventionally referred to as an Allied occupation, it was overwhelmingly an American affair. Unlike postwar Germany (and Korea), defeated Japan was not divided into separate zones of occupation by the different Allied powers. A multinational Far Eastern Commission was eventually established in Washington, D.C., and a four-power Allied Council for Japan was sent to Tōkyō, which included British, Chinese, and Soviet representatives, but a single, unified supreme commander for the Allied powers (SCAP) was appointed for the entire region. The officer assigned this command was the senior American general Douglas MacArthur (1880–1964), who set up his headquarters in the Daiichi building in Tōkyō at the end of August 1945. Most of the occupation personnel were also American.

President Truman initially instructed General MacArthur that inside defeated Japan, "your authority is supreme," and MacArthur envisioned his own role in Japan as nothing less than "a sovereign."[2] MacArthur took a grandly imperious view of his position as a kind of military proconsul presiding over postwar Japan, and he was fond of claiming that he had some special understanding of the "Oriental mind" – based, presumably, on his early years of experience living in the Philippines. Actually, the Southeast Asian and largely Catholic Filipinos are quite different from the East Asian Japanese, and MacArthur had very little real familiarity with Japan. Nevertheless, MacArthur's paternalistic attitude did generate some well-intentioned efforts to benefit the Japanese people. This was crucial because initially, amid the desolation of Japan's bombed-out cities, there were desperate shortages of almost everything. Food was rationed, but the rations were less than the minimum normal nutritional requirements necessary to sustain life. Nearly everyone was forced, therefore, to turn to illegal black markets just to get enough food to survive. Black marketeering was so pervasive that one magazine observed with dark humor in 1948 that "the only people who are not living illegally are those in jail."[3] MacArthur, however, responded quickly to the emergency by requesting relief supplies of food and medicine, which undoubtedly saved many lives, even though it could not begin to eliminate all the hardships of the early postwar years. MacArthur also seems to have felt some empathy for the Japanese emperor.

At the time of Japan's surrender, American opinion was seriously divided over the question of how thoroughly Japan would have to be forcibly reconstructed so that it would no longer be a threat to world peace. Some felt that the old, militaristic Japan would have to be almost completely obliterated, and a great many of the Allies felt that Japan should quite properly be punished for its wartime aggression. Initially, plans were drawn up to dismantle Japan's remaining industrial plants and ship them abroad as war reparations. All of Japan's overseas colonial possessions, including Korea, Taiwan, and Manchuria (which had not technically been a colony but had been effectively dominated by the Japanese), were liberated, and some six and a half million Japanese people were returned from overseas to the home islands.

War crime trials also soon began, intended to punish specific alleged culprits. Twenty-eight Class A prisoners were charged with major "crimes against peace" and tried by the International Military Tribunal for the Far East. Seven of these were convicted and sentenced to death by hanging. In addition (not counting those captured by the Soviet Union and Chinese Communists), some fifty-seven hundred other Japanese were tried by Allied international military tribunals, most of whom were accused of Class C, or conventional war crimes, such as mistreatment of prisoners. Of these, 4,405 were convicted and 984 executed. Beyond the punishment of specific war criminals, during the first three years of the occupation, more than two hundred thousand former military officers, politicians, and business leaders were also purged by the occupation authorities.

Many Americans felt that the individual most responsible for the war in the Pacific had been the Japanese emperor himself. The U.S. Senate passed a resolution in 1945 calling for the emperor also to be tried as a war criminal. In January

1946, however, General MacArthur cabled Washington from Tōkyō with a forceful assertion of the idea that putting the emperor on trial for war crimes would be counterproductive and would probably even provoke guerrilla warfare against the Allied occupation. A plausible argument could be made that the emperor of Japan had always been more a symbol of the nation than an active ruler; that the emperor's individual personal responsibility for specific government policies, including military action, had been limited; and that, precisely as a symbol of Japan, the prestige of the throne could be wielded now in the cause of peace and stability just as easily as it previously had been for war. In the end, MacArthur's position prevailed. Not only was the institution of the emperor preserved, but the same wartime Shōwa Emperor ("Hirohito") was allowed to remain seated on the chrysanthemum throne, and the question of his war guilt was largely forgotten.

Even after the surrender, the Japanese government continued to function and handle routine administration. SCAP's authority was ultimately final, but technically, the occupation authorities were there only in a supervisory capacity. In spring 1946, Japan conducted its first postwar election, which was also the first ever in which women were allowed to vote. Yoshida Shigeru (1878–1967) became prime minister, and he would continue to play a leading role throughout the occupation era. The story goes that Yoshida began his first cabinet meeting with the observation that it might be possible for Japan to lose the war and still win the peace.[4]

SCAP's ability to supervise the details of postwar Japan was handicapped by a scarcity of competent Japanese language speakers and of specialists familiar with Japanese culture. During the war, a number of crash courses in Japanese language training had sprung up in the United States. Soon after the Japanese struck Pearl Harbor, for example, Harvard University decided to offer elementary intensive Japanese language instruction in the spring semester of 1942, instead of waiting for the normal beginning of the academic year in September. Its teachers were "stunned when we found close to a hundred students cramming the small classroom" instead of "the usual five or ten." At the start of World War II, the U.S. Navy had only twelve officers who could speak Japanese, but by the end of the war, the U.S. Navy Japanese Language School alone had graduated eleven hundred new translators.[5] Even so, the number of fluent Japanese speakers among the occupation personnel was limited. This made the occupation authorities heavily reliant on English-speaking translators provided by the Japanese Central Liaison Office and opened the door for accidental, or occasionally perhaps even deliberate, misunderstandings.

Nonetheless, SCAP had both the leverage and determination to prod the Japanese Diet (the legislature) into making sweeping reforms that would have been otherwise entirely unthinkable. Because of the Roosevelt era New Deal background of many Americans at the end of World War II, the initial thrust of these reforms emphasized the unionization of factory labor, farmland redistribution, trust busting, and equality of rights. For example, a trade union law was passed in December 1945 that guaranteed Japanese workers the right to organize, strike, and engage in collective bargaining. Antimonopoly and antitrust laws were passed, which forced the breakup of the giant *zaibatsu*. A 1946 farmland reform law prohibited absentee landlordism and strictly limited the amount of farmland that could be rented out to tenant farmers. This land reform, combined with rapid urbanization, was of fundamental importance in finally completing the almost total dissolution of the traditional rural social order. Political prisoners, including Communists, were released from jail. State *Shintō* religion was also disestablished, the emperor renounced his claim to be a manifest deity, and the principle of religious freedom was proclaimed.

Not content with specific new laws or policies, a conviction began to grow that Japan needed an entirely new constitution to replace the nineteenth-century Meiji era document. Since official Japanese proposals for constitutional revision did not go far enough to suit the occupation authorities (whereas some unofficial Japanese proposals went too far, threatening, for example, to eliminate the emperor), the Americans stepped in and wrote the new constitution themselves, originally in English. A small team from the Government Section of SCAP drafted it in roughly a week (February 4–12, 1946) of intense effort, based on guidelines sketched out for them by General MacArthur. After a few revisions, this new constitution was approved by the Japanese Diet in November 1946 and took effect in May 1947. It is still in effect today.

Although, to a large extent, the Japanese emperor had really always only been something of a figurehead, his once theoretically supreme authority was now officially reduced in the new constitution to being merely a "symbol of the State." Sovereign power was now vested, instead, in "the people." Japan became a genuine Western-style democracy, where all citizens twenty years of age and older are eligible to vote. This includes women – a right that was not introduced in France until 1945 and in Switzerland until as late as the 1970s.[6] Despite the American authorship of this document, a British-style parliamentary system was maintained rather than an American-style presidency. Unlike the prewar Japanese system, however, under which the prime minister had been chosen by the emperor (or more accurately, by senior statesmen in the name of the emperor), the postwar prime minister is now responsible to, and chosen by, the Diet. The former upper House of Peers, and the peerage itself, were eliminated and replaced by an Upper House filled with elected councilors.

Because the prime minister was now chosen by the legislators, this meant that he was usually the head of the leading party in the Diet. In practice, until August 2009, this leading party nearly always was the Liberal Democratic Party (LDP). Despite the continued existence of multiple opposition parties, from the original formation of the LDP in 1955 until 2009, with only one brief exception in the mid-1990s, the LDP was effectively the permanent ruling party in Japan. In other words, postwar Japan experienced a peculiar form of multiparty democracy in which the same one party nearly always won. The explanation for this seemingly odd situation is that the main opposition to the ruling LDP – which, despite its somewhat misleading name, is actually the more conservative major party – usually came from the Socialists. Although these Socialists did enjoy a fairly solid core constituency, because they rejected the mutual security treaty with the United

States and held to a generally Marxist line during the cold war years, their popular appeal was also always relatively limited. In contrast, the LDP long delivered undeniable peace and prosperity and promised benefits for nearly everyone.

Since LDP rule was so entrenched, this meant that the real politics of postwar Japan commonly involved factions within the LDP, resulting in the prime minister often being chosen through deals struck between various faction leaders. Also, because LDP members frequently had to compete against each other to get elected, election campaigns remained expensive, and corruption scandals became shockingly endemic. The LDP provided nineteen consecutive prime ministers until 1993, but in that year, when the LDP was rocked by yet another scandal involving the head of its largest faction (who was arrested and accused of taking fifty million dollars in illegal campaign contributions), the LDP splintered. In August 1993, a coalition of seven different political parties put into office the first non-LDP prime minister in thirty-eight years. This man also enjoyed the highest popularity rating of any Japanese prime minister since World War II. His government was, however, paralyzed by disagreements between the wildly divergent blocs that formed its coalition, and when he, too, soon became embroiled in accusations of campaign contribution irregularities, he resigned in April 1994, after only eight months in office. The next prime minister survived in office only two months. Then, in June 1994, a bizarre three-party coalition bringing the conservative LDP together with the Socialists provided Japan with its first Socialist prime minister since 1948. By January 1996, however, the LDP was back in power, and once again, all subsequent Japanese prime ministers were, for many years, drawn from the ranks of the LDP. By 2009, however, after Japan's long-stagnant economy had been further afflicted by a major global recession, criticism of the apparently ineffective LDP economic policies combined with a loss of LDP appeal to younger voters led to a convincing LDP electoral defeat at the hands of the opposition Democratic Party. Whether this 2009 election will truly mark the end of the LDP's long reign, or merely be another brief interruption, only time will tell.

Japan's postwar constitution unintentionally, therefore, produced a long-sustained and rather unusual one-and-a-half-party form of parliamentary democracy. More deliberately, it also enshrined an imposing array of new popular rights, reflecting the American New Deal thinking of the 1940s. These included the rights to social welfare and security, public health, minimum standards of living, and gender equality. In an attempt to promote so-called democratic (or at least, less patriarchal) ideals, during the 1950s, central and local Japanese government agencies, together with certain private organizations, conducted a campaign to encourage Japanese families to, among other things, rotate the family bathing order so that the father did not always get to bathe first.[7]

The most remarkable feature of Japan's postwar constitution is surely Article 9, which asserts that "the Japanese people forever renounce war as a sovereign right of the nation" and flatly states that military forces "will never be maintained." This seems to have originally been MacArthur's idea and is entirely in keeping with the initial concern of the occupation authorities to prevent Japan from ever again becoming a threat to world peace. Ironically, however, many Americans soon began to regret this sweeping degree of Japanese demilitarization, as Japan quickly turned from being an enemy during World War II into an important American ally in the cold war against communism. MacArthur himself helped Japan create a new police reserve, which later became the Self-Defense Forces. Despite an absolute constitutional prohibition, postwar Japan actually did eventually come to invest fairly heavily in self-defense capability. Yet, in the aftermath of World War II, many Japanese sincerely felt deep revulsion for the militarism that had led them to disaster in 1945, and postwar Japan has genuinely remained an almost uniquely pacifistic country.[8]

The early occupation reforms had begun in the lingering afterglow of U.S. president Roosevelt's liberal New Deal and emphasized such things as the release of political prisoners and the passage of a trade union law. But in February 1947, SCAP intervened to prevent a general strike that had been organized by a coalition of Japanese labor unions. With the mounting tensions of the cold war, and a Socialist victory in the April 1947 Japanese elections, a "reverse course" in American policy has sometimes been detected. Certainly the overriding American strategic concern was shifting rapidly from preventing a militaristic Japan from ever again becoming a threat to world peace to the global containment of communism. Because a strong, capitalist, and democratic Japan might contribute to that cold war effort, plans to make Japan pay war reparations were abandoned by 1948 (although Japan did eventually make some quite substantial payments anyway).

At first, there had been some expectation that the postwar occupation might continue for a very long time, but MacArthur believed that a prolonged military occupation would be counterproductive. Work on a peace treaty to end the occupation began as early as 1950. The resulting treaty was officially signed in San Francisco in September 1951. In a revealing indication of the extent to which postwar Japan was now firmly in the American-oriented cold war camp, neither the Soviet Union nor the People's Republic of China attended the peace ceremonies, and a separate peace between Japan and China would not be concluded until 1972. Nevertheless, the San Francisco Peace Treaty took effect on April 28, 1952, officially ending the postwar occupation. In June, the Shōwa Emperor was able to report the restoration of Japanese independence to the sun goddess Amaterasu at the imperial shrine in Ise.

The official end of the occupation did not mean the end of the American military presence. Under the terms of a mutual security agreement, the United States assumed much of the responsibility for the military defense of Japan and was allowed to maintain bases on the Japanese home islands as well as outright American control over the island of Okinawa (until 1972). In 1960, the revision and extension of this U.S.-Japan Security Treaty provoked the largest political demonstrations in Japanese history, which forced the cancellation of a planned visit to Japan by U.S. president Dwight D. Eisenhower. The American military presence continues today, and the American-drafted constitution still stands. Since 1945, in fact, Japan has remained one of the staunchest American allies in the world. After Japan regained her independence, though, in 1957 the sentences of war criminals of all classes were commuted, and for many years after 1954,

Japanese prime ministers were frequently men who had once been purged by the occupation.

Economic Recovery and the "Developmental State"

For many people in Japan, the first winter after the end of World War II was the hardest. As a result of wartime firebombing, millions of persons were homeless and obliged to sleep in subway stations or whatever other improvised shelter they could find. Industrial production stood at a fraction of its prewar levels, and some five million Japanese were unemployed. Japan recovered only very slowly from this devastation. Recovery had scarcely even begun by the end of the occupation. Real per capita gross national product (GNP) in Japan did not regain its pre–World War II level until 1953.[9] The difficulty of Japan's economic recovery was compounded by the almost complete lack of industrial raw materials in the home islands. The outbreak of the Korean War in 1950 – during the fighting of which United Nations forces used Japan for invaluable forward bases – sparked a minor boom in the Japanese economy, but it would not be until the end of the 1950s that the Japanese economy really took off.

From 1955 until 1973, then, the average annual growth in Japan's GNP exceeded 10 percent. In two decades, from 1950 to 1970, Japan's GNP multiplied some twenty times. By 1968, Japan had passed West Germany to become the world's third largest economy. At the same time, the industrial sector of Japan's economy finally became one of the most developed on earth. In the 1950s, for consumers in America, the label "made in Japan" had still been synonymous with "cheap." But Japan moved swiftly from its initial base in textiles and other light industries to more advanced consumer electronics. The transistor, for example, was invented by Bell Laboratories in 1948, and during the 1950s, Japan's Sony Corporation adapted this new technology to create a whole new generation of lightweight portable radios. As a result, Japan soon dominated the world market for transistor radios. Not content with stopping there, Japanese corporations moved on to become major producers of ever larger and more sophisticated products. The first Japanese Toyota Toyopet automobiles were unloaded in the United States in 1957 (see Figure 10.1). By 1981, Japan had become the world's largest automaker and an authentic global economic superpower.

One reason for Japan's remarkable postwar economic success may have been the total devastation of the war itself, which provided a clean slate from which to begin with the latest technologies and newest facilities, obtained through generous (though not free) agreements for technology transfer from the United States and other developed countries. The transistor radio is one such classic example of technology transfer. Japan also enjoyed the immense advantage of relatively unrestricted export access to the huge American consumer market, although Japan was hardly alone in that position. But Japan also had the benefit of well-trained and experienced human capital surviving from before the war, and much of the credit for Japan's success is certainly due simply to the hard work and determination of the Japanese people.

Figure 10.1. The Toyota Toyopet, shown arriving in San Francisco in 1957, was Japan's first export automobile. © Bettmann/Corbis.

In the early postwar years, there was a general popular consensus in Japan about the importance of economic growth as a national priority. Partly as a result of occupation-imposed reforms such as farmland redistribution and the breakup of the *zaibatsu*, it also happened that during its period of rapid economic growth, Japan was the industrialized nation with the most equal income distribution in the world (although by the end of the twentieth century, this had become less true). The postwar Japanese population was overwhelmingly middle class.[10] Some uniquely Japanese features of the postwar economy were also notably egalitarian. These included an expectation of secure lifetime employment (at least for the fortunate employees of larger corporations) and pay based mostly on seniority. This restricted individual career mobility and scope for personal ambition, but also limited competition between coworkers and allegedly encouraged a spirit of cooperation. So-called bottom-up decision making allowed even low-ranking managers a say in formulating corporate policy, while top executives typically worked their way up through the ranks at their companies and remained content with relatively modest salaries (as well as high income tax rates).

Another critical element in Japan's industrial growth was the relative abundance of capital for investment. This was possible because of Japan's exceptionally high rates of personal savings. While the Japanese inclination to save was certainly encouraged by specific government tax policies, some analysts are also, more controversially, inclined to credit something in Confucian culture. This is debatable, but it is a fact that high savings rates have been a strikingly common characteristic throughout modern East Asia.

Although their effectiveness may also be disputed, deliberate government policies were a factor, too. Japan was the original East Asian "developmental state." In the 1970s, Japanese officials openly described their country as having a "plan-oriented market economy."[11] A little historical background helps explain this situation. Following the initial period of state-fostered industrialization in the late nineteenth-century Meiji era, Japan had moved in the direction of Anglo-American-style laissez-faire market capitalism. But the economic deadlock of the 1920s, the bank panic of 1927, and then the onset of the Great Depression had given birth to an impulse in Japan toward so-called industrial rationalization. This involved an odd mix of influences, ranging from American-style efficiency experts to Soviet Russian–style five-year plans, but most especially, it focused on the German model. In 1930, for example, a Japanese bureaucrat named Kishi Nobusuke (1896–1987) spent seven months in Berlin studying industrial rationalization. In Japan, such rationalization was interpreted to mean replacing supposedly excessive competition with cooperation. Kishi Nobusuke subsequently served as a deputy director in the Industrial Department of Manchukuo (the principal laboratory for Japan's prewar experiment with state-led industrialization) in the 1930s and then later as the home government's minister of commerce and industry during World War II. After the war, Kishi was temporarily imprisoned as a war crimes suspect, but following his release, he served as prime minister in 1957–1960, at the beginning of Japan's postwar economic "miracle."[12]

The state-guided capitalism that became characteristic of post–World War II Japan was, however, in some ways a curious hybrid of the prewar Japanese experience with postwar Allied occupation practices. As SCAP began to shift its priorities toward economic reconstruction, for example, by 1947 the occupation authorities were deliberately promoting strategic industries in Japan, using such tools as the allocation of resources, loans from the Reconstruction Finance Bank, and direct government subsidies. Although SCAP had broken up the *zaibatsu* and purged former military officers, politicians, and business leaders, relatively few Japanese bureaucrats were purged after World War II, and the level of bureaucratic control, ironically, reached an all-time peak during the American-led occupation.[13]

The prewar Ministry of Commerce and Industry (which had been reorganized during World War II as the Ministry of Munitions) was reorganized yet again in 1949, during the occupation, as the Ministry of International Trade and Industry (MITI). In the late 1950s, MITI began to target designated key sectors of industry, such as oil refining, petrochemicals, and electronics, for deliberate development. To promote such targeted industries, MITI could directly approve credit for low-interest loans from the Japan Development Bank or the Japan Export Import Bank, and also offer outright government subsidies or tax breaks on such things as the portion of corporate income derived from exports. MITI also controlled access to foreign technology and foreign exchange and held licensing authority over key industries. To protect strategic industries from foreign competition, the government sometimes also resorted to outright quotas on imports. Import quotas on foreign-made automobiles were in effect until 1965, for example.

Aside from initially limiting imported foreign manufactured goods, Japan has also even more consistently remained stubbornly resistant to foreign direct investment. Even after decades of economic liberalization, at the beginning of the twenty-first century, in 2001, foreign direct investment in Japan was still only 0.4 percent of gross domestic product (GDP).[14] This reluctance to accept foreign investment meant that Japan has been heavily reliant on domestic sources of capital, and because the Japanese stock market, as of 1963, provided only about 10 percent of the total necessary capital, most of the money for Japan's early postwar industrial growth came in the form of bank loans. Because the Bank of Japan, the ultimate source of much of the lending, was under the supervision of the Ministry of Finance, this meant that there was a degree of indirect government supervision over most investment decisions. Perhaps even more important than government guidance, however, was the fact that, since Japanese industry obtained so much of its capital from bank loans, Japanese firms were under relatively little pressure to attract stock market investors by showing regular quarterly profit increases and were free to concentrate more on long-term growth, market share, and stability.

In the meantime, perhaps reflecting the key role played by banks in this postwar system, giant new bank-centered enterprise groups known as *keiretsu* took shape, notably around the Fuji, Sanwa, Daiichi, Mitsui, Mitsubishi, and Sumitomo banks. These *keiretsu* typically consisted of one large bank, one general trading company, and several industrial firms. They differed from the prewar *zaibatsu* in that they no longer had central boards or holding companies and functioned instead as networks of mutual stock ownership and financing and preferred (or even obligatory) trading partners.

These enterprise groups then competed fiercely with each other, in what was, despite some bureaucratic government guidance, clearly a predominantly capitalist economy. Bureaucratic administration of the economy had in fact peaked during the occupation years and tended to decline thereafter. As early as 1951, tax concessions began to replace direct government subsidies as a tool for the promotion of industrial development. Significant liberalization of the Japanese economy began around 1961, and vaguer (and more easily disregarded) administrative guidance replaced direct bureaucratic controls. By the 1980s, Japan actually had a proportionately much smaller central and local government bureaucracy than the United States or most other industrialized democracies.[15]

Trade Wars and the End of the Japanese Miracle

The success of the Japanese economic miracle was so spectacular that in 1979, an influential book was published with the unsettling title *Japan as Number One: Lessons for America*.[16] Per capita income in Japan actually passed the United States in 1988 (although it has since sunk again below the U.S. level, and a meaningful comparative standard of living is, in any case, more difficult to measure). By the end of the 1980s, Japan appeared seriously poised to emerge as the world's foremost economy. By 1991, Japan had become the world's leading donor of foreign aid, and Japan had also eclipsed the United States as a source of foreign investment in Asia.

While some Americans looked to the Japanese model for possible lessons, other Americans simply felt that the playing field was unfairly skewed against them. Japan, it was alleged, was practicing predatory neomercantilist, or protectionist, trade policies. Though the United States had for decades provided Japan with military protection and free access to the American consumer market, Japan supposedly had not reciprocated by opening its own domestic market to foreign products. The 1980s became a decade of often highly emotionally charged trade wars between Japan and its leading allies. Tensions between Japan and the United States were reflected in books such as Clyde Prestowitz's *Trading Places: How We Allowed Japan to Take the Lead*, with its disturbing first chapter title: "The End of the American Century."[17]

One difficulty with accusations of unfair trading practices was that by the 1980s, most of Japan's early postwar protectionist restrictions had already been lifted (except in the sensitive category of food), yet the Japanese market remained strangely resistant to penetration by foreign products. A partial explanation for this may have been the dense networks of preferred customers and preferential business relationships within the Japanese system, and the complicated distribution patterns involving numerous middlemen and many small, mom-and-pop stores. At the end of the twentieth century, half of all Japan's retail outlets still had no more than two employees. Determined to force the issue, however, in 1988, the U.S. Congress passed an omnibus trade law containing a so-called Super 301 provision calling for the citation of unfair trading partners. Even earlier, in September 1985, finance ministers from the United States, Great Britain, France, Germany, and Japan met at the Plaza Hotel in New York to develop a plan to reduce the American trade deficit by decreasing the currency exchange value of the dollar, which would make American exports (priced in dollars) cheaper and theoretically therefore more competitive. The resulting Plaza Accord caused the value of the Japanese yen (which had earlier been fixed at 360 to the dollar from the time of the Allied occupation until 1971) to soar from 239 per dollar to as high as 79 yen per dollar by 1995.

In Japan, officials responded to the trade wars of the 1980s with much talk about the need to internationalize and adjust to meet world standards and expectations. Curiously paralleling this, however, was also a revived interest in Japanese national identity (called *Nihonjinron* or "discourses on Japanese people"). Japan was popularly imagined as possessing a unique culture that could be traced back to Stone Age origins, and there was even a somewhat resurgent spirit of Japanese nationalism, exemplified by a 1989 Ministry of Education requirement that schools fly the "Rising Sun" national flag and sing the national anthem during ceremonies. Although the simultaneous calls for internationalization and reawakened interest in Japaneseness were seemingly contradictory impulses, the contradiction is partially explained by the emerging conceit that Japan's exceptional economic success was just exactly because of Japan's unique national character.[18]

As Japan had prospered, aspects of allegedly traditional Japanese culture, such as a preference for family-style groupings (for example, viewing the business as a fictive family), a preference for harmony over competition, decision making by consensus, and others, had come to be celebrated (by some) as reasons for Japan's success. "Spiritual training," which had been to some extent discredited by defeat in World War II, saw a revival by the early 1970s. Many companies instituted spiritual training programs for their employees, in which trainees built character by enduring physical labor, military-style exercises, long hikes, and sitting in Zen meditation.[19]

The Japanese had good reason to feel somewhat self-satisfied by the late 1980s. A new era literally then began in 1989 with the death of the Shōwa Emperor (Hirohito) in January, after a lengthy sixty-three-year reign. The new emperor's reign period is called Heisei, which means "achieving peace." This new era almost immediately encountered difficulties, however. The 1985 Plaza Accord had sharply increased the exchange value of the yen, but for a few years, Japanese industry had been able to successfully compensate for the increased relative cost of its exports with accelerated investments. This, however, led to inflated asset values and a bubble economy. The Japanese stock market soared, and real estate prices reached fantastic levels. By the late 1980s, the land on which the imperial palace stands in downtown Tōkyō was equal in value to all of California, and a popular joke claimed that if you were to fold the largest denomination of currency the Japanese government issued – the ten thousand yen note – as tightly as possible and drop it in the pricey Ginza district of Tōkyō, it would not pay for the cost of the ground it covered.[20]

Almost inevitably, these real estate and stock market bubbles eventually burst. It happened in 1990. Commercial real estate prices in Japan's major cities fell by as much as 85 percent, and as of 1992, the Nikkei stock index was down 60 percent from its 1989 high. This left Japan with much excess industrial capacity and enormous bad debts. By the early twenty-first century, Japanese banks may have held as much as a hundred trillion yen in problem debt, or nearly 20 percent of GDP. The former exhilarating rates of economic growth seem unlikely now to ever return. Japan's quandary is that it can produce more than its own domestic market can consume, and with the rise of new rival Asian manufacturing powers (such as China) and the "hollowing" of Japan's own manufacturing due to the transfer of production overseas, export-led growth can no longer generate the kind of dynamic expansion of the Japanese economy it once did.

If the Japanese economy is stagnant, the Japanese population is also graying. The combination of a less-than-replacement birthrate with the longest average life expectancy in the world makes Japan now the most rapidly aging society on earth. The Japanese workforce peaked in size in 1998, and there are dire predictions that the population may even decline by as much as half over the next century. That Japanese society also remains resistant to large-scale immigration and the creation of new Japanese citizens via naturalization does not augur well for any resumption of miraculous rates of growth.

As it happened, the apparent end of the Japanese miracle also coincided with the fall of the Berlin Wall in 1989 and the lowering of the red flag of the Soviet Union over the Kremlin walls in Moscow for the last time in 1991. The former Soviet bloc dissolved, and the world's largest remaining communist country, China, which had already begun experimenting with a market economy years earlier, by the 1990s sometimes seemed even more capitalistic than the capitalists themselves. With the end of the cold war, deregulation, privatization, free trade, and globalization were everywhere the fashion. An important milestone in this post–cold war age of globalization was the creation of a new World Trade Organization (WTO) in 1995. Fueled by the Internet and other new information technologies, in the 1990s, the U.S. economy embarked on what has been called the longest sustained peacetime expansion in American history. American self-confidence was resurgent, and Japan seemed more subdued.

Japan and Globalization

Despite the end of dramatic economic growth rates, Japan today is still a prosperous, highly developed, thoroughly modern society – in many ways a very attractive place to live. Unrestrained economic development in the early postwar years had incurred costs, or downsides, of its own, such as making Japan one of the most heavily polluted countries on earth. A growing awareness of the dangers of pollution, and civic activism, brought new controls and regulations in the 1970s and the beginning of environmental improvements. Some relaxation of the intense pressure for constant economic growth since the 1990s may also make it easier simply to enjoy life a little.

Unlike as recently as the end of World War II, Japan is now an overwhelmingly urban society with roughly 80 percent of the Japanese people living in cities. These Japanese cities are generally very pleasant places, too. Among them, Tōkyō may have already been the largest city in the world by the eighteenth century, and if it perhaps has more recently been surpassed in size by Mexico City, it is still a vast metropolis that is home to some thirty million people. Apart from a few scattered clusters of skyscrapers, however, the Tōkyō skyline is relatively unremarkable and undistinguished. The city has been described as resembling a (seemingly) endless series of urban villages, each centering around a shopping arcade and connected by a remarkably efficient network of subway lines. Thanks to the American firebombing in 1945, and relentless construction, it is almost entirely new.

Tōkyō is new, modern, and generally "Western" in appearance. Japan had, of course, already begun self-consciously Westernizing in the late nineteenth century. The American-led postwar occupation greatly accelerated the pace of what was now often specifically American influence. During the cold war, as a bamboo curtain divided East Asia, it was the portions of East Asia that, like Japan, looked farther east – across the Pacific toward the United States – that proved especially dynamic. On balance, it is possible to argue plausibly that the American presence has been generally beneficial and that "most people in East Asia are far better off today than they would have been if the Americans had stayed home."[21] Beyond the indisputably growing economic interconnectedness of the Pacific Rim, there has also been a fair amount of cultural Americanization.

If Japan today is, in many ways, just another modern, industrialized, Western society, its face is often specifically American. Baseball is enormously popular in Japan. In 2007, when the premier of the People's Republic of China visited Japan in an effort to improve Sino-Japanese relations, one of his more publicized activities was to play a game of softball at a Japanese university. If McDonald's fast-food restaurants are the epitome of modern American popular culture, after the opening of the first Tōkyō outlet in 1971, McDonald's became the top restaurant in Japan by customer volume (with Kentucky Fried Chicken as number two) and so much a part of Japanese culture that according to an often-told (and possibly not even apocryphal) story, young Japanese on vacation in the United States have sometimes been "pleasantly surprised" to discover that there are McDonald's in America, too.[22] There had already been coffee shops lining the streets of Japanese cities long before the appearance of the American Starbucks chain, but after the explosive expansion of Starbucks, the world's busiest Starbucks was soon located in Tōkyō.[23] Tōkyō Disneyland opened in 1984, and before long, the Japanese were spending more money at that attraction than Americans themselves were spending at either the California or the Florida Disney theme parks.[24] The rising tide of American pop culture even threatened to swamp Japan's own native culture, to the alarm of some cultural conservatives. In the mid-1980s, for example, there was a flap in the Japanese media when it was reported that young Japanese were forgetting how to use chopsticks. (The use of chopsticks, called *hashi* in Japanese and *kuaizi* in Chinese, is another – minor, but in its own way symbolic – East Asian cultural marker. In Greater China, at least, chopsticks remain entirely unthreatened by knives and forks, and they are actually still quite common in Japan, too.)

Yet, if "Japan is unmistakably westernized," it is also true that "Westerners who visit Japan do not necessarily find what they see familiar."[25] Not only are individual Western influences sometimes modified in the process of domestication, but the juxtaposition of influences, sometimes from totally different sources, can also be unexpected. Not all the Western influences are American, either. For example, during the early years of the postwar occupation, in spite of the overwhelming American military presence at that time, Japanese translations of books from French, German, Russian, and British authors each outnumbered those from American writers.[26] French, rather than English, has been the standard international language used by the postwar Japanese post office. And even though the current Japanese constitution was actually written by Americans, as mentioned previously, Japan still has a British-style parliamentary system, and the Japanese also drive on the left-hand side of the street, British style.

If McDonald's is the leading restaurant in Japan, that is mainly because most restaurants in Japan are small, independent operations, not large corporate chains. The vast majority of restaurants are actually (modern) Japanese style. There are also Chinese, Italian, French, Indian, and other restaurants. Baseball and golf are genuinely popular, but *sumō* wrestling also retains a following. Many Japanese homes still have floors with tatami matting rather than solid Western-style floors. It is not uncommon for Japanese people to dress occasionally in semi-traditional-style kimono, and significant numbers of people actually do practice such traditions as the tea ceremony or the art of flower arranging (ikebana). Precisely because Japan did take a conservative approach to modernization, the Japanese have sometimes quite self-consciously preserved elements of tradition. Visitors to Japan frequently find themselves presented with an explicit choice between "Japanese style" or "Western style" (*Wafū* or *Yōfū*). Despite the almost universal study of English as a second language in Japan, moreover, although there are now many Japanese who are genuinely fluent in English, English is still not really very widely spoken on the street. In other words, despite all the modernization, Westernization, and Americanization, Japan remains, somehow, Japanese.

Moreover, if Japan today is culturally globalizing – which some interpret to mean Americanizing – Japan has become a major alternative center of globalizing influences in its own right. This includes, but is not limited to, the material products of Japanese industry. Concealed beneath the superficial stagnation of the Japanese economy since 1990, there has been a huge spike in Japanese investment elsewhere in Asia. The number of Japanese companies operating in China, for example, increased by a factor of fifteen in the decade between 1988 and 1997.[27] Japanese brands, such as Sony, Panasonic, Nintendo, Nissan, Isuzu, Mitsubishi, Honda, Toyota, and Lexus, are all globally familiar and world-renowned for quality. Beyond these industrial products, moreover, Japan also exerts a powerful cultural attraction. One recent English-language book, *The Sushi Economy*, takes the consumption of Japanese sushi (vinegared rice with fresh seafood and other delicacies) as an index of globalization.[28] Douglas McGray has even suggested that Japan may become the next cultural superpower – a center of global "cool."[29]

The Japanese children's television program *The Mighty Morphin Power Rangers* was being shown in eighty different countries as of the mid-1990s and at its peak claimed to be the most watched children's show in the world.[30] A majority of the world's animated cartoons are now made in Japan, and the specifically Japanese style called anime has attracted something of a global cult following (familiar titles include *Sailor Moon*, *Speed Racer*, *Astro Boy*, and *Doraemon*). Despite sometimes bitter lingering memories of early-twentieth-century Japanese imperialism (South Korea, for example, officially prohibited the importation of Japanese popular culture products until 1998), Japanese pop culture has made special inroads among young Asians. Hello Kitty and karaoke have been infinitely more popular in East Asia than they have been in the West, and Japanese video games, TV programs, and pop music can be found everywhere. The fiction of the Japanese novelist Murakami Haruki, although translated into some fifteen languages and popular worldwide, seems to resonate especially with East Asians. Nearly three million copies of his books were in print in the People's Republic of China alone as of 2005. Yet despite his often overtly global, Westernized, and cosmopolitan themes, Murakami's writing "brings Japan to the world every bit as much as the other way around."[31]

In Taipei, the capital of Taiwan, the first major skyscraper ever constructed was the Mitsukoshi building – a Japanese department store. Although it has since been eclipsed by the newer Taipei 101, which, for a few years in the early twenty-first century, was the tallest skyscraper on the planet, the Mitsukoshi building still towers over the skyline of the old Taipei city center. Japanese cultural influences on Taiwan began to surge especially in the 1980s. By mid-decade, Japanese-language publications in Taiwan were outselling those written in English, and despite a continuing official ban on Japanese songs and movies, 31 percent of all Taiwan's video rentals were Japanese productions.[32] One twenty-first-century Taipei restaurant advertises authentic Japanese-style curry. Curry originated as an Indian-style dish that was much popularized by the British, and in prepackaged form, it became a staple of the modern Japanese diet, widely available in coffee shops and inexpensive Japanese restaurants. Like the Japanese-style curry that was being marketed in Taipei, a similar process of hybridization is actually at the core of much cultural globalization (see Figure 10.2).

Many modern Japanese products were arguably, in some sense, originally Western ideas – including everything from automobiles to transistors, pop music videos, and cartoons – that now merely happen to be manufactured in Japan. This might simply be taken as further evidence of the Westernization of Japan, except that these things are often given a Japanese twist in the process and sometimes then even return to influence the West. The Japanese word *anime* (pronounced "ah-nee-may"), for example, comes from the English "animation." This nicely illustrates the often complex crosscurrents of cultural globalization.

Jūdō was, of course, originally a Japanese martial art, and even today, even as practiced in the United States, it still usually involves a certain amount of Japanese-style clothing, ritual, and Japanese-language vocabulary. Yet it was, from the start, a modern hybrid. It was invented in the 1880s (based on older styles of weaponless combat) by Japan's first member of the International Olympic Committee. It may have been inspired in part by the ancient Chinese Daoist philosophy of yielding – "using the soft to conquer the hard" – but it was also inspired by modern European ideas concerning sport and the importance of physical exercise. With its acceptance as an Olympic sport in 1960, *Jūdō* became increasingly international. By the end of the twentieth century, there were more *Jūdō* practitioners in Europe than in Japan, Europeans were competing for the majority of A-level titles, and the official languages of the International Judo Federation were English and French, not Japanese.[33]

The British colony of Hong Kong, located on the coast of China, experienced an invasion of modern Japanese pop music during the 1980s. This music included both the original Japanese-language versions and local Cantonese-language covers of Japanese songs. At one point in 1989, for example, there were four different roughly simultaneous Hong Kong covers of the same Japanese song. In the 1990s, this Japanese boom was followed by something of a counterreaction and an assertion of native Hong Kong musical talent. Cantonese covers of Japanese songs became less common in the 1990s, although original Japanese music remained popular. Most recently, though, a hybridization of pop music seems to be the trend.[34]

Figure 10.2. The Taipei 101, in Taiwan, was the tallest skyscraper in the world from 2003 to 2009. The white sign prominent on the street in the right foreground of this picture advertises (in Chinese) "Japanese-style Ramen [Noodles]." This is an interesting example not only of modern Japanese popular culture influences on Taiwan (and Greater China) but also – since Ramen noodles are actually a modern Japanese adaptation of what was once originally a Chinese dish – of Chinese influences on Japan. Dried instant Ramen noodles have also now become an inexpensive staple of the worldwide diet, illustrating the sometimes surprisingly complex, circular patterns of what we call globalization. © Louie Psihoyos/Corbis.

As one final illustration of the complicated patterns in which global and local, traditional and new, intertwine in the formation of modern pop culture, something called *enka*-style music is often considered to be the very embodiment of native popular (as opposed to elite) Japanese musical traditions. Yet *enka* actually combines modern Western instruments with Japanese scales and techniques, and although the word *enka* can be traced as far back as the 1880s, the familiar *enka* style did not really emerge until the 1920s or even later. Despite its popular association with the "soul of the Japanese," moreover, such non-Japanese artists as Teresa Teng (Deng Lijun, 1953–1995) have also been described as *enka* singers. Teresa Teng frequently recorded in Japanese – but more commonly in her native Mandarin Chinese. Teresa (notice also the borrowed Western-language first name) was a "mainlander" Chinese, born and raised on Taiwan, whose clear, sweet voice and numerous hit tunes played a role that "cannot be underestimated" in reintroducing modern Western-style commercial pop music to the mainland People's Republic of China, as it began to emerge from Maoist isolationism after 1978. She remains, even after her tragic premature death from asthma in 1995, one of the most beloved pop singers in the entire Chinese-speaking world. Somehow she managed to simultaneously combine being a singer from Taiwan who was quintessentially Chinese with also being both Western style and Japanese style.[35]

The world increasingly interpenetrates. Globalization operates across national borders (which, however, still remain important) in complex, swirling patterns. Japan, which has been called the first non-Western society on earth to successfully modernize, remains perhaps overall the most successful. Yet, although it is difficult to define or explain precisely what this means, Japan somehow also remains uniquely Japanese.

For Further Reading

The postwar Allied occupation of Japan is covered by John W. Dower, *Embracing Defeat: Japan in the Wake of World War II* (New York: W. H. Norton, 1999). For a critical look at the prosecutions of Japanese defendants for war crimes, see Richard H. Minear, *Victors' Justice: The Tokyo War Crimes Trial* (Princeton University Press, 1971).

On postwar Japanese politics, see Takeshi Ishida and Ellis S. Krauss, eds., *Democracy in Japan* (University of Pittsburgh Press, 1989), and Tetsuya Kataoka, ed., *Creating Single-party Democracy: Japan's Postwar Political System* (Stanford, CA: Hoover Institution Press, 1992).

The classic study of Japan's postwar economic recovery is Chalmers Johnson, *MITI and the Japanese Miracle: The Growth of Industrial Policy, 1925–1975* (Stanford University Press, 1982).

For contemporary Japanese life, see Theodore C. Bestor, *Neighborhood Tokyo* (Stanford University Press, 1989); Edward Seidensticker, *Tokyo Rising: The City since the Great Earthquake* (Cambridge, MA: Harvard University Press, 1991); and Christine R. Yano, *Tears of Longing: Nostalgia and the Nation in Japanese Popular Song* (Cambridge, MA: Harvard University Asia Center, 2002).

On Japanese pop culture and globalization, see Harumi Befu and Sylvie Guichard-Anguis, eds., *Globalizing Japan: Ethnography of the Japanese Presence in Asia, Europe, and America* (London: RoutledgeCurzon, 2001); Timothy J. Craig, ed., *Japan Pop! Inside the World of Japanese Popular Culture* (Armonk, NY: M. E. Sharpe, 2000); and Joseph J. Tobin, ed., *Re-made in Japan: Everyday Life and Consumer Taste in a Changing Society* (New Haven, CT: Yale University Press, 1992).

11 Korea since 1945

The Korean War

The cold war first erupted into heated conflict on the Korean peninsula, and it is most especially in Korea that the cold war lingers on still today, long after it has passed into history almost everywhere else. The first great global crisis of the cold war era, the Korean War, was a direct consequence of Allied dispositions at the end of World War II. During World War II, the U.S. State Department had contemplated plans for a four-power trusteeship to administer the Korean peninsula following its postwar liberation from Japanese colonial rule. President Roosevelt briefly discussed such plans with the Soviet leader Joseph Stalin at their wartime Yalta conference – President Roosevelt suggesting that such a trusteeship might need to continue for some twenty or thirty years. But Korea received so little wartime American attention that the U.S. Secretary of State reportedly even had to ask a subordinate in 1945 where Korea is.[1] Japan surrendered sooner than many people had anticipated, leaving the United States almost totally unprepared for any immediate action in Korea. Meanwhile, Soviet Russian troops had already entered the peninsula from the north on August 9, 1945, during the final days of World War II. The first U.S. occupation forces in Korea did not arrive in the south until September 8, a full month later. The arriving American GIs found, as one report to the State Department concluded on September 15, "a powder keg ready to explode at the application of a spark."[2]

Amid the gathering signs of what would soon become an open cold war rivalry between the two former World War II Allies, the United States and the Soviet Union, there was a not unreasonable fear in Washington that the Soviets might press their early advantage to overrun the entire Korean peninsula. A joint partition of Korea was therefore hastily arranged, and it was actually the U.S. Pentagon that somewhat arbitrarily decided on the thirty-eighth parallel – a mere line on a Pentagon office wall map, reflecting no particular preexisting cultural or geographic conditions – as the point of division between the U.S. and Soviet zones.[3] Meanwhile, throughout the Korean peninsula, so-called People's Committees had quickly organized themselves in the wake of Japan's surrender. Given the bitter poverty of most Korean peasants, and the taint of collaboration with Japanese colonial rule that, to some degree or another, unavoidably haunted almost all of the preexisting Korean elite, American forces in southern Korea were chiefly concerned to identify and give their support to Korean leaders who would be reliably anti-communist. Some of the most likely candidates were found among returning Korean nationalists who had evaded cooperation with the Japanese by living for extended periods in exile abroad. Most notable among these was Syngman Rhee (Yi Sŭng-man, 1875–1965), who now came home to Korea after thirty-five years in the United States.

After the attempt to negotiate a trusteeship with the Soviet Union failed, the United States appealed to the newly formed United Nations (UN), and in May 1948, the UN supervised the first general democratic election in Korean history. This was conducted only in the southern, U.S.-occupied zone. The newly elected Korean National Assembly then selected Syngman Rhee to serve as the first president in July, and on August 15, 1948, the establishment of the Republic of Korea (commonly known as South Korea) was formally proclaimed. Less than a month later, on September 9, a rival Democratic People's Republic of Korea (North Korea) was created in the north. Kim Il Sung (Kim Il-sŭng, 1912–1994), who had returned after World War II from his own period of anti-Japanese exile in the Soviet Union, was designated premier (later, president). By early 1949, both the Soviet Union and the United States had withdrawn their troops from Korea, and the postwar Allied military occupation of Korea was over.

Despite the sharp ideological opposition between these two new Korean governments, few Korean people saw this north-south division as at all natural or desirable, or expected it to be permanent. Many were quite eager to reunify their nation. There were, consequently, several exchanges of gunfire and mutual provocations over the next few years, but the superpower patrons of these two rival Korean governments, the United States and the Soviet Union, were both anxious to avoid being dragged into any new World War III with each other and acted to restrain their respective protégés.

However, as a Communist victory in China's civil war grew increasingly more certain, in the end (despite substantial U.S. noncombatant assistance to Chiang Kai-shek's Chinese Nationalists), the United States declined to actively intervene in the fighting on the Chinese mainland. After Chiang Kai-shek's Nationalist government retreated to the island of Taiwan in 1949, for a time, there were even some indications that President Truman might terminate U.S. support for Chiang. In a speech at the National Press Club on January 12, 1950, Secretary of State Dean Acheson publicly described America's defensive perimeter in Asia in such a way as to seemingly pointedly leave out both Taiwan and Korea. All these signs seemed to be indications that the United States might not actively intervene in a Korean civil war, either, or be willing to shed vast quantities of American blood to prevent a forcible North Korean reunification of the peninsula. In 1950, therefore, Joseph Stalin finally gave his approval to Kim Il Sung's ambitious plan of attack – with the understanding that there would be no active Russian participation. In hindsight, this was obviously an enormous miscalculation. What the various Communist leaders did not realize was that the political backlash in the United States over the perceived "loss of China" was actually hardening American political resolve to contain the spread of communism and prevent any further such losses.

South Korea had a larger population than the north – approximately two-thirds of Korea's total – but most of Korea's existing heavy industry was located in the north. The northern military forces were also better equipped, with 242 new Soviet Russian–made T-34 tanks and a small combat air force, in opposition to which the south could field no tanks at all and only a handful of training aircraft. In addition, as many as one hundred thousand North Korean soldiers had previous combat experience fighting with the Chinese Communist forces during China's civil war. These troops were already battle hardened, and their service in the Chinese Communist cause also established an ominous burden of debt that the Chinese Communists might have felt obliged to repay. Despite these northern advantages, at the time, few people in the south realized how inadequate their own military forces actually were.

In the early morning hours before dawn on June 25, 1950, North Korean forces staged a massive offensive south across the line of the thirty-eighth parallel. President Truman was home in Independence, Missouri, at the time, and it was Secretary of State Acheson who made the initial decision to engage American troops in the defense of South Korea. With characteristic determination, however, President Truman fully committed U.S. forces in Korea and ordered the American Seventh Fleet into the Taiwan Straits to prevent a possible Communist invasion of Taiwan, as well. As a permanent member of the UN's Security Council, the Soviet Union would have ordinarily been in a position to veto any intervention by the UN, but it happened that the Soviets were just then boycotting the UN (from January to August 1950) because China's UN seat was still being held by Chiang Kai-shek's Republic of China (now on Taiwan) rather by Mao Zedong's People's Republic (on the mainland). As a result, the UN was able to react quickly and decisively to condemn the North Korean attack. The defense of South Korea became a UN action. Eventually, some fifteen counties would contribute soldiers to the war effort, although by far the largest foreign contingent came from the United States, and the American general Douglas MacArthur (then still supreme commander for the Allied powers in Japan) assumed overall command.

The South Korean capital, Seoul, was only sixty miles south of the thirty-eighth parallel, and Seoul fell to northern forces in just three days. By the third week of the war, over half of South Korea had been captured by northern armies. With only light, handheld weapons to confront the northern armored vehicles, the first American units that engaged the enemy also fell back quickly. Eventually, however, UN forces were able to dig in and hold a defensive perimeter of about fifty square miles around the southeastern Korean port city of Pusan, which provided an essential base for resupply and the buildup for a counteroffensive. By about mid-August, the balance of firepower had shifted, with the UN increasingly having a large advantage in heavy weapons, especially airpower. By the end of active combat, UN aircrews had flown over a million sorties against the north.

Next, in a daring gamble, General MacArthur staged an amphibious landing farther up the west coast at Inch'ŏn, on September 15. Inch'ŏn is an important port city, serving the southern capital Seoul, but it has no nice sandy beaches, and features one of the world's most extreme tidal ranges. At low tide, an amphibious invasion must confront miles of mudflats. Inch'ŏn could very easily have become a deathtrap for the UN soldiers, and MacArthur decided to strike there anyway against much advice – but he was fortunate, this time. Inch'ŏn turned out to be perhaps the single greatest triumph in General MacArthur's long and distinguished military career. A mighty invasion armada consisting of 261 ships put the American X Corps ashore with the loss of only 536 men. By the end of September, the North Korean forces had been driven back to the place from which they had started, across the thirty-eighth parallel.

Encouraged by this success, UN forces then proceeded from the containment of communism to its rollback. Even before the Inch'ŏn landings, President Truman had authorized General MacArthur to continue his advance into North Korea – as long as there was no sign of intervention by either the Soviet Union or the People's Republic of China. This time, it was the anti-communist world leaders who miscalculated.

On September 30, the first South Korean troops passed north across the thirty-eighth parallel. On October 2, the Chinese premier (Zhou Enlai) formally notified the Indian ambassador that China would intervene if any American troops crossed the parallel. Because the United States did not recognize the People's Republic of China and had no direct communications with it, indirect diplomacy was the only possible way to signal China's intentions. Although this Chinese message was repeated through several channels, it was evidently not taken seriously. On October 7, the American First Cavalry crossed the thirty-eighth parallel heading into North Korea. On October 19, the North Korean capital fell, and by October 26, advanced units of the UN forces had reached as far as the Yalu River, which marks the border between Korea and China. A few days earlier, on October 15, at an historic meeting on Wake Island, General MacArthur personally assured President Truman that there was "very little" chance of Chinese intervention in the war. Even if the Chinese did intervene, MacArthur boasted that they would be easily crushed in what he predicted would be "the greatest slaughter in the history of mankind."[4]

The very next day, on October 16, Chinese so-called volunteers began crossing the Yalu River headed in the opposite direction, undetected by UN observers. Given the vast disparity in military firepower between the United States and China at that time (this was, furthermore, a People's Republic of China that was still scarcely a year old), China's decision to enter the war was also an enormous gamble. At the time of Chinese entry, "as many as two-thirds of some infantry units" did not have even small arms. Even at the end of active combat in Korea, despite receiving new supplies from the Soviet Union, the Chinese were still only equipped with a motley assortment of weapons from ten different countries, with captured American weapons (26%) still apparently outnumbering those obtained from the Soviet Union (20%).[5] It was therefore not an easy decision for the Chinese leaders to commit themselves to combat with the powerful American armed forces, especially after Joseph Stalin belatedly informed them that the Soviet Union would not provide air support. But Mao Zedong was confident in his doctrine of "people's war," which relied on resources of manpower rather than technology. On October 26 – the same day that UN troops began to arrive on the banks of the Yalu River – Chinese People's Volunteers struck at South Korean columns, hitting American forces a few days later, on November 1, and overrunning U.S. cavalry positions at Unsan. After this, however, the Chinese withdrew again into concealment in North Korea's rugged terrain, and although the American president and Joint Chiefs of Staff were cautious and anxious to avoid a major war with China, General MacArthur remained confident and inclined to downplay the Chinese intervention as merely token interference.

MacArthur, in fact, felt optimistic enough to launch a "home by Christmas" offensive on November 24, in an effort to finish the war quickly. What MacArthur did not realize was that some two hundred thousand Chinese soldiers lay hidden in the mountains separating the two main UN columns in the east and west. On November 27, the Chinese struck in full force. Within a week, the center of the UN line had fallen back again some fifty miles. By January 4, 1951, the South Korean capital at Seoul had fallen to the enemy for a second time.

General MacArthur seems to have felt at this point that the best military response to Chinese intervention in Korea would be to escalate the war by taking the offensive to the Chinese homeland. President Truman and the Joint Chiefs, however, sensibly enough, did not relish the idea of turning a limited, if nasty, war in Korea into a general World War III. China's lack of industry would have rendered attempts to bomb it into rubble futile, and China's vast population and extensive land area (coupled with the Chinese Communists' considerable prior experience at guerrilla warfare) would have drawn any American ground invasion of China into a costly quagmire – and there was always the danger of sparking a true World War with the rival superpower, the Soviet Union. When President Truman ordered that all future public statements concerning the Korean War be cleared through the State Department, General MacArthur proceeded to violate this presidential directive repeatedly. MacArthur's complaint was that the restraints being imposed on his war effort by civilian politicians were preventing him from winning total victory. In March 1951, MacArthur even wrote a letter endorsing the idea of "unleashing" Chiang Kai-shek's Nationalist Chinese from Taiwan to open a second front against the Chinese Communists. When this letter was read aloud on the floor of the U.S. House of Representatives, the U.S. president viewed it as outright insubordination, and on April 11, President Truman officially relieved General MacArthur of his command.

The bloodiest phase of the combat in Korea was still yet to come, but by June 1951, the war had reached an effective stalemate not far from its original starting point at the thirty-eighth parallel. Cease-fire talks began, and a truce was declared on July 27, 1953. The war in Korea had cost the United States some thirty-three thousand lives. China lost roughly eight hundred thousand, including Chairman Mao's own son. The conflict left a staggering three million Koreans

Figure 11.1. "With her brother on her back a war weary Korean girl tiredly trudges by a stalled M-26 tank, at Haengju, Korea," June 9, 1951. National Archives.

killed, wounded, or missing – one out of every ten (see Figure 11.1). In the north, the war provided Kim Il Sung with an opportunity to further consolidate his power. In South Korea, it helped pave the way for three decades of authoritarian military rule. In China, the war greatly increased the prestige of the infant People's Republic, which had taken on the world's leading military superpower and not been clearly defeated. To the present day, two mutually hostile Koreas still confront each other across a heavily fortified demilitarized zone (DMZ). An official end to the war has yet to be arranged. The United States still has some thirty-eight thousand troops stationed in South Korea. And ironically, the (by now only nominally communist) People's Republic of China now has much closer relations with South Korea than it does with the strange, isolated Korean communist regime in the north.

North Korea

In the immediate aftermath of the war, with substantial Soviet assistance, and through energetic mass mobilization of its population, the Democratic People's Republic of Korea recovered from the extensive destruction surprisingly quickly. For many years, the North Korean economy even appeared to be more vigorous than that of the south. But the North Koreans were reluctant to fully acknowledge the massive contribution that had been made by China in saving them from defeat during the war, or the important Soviet role in establishing Kim Il Sung as leader in the first place, and North Korea quickly began charting a resolutely independent course. After the death of Joseph Stalin in 1953, this independent streak became even more pronounced, and after the split between Russia and China in 1960, North Korean independence became extreme. Soviet assistance dwindled. After the final collapse of the Soviet Union in the 1990s, while much of the rest of the world entered a new post–cold war era of globalization, North Korea's independence (another word for which is *isolation*) became almost total.

During the period when Korea was a Japanese colony, Kim Il Sung had grown up on the other side of the border, in Manchuria, where there was a large Korean population. There Kim became the leader of a small (fifty to three hundred men) anti-Japanese guerilla band, operating in cooperation with the growing forces of the Chinese Communists. Overwhelming conventional Japanese military advantage eventually forced Kim's guerillas to retreat to bases in the Soviet Union in 1941, where Kim spent the remainder of World War II. After Japan's surrender, Kim returned to Korea along with Soviet Russian forces, where, initially very much as a Soviet protégé, he overcame all challengers for leadership of the North Korean Communists. Once in power, and after his disastrously failed attempt to conquer the south and reunify Korea, he developed his own unique philosophy of *Juche*, or "self-reliance," beginning around 1955. *Juche* became the core ideology of North Korea, to a large extent replacing orthodox Marxism. This ideology was then drummed into the entire population through morning-to-night loudspeaker broadcasts and obligatory political study sessions. The growing personality cult of the Great Leader Kim Il Sung "became a kind of secular religion" in which Kim Il Sung performed the role of "a living sage-king or god."[6]

Although it is in some ways obviously a Stalinist-style regime, the Democratic People's Republic of Korea is also quite unique. Images of the Great Leader Kim Il Sung are everywhere, and by the end of the twentieth century, there were over thirty-five thousand monuments in relatively small North Korea.[7] The patriarchal Korean Confucian legacy, and even patterns of premodern ancestor worship, allegedly underlay the extreme form of personality cult that developed around Kim Il Sung.[8] This Korean personality cult echoes the similar cults of Stalin and Mao Zedong, but Kim magnified the impulse even further, turning North Korea into a somewhat bizarre form of "socialist monarchy," in which supreme leadership actually became hereditary. Leadership passed from Kim Il Sung to his son Kim Jong Il (Kim Chŏng-il, 1941–) after the father's death in 1994. When Kim Jong Il's own health became uncertain in 2009, his third son was officially designated heir.

Despite the Democratic People's Republic of Korea's early achievements in economic development, these eventually gave way to stagnation and decay. Available resources were diverted to military applications, which, by the late 1960s, consumed some 30 percent of the total national budget.[9] In 1995–1996, serious erosion problems stemming from years of poor land management, combined with the declining availability of fertilizer and a lack of electric power for irrigation pumps, as well as some bad weather, resulted in a truly massive famine that even North

Korea could not conceal. Perhaps as many as a million people died from malnutrition (in a country that today has a total population of less than twenty-three million).

Tensions between North and South Korea, meanwhile, remain high. The DMZ between the two Koreas is one of the most heavily fortified areas in the world and remains a potential flashpoint. There continue to be periodic incidents. In 1983, for example, seventeen top South Korean officials were killed, and the president himself only narrowly escaped death, when North Korean commandoes detonated a bomb during their visit to Rangoon, Burma. Most alarmingly, in the early 1990s, North Korea actively embarked on a program to develop an atomic bomb.

In connection with a temporary thaw in relations with the south, in 1992, inspections of North Korean sites by the International Atomic Energy Agency began to be permitted. These inspections had no sooner begun than they were interrupted again the following year, however, and tensions escalated until North Korea announced that any further international sanctions would be considered an act of war. For the moment, this showdown was defused by a dramatic visit to North Korea by former U.S. president Jimmy Carter, who managed to extract an agreement to resume talks. Under the terms of the resulting Agreed Framework, North Korea agreed to halt its nuclear program in exchange for a U.S. promise to supply fuel and to help North Korea develop light-water reactors that could not be put to military uses. In 2002, however, North Korea once again expelled its inspectors, withdrew from the Nuclear Nonproliferation Treaty, and openly began trying to develop atomic weapons – in 2006, apparently actually exploding a small nuclear test device.

During his State of the Union address in 2002, then U.S. president George W. Bush famously designated North Korea part of what he called an "Axis of Evil," together with Iraq and Iran. Because the United States soon thereafter intervened militarily in Iraq to promote regime change, deposing the Iraqi dictator Saddam Hussein, this verbal American linkage of North Korea with Iraq and Iran presumably only further fueled North Korean paranoia. Although the People's Republic of China – almost the only foreign country having any leverage at all over North Korea – has stepped in with efforts to organize six-party talks (involving the United States, China, Russia, Japan, and both North and South Korea), tensions with the unpredictable northern regime continue to simmer. China, despite its now greater cultural and commercial interests in South Korea, like all of North Korea's other neighbors and the entire world has good reason for concern about the future of the North Korean state.

South Korea: Syngman Rhee and the First Republic (1948–1960)

The Republic of Korea (South Korea) was founded in 1948 as a constitutional democracy, but democracy in South Korea did not exactly flourish immediately or without qualification. On the basis of a series of major constitutional revisions, and a couple of military coups, South Korea has gone through a succession of what are known as six different "Republics" since 1948, the most recent of which began in 1987. The first president of the First Republic, Syngman Rhee, soon began displaying allegedly authoritarian inclinations. On one occasion, he literally locked up members of the National Assembly until they voted as he desired.[10] Although Syngman Rhee was an undoubted Korean patriot and nationalist hero, he had spent most of his adult life in exile in the United States, where he had obtained a PhD in political science from Princeton. He also had an Austrian wife. This all made him something of a stranger in his own land.

His new country had been plunged almost immediately after its formation into a devastating war with the north. Even after the end of active combat, in the 1950s, South Korea long remained one of the poorest countries on earth. Even Communist North Korea appeared more economically successful than South Korea until as late as the mid-1970s. A U.S.-backed program of compulsory land redistribution did, however, finally destroy the power base of the old Korean *Yangban* aristocracy. This was arguably essential because the modernizing capacity – even the tax-collecting ability – of the late premodern Chosŏn Dynasty had been severely hobbled by the dominance of that landowning-bureaucratic *Yangban* elite. According to data collected during the subsequent Japanese colonial period, more than three-quarters of all Korean farmers were still tenant farmers who leased part, or all, of their fields. A postcolonial 1949 land distribution law finally limited landholdings to 7.5 acres, but even then, it took the mass disruption of the Korean War before this reform could be fully implemented. The tenant-farming rate in South Korea then plunged rapidly from 49 percent to only 7 percent. The Korean War, therefore, finally completed the elimination of the traditional social and economic order in Korea. Korean society was transformed from a highly polarized hierarchy to a relatively egalitarian community – a feature that postwar South Korea also had in common with both postwar Japan and Taiwan.[11]

Even so, the South Korean economy long remained stagnant and heavily reliant on American aid. Between the end of World War II and the mid-1970s, the United States provided more aid to South Korea per capita than to any other country in the world, except Israel and South Vietnam. In the decade following the Korean War, American aid amounted to almost 80 percent of Korea's fixed capital formation.[12]

Allegations of large-scale fraud in the 1960 presidential elections – during which Syngman Rhee claimed to have won almost 90 percent of the vote – ignited student protests. When police in Seoul fired into a crowd outside the presidential office building, killing some 186 student demonstrators, university professors joined the protests, U.S. backing for President Rhee was withdrawn, the Korean army refused to intervene on his behalf, and on April 26, the aging President Rhee was obliged to resign and retire to resumed exile in Hawai'i. After Rhee's resignation, there followed nine months of freewheeling democracy – or leftist anarchy, as others saw it – until a junta from the Military Academy led by Major General Park Chung Hee (Pak Chŏng-hŭi, 1917–1979) stepped in and staged a military coup in the middle of the night on May 16, 1961 (see Figure 11.2).

The military junta then established a Supreme Council for National Reconstruction, suspended the constitution, banned political activities and demonstrations,

Figure 11.2. South Korean president Park Chung Hee, 1961. Rene Burri. Magnum Photos.

imposed censorship, and closed down most of Seoul's daily newspapers. For the next thirty-two years, from 1961 until 1993, South Korea would be led in a more or less authoritarian fashion by military men. It was Park Chung Hee's government that also, however, and to its undeniable credit, for the first time firmly set Korea's sights on modern economic development, transformed the Republic of Korea into a classic East Asian–style developmental state, and launched South Korea's dramatically successful period of economic takeoff.

Park Chung Hee and the Industrialization of South Korea

Park Chung Hee, who presided over South Korea from 1961 until his assassination in 1979, had attended a Japanese military academy during the period of Japanese colonial rule and served as a second lieutenant in the Japanese army in Manchuria during World War II. In Manchukuo, Park encountered the wartime Japanese developmental state model in its most extreme form. Earlier, nineteenth-century, Meiji era Japanese success at "enriching the country and strengthening the army" also became an inspiration for Park's Korea, and the exact same Meiji period slogan (written with four Chinese characters that are pronounced "puguk kangbyong" in Korean and "fukoku kyōhei" in Japanese) was even invoked.[13] The roots of a developmental state system – one that could be harsh and exploitative but that also really did deliver rapid rates of industrial growth – had in fact already been planted in Korean soil during the Japanese colonial period.[14] Despite the fact that fifteen years elapsed between the end of Japanese rule in 1945 and the resumption of certain similar developmental patterns under Park Chung Hee, it is probably no coincidence that South Korea's approach to economic development more closely paralleled Japan's model than anywhere else in East Asia did, or that in some ways it more closely resembled the prewar rather than the post–World War II Japanese model.[15]

After seizing power, during his first months in office, Park Chung Hee established an Economic Planning Board and announced a five-year plan for economic development. As this first five-year plan was being implemented, beginning in 1962, banking was also placed under the control of the Ministry of Finance and the state-run Bank of Korea. By 1970, 96 percent of all South Korean financial assets were government controlled.[16] This meant that in addition to tax incentives and control over licenses and permits as tools for promoting planned industrialization, the government also held critical control over investment capital. Low-interest bank loans (often even at negative real interest rates – the average net cost to business of loans for heavy industry in the 1970s has been estimated at minus 6.7%[17]) allocated by the government then became a key tool in promoting industrialization.

Such loans were vital to the development of what would become South Korea's distinctively huge *chaebŏl*, or conglomerates. The Korean word *chaebŏl* is written with the same two Chinese characters as the Japanese word *zaibatsu*, and the two are somewhat similar phenomena: essentially, holding companies controlling a range of highly diversified enterprises. Among the largest and best-known Korean *chaebŏl* are Samsung, Hyundai, and LG. These *chaebŏl* were nearly all new after World War II and remained largely family owned and managed. The founder of Hyundai, for example, had begun life working at the docks at the port of Inch'ŏn in the 1930s and as an errand boy at a rice mill in Seoul. In 1940, he bought an auto repair shop. After World War II, he developed construction contracts with the U.S. military, eventually including such activities as highway construction for the Americans in Thailand and dredging in Vietnam. By the early 1970s, Hyundai was building the largest shipyard in the world in South Korea (at Ulsan).[18]

Some of these *chaebŏl* became quite astonishingly huge. As of 1991, sales of South Korea's largest five *chaebŏl* amounted to almost 50 percent of total gross national product (GNP). In that year, Samsung's share of Korea's GNP alone was equal to the combined total share of the largest twenty American companies in the U.S.[19] They also became remarkably all encompassing: "The typical Hyundai worker drives a Hyundai car, lives in a Hyundai apartment, gets his mortgage from Hyundai credit, receives health care at Hyundai hospital, sends his kids to school on Hyundai loans or scholarships, and eats his meals at Hyundai cafeterias."[20] If the *chaebŏl* had the economic resources to extend credit to their employees, though, they themselves needed large infusions of outside investment capital. Like the pre–World War II Japanese *zaibatsu* and the postwar Japanese *keiretsu*, the South Korean *chaebŏl* had highly diversified interests, but unlike the Japanese *keiretsu*, the Korean *chaebŏl* were generally not linked to major banks and were therefore ultimately dependent on outside financing. Because they also normally wished to retain ownership and management privately in the hands of a single family, moreover, Korean *chaebŏl* were usually also reluctant to go public on the stock market. Hyundai Engineering and Construction, for example, made its first public offering of 30 percent of its stock shares in 1984 only after twenty-seven official government requests and attention in the National Assembly.[21] Instead of coming from the stock market, therefore, most capital investment has come in the form of bank loans. Because banking was substantially controlled by the government, these bank loans, together with licensing authority, became the key instruments of the South Korean developmental state.

This heavy reliance on bank financing also encouraged South Korean companies to become far more heavily indebted than their counterparts in, for example, Taiwan or the United States. Such debt did not appear threatening at first because, together with government control over the allocation of capital, the government also assumed much of the investment risk. It could be safely assumed that favored *chaebŏl* would never be allowed to go bankrupt. An absolutely critical distinction that set South Korea apart from much of the rest of the developing world, however, was not so much this so-called crony capitalism but the fact that at least initially, the government was simultaneously also able to demand very high standards of performance and productive discipline from the *chaebŏl*.[22] As these *chaebŏl* increasingly became "too big to fail," however, and under subsequent South Korean presidents with less determination and prestige than Park Chung Hee, in the long run, these features of the Korean economy would become problems. In the short term, though, the system seemed to work splendidly. From 1965 to 1990, the Republic of Korea had the second fastest growing economy in the world, after Taiwan.

Park's strategic ambition was not so much to transform Korea into a consumer paradise as to make South Korea a rich country with a strong army. A commitment to the buildup of steel and heavy industrial production, therefore, in spite of Korea's lack of any obvious comparative market advantage in those sectors, became a distinguishing feature of South Korea's approach. As always in South Korea, a major consideration was the ever-looming threat of invasion from the north. Park Chung Hee felt a deep, and not unreasonable, desire to avoid being entirely dependant on the United States for military protection, and therefore regarded it as essential for South Korea to develop an industrial base that might ensure its own self-defense capability. Especially by the early 1970s, as the United States began transferring its official recognition from the Republic of China on Taiwan to the People's Republic of China on the mainland and disengaging from the war in Vietnam, and as President Richard Nixon announced plans to reduce the American troop presence in Korea, Park increasingly aspired to make Korea self-sufficient in heavy industry. Steel production, chemicals, automobile construction, shipbuilding, machine tools, and electronics were strongly promoted. Hyundai Motors, for example, opened in 1967 with technical assistance from Mitsubishi and other foreign experts, and began producing an automobile of its own design in 1975. Hyundai cars began being exported to the American market in 1986. By the mid-1990s, South Korea was the fifth largest auto maker in the world.

Park Chung Hee had come to power in a military coup, but Park then won election as president in reasonably democratic popular votes in 1963, 1967, and 1971. In the 1971 election, however, an opposition candidate managed to take 45 percent of the vote. Apparently feeling threatened by the strength of the opposition, as well as by the changing international situation of the early 1970s, Park declared martial law, dissolved the National Assembly, and had a new constitution drafted. These 1972 "revitalizing" reforms (the Korean term is *Yushin*, which is written with the same two characters – ultimately derived from the Confucian Classic the *Book of Odes* – as the term conventionally translated "restoration" in the 1868 Japanese "Meiji Restoration") made the South Korean government significantly more authoritarian. Direct popular election of the president ended, and the president was thereafter selected by an electoral college, one-third of whose members were appointed by the president. Political power was heavily concentrated in the president, who also had the power to appoint cabinet ministers, judges, governors, university presidents, and ranking military officers, to dissolve the National Assembly, and to issue orders having something of the force of law.

Park Chung Hee's South Korean version of the developmental state was, as we have seen, influenced by Japanese models, and the first generation of postwar Korean leaders had mostly been educated under Japanese rule. Many were fluent in the Japanese language. After South Korea reestablished formal diplomatic relations with Japan in 1965, moreover, Japan quickly became South Korea's largest trading partner. But if history explains Korea's close connections with Japan, it also explains deep Korean feelings of bitterness toward their former colonial masters and an understandable desire to assert Korea's own independent national identity. Japanese cultural products were officially banned in South Korea until as late as 1998, and although generic modern Japanese appliances such as TVs might be acceptable, Japanese automobiles were totally excluded. Japanese-language education was also banned in Korea (and not reintroduced into Korean high schools until 1973).

In contrast to Japanese influences, the American presence was not only also very strong but sometimes more welcome, especially in the early years. The Korean army, which long remained under overall U.S. supreme command, was a particularly intense focal point of American influence. As army officer and future president Roh Tae Woo (No T'ae-u, 1932–) later reminisced, "When our Military Academy was founded, all our textbooks were translations of West Point textbooks – some of them were still in English. At first two-thirds of the faculty were American officers. . . . Our cadets were one of the first groups in Korea to study Western institutions this thoroughly."[23] Partly because of its familiarity from American military bases, Spam (a distinctive American brand of precooked canned meat) became rather uniquely popular in Korea, and American pop culture has become pervasive in the age of globalization, as we will examine further later.

In addition, although it is not specifically an American influence, Christianity has also flourished more spectacularly in Korea than anywhere else in East Asia.

The Christian success in Korea may be partially due to a link between Christian churches and anti-Japanese Korean nationalism during the colonial era, and also to Christian support for the causes of democracy and human rights in the authoritarian South Korea of the 1960s–1980s. In Korea, Christmas has been a national holiday since 1945, and by the end of the twentieth century, Christianity – especially of the Evangelical Protestant variety – could be called the dominant religion in the Republic of Korea. More than a quarter of the South Korean people are Christians.[24]

Democratization and Globalization

On October 26, 1979, after dinner in a Korean CIA (KCIA) building located near the presidential Blue House in Seoul, President Park Chung Hee was shot to death by his dinner companion, the head of the KCIA – apparently because of a disagreement over how to control recent student and labor unrest. Following the assassination of President Park, on December 12, a gun battle erupted in the streets of Seoul between opposing detachments of South Korean soldiers, which ended with an attack on the Ministry of Defense and the arrest of the defense minister and the martial law commander, ostensibly in connection with President Park's murder. This was the beginning of yet another military coup, this time orchestrated by Major General Chun Doo Hwan (Chŏn Tu-hwan, 1931–). As General Chun gathered the reins of power into his own hands, in May 1980, he declared martial law, closed all universities, and suspended the National Assembly. This sparked protests, notably in the southwestern Korean city of Kwangju. University students were joined in the streets by citizens, and for a few days, the demonstrators controlled the city. Army special forces were sent in, however, and the disturbance was crushed – with 191 officially acknowledged deaths. Chun's government assumed control over all Korean television networks and began large-scale purges of the bureaucracy.

The climate of world opinion in the 1980s was very different from when Park Chung Hee had seized power in a military coup twenty years before, however. In the Philippines, long-standing dictator Ferdinand Marcos was toppled by a "people power" movement in 1986. In Taiwan, martial law would be lifted, and a successful transition from single-party rule to multiparty democracy began in 1987. By the 1980s, South Korea was also no longer an impoverished, war-ravaged developing country but a successfully industrialized economic powerhouse, and the expectation was widespread among Korean people that democratization should also be part of this modernization process. Students, in particular, clamored for democracy. Korean workers, whose low wages had helped make Korean industry globally competitive, were increasingly organized and active in demanding pay raises. In the single year 1987, there were 3,749 labor disputes in South Korea – more than in the entire previous history of the republic.[25]

In 1987, with international attention newly focused on South Korea because of the upcoming 1988 Seoul Olympics, a brutal military crackdown against student demonstrations would have been especially awkward, and weeks of clashes between rock-throwing students and teargas-firing police that year finally ended with Chun Doo Hwan's hand-picked successor, Roh Tae Woo, making significant concessions to the demonstrators. In June 1987, Roh publicly promised, among other things, a direct popular presidential election and the release of political prisoners. In December, the promised presidential election duly occurred. Because there were five serious contenders, the ruling party candidate, Roh Tae Woo – President Chun Doo Hwan's chosen successor and yet another army general – was able to win the election with less than 37 percent of the vote. Nevertheless, he became South Korea's first democratically elected president in years.

Another milestone was passed in 1992 with the election of Korea's first civilian president in three decades (Kim Young Sam, 1927–). During the 1992 election campaign, all three major candidates had pledged to reduce the level of government intervention in the economy, and the incoming president's new administration was committed to economic liberalization, deregulation, and globalization. As a former dissident (who had, however, now compromised and allied with the ruling party), this new president was also anxious to promote democratizing reforms after he took office in 1993. It is worth noting that his vision of democracy was still strikingly Confucian, however, emphasizing the collective good of the community over selfish individual interests, harmony, national discipline, and the quintessentially Confucian ideal of leadership by virtuous example.[26] In keeping with the goal of implementing democratic reforms, in 1995, former presidents Chun Doo Hwan and Roh Tae Woo were both arrested and placed on trial on charges of mutiny and treason for their role in the 1980 military coup and the Kwangju massacre. Both were convicted, and former president Chun was sentenced to death, although that was commuted to life in prison, and he was eventually pardoned in 1997.

In the early 1990s, the new South Korean administration also made a formal policy commitment to globalization and the dismantling of the Korean developmental state. By the 1990s, the old model of state-guided capitalism was increasingly out of fashion, and it was arguably also starting to become counterproductive. The United States and other trading partners were beginning to apply serious pressure on South Korea to open its own domestic markets, while even cheaper-labor rival exporting counties (such as China) were beginning to undercut Korea's competitive edge in cost – just as Korea's own workers' wages were belatedly beginning to shoot up. The idea was that Korea might benefit if market inefficiencies resulting from protectionism and tight government regulation could be eliminated. The lengthy series of South Korean government five-year economic plans now came to an end, and in 1994, the Economic Planning Board was merged into a new superministry (called the Ministry of Finance and Economy). South Korea also opened up diplomatically, becoming a member of the United Nations in 1991 and normalizing relations with the Soviet Union in 1990 and with the People's Republic of China in 1992. In 1998, South Korea finally even agreed to begin gradually lifting its ban on the importation of Japanese cultural products, starting with movies and cartoons.

Initially, cheap labor had been South Korea's principal comparative advantage in the global marketplace, and domestic austerity had been strongly encouraged.

Neon lights were banned under President Park Chung Hee, and television broadcasts (except for the U.S. Armed Forces network) were only in black and white. Until 1982, a midnight–4:00 A.M. curfew was in effect. Imports of foreign consumer goods were often restricted, and buying foreign was discouraged as being unpatriotic. To protect the domestic automobile industry, the import of finished automobiles was prohibited until 1987. But by the 1980s, things had begun to seriously change. In the space of a single generation, South Korea had moved dramatically from what had still been a poor and largely peasant society in the 1940s–1950s to a modern, industrialized, and increasingly affluent urban middle-class society. Something like 42 percent of the South Korean people now lived in the single metropolis of Seoul. These new Korean people were not merely urban but also modern and sophisticated. Seoul boasted strikingly high concentrations of PhDs and especially high levels of broadband computer Internet connections. Koreans were the first in East Asia, for example, to digitalize the Buddhist scriptures for CD-ROM distribution.[27] In the 1990s, Korea also became a net investor nation, investing more money abroad than it received.[28]

With the boom of the 1980s, wages went up sharply, automobiles began to fill the once nearly empty streets, and import restrictions finally began to be lifted. Beginning in 1989, for the first time, passports became easily available to South Koreans wishing to leave the country, and foreign travel has since become much more common. Koreans increasingly are inclined to make purchases based on judgments of price and quality rather than for patriotic national considerations. Large Western discount stores such as the American Wal-Mart and the French Carrefour made their appearance, and American music, movies, and cola became the rage among young Koreans. Popular sports, with the exception of the Korean martial art *t'aekwŏndo*, are now almost exclusively Western style. As late as 1995, there had still been only twenty-six golf courses in all of South Korea, but a decade later there were nearly a thousand.[29]

In 1996, it was estimated that 58 percent of South Koreans ate at Western-style restaurants, and 40 percent said they preferred sleeping on Western-style beds instead of on the floor, Korean style. It remains noteworthy, though, that a sizeable majority of Koreans apparently still do not prefer Western-style beds. Through a process of selective amnesia, the foreign origins of many of those originally Western items that have been widely accepted, such as computers, blue jeans, and modern commercial pop music, can be conveniently forgotten, while special emphasis can simultaneously be placed on the relative handful of remaining distinctive Korean national cultural markers, such as the eating of *kimch'i* (spicy Korean pickled cabbage) and speaking the Korean language.[30] Those non-Korean items that remain conspicuously foreign, meanwhile, may still not be very enthusiastically welcomed. The first McDonald's opened in Seoul in 1988, for example, but McDonald's has grown more slowly in South Korea than elsewhere in East Asia. One reason for this may be because the hamburger does not fit easily into preexisting Korean food categories, which typically consist of "dishes" served to accompany rice. But this should be equally true of many other East Asian cuisines and is not an entirely adequate explanation for South Korean resistance to McDonald's. As citizens of a relatively small country with strong recent memories of foreign colonial domination and attempted forced assimilation, Koreans may understandably be particularly sensitive to fears of foreign cultural imperialism and the possible loss of Korean national identity.[31] As late as 1993, South Korea – "alone in Asia" – still refused to allow the then phenomenally popular American pop star Michael Jackson to perform there.[32]

Despite the fact that few countries in the world had made as public a commitment to the ideal of globalization as South Korea did in the early 1990s, by the end of that particular president's term in office (1993–1998), the Republic of Korea's global competitiveness rankings had actually declined. In 1997, South Korea was even obliged to accept the largest bailout (fifty-eight billion dollars) thus far in the history of the International Monetary Fund (IMF) to avoid "financial meltdown."[33] The paradox of eager globalization combined with conspicuous failure may have been less due to any inherent defects in the globalization model, however, than it was simply the result of a combination of unfortunate circumstances with remaining serious imperfections in the globalizing reform process in Korea.

While the *chaebŏl* had continued to grow in size in the 1980s–1990s, liberalization of the economy and deregulation made it simultaneously harder for the government to impose any discipline on them. At the same time, the need of politicians for "donations" gave businesses increased leverage over the government itself. In 1995, for example, reformist prosecutors uncovered a secret slush fund of 285 million dollars that had been accumulated by former president Chun Doo Hwan. In the 1990s, deregulation of Korea's financial systems in the name of globalization also brought in a flood of mostly short-term foreign debt, and Korean banks, accustomed to never having to make careful risk assessments because it was assumed they could always rely on government bailouts, permitted some rather dubious investments. Unfortunate circumstances made their appearance at this point, as speculation involving Thailand's currency (known as the baht) in July 1997 touched off a devastating financial crisis that swept across much of Southeast Asia. Most of Confucian East Asia (notably the People's Republic of China) proved relatively immune to this so-called Asian flu, but South Korea found itself badly exposed. The Korean stock market lost half its value, and by 1998, some twenty thousand Korean firms had gone bankrupt, including ten of the top thirty *chaebŏl*.

This was clearly very bad news, but under the pressure of this crisis and IMF supervision, South Korea moved forward quickly with economic liberalization. Although the total number of economic regulations was cut in half, supervisory financial regulations were also effectively tightened. *Chaebŏl* were pushed to become more transparent in their business operations, divest themselves of large numbers of peripheral subsidiaries, and lower their debt-to-asset ratios. Foreign direct investment in Korea was made easier, and even outright foreign acquisition of Korean firms was permitted. The recovery was rapid and successful enough that Korea was able to pay back what it owed the IMF in three and a half years rather than the anticipated four.

Meanwhile, in 1997, opposition party candidate Kim Dae Jung (1924–2009) won the presidential election, marking the first democratic transfer of power to the political opposition in the history of the Republic of Korea. With the start of the new millennium, it would appear that South Korea's democracy, as well as its market economy, have both matured considerably. In June 2000, President Kim Dae Jung flew to P'yŏngyang, where he was received surprisingly graciously by North Korean leader Kim Jong Il. That same year, President Kim was awarded the Nobel Peace Prize for his contributions to peace and democracy and to reconciliation with the north.

In the twenty-first century, a so-called Korean wave of excitement for South Korean television programming (dubbed, for example, into Mandarin Chinese), movies, music, and other pop cultural items, as well as for the material products of Korean industry, such as cell phones and automobiles, has swept across much of Asia. In the Chinese-speaking world, South Korean pop culture imports currently seem hotter even than Japanese products. History, of course, never ends, and there will continue to be difficulties and uncertainties – in 2009, for example, there was a renewed nuclear scare involving North Korea, and a former South Korean president, hounded by accusations of bribery, tragically committed suicide by jumping off a cliff. Whatever the future may bring, however, there can be no doubt that the Republic of Korea has made truly stunning achievements in the little more than half a century since it was born in 1948.

For Further Reading

For introductory overviews, see Don Oberdorfer, *The Two Koreas: A Contemporary History* (New York: Basic Books, [1997] 2001), and Michael Edson Robinson, *Korea's Twentieth-century Odyssey: A Short History* (Honolulu: University of Hawai'i Press, 2007).

A riveting journalistic account of the Korean War is David Halberstam, *The Coldest Winter: America and the Korean War* (New York: Hyperion, 2007).

On North Korea, see chap. 8 of Bruce Cumings, *Korea's Place in the Sun: A Modern History* (New York: W. W. Norton, 1997); Han S. Park, ed., *North Korea: Ideology, Politics, Economy* (Englewood Cliffs, NJ: Prentice Hall, 1996); and Dae-Sook Suh, *Kim Il Sung: The North Korean Leader* (New York: Columbia University Press, 1988).

Concerning South Korea's dramatic economic takeoff, see Alice H. Amsden, *Asia's Next Giant: South Korea and Late Industrialization* (New York: Oxford University Press, 1989); John Lie, *Han Unbound: The Political Economy of South Korea* (Stanford University Press, 1998); and Meredith Woo-Cumings, ed., *The Developmental State* (Ithaca, NY: Cornell University Press, 1999).

On contemporary Korea more generally, see Robert E. Buswell Jr. and Timothy S. Lee, eds., *Christianity in Korea* (Honolulu: University of Hawai'i Press, 2006); Mark L. Clifford, *Troubled Tiger: Businessmen, Bureaucrats, and Generals in South Korea* (Armonk, NY: M. E. Sharpe, 1994); and Carter J. Eckert, "Korea's Transition to Modernity: A Will to Greatness," in *Historical Perspectives on Contemporary East Asia*, ed. Merle Goldman and Andrew Gordon (Cambridge, MA: Harvard University Press, 2000).

For Korea in the age of globalization, see Young Whan Kihl, *Transforming Korean Politics: Democracy, Reform, and Culture* (Armonk, NY: M. E. Sharpe, 2005); Samuel S. Kim, ed., *Korea's Globalization* (Cambridge University Press, 2000); and James Lewis and Amadu Sesay, eds., *Korea and Globalization: Politics, Economics and Culture* (London: RoutledgeCurzon, 2002).

12 China since 1945

The Chinese Civil War

Although China was one of the "victors" in World War II, conditions in war-ravaged China did not noticeably improve after Japan's defeat. Instead, the catastrophic inflation, corruption, and black marketeering that had begun during the World War only continued, or even became worse, while the off-again, on-again civil war between the Chinese Nationalists and Communists entered its final phase. In the first months after the war, the U.S. ambassador did succeed in bringing Mao Zedong and Chiang Kai-shek together for face-to-face negotiations. It was Mao's first ride in an airplane. The American hope was to prevent full-scale civil war and promote democracy in China, and for that purpose, in late 1945, President Truman appointed one of America's most distinguished military leaders and statesmen, General George C. Marshall (1880–1959), as a special envoy to China. General Marshall remained in China for a little over a year (December 1945–January 1947), and on his departure, he was able to express cautious optimism that a new Chinese constitution, and democratic elections scheduled for late 1947, might hold.

But General Marshall also expressed concern that efforts at reaching a peace settlement were being frustrated by extremists on both sides. In fact, the bitter antagonism between the Chinese Nationalists and Communists ultimately proved too deep to sustain the uneasy truce. The problems of postwar China in general, moreover, were proving stubbornly intractable. On the island of Taiwan, for example – recently returned to Chinese rule following Japan's surrender – residual damage from World War II, Nationalist Chinese government economic policies that restricted the operations of a free market, and the circulation of excessive amounts of currency all combined to foster high unemployment, shortages of goods, and out-of-control inflation. When police investigators attempted to confiscate suspected contraband cigarettes from a middle-aged female street vendor in the provincial capital, Taipei (Taibei in the mainland's newer pinyin spelling system), resulting in a scuffle that killed a bystander, Taiwan erupted into a major, islandwide rebellion on February 28, 1947. The rebellion was crushed by

Nationalist government troops, resulting in the deaths of thousands of Taiwanese.[1] This February 28 Incident left a long-festering wound (which was, furthermore, long publicly unmentionable in Taiwan) in relations between the Taiwanese people and the ruling Chinese Nationalist government on the island.

Meanwhile, although the Soviet Union did not enter the war against Japan until just six days before Japan's surrender, that was still sufficient time for the Soviets to overrun Manchuria at the end of World War II. The Soviets then occupied Manchuria for about a year, retained control over Port Arthur and the China Eastern Railway (running across Manchuria) until 1954, and extracted hundreds of millions of dollars' worth of war reparations from the region. Many Chinese later grumbled about this Soviet looting, but in the short term, the massive Soviet military presence definitely gave a boost to the Chinese Communists. The Russians turned over to the Chinese Communists some three-quarters of a million captured rifles, eighteen thousand machine guns, and four thousand pieces of artillery.[2] Manchuria then became the launching pad for the Chinese Communist military reunification of China.

The United States was simultaneously, of course, providing very substantial aid to Chiang Kai-shek's Nationalists. The Nationalist armies were initially larger and better equipped than the Communist Red Army (later known as the People's Liberation Army), but the Nationalists fought a static defensive war and were outmaneuvered and defeated unit by unit. In the process, huge amounts of men and material were captured by the Communists. As the Communist offensive began to accelerate in 1948, the last senior American advisor to Chiang Kai-shek's military even complained that "the Communists had more of our equipment than the Nationalists did." Mao Zedong was fond of joking that Chiang Kai-shek "was our supply officer."[3]

Events now began to unfold quickly. Beijing fell to the Communists in January 1949, and by April, the Red Army, coming down from the north, was staging assaults across the Yangzi River into south China. Chiang Kai-shek retreated with some two million followers to the island of Taiwan (where the Republic of China at least nominally survives to the present day), and on October 1, 1949, Mao Zedong stood on Tiananmen – the old Gate of Heavenly Peace rather than the new Tiananmen Square, which did not yet exist – and proclaimed the establishment of a new country, called the People's Republic of China (PRC).

Chairman Mao's New China

Despite the revolutionaries' considerable resentment at what they remembered as a century of Chinese national humiliation under the hands of Western imperialists, Westerners in China were not all immediately expelled after the Communist takeover. The American president, furthermore, even briefly contemplated recognizing the new People's Republic. But following the outbreak of war in Korea in 1950, the United States firmly recommitted itself to support for Chiang Kai-shek's Nationalist Republic of China on Taiwan, recognizing it as the only legitimate government of China, and the containment of communism emerged as the American grand design. Cold war alignments now rapidly hardened. The new PRC, for its part, adopted a policy of "leaning to one side" by cultivating relatively cordial relations with the Soviet Union. In December 1949, Mao Zedong went to Moscow on his first ever trip abroad to participate in the celebrations surrounding Joseph Stalin's seventieth birthday. Mao was kept waiting and felt insufficiently well treated, but he did obtain a three hundred million dollar loan, and a (short) period of Soviet assistance to China began that "has been characterized as the largest technology transfer in history."[4]

Following a dozen years of world war and civil war, compounded by decades of previous warlordism and national disintegration, the most urgent immediate priority for the new China was simply to restore order. A new, unified national currency was introduced, known as the *renminbi* (the "people's money"; also known, more generically, as the *yuan*), and using some high-profile executions of currency speculators as well as the establishment of fixed commodity prices, raging inflation was finally brought under control. The new Communist rulers of China had no intention of merely restoring the status quo, however. The Communist victory in 1949 owed much to the mass mobilization of popular sentiments of patriotic nationalism to save China from foreign threats, perceived or real, but the Communist leaders were also sincerely committed Marxists and were determined to carry through a Marxist social revolution.

This presented some serious challenges. Although a striking number of early top Chinese Communist leaders had studied in Europe or the Soviet Union, by 1949, the overwhelming majority of party members and cadres (persons in leadership positions) were very poorly educated and unfamiliar with the wider world beyond China. Marxist theory taught that historical progress is driven by class struggle through a regular series of stages, defined in terms of modes of production. The most relevant of these stages were supposed to be the transition from feudalism to capitalism, and then (in the future) from capitalism to communism. Theoretically, therefore, communism was expected to emerge out of the most advanced stage of industrialized capitalism, as a result of class struggle between factory workers (the proletariat) and factory owners. The glaring problem for China, of course, was that factories and factory workers were both quite sparse in the China of 1949. According to theory, China was not yet capitalist but rather still feudal.

Actually, however, conditions in China bore little real resemblance to medieval European feudalism either, and there were some difficulties in applying the feudal model. Tweaking the general theory to better fit Chinese conditions, the specific formula that the Chinese Communists developed was that China was "semi-feudal, semi-colonial." The Marxist revolutionary solution to semi-colonialism, then, was to rise up as a nation and drive out the foreign imperialist exploiters, while the prescription for semi-feudalism was for poor peasants also to rise up, denounce their landlord exploiters, and confiscate and redistribute their land. After the Chinese Communist victory in 1949, anti-landlord struggle sessions were therefore duly encouraged in every village.

The Marxist idea that class exploitation of tenant farmers by landlords was the underlying reason for China's poverty not only came as surprising news to many Chinese farmers but, in many parts of China, it also "distorted reality." In one north Chinese county that has been carefully studied by recent American scholars, for example, 80 percent of the farm households had previously already been owner cultivators (rather than tenant farmers), recognized existing social divisions had been primarily between families rather than between classes, and there had been a general community-wide spirit of unity in patriotic resistance against Japan, and support for the underground Communist Party, during the war. Now, however, "suddenly unity was to yield to something called class struggle."[5]

The new class categories that were now obligatorily applied to everyone in China were inevitably therefore often somewhat arbitrary, but land redistribution was nonetheless extensively carried out across the countryside. This was a revolutionary action, but in theory it corresponded to the transition from feudalism to capitalism – what was called the bourgeois-democratic stage of the revolution – rather than from capitalism to communism. Even after redistribution, the land was still personal private property. Similar land redistribution programs (without the violent struggle) were promoted by U.S. advisors in Taiwan, Japan, and South Korea as a way of diminishing the appeal of communism. In theory, furthermore, the subsequent transition from this bourgeois-democratic stage to full-blown communism might still take a long time. But Mao Zedong was impatient. No sooner was the land reform completed, by about 1952, than Mao was ready to initiate the "transition to socialism." Collectivized farming, for example, began to be promoted.

Although Mao had led what was undeniably a rural "peasant revolution," modern socialist industrialization nonetheless remained a cherished Communist goal. A Soviet Russian model for the development of heavy industry in China was soon adopted, based on centralized planning and a series of Stalinist-style five-year plans, the first of which was implemented in 1953. Although production statistics from China, particularly those from the Mao era, are not always reliable, this first five-year plan does seem to have unleashed considerable real industrialization. Meanwhile, during another visit to Moscow in 1957 on the occasion of the fortieth anniversary of the Bolshevik revolution, Mao was encouraged by the pioneering launch of the Soviet space satellite Sputnik to declare that "the east wind was prevailing over the west wind." It was possible, then, to believe that communism was ascendant throughout the world and was the inevitable future of all mankind. Mao was inspired enough by the Soviets' announced goal of overtaking the U.S. economy in fifteen years to call for China overtaking Great Britain in that same length of time.[6]

The Great Leap Forward and the Cultural Revolution

Mao's visit to Moscow may have also struck a spark of Chinese nationalistic competitive rivalry with the Russians, however. Mao very soon began to contemplate significant departures from the Soviet Russian model. Mao's flash of originality was the idea that industrialization, and economic takeoff, could be achieved through people power, in the form of mass mobilization of labor through "spontaneous" popular enthusiasm rather than necessarily through the introduction of new technologies, capital investment, or elitist technocratic Soviet-style centralized planning. Mao, who was particularly fond of a story about a crazy old man who nonetheless eventually moved an entire mountain, bit by bit, was convinced that if sufficiently motivated and determined, people can achieve seemingly impossible goals. This Maoist faith in the capacity of human willpower to overcome all obstacles underlay what came to be known as the Great Leap Forward, beginning in 1958.

The ability to whip up popular enthusiasm and mobilize mass participation is perhaps the single most distinguishing feature of Mao's approach to politics, and one that makes it distinctly modern – there is nothing very "traditional" about Maoism. In addition to energizing an economic takeoff, the expectation was that Mao's Great Leap Forward would also achieve the transition to genuine communism, because newly organized rural people's communes were to become the basic organizational unit in the countryside. Economies of scale were to be achieved on an industrial, or more especially military, model. Much of the language was certainly militaristic. Farmers were to be organized into production brigades, which were divided into platoons and supervised by battalions. Women, too, were to join the labor force, being liberated from their household chores by collective nurseries and mess halls.

The Great Leap Forward was announced in early 1958, the first experimental commune was established in April, and by early autumn, nearly all rural China had been convulsed by a wave of literal communization. For a time, even the most cautious of China's leaders were swept away by Mao's enthusiasm for rapid socialist development. But the Great Leap Forward quickly turned into a great disaster. The most notorious examples of this were the so-called backyard steel furnaces that were intended to double China's steel and iron production in a single year. As many as ninety million people were mobilized for some degree of participation in smelting steel, but because there was no coordinated planning, most of these people had no experience in steel production, and their equipment was necessarily hastily improvised, the actual results were disappointing.

Even more serious was the disaster in agriculture. Because private ownership was now forbidden, many farmers apparently simply killed their livestock rather than turn it over to the collective. Many felt little incentive to work hard on the new communal farms. Encouraged to believe that the problem now would be what to do with overproduction, and diverted and exhausted by various other mobilization campaigns, farmers sometimes allowed crops to rot unharvested in the fields. In other cases, the yields themselves were meager because of excessive faith in the idea that planting seeds deeper and closer together would increase production. The law of unintended consequences also took its toll: a massive Maoist campaign to kill sparrows, as pests, led to plagues of insects that had previously been eaten by those sparrows. Other Maoist mass mobilization campaigns caused deforestation, soil erosion, and environmental damage. Although the Great Leap Forward began in early 1958 amid great popular enthusiasm, by fall 1958, serious shortages were already becoming apparent. It is now estimated that at least fifteen million people – and possibly many more – died of malnutrition during the famine caused by the Great Leap Forward in the years 1958–1962.[7]

Because Mao sometimes encouraged criticism, but also sometimes lashed out unpredictably at anyone who disagreed with him, the people around Mao were reluctant to tell him anything he did not want to hear. Natural human ambition to always appear successful may have also contributed an incentive to submit glowing but false reports. It should be remembered, too, that this was still a China that was largely pre-television and pre-telephone (to say nothing of pre-Internet) – a land where communications were still very poorly developed. Almost no one at the time seems to have fully comprehended the true extent of the disaster, but it was nonetheless soon clear that something had gone wrong, and even Mao came to endorse more realistic corrective measures – but not happily.

At a party meeting held at a retreat on Lu Mountain (Lushan) in 1959, the defense minister, a hero of the Korean War, dared to offer a critique, in a private letter to Mao, of the Great Leap Forward as a violation of the basic laws of economics. Mao had this criticism publicly circulated at the meeting, however, and strongly denounced it. Even as the hardships caused by the Great Leap Forward were becoming unmistakable, Mao's prestige was still unchallengeable. Mao won this showdown, and the defense minister was purged as a "bourgeois element." Mao did, however, now step down as the head of the Chinese government (while retaining his more powerful position as chairman of the Communist Party), and more pragmatic leaders did begin to introduce measures to restore the economy. Over the next few years, Mao was seen so seldom in public that some observers in the West began to speculate that he might even be dead.

But Mao was not dead, and he was apparently growing suspicious that "revisionists" and "capitalist roaders" (contemporary jargon for persons taking the road back to capitalism) in high positions in the PRC were sabotaging his revolution. This suspicion set the stage for Mao's next, and last, great campaign, which is known as the Great Proletarian Cultural Revolution.[8] The prelude to this Cultural Revolution actually began with a theatrical play about an historical Ming Dynasty official who was dismissed by a despotic emperor, written by a certain vice mayor of Beijing, which was widely interpreted as a thinly veiled allegorical criticism of Mao (as the despotic emperor). Mao responded by orchestrating a campaign to criticize the play, forcing its author to publish a self-criticism and confession by the end of 1965.

By spring 1966, Mao, his wife, and a circle of radical followers were encouraging young students to take to the streets to promote a Maoist vision of revolution. Mao famously told the students, "It is right to rebel." Many of the students organized themselves into groups called Red Guards, the first of which appeared at a Beijing middle school in May 1966. By June, classes in China's schools had been suspended, and millions of students were released to join the action. They were given free rail transportation, and many went to Beijing in the hope of catching a glimpse of the "big red sun," Chairman Mao.

To the extent that the Cultural Revolution was cultural, it represented a rejection of the old feudal (i.e., traditional) and bourgeois (i.e., Western) influences in art, literature, and culture generally (including such things as Western-style haircuts and cosmetics for women), and an attempt to replace these with a new socialist culture, of which the repeated performance of a handful of approved revolutionary model operas was perhaps the most conspicuous example. The main thrust of the Cultural Revolution may be viewed, however, as a power struggle through which Mao intended to regain control over the direction of his revolution.

On July 17, 1966, the seventy-three-year-old Mao Zedong electrified the youth of China by swimming several miles down the Yangzi River. He then returned to Beijing to attack the party leadership in a Central Committee meeting on July 21. Persons in leadership positions throughout China who were not perceived as being sufficiently Maoist were denounced and publicly struggled against, with the Red Guards serving as the shock troops in this attack. Most prominent among the victims were the president of the PRC (the head of China's government) and another senior leader named Deng Xiaoping. By 1968, the president of the People's Republic had been formally expelled from the Communist Party. He died of pneumonia, lying naked on his cement prison floor, an "enemy of the people," the following year, in 1969.[9] The other top-ranking target of the Cultural Revolution, Deng Xiaoping, was comparatively fortunate. Deng, too, was purged, and Deng endured three years of struggle sessions and solitary confinement and then three more years of internal exile under house arrest, working in a tractor repair factory in southeast China.[10] But Deng survived, was eventually rehabilitated, and made an historic comeback.

The Cultural Revolution brought a radical shakeup of the power structure in the People's Republic of China. By 1969, almost half of the original Politburo members, and more than half of the original Central Committee members, had been purged. However, ever more radical Red Guard factions were also dragging China ever deeper into chaos. Increasingly, there was even some actual combat between armed factions. Finally, beginning in September 1967, Mao called on the People's Liberation Army to step in and restore order. Beginning in 1968, and continuing until Mao's death in 1976, more than twelve million students were "sent down" to remote rural villages. This was intended both to break up the student concentrations and to acquaint elitist student intellectuals with a taste of hard peasant life. By now, the active phase of the Cultural Revolution was over.

Nixon and Mao

Meanwhile, ironically enough, changing world conditions were leading to a dramatic thaw in relations between the United States and China. Mao had once dismissed U.S. "imperialism" as a "paper tiger" and leaned toward the Soviet Union, but his relationship with Joseph Stalin had also always been distant and rocky, and after Stalin died in 1953, China's relations with the Soviet Union deteriorated rapidly. Beijing denounced the Soviets for revisionism and betrayal of the revolution, while Moscow criticized ultra-radical Chinese Maoists for their extremism. In 1960, there was a complete rupture, and the Soviets withdrew all aid and advisors from China. In 1962, the Soviets supported the Indian side in a minor war between India and China. In 1968, Moscow sent troops into Czechoslovakia and openly asserted Moscow's right to intervene in, and the limited independent sovereignty of, other countries within the Socialist bloc. By this time, the Russians also seemed to be the dominant external supporters of the Communist cause in Vietnam, to China's south. The Chinese therefore increasingly felt surrounded with, and threatened by, Russians.

To the north, China and the Soviet Union shared the longest land border in the world – some 4,150 miles. Along this frontier there was a massive Soviet military buildup, with the number of Soviet divisions deployed along the border with China increasing from twenty-five in 1969 to forty-five in 1973. During these years, there were a large number of border incidents, the most serious of which occurred in March 1969 at Damansky Island (called Zhenbao in Chinese) in the Ussuri River, which separates northeastern Manchuria from the Soviet Union. This appears to have begun with a Chinese ambush that killed thirty Soviet soldiers. The Soviets responded by introducing tanks and heavy artillery and pounding away at the island and the Chinese shore. A few weeks later, when the Soviet premier tried to telephone Mao Zedong, the Chinese operator hung up on him and would not put his call through.[11] Around this time, Moscow seems to have seriously contemplated waging a preemptive war on China, especially to take out fledgling Chinese nuclear facilities. In view of all these developments, by 1969, many of China's leaders had come to view the Soviet Union as a greater military threat to China than the United States. The preconditions were therefore set on the Chinese side for détente, or a relaxation of tensions, with the United States.

On the American side, the United States had continued to recognize Chiang Kai-shek's Republic of China on the island of Taiwan as the only legitimate government of all China ever since 1949. There were no direct communications between the United States and the PRC (although, after 1954, representatives of the United States and the People's Republic did conduct some limited negotiations in third countries, notably in Warsaw in communist Poland, concerning such pressing issues as exchanges of prisoners of war), and Americans were flatly not permitted to travel to mainland China. In 1969, moreover, the United States had a new president, Richard M. Nixon (1913–1994), who had built much of his early career on vigorous opposition to communism. Nixon was also, however, a brilliant geopolitical realist. As would become clear later, breaking the ice with China was a magnificently effective strategic gambit in Washington's global cold war rivalry with Moscow. In addition, the United States was then mired in a deeply unpopular war in Vietnam. By 1969, there were 541,000 U.S. troops in Vietnam, and something like one American in Saigon (the South Vietnamese capital) for every fifteen Vietnamese. Yet there was still no end to the war in sight. China appeared to be the only country that might be able to provide some leverage to help the United States extricate itself from Vietnam – and a breakthrough with China would, in any case, shift the spotlight from the unfortunate situation in Vietnam to a new American diplomatic triumph.

Figure 12.1. U.S. president Richard M. Nixon meets Chairman Mao Zedong, February 29, 1972. The Nixon Library at College Park/National Archives.

Both Mao and Nixon were therefore ready to relax the Sino-American confrontation, and an opportunity presented itself in 1971 in the form of so-called ping-pong diplomacy. During the most feverish years of the Cultural Revolution, China had simply not participated in any international athletic events. With Mao's approval, however, a Chinese team attended the 1971 World Table Tennis Championship being held in Japan. Friendly relations between the U.S. and Chinese ping-pong teams prompted an invitation (with top-level approval) to the American team to visit China. A year later, the Chinese team reciprocated with a visit to the United States – becoming the first visitors to America from mainland China in twenty-three years.

Secret negotiations between the Nixon administration and Beijing began, and for a stunning week in February 1972, President Nixon went to China (see Figure 12.1).[12] Aside from the deep ideological divide between communist China and capitalist America, the biggest and most thorny diplomatic issue was the problem of Taiwan. Because both Beijing and Taipei (the capital of Taiwan, where Chiang Kai-shek was still alive and still president at the time of the Nixon trip) insisted that they were the only legitimate government of all China, the United States delicately sidestepped the issue in the resulting formal document known as the Shanghai Communiqué. This document acknowledged that Chinese people on both Taiwan and the mainland were in agreement that there is only one China, and that Taiwan is a part of it, and expressed the desire that this issue be settled peacefully by the Chinese themselves. The Shanghai Communiqué also affirmed the American intention of progressively withdrawing U.S. military forces from Taiwan.

Despite this breakthrough in 1972, the United States did not officially switch recognition from the Republic of China on Taiwan (Taipei) to the PRC on the mainland (Beijing) until 1979. Even after that, the U.S. Congress, which does not always docilely follow the lead of the White House, almost immediately passed a new Taiwan Relations Act, committing the United States to a high level of continued support for Taiwan (despite official U.S. nonrecognition after 1979). Nonetheless, the 1970s marked the beginning of a new era of friendly feelings between the United States and China.

Deng Xiaoping and "Market-Leninism"

This was a China, moreover, that was also now rapidly beginning to be transformed almost beyond recognition. On September 9, 1976, Chairman Mao Zedong, who had long been ill with Lou Gehrig's disease, died. In the wake of Mao's death, there was an alleged attempt by Mao's wife and three of her ultra-radical colleagues – the Gang of Four – to seize power. Instead, senior military figures staged a preemptive countercoup. On the night of October 6, elite troops from the State Council Home Guard and PLA unit 8341 – commanded by Mao's own former personal body guard – arrested the Gang of Four in their homes in the Communist Party leadership compound known as Zhongnanhai, adjacent to the old imperial palace in Beijing. Although there was apparently some fighting involving the Worker's Militia in Shanghai, the Worker's Militia in Beijing surrendered without a struggle, and the coup succeeded fairly smoothly, although it was not publicly announced for several weeks.[13]

Power therefore passed not to Mao's wife and the Gang of Four but to Mao's own handpicked successor (Hua Guofeng, 1921–2008). This was a still relatively young man who had been plucked out of relative obscurity during the Cultural Revolution, and his mandate was therefore based almost entirely on continuing Mao's legacy. Mao's alleged deathbed testimonial, "With you in charge, I'm at ease," was heavily publicized in his support. The problem with relying on Mao's legacy, however, was that after the Cultural Revolution and Mao's death, China was swept with a wave of disillusionment and something of an inevitable counterreaction. Over time, some three million people who had been purged during the Cultural Revolution were restored to public life. Horror stories of some of the worst excesses of the Cultural Revolution, described as the "literature of the wounded," were permitted to be publicly aired. The senior surviving victim of the Cultural Revolution, Deng Xiaoping – who had joined the Chinese Communist Party (CCP) in the 1920s, participated in the Long March, and been one of the top PRC leaders in 1950s – was not only still alive but also already promoting a relatively appealing program of economic and technological reform.

The Gang of Four, rather than Mao himself (who continued to receive a more conditional public veneration), were blamed for most of the excesses of the Cultural Revolution and were soon placed on a televised show trial. Mao's wife, a former actress, put up a spirited self-defense but was condemned anyway and spent the rest of her life in prison. By 1978, Deng Xiaoping, representing the economic reform faction, had risen to supreme power. Partly because of a conscious desire to avoid a Mao-style cult of personality, and to promote a more collective decision-making process, Deng did not take any top offices or titles for himself, but from this time until his death in 1997, Deng was China's acknowledged paramount leader. Despite his stature, however, Deng never enjoyed the kind of concentrated prestige and power that Mao had once wielded. There also remained considerable differences of opinion among China's top leaders, and even among the reformers, it was still felt necessary to cautiously grope their way forward.

The goal of the economic reformers was, very simply, to raise China's standard of living. They had no particular sweeping master plan for achieving this, though, and one of their slogans famously compared reform to wading "across a river by groping for stones." They proceeded, necessarily, through improvisation, and the economic reforms actually began with unauthorized local initiatives in the agricultural sector. In 1979, one commune responded to a drought situation by drawing up individual contracts and basing pay on productivity. The practice quickly spread, despite some criticism from local Communist Party leaders, and turned into a general nationwide abandonment of the communes and a return to the family farm, or individual household, as the basic agricultural unit.

Reform of the state-run industrial sector presented a much more complicated problem. China's leaders were especially reluctant to throw large numbers of work-ers out of their jobs by closing down even the most unproductive state-run factories. It was easier simply to authorize new enterprises outside the existing state-run sec-tor – but the surging growth of this new entrepreneurship then quickly threatened to overwhelm the state-run share. By about 1992, China had become a predomi-nantly market economy. Beginning in 1997, within a five-year period, China actu-ally did lay off more than twenty-five million workers from state-owned enterprises, as it tackled the thorny problem of market-based economic reform. By the early twenty-first century, the former China bureau chief of the *Financial Times* could actually marvel that "China today is a great deal less socialist than any country in Europe."[14]

For orthodox Communists, some form of collective ownership of the means of production is supposed to be fundamental. The Chinese translation of the (originally foreign) word *communism – gongchan-zhuyi* – literally means "collective production-ism." This emphasis on collective ownership was partly an egalitar-ian ideal, but, theoretically at least, large-scale collective ownership might also enable comprehensive centralized planning and enormous economies of scale, and seemingly did have a rational "scientific" aspect. In historical practice, however, the performance of communist economies in the twentieth century was fairly uni-formly less than spectacular, and Deng Xiaoping and the Chinese reformers were open to experimentation. Deng's most distinguishing personal characteristic was pragmatism: he was widely quoted in the English-language press as saying that it does not matter whether a cat is black or white as long as it catches mice, and "seek truth through facts" became the slogan that the reformers themselves heavily promoted in China. Market forces, the pursuit of profit, and even stock exchanges gradually came to be tolerated. To the extent that some Marxist theoretical justification was still necessary for all this apparently capitalist behavior, it eventually came to be argued that because China was still necessarily only in the "initial stages of socialism," a little capitalism was only to be expected.[15]

Serious interest in Marxism has, in any case, largely melted away in China since Mao's death. It remains significant, nonetheless, that the new market economy emerged "not *on the ruins*" of communism – sweepingly replacing it – but from inside those ruins. New developments were, necessarily, partially shaped by preexisting institutions, habits, and expectations, in an ongoing process of evolutionary transformation.[16] As one consequence, actual legal private ownership of property has been slow to develop in China. Many of the new skyscrapers in Shanghai, for example, have been built by Hong Kong investors who merely leased the land from the municipal government, which still owns it. Perhaps the most glaring historical legacy is that a third of private business owners in China are now actually Communist Party members, and even though it has become common to joke that the acronym CCP really should now stand for "Chinese Capitalist Party," the (still so-called) Communist Party does remain the sole ruling party.

Critics initially objected that China's gradual, piecemeal, hybrid approach to economic reform could not possibly succeed, comparing it to trying to leap over the Grand Canyon in series of small jumps rather than one big leap, but in practice it actually seems to have been more effective than the big-bang sudden shock therapy reform that was attempted in the former Soviet Union, where gross domestic product (GDP) actually contracted sharply after the initial privatization in the 1990s. According to American Central Intelligence Agency estimates of purchasing power parity, by 2008, the real size of China's GDP was three and a half times that of Russia, although the Russian economy had originally been much more developed.[17] (China, of course, also has a much larger total population than Russia.)

In terms of sheer economic growth, the market-based reforms in China since 1978 have been spectacularly successful. Although most Chinese people remain poor by the standards of the world's most developed countries, some four hundred million Chinese people have been lifted out of the direst poverty, and China's major cities have been utterly transformed. By the end of the twentieth century, China had more television sets than any other country in the world. By the start of the twenty-first century, in 2001, China had the most cell phones in the world. There is now more Internet use in China than in any other single country, and in December 2008, China actually passed the United States to become the world's largest market for automobile sales (although this was, initially at least, mainly because of a slump in U.S. car sales owing to a recession). By 2006, China had also become the world's third largest market for luxury goods.[18]

It is an astonishing paradox that one of world's few remaining major communist countries also boasts perhaps the world's most booming capitalist economy. The explanation, of course, is that China is not really very communist in any meaningful sense anymore. The reasons for China's rapid economic takeoff were chiefly the relaxation of central controls; a widespread and obsessive focus on economic growth and money making; a huge, relatively well educated and eager labor supply; and generous foreign investment. Opening up to foreign trade and investment was critical. Under Chairman Mao, Marxist theories concerning the economic function of imperialism had combined with the memory of a century of perceived national humiliation at the hands of foreigners to put a high priority on national self-sufficiency and independence – and corresponding isolationism. That independence and isolationism, ironically, then shut China out of the opportunities for export-led economic growth that became a major reason for the economic "miracles" elsewhere in non-communist East Asia. Under Deng Xiaoping, China opened up again.

Indeed, one significant difference between China in the era of market-based economic reform and the developmental state model as seen in Japan and South Korea may actually be China's greater openness to foreign investment. Both Japan and South Korea had promoted exports while simultaneously keeping direct foreign investment in their own economies limited. As of 2003, the foreign direct investment to GDP ratio in China was 35 percent, compared to only 2 percent in Japan. One possibly negative consequence for China of this heavy reliance on direct foreign investment, though, is that an estimated 70 percent of all the value added to China's exports accrues to foreign rather than to Chinese component makers, brand owners, distributors, and others. Much of the profits, in other words, go to foreigners.[19]

In some respects, post-Mao China ironically seems to be returning to China's late-nineteenth and early-twentieth-century pattern, even down to the reappearance of something like the old treaty ports in the modified new form of special economic zones (SEZs). Four of these SEZs were initially approved in 1979 (Shenzhen, Shantou, Zhuhai, and Xiamen, all in the southeast), on the model of export processing zones elsewhere in East Asia (such as those established in Taiwan beginning in 1966), and offering low taxes and other economic incentives. The SEZ at Shenzhen, near Hong Kong, in particular, then exploded from rural rice paddies into a bustling city that is now home to some twelve million people.

China's new openness brought in not only foreign investment but also foreign ideas. To hard-line critics, the reformers explained that when a window is opened, it is impossible to prevent a few flies from coming in. Other Chinese people actively welcomed the fresh air, however. For some, this rediscovery of the outside world was an exciting time of new possibilities. If the May Fourth era in the early twentieth century had been China's first great experience with modern internationalism, this was now a second age of globalization. But if "science and democracy" had been the original May Fourth slogan, it was now the science half of the equation that was most enthusiastically promoted. Science has been embraced as a guide to modernization in post-Mao China, and China since 1978 has actively "become a technocracy," where most middle- and top-level leaders now have technical training in either engineering or the natural sciences. Amazingly, at the start of the twenty-first century, every one of China's highest leaders – the nine members of the Politburo Standing Committee – were trained engineers. One of the first concrete results of this new enthusiasm for Western science, ironically enough, turned out to be China's controversial one-child policy (much criticized by some in the West), which was literally advocated by rocket scientists beginning in the late 1970s.[20]

China's economic growth has been largely fueled by new investment (and not exclusively foreign investment, either, since China's own domestic savings rate is nearly 50%, and by 2008, China was holding an estimated two trillion U.S. dollars in foreign exchange reserves) rather than dramatic improvements in productivity. China's efficiency in the use of resources such as oil and water remains low compared to advanced industrialized nations, and China's prohibition of independent labor unions has also helped keep wages low. As a consequence, China's economic success has been accompanied by some highly unattractive features such as sweatshops, official corruption, and horrific environmental pollution.

In 2007, China passed the United States to become the world's largest emitter of greenhouse gases. Corruption and abuses of authority have become endemic. To mention only one case, in 2004, some ten thousand farmers in Fujian Province signed petitions calling for the dismissal of local officials. In one of the affected townships, it appears that land use compensation amounting to 240 million yuan had been diverted by officials, without consulting the farmers, for the construction of a new technological zone rather than being distributed among the people who had previously tilled the land. In compensation, the farmers were given only 800 yuan per year as a dividend and an additional 840 yuan per year to purchase the food they could no longer grow themselves on their no-longer-available farmland.[21]

If the economic reforms undeniably opened up new entrepreneurial opportunities for some people, they also took away most of the old guarantees for others. China's Mao era social safety nets quickly evaporated. Rapid urbanization also created a huge underclass of migrant workers, who often face discrimination and harsh working and living conditions. It is also widely alleged that gender discrimination has actually gotten worse under the market-based reforms, as old patriarchal prejudices revive. Women are often the first to be laid off by unprofitable and over-staffed state industries and the last to be hired for new employment opportunities (while the less desirable sweatshops, on other hand, often prefer to employ young girls). In 1978, on the eve of the market-based reforms, more than 11 percent of the Central Committee members and their alternates had been women, but by 1994, the proportion of women at that level of power had fallen to only 7.5 percent.[22]

Meanwhile, the era of good feelings between China and the United States that was ushered in by President Nixon's visit in 1972 had come under various new strains, including the growing trade imbalance, U.S. concern that China was helping Pakistan develop nuclear weapons, and a newly emerging concern for human rights issues. The fall of the Berlin Wall in 1989, and subsequent collapse of the Soviet Union, terminated the cold war anti-Soviet convergence of strategic interests between China and the United States, and the almost simultaneous Tiananmen massacre in Beijing ended any illusions some Americans may have entertained that China was happily on its way to becoming a capitalist democracy just like the United States.

Tiananmen

After Deng Xiaoping became China's paramount leader, he engineered the installation of a (relatively) younger generation of reformers in China's top offices. In the
early 1980s, one of these men, Hu Yaobang (1915–1989), was Deng's designated
successor and, as secretary general of the Communist Party, the highest ranking
person in China. But in the winter of 1986–1987, Hu Yaobang was accused by
hard-liners of being too sympathetic to student demonstrators and the allegedly
insidious influences of "bourgeois liberalization," and Hu was compelled to step
down. Hu Yaobang was simply replaced, however, as secretary general by another
reformer and Deng protégé, Zhao Ziyang (1919–2005), and this attempted hard-
line crackdown on bourgeois liberalization proved to be somewhat abortive.

On the morning of April 15, 1989, former secretary General Hu Yaobang died
in the hospital following a heart attack. Later that same afternoon, mourners began
appearing in Tiananmen Square. Their laments for Hu Yaobang offered a pointed
criticism of the hard-liners. As one anonymous couplet that appeared on a poster
phrased it,

> Those who should have died live,
> Those who should have lived have died.[23]

By the time of Hu Yaobang's funeral, two hundred thousand student demonstrators
had gathered in Tiananmen Square. Their demonstrations continued on after the
funeral and increasingly included calls for political reforms to complement the
existing market-based economic reforms.

An anonymous *People's Daily* editorial on April 26 threatened the students with
harsh reprisals, but the students responded, instead, with defiance. The next day,
students staged a huge march on Tiananmen Square from the university campuses
in Beijing's northwestern suburbs. The students broke through police barricades
and were cheered on by spectators. Because the original 1919 May Fourth student
demonstrations against the Versailles peace treaty had started at Tiananmen, on
May 4, 1989, there was another particularly large student march on Tiananmen
Square, in commemoration of the seventieth anniversary of the May Fourth Movement. One Uighur student read a "New May Fourth Manifesto" in the square. On
May 13, a smaller group of students began a permanent occupation of the square
and a hunger strike. Some of the students claimed that they had consciously chosen
to take a nonviolent approach, and a hunger strike was a particularly convincing
way of demonstrating self-sacrificing sincerity because it threatened to hurt no one
except themselves.

Such massive student demonstrations would have been potent symbols at any
time, but their effect was incalculably magnified now because they just happened
to coincide with the first Sino-Soviet summit meeting in three decades. On May
16, the leader of the Soviet Union arrived in Beijing from Moscow, trailed by
over a thousand foreign journalists. As a result of all the resulting world media
attention, the student demonstrations in Tiananmen Square became the best-
covered political event in the history of the PRC (at least until the 2008 Beijing

Olympics). By May 17, there were a million demonstrators in the hundred-acre Tiananmen Square, and their demonstrations completely upstaged the supposedly historic Sino-Soviet summit.

On May 18, Secretary General Zhao Ziyang visited some student hunger strikers recovering in a Beijing hospital and assured them that "the aims of the Party and government are the same as your aims." But at a meeting of party elders with top officials that very same day, Deng Xiaoping pointedly asked, "What other country in the world would watch more than a month of marches and demonstrations in its capital and do nothing about it?" A decision was reached at that meeting to impose martial law.[24] After the Sino-Soviet summit meeting and the departure of the Russian leader, live satellite television broadcasts were ordered terminated, and on May 20, martial law was formally declared. An ultimatum was issued to the demonstrators: disperse immediately or be dispersed by force. When troops attempted to move toward the square, however, they were stopped by human barricades formed by the citizens of Beijing. One column of soldiers even turned around, its commanding officer promising never to return. This first attempt to use the army to clear the square failed.

At the time, many people in the Communist Party itself were apparently sympathetic to the students. It has been claimed that as many as eight hundred thousand Communist Party members actively participated in demonstrations in 123 cities in China in 1989.[25] Sympathizers included even the highest-ranking person in China, the secretary general of the Communist Party Zhao Ziyang. Zhao did not attend the meeting declaring martial law, and he eventually went in person to the square. There, shedding tears, Zhao admitted that he had come too late. On May 25, the CCP secretary general Zhao Ziyang was placed under house arrest, where he remained until his death in 2005.[26]

Student grievances in 1989 included, especially, criticism of widespread official corruption, the often numbing bureaucratic arbitrariness of life in the PRC, the stifling lack of personal freedoms, and frustration with a reform process that had apparently stalled. Another highly potent, although perhaps less noble, motivation was the acute realization that college-educated professionals in China – who were assigned jobs by the state at fixed state salaries (which at that time were also being further rapidly squeezed by inflation) – had been largely left out of the new opportunities for profit making in the market-based reform era, which were mostly being realized by more entrepreneurial types. One 1988 survey actually concluded that the average college graduate earned less than someone who had not attended college![27] Private barbers, it was grumbled, now made more money than surgeons, and waitresses in the big hotels were making more than university professors.

The 1980s were also a time of revived May Fourth-style Chinese student fascination with things Western – particularly, now, American things. The *Goddess of Democracy* statue that was erected in Tiananmen Square was inspired by, although not an exact copy of, the American *Statue of Liberty*. One of the banners hung in Tiananmen Square proclaimed, "Give me liberty or give me death," a direct allusion to the American Revolution. A Western-influenced rock and roll song, Cui Jian's "I Have Nothing" (*Yi wu suoyou*), became the "unofficial anthem" of the Tiananmen demonstrations. At the time, someone also even publicly (though anonymously) observed that the inevitable death of capitalism predicted by Karl Marx a century earlier had not only not happened yet but that the capitalist countries "have turned out to be remarkably healthy," whereas those countries that had taken the socialist cure were "feeling listless and sick to the marrow of their bones."[28]

These were the critical final years when the cold war was drawing to a close, and there were nearly simultaneous democracy movements in several other parts of the world. "People power" successfully brought down the Filipino dictator Ferdinand Marcos in 1986, student demonstration in South Korea led to a democratic presidential election in 1987, and in the same year, Taiwan repealed its martial law and legalized the formation of opposition parties, becoming a genuine multiparty democracy. In 1989, the Berlin Wall fell, beginning the unraveling of the Soviet bloc in Eastern Europe and the collapse of the Soviet Union. But the 1989 Tiananmen Square demonstrations in China ended very differently.

The Australian scholar Geremie Barmé has argued that extremists on both sides shouted down more moderate voices, eliminating the possibility of a compromise and making violent confrontation increasingly unavoidable. One student leader allegedly confessed to a desire for the creation of martyrs, telling an American journalist on May 28:

> My fellow students keep asking me, "what should we do next?" . . . I feel so sad, because how can I tell them that what we are actually hoping for is bloodshed. . . . Only when the square is awash with blood will the people of China open their eyes. Only then will they really be united. But how can I explain any of this to my fellow students?[29]

On the government side, senior leaders were already looking at developments in Eastern Europe as a negative example that they wanted to avoid in China. Deng Xiaoping, who had been a principal target of Red Guard student activism during the Cultural Revolution in the 1960s, distrusted student movements. Deng was a reformer and a pragmatist, but he was also a lifelong Communist and one time close associate of Mao Zedong, not a liberal democrat. His tolerance had limits. Mao, perceptively, once compared Deng to "a ball of cotton with a pin inside."[30] And above all, senior Communist leaders, including Deng Xiaoping, were determined to maintain control.

In the darkness of early Sunday morning, June 4, thousands of fully armed combat troops from the Twenty-seventh Army, brought in from outside of Beijing for this purpose, and backed by mainline battle tanks and armored personnel carriers, assaulted Tiananmen Square. Around 1:00 A.M., an armored personnel carrier toppled the *Goddess of Democracy* statue, and at 4:30 A.M., the remaining students, after taking a voice vote, withdrew from the square. Hundreds – perhaps thousands – of people had been killed (nearly all of them in the approaches to Tiananmen Square rather than in the square itself), and in the aftermath, the city seethed with discontent, as tanks ominously patrolled the boulevards. For a time, China appeared poised on the brink of civil war.

Debate within the highest reaches of the Communist Party continued until June 7, when a resolution was reached to expel so-called counterrevolutionary elements. On June 8, the Twenty-seventh Army was pulled out of Beijing, and on June 9, the New China News Agency was able to report that all seven major military zones in China had declared their support for the decision to crack down. The danger of civil war had been averted, and the CCP had reasserted control. But the cost was high. Many Western observers concluded that the massacre had stripped the CCP of all shreds of legitimacy. Certainly the pervasive image of China's government in American public opinion since 1989 has been of brutal repression. Since 1989, in China itself, however, the Communist Party has managed to stay in power, suppress unwelcome memories, restart the market-based economic reforms, and deliver surging prosperity. By 2008, a Pew Research Center survey found that China's rate of popular national satisfaction was the highest in the world, with 86 percent of the Chinese people expressing satisfaction with the direction of their country.[31]

Greater China

China's recent economic development has been largely fueled by foreign investment, but a surprising peculiarity of this foreign investment is that much of it – by some estimates perhaps even as much as 80 percent – has come from Chinese people.[32] There are some thirty to thirty-five million overseas Chinese (*Huaqiao*) who live scattered around the world, in neither the PRC nor Taiwan, and who have been important sources of investment in China. In some cases, also, there are PRC-born people who have lived abroad long enough to obtain foreign passports or residency permits that, somewhat artificially, qualify them for privileged treatment as "foreign" investors in China. In addition, though, and most pertinently, there are also three predominantly Chinese territories outside the mainland PRC that together comprise a kind of Greater China: Taiwan, Hong Kong, and Singapore. British colonial Hong Kong, especially, proved critical to the early stages of China's market-based reforms, serving as China's single largest source of foreign direct investment. After Hong Kong reverted to Chinese rule in 1997, Taiwan then replaced it as the major source of foreign investment. Singapore, although less directly relevant, also merits mention.

Greater China and the overseas Chinese have provided an often underappreciated "secret weapon" in China's economic takeoff. As Chinese-language speakers who have, if not family members currently living in China, at least ancestral ties to China, they enjoy certain natural advantages in doing business there. This Greater China has demonstrated a dynamic synergy that is, furthermore, not merely limited to economic stimulation but also has cultural dimensions. For example, in 1989, nine out of the ten top hit songs in Shanghai came from either Hong Kong or Taiwan.[33] Despite such cross-fertilization, however, all four of these Chinese places – the PRC, Taiwan, Hong Kong, and Singapore – are also significantly different from each other, making them interesting places to explore in their own right.

Singapore

Singapore is the most remote from the PRC of these three Chinese territories (and also the smallest), occupying land geographically located in Southeast Asia that has never been part of any country based on mainland China. Singapore also has a larger proportion of non-Chinese people in its population mix than any of the others. Singapore is, accordingly, frequently not even mentioned in discussions of Greater China. Still, about three-quarters of the people in Singapore are ethnic Chinese; Singapore has sometimes been explicitly held up in China as a model for the post-Mao PRC; and since the 1990s, large numbers of Chinese officials have visited Singapore for training. Although it is more peripheral than either Hong Kong or Taiwan, therefore, Singapore is not entirely irrelevant. It is also a spectacularly successful modern place, with, as noted in the introduction, a per capita GDP in 2008 greater than that of the United States.

Singapore's importance has always been a function of geography. Singapore is located on a tiny island, some twenty-six by seventeen miles in total area, at the southern tip of the Malay peninsula. There it occupies an excellent position from which to dominate the narrow straits of water between the Malay peninsula and the island of Sumatra that has been a principal gateway for shipping coming from the west into the Pacific Ocean for many centuries. As testimony to its strategic location, Singapore is today the world's busiest container port. This tiny island was still almost entirely uninhabited, however, when the British East India Company first established a base there in 1819.

As the British gradually incorporated Malaya into their empire, large numbers of Chinese people, together with somewhat smaller numbers of Indians, moved into the region to participate in its economic development. After World War II, as part of the general worldwide postwar decolonization movement, British Malaya gained independence in 1957. The problem was that by this time, ethnic Chinese were an absolute majority of the population rather than the supposedly native Malays. The resulting ethnic tensions were severe, and because the Chinese population was especially concentrated on the island and in the city of Singapore, these tensions were partially resolved by allowing Singapore to split from Malaysia in 1965, becoming an independent city-state.

Even after independence, Singapore still faced serious challenges. It was necessary to forge a new national identity for an entirely new, and very small, country with a mixed, although predominantly Chinese, population. The economic outlook was also uncertain on an island where the British naval base had previously been the largest employer. Through low taxes, the aforementioned choice location, a skilled and hardworking English-speaking population (English is the only language that all the multiethnic Singaporeans are expected to be able to speak), and the embrace of international trade, Singapore prospered. Yet one analyst concludes that "Singapore became rich because it was already relatively rich, and because it had good policies"; that is, Singapore's prosperity was rooted in a lengthy colonial prehistory of active participation in world trade, which was modified after the end of British rule to include a particularly active new role for government. If markets and global capitalism were essential components in Singapore's success story, after independence, Singapore also had a notably interventionist government. "Singapore," it has been said, "is prominent as a country where planning succeeded."[34]

Singapore became perhaps the most Westernized place in Southeast Asia, yet it also, paradoxically, became something of a self-conscious spokesman for so-called Asian values and a leading example of allegedly Confucian benevolent authoritarianism. An antiseptic, relatively crime-free environment was achieved through unusually strict measures such as a stiff U.S. $50 fine for spitting in public, a fine for not flushing public toilets after use, a long-standing (now slightly modified) prohibition on chewing gum, a ban on nudity, and a particularly high rate of capital punishment. Despite maintaining many of the forms of political democracy, moreover, an internal security act that was intended to suppress the threat of communism also suppressed most other political opposition to the ruling People's Action Party (PAP). The PAP long enjoyed a total monopoly on seats in parliament and still continues to limit the political opposition to a token presence. Private ownership of television satellite dishes is illegal, computer Web sites and blogs must register with the government, and there is a ban on political content in the run-up to elections. It is, perhaps, little wonder that Singapore has sometimes been invoked as a model by certain leaders of the post-Mao PRC. Despite the authoritarianism, however, and deliberate government promotion of economic growth (which evidently must have been more supportive of business than constraining of it), in 2009, the free-enterprise-oriented Heritage Foundation named Singapore the second freest economy in the entire world.[35]

Hong Kong

The world's number one freest economy, then, is Hong Kong (according to the Heritage Foundation, for the fifteenth consecutive year in 2009). Hong Kong is a bustling bastion of capitalism and cosmopolitanism. It enjoys a longer average life expectancy than the United States and is a member of that exclusive club of territories with the world's highest per capita incomes. But Hong Kong is also now a special administrative region (SAR) of the PRC.

Hong Kong (in Mandarin, *Xiang'gang*, "Fragrant Harbor"), like Singapore, began life as a British colony. In the early nineteenth century, there had been literally almost nothing on the island, apart from a scattering of Chinese villagers. When the island was originally won from China at the time of the first Opium War in 1842, it was still such an empty rock that the British foreign secretary, Lord Palmerston, notoriously dismissed the apparently worthless acquisition as "a barren island, which will never be a mart of trade."[36] To the original island, Kowloon peninsula (on the mainland across from the island) was added in 1860, and in 1898, an additional 365.5 square miles were leased for ninety-nine years, which came to be known as the New Territories.

Soon after the British acquisition, Chinese people began migrating there in large numbers, in search of economic opportunity. Chinese people now make up some 95 percent of Hong Kong's total population. Aside from its splendid natural

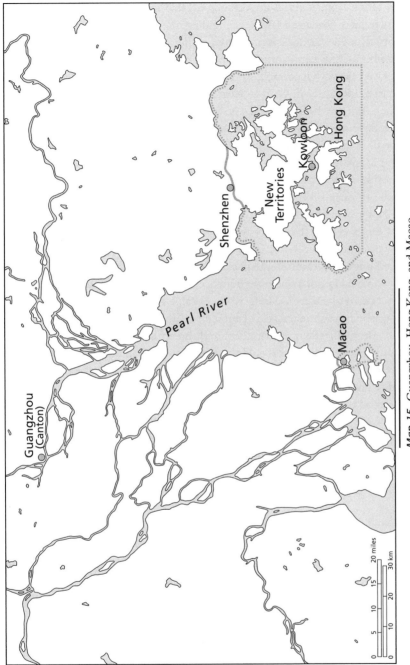

Map 15. Guangzhou, Hong Kong, and Macao

333

harbor, Hong Kong's initial importance derived mostly from its location, across from Portuguese Macao and near the mouth of the river that leads up to Guangzhou (Canton). But Guangzhou lost its monopoly on Western maritime trade at the very moment the British first acquired Hong Kong. Therefore, although British Hong Kong always fared well enough, for the first century of British rule, it remained of secondary importance in China – even for the British – to the great treaty port of Shanghai. As Lord Kadoorie once observed, comparing Hong Kong to Shanghai in the days before World War II, Hong Kong was "a nice quiet little place."[37]

That all changed in 1949, when mainland China began to retreat into self-imposed Maoist isolation. Shanghai moldered for decades after 1949, and much of its business talent fled immediately. Some went to New York, some to Taiwan, and some to various other places, but a disproportionate number came to Hong Kong. Hong Kong remains even today very much an in-migrant society – at the start of the twenty-first century, only about half the people in Hong Kong had actually been born there – although these in-migrants are overwhelmingly Chinese and predominantly Cantonese speaking. Some of these in-migrants came with money, some had prior business experience, but they nearly all brought an anxious, energetic drive to succeed. Hong Kong became a particularly fast-paced society, and flourished as a little enclave of capitalism on the shores of Communist China.

Then, after Chairman Mao's death and the onset of Deng Xiaoping's market-based reforms in the late 1970s, Hong Kong found itself uniquely well positioned to serve as the main doorway through which the outside world reentered China. Most foreign investment in China was soon flowing through Hong Kong (even if it did not all originate there), and before long, a majority of Hong Kong factory workers were actually working on the other side of the border in new factories built in the People's Republic. Much of neighboring Guangdong Province and the Pearl River delta were rapidly transformed into a giant extension of Hong Kong, and Hong Kong entered now into its greatest boom era. Even while still a British colony, per capita income in Hong Kong surpassed that of Great Britain in the 1990s.

Despite Hong Kong's free and prosperous capitalist economy, however, British Hong Kong was not a democracy; that is, there was no representative self-government. British Hong Kong was, instead, a direct Crown colony, whose governors – most of them career Foreign Service bureaucrats – were all appointed from London. The first direct popular democratic election in Hong Kong's history, for eighteen of the sixty seats in the relatively weak Legislative Council (the remainder of the seats being either appointed or chosen by narrow professional and industrial groups), was not held until 1991. But the last British colonial governor (and the first who was a professional politician), Christopher Patten (now Lord Patten, 1944–), came into office in 1992 determined to promote a greater degree of democratization, and he succeeded to the extent that by 1995, for the first time, the Legislative Council was wholly elected, though still partially indirectly.[38]

In the meantime, though, people in Hong Kong had always been conscious of living in a "borrowed place," as the famous phrase put it. Although Hong Kong island had supposedly been awarded to Britain forever, it had been granted under duress in a moment of Chinese weakness, and remained a sore point in China's memory. The majority of Hong Kong's land area, the New Territories, had merely been leased. That ninety-nine-year lease was due to expire in 1997, and in anticipation of that date, British prime minister Margaret Thatcher (1925–) visited Beijing in 1982 in the hope of negotiating an extension. Deng Xiaoping and the Beijing authorities flatly refused to consider any continuation of British administration, however, and the final outcome was a 1984 Sino-British Joint Declaration, under the terms of which all of Hong Kong would revert to Chinese rule at the expiration of the lease. But Beijing also made a significant concession: Hong Kong would become a special administrative region of the People's Republic, and would be allowed to keep its own distinctive capitalist society for at least fifty years, under the formula "one country, two systems" (a formula that PRC authorities also hoped might be used to lure Taiwan back to the motherland).

So at midnight on June 30, 1997, the Union Jack was hauled down for the last time, and 156 years of British colonial rule in Hong Kong finally came to an end. Though officially part of China now, Hong Kong nonetheless does retain a high degree of autonomy. English is still one of its two official languages, the border with the PRC is still monitored, and although pictures of Queen Elizabeth were removed from the coins (paper money in Hong Kong, as befits such a showcase of private capitalism, is actually issued by banks rather than by the government), Hong Kong retains its own separate money system, known as the Hong Kong dollar. Since 1997, Hong Kong has generally continued to become ever more prosperous, and it remains a uniquely cosmopolitan success story: "Asia's World City," a place where you can find British-style double-decker buses, a large Indian merchant community, an impressive Islamic mosque near the heart of the Kowloon tourist district, a distinctive local Cantonese version of Chinese cuisine (featuring such delicacies as dim sum), and even a new Disneyland. As a still relatively free and uncontrolled society, Google Internet searches in Hong Kong are uncensored, and Hong Kong is also the only place in China today where the Tiananmen massacre can be openly commemorated.

Taiwan

In 1974, the last surviving, unsurrendered Japanese imperial army soldier from World War II was discovered on a remote Indonesian island in the Pacific, after having hidden in the jungle there for three decades, beginning each day with worship of the Shōwa Emperor. Ironically enough, this ultraloyal Japanese soldier originally came from Taiwan rather than from one of the Japanese home islands. Nor was he "Taiwanese" as that term is narrowly understood; he was instead an aborigine from the Ami tribe on Taiwan. His Japanese name was Nakamura Akio, his Chinese name was Lee Kuang-huei, and his Ami tribal name was Suniyon.[39] His story nicely encapsulates some of the complexities of Taiwan's thorny identity problem.

To compound this complexity, incredible though it may seem, a higher percentage of the population on Taiwan today is actually conventionally considered to be ethnic Han Chinese (98%) than on mainland China itself (where, officially, 91.5% of the population is ethnic Chinese, and the real proportion is probably even lower). Taiwan's government still calls itself the Republic of China, it still flies the old national flag of the Chinese Republic, "China Airlines" is still the English name of Taiwan's national flag carrier, and Taiwan still actively uses the old Chinese Nationalist calendar that counts all dates from the founding of the Chinese Republic on the mainland in 1912 (making, for example, the year 2000 of our so-called "common era" the year 89 on Taiwan). For most of Taiwan's history since 1945, furthermore, it has been ruled by the Chinese Nationalist Party. Because Taiwan never conducted a communist revolution against allegedly feudal Chinese tradition (as mainland China did so strenuously in the 1950s–1960s), an argument can even plausibly be made that Taiwan has maintained more continuity with certain aspects of Chinese traditional culture (such as religion, respect for Confucian values, and the full form of the Chinese writing system) than the mainland PRC has. In perhaps the ultimate paradox, on Taiwan itself it was actually illegal to advocate Taiwan's independence (from China) until 1992! Yet, on the other hand, Taiwan has also really never been a part of the People's Republic of China (administered from Beijing since 1949), and there is a sizable segment of the population on Taiwan that does deny that they are Chinese.

This bewildering situation is explained by history. There are aborigines on the island, though today they only make up about 2 percent of the population, essentially for the same reason that there are also still aboriginal populations in many of the more remote corners of mainland China. Taiwan was simply one of China's last frontiers. Although Taiwan is only about a hundred miles from mainland China, the area on the mainland adjacent to Taiwan was one of the last parts of China proper to be extensively settled by Chinese people. The Taiwan straits are narrow, but navigating those straits in the age of sail was hazardous because of shallows, strong currents, and often adverse winds. There are relatively few good natural harbors on Taiwan's west coast, and it is a highly mountainous, jungle-covered, tropical and subtropical island with limited appeal to early Chinese settlers. Therefore, although there was certainly some Chinese contact from fairly early times, as late as the mid-sixteenth century, Chinese sailors landing on the island to trade with the aborigines reported it "uninhabitable."[40] Obviously, of course, this was an exaggeration: there clearly already were inhabitants, and there had been for thousands of years. These were the aborigines, who were themselves culturally diverse, speaking numerous different languages but with broad linguistic and cultural ties to many of the other island peoples of Southeast Asia.

In the seventeenth century, the Dutch established an outpost on the southwest coast of Taiwan (1624–1662), but the Dutch were soon driven off by Chinese pirates (see Chapter 6). In 1683, this independent Chinese pirate lair was then conquered by the Qing Dynasty, and for the first time, Taiwan officially became part of an empire based in China. Over the next two centuries, the island came to be more extensively settled by in-migrants from southeastern coastal China. The largest group came from Fujian Province, directly across the straits. These settlers spoke a dialect of Chinese known as Southern Min, which is today most commonly simply called Taiwanese. They now make up roughly three-quarters of the population of Taiwan and are the so-called "Taiwanese" (also called Hoklo) in the narrow sub-ethnic sense. Another significant in-migrant group, however, were the Hakka, who came from farther south in Guangdong Province. The Hakka dialect is significantly different from Taiwanese, and Hakka people make up roughly 10 percent of the present population of Taiwan.

Taiwan's history also has a significant Japanese layer because after the Qing Dynasty was defeated by Japan in war in 1895, the island was ceded to Japan and became modern Japan's first overseas imperial colony. Despite an armed insurgency against Japanese occupation that may have lasted as long as twenty years, Japanese rule was eventually consolidated, and – at least compared to other parts of Japan's colonial empire – it was relatively benign. The current presidential palace in Taipei, where the president of the Republic of China now has his office, was constructed by the Japanese. By World War II, most Taiwanese were probably at least functionally literate in the Japanese language, and many were quite fluent in Japanese. Few, on the other hand, would have learned to speak the Mandarin that is the most common dialect on the Chinese mainland (except for the southeast coast) and that has been the favored language of modern Chinese nation building.

In 1945, Japan lost World War II, and Taiwan was returned to Chinese rule – but a China that was now Chiang Kai-shek's Nationalist Republic rather than the Manchu-ruled Qing Empire. Four years later, the Chinese Nationalists lost their civil war with the Chinese Communists, and Chiang Kai-shek, the central government of the Republic of China, and roughly two million other refugees retreated in 1949 to the island of Taiwan (and also a number of other, much smaller off-shore islands such as the Pescadores, Quemoy [Mandarin: Jinmen], and Matsu), where the Republic of China has been maintained, at least in name, until the present day. Chiang Kai-shek remained president until his death in 1975, and the government in Taipei long continued to claim that it was the only legitimate government of all China. Until about 1990, Taipei even refused to officially acknowledge the existence of the PRC, referring instead simply to "communist bandits."

The United States supported this claim and also continued to officially recognize the government in Taipei as the legitimate government of China until 1979 (although no one anywhere, of course, ever pretended that the island of Taiwan, by itself, was the whole of China). Because both Taipei and Beijing insisted that they were the only legitimate government of a unitary China that included both the mainland and Taiwan, dual recognition was not a diplomatic option. The resulting "one China" formula turned out to be very awkward for Taiwan, however, because, when forced to choose, most of the world eventually opted to recognize the Beijing-based PRC. Great Britain recognized the PRC in 1950, soon after its formation, France recognized it in 1964, Canada established diplomatic relations in 1970, and by 1979, even the United States had formally switched its recognition from Taipei to Beijing. Today, the only European state that still officially recognizes the Republic of China on Taiwan is the Vatican. China's seat in the United Nations was eventually awarded to Beijing, as was China's position in most other international organizations, leaving Taiwan in considerable formal diplomatic isolation (although it still enjoys widespread informal relations).

The split between mainland China and Taiwan is therefore very much a still unresolved holdover from the mid-twentieth-century civil war between the Chinese Communists and Nationalists. The PRC absolutely does claim the territory as a "renegade province," many citizens of the PRC do feel very strongly about the issue, and tensions between Taiwan and the PRC have sometimes run quite high. However, when people speak of friction between mainlanders and Taiwanese, this sometimes does not refer to the actual mainland PRC, but rather to the group of "mainlanders" who fled to the island of Taiwan in 1949 together with Chiang Kai-shek. These mainlanders on Taiwan make up roughly 14 percent of the island's population, yet they long dominated the government, the military, and some of the larger businesses. For decades, some Taiwanese felt oppressed by this continuing mainlander rule on the island. This domestic friction, furthermore, may have played a role in the development of the Taiwan independence movement.

On Taiwan, the Chinese Nationalist government promoted Mandarin as the National Language (*Guoyu*), and for a long time required that only Mandarin be spoken in public, even though it is not the mother tongue of the majority of people on the island. Schools on Taiwan taught Chinese history (although with communism long censored out), and under the rule of the Chinese Nationalist Party, the government on Taiwan for a long time even tried to promote a kind of Chinese national identity on the island. At the other extreme, however, from the time Taiwan first reverted to Chinese rule in 1945, some of the Taiwanese inhabitants – especially members of the old Taiwanese elite – felt alienated from the new mainlander-dominated government. The lasting memory of the February 28, 1947, islandwide rebellion and massacre of Taiwanese by the Nationalist military governor, in particular, opened a deep and lasting rift between many Taiwanese and the Chinese Nationalist government (see the beginning of this chapter). The prolonged period of martial law, which remained in force from 1948 until 1987, the anti-communist white terror of the 1950s, and continued suppression of political opposition to the ruling Nationalist Party further contributed to simmering resentment.[41]

Despite these problems, however, Taiwan also quickly became a spectacular example of an East Asian "economic miracle," and the first genuine multiparty democracy in Chinese history. When the Nationalist central government first retreated to the island in 1949, Taiwan was war torn, overrun with refugees, and suffering from extremely high unemployment and inflation. By introducing the New Taiwan Dollar (NT) to replace the old currency, and other measures, the government successfully tamed inflation, reducing the inflation rate from a staggering 3,000 percent in early 1949 to only 8.8 percent by 1952.[42] The government also took swift and effective action to end the corruption and warlordism that had plagued the Republic of China on the mainland for so many years, and finally carried out the long-promised farmland redistribution program, under the old Nationalist slogan "land to the tillers." The former Taiwanese landlords were deprived of their landholdings, but compensated with bonds and stock in government-owned enterprises.

In the 1950s, Taiwan's economic policies emphasized the typical postcolonial developing-world approach known as import substitution, which essentially meant promoting domestically manufactured substitutes for foreign imports and artificially protecting them with a wall of high import taxes, outright restrictions, and currency controls. But Taiwan then became one of the first developing economies in the world to move away from the import substitution model and concentrate instead on export-led growth, beginning in the early 1960s. Government incentives played a role in this, such as tax rebates for exporters and the establishment of special duty-free export-processing zones beginning in 1966. In the long run, however, Taiwan's economic takeoff was also accompanied by a process of general deregulation and privatization. In 1952, for example, the government was responsible for 57 percent of Taiwan's industrial production, but by 1987, that figure had fallen to only 14 percent.[43] In striking contrast to South Korea or Japan, where the developmental model featured giant conglomerates with close ties to the government, in Taiwan, the source of economic dynamism turned out overwhelmingly to be the independent, small, often literally family-run "Chinese-style" firm. Ninety-four percent of Taiwan's total production was attributable to small enterprises with fewer than fifty employees.[44]

As a consequence of the small scale of these enterprises, Taiwan, unlike South Korea or Japan, has not been globally competitive in major heavy industries such as automobile manufacturing. But the flexibility of its many small companies, correspondingly, also allowed Taiwan to become a powerhouse in information technology – especially strong in such items as laptop computers. For much of the 1970s and 1980s, Taiwan enjoyed the fastest-developing economy on earth. In a single generation, Taiwan leaped from what had still been a largely preindustrial peasant economy in 1949 to a modern center of economic globalization. Most recently, Taiwan has begun outsourcing much of the actual manufacturing process to cheaper-labor factories on mainland China, and Taiwan has emerged as a major source of foreign investment in its own right.

Taiwan's newfound prosperity, meanwhile, brought a general improvement in the quality of life on the island. The capital city, Taipei, once had the reputation of being a "gray city." The old Japanese-style colonial era buildings made of unpainted, weathered wood had been torn down and were often replaced by rather ugly naked concrete. More recently, however, Taipei has become increasingly attractive. Especially as a new subway system came on-line in the mid-1990s, Taipei now has all the conveniences of a thoroughly modern city. In the towering building known as Taipei 101 – just across the street from the somewhat older World Trade Center, and for a few years in the early twenty-first century the world's tallest skyscraper – shoppers can stroll leisurely from a high-end luxury Armani store to a Cartier store, and then to Fendi, Gucci, Prada, Tiffany, Versace, Louis Vuitton, and so forth.

Following Taiwan's successful economic takeoff, Taiwan also managed the transition to genuine democracy. Since 1949, there had always been at least some of the trappings of democracy on Taiwan, but until 1969, there were only local elections, and until as late as the start of the 1990s, most seats at the national level were simply never up for reelection. This was because they were still held by representatives of constituencies on mainland China, chosen before 1949, whose continued existence was tied to Taipei's claim to be the legitimate government of all China. Also, until September 1986 (when the first true opposition party – the Democratic Progressive Party, or DPP – was formed), Taiwan was always effectively a single-party state. This single ruling party, the Chinese Nationalist Party, had, moreover, been reorganized in 1924 as an explicitly Leninist-model revolutionary party. However, as part of Dr. Sun Yat-sen's legacy, this Nationalist Party had also simultaneously always been officially committed to an ultimate goal of transition to democracy. Since 1927, under Chiang Kai-shek, it had also always been staunchly anti-communist.[45]

By the 1980s, a majority of Taiwan's population was comfortably middle class, and many, moreover, were well educated, intimately familiar with conditions in Japan and the United States, and increasingly inclined to demand the right to participate in political decision making. That there were significant domestic issues and internal dissatisfactions undoubtedly helped fuel this politicization. There also seems to have simply been something in the global zeitgeist, or spirit of the times, in the late 1980s that favored democratization. We have already examined the democratization of South Korea in 1987 and the Tiananmen Square demonstrations in Beijing in 1989. Finally, a generous share of the credit for Taiwan's successful transition to democracy must also go to the leaders of the ruling Nationalist Party, especially President Chiang Ching-kuo (Jiang Jingguo, 1910–1988; see Figure 12.2), Chiang Kai-shek's son and heir, who flatly refused to authorize arrests when told of the (then still technically illegal) formation of the DPP in 1986. "'It is easy to use power,' he told an aid, 'but it is hard to know when not to use it.'"[46] In the following year, 1987, President Chiang Ching-kuo's administration formally repealed martial law, legalized the formation of opposition parties, lifted some of the existing restrictions on the press, and permitted indirect travel (through another country) to mainland China.

In this sudden new age of multiparty democracy, a number of political parties formed, but the most important was always the DPP, and Taiwan seems increasingly to be stabilizing and consolidating into a primarily two-party system, with the DPP and the Nationalist Party as the two major alternatives. As a political party that originated among Taiwanese dissidents deeply resentful of long-standing mainlander rule through the Chinese Nationalist Party, from the beginning, the DPP was associated with a platform calling for Taiwan independence, even though advocating independence remained illegal on Taiwan until 1992. In 2000, the DPP candidate, Chen Shuibian (1950–), actually won the presidential election. This was a truly epochal milestone: the first peaceful democratic transfer of power from one political party to another in Chinese history. Chen won the election with only 39.3 percent of the vote, however, thanks to a three-way split within the opposing Nationalist Party. In 2004, Chen Shuibian won reelection for a second four-year term with a slim majority.

Figure 12.2. Chiang Ching-kuo (center), the son of Chiang Kai-shek and future president of Taiwan, as Taiwan's defense minister meets with U.S. president John F. Kennedy in the White House, 1963. © Bettmann/Corbis.

As president, although his popular mandate for promoting Taiwan independence was always somewhat qualified, and the real danger of provoking war with the mainland made it necessary for him to proceed with caution, Chen Shuibian did begin gingerly advancing some measures to promote the DPP agenda and to reject the legacy of Chiang Kai-shek and the Chinese Nationalist Party. Notably, the word *China* was dropped from the name of several state-run organizations in Taiwan, and in 2007, the Chiang Kai-shek Memorial in downtown Taipei was officially renamed the Taiwan Democracy Memorial Hall. Not only were these moves controversial, however, but during his second term, President Chen and his party also became beleaguered by accusations of corruption and incompetence. In November 2008, the by then ex-president Chen was arrested and handcuffed, placed on trial for corruption, and eventually sentenced to life in prison.

Meanwhile, in the March 2008 presidential elections, the Nationalist Party candidate Ma Ying-jeou (Ma Yingjiu, 1950–) convincingly won back the presidency with 58.5 percent of the vote. President Ma is considered to be a mainlander, born in Hong Kong. He holds a doctorate in law from Harvard University in the United States and speaks English fluently. His election, and former president Chen's disgrace, at least temporarily has considerably reduced the tensions between Taiwan and the PRC and has taken some of the wind out of the sails of the Taiwan independence movement. The former name of the Chiang Kai-shek Memorial in Taipei was officially restored in 2009, and Chiang Kai-shek's reputation in general currently seems to be somewhat on the rebound.[47]

Since the time during the Korean War when President Truman committed the U.S. Navy to "neutralizing" the Taiwan Straits in 1950, Taiwan has enjoyed a consistently close relationship with the United States. Many of Taiwan's leaders have been educated at American universities, the motion pictures advertised on giant billboards at Taipei's many movie theaters have long been disproportionately Hollywood movies (and Taiwan's best-known motion picture director, Ang Lee [Li An, 1954-] is a familiar figure in Hollywood), a substantial amount of the pop music heard in Taiwan is in English (and even the Chinese-language songs are mostly modern and Western style), many young Taiwanese have grown up drinking cola more often than tea, and since the opening of the first McDonald's restaurant on Taiwan in 1984, McDonald's has become a familiar feature of daily life throughout the island. Yet the Japanese influence on Taiwan also remains strong. And paradoxically, even while President Chen Shuibian and the DPP were trying to promote a Taiwan independence agenda and tensions between Taipei and Beijing were most elevated, Taiwan's economic and cultural reintegration with mainland China was also simultaneously rapidly accelerating.

Prior to the democratization of Taiwan in 1987, it had been flatly illegal for people from Taiwan to go to mainland China. Thereafter, however, they began doing so in ever growing numbers. The PRC has now become Taiwan's largest market, and after Hong Kong reverted to Chinese rule in 1997, Taiwan emerged to become the PRC's new leading source of foreign investment. Today, something like a million Taiwan people (out of a total population of only twenty-three million) actually live on mainland China, operating some one hundred thousand businesses there. As of 2002, it was estimated that more than 70 percent of all the electronics products made in the PRC were produced by Taiwan-invested businesses.[48] Taiwan, in other words, has become a critical component in the PRC's recent economic surge.

At the same time, the degree of cultural reintegration is also striking. The Mandarin language that is spoken in Taiwan is nearly identical to the Mandarin spoken in the PRC, and even the so-called Taiwanese dialect also originated on the adjacent mainland province. Naturally, there are local variations. When someone in Taiwan, for example, says that something gives them the flu (or "a cold," *ganmao*), it usually means that they are turned off by it, whereas in mainland China, the same slang expression can mean the exact opposite: that they are enthusiastic about it. In general, though, Taiwan and mainland China literally speak the same languages. Chinese-language pop music from Taiwan, as well as from Hong Kong, has tended to dominate the post-reform mainland market. Joint-production movies and other pop culture entertainments have recently proliferated. It is not uncommon now to see television programs that are set in both Taiwan and China, with characters flying back and forth. For example, the entertaining 2007 romantic comedy TV serial *Corner with Love* (*Zhuan jiao yu dao ai*) featured a young vendor of distinctively Taiwanese-style oyster omelets from Taipei's Shilin night market who went to Shanghai, China, in pursuit of his dream of becoming an artist, only to accidentally fall in love there with a wealthy Chinese girl. While no political solution to the Taiwan problem is anywhere in sight yet, it may therefore be argued that Taiwan has become a successful example of Chinese modernization in its own right, and is also actively playing an important role in the continuously unfolding story of the People's Republic of China.

China and Globalization

Mainland China's experiment with market-based economic reforms had seemingly become stalled by the mid-1980s, and the shocking events in Tiananmen Square in 1989 ushered in a climate of political chill. But Deng Xiaoping then performed a high-profile "southern tour" of the SEZs in the early 1990s, pronouncing that China should not fear a little capitalism, and this succeeded in explosively restarting the economic reform process. By the early 1990s, China had successfully completed its transition to a predominantly market economy, and since then, China's economy has continued to surge. For the China bureau chief of the *Financial Times*, the balance first clearly shifted from "how the world was affecting China" to how "China was affecting the world" in 2004, when manhole covers abruptly began being stolen from around the planet – 150 from the streets of Chicago, Illinois, in one month alone – to supply the voracious demand of China's industry for scrap metal.[49] China's growing global economic clout is nowhere more starkly illuminated than by the estimate that in the decade ending in 2008, China invested about one trillion U.S. dollars in American government bonds and other U.S. debt. China passed Japan in late 2008 to become the largest single holder of U.S. government debt.

Economic growth and international integration have not yet triggered democratization in China, however, frustrating any easy assumption that democratization must be an inescapable component of the post–cold war globalization process. It is even possible that instead, by making it appear successful, the economic reforms may actually buttress continued Communist Party rule. Certainly that was Deng Xiaoping's intention, and his great gamble. China's current president, Hu Jintao (1942–), did affirm a commitment to democracy and rule by law shortly after coming to power in 2002. But even Mao Zedong himself had also sometimes invoked the word *democracy*. After the establishment of the PRC in 1949, eight so-called democratic parties were kept on display, yet they were unmistakably subordinate to the Communist Party and dependent on state funding rather than being genuine opposition parties. The PRC has never tolerated any more than token political opposition or embraced the idea of direct popular multiparty elections. Voting by ordinary citizens remains limited to the lowest administrative level – the some 680,000 village administration committees. Despite its new openness, which for the most part is real enough, China still holds the world's largest number of journalists in prison, and the number of people in reeducation-through-labor camps has reportedly even increased since the early 1990s.[50] The Internet is also monitored, in what is sometimes jokingly called the "Great Firewall of China." Although this Internet censorship is easily enough sidestepped by determined Web surfers, it probably does effectively channel the majority of casual browsers to politically safe Web sites.

Nonetheless, the leadership succession in China has been regularized and stabilized. China's current president, Hu Jintao, represents the third generation of top leaders after Mao Zedong (the fourth if you count Mao himself, and the fifth if you include Hua Guofeng's brief interim tenure at the top), and if China's new leaders are mostly not particularly charismatic, they are also mostly not remarkably objectionable either. The current premier (Wen Jiabao, 1942–) even came to be widely perceived as a caring and beloved leader when he boarded a plane for Sichuan within two hours of a terrible earthquake there in May 2008, to direct disaster relief. One of the biggest grievances leading up to the Tiananmen Square demonstrations in 1989 had been that college-educated professionals felt excluded from the profit-making opportunities provided by market-based reforms. Since 1989, however, some observers believe that college-educated professionals in China have been specifically targeted for economic rewards and have accordingly become increasingly content and satisfied with the status quo.[51] Half of all college students in China are now applying to join the Communist Party, and party membership has grown, reaching some seventy-three million by 2003. This recent growth in CCP membership, of course, has little to do with serious belief in Marxism and much to do with the CCP being the sole ruling party.

China today does face a considerable number of daunting problems, which could very conceivably converge into some cataclysmic perfect storm that might overwhelm the PRC. Major problems include the exhaustion of China's natural resources, growing economic inequality, and endemic corruption. Perhaps the single most frightening problem is China's rapidly dwindling water supply, particularly in north China, where the water table is plummeting alarmingly. In general, ultra-high-speed industrialization on China's enormous scale has had a predictably horrific effect on the environment. In one 2007 survey of the environmental livability of seventy-two world cities, Beijing was ranked the absolute worst. China already burns about one-third of the entire planet's coal usage – two billion tons each year – and coal consumption in China is still increasing at a rate of 10 percent annually. Yet China's leaders are also aware of these problems, and there have already been some discernable improvements. China, for example, has implemented higher fuel-efficiency standards for automobiles than the United States, its solar energy industry is the fastest growing in the world, and its wind-turbine energy production is also developing spectacularly.[52]

Although there has not been a military elite in China since the Bronze Age (with the exception, perhaps, of the Manchu banner men during the Qing Dynasty), and something in the prevailing traditional Confucian ethos arguably did privilege civilian literary accomplishments over feats of arms, it is nonetheless also true that war has actually been as much a part of Chinese history as it has in almost any other country. China today shares land borders with fourteen different countries and has territorial disputes with several. Yet China today has nonetheless deliberately charted a course of development that it advertises as a "peaceful rise" – a rise, that is, based not on predatory mercantilism or military expansionism, but on the promise of universally shared prosperity. In its implementation, this has included the cultivation of friendly relations with many countries, including even such mutual rivals as both Pakistan and India and North and South Korea, and also with some of America's closest allies, such as Japan, Australia, the European Union, and Israel, as well as with regimes that are perceived as hostile toward U.S. interests such as Hugo Chavez's Venezuela.

China is increasingly becoming integrated into global systems and institutions, such as the World Trade Organization, and playing by accepted international rules and standards. The sweeping transformation China has undergone has sometimes come with breathtaking swiftness. The first television commercials in the PRC, for example, were not broadcast until 1979, and early commercial efforts sometimes produced laughable advertisements for such products as cement mixers, having obviously limited appeal to individual consumers. The initial Chinese attempts to crack the American consumer market also brought some hilariously poorly chosen English brand names such as Pansy brand men's underwear, White Elephant brand batteries, and Maxipuke playing cards (*pu ke* being the Chinese transliteration of the English word *poker*).[53] But the Chinese have rapidly become more sophisticated, have plugged into the new communications technologies, and are increasingly meeting world standards.

In 1984, China had no golf courses, but by 2007, China had the fifth greatest number of golf courses in the world (and an absolute majority of the world's golf club heads are now made in China). Western-style classical music is arguably now more genuinely flourishing in the PRC than it is in the United States (and China also dominates world production of pianos and violins). Christianity, amazingly enough, has also been booming in the PRC for a generation now, and there are already a great many more Christians in "communist" China than there are in America's long-favored cold war protégé, Japan.

Much of this dramatic transformation can legitimately be said to represent the triumph not just of an international, or even a Western, but of a specifically American model. Both China's current president and premier have children who have studied in the United States (and Taiwan's new president, Ma Ying-jeou, has a doctorate from Harvard). One of Deng Xiaoping's grandsons is a U.S. citizen. English is the preferred language of international communication, and it is not uncommon to overhear a German businessman in China, for example, conversing with his Chinese counterparts in English. At the end of the twentieth century, the world's largest and busiest McDonald's restaurant was in Tiananmen Square. In the early twenty-first century, China became the American National Basketball Association's (NBA) second largest market outside the United States. The most popular brand of automobile in China is the American General Motors (GM) – even as GM has been struggling in the United States itself. In 2009, the Mattel toy company opened the world's first store with an entirely Barbie doll theme in Shanghai.

Yet as modern global culture merges and blends into China, it also sometimes takes odd twists – such things as pictures of Mao Zedong being treated to Andy Warhol–style pop art techniques. The results can sometimes be unintentionally comic, such as when the secretary general of the Chinese Communist Party urged members of the Politburo to watch the Hollywood movie *Titanic*, praising, among other things, its portrayal of class conflict.[54] There have been some notably popular Mao-themed consumer fads in the newly commercialized PRC, and Mao's picture, ironically enough, remains conspicuous on the Chinese money itself.

The first major political manifestation of the new Internet technology in China came in the form of a newly invented "traditional" Chinese religion. On the tenth anniversary of the Tiananmen Square demonstrations, in April 1999, ten thousand followers of a new religion called Falun Gong suddenly materialized out of nowhere to demonstrate in front of the Communist Party leadership compound, northwest of Tiananmen Square in Beijing. This Falun Gong was a variant of traditional Chinese therapeutic Qigong exercises, combined with Buddhism, that was founded in 1992. Its followers used computer Web sites and cell phones to mobilize this impressive mass demonstration in 1999, which they evidently hoped would win greater toleration of Falun Gong from the authorities in Beijing. The attempt backfired, however, because party leaders panicked instead and ordered a harsh and continuing crackdown on Falun Gong as a supposedly dangerous cult. Other unofficial political uses of the new Internet and cell phone technologies since then have chiefly been to coordinate large-scale popular demonstrations of anti-Japanese patriotic nationalism. In one case, an Internet campaign was also used to force the closure of an American Starbucks coffee shop inside the Forbidden City in Beijing. The new communications technologies, in other words, often serve indigenous agendas as well as linking China to the outside world.

History may not exactly repeat itself, either as tragedy or as farce, but it does pile up, and it seems impossible to ever entirely escape from beneath the weight of the past. Globalization in China has therefore not been a simple one-directional process of Americanization or Westernization but a much more complicated multidirectional process of action and reaction, shaped by both the preexisting situation and the swirling patterns of international trends. In China, for example, one of the banners unfurled in Tiananmen Square in 1989 read "Give Me Liberty or Give Me Death" – a direct reference to the American Revolution. But the Tiananmen demonstrators also consciously invoked memories of the French Revolution, of China's own May Fourth Movement, and of world figures such as Mahatma Gandhi as well as the American Martin Luther King Jr. For the *Goddess of Democracy* statue, the young students from the Central Academy of Fine Arts who actually designed the statue explicitly rejected a suggestion simply to copy the American *Statue of Liberty* in favor of creating "a new work of universal appeal" (see Figure 12.3). As it happened, this was influenced by their prior training in the style of Soviet Russian revolutionary realism. The head of the *Goddess of Democracy* statue was therefore, ironically, inspired more by a monumental statue of *A Worker and Collective Farm Woman* from the Soviet Pavilion at the 1937 Paris World's Fair than by the *Statue of Liberty* in New York City harbor. Other influences were more specifically East Asian: Chinese student demonstrators got the idea of wearing white headbands with slogans from South Korean student demonstrators, who adapted the practice from a Japanese samurai tradition indicating a willingness to fight to the death.[55]

Figure 12.3. Constructing the *Goddess of Democracy* statue in Tiananmen Square, Beijing, 1989. Stuart Franklin. Magnum Photos.

In the new the age of globalization, as the tide of Marxist revolution against "feudal" tradition has receded, there has even been a certain amount of conscious revival of, and renewed pride in, premodern Chinese traditions. Even when China presents itself in specifically modern Westernized terms, moreover, as in the case of the 2008 Beijing Olympics (which, despite some supposedly Chinese flourishes and trappings, was a thoroughly modern Western-style event), or in the many factories mass-producing golf clubs, computers, and toys, as China's global economic profile rises, it is only to be expected that China itself will become more of a center of globalizing influences. In fact, China is already coming to be seen as representing an attractive possible alternative model for some parts of the developing world, where – especially in Asia, Africa, and Latin America – China has suddenly become a major force for export growth. In 2009, for example, China passed the United States to become Brazil's largest trading partner. Despite globalization – indeed, because of globalization – China is becoming globally more important.

For Further Reading

A careful study of the Chinese Nationalist defeat on the mainland in 1949 is Suzanne Pepper, *Civil War in China: The Political Struggle, 1945–1949* (Berkeley: University of California Press, 1978).

For Chairman Mao's revolutionary China, see Edward Friedman, Paul G. Pickowicz, and Mark Selden, *Chinese Village, Socialist State* (New Haven, CT: Yale University Press, 1991), and Maurice Meisner, *Mao's China and After: A History of the People's Republic* (New York: Free Press, [1977] 1986). Personal accounts of life in Mao's China are numerous and include Jung Chang, *Wild Swans: Three Daughters of China* (New York: Anchor Books, 1992), and Heng Liang and Judith Shapiro, *Son of the Revolution* (New York: Vintage Books, 1984). The best account of the Nixon visit is Margaret MacMillan, *Nixon and Mao: The Week That Changed the World* (New York: Random House, 2007).

On the Deng Xiaoping era and economic reforms, see Richard Baum, *Burying Mao: Chinese Politics in the Age of Deng Xiaoping* (Princeton University Press, 1994), and David L. Wank, *Commodifying Communism: Business, Trust, and Politics in a Chinese City* (Cambridge University Press, 1999). The Deng era origins of China's controversial one-child policy are examined in Susan Greenhalgh, *Just One Child: Science and Policy in Deng's China* (Berkeley: University of California Press, 2008).

A superb collection of documents relating to the Tiananmen democracy movement is Minzhu Han (pseudonym), ed., *Cries for Democracy: Writings and Speeches from the 1989 Chinese Democracy Movement* (Princeton University Press, 1990). Another important (and clandestinely released) documentary collection on the events in Tiananmen Square, which purports to include transcripts of discussions among China's top leaders, is Liang Zhang (pseudonym), compiler, *The Tiananmen Papers*, ed. Andrew J. Nathan and Perry Link (New York: PublicAffairs, 2001).

Concerning Greater China, see Willem Van Kemenade, *China, Hong Kong, Taiwan, Inc.*, trans. Diane Webb (New York: Vintage Books, 1998). A good comprehensive history of Hong Kong is Frank Welsh, *A Borrowed Place: The History of Hong Kong* (New York: Kodansha International, 1993). For Taiwan, see Murray A. Rubinstein, ed., *Taiwan: A New History* (Armonk, NY: M. E. Sharpe, 1999). On the Chinese Nationalist government in Taiwan, see Jay Taylor, *The Generalissimo's Son: Chiang Ching-kuo and the Revolutions in China and Taiwan* (Cambridge, MA: Harvard University Press, 2000). On Taiwanese identity, see Alan M. Wachman, *Taiwan: National Identity and Democratization* (Armonk, NY: M. E. Sharpe, 1994). Johanna Menzel Meskill skillfully tells the story of Taiwan's early settlement in *A Chinese Pioneer Family: The Lins of Wu-feng, Taiwan, 1729–1895* (Princeton University Press, 1979).

On globalization and recent Chinese culture, see Geremie R. Barmé, *In the Red: On Contemporary Chinese Culture* (New York: Columbia University Press, 1999), and Doug Guthrie, *China and Globalization: The Social, Economic, and Political Transformation of Chinese Society* (New York: Routledge, 2006).

For astute assessments of the current situation, see James Kynge, *China Shakes the World: A Titan's Rise and Troubled Future – and the Challenge for America* (Boston: Houghton Mifflin, 2006), and David M. Lampton, *The Three Faces of Chinese Power: Might, Money, and Minds* (Berkeley: University of California Press, 2008).

Afterword

In the current age of globalization, some of the most far-flung regions of the planet now sometimes seem to have more in common with each other than they do with their own traditional pasts. In an important sense, it may truly be said that there is already a single common, worldwide human civilization. At the same time, the nation-state remains very much the basic building block of the world community, and separate national identities also remain strong. And paradoxically, in this new age of globalization, certain more narrowly local identities have also sometimes resurfaced with unexpectedly renewed urgency. As Benjamin Barber observes, "a world that is coming together pop culturally and commercially is a world whose discrete subnational ethnic and religious and racial parts are also far more in evidence." Old local dialects, languages, and identities have reawakened. Catalonia, for example, now "integrates itself into Europe precisely by segregating itself from Spain."[1]

Inside China, the market-based reforms of the Deng Xiaoping era were all about the loosening of central controls and decentralization, to the point that it became, bizarrely enough, not unheard of for Chinese provinces to restrict imports from other Chinese provinces even while their barriers to international foreign trade were being steadily dismantled. China's ability to remain a unified country was even cast into some doubt.[2] There has been some revival of old regional identities in China, and not merely in the more obvious extreme cases of Tibet or Uighur-inhabited Eastern Turkestan (Xinjiang), but even within the ethnic Han Chinese majority culture of China proper.[3] Local dialects that were long submerged under Mandarin have more recently sometimes been proudly reflaunted.

Multiple layers of culture and identity quite normally coexist, either with or without friction. In the tiny but illuminating case of identity-challenged Taiwan, for example, we find a successful, modern, thoroughly Westernized society that has long enjoyed a particularly close connection with the United States, but where the Japanese influence has also been especially strong. In Taiwan, as well, elements of mainstream Chinese traditional civilization (such as religion) have flourished, arguably even more vigorously sometimes than in mainland China itself, while at the same time, there is also undeniably a uniquely local Taiwanese culture. Taiwan is simultaneously a "world citizen" poised on the "cutting edge of globalization"[4] and a place where visitors who manage to escape the cocoon of their Western-style hotels to wander the streets and night markets will also still immediately realize that, like Dorothy in *The Wizard of Oz*, they are not in Kansas anymore.

If the global and the local have both garnered new attention, however, and the nation-state still endures as the basic unit of world identity, what of such larger intermediate-level cultural areas (what used to be called "civilizations") as East Asia? Is East Asia still relevant today? Many observers might suppose not, and to some extent, it is certainly true that East Asia is not as cohesive a region as it once was. There can no longer be any possibility of a self-contained and (even relatively) closed East Asian world. The cold war in particular split East Asia into two major divisions, with a bamboo curtain separating those communist countries aligned with the Soviet Union from those other countries that were aligned with the Western democracies. Both halves of this cold war–torn East Asia were, furthermore, at least partially and imperfectly, transformed along the lines of their respective different ideological models (both of which, moreover – communism and democratic capitalism alike – despite their apparently stark opposition, can be traced to European origins). Beneath the surface of this mesmerizing story of global cold war polarization, however, and unnoticed by many people at the time, it has been suggested that perhaps the most truly significant long-term development of the entire cold war era really was the economic rise of East Asia.[5]

East Asian success might simply be interpreted merely as an extension, or as a further example, of the triumph of the Western capitalist model at the end of the cold war, but it remains to be explained, then, why East Asia alone was so uniquely successful. In 1993, for example, the World Bank calculated the odds of such economic success being concentrated in the East Asian region at 1 in 10,000.[6] Some analysts have even invoked a "Confucian work ethic" to explain this East Asian "miracle."[7] While there are good reasons for maintaining a healthy dose of skepticism concerning any simplistic Confucian explanations for East Asian dynamism – starting with the fact that Confucianism itself is a rather nebulous concept – East Asian success nonetheless has been exceptional, and it does suggest, at least, that East Asia deserves to be taken seriously. East Asia, North America, and Europe may well be the three greatest centers of global wealth and power in the early twenty-first century.

With the end of the cold war, moreover, and mainland China's reemergence from isolationism and subsequent spectacular economic takeoff, East Asia is much less divided than it once was in the 1950s to 1970s. East Asia may have even actually regained some coherence as a region. Although sales access to the enormous U.S. consumer market was once perhaps the most essential key to early export-led Pacific Rim economic growth, the East Asian nations have all more recently become each other's largest trading partners, and often also enthusiastic consumers of each other's modern pop culture. This in no way diminishes their accelerating participation in the larger global community, nor does it eliminate internal East Asian rivalries such as those between China and Japan, Korea and

Japan, North Korea and South Korea, or Taiwan and the People's Republic of China (PRC). American GM brand automobiles are currently more popular in the PRC than Japanese brands, and recent flare-ups of popular Chinese nationalist fury have most commonly been directed at still bitter memories of Japanese aggression during World War II. Conversely, some Japanese understandably feel considerable apprehension about the rising Chinese giant nearby on the mainland. The relationship between Taiwan and the PRC remains a potential flash point that could erupt into war. And for North Korea, the cold war still does not appear to have ended. In this potentially highly unstable security environment, the continuing presence of American power remains a welcome stabilizing influence that few East Asians are really eager to see disappear anytime soon. Throughout much of East Asia, moreover, American pop culture is only increasing its reach and influence.

Yet the economic and cultural reintegration of East Asia has also been considerable, and over the entire region, the ghost, not so much of Confucius as of the entire East Asian past, hovers, often invisibly but nonetheless powerfully, in the form of the extensively shared vocabulary among the various East Asian languages. China (including Greater China), Japan, and Korea are very different places, but they also literally share many of the same words and ideas. Globalization, so far, has certainly not eliminated all local differences, and it may be that East Asia's remarkable economic success in recent decades, and more recent post–cold war regional reconnections, means that East Asia's relevance as a region has not only not entirely vanished into history but could even be increasing.

Notes

Introduction: What Is East Asia?

1. The top five national economies in 2008 (not counting the European Union as a "nation"), based on estimates of their actual size, were the United States, China, Japan, India, and Germany. See the Central Intelligence Agency (CIA), "World Fact Book," country comparison: GDP (purchasing power parity), https://www.cia.gov/library/publications/the-world-factbook/.
2. P. Bairoch, "International Industrialization Levels from 1750 to 1980," *Journal of European Economic History* 11, no. 2 (1982): 296, table 10.
3. Tsuen-Hsuin Tsien, *Written on Bamboo and Silk: The Beginnings of Chinese Books and Inscriptions* (University of Chicago Press, 1962), p. 2.
4. CIA, "World Fact Book" country comparison: GDP-per capita (purchasing power parity).
5. M. W. Lewis and K. E. Wigen, *The Myth of Continents: A Critique of Metageography* (Berkeley: University of California Press, 1997), pp. 16, 21, 53–55. The statistics are from R. B. Marks, *The Origins of the Modern World: A Global and Ecological Narrative from the Fifteenth to the Twenty-first Century*, 2nd ed. (Lanham, MD: Rowman and Littlefield, 2007), pp. 80–81.
6. A. H. Brodrick, *Little China: The Annamese Lands* (London: Oxford University Press, 1942).
7. Guo Maoqian (fl. 1264–1269 CE), ed., *Yuefu shiji* (Collected Music Bureau Poetry) (Taibei: Taiwan Zhonghua shuju, 1965), 44.1a.
8. D. Yen-ho Wu, "The Construction of Chinese and Non-Chinese Identities," in Wei-ming Tu, ed., *The Living Tree: The Changing Meaning of Being Chinese Today* (Stanford University Press, 1994), p. 150.
9. E. H. Schafer, "The *Yeh Chung Chi*," *T'oung Pao* 76, nos. 4–5 (1990): 147–149. See also J. Fitzgerald, "The Nationless State: The Search for a Nation in Modern Chinese Nationalism," in *Chinese Nationalism*, ed. J. Unger (Armonk, NY: M. E. Sharpe, 1996), p. 67.
10. Y. Pines, "Beasts or Humans: Pre-Imperial Origins of the 'Sino-Barbarian' Dichotomy," in *Mongols, Turks, and Others: Eurasian Nomads and the Sedentary World*, ed. R. Amitai and M. Biran (Leiden, Netherlands: Brill, 2005), p. 62.
11. Fang Xuanling, ed., *Jin shu* (The Dynastic History of the Jin) (644 CE) (Beijing: Zhonghua shuju, 1974), 28.844.

12. W. G. Aston, trans., *Nihongi: Chronicles of Japan from the Earliest Times to* A.D. *697* (Rutland, VT: Charles E. Tuttle, [1896] 1972), vol. I, p. 1, note 1. See also C. Holcombe, *The Genesis of East Asia, 221* B.C.–A.D. *907* (Honolulu: University of Hawai'i Press, 2001), pp. 72–73.

13. For tea, see D. Keene, *Yoshimasa and the Silver Pavilion: The Creation of the Soul of Japan* (New York: Columbia University Press, 2003), pp. 139–151. For sushi, see S. Issenberg, *The Sushi Economy: Globalization and the Making of a Modern Delicacy* (New York: Gotham Books, 2007), p. xxi. For *Jūdō*, see Inoue Shun, "The Invention of the Martial Arts: Kanō Jigorō and Kōdōkan Judo," in *Mirror of Modernity: Invented Traditions of Modern Japan*, ed. S. Vlastos (Berkeley: University of California Press, 1998), pp. 163–173. For the nation-state, see T. Morris-Suzuki, "A Descent into the Past: The Frontier in the Construction of Japanese Identity," in *Multicultural Japan: Palaeolithic to Postmodern*, ed. D. Denoon et al. (Cambridge University Press, 1996), p. 82.

14. A. B. Woodside, *Vietnam and the Chinese Model: A Comparative Study of Nguyên and Ch'ing Civil Government in the First Half of the Nineteenth Century* (Cambridge, MA: Harvard University Press, 1971), p. 120.

15. K. W. Taylor, "Surface Orientations in Vietnam: Beyond Histories of Nation and Region," *Journal of Asian Studies* 57, no. 4 (1998): 966.

Chapter 1. The Origins of Civilization in East Asia

1. Technically, the emperor only denied that he was a "manifest deity" and did not renounce the claim to descent from the sun goddess. See J. W. Dower, *Embracing Defeat: Japan in the Wake of World War II* (New York: W. H. Norton, 1999), p. 316.

2. D. E. Mungello, *Curious Land: Jesuit Accommodation and the Origins of Sinology* (Honolulu: University of Hawai'i Press, 1985), pp. 144, 179.

3. Ping-ti Ho, *The Cradle of the East: An Inquiry into the Indigenous Origins of Techniques and Ideas of Neolithic and Early Historic China, 5000–1000* B.C. (Chinese University of Hong Kong, 1975).

4. A. Sherratt, "The Trans-Eurasian Exchange: The Prehistory of Chinese Relations with the West," in *Contact and Exchange in the Ancient World*, ed. V. H. Mair (Honolulu: University of Hawai'i Press, 2006), pp. 32, 53.

5. S. M. Nelson, "The Politics of Ethnicity in Prehistoric Korea," in *Nationalism, Politics, and the Practice of Archaeology*, ed. P. L. Kohl and C. Fawcett (Cambridge University Press, 1995), p. 221.

6. N. Ostler, *Empires of the Word: A Language History of the World* (New York: HarperCollins, 2005), p. xix.

7. A. P. Smyth, "The Emergence of English Identity, 700–1000," in *Medieval Europeans: Studies in Ethnic Identity and National Perspectives in Medieval Europe*, ed. A. P. Smyth (New York: St. Martin's Press, 1998), p. 25.

8. See J. DeFrancis, *The Chinese Language: Fact and Fantasy* (Honolulu: University of Hawai'i Press, 1984), pp. 54–58.

9. S. R. Ramsey, *The Languages of China* (Princeton University Press, 1987), pp. 21, 24.

10. Chen Shou (233–297 CE), *Sanguo zhi* (*Chronicles of the Three Kingdoms*) (Beijing: Zhonghua shuju, 1959), 30.852.

11. P. Bellwood, *Prehistory of the Indo-Malaysian Archipelago* (1985; Honolulu: University of Hawai'i Press, 1997), pp. 97, 110; J. Norman and Tsu-lin Mei, "The Austroasiatics in Ancient South China: Some Lexical Evidence," *Monumenta Serica* 32 (1976).

12. B. G. Trigger, *Understanding Early Civilizations: A Comparative Study* (Cambridge University Press, 2003), pp. 600–602.

13. A. R. Millard, "The Infancy of the Alphabet," *World Archaeology* 17, no. 3 (1986): 394–396.

14. W. C. Hannas, *Asia's Orthographic Dilemma* (Honolulu: University of Hawai'i Press, 1997), p. 28.

15. I. Morris, *The World of the Shining Prince: Court Life in Ancient Japan* (1964; Harmondsworth, UK: Penguin Books, 1985), p. 207.

16. I. Smits, "The Way of the Literati: Chinese Learning and Literary Practice in Mid-Heian Japan," in *Heian Japan, Centers and Peripheries*, ed. M. Adolphson, E. Kamens, and S. Matsumoto (Honolulu: University of Hawai'i Press, 2007), p. 106; P. Kornicki, *The Book in Japan: A Cultural History from the Beginnings to the Nineteenth Century* (Leiden, Netherlands: Brill, 1998), p. 382; D. Keene, "The Sino-Japanese War of 1894–95 and Its Cultural Effects in Japan," in *Tradition and Modernization in Japanese Culture*, ed. D. H. Shively (Princeton University Press, 1971), pp. 167–172.

17. J. Stanlaw, "'For Beautiful Human Life': The Use of English in Japan," in *Re-made in Japan: Everyday Life and Consumer Taste in a Changing Society*, ed. J. J. Tobin (New Haven, CT: Yale University Press, 1992), pp. 61–62.

18. Kichung Kim, *An Introduction to Classical Korean Literature: From Hyangga to P'ansori* (Armonk, NY: M. E. Sharpe, 1996), p. 5.

19. Hannas, *Asia's Orthographic Dilemma*, p. 183.

20. L. Febvre and H. J. Martin, *The Coming of the Book: The Impact of Printing, 1450–1800*, trans. D. Gerard (1958; London: NLB, 1976), p. 249.

21. Kwang-chih Chang, *Shang Civilization* (New Haven, CT: Yale University Press, 1980), pp. 38–39, 42–52.

22. S. Allan, "Erlitou and the Formation of Chinese Civilization: Toward a New Paradigm," *Journal of Asian Studies* 66, no. 2 (2007).

23. *Shoku Nihongi (Continued Chronicles of Japan)* (797 CE), Shin Nihon koten bungaku taikei 12 (Tōkyō: Iwanami shoten, 1989), 4.124–127.

24. Trigger, *Understanding Early Civilizations*, p. 79.

Chapter 2. The Formative Era

1. Han Yu (768–824 BCE), "Yuan dao" (Essentials of the Moral Way), in *Han Changli quanji* (Beijing: Zhongguo shudian, 1991), 11.174. Here *Yi* is translated as "foreign" and *Zhongguo* as "Chinese." For a slightly variant translation, see W. T. de Bary and I. Bloom, eds., *Sources of Chinese Tradition*, vol. 1. *From Earliest Times to 1600*, 2nd ed. (New York: Columbia University Press, 1999), p. 572.

2. Y. Pines, *Envisioning Eternal Empire: Chinese Political Thought of the Warring States Era* (Honolulu: University of Hawai'i Press, 2009), pp. 20, 29–30.

3. L. M. Jensen, *Manufacturing Confucianism: Chinese Traditions and Universal Civilization* (Durham, NC: Duke University Press, 1997), p. 5.

4. All quotations from Zhou period texts in this chapter are from de Bary and Bloom, *Sources of Chinese Tradition*.

5. P. Duus, *The Abacus and the Sword: The Japanese Penetration of Korea, 1895–1910* (Berkeley: University of California Press, 1995), p. 31n5.

6. *Shoku Nihongi*, 20.182–183.

7. G. B. Sansom, *Japan: A Short Cultural History* (Stanford University Press, [1931] 1978), p. 109.

8. H. Ooms, *Imperial Politics and Symbolics in Ancient Japan: The Tenmu Dynasty, 650–800* (Honolulu: University of Hawai'i Press, 2009), pp. 165–168, and frequent references to Daoism.

9. D. E. Mungello, *The Great Encounter of China and the West, 1500–1800* (Lanham, MD: Rowman and Littlefield, 1999), pp. 89–90.

10. R. J. Samuels, *"Rich Nation Strong Army": National Security and the Technological Transformation of Japan* (Ithaca, NY: Cornell University Press, 1994), p. 35.

11. See R. D. Sawyer, "Military Writings," in *A Military History of China*, ed. D. A. Graff and R. Higham (Boulder, CO: Westview Press, 2002). See also R. D. Sawyer and Mei-chün Sawyer, trans., *The Seven Military Classics of Ancient China* (New York: Basic Books, [1993] 2007).

12. A. I. Johnston, *Cultural Realism: Strategic Culture and Grand Strategy in Chinese History* (Princeton University Press, 1995), pp. 107–108.

13. Sima Qian (145–90? BCE), *Shi ji* (Records of the Grand Historian) (Beijing: Zhonghua shuju, 1959), 6.245.

14. Chun-shu Chang, *The Rise of the Chinese Empire, vol. 1. Nation, State, and Imperialism in Early China, ca. 1600* B.C.–A.D. *8* (Ann Arbor: University of Michigan Press, 2007), p. 58.

15. D. Bodde, "The State and Empire of Ch'in," in *The Cambridge History of China, vol. 1. The Ch'in and Han Empires, 221* B.C.–A.D. *220*, ed. D. Twitchett and M. Loewe (Cambridge University Press, 1986), p. 50.

16. *Lü shi chunqiu, jinzhu jinyi* (The Spring and Autumn of Master Lü, Newly Annotated and Newly Interpreted) (ca. 239 BCE) (Taibei: Taiwan shangwu yinshuguan, 1989), 13.350; Sima Qian, *Shi ji*, 6.238–239.

17. M. J. Puett, *To Become a God: Cosmology, Sacrifice, and Self-Divinization in Early China* (Cambridge, MA: Harvard University Press, 2002), pp. 225, 240.

18. de Bary and Bloom, *Sources of Chinese Tradition*, pp. 228–231.

19. Chang, *Rise of the Chinese Empire*, vol. 1, p. 246.

20. See S. A. Queen, *From Chronicle to Canon: The Hermeneutics of the Spring and Autumn, According to Tung Chung-shu* (Cambridge University Press, 1996), p. 115.

21. B. Watson, trans., *Courtier and Commoner in Ancient China: Selections from the* History of the Former Han *by Pan Ku* (New York: Columbia University Press, 1974), pp. 192–193.

22. Feng Yan, *Feng shi wenjian ji, jiaozhu* (A Record of what Mr. Feng Heard and Saw, Revised and Annotated) (ca. 800 CE) (Beijing: Zhonghua shuju, 1958), 2.8.

23. Fan Ye (398–445 CE), *Hou-Han shu* (Dynastic History of the Later Han) (Beijing: Zhonghua shuju, 1965), 84.2801.

24. See H. L. Goodman, *Ts'ao P'i Transcendent: The Political Culture of Dynasty-Founding in China at the End of the Han* (Seattle: Scripta Serica, 1998).

25. *Jin shu*, 69.1848.

Chapter 3. The Age of Cosmopolitanism

1. The Sixteen Kingdoms were Former Zhao (or Han), Later Zhao, Former Yan, Former Qin, Later Yan, Later Qin, Southern Yan, Xia, Former Liang, Shu (or Cheng-Han), Later Liang, Western Qin, Southern Liang, Western Liang, Northern Liang, and Northern Yan.

2. The Five Hu peoples were the Xiongnu, the Xianbei, the Di, the Qiang, and the Jie.

3. See D. A. Graff, *Medieval Chinese Warfare, 300–900* (London: Routledge, 2002), pp. 41–42.

4. *Jin shu*, 101.2649.

5. Sun Sheng (4th century), *Jin yang qiu* (Annals of Jin), quoted in Liu Yiqing (403–444 CE), *Shishuo xinyu, jiaojian* (A New Account of Tales of the World, Revised Commentary), (Hong Kong: Zhonghua shuju, 1987), A.97 (chap. 3, no. 12). Translated slightly differently in R. B. Mather, trans., *Shih-shuo Hsin-yü: A New Account of Tales of the World* (Minneapolis: University of Minnesota Press, 1976), p. 86, no. 12, note 1.

6. For the imperial library, see Xiaofei Tian, *Beacon Fire and Shooting Star: The Literary Culture of the Liang (502–557)* (Cambridge, MA: Harvard University Asia Center, 2007), p. 95. For the *Wen xuan*, see D. R. Knechtges, "Culling the Weeds and Selecting Prime

Blossoms: The Anthology in Early Medieval China," in *Culture and Power in the Reconstitution of the Chinese Realm, 200–600*, ed. S. Pearce, A. Spiro, and P. Ebrey (Cambridge, MA: Harvard University Press, 2001), pp. 206, 239.

7. Liu Shufen, "Jiankang and the Commercial Empire of the Southern Dynasties: Change and Continuity in Medieval Chinese Economic History," in Pearce et al., *Culture and Power*, pp. 35 and 254n2.

8. B. Ward-Perkins, *The Fall of Rome and the End of Civilization* (Oxford University Press, 2005), p. 87.

9. Seng You (435–518 CE), *Hong ming ji* (Collection Expanding Illumination) (Taibei: Taiwan Zhonghua shuju, 1983), epilogue, 14.9b. Here translating *Xia* and *Hua* as "China" and *Rong* and *Yi* as "barbarian."

10. Wei Shou, *Wei shu* (Dynastic History of the [Northern] Wei) (554 CE) (Beijing: Zhonghua shuju, 1974), 97.2142.

11. Yu Xin (513–581), in Zhang Zhuo (early eighth century), *Chao ye qian zai* (The Whole Record of Court and Country), preserved in *Taiping guangji* (Extensive Records [Assembled during] the Taiping Era) (978 CE) (Beijing: Zhonghua shuju, 1981), 198.1483.

12. See J. Holmgren, "The Composition of the Early Wei Bureaucratic Elite as Background to the Emperor Kao-tsu's Reforms (423–490 AD)," *Journal of Asian History* 27 (1993): 115–116.

13. Wang Tong (ca. 584–617 CE), *Wenzhongzi zhongshuo* (Master Wenzhong's [i.e., Wang Tong's] Discourses on the Mean) (Taibei: Taiwan Zhonghua shuju, 1965), 4.3a.

14. A. F. Wright, "The Sui Dynasty (581–617)," in *The Cambridge History of China*, vol. 3. *Sui and T'ang China, 589–906, Part 1*, ed. D. Twitchett (London: Cambridge University Press, 1979), p. 49.

15. Li Baiyao (565–648 CE), *Bei-Qi shu* (Dynastic History of the Northern Qi) (Beijing: Zhonghua shuju, 1972), 50.693.

16. A. L. Juliano and J. A. Lerner, eds., *Monks and Merchants: Silk Road Treasures from Northwest China, Gansu and Ningxia, 4th–7th Century* (New York: Harry N. Abrams, 2001), pp. 98–100.

17. A. E. Dien, *Six Dynasties Civilization* (New Haven, CT: Yale University Press, 2007), pp. 71–75; M. E. Lewis, *China between Empires: The Northern and Southern Dynasties* (Cambridge, MA: Harvard University Press, 2009), p. 105.

18. Lewis, *China between Empires*, pp. 196–204; S. R. Bokenkamp, *Ancestors and Anxiety: Daoism and the Birth of Rebirth in China* (Berkeley: University of California Press, 2007), pp. 171–172, 182.

19. Huijiao, *Gao seng zhuan* (Biographies of Eminent Monks) (ca. 530 CE) (Taibei: Huiwentang, 1987), 10.240.

20. See J. A. Millward, *Eurasian Crossroads: A History of Xinjiang* (New York: Columbia University Press, 2007).

21. Mouzi, "Lihuo lun" (On Disposing of Error), *Hong ming ji*, 1.9b.

22. The estimate is from P. L. Swanson, *The Foundations of T'ien-T'ai Philosophy: The Flowering of the Two Truths Theory in Chinese Buddhism* (Berkeley, CA: Asian Humanities Press, 1989), p. 44.

23. Li Yanshou, *Nan shi* (History of the Southern Dynasties) (ca. 629 CE) (Beijing: Zhonghua shuju, 1975), 70.1721–1722.

24. W. G. Aston, trans., *Nihongi: Chronicles of Japan from the Earliest Times to A.D. 697* (Rutland, VT: Charles E. Tuttle, [1896] 1972), vol. II, pp. 66–67.

25. S. M. Nelson, *The Archaeology of Korea* (Cambridge University Press, 1993), p. 147.

26. Hsu Cho-yun (Xu Zhuoyun) and K. M. Linduff, *Western Chou Civilization* (New Haven, CT: Yale University Press, 1988), p. 201.

27. *A Study of the Parhae Kingdom* (*Parhae ko*), by Yu Tŭk-kong (1748–1807).

28. G. Ledyard, "Galloping Along with the Horseriders: Looking for the Founders of Japan," *Journal of Japanese Studies* 1, no. 2 (1975): 231.

29. Choi Jongtaik, "The Development of the Pottery Technologies of the Korean Peninsula and Their Relationship to Neighboring Regions," in *Early Korea 1: Reconsidering Early Korean History through Archaeology*, ed. M. E. Byington (Seoul: Korea Institute, Harvard University, 2008), pp. 157, 176–187.

30. See Hyung Il Pai, *Constructing "Korean" Origins: A Critical Review of Archaeology, Historiography, and Racial Myth in Korean State-Formation Theories* (Cambridge, MA: Harvard University Asia Center, 2000), pp. 122–126.

31. The current text of the *Chronicles of the Three Kingdoms* actually reads "Yemayi," but this appears to be a garbling of the original. See W. W. Farris, *Sacred Texts and Buried Treasures: Issues in the Historical Archaeology of Ancient Japan* (Honolulu: University of Hawai'i Press, 1998), p. 22.

32. Kwon Oh Young, "The Influence of Recent Archaeological Discoveries on the Research of Paekche History," in Byington, *Early Korea 1*, pp. 97–102.

33. H. Ooms, *Imperial Politics and Symbolics in Ancient Japan: The Tenmu Dynasty, 650–800* (Honolulu: University of Hawai'i Press, 2009), pp. 102–103.

34. See M. J. Seth, *A Concise History of Korea: From the Neolithic Period through the Nineteenth Century* (Lanham, MD: Rowman and Littlefield, 2006), p. 8.

35. J. M. Kitagawa, *On Understanding Japanese Religion* (Princeton University Press, [1979] 1987), pp. 71, 117–126.

36. See J. R. Piggott, *The Emergence of Japanese Kingship* (Stanford University Press, 1997), pp. 91–92, 127.

37. Aston, *Nihongi*, vol. II, p. 131.

Chapter 4. The Creation of a Community: China, Korea, and Japan (Seventh–Tenth Centuries)

1. P. Kennedy, *The Rise and Fall of the Great Powers: Economic Change and Military Conflict from 1500 to 2000* (New York: Random House, 1987), pp. xvi, 515.

2. H. J. Wechsler, *Mirror to the Son of Heaven: Wei Cheng at the Court of T'ang T'ai-tsung* (New Haven, CT: Yale University Press, 1974), p. 31.

3. A. Eisenberg argues that the Tang founder actively anticipated such deadly competition between his sons in chapter 6 of *Kingship in Early Medieval China* (Leiden, Netherlands: Brill, 2008).

4. Wen Daya, *Da-Tang chuangye qiju zhu* (Diary of the Founding of Great Tang) (ca. 626 CE) (Shanghai: Shanghai guji chubanshe, 1983), 1.2.

5. See Yihong Pan, *Son of Heaven and Heavenly Qaghan: Sui-Tang China and Its Neighbors* (Bellingham: Western Washington University, 1997), pp. 179–181.

6. Xuanzang (ca. 596–664 CE) and Bianji (620–648 CE), *Da-Tang xiyu ji* (A Record of the Western Regions in Great Tang) (Taibei: Xinwenfeng chuban gongsi, 1987), 1.78.

7. M. S. Abramson, *Ethnic Identity in Tang China* (Philadelphia: University of Pennsylvania Press, 2008), p. xi.

8. Du You, *Tong dian* (Comprehensive Canons) (801 CE) (Beijing: Zhonghua shuju, 1984), 146.763, panel a.

9. Lu Fahe's biography is in *Bei-Qi shu*, 32.427–431.

10. A. E. Dien, "Civil Service Examinations: Evidence from the Northwest," in *Culture and Power in the Reconstitution of the Chinese Realm, 200–600*, ed. S. Pearce, A. Spiro, and P. Ebrey (Cambridge, MA: Harvard University Press, 2001), pp. 99–121.

11. C. Benn, *China's Golden Age: Everyday Life in the Tang Dynasty* (Oxford University Press, 2002), p. 255.

12. Yuan Zhen, *Yuan shi changqing ji* (The Works of Mr. Yuan [Zhen], Collected in the Changqing Era [821–825 CE]) (Taibei: Taiwan Zhonghua shuju, 1965), 51.1b.

13. Wang Qinruo et al., ed., *Cefu yuangui* (The Great Tortoise of Archives) (ca. 1012 CE) (Taibei: Taiwan Zhonghua shuju, 1981), 160.1932. Entry dated 835 CE.

14. Ouyang Xiu and Song Qi, *Xin Tang shu* (New Dynastic History of the Tang) (1060 CE) (Beijing: Zhonghua shuju, 1975), 135.4576.

15. R. H. Sharf, *Coming to Terms with Chinese Buddhism: A Reading of the* Treasure Store Treatise (Honolulu: University of Hawai'i Press, 2002), pp. 7–9.

16. H. Dumoulin, *Zen Buddhism: A History*, vol. 1. *India and China*, trans. J. W. Heisig and P. Knitter (New York: Macmillan, 1988), p. 85.

17. S. Owen, *The Great Age of Chinese Poetry: The High T'ang* (New Haven, CT: Yale University Press, 1981), p. 292.

18. See E. G. Pulleyblank, *The Background of the Rebellion of An Lu-shan* (London: Oxford University Press, 1955).

19. M. R. Drompp, *Tang China and the Collapse of the Uighur Empire: A Documentary History* (Leiden, Netherlands: Brill, 2005), pp. 20–38.

20. Abramson, *Ethnic Identity in Tang China*, pp. 179–191.

21. Han Yu (768–824 CE), "Yu Meng Shangshu shu" (Letter to Minister Meng [Jian]), in *Han Changli quanji*, 18.268.

22. Wen Tingyun (mid-ninth century), "Ganzhuanzi" (Master Dried Re-cooked Meat), extracted in *Taiping guangji*, 243.1875–1879.

23. R. M. Hartwell, "Demographic, Political, and Social Transformations of China, 750–1550," *Harvard Journal of Asiatic Studies* 42, no. 2 (1982): 366.

24. Iryŏn, *Samguk yusa* (Memorabilia from the Three [Korean] Kingdoms) (1280 CE), 4; T.49.1002.

25. Kim Pu-sik, *Samguk sagi* (Historical Record of the Three [Korean] Kingdoms) (1145 CE) (Seoul: Hongsin munhwasa, 1994), vol. 1, p. 413 (Koguryŏ Basic Annals 10).

26. Chŏng In-ji, *Koryŏ sa* (History of Koryŏ) (1451 CE) (Seoul: Kyŏngin munhwasa, 1981), 2.15b. Fourth of "Ten Injunctions." Translated more freely in P. H. Lee, ed., *Sourcebook of Korean Civilization*, vol. 1. *From Early Times to the Sixteenth Century* (New York: Columbia University Press, 1993), p. 264.

27. *Sui shu*, 81.1827.

28. J. R. Piggott, *The Emergence of Japanese Kingship* (Stanford University Press, 1997), pp. 96–99.

29. H. Ooms, *Imperial Politics and Symbolics in Ancient Japan: The Tenmu Dynasty, 650–800* (Honolulu: University of Hawai'i Press, 2009), p. 51.

30. *Ryō no gige* (Commentary to the [Yōrō] Administrative Code [of 718 CE]), Shintei zōho kokushi taikei (fukyūban) (833 CE) (Tōkyō: Yoshikawa kōbunkan, 1972), 6.205.

31. Sugawara no Michizane, compiler, *Ruijū kokushi* (Categorized National Histories), Shintei zōho kokushi taikei (ca. 892 CE) (Tōkyō: Yoshikawa kōbunkan, 1965), 107.59.

32. *Honchō monzui, chūshaku* (The Annotated Essential Literature of Our Dynasty), attributed to Fujiwara no Akihira (989–1066 CE), ed. Kakimura Shigematsu (ca. 1037–45 CE) (Tōkyō: Fuzambō, 1968), 9.210.

33. *Honchō monzui*, 2.285.

34. B. L. Batten, "Cross-border Traffic on the Kyushu Coast, 794–1086," in *Heian Japan, Centers and Peripheries*, ed. M. Adolphson, E. Kamens, and S. Matsumoto (Honolulu: University of Hawai'i Press, 2007), pp. 358–360.

35. W. W. Farris, *Population, Disease, and Land in Early Japan, 645–900* (Cambridge, MA: Harvard University Press, 1985), chap. 2.

36. On early printing, and its massive scale and Buddhist function in this case, see T. H. Barrett, *The Woman Who Discovered Printing* (New Haven, CT: Yale University Press, 2008), p. 94.

37. For Japan, see W. R. LaFleur, *The Karma of Words: Buddhism and the Literary Arts in Medieval Japan* (Berkeley: University of California Press, 1983), pp. 9–14.

38. W. H. McCullough, "The Heian Court, 794–1070," in *The Cambridge History of Japan*, vol. 2. *Heian Japan*, ed. D. H. Shively and W. H. McCullough (Cambridge University Press, 1999), p. 70.

39. *The Pillow Book of Sei Shōnagon*, trans. I. Morris (early 11th century) (Baltimore: Penguin Books, 1967), p. 263.

40. *Shoku Nihon kōki* (The Later Chronicles of Japan, Continued), Kokushi taikei (869 CE) (Tōkyō: Keizai zasshisha, 1897), 8.255.

41. McCullough, "Heian Court," pp. 61–62.

42. M. Collcutt, "Lanxi Daolong (1213–1278) at Kenchōji: Chinese Contributions to the Making of Medieval Japanese Rinzai Zen," in *Tools of Culture: Japan's Cultural, Intellectual, Medical, and Technological Contacts in East Asia, 1000–1500s*, ed. A. E. Goble, K. R. Robinson, and H. Wakabayashi (Ann Arbor, MI: Association for Asian Studies, 2009), pp. 135–138.

Chapter 5. Mature Independent Trajectories (Tenth–Sixteenth Centuries)

1. A pioneering study of Xi Xia is R. W. Dunnell, *The Great State of White and High: Buddhism and State Formation in Eleventh-century Xia* (Honolulu: University of Hawai'i Press, 1996).

2. Wang Gungwu, *The Nanhai Trade: The Early History of Chinese Trade in the South China Sea* (Singapore: Times Academic Press, [1958] 1998), pp. 16–17, 25.

3. Le Tac, *Annam chi luoc* (A Brief Chronicle of Vietnam) (1340 CE) (Beijing: Zhonghua shuju, 1995), 16.381.

4. D. C. Wright, *From War to Diplomatic Parity in Eleventh-Century China: Sung's Foreign Relations with Kitan Liao* (Leiden, Netherlands: Brill, 2005), pp. 36–37.

5. N. Standen, *Unbounded Loyalty: Frontier Crossing in Liao China* (Honolulu: University of Hawai'i Press, 2007), p. 182.

6. P. K. Bol, "Chao Ping-wen (1159–1232): Foundations for Literati Learning," in *China under Jurchen Rule: Essays on Chin Intellectual and Cultural History*, ed. H. C. Tillman and S. H. West (Albany: State University of New York Press, 1995), p. 127; H. C. Tillman, "Confucianism under the Chin and the Impact of Sung Confucian Tao-hsüeh," in Tillman and West, *China under Jurchen Rule*, pp. 88–89.

7. R. Trauzettel, "Sung Patriotism as a First Step toward Chinese Nationalism," in *Crisis and Prosperity in Sung China*, ed. J. W. Haeger (Tucson: University of Arizona Press, 1975).

8. See M. Elvin, *The Pattern of the Chinese Past: A Social and Economic Interpretation* (Stanford University Press, 1973), part two.

9. Tansen Sen, *Buddhism, Diplomacy, and Trade: The Realignment of Sino-Indian Relations, 600–1400* (Honolulu: University of Hawai'i Press, 2003), pp. 232–233.

10. Shiba Yoshinobu, "Sung Foreign Trade: Its Scope and Organization," in *China among Equals: The Middle Kingdom and Its Neighbors, 10th–14th Centuries*, ed. M. Rossabi (Berkeley: University of California Press, 1983), p. 106.

11. P. F. Souyri, *The World Turned Upside Down: Medieval Japanese Society*, trans. Käthe Roth (New York: Columbia University Press, [1998] 2001), pp. 148–149.

12. F. W. Mote, *Imperial China: 900–1800* (Cambridge, MA: Harvard University Press, 1999), p. 165.

13. R. Hartwell, "A Revolution in the Chinese Iron and Coal Industries during the Northern Sung, 960–1126 A.D.," *Journal of Asian Studies* 21, no. 2 (1962): 155; Elvin, *Pattern of the Chinese Past*, pp. 85–86.

14. B. K. So, "Legitimizing New Political Order Legally: Legal Reforms in Northern Song China," in *The Legitimation of New Orders: Case Studies in World History*, ed. P. Y. Leung (Hong Kong: Chinese University Press, 2007), p. 38.

15. The system in its final form, under the Qing Dynasty, is detailed in Ichisada Miyazaki, *China's Examination Hell: The Civil Service Examinations of Imperial China*, trans. C. Schirokauer (New Haven, CT: Yale University Press, [1963] 1981).

16. P. B. Ebrey, *The Inner Quarters: Marriage and the Lives of Chinese Women in the Sung Period* (Berkeley: University of California Press, 1993), pp. 5–6, 267–270.

17. W. T. de Bary, *East Asian Civilizations: A Dialogue in Five Stages* (Cambridge, MA: Harvard University Press, [1988] 1994), p. 62.

18. L. A. Walton, *Academies and Society in Southern Sung China* (Honolulu: University of Hawai'i Press, 1999), pp. 102–103.

19. A. Welter, "A Buddhist Response to the Confucian Revival: Tsan-ning and the Debate over Wen in the Early Sung," in *Buddhism in the Sung*, ed. P. N. Gregory and D. A. Getz Jr. (Honolulu: University of Hawai'i Press, 1999), pp. 37, 48–50.

20. "The Great Learning," in *The Four Books*, trans. J. Legge (repr., Taipei: Culture, 1979), pp. 4–7. Emphasis from original translation.

21. E. L. Davis, *Society and the Supernatural in Song China* (Honolulu: University of Hawai'i Press, 2001), pp. 3–8.

22. Wontack Hong, *Korea and Japan in East Asian History: A Tripolar Approach to East Asian History* (Seoul: Kudara International, 2006), p. 275, margin.

23. See M. Rossabi, *Khubilai Khan: His Life and Times* (Berkeley: University of California Press, 1988).

24. Hok-Lam Chan, "The 'Song' Dynasty Legacy: Symbolism and Legitimation from Han Liner to Zhu Yuanzhang of the Ming Dynasty," *Harvard Journal of Asiatic Studies* 68, no. 1 (2008): 117. On the choice of the name "Ming," see p. 123.

25. J. Larner, *Marco Polo and the Discovery of the World* (New Haven, CT: Yale University Press, 1999), pp. 153–160.

26. P. D. Curtin, *Cross-cultural Trade in World History* (Cambridge University Press, 1984), p. 121.

27. A. I. Johnston, *Cultural Realism: Strategic Culture and Grand Strategy in Chinese History* (Princeton University Press, 1995), pp. 27, 184.

28. P. C. Perdue, *China Marches West: The Qing Conquest of Central Asia* (Cambridge, MA: Harvard University Press, 2005), pp. 57–60.

29. See L. Levathes, *When China Ruled the Seas: The Treasure Fleet of the Dragon Throne, 1405–1433* (New York: Oxford University Press, 1994).

30. C. Chang, *The Development of Neo-Confucian Thought*, 2 vols. (New York: Bookman Associates, 1962), pp. 2.35, 2.44, 2.52–55, 2.64–65. (Wang Yangming is here referred to by an alternate name, and older spelling, "Wang Shou-jen.")

31. G. Ledyard, "Yin and Yang in the China-Manchuria-Korea Triangle," in Rossabi, *China among Equals*, p. 343.

32. P. H. Lee, ed., *Sourcebook of Korean Civilization, vol. 1: From Early Times to the Sixteenth Century* (New York: Columbia University Press, 1993), p. 284.

33. R. E. Buswell Jr., trans., *The Korean Approach to Zen: The Collected Works of Chinul* (Honolulu: University of Hawai'i Press, 1983), p. 38.

34. M. J. Seth, *A Concise History of Korea: From the Neolithic Period through the Nineteenth Century* (Lanham, MD: Rowman and Littlefield, 2006), pp. 104–106.

35. Ibid., p. 177.

36. M. Deuchler, *The Confucian Transformation of Korea: A Study of Society and Ideology* (Cambridge, MA: Harvard University Press, 1992), p. 134.

37. Yŏng-ho Ch'oe, "Private Academies and the State in Late Chosŏn Korea," in *Culture and the State in Late Chosŏn Korea*, ed. J. K. Haboush and M. Deuchler (Cambridge, MA: Harvard University Asia Center, 1999), p. 28, table 1.

38. J. K. Haboush, "The Confucianization of Korean Society," in *The East Asian Region: Confucian Heritage and Its Modern Adaptation*, ed. G. Rozman (Princeton University Press, 1991), pp. 84–86.

39. On samurai, see W. W. Farris, *Heavenly Warriors: The Evolution of Japan's Military, 500–1300* (Cambridge, MA: Harvard University Press, 1992); K. F. Friday, *Hired Swords:*

The Rise of Private Warrior Power in Early Japan (Stanford University Press, 1992); and Takeuchi Rizō, "The Rise of the Warriors," in Shively and McCullough, *Heian Japan.*

40. H. P. Varley, *Warriors of Japan as Portrayed in the War Tales* (Honolulu: University of Hawai'i Press, 1994), p. 5.

41. W. H. McCullough, "The Capital and Its Society," in Shively and McCullough, *Heian Japan*, p. 125.

42. Kitagawa Hiroshi and B. T. Tsuchida, trans., *The Tale of the Heike* (University of Tokyo Press, 1975), p. 18.

43. See J. P. Mass, "The Emergence of the Kamakura *Bakufu*," in *Medieval Japan: Essays in Institutional History*, ed. J. W. Hall and J. P. Mass (Stanford University Press, 1974).

44. H. Ooms, *Imperial Politics and Symbolics in Ancient Japan: The Tenmu Dynasty, 650–800* (Honolulu: University of Hawai'i Press, 2009), pp. xvi, 269n5.

45. See Souyri, *World Turned Upside Down*, chap. 6.

46. Ibid., p. 79.

47. Hayashiya Tatsusaburō, "Kyoto in the Muromachi Age," in *Japan in the Muromachi Age*, ed. J. W. Hall and Toyoda Takeshi (Berkeley: University of California Press, 1977), p. 22.

48. M. E. Berry, *The Culture of Civil War in Kyoto* (Berkeley: University of California Press, 1994), p. 29.

49. D. Keene, *Yoshimasa and the Silver Pavilion: The Creation of the Soul of Japan* (New York: Columbia University Press, 2003), esp. pp. 145–146.

50. Father Alessandro Valignano, quoted in C. R. Boxer, *The Christian Century in Japan, 1549–1650* (Berkeley: University of California Press, 1967), p. 75.

Chapter 6. Early Modern East Asia (Sixteenth–Eighteenth Centuries)

1. A. Woodside, *Lost Modernities: China, Vietnam, Korea, and the Hazards of World History* (Cambridge, MA: Harvard University Press, 2006), pp. 3–4.

2. See P. Duus, *Feudalism in Japan*, 2nd ed. (New York: Alfred A. Knopf, 1969).

3. T. Brook, *The Confusions of Pleasure: Commerce and Culture in Ming China* (Berkeley: University of California Press, 1998), pp. 211–212.

4. W. T. Rowe, *China's Last Empire: The Great Qing* (Cambridge, MA: Harvard University Press, 2009), pp. 123-124.

5. C. Clunas, *Empire of Great Brightness: Visual and Material Cultures of Ming China, 1368–1644* (Honolulu: University of Hawai'i Press, 2007), p. 67. For the abacus, see p. 119.

6. R. Huang, *1587, a Year of No Significance: The Ming Dynasty in Decline* (New Haven, CT: Yale University Press, 1981), p. 163.

7. C. Clunas, *Superfluous Things: Material Culture and Social Status in Early Modern China* (Honolulu: University of Hawai'i Press, [1991] 2004), pp. 58–59. For sea slugs, see B. W. Andaya, "Oceans Unbounded: Transversing Asia across 'Area Studies,'" *Journal of Asian Studies* 65, no. 4 (2006): 675–676.

8. L. E. Eastman, *Family, Field, and Ancestors: Constancy and Change in China's Social and Economic History, 1550–1949* (New York: Oxford University Press, 1988), p. 124.

9. For firearms, see M. J. Chaiklin, *Cultural Commerce and Dutch Commercial Culture: The Influence of European Material Culture on Japan, 1700–1850* (Leiden, Netherlands: CNWS, 2003), p. 149. For Saint Francis Xavier, see C. R. Boxer, *The Christian Century in Japan, 1549–1650* (Berkeley: University of California Press, 1967), pp. 36–37.

10. P. D. Curtin, *Cross-cultural Trade in World History* (Cambridge University Press, 1984), p. 150.

11. A. G. Frank, *ReOrient: Global Economy in the Asian Age* (Berkeley: University of California Press, 1998), pp. xxiii, 5, 142–143.

12. L. Blussé, *Visible Cities: Canton, Nagasaki, and Batavia and the Coming of the Americans* (Cambridge, MA: Harvard University Press, 2008), pp. 23–24.

13. See J. E. Wills Jr., "The Seventeenth-century Transformation: Taiwan under the Dutch and the Cheng Regime," in *Taiwan: A New History*, ed. M. A. Rubinstein (Armonk, NY: M. E. Sharpe, 1999).

14. Chun-shu Chang and S. Hsueh-lun Chang, *Crisis and Transformation in Seventeenth-century China: Society, Culture, and Modernity in Li Yü's World* (Ann Arbor: The University of Michigan Press, [1992] 1998), p. 289.

15. J. D. Spence, *The Memory Palace of Matteo Ricci* (Harmondsworth, UK: Penguin Books, 1983), pp. 96, 149, 152.

16. Boxer, *Christian Century*, pp. 134–135.

17. See W. W. Appleton, *A Cycle of Cathay: The Chinese Vogue in England during the Seventeenth and Eighteenth Centuries* (New York: Octagon Books, [1951] 1979); D. E. Mungello, *The Great Encounter of China and the West, 1500–1800* (Lanham, MD: Rowman and Littlefield, 1999), chaps. 4–5; and A. Reichwein, *China and Europe: Intellectual and Artistic Contacts in the Eighteenth Century*, trans. J. C. Powell (New York: Alfred A. Knopf, 1925).

18. Chang and Chang, *Crisis and Transformation*. The quote is from p. 2.

19. Brook, *Confusions of Pleasure*, p. 220.

20. Chang and Chang, *Crisis and Transformation*, p. 273.

21. F. Wakeman Jr., *The Great Enterprise: The Manchu Reconstruction of Imperial Order in Seventeenth-century China* (Berkeley: University of California Press, 1985), vol. I, p. 42, n43.

22. See P. K. Crossley, *The Manchus* (Oxford: Blackwell, 1997).

23. P. Berger, *Empire of Emptiness: Buddhist Art and Political Authority in Qing China* (Honolulu: University of Hawai'i Press, 2003), p. 97.

24. P. C. Perdue, *China Marches West: The Qing Conquest of Central Asia* (Cambridge, MA: Harvard University Press, 2005), p. 285.

25. E. J. M. Rhoads, *Manchus and Han: Ethnic Relations and Political Power in Late Qing and Early Republican China, 1861–1928* (Seattle: University of Washington Press, 2000), pp. 89–90. For differences between Manchu and Chinese, see pp. 52–63.

26. L. Hostetler, *Qing Colonial Enterprise: Ethnography and Cartography in Early Modern China* (University of Chicago Press, 2001), chap. 2.

27. J. D. Spence, *To Change China: Western Advisers in China 1620–1960* (Boston: Little, Brown, 1969), chap. 1.

28. R. B. Marks, *The Origins of the Modern World: A Global and Ecological Narrative from the Fifteenth to the Twenty-first Century*, 2nd ed. (Lanham, MD: Rowman and Littlefield, 2007), p. 106; P. Bairoch, "International Industrialization Levels from 1750 to 1980," *Journal of European Economic History* 11, no. 2 (1982): 296, table 10.

29. See B. Cumings, *Korea's Place in the Sun: A Modern History* (New York: W. W. Norton, 1997), p. 48.

30. K. M. Swope, *A Dragon's Head and A Serpent's Tail: Ming China and the First Great East Asian War, 1592–1598* (Norman, OK: University of Oklahoma Press, 2009), pp. 3–4.

31. The expression is credited to W. E. Griffis's book *Corea, the Hermit Nation* (New York: Scribner, 1882).

32. J. K. Haboush, "Constructing the Center: The Ritual Controversy and the Search for a New Identity in Seventeenth-century Korea," in *Culture and the State in Late Chosŏn Korea*, ed. J. Kim Haboush and M. Deuchler (Cambridge, MA: Harvard University Asia Center, 1999), p. 70.

33. D. Baker, "A Different Thread: Orthodoxy, Heterodoxy, and Catholicism in a Confucian World," in Haboush and Deuchler, *Culture and the State*. For saints, see the introduction to ibid., p. 13.

34. Luis Frois, quoted in G. Elison, "The Cross and the Sword: Patterns of Momoyama History," in *Warlords, Artists, and Commoners: Japan in the Sixteenth Century*, ed. G. Elison and B. L. Smith (Honolulu: University of Hawai'i Press, 1981), p. 66.

35. A good study of this remarkable man's career is M. E. Berry, *Hideyoshi* (Cambridge, MA: Harvard University Press, 1982).

36. Blussé, *Visible Cities*, pp. 24, 48.

37. Chaiklin, *Cultural Commerce*, pp. 102, 149–172.

38. M. B. Jansen, *China in the Tokugawa World* (Cambridge, MA: Harvard University Press, 1992), p. 4.

39. See Tetsuo Najita, *Visions of Virtue in Tokugawa Japan: The Kaitokudō Merchant Academy of Osaka* (University of Chicago Press, 1987).

40. J. L. McClain and J. M. Merriman, "Edo and Paris: Cities and Power," in *Edo and Paris: Urban Life and the State in the Early Modern Era*, ed. J. L. McClain, J. M. Merriman, and U. Kaoru (Ithaca, NY: Cornell University Press, 1994), pp. 12–13.

41. See D. H. Shively, "*Bakufu* versus *Kabuki*," in *Studies in the Institutional History of Early Modern Japan*, ed. J. W. Hall and M. Jansen (Princeton University Press, [1955] 1968).

42. D. Keene, *World within Walls: Japanese Literature of the Pre-Modern Era, 1600–1867* (New York: Grove Press, 1976), p. 266.

43. M. E. Berry, *Japan in Print: Information and Nation in the Early Modern Period* (Berkeley: University of California Press, 2006), p. 31.

44. T. C. Smith, *Native Sources of Japanese Industrialization, 1750–1920* (Berkeley: University of California Press, 1988), p. 25.

45. T. Makoto, "Festivals and Fights: The Law and the People of Edo," in McClain et al., *Edo and Paris*, p. 404.

Chapter 7. The Nineteenth-century Encounter of Civilizations

1. D. R. Headrick, *The Tentacles of Progress: Technology Transfer in the Age of Imperialism, 1850–1940* (New York: Oxford University Press, 1988), pp. 49, 90.

2. H. James, *The End of Globalization: Lessons from the Great Depression* (Cambridge, MA: Harvard University Press, 2001), p. 12.

3. C. Clunas, *Superfluous Things: Material Culture and Social Status in Early Modern China* (Honolulu: University of Hawai'i Press, [1991] 2004), p. 66; F. Dikötter, *Exotic Commodities: Modern Objects and Everyday Life in China* (New York: Columbia University Press, 2006), p. 34.

4. K. Pomeranz, *The Great Divergence: China, Europe, and the Making of the Modern World Economy* (Princeton University Press, 2000), pp. 61–62.

5. R. B. Marks, *The Origins of the Modern World: A Global and Ecological Narrative from the Fifteenth to the Twenty-first Century*, 2nd ed. (Lanham, MD: Rowman and Littlefield, 2007), pp. 108–112.

6. Quoted in S. W. Mintz, *Sweetness and Power: The Place of Sugar in Modern History* (New York: Viking, 1985), p. 116.

7. E. J. Hobsbawm, *The Age of Empire, 1875–1914* (New York: Vintage Books, 1989), p. 59.

8. Pomeranz, *Great Divergence*, pp. 17, 121–122, 138–142.

9. R. Fortune, *A Residence among the Chinese: Inland, on the Coast, and at Sea* (Taipei: Ch'eng Wen, [1857] 1971), pp. 98–99.

10. P. C. Perdue, *China Marches West: The Qing Conquest of Central Asia* (Cambridge, MA: Harvard University Press, 2005), pp. 552–555.

11. A. P. Dudden, *The American Pacific: From the Old China Trade to the Present* (New York: Oxford University Press, 1992), pp. 5–6.

12. See P. W. Fay, *The Opium War, 1840–1842: Barbarians in the Celestial Empire in the Early Part of the Nineteenth Century and the War by Which They Forced Her Gates Ajar* (New York: W. W. Norton, 1975).

13. F. Welsh, *A Borrowed Place: The History of Hong Kong* (New York: Kodansha International, 1993), pp. 310, 318–319.

14. M. S. Erbaugh, "The Secret History of the Hakkas: The Chinese Revolution as a Hakka Enterprise," in *China Off Center: Mapping the Margins of the Middle Kingdom*, ed. S. D. Blum and L. M. Jensen (Honolulu: University of Hawai'i Press, 2002), pp. 186–188. On Hakka origins, see Sow-Theng Leong, *Migration and Ethnicity in Chinese History: Hakkas, Pengmin, and Their Neighbors*, ed. T. Wright (Stanford University Press, 1997).

15. See J. D. Spence, *God's Chinese Son: The Taiping Heavenly Kingdom of Hong Xiuquan* (New York: W. W. Norton, 1996).

16. S. Y. Teng, *The Taiping Rebellion and the Western Powers: A Comprehensive Survey* (Taipei: Rainbow-Bridge, 1972), pp. 212–213.

17. I. C. Y. Hsü, *The Ili Crisis: A Study of Sino-Russian Diplomacy, 1871–1881* (Oxford University Press, 1965), pp. 12–15, 18, 22–44.

18. Quoted in P. K. Cheng, M. Lestz, and J. D. Spence, eds., *The Search for Modern China: A Documentary Collection* (New York: W. W. Norton, 1999), pp. 100–103.

19. A classic study is M. C. Wright, *The Last Stand of Chinese Conservatism: The T'ung-Chih Restoration, 1862–1874* (Stanford University Press, 1957).

20. See P. A. Cohen, *Discovering History in China: American Historical Writing on the Recent Chinese Past* (New York: Columbia University Press, 1984), p. 39.

21. Wang Tao, quoted in W. T. de Bary, Wing-tsit Chan, and C. Tan, *Sources of Chinese Tradition*, vol. 2 (New York: Columbia University Press, 1960), pp. 55–59.

22. J. D. Spence, *The Gate of Heavenly Peace: The Chinese and Their Revolution, 1895–1980* (New York: Penguin Books, 1981), p. 43.

23. L. E. Eastman, *Family, Fields, and Ancestors: Constancy and Change in China's Social and Economic History, 1550–1949* (New York: Oxford University Press, 1988), p. 184.

24. R. Murphey, *The Outsiders: The Western Experience in India and China* (Ann Arbor: University of Michigan Press, 1977), pp. 122, 192; Welsh, *A Borrowed Place*, p. 235.

25. Hsü, *The Ili Crisis*, p. 14.

26. N. R. Clifford, *Spoilt Children of Empire: Westerners in Shanghai and the Chinese Revolution of the 1920s* (Hanover, NH: Middlebury College Press, 1991), p. 68.

27. F. Wakeman Jr., *Policing Shanghai, 1927–1937* (Berkeley: University of California Press, 1995), pp. 34–35.

28. See D. Wolff, *To the Harbin Station: The Liberal Alternative in Russian Manchuria, 1898–1914* (Stanford University Press, 1999).

29. J. Davids, ed., *American Diplomatic and Public Papers: The United States and China, Series III – The Sino-Japanese War to the Russo-Japanese War, 1894–1905* (Wilmington, DE: Scholarly Resources, 1981), vol. V (Boxer Uprising), document 15, p. 40. On the Boxers, see P. A. Cohen, *History in Three Keys: The Boxers as Event, Experience, and Myth* (New York: Columbia University Press, 1997), and J. W. Esherick, *The Origins of the Boxer Uprising* (Berkeley: University of California Press, 1987).

30. M. Deuchler, *Confucian Gentlemen and Barbarian Envoys: The Opening of Korea, 1875–1885* (Seattle: University of Washington Press, 1977), p. 27.

31. Key-Hiuk Kim, *The Last Phase of the East Asian World Order: Korea, Japan, and the Chinese Empire, 1860–1882* (Berkeley: University of California Press, 1980), p. 40.

32. See P. Duus, *The Abacus and the Sword: The Japanese Penetration of Korea, 1895–1910* (Berkeley: University of California Press, 1995), pp. 101, 108–118.

33. See M. E. Robinson, *Cultural Nationalism in Colonial Korea, 1920–1925* (Seattle: University of Washington Press, 1988), chapter 1.

34. See M. B. Jansen, *Sakamoto Ryōma and the Meiji Restoration* (New York: Columbia University Press, [1961] 1994), pp. 41–43.

35. T. C. Smith, *Native Sources of Japanese Industrialization, 1750–1920* (Berkeley: University of California Press, 1988), p. 11, and chap. 7.

36. M. B. Jansen, *The Making of Modern Japan* (Cambridge, MA: Harvard University Press, 2000), pp. 337–339.

37. T. Morris-Suzuki, "A Descent into the Past: The Frontier in the Construction of Japanese Identity," in *Multicultural Japan: Palaeolithic to Postmodern*, ed. D. Denoon, M. Hudson, G. McCormack, and T. Morris-Suzuki (Cambridge University Press, 1996).

38. See D. Keene, "The Sino-Japanese War of 1894–95 and Its Cultural Effects in Japan," in *Tradition and Modernization in Japanese Culture*, ed. D. H. Shively (Princeton University Press, 1971), pp. 169–172.

39. H. M. Hopper, *Fukuzawa Yūkichi: From Samurai to Capitalist* (New York: Pearson Longman, 2005), pp. 121–122.

40. I. P. Hall, *Mori Arinori* (Cambridge, MA: Harvard University Press, 1973), pp. 3–6, 189–195.

41. C. Gluck, *Japan's Modern Myths: Ideology in the Late Meiji Period* (Princeton University Press, 1985), pp. 23, 27.

42. M. B. Jansen, "The Ruling Class," in *Japan in Transition: From Tokugawa to Meiji*, ed. M. B. Jansen and G. Rozman (Princeton University Press, 1986), pp. 89–90.

43. D. H. Shively, "The Japanization of the Middle Meiji," in *Tradition and Modernization in Japanese Culture*, ed. D. H. Shively (Princeton University Press, 1971), p. 85.

44. "Imperial Rescript on Education," in *The Japan Reader 1: Imperial Japan, 1800–1945*, ed. J. Livingston, J. Moore, and F. Oldfather (New York: Pantheon Books, 1973), p. 154.

45. T. C. Smith, *Political Change and Industrial Development in Japan: Government Enterprise, 1868–1880* (Stanford University Press, 1955), pp. 26, 30–31, 34–53, 102–103; E. H. Norman, *Japan's Emergence as a Modern State: Political and Economic Problems of the Meiji Period* (New York: Institute of Pacific Relations, 1940), pp. 117–133; E. S. Crawcour, "Economic Change in the Nineteenth Century," in *The Economic Emergence of Modern Japan*, ed. K. Yamamura (Cambridge University Press, 1997), pp. 41–44, 48–49.

46. R. J. Samuels, *"Rich Nation Strong Army": National Security and the Technological Transformation of Japan* (Ithaca, NY: Cornell University Press, 1994), pp. 84–88.

47. Smith, *Native Sources of Japanese Industrialization*, pp. 42–46.

48. W. D. Wray, "Shipping: From Sail to Steam," in Jansen and Rozman, *Japan in Transition*, pp. 249, 254–259.

49. Akira Iriye, *China and Japan in the Global Setting* (Cambridge, MA: Harvard University Press, 1992), p. 20; W. G. Beasley, *Japanese Imperialism, 1894–1945* (Oxford: Clarendon Press, [1987] 1991), p. 25.

50. S. B. Hanley, "The Material Culture: Stability in Transition," in Jansen and Rozman, *Japan in Transition*, pp. 463, 467–469; E. Seidensticker, *Low City, High City: Tokyo from Edo to the Earthquake* (New York: Alfred A. Knopf, 1983), pp. 42–44, 47–48.

Chapter 8. The Age of Westernization (1900–1929)

1. M. Elvin, "The Collapse of Scriptural Confucianism," in *Another History: Essays on China from a European Perspective* (Canberra, Australia: Wild Peony, [1990] 1996), p. 355.

2. Tze-ki Hon, "Zhang Zhidong's Proposal for Reform: A New Reading of the *Quanxue pian*," in *Rethinking the 1898 Reform Period: Political and Cultural Change in Late Qing China*, ed. R. E. Karl and P. Zarrow (Cambridge, MA: Harvard University Asia Center, 2002), pp. 78–79, 86, 91–98.

3. L. Ou-fan Lee, *Shanghai Modern: The Flowering of a New Urban Culture in China, 1930–1945* (Cambridge, MA: Harvard University Press, 1999), p. 44.

4. E. P. Young, "China in the Early Twentieth Century: Tasks for a New World," in *Histori-cal Perspectives on Contemporary East Asia*, ed. M. Goldman and A. Gordon (Cambridge, MA: Harvard University Press, 2000), p. 190.

5. E. J. M. Rhoads, "The Assassination of Governor Enming and Its Effect on Manchu-Han Relations in Late Qing China," in *China's Republican Revolution*, ed. Etō Shinkichi and H. Z. Schiffrin (University of Tokyo Press, 1994), pp. 3, 6, 12, 22–23n29.

6. L. Greenfeld, *Nationalism: Five Roads to Modernity* (Cambridge, MA: Harvard University Press, 1992), pp. 6–7, 47. A particularly influential study is B. Anderson, *Imagined Communities: Reflections on the Origin and Spread of Nationalism* (London: Verso, [1983] 1991).

7. T. Morris-Suzuki, "A Descent into the Past: The Frontier in the Construction of Japanese Identity," in *Multicultural Japan: Palaeolithic to Postmodern*, ed. D. Denoon et al. (Cambridge University Press, 1996), p. 88.

8. L. H. Liu, *Translingual Practice: Literature, National Culture, and Translated Modernity – China, 1900–1937* (Stanford University Press, 1995), appendix B, p. 292.

9. M.-C. Bergère, *Sun Yat-sen*, trans. J. Lloyd (Stanford University Press, [1994] 1998), pp. 6, 31.

10. E. A. McCord, *The Power of the Gun: The Emergence of Modern Chinese Warlordism* (Berkeley: University of California Press, 1993), p. 46.

11. J. W. Esherick, "Founding a Republic, Electing a President: How Sun Yat-sen Became *Guofu*," in Etō and Schiffrin, *China's Republican Revolution*, p. 146.

12. F. Dikötter, *Exotic Commodities: Modern Objects and Everyday Life in China* (New York: Columbia University Press, 2006), pp. 1, 4, 10, 30–31, 56, 90, 104, 111, 178, 252.

13. Lu Hsun (Lu Xun), "A Madman's Diary," in *Selected Stories of Lu Hsun*, trans. Yang Hsien-yi and G. Yang (Peking: Foreign Language Press, [1918] 1972), p. 10.

14. V. Goossaert, "1898: The Beginning of the End for Chinese Religion?" *Journal of Asian Studies* 65, no. 2 (2006): 308.

15. P. Bairoch, "International Industrialization Levels from 1750 to 1980," *Journal of European Economic History* 11, no. 2 (1982): 296, table 10.

16. S. Cochran, "Transnational Origins of Advertising in Early Twentieth-century China," in *Inventing Nanjing Road: Commercial Culture in Shanghai, 1900–1945*, ed. S. Cochrane (Ithaca, NY: Cornell University East Asia Program, 1999).

17. H. Harrison, *China: Inventing the Nation* (London: Arnold, 2001), pp. 158–160.

18. M. B. Jansen, *The Making of Modern Japan* (Cambridge, MA: Harvard University Press, 2000), p. 531.

19. Tse-tsung Chow, *The May Fourth Movement: Intellectual Revolution in Modern China* (Stanford University Press, 1960), pp. 35–40, 42n.

20. J. P. Harrison, *The Long March to Power: A History of the Chinese Communist Party, 1921–72* (New York: Praeger, 1972), p. 23.

21. W. Wei, "'Political Power Grows Out of the Barrel of a Gun': Mao and the Red Army," in *A Military History of China*, ed. D. A. Graff and R. Higham (Boulder, CO: Westview Press, 2002), pp. 231, 234–236.

22. E. Snow, *Red Star Over China* (New York: Grove Press, [1938] 1968), p. 155.

23. See M. L. Cohen, "Cultural and Political Inventions in Modern China: The Case of the Chinese 'Peasant,'" in *China in Transformation*, ed. Tu Wei-ming (Cambridge, MA: Harvard University Press, 1994); B. I. Schwartz, *Chinese Communism and the Rise of Mao* (Cambridge, MA: Harvard University Press, [1951] 1979), pp. 197–199.

24. J. Fitzgerald, *Awakening China: Politics, Culture, and Class in the Nationalist Revolution* (Stanford University Press, 1996), p. 163.

25. J. H. Fincher, *Chinese Democracy: The Self-government Movement in Local, Provincial, and National Politics, 1905–1914* (New York: St. Martin's Press, 1981), p. 223.

26. F. Wakeman Jr., *Policing Shanghai, 1927–1937* (Berkeley: University of California Press, 1995), pp. 124, 259; P. M. Coble Jr., *The Shanghai Capitalists and the Nationalist Government, 1927–1937* (Cambridge, MA: Harvard University Press, [1980] 1986), p. 39.

27. G. McCormack, *Chang Tso-lin in Northeast China, 1911–1928: China, Japan, and the Manchurian Idea* (Stanford University Press, 1977), pp. 120–122.

28. Jui-te Chang, "The National Army from Whampoa to 1949," in Graff and Higham, *Military History of China*, p. 195.

29. M. Atkins, *Informal Empire in Crisis: British Diplomacy and the Chinese Customs Succession, 1927–1929* (Ithaca, NY: Cornell University East Asia Program, 1995), pp. 15, 22.

30. R. Mitter, *A Bitter Revolution: China's Struggle with the Modern World* (Oxford University Press, 2004), pp. 149, 155.

31. Ki-baik Lee, *A New History of Korea*, trans. E. W. Wagner (Cambridge, MA: Harvard University Press, 1984), p. 317.

32. P. Duus, *The Abacus and the Sword: The Japanese Penetration of Korea, 1895–1910* (Berkeley: University of California Press, 1995), pp. 319, 328.

33. M. B. Jansen, "Japanese Imperialism: Late Meiji Perspectives," in *The Japanese Colonial Empire, 1895–1945*, ed. R. H. Myers and M. R. Peattie (Princeton University Press, 1984), p. 78; C. J. Eckert, "Korea's Transition to Modernity: A Will to Greatness," in Goldman and Gordon, *Historical Perspectives*, pp. 136–137.

34. M. E. Robinson, *Cultural Nationalism in Colonial Korea, 1920–1925* (Seattle: University of Washington Press, 1988), pp. 43–46.

35. M. E. Robinson, *Korea's Twentieth-century Odyssey: A Short History* (Honolulu: University of Hawai'i Press, 2007), pp. 90–91.

36. M. R. Peattie, "Japanese Attitudes toward Colonialism, 1895–1945," in Myers and Peattie, *Japanese Colonial Empire*, pp. 96–98.

37. E. I-te Chen, "The Attempt to Integrate the Empire: Legal Perspectives," in Myers and Peattie, *Japanese Colonial Empire*, p. 242n3.

38. W. G. Beasley, *Japanese Imperialism, 1894–1945* (Oxford: Clarendon Press, [1987] 1991), pp. 152–153.

39. B. Cumings, *Korea's Place in the Sun: A Modern History* (New York: W. W. Norton, 1997), p. 175.

40. E. Seidensticker, *Low City, High City: Tokyo from Edo to the Earthquake* (New York: Alfred A. Knopf, 1983), pp. 95, 101, 110–113, 166.

41. S. B. Hanley, "The Material Culture: Stability in Transition," in *Japan in Transition: From Tokugawa to Meiji*, ed. M. B. Jansen and G. Rozman (Princeton University Press, 1986), pp. 460, 463.

42. D. H. Shively, "The Japanization of the Middle Meiji," in *Tradition and Modernization in Japanese Culture*, ed. D. H. Shively (Princeton University Press, 1971), p. 77.

43. E. S. Crawcour, "Industrialization and Technological Change, 1885–1920," in *The Economic Emergence of Modern Japan*, ed. K. Yamamura (Cambridge University Press, 1997), p. 52.

44. M. Hane, *Peasants, Rebels, and Outcastes: The Underside of Modern Japan* (New York: Pantheon Books, 1982), p. 34.

45. T. Nakamura, "Depression, Recovery, and War, 1920–1945," in Yamamura, *Economic Emergence of Modern Japan*, p. 118.

46. C. Gluck, *Japan's Modern Myths: Ideology in the Late Meiji Period* (Princeton University Press, 1985), p. 12.

47. E. T. Atkins, "Can Japanese Sing the Blues? 'Japanese Jazz' and the Problem of Authenticity," in *Japan Pop! Inside the World of Japanese Popular Culture*, ed. T. J. Craig (Armonk, NY: M. E. Sharpe, 2000), pp. 35, 37.

48. R. H. Mitchell, *Censorship in Imperial Japan* (Princeton University Press, 1983), pp. 196–199.

49. See R. T. Takaki, *Strangers from a Different Shore: A History of Asian Americans*, rev. ed. (Boston: Little, Brown, 1998), pp. 208–210.

50. W. F. Morton, *Tanaka Giichi and Japan's China Policy* (New York: St. Martin's Press, 1980), pp. 130–134, 149–150, 158–160.

Chapter 9. The Dark Valley (1930–1945)

1. See M. A. Barnhart, *Japan Prepares for Total War: The Search for Economic Security, 1919–1941* (Ithaca, NY: Cornell University Press, 1987).

2. Saburō Ienaga, *The Pacific War, 1931–1945* (New York: Pantheon Books, [1968] 1978), pp. 19–32.

3. J. W. Dower, *War without Mercy: Race and Power in the Pacific War* (New York: Pantheon Books, 1986), pp. 221–222, 238.

4. B.-A. Shillony, *Revolt in Japan: The Young Officers and the February 26, 1936 Incident* (Princeton University Press, 1973), pp. 32–36.

5. S. Pao-San Ho, "Colonialism and Development: Korea, Taiwan, and Kwantung," in *The Japanese Colonial Empire, 1895–1945*, ed. R. H. Myers and M. R. Peattie (Princeton University Press, 1984), p. 352.

6. G. McCormack, *Chang Tso-lin in Northeast China, 1911–1928: China, Japan, and the Manchurian Idea* (Stanford University Press, 1977), p. 8, table 1.

7. W. G. Beasley, *Japanese Imperialism, 1894–1945* (Oxford: Clarendon Press, [1987] 1991), pp. 212–217.

8. M. R. Peattie, *Ishiwara Kanji and Japan's Confrontation with the West* (Princeton University Press, 1975), pp. 32, 56–58, 96–107, 120–123, 319–320.

9. L. Young, *Japan's Total Empire: Manchuria and the Culture of Wartime Imperialism* (Berkeley: University of California Press, 1998), chap. 3.

10. On Xinjing, see D. D. Buck, "Railway City and National Capital: Two Faces of the Modern in Changchun," in *Remaking the Chinese City: Modernity and National Identity, 1900–1950*, ed. J. W. Esherick (Honolulu: University of Hawai'i Press, 2000).

11. Young, *Japan's Total Empire*, pp. 246–247.

12. Prasenjit Duara, *Sovereignty and Authenticity: Manchukuo and the East Asian Modern*. (Lanham, MD: Rowman and Littlefield, 2003), pp. 73, 77.

13. See C. D. Musgrove, "Building a Dream: Constructing a National Capital in Nanjing, 1927–1937," in Esherick, *Remaking the Chinese City*.

14. W. C. Kirby, "The Nationalist Regime and the Chinese Party-State, 1928–1958," in *Historical Perspectives on Contemporary East Asia*, ed. M. Goldman and A. Gordon (Cambridge, MA: Harvard University Press, 2000), p. 227.

15. See J. Taylor, *The Generalissimo's Son: Chiang Ching-kuo and the Revolutions in China and Taiwan* (Cambridge, MA: Harvard University Press, 2000).

16. W. C. Kirby, *Germany and Republican China* (Stanford University Press, 1984), pp. 3–5, 262.

17. L. E. Eastman, "Nationalist China during the Nanking Decade, 1927–1937," in *The Nationalist Era in China, 1927–1949*, ed. L. E. Eastman, J. Ch'en, S. Pepper, and L. P. Van Slyke (Cambridge University Press, 1991), p. 9.

18. L. E. Eastman, *Seeds of Destruction: Nationalist China in War and Revolution, 1937–1949* (Stanford University Press, 1984), pp. 10, 41.

19. J. P. Harrison, *The Long March to Power: A History of the Chinese Communist Party, 1921–72* (New York: Praeger, 1972), pp. 19–20.

20. A. Dirlik, *The Origins of Chinese Communism* (New York: Oxford University Press, 1989), pp. 253–273.

21. J. T. Dreyer, *China's Political System: Modernization and Tradition*, 4th ed. (New York: Pearson Longman, 2004), p. 66.

22. E. Snow, *Red Star over China* (New York: Grove Press, [1938] 1968), pp. 165–166.

23. M. Meisner, *Mao's China and After: A History of the People's Republic* (New York: Free Press, [1977] 1986), pp. 43–47.

24. H. E. Salisbury, *The Long March: The Untold Story* (New York: McGraw-Hill, 1985), pp. 10–11.

25. J. D. Spence, *Mao Zedong* (New York: Viking, 1999), pp. 82–86.

26. See I. Chang, *The Rape of Nanking: The Forgotten Holocaust of World War II* (New York: Penguin Books, 1997).

27. T. H. White and A. Jacoby, *Thunder out of China* (New York: William Sloan Associates, [1946] 1961), pp. 70–72.

28. S. Pepper, *Civil War in China: The Political Struggle, 1945–1949* (Berkeley: University of California Press, 1978), p. 95.

29. J. H. Boyle, *China and Japan at War, 1937–1945: The Politics of Collaboration* (Stanford University Press, 1972), pp. 351–352, 361–362.

30. Barnhart, *Japan Prepares for Total War*, pp. 91, 95–96, 101–104.

31. T. R. H. Havens, *Valley of Darkness: The Japanese People and World War Two* (Lanham, MD: University Press of America, 1986), pp. 16, 18, 50.

32. Mikiso Hane, *Modern Japan: A Historical Survey* (Boulder, CO: Westview Press, 1986), p. 297.

33. M. Hastings, *Retribution: The Battle for Japan, 1944–45* (New York: Alfred A. Knopf, 2008), p. 26.

34. M. S. Gallicchio, *The Cold War Begins in Asia: American East Asian Policy and the Fall of the Japanese Empire* (New York: Columbia University Press, 1988), pp. 73–74.

35. See J. W. Dower, *Embracing Defeat: Japan in the Wake of World War II* (New York: W. H. Norton, 1999), pp. 33–39.

36. D. W. White, *The American Century: The Rise and Decline of the United States as a World Power* (New Haven, CT: Yale University Press, 1996), p. 56.

Chapter 10. Japan since 1945

1. See, for example, O. Statler, *Japanese Inn* (Honolulu: University of Hawai'i Press, [1961] 1982), pp. 3, 321–333, and "About the Author."

2. W. Manchester, *American Caesar: Douglas MacArthur, 1880–1964* (Boston: Little, Brown, 1978), pp. 470–471.

3. J. W. Dower, *Embracing Defeat: Japan in the Wake of World War II* (New York: W. H. Norton, 1999), pp. 96–97.

4. M. B. Jansen, *The Making of Modern Japan* (Cambridge, MA: Harvard University Press, 2000), p. 676.

5. E. O. Reischauer, *My Life between Japan and America* (New York: Harper and Row, 1986), p. 91; E. Terry, *How Asia Got Rich: Japan, China, and the Asian Miracle* (Armonk, NY: M. E. Sharpe, 2002), p. 353.

6. T. J. Pempel, "Prerequisites for Democracy: Political and Social Institutions," in *Democracy in Japan*, ed. T. Ishida and E. S. Krauss (University of Pittsburgh Press, 1989), p. 21.

7. A. Gordon, "Society and Politics from Transwar through Postwar Japan," in *Historical Perspectives on Contemporary East Asia*, ed. M. Goldman and A. Gordon (Cambridge, MA: Harvard University Press, 2000), pp. 279–280.

8. See M. Harries and S. Harries, *Sheathing the Sword: The Demilitarization of Japan* (New York: Macmillan, 1987), p. 307.

9. Yutaka Kosai, "The Postwar Japanese Economy, 1945–1973," in *The Economic Emergence of Modern Japan*, ed. K. Yamamura (Cambridge University Press, 1997), p. 159.

10. Ibid., p. 177.

11. C. Johnson, *MITI and the Japanese Miracle: The Growth of Industrial Policy, 1925–1975* (Stanford University Press, 1982), p. 10.

12. Ibid., pp. 45–46, 102–106, 108–109, 130–132.

13. Ibid., pp. 41, 44, 176.

14. R. Katz, *Japanese Phoenix: The Long Road to Economic Revival* (Armonk, NY: M. E. Sharpe, 2003), p. 166.

15. E. S. Krauss, "Politics and the Policymaking Process," in Ishida and Krauss, *Democracy in Japan*, p. 50.

16. E. F. Vogel, *Japan as Number One: Lessons for America* (Cambridge, MA: Harvard University Press, 1979).

17. C. V. Prestowitz Jr., *Trading Places: How We Allowed Japan to Take the Lead* (New York: Basic Books, 1988).

18. G. McCormack, "*Kokusaika*: Impediments in Japan's Deep Structure," in *Multicultural Japan: Palaeolithic to Postmodern*, ed. D. Denoon et al. (Cambridge University Press, 1996), pp. 274–276.

19. See T. P. Rohlen, "'Spiritual Education' in a Japanese Bank," in *Japanese Culture and Behavior: Selected Readings*, ed. T. Sugiyama Lebra and W. P. Lebra (Honolulu: University of Hawai'i Press, [1973] 1986).

20. E. Seidensticker, *Tokyo Rising: The City since the Great Earthquake* (Cambridge, MA: Harvard University Press, 1991), p. 337.

21. W. I. Cohen, *The Asian American Century* (Cambridge, MA: Harvard University Press, 2002), p. 32.

22. B. R. Barber, *Jihad vs. McWorld: How Globalism and Tribalism Are Reshaping the World* (New York: Ballantine Books, 1996), p. 18; E. Ohnuki-Tierney, "McDonald's in Japan: Changing Manners and Etiquette," in *Golden Arches East: McDonald's in East Asia*, ed. J. L. Watson (Stanford University Press, 1997), p. 181.

23. Cohen, *Asian American Century*, p. 44.

24. M. Y. Brannen, "'Bwana Mickey': Constructing Cultural Consumption at Tokyo Disneyland," in *Re-made in Japan: Everyday Life and Consumer Taste in a Changing Society*, ed. Joseph J. Tobin (New Haven, CT: Yale University Press, 1992), pp. 216–217.

25. J. J. Tobin, "Introduction: Domesticating the West," in Tobin, *Re-made in Japan*, p. 4.

26. Dower, *Embracing Defeat*, p. 182.

27. Terry, *How Asia Got Rich*, pp. 230–231.

28. S. Issenberg, *The Sushi Economy: Globalization and the Making of a Modern Delicacy* (New York: Gotham Books, 2007).

29. D. McGray, "Japan's Gross National Cool (Globalization at Work)," *Foreign Policy* (May 2002).

30. A. Allison, "Sailor Moon: Japanese Superheroes for Global Girls," in *Japan Pop! Inside the World of Japanese Popular Culture*, ed. T. J. Craig (Armonk, NY: M. E. Sharpe, 2000), p. 264.

31. M. Hillenbrand, "Murakami Haruki in Greater China: Creative Responses and the Quest for Cosmopolitanism," *Journal of Asian Studies* 68, no. 3 (2009): 718–719, 739.

32. L. Ching, "Imaginings in the Empires of the Sun: Japanese Mass Culture in Asia," in *Contemporary Japan and Popular Culture*, ed. J. W. Treat (Honolulu: University of Hawai'i Press, 1996), pp. 171, 179–180.

33. S. Frühstück and W. Manzenreiter, "Neverland Lost: Judo Cultures in Austria, Japan, and Elsewhere Struggling for Cultural Hegemony," in *Globalizing Japan: Ethnography of the Japanese Presence in Asia, Europe, and America*, ed. H. Befu and S. Guichard-Anguis (London: RoutledgeCurzon, 2001), pp. 86–87.

34. Masashi Ogawa, "Japanese Popular Music in Hong Kong: Analysis of Global/Local Cultural Relations," in Befu and Guichard-Anguis, *Globalizing Japan*, pp. 123–125, 129.

35. C. R. Yano, *Tears of Longing: Nostalgia and the Nation in Japanese Popular Song* (Cambridge, MA: Harvard University Asia Center, 2002), pp. 3–4, 9 (Teng is here spelled in

Japanese, rather than Chinese, as "Ten"), 28–44; A. F. Jones, *Like a Knife: Ideology and Genre in Contemporary Chinese Popular Music* (Ithaca, NY: Cornell University East Asia Program, 1992), p. 16.

Chapter 11. Korea since 1945

1. M. S. Gallicchio, *The Cold War Begins in Asia: American East Asian Policy and the Fall of the Japanese Empire* (New York: Columbia University Press, 1988), p. 5.
2. B. Cumings, *Korea's Place in the Sun: A Modern History* (New York: W. W. Norton, 1997), p. 192.
3. Gallicchio, *Cold War Begins in Asia*, p. 75; D. Oberdorfer, *The Two Koreas: A Contemporary History*, rev. and updated ed. (New York: Basic Books, [1997] 2001), p. 6.
4. D. Halberstam, *The Coldest Winter: America and the Korean War* (New York: Hyperion, 2007), pp. 366–367.
5. P. West, "Confronting the West: China as David and Goliath in the Korean War," *Journal of American-East Asian Relations* 2, no. 1 (1993): 12, 16.
6. C. J. Eckert, "Korea's Transition to Modernity: A Will to Greatness," in *Historical Perspectives on Contemporary East Asia*, ed. M. Goldman and A. Gordon (Cambridge, MA: Harvard University Press, 2000), p. 146.
7. S. S. Kim, "Korea's *Segyehwa* Drive: Promise versus Performance," in *Korea's Globalization*, ed. S. S. Kim (Cambridge University Press, 2000), p. 277.
8. I. Göthel, "*Juche* and the Issue of National Identity in the DPRK of the 1960s," in *North Korea: Ideology, Politics, Economy*, ed. Han S. Park (Englewood Cliffs, NJ: Prentice Hall, 1996), pp. 25–27.
9. Dae-Sook Suh, *Kim Il Sung: The North Korean Leader* (New York: Columbia University Press, 1988), pp. 219–220.
10. C. J. Eckert, Ki-baik Lee, Young Ick Lew, M. Robinson, and E. W. Wagner, *Korea Old and New: A History* (Seoul: Ilchokak, 1990), pp. 349–350.
11. J. Lie, *Han Unbound: The Political Economy of South Korea* (Stanford University Press, 1998), pp. 11–13.
12. Eckert et al., *Korea Old and New*, p. 396.
13. Young Whan Kihl, *Transforming Korean Politics: Democracy, Reform, and Culture* (Armonk, NY: M. E. Sharpe, 2005), p. 71.
14. Atul Kohli, "Where Do High-Growth Political Economies Come From? The Japanese Lineage of Korea's 'Developmental State,'" in *The Developmental State*, ed. M. Woo-Cumings (Ithaca, NY: Cornell University Press, 1999).
15. E. F. Vogel, *The Four Little Dragons: The Spread of Industrialization in East Asia* (Cambridge, MA: Harvard University Press, 1991), pp. 48–54.
16. Lie, *Han Unbound*, p. 71.
17. Cumings, *Korea's Place in the Sun*, p. 317.
18. M. L. Clifford, *Troubled Tiger: Businessmen, Bureaucrats, and Generals in South Korea* (Armonk, NY: M. E. Sharpe, 1994), pp. 115–118.
19. K. J. Fields, *Enterprise and the State in Korea and Taiwan* (Ithaca, NY: Cornell University Press, 1995), pp. 7, 96.
20. M. Woo-Cumings, Introduction to *Developmental State*, p. 18.
21. Clifford, *Troubled Tiger*, p. 231.
22. A. H. Amsden, *Asia's Next Giant: South Korea and Late Industrialization* (New York: Oxford University Press, 1989), pp. 145–147.
23. F. Gibney, *The Pacific Century: America and Asia in a Changing World* (New York: Charles Scribner's Sons, 1992), p. 396.
24. J. H. Grayson, "A Quarter-Millennium of Christianity in Korea," in *Christianity in Korea*, ed. R. E. Buswell Jr. and T. S. Lee (Honolulu: University of Hawai'i Press, 2006), pp. 15–17, 21–22.

25. Kihl, *Transforming Korean Politics*, p. 96.

26. Ibid., pp. 108, 110.

27. Jong-myung Kim, "The *Tripiṭaka Koreana*: Its Computerization and Significance for the Cultural Sciences in a Modern Globalizing World," in *Korea and Globalization: Politics, Economics, and Culture*, ed. J. Lewis and A. Sesay (London: RoutledgeCurzon, 2002), pp. 154–155.

28. Eun Mee Kim, "Globalization of the South Korean *Chaebol*," in Kim, *Korea's Globalization*, pp. 109–110.

29. Byong-suh Kim, "Modernization and the Explosive Growth and Decline of Korean Protestant Religiosity," in Buswell and Lee, *Christianity in Korea*, p. 325.

30. Jeong Duk Yi, "Globalization and Recent Changes to Daily Life in the Republic of Korea," in Lewis and Sesay, *Korea and Globalization*, pp. 11, 16–19, 24, 32.

31. Sangmee Bak, "McDonald's in Seoul: Food Choices, Identity, and Nationalism," in *Golden Arches East: McDonald's in East Asia*, ed. J. L. Watson (Stanford University Press, 1997), pp. 138–140, 151, 157, 159.

32. Clifford, *Troubled Tiger*, p. 8.

33. S. S. Kim, "Korea and Globalization (*Segyehwa*): A Framework for Analysis" and "Korea's *Segyehwa* Drive," in Kim, *Korea's Globalization*, pp. 2, 247–252.

Chapter 12. China since 1945

1. Lai Tse-han, R. H. Myers, and Wei Wou, *A Tragic Beginning: The Taiwan Uprising of February 28, 1947* (Stanford University Press, 1991), pp. 80–89, 102ff, 159–160.

2. J. D. Spence, *Mao Zedong* (New York: Viking, 1999), pp. 103–104.

3. D. Halberstam, *The Coldest Winter: America and the Korean War* (New York: Hyperion, 2007), p. 235.

4. A. J. Nathan and R. S. Ross, *The Great Wall and the Empty Fortress: China's Search for Security* (New York: W. W. Norton, 1997), p. 39.

5. E. Friedman, P. G. Pickowicz, and M. Selden, *Chinese Village, Socialist State* (New Haven, CT: Yale University Press, 1991), pp. 14, 81–82.

6. F. C. Teiwes and W. Sun, *China's Road to Disaster: Mao, Central Politicians, and Provincial Leaders in the Unfolding of the Great Leap Forward, 1955–1959* (Armonk, NY: M. E. Sharpe, 1999), pp. 70–71.

7. One journalistic exposé of this tragedy is J. Becker, *Hungry Ghosts: Mao's Secret Famine* (New York: Free Press, 1996).

8. There are now numerous firsthand accounts of the Cultural Revolution. One particularly popular memoir of growing up in Mao's China is Jung Chang, *Wild Swans: Three Daughters of China* (New York: Anchor Books, 1992).

9. A. F. Thurston, *Enemies of the People: The Ordeal of the Intellectuals in China's Great Cultural Revolution* (Cambridge, MA: Harvard University Press, 1988), pp. 151–153.

10. D. S. G. Goodman, *Deng Xiaoping and the Chinese Revolution: A Political Biography* (London: Routledge, 1994), pp. 77–78.

11. P. Tyler, *A Great Wall: Six Presidents and China: An Investigative History* (New York: Century Foundation, 1999), pp. 47–49, 59–60.

12. See M. MacMillan, *Nixon and Mao: The Week That Changed the World* (New York: Random House, 2007).

13. R. Baum, *Burying Mao: Chinese Politics in the Age of Deng Xiaoping* (Princeton University Press, 1994), p. 41.

14. J. Kynge, *China Shakes the World: A Titan's Rise and Troubled Future – and the Challenge for America* (Boston: Houghton Mifflin, 2006), p. 99.

15. J. Gittings, *The Changing Face of China: From Mao to Market* (Oxford University Press, 2005), pp. 104–105.

16. D. Stark, cited in D. L. Wank, *Commodifying Communism: Business, Trust, and Politics in a Chinese City* (Cambridge University Press, 1999), p. 32n22.

17. Central Intelligence Agency, "World Fact Book," country comparison: GDP (purchasing power parity), https://www.cia.gov/library/publications/the-world-factbook/.

18. D. M. Lampton, *The Three Faces of Chinese Power: Might, Money, and Minds* (Berkeley: University of California Press, 2008), p. 84.

19. Ibid., pp. 89, 97–98, 114–115.

20. S. Greenhalgh, *Just One Child: Science and Policy in Deng's China* (Berkeley: University of California Press, 2008), pp. 76, 308, 332–334; J. T. Dreyer, *China's Political System: Modernization and Tradition*, 4th ed. (New York: Pearson Longman, 2004), p. 136, figure 6.2.

21. W. Wo-lap Lam, *Chinese Politics in the Hu Jintao Era: New leaders, New Challenges* (Armonk, NY: M. E. Sharpe, 2006), p. 89.

22. N. D. Kristof and S. Wudunn, *China Wakes: The Struggle for the Soul of a Rising Power* (New York: Vintage Books, 1995), p. 222.

23. Han Minzhu (pseudonym), ed., *Cries for Democracy: Writings and Speeches from the 1989 Chinese Democracy Movement* (Princeton University Press, 1990), p. 6.

24. Zhang Liang (pseudonym), compiler, *The Tiananmen Papers*, ed. A. J. Nathan and P. Link (New York: PublicAffairs, 2001), pp. 199, 204.

25. Baum, *Burying Mao*, p. 276.

26. Zhao Ziyang's memoirs have been published as *Prisoner of the State: The Secret Journal of Zhao Ziyang*, trans. and ed. Bao Pu, R. Chiang, and A. Ignatius (New York: Simon and Shuster, 2009).

27. L. Feigon, *China Rising: The Meaning of Tiananmen* (Chicago: Ivan R. Dee, 1990), p. 110.

28. Han, *Cries for Democracy*, p. 166.

29. G. R. Barmé, *In the Red: On Contemporary Chinese Culture* (New York: Columbia University Press, 1999), pp. 329–333, 338.

30. O. Schell, *Discos and Democracy: China in the Throes of Reform* (New York: Anchor Books, 1989), p. 251.

31. "The 2008 Pew Global Attitudes Survey in China: The Chinese Celebrate Their Roaring Economy, as They Struggle with Its Costs," http://www.pewglobal.org, under "Reports."

32. Wank, *Commodifying Communism*, p. 228.

33. A. F. Jones, "The Politics of Popular Music in Post-Tiananmen China," in *China Off Center: Mapping the Margins of the Middle Kingdom*, ed. S. D. Blum and L. M. Jensen (Honolulu: University of Hawai'i Press, 2002), p. 302.

34. W. G. Huff, *The Economic Growth of Singapore: Trade and Development in the Twentieth Century* (Cambridge University Press, 1994), pp. 4, 366–369.

35. "2009 Index of Economic Freedom," http://www.heritage.org/index.

36. F. Welsh, *A Borrowed Place: The History of Hong Kong* (New York: Kodansha International, 1993), p. 1.

37. K. Rafferty, *City on the Rocks: Hong Kong's Uncertain Future* (London: Penguin Books, 1991), p. 139.

38. For the governor's own perspective, see C. Patten, *East and West: China, Power, and the Future of Asia* (New York: Times Books, 1998).

39. Chih-huei Huang, "The *Yamatodamashi* of the Takasago Volunteers of Taiwan: A Reading of the Postcolonial Situation," in *Globalizing Japan: Ethnography of the Japanese Presence in Asia, Europe, and America*, ed. H. Befu and S. Guichard-Anguis (London: RoutledgeCurzon, 2001), pp. 223–224.

40. Wen-hsiung Hsu, "From Aboriginal Island to Chinese Frontier: The Development of Taiwan before 1683," in *China's Island Frontier: Studies in the Historical Geography of Taiwan*, ed. R. G. Knapp (Taipei: SMC, [1980] 1995), pp. 5–11.

41. On "The Origins of Taiwanese Identity," see A. M. Wachman, *Taiwan: National Identity and Democratization* (Armonk, NY: M. E. Sharpe, 1994), pp. 91–124. On martial law and

the "white terror," see P. Chen-main Wang, "A Bastion Created, a Regime Reformed, an Economy Reengineered, 1949–1970," in *Taiwan: A New History*, ed. M. A. Rubinstein (Armonk, NY: M. E. Sharpe, 1999), pp. 323, 330.

42. Wang, "A Bastion Created," p. 324.

43. J. S. Prybyla, "Economic Developments in the Republic of China," in *Democracy and Development in East Asia: Taiwan, South Korea, and the Philippines*, ed. T. W. Robinson (Washington, DC: AEI Press, 1991), p. 54.

44. W. McCord, *The Dawn of the Pacific Century: Implication for Three Worlds of Development* (New Brunswick, NJ: Transaction, [1991] 1993), p. 44.

45. Hung-mao Tien, *The Great Transition: Political and Social Change in the Republic of China* (Stanford, CA: Hoover Institution Press, 1989), pp. 1–2, 64.

46. J. Taylor, *The Generalissimo's Son: Chiang Ching-kuo and the Revolutions in China and Taiwan* (Cambridge, MA: Harvard University Press, 2000), pp. 405–407.

47. For a relatively favorable new biography, see J. Taylor, *The Generalissimo: Chiang Kai-shek and the Struggle for Modern China* (Cambridge, MA: Harvard University Press, 2009).

48. Lampton, *Three Faces of Chinese Power*, p. 97.

49. Kynge, *China Shakes the World*, pp. xii–xiii.

50. Lam, *Chinese Politics in the Hu Jintao Era*, pp. 150, 153.

51. J. Unger, "China's Conservative Middle Class," *Far Eastern Economic Review* 169, no. 3 (2006).

52. J. Fallows, *Postcards from Tomorrow Square: Reports from China* (New York: Vintage Books, 2009), pp. 188–192, 205, 240.

53. R. E. Stross, *Bulls in the China Shop and Other Sino-American Business Encounters* (New York: Pantheon Books, 1990), p. 244.

54. Barmé, *In the Red*, p. 349.

55. For the *Goddess of Democracy* statue, see Han, *Cries for Democracy*, pp. 343–344. For headbands, see O. Schell, *Mandate of Heaven: A New Generation of Entrepreneurs, Dissidents, Bohemians, and Technocrats Lays Claim to China's Future* (New York: Simon and Schuster, 1994), p. 82.

Afterword

1. B. R. Barber, *Jihad vs. McWorld: How Globalism and Tribalism Are Reshaping the World* (New York: Ballantine Books, 1996), pp. 11, 170–179.

2. D. S. G. Goodman, "The Politics of Regionalism: Economic Development, Conflict and Negotiation," in *China Deconstructs: Politics, Trade, and Regionalism*, ed. D. S. G. Goodman and G. Segal (London: Routledge, 1994), pp. 1, 6–7.

3. See E. Friedman, "Reconstructing China's National Identity," in *National Identity and Democratic Prospects in Socialist China* (Armonk, NY: M. E. Sharpe, 1995), pp. 102–108.

4. R. Schriver and M. Stokes, "Taiwan's Liberation of China," *Current History* 107, no. 710 (2008): 280.

5. C. Johnson, Foreword to E. Terry, *How Asia Got Rich: Japan, China, and the Asian Miracle* (Armonk, NY: M. E. Sharpe, 2002), p. ix.

6. World Bank, *The East Asian Miracle: Economic Growth and Public Policy* (New York: Oxford University Press, 1993), pp. 1–2. In its definition of *East Asia*, the World Bank included the somewhat less prosperous (and culturally almost entirely unrelated) Southeast Asian newly industrializing economies and excluded China, which was then still in the early stages of its market-based reform.

7. See W. McCord, *The Dawn of the Pacific Century: Implication for Three Worlds of Development* (New Brunswick, NJ: Transaction, 1993), pp. 28–29, 105–107, 183–184. McCord himself favors structural and policy explanations over those rooted in cultural differences.

Bibliography

Abramson, Marc S. *Ethnic Identity in Tang China*. Philadelphia: University of Pennsylvania Press, 2008.

Adshead, Samuel Adrian M. *T'ang China: The Rise of the East in World History*. New York: Palgrave Macmillan, 2004.

Allan, Sarah. "Erlitou and the Formation of Chinese Civilization: Toward a New Paradigm." *Journal of Asian Studies* 66, no. 2 (2007).

Allan, Sarah, ed. *The Formation of Chinese Civilization: An Archaeological Perspective*. New Haven, CT: Yale University Press, 2005.

Allison, Anne. "Sailor Moon: Japanese Superheroes for Global Girls." In *Japan Pop! Inside the World of Japanese Popular Culture*. Edited by Timothy J. Craig. Armonk, NY: M. E. Sharpe, 2000.

Ames, Roger T. *The Art of Rulership: A Study of Ancient Chinese Political Thought*. Albany: State University of New York Press, 1994.

Amino Yoshihiko. "Emperor, Rice, and Commoners." In *Multicultural Japan: Palaeolithic to Postmodern*. Edited by Donald Denoon et al. Cambridge: Cambridge University Press, 1996.

Amsden, Alice H. *Asia's Next Giant: South Korea and Late Industrialization*. New York: Oxford University Press, 1989.

Andaya, Barbara Watson. "Oceans Unbounded: Transversing Asia across 'Area Studies.'" *Journal of Asian Studies* 65, no. 4 (2006).

Anderson, Benedict. *Imagined Communities: Reflections on the Origin and Spread of Nationalism*. London: Verso, 1991.

Appleton, William W. *A Cycle of Cathay: The Chinese Vogue in England during the Seventeenth and Eighteenth Centuries*. New York: Octagon Books, 1979.

Asakawa, Kan'ichi. *The Early Institutional Life of Japan: A Study in the Reform of 645* A.D. New York: Paragon, 1963.

Aston, W. G., trans. *Nihongi: Chronicles of Japan from the Earliest Times to* A.D. *697*. Rutland, VT: Charles E. Tuttle, [1896] 1972.

Atkins, E. Taylor. "Can Japanese Sing the Blues? 'Japanese Jazz' and the Problem of Authenticity." In *Japan Pop! Inside the World of Japanese Popular Culture*. Edited by Timothy J. Craig. Armonk, NY: M. E. Sharpe, 2000.

Atkins, Martyn. *Informal Empire in Crisis: British Diplomacy and the Chinese Customs Succession, 1927–1929*. Ithaca, NY: Cornell University East Asia Program, 1995.

Backus, Charles. *The Nan-Chao Kingdom and T'ang China's Southwestern Frontier*. Cambridge: Cambridge University Press, 1981.

Bairoch, Paul. "International Industrialization Levels from 1750 to 1980." *Journal of European Economic History* 11, no. 2 (1982).

Bak, Sangmee. "McDonald's in Seoul: Food Choices, Identity, and Nationalism." In *Golden Arches East: McDonald's in East Asia*. Edited by James L. Watson. Stanford, CA: Stanford University Press, 1997.

Baker, Don. "A Different Thread: Orthodoxy, Heterodoxy, and Catholicism in a Confucian World." In *Culture and the State in Late Chosŏn Korea*. Edited by JaHyun Kim Haboush and Martina Deuchler. Cambridge, MA: Harvard University Asia Center, 1999.

Balazs, Etienne. *Chinese Civilization and Bureaucracy*. Translated by H. M. Wright. New Haven, CT: Yale University Press, 1964.

Bamba, Nobuya. *Japanese Diplomacy in a Dilemma: New Light on Japan's China Policy, 1924–1929*. Vancouver: University of British Columbia Press, 1972.

Barber, Benjamin R. *Jihad vs. McWorld: How Globalism and Tribalism Are Reshaping the World*. New York: Ballantine Books, 1996.

Barfield, Thomas J. *The Perilous Frontier: Nomadic Empires and China, 221 BC to AD 1757*. Cambridge, MA: Blackwell, 1989.

Barmé, Geremie R. *In the Red: On Contemporary Chinese Culture*. New York: Columbia University Press, 1999.

Barnes, Gina L. *China, Korea, and Japan: The Rise of Civilization in East Asia*. London: Thames and Hudson, 1993.

———. *State Formation in Japan: Emergence of a 4th-century Ruling Elite*. London: Routledge, 2007.

Barnhart, Michael A. *Japan Prepares for Total War: The Search for Economic Security, 1919–1941*. Ithaca, NY: Cornell University Press, 1987.

Barrett, Timothy H. *The Woman Who Discovered Printing*. New Haven, CT: Yale University Press, 2008.

Batten, Bruce L. "Cross-border Traffic on the Kyushu Coast, 794–1086." In *Heian Japan, Centers and Peripheries*. Edited by Mikael Adolphson, Edward Kamens, and Stacie Matsumoto. Honolulu: University of Hawai'i Press, 2007.

———. "Foreign Threat and Domestic Reform: The Emergence of the Ritsuryō State." *Monumenta Nipponica* 41, no. 2 (1986).

———. "Provincial Administration in Early Japan: From Ritsuryō kokka to Ōchō kokka." *Harvard Journal of Asiatic Studies* 53, no. 1 (1993).

Baum, Richard. *Burying Mao: Chinese Politics in the Age of Deng Xiaoping*. Princeton, NJ: Princeton University Press, 1994.

Beasley, W. G. *Japanese Imperialism, 1894–1945*. Oxford: Clarendon Press, 1991.

Becker, Jasper. *The Chinese: An Insider's Look at the Issues Which Affect and Shape China Today*. Oxford: Oxford University Press, 2000.

———. *Hungry Ghosts: Mao's Secret Famine*. New York: Free Press, 1996.

Beckwith, Christopher I. *The Tibetan Empire in Central Asia: A History of the Struggle for Great Power among Tibetans, Turks, Arabs, and Chinese during the Early Middle Ages*. Princeton, NJ: Princeton University Press, 1987.

Bellah, Robert. *Tokugawa Religion: The Cultural Roots of Modern Japan*. New York: Free Press, [1957] 1985.

Bellwood, Peter. *Prehistory of the Indo-Malaysian Archipelago*. Honolulu: University of Hawai'i Press, [1985] 1997.

Benn, Charles. *China's Golden Age: Everyday Life in the Tang Dynasty*. Oxford: Oxford University Press, 2002.

Bentley, Jerry H. *Old World Encounters: Cross-cultural Contacts and Exchanges in Pre-modern Times*. New York: Oxford University Press, 1993.

Berger, Patricia. *Empire of Emptiness: Buddhist Art and Political Authority in Qing China*. Honolulu: University of Hawai'i Press, 2003.

Bergère, Marie-Claire. *Sun Yat-sen*. Translated by Janet Lloyd. Stanford, CA: Stanford University Press, 1998.

Berry, Mary Elizabeth. *The Culture of Civil War in Kyoto*. Berkeley: University of California Press, 1994.

———. *Hideyoshi*. Cambridge, MA: Harvard University Press, 1982.

———. *Japan in Print: Information and Nation in the Early Modern Period*. Berkeley: University of California Press, 2006.

Best, Jonathan W. "Diplomatic and Cultural Contacts between Paekche and China." *Harvard Journal of Asiatic Studies* 42, no. 2 (1982).

———. *A History of the Early Korean Kingdom of Paekche: Together with an Annotated Translation of the Paekche Annals of the Samguk sagi*. Cambridge, MA: Harvard University Asia Center, 2006.

Bestor, Theodore C. *Neighborhood Tokyo*. Stanford, CA: Stanford University Press, 1989.

Bingham, Woodbridge. *The Founding of the T'ang Dynasty: The Fall of Sui and Rise of T'ang, a Preliminary Survey*. New York: Octagon Books, [1941] 1970.

Blussé, Leonard. *Visible Cities: Canton, Nagasaki, and Batavia and the Coming of the Americans*. Cambridge, MA: Harvard University Press, 2008.

Bokenkamp, Stephen R. *Ancestors and Anxiety: Daoism and the Birth of Rebirth in China*. Berkeley: University of California Press, 2007.

Bol, Peter K. *"This Culture of Ours": Intellectual Transitions in T'ang and Sung China*. Stanford, CA: Stanford University Press, 1992.

Borgen, Robert. *Sugawara no Michizane and the Early Heian Court*. Cambridge, MA: Harvard University Press, 1986.

Boxer, Chester Ralph. *The Christian Century in Japan, 1549–1650*. Berkeley: University of California Press, 1967.

Boyle, John Hunter. *China and Japan at War, 1937–1945: The Politics of Collaboration*. Stanford, CA: Stanford University Press, 1972.

Brannen, Mary Yoko. "'Bwana Mickey': Constructing Cultural Consumption at Tokyo Disneyland." In *Re-made in Japan: Everyday Life and Consumer Taste in a Changing Society*. Edited by Joseph J. Tobin. New Haven, CT: Yale University Press, 1992.

Brodrick, Alan Houghton. *Little China; the Annamese Lands*. London: Oxford University Press, 1942.

Brook, Timothy. *The Confusions of Pleasure: Commerce and Culture in Ming China*. Berkeley: University of California Press, 1998.

Buck, David D. "Railway City and National Capital: Two Faces of the Modern in Changchun." In *Remaking the Chinese City: Modernity and National Identity, 1900–1950*. Edited by Joseph W. Esherick. Honolulu: University of Hawai'i Press, 2000.

Buswell, Robert E., Jr., trans. *The Korean Approach to Zen: The Collected Works of Chinul*. Honolulu: University of Hawai'i Press, 1983.

Cahill, James. *Chinese Painting*. New York: Rizzoli, [1960] 1985.

Campany, Robert Ford. *Making Transcendents: Ascetics and Social Memory in Early Medieval China*. Honolulu: University of Hawai'i Press, 2009.

Carter, Thomas Francis. *The Invention of Printing in China and Its Spread Westward*. Revised by L. Carrington Goodrich. New York: Ronald Press, [1925] 1955.

Chaiklin, Martha J. *Cultural Commerce and Dutch Commercial Culture: The Influence of European Material Culture on Japan, 1700–1850*. Leiden, Netherlands: CNWS, 2003.

Chaffee, John W. *The Thorny Gates of Learning in Sung China: A Social History of the Examinations*. New edition. Binghamton: State University of New York Press, 1995.

Chan, Hok-Lam. "The 'Song' Dynasty Legacy: Symbolism and Legitimation from Han Liner to Zhu Yuanzhang of the Ming Dynasty." *Harvard Journal of Asiatic Studies* 68, no. 1 (2008).

Chang, Carson. *The Development of Neo-Confucian Thought*. 2 vols. New York: Bookman Associates, 1962.

Chang, Chun-shu. *The Rise of the Chinese Empire*. 2 vols. Ann Arbor: University of Michigan Press, 2007.

Chang, Chun-shu, and Shelley Hsueh-lun Chang. *Crisis and Transformation in Seventeenth-century China: Society, Culture, and Modernity in Li Yü's World*. Ann Arbor: University of Michigan Press, 1998.

———. *Redefining History: Ghosts, Spirits, and Human Society in P'u Sung-ling's World, 1640–1715*. Ann Arbor: University of Michigan Press, 1998.

Chang, Iris. *The Rape of Nanking: The Forgotten Holocaust of World War II*. New York: Penguin Books, 1997.

Chang, Jui-te. "The National Army from Whampoa to 1949." In *A Military History of China*. Edited by David A. Graff and Robin Higham. Boulder, CO: Westview Press, 2002.

Chang, Jung. *Wild Swans: Three Daughters of China*. New York: Anchor Books, 1992.

Chang, Kwang-chih. *The Archaeology of Ancient China*. 4th edition. New Haven, CT: Yale University Press, 1986.

———, ed. *Food in Chinese Culture: Anthropological and Historical Perspectives*. New Haven, CT: Yale University Press, 1977.

———. *Shang Civilization*. New Haven, CT: Yale University Press, 1980.

Ch'en, Ch'i-yün (Chen Qiyun). *Hsün Yüeh (A.D. 148–209): The Life and Reflections of an Early Medieval Confucian*. Cambridge: Cambridge University Press, 1975.

Chen, Edward I-te. "The Attempt to Integrate the Empire: Legal Perspectives." In *The Japanese Colonial Empire, 1895–1945*. Edited by Ramon H. Myers and Mark R. Peattie. Princeton, NJ: Princeton University Press, 1984.

Chen, Jo-shui. "Empress Wu and Proto-feminist Sentiments in T'ang China." In *Imperial Rulership and Cultural Change in Traditional China*. Edited by Frederick P. Brandauer and Chun-chieh Huang. Seattle: University of Washington Press, 1994.

———. *Liu Tsung-yüan and Intellectual Change in T'ang China, 773–819*. Cambridge: Cambridge University Press, 1992.

Ch'en, Kenneth K. S. *Buddhism in China: A Historical Survey*. Princeton, NJ: Princeton University Press, 1964.

Chen, Sanping. "A-gan Revisited – the Tuoba's Cultural and Political Heritage." *Journal of Asian History* 30, no. 1 (1996).

Cheng, Pei-kai, Michael Lestz, and Jonathan D. Spence, eds. *The Search for Modern China: A Documentary Collection*. New York: W. W. Norton, 1999.

Ching, Leo. "Imaginings in the Empires of the Sun: Japanese Mass Culture in Asia." In *Contemporary Japan and Popular Culture*. Edited by John Whittier Treat. Honolulu: University of Hawai'i Press, 1996.

Ch'oe, Yŏng-ho. "Private Academies and the State in Late Chosŏn Korea." In *Culture and the State in Late Chosŏn Korea*. Edited by JaHyun Kim Haboush and Martina Deuchler. Cambridge, MA: Harvard University Asia Center, 1999.

Choi, Jongtaik. "The Development of the Pottery Technologies of the Korean Peninsula and Their Relationship to Neighboring Regions." In *Early Korea 1: Reconsidering Early Korean History through Archaeology*. Edited by Mark E. Byington. Seoul: Korea Institute, Harvard University, 2008.

Chow, Tse-tsung. *The May Fourth Movement: Intellectual Revolution in Modern China*. Stanford, CA: Stanford University Press, 1960.

Ch'ü, T'ung-tsu. "Chinese Class Structure and Its Ideology." In *Chinese Thought and Institutions*. Edited by John K. Fairbank. Chicago, IL: University of Chicago Press, 1957.

———. *Local Government in China under the Ch'ing*. Stanford, CA: Stanford University Press, [1962] 1978.

Clifford, Mark L. *Troubled Tiger: Businessmen, Bureaucrats, and Generals in South Korea*. Armonk, NY: M. E. Sharpe, 1994.

Clifford, Nicholas R. *Spoilt Children of Empire: Westerners in Shanghai and the Chinese Revolution of the 1920s*. Hanover, NH: Middlebury College Press, 1991.

Clunas, Craig. *Empire of Great Brightness: Visual and Material Cultures of Ming China, 1368–1644*. Honolulu: University of Hawai'i Press, 2007.

_____. *Superfluous Things: Material Culture and Social Status in Early Modern China*. Honolulu: University of Hawai'i Press, [1991] 2004.

Coble, Parks M., Jr. *The Shanghai Capitalists and the Nationalist Government, 1927–1937*. Cambridge, MA: Harvard University Press, 1986.

Cochran, Sherman. "Transnational Origins of Advertising in Early Twentieth-century China." In *Inventing Nanjing Road: Commercial Culture in Shanghai, 1900–1945*. Edited by Sherman Cochran. Ithaca, NY: Cornell University East Asia Program, 1999.

Cohen, Myron L. "Cultural and Political Inventions in Modern China: The Case of the Chinese 'Peasant.'" In *China in Transformation*. Edited by Tu Wei-ming. Cambridge, MA: Harvard University Press, 1994.

Cohen, Paul A. *Discovering History in China: American Historical Writing on the Recent Chinese Past*. New York: Columbia University Press, 1984.

_____. *History in Three Keys: The Boxers as Event, Experience, and Myth*. New York: Columbia University Press, 1997.

Cohen, Warren I. *The Asian American Century*. Cambridge, MA: Harvard University Press, 2002.

_____. *East Asia at the Center: Four Thousand Years of Engagement with the World*. New York: Columbia University Press, 2001.

Collcutt, Martin. *Five Mountains: The Rinzai Zen Monastic Institution in Medieval Japan*. Cambridge, MA: Council on East Asian Studies, Harvard University, 1981.

_____. "Lanxi Daolong (1213–1278) at Kenchōji: Chinese Contributions to the Making of Medieval Japanese Rinzai Zen." In *Tools of Culture: Japan's Cultural, Intellectual, Medical, and Technological Contacts in East Asia, 1000–1500s*. Edited by Andrew Edmund Goble, Kenneth R. Robinson, and Haruko Wakabayashi. Ann Arbor, MI: Association for Asian Studies, 2009.

Conroy, Hilary. *The Japanese Seizure of Korea, 1868–1910: A Study of Realism and Idealism in International Relations*. Philadelphia: University of Pennsylvania Press, 1960.

Craig, Albert. "The Restoration Movement in Chōshū." In *Studies in the Institutional History of Early Modern Japan*. Edited by John W. Hall and Marius Jansen. Princeton, NJ: Princeton University Press, [1959] 1968.

Cranston, Edwin A. "Asuka and Nara Culture: Literacy, Literature, and Music." In *The Cambridge History of Japan*, vol. 1. *Ancient Japan*. Edited by Delmer M. Brown. Cambridge: Cambridge University Press, 1993.

Crawcour, E. Sydney. "Economic Change in the Nineteenth Century." In *The Economic Emergence of Modern Japan*. Edited by Kozo Yamamura. Cambridge: Cambridge University Press, 1997.

_____. "Industrialization and Technological Change, 1885–1920." In *The Economic Emergence of Modern Japan*. Edited by Kozo Yamamura. Cambridge: Cambridge University Press, 1997.

Creel, Herrlee G. *The Origins of Statecraft in China, vol. 1: The Western Chou Empire*. Chicago, IL: University of Chicago Press, 1970.

Croll, Elisabeth J. *Feminism and Socialism in China*. London: Routledge and Kegan Paul, 1980.

Crossley, Pamela Kyle. *The Manchus*. Oxford: Blackwell, 1997.

Crowley, James B. *Japan's Quest for Autonomy: National Security and Foreign Policy, 1930–1938*. Princeton, NJ: Princeton University Press, 1966.

Cumings, Bruce. *Korea's Place in the Sun: A Modern History*. New York: W. W. Norton, 1997.

Curtin, Philip D. *Cross-cultural Trade in World History*. Cambridge: Cambridge University Press, 1984.

Dardess, John W. *Conquerors and Confucians: Aspects of Political Change in Late Yüan China*. New York: Columbia University Press, 1973.

Davis, Edward L. *Society and the Supernatural in Song China.* Honolulu: University of Hawai'i Press, 2001.

de Bary, Wm. Theodore. *East Asian Civilizations: A Dialogue in Five Stages.* Cambridge, MA: Harvard University Press, [1988] 1994.

de Bary, Wm. Theodore, and Irene Bloom, eds. *Sources of Chinese Tradition,* vol. 1. *From Earliest Times to 1600.* 2nd edition. New York: Columbia University Press, 1999.

de Bary, Wm. Theodore, Wing-tsit Chan, and Chester Tan, eds. *Sources of Chinese Tradition.* Vol. 2. New York: Columbia University Press, 1960.

de Crespigny, Rafe. *Generals of the South: The Foundation and Early History of the Three Kingdoms State of Wu.* Faculty of Asian Studies Monographs 16. Canberra: Australian National University, 1990.

DeFrancis, John. *The Chinese Language: Fact and Fantasy.* Honolulu: University of Hawai'i Press, 1984.

Deng, Xiaonan. "Women in Turfan during the Sixth to Eighth Centuries: A Look at Their Activities outside the Home." *Journal of Asian Studies* 58, no. 1 (1999).

Deuchler, Martina. *Confucian Gentlemen and Barbarian Envoys: The Opening of Korea, 1875–1885.* Seattle: University of Washington Press, 1977.

———. *The Confucian Transformation of Korea: A Study of Society and Ideology.* Cambridge, MA: Harvard University Press, 1992.

Di Cosmo, Nicola. *Ancient China and Its Enemies: The Rise of Nomadic Power in East Asian History.* Cambridge: Cambridge University Press, 2002.

Dien, Albert E. "Civil Service Examinations: Evidence from the Northwest." In *Culture and Power in the Reconstitution of the Chinese Realm, 200–600.* Edited by Scott Pearce, Audrey Spiro, and Patricia Ebrey. Cambridge, MA: Harvard University Press, 2001.

———. *Six Dynasties Civilization.* New Haven, CT: Yale University Press, 2007.

———, ed. *State and Society in Early Medieval China.* Stanford, CA: Stanford University Press, 1990.

Dikötter, Frank. *Exotic Commodities: Modern Objects and Everyday Life in China.* New York: Columbia University Press, 2006.

Dirlik, Arif. *The Origins of Chinese Communism.* New York: Oxford University Press, 1989.

Dore, Ronald P. *Taking Japan Seriously: A Confucian Perspective on Leading Economic Issues.* Stanford, CA: Stanford University Press, 1987.

———. "Talent and the Social Order in Tokugawa Japan." In *Studies in the Institutional History of Early Modern Japan.* Edited by John W. Hall and Marius Jansen. Princeton, NJ: Princeton University Press, [1962] 1968.

Dower, John W. *Embracing Defeat: Japan in the Wake of World War II.* New York: W. H. Norton, 1999.

———. *War without Mercy: Race and Power in the Pacific War.* New York: Pantheon Books, 1986.

Dreyer, June Teufel. *China's Political System: Modernization and Tradition.* 4th edition. New York: Pearson Longman, 2004.

Drompp, Michael R. *Tang China and the Collapse of the Uighur Empire: A Documentary History.* Leiden, Netherlands: Brill, 2005.

Duara, Prasenjit. *Sovereignty and Authenticity: Manchukuo and the East Asian Modern.* Lanham, MD: Rowman and Littlefield, 2003.

Dudden, Arthur Power. *The American Pacific: From the Old China Trade to the Present.* New York: Oxford University Press, 1992.

Dumoulin, Heinrich. *Zen Buddhism: A History,* vol. 1. *India and China.* Translated by James W. Heisig and Paul Knitter. New York: Macmillan, 1988.

Dunne, George H. *Generation of Giants: The Story of the Jesuits in China in the Last Decades of the Ming Dynasty.* Notre Dame, IN: University of Notre Dame Press, 1962.

Dunnell, Ruth W. *The Great State of White and High: Buddhism and State Formation in Eleventh-century Xia.* Honolulu: University of Hawai'i Press, 1996.

Duus, Peter. *The Abacus and the Sword: The Japanese Penetration of Korea, 1895–1910.* Berkeley: University of California Press, 1995.

_____. *Feudalism in Japan.* 2nd edition. New York: Alfred A. Knopf, 1969.

Earhart, H. Byron. *Religions of Japan: Many Traditions within One Sacred Way.* San Francisco: Harper and Row, 1984.

Eastman, Lloyd E. *Family, Fields, and Ancestors: Constancy and Change in China's Social and Economic History, 1550–1949.* New York: Oxford University Press, 1988.

_____. "Nationalist China during the Nanking Decade, 1927–1937." In *The Nationalist Era in China, 1927–1949.* Edited by Lloyd E. Eastman, Jerome Ch'en, Suzanne Pepper, and Lyman P. Van Slyke. Cambridge: Cambridge University Press, 1991.

_____. *Seeds of Destruction: Nationalist China in War and Revolution, 1937–1949.* Stanford, CA: Stanford University Press, 1984.

Eberhard, Wolfram. *Conquerors and Rulers: Social Forces in Mediaeval China.* Leiden, Netherlands: E. J. Brill, 1952.

Ebrey, Patricia Buckley. *The Aristocratic Families of Early Imperial China: A Case Study of the Po-Ling Ts'ui Family.* Cambridge: Cambridge University Press, 1978.

_____. *The Inner Quarters: Marriage and the Lives of Chinese Women in the Sung Period.* Berkeley: University of California Press, 1993.

Ebrey, Patricia Buckley, and Peter N. Gregory, eds. *Religion and Society in T'ang and Sung China.* Honolulu: University of Hawai'i Press, 1993.

Ebrey, Patricia Buckley, Anne Walthall, and James B. Palais. *East Asia: A Cultural, Social, and Political History.* Boston: Houghton Mifflin, 2006.

Eckert, Carter J. "Korea's Transition to Modernity: A Will to Greatness." In *Historical Perspectives on Contemporary East Asia.* Edited by Merle Goldman and Andrew Gordon. Cambridge, MA: Harvard University Press, 2000.

Eckert, Carter J., Ki-baik Lee, Young Ick Lew, Michael Robinson, and Edward W. Wagner. *Korea Old and New: A History.* Seoul: Ilchokak, 1990.

Eisenberg, Andrew. *Kingship in Early Medieval China.* Leiden, Netherlands: Brill, 2008.

Elison, George. "The Cross and the Sword: Patterns of Momoyama History." In *Warlords, Artists, and Commoners: Japan in the Sixteenth Century.* Edited by George Elison and Bardwell L. Smith. Honolulu: University of Hawai'i Press, 1981.

Elman, Benjamin A. "Political, Social, and Cultural Reproduction via Civil Service Examinations in Late Imperial China." *Journal of Asian Studies* 50, no. 1 (1991).

Elvin, Mark. "The Collapse of Scriptural Confucianism." In *Another History: Essays on China from a European Perspective.* Canberra, Australia: Wild Peony, 1996.

_____. *The Pattern of the Chinese Past: A Social and Economic Interpretation.* Stanford, CA: Stanford University Press, 1973.

_____. *The Retreat of the Elephants: An Environmental History of China.* New Haven, CT: Yale University Press, 2004.

Erbaugh, Mary S. "The Secret History of the Hakkas: The Chinese Revolution as a Hakka Enterprise." In *China Off Center: Mapping the Margins of the Middle Kingdom.* Edited by Susan D. Blum and Lionel M. Jensen. Honolulu: University of Hawai'i Press, 2002.

Esherick, Joseph W. "Founding a Republic, Electing a President: How Sun Yat-sen Became Guofu." In *China's Republican Revolution.* Edited by Etō Shinkichi and Harold Z. Schiffrin. Tokyo: University of Tokyo Press, 1994.

_____. *The Origins of the Boxer Uprising.* Berkeley: University of California Press, 1987.

Fairbank, John King. *Trade and Diplomacy on the China Coast: The Opening of the Treaty Ports, 1842–1854.* Stanford, CA: Stanford University Press, [1953] 1969.

Fairbank, John K., Edwin O. Reischauer, and Albert M. Craig. *East Asia: Tradition and Transformation.* Revised edition. Boston: Houghton Mifflin, 1989.

Fallows, James. *Looking at the Sun: The Rise of the New East Asian Economic and Political System.* New York: Pantheon Books, 1994.

_____. *Postcards from Tomorrow Square: Reports from China.* New York: Vintage Books, 2009.

Farmer, Edward L. *Early Ming Government: The Evolution of Dual Capitals*. Cambridge, MA: East Asian Research Center, Harvard University, 1976.

Farris, William Wayne. "Ancient Japan's Korean Connection." *Korean Studies* 20 (1996).

———. *Heavenly Warriors: The Evolution of Japan's Military, 500–1300*. Cambridge, MA: Harvard University Press, 1992.

———. *Population, Disease, and Land in Early Japan, 645–900*. Cambridge, MA: Harvard University Press, 1985.

———. *Sacred Texts and Buried Treasures: Issues in the Historical Archaeology of Ancient Japan*. Honolulu: University of Hawai'i Press, 1998.

Faure, Bernard. *The Will to Orthodoxy: A Critical Genealogy of Northern Chan Buddhism*. Translated by Phyllis Brooks. Stanford, CA: Stanford University Press, 1997.

Fay, Peter Ward. *The Opium War, 1840–1842: Barbarians in the Celestial Empire in the Early Part of the Nineteenth Century and the War by Which They Forced Her Gates Ajar*. New York: W. W. Norton, 1975.

Febvre, Lucien, and Henri-Jean Martin. *The Coming of the Book: The Impact of Printing, 1450–1800*. Translated by David Gerard. London: NLB, [1958] 1976.

Feigon, Lee. *China Rising: The Meaning of Tiananmen*. Chicago, IL: Ivan R. Dee, 1990.

Feuerwerker, Albert. *Rebellion in Nineteenth-century China*. Ann Arbor: Center for Chinese Studies, University of Michigan, 1975.

Fields, Karl J. *Enterprise and the State in Korea and Taiwan*. Ithaca, NY: Cornell University Press, 1995.

Fincher, John H. *Chinese Democracy: The Self-government Movement in Local, Provincial and National Politics, 1905–1914*. New York: St. Martin's Press, 1981.

Fitzgerald, John. *Awakening China: Politics, Culture, and Class in the Nationalist Revolution*. Stanford, CA: Stanford University Press, 1996.

———. "The Nationless State: The Search for a Nation in Modern Chinese Nationalism." In *Chinese Nationalism*. Edited by Jonathan Unger. Armonk, NY: M. E. Sharpe, 1996.

Foltz, Richard C. *Religions of the Silk Road: Overland Trade and Cultural Exchange from Antiquity to the Fifteenth Century*. New York: St. Martin's Press, 1999.

Fortune, Robert. *A Residence among the Chinese: Inland, on the Coast, and at Sea*. Taipei: Ch'eng Wen, [1857] 1971.

Frank, Andre Gunder. *ReOrient: Global Economy in the Asian Age*. Berkeley: University of California Press, 1998.

Franke, Herbert, and Denis Twitchett, eds. *The Cambridge History of China*, vol. 6. *Alien Regimes and Border States, 907–1368*. Cambridge: Cambridge University Press, 1994.

Friday, Karl F. *Hired Swords: The Rise of Private Warrior Power in Early Japan*. Stanford, CA: Stanford University Press, 1992.

Friedman, Edward. "Reconstructing China's National Identity." In *National Identity and Democratic Prospects in Socialist China*. Armonk, NY: M. E. Sharpe, 1995.

Friedman, Edward, Paul G. Pickowicz, and Mark Selden. *Chinese Village, Socialist State*. New Haven, CT: Yale University Press, 1991.

Frühstück, Sabine, and Wolfram Manzenreiter. "Neverland Lost: Judo Cultures in Austria, Japan, and Elsewhere Struggling for Cultural Hegemony." In *Globalizing Japan: Ethnography of the Japanese Presence in Asia, Europe, and America*. Edited by Harumi Befu and Sylvie Guichard-Anguis. London: RoutledgeCurzon, 2001.

Fung, Yu-lan. *A Short History of Chinese Philosophy*. Edited by Derk Bodde. New York: Free Press, 1948.

Gallicchio, Marc S. *The Cold War Begins in Asia: American East Asian Policy and the Fall of the Japanese Empire*. New York: Columbia University Press, 1988.

Gardiner, Kenneth H. J. *The Early History of Korea: The Historical Development of the Peninsula up to the Introduction of Buddhism in the Fourth Century* A.D. Honolulu: University of Hawai'i Press, 1969.

Gelber, Harry G. *Opium, Soldiers, and Evangelicals: England's 1840–42 War with China, and Its Aftermath*. New York: Palgrave Macmillan, 2004.

Gernet, Jacques. *Buddhism in Chinese Society: An Economic History from the Fifth to the Tenth Centuries*. Translated by Franciscus Verellen. New York: Columbia University Press, [1956] 1995.

———. *Daily Life in China on the Eve of the Mongol Invasion, 1250–1276*. Translated by H. M. Wright. Stanford, CA: Stanford University Press, [1959] 1970.

Gibney, Frank. *The Pacific Century: America and Asia in a Changing World*. New York: Charles Scribner's Sons, 1992.

Gittings, John. *The Changing Face of China: From Mao to Market*. Oxford: Oxford University Press, 2005.

Gluck, Carol. *Japan's Modern Myths: Ideology in the Late Meiji Period*. Princeton, NJ: Princeton University Press, 1985.

Goodman, David S. G. *Deng Xiaoping and the Chinese Revolution: A Political Biography*. London: Routledge, 1994.

———. "The Politics of Regionalism: Economic Development, Conflict and Negotiation." In *China Deconstructs: Politics, Trade, and Regionalism*. Edited by David S. G. Goodman and Gerald Segal. London: Routledge, 1994.

Goodman, Howard L. *Ts'ao P'i Transcendent: The Political Culture of Dynasty-Founding in China at the End of the Han*. Seattle, WA: Scripta Serica, 1998.

Goossaert, Vincent. "1898: The Beginning of the End for Chinese Religion?" *Journal of Asian Studies* 65, no. 2 (2006).

Gordon, Andrew. "Society and Politics from Transwar through Postwar Japan." In *Historical Perspectives on Contemporary East Asia*. Edited by Merle Goldman and Andrew Gordon. Cambridge, MA: Harvard University Press, 2000.

Göthel, Ingeborg. "Juche and the Issue of National Identity in the DPRK of the 1960s." In *North Korea: Ideology, Politics, Economy*. Edited by Han S. Park. Englewood Cliffs, NJ: Prentice Hall, 1996.

Graff, David A. *Medieval Chinese Warfare, 300–900*. London: Routledge, 2002.

Graff, David A., and Robin Higham, eds. *A Military History of China*. Boulder, CO: Westview Press, 2002.

Graham, Angus C. *Disputers of the Tao: Philosophical Argument in Ancient China*. La Salle, IL: Open Court, 1989.

Grayson, James Huntley. "A Quarter-Millennium of Christianity in Korea." In *Christianity in Korea*. Edited by Robert E. Buswell Jr. and Timothy S. Lee. Honolulu: University of Hawai'i Press, 2006.

Greenberg, Michael. *British Trade and the Opening of China, 1800–42*. Cambridge: Cambridge University Press, 1951.

Greenfeld, Liah. *Nationalism: Five Roads to Modernity*. Cambridge, MA: Harvard University Press, 1992.

Greenhalgh, Susan. *Just One Child: Science and Policy in Deng's China*. Berkeley: University of California Press, 2008.

Grieder, Jerome B. *Hu Shih and the Chinese Renaissance: Liberalism in the Chinese Revolution, 1917–1937*. Cambridge, MA: Harvard University Press, 1970.

Groner, Paul. *Saichō: The Establishment of the Japanese Tendai School*. Seoul: Berkeley Buddhist Studies Series, 1984.

Grossberg, Kenneth A. *Japan's Renaissance: The Politics of the Muromachi Bakufu*. Ithaca, NY: Cornell University Press, [1981] 2000.

Guisso, R. W. L. *Wu Tse-t'ien and the Politics of Legitimation in T'ang China*. Bellingham: Western Washington University, 1978.

Guthrie, Doug. *China and Globalization: The Social, Economic, and Political Transformation of Chinese Society*. New York: Routledge, 2006.

Haboush, JaHyun Kim. "The Confucianization of Korean Society." In *The East Asian Region: Confucian Heritage and Its Modern Adaptation*. Edited by Gilbert Rozman. Princeton, NJ: Princeton University Press, 1991.

_____. "Constructing the Center: The Ritual Controversy and the Search for a New Identity in Seventeenth-century Korea." In *Culture and the State in Late Chosŏn Korea*. Edited by JaHyun Kim Haboush and Martina Deuchler. Cambridge, MA: Harvard University Asia Center, 1999.

Hackett, Roger F. *Yamagata Aritomo in the Rise of Modern Japan, 1838–1922*. Cambridge, MA: Harvard University Press, 1971.

Halberstam, David. *The Coldest Winter: America and the Korean War*. New York: Hyperion, 2007.

Hall, Ivan Parker. *Mori Arinori*. Cambridge, MA: Harvard University Press, 1973.

Hall, John Whitney. "The Castle Town and Japan's Modern Urbanization." In *Studies in the Institutional History of Early Modern Japan*. Edited by John W. Hall and Marius Jansen. Princeton, NJ: Princeton University Press, [1955] 1968.

_____. *Government and Local Power in Japan, 500 to 1700: A Study Based on Bizen Province*. Princeton, NJ: Princeton University Press, 1966.

Han, Minzhu (pseudonym), ed. *Cries for Democracy: Writings and Speeches from the 1989 Chinese Democracy Movement*. Princeton, NJ: Princeton University Press, 1990.

Hane, Mikiso. *Modern Japan: A Historical Survey*. Boulder, CO: Westview Press, 1986.

_____. *Peasants, Rebels, and Outcastes: The Underside of Modern Japan*. New York: Pantheon Books, 1982.

Hanley, Susan B. "The Material Culture: Stability in Transition." In *Japan in Transition: From Tokugawa to Meiji*. Edited by Marius B. Jansen and Gilbert Rozman. Princeton, NJ: Princeton University Press, 1986.

Hannas, Wm. C. *Asia's Orthographic Dilemma*. Honolulu: University of Hawai'i Press, 1997.

Harries, Meirion, and Susie Harries. *Sheathing the Sword: The Demilitarization of Japan*. New York: Macmillan, 1987.

Harrison, Henrietta. *China: Inventing the Nation*. London: Arnold, 2001.

Harrison, James Pinckney. *The Long March to Power: A History of the Chinese Communist Party, 1921–72*. New York: Praeger, 1972.

Hartman, Charles. *Han Yü and the T'ang Search for Unity*. Princeton, NJ: Princeton University Press, 1986.

Hartwell, Robert M. "Demographic, Political, and Social Transformations of China, 750–1550." *Harvard Journal of Asiatic Studies* 42, no. 2 (1982).

_____. "A Revolution in the Chinese Iron and Coal Industries during the Northern Sung, 960–1126 A.D." *Journal of Asian Studies* 21, no. 2 (1962).

Hastings, Max. *Retribution: The Battle for Japan, 1944–45*. New York: Alfred A. Knopf, 2008.

Havens, Thomas R. H. *Valley of Darkness: The Japanese People and World War Two*. Lanham, MD: University Press of America, 1986.

Hayashiya, Tatsusaburō. "Kyoto in the Muromachi Age." In *Japan in the Muromachi Age*. Edited by John Whitney Hall and Toyoda Takeshi. Berkeley: University of California Press, 1977.

Headrick, Daniel R. *The Tentacles of Progress: Technology Transfer in the Age of Imperialism, 1850–1940*. New York: Oxford University Press, 1988.

Hendry, Joy. "Japan: The Anthropology of Modernity." In *Asia's Cultural Mosaic: An Anthropological Introduction*. Edited by Grant Evans. New York: Prentice Hall, 1993.

Henthorn, William E. *A History of Korea*. New York: Free Press, 1971.

Hesselink, Reinier H. "The Introduction of the Art of Mounted Archery into Japan." *Transactions of the Asiatic Society of Japan, Fourth Series* 6 (1991).

_____. *Prisoners from Nambu: Reality and Make-Believe in 17th-century Japanese Diplomacy*. Honolulu: University of Hawai'i Press, 2002.

Hessler, Peter. *Oracle Bones: A Journey between China's Past and Present.* New York: Harper-Collins, 2006.

Hevia, James Louis. *Cherishing Men from Afar: Qing Guest Ritual and the Macartney Embassy of 1793.* Durham, NC: Duke University Press, 1995.

Hewitt, Duncan. *China: Getting Rich First, a Modern Social History.* New York: Pegasus, 2008.

Hillenbrand, Margaret. "Murakami Haruki in Greater China: Creative Responses and the Quest for Cosmopolitanism." *Journal of Asian Studies* 68, no. 3 (2009).

Hinton, William. *Fanshen: A Documentary of Revolution in a Chinese Village.* New York: Vintage Books, 1966.

Hirschmeier, Johannes. *The Origins of Entrepreneurship in Meiji Japan.* Cambridge, MA: Harvard University Press, 1964.

Ho, Ping-ti. *The Cradle of the East: An Inquiry into the Indigenous Origins of Techniques and Ideas of Neolithic and Early Historic China, 5000–1000* B.C. Hong Kong: Chinese University of Hong Kong, 1975.

Ho, Samuel Pao-San. "Colonialism and Development: Korea, Taiwan, and Kwantung." In *The Japanese Colonial Empire, 1895–1945.* Edited by Ramon H. Myers and Mark R. Peattie. Princeton, NJ: Princeton University Press, 1984.

Hobsbawm, Eric J. *The Age of Empire, 1875–1914.* New York: Vintage Books, 1989.

Holcombe, Charles. *The Genesis of East Asia, 221* B.C.–A.D. *907.* Honolulu: University of Hawai'i Press, 2001.

Holmgren, Jennifer. *Chinese Colonization of Northern Vietnam: Administrative Geography and Political Development in the Tongking Delta, First to Sixth Centuries* A.D. Canberra: Australian National University, 1980.

———. "The Composition of the Early Wei Bureaucratic Elite as Background to the Emperor Kao-tsu's Reforms (423–490 A.D.)." *Journal of Asian History* 27 (1993).

Holzman, Donald. *Poetry and Politics: The Life and Works of Juan Chi,* A.D. *210–263.* Cambridge: Cambridge University Press, 1976.

Hon, Tze-ki. "Zhang Zhidong's Proposal for Reform: A New Reading of the Quanxue pian." In *Rethinking the 1898 Reform Period: Political and Cultural Change in Late Qing China.* Edited by Rebecca E. Karl and Peter Zarrow. Cambridge, MA: Harvard University Asia Center, 2002.

Hong, Wontack. *Korea and Japan in East Asian History: A Tripolar Approach to East Asian History.* Seoul: Kudara International, 2006.

———. *Paekche of Korea and the Origin of Yamato Japan.* Seoul: Kudara International, 1994.

Hopper, Helen M. *Fukuzawa Yūkichi: From Samurai to Capitalist.* New York: Pearson Longman, 2005.

Hostetler, Laura. *Qing Colonial Enterprise: Ethnography and Cartography in Early Modern China.* Chicago, IL: University of Chicago Press, 2001.

Howland, D. R. *Borders of Chinese Civilization: Geography and History at Empire's End.* Durham, NC: Duke University Press, 1996.

Hsia, Chih-tsing (C. T.). *The Classic Chinese Novel: A Critical Introduction.* New York: Columbia University Press, 1968.

Hsiao, Kung-chuan. *A History of Chinese Political Thought,* vol. 1. *From the Beginnings to the Sixth Century* A.D. Translated by F. W. Mote. Princeton, NJ: Princeton University Press, 1979.

Hsu, Cho-yun (Xu Zhuoyun). *Ancient China in Transition: An Analysis of Social Mobility, 722–222* B.C. Stanford, CA: Stanford University Press, [1965] 1977.

Hsu, Cho-yun (Xu Zhuoyun), and Katheryn M. Linduff. *Western Chou Civilization.* New Haven, CT: Yale University Press, 1988.

Hsü, Immanuel C. Y. *The Ili Crisis: A Study of Sino-Russian Diplomacy, 1871–1881.* Oxford: Oxford University Press, 1965.

———. *The Rise of Modern China.* 6th ed. New York: Oxford University Press, 2000.

Hsu, Wen-hsiung. "From Aboriginal Island to Chinese Frontier: The Development of Taiwan before 1683." In *China's Island Frontier: Studies in the Historical Geography of Taiwan*. Edited by Ronald G. Knapp. Taipei: SMC, [1980] 1995.

Hu, Shih. "The Indianization of China: A Case Study in Cultural Borrowing." In *Independence, Convergence, and Borrowing in Institutions, Thought, and Art*. Cambridge, MA: Harvard University Press, 1937.

Huang, Chih-huei. "The Yamatodamashi of the Takasago Volunteers of Taiwan: A Reading of the Postcolonial Situation." In *Globalizing Japan: Ethnography of the Japanese Presence in Asia, Europe, and America*. Edited by Harumi Befu and Sylvie Guichard-Anguis. London: RoutledgeCurzon, 2001.

Huang, Ray. *China: A Macro History*. Armonk, NY: M. E. Sharpe, 1990.

———. *1587, a Year of No Significance: The Ming Dynasty in Decline*. New Haven, CT: Yale University Press, 1981.

Hucker, Charles O. *China's Imperial Past: An Introduction to Chinese History and Culture*. Stanford, CA: Stanford University Press, 1975.

Hudson, Mark J. *Ruins of Identity: Ethnogenesis in the Japanese Islands*. Honolulu: University of Hawai'i Press, 1999.

Huff, W. G. *The Economic Growth of Singapore: Trade and Development in the Twentieth Century*. Cambridge: Cambridge University Press, 1994.

Hur, Nam-lin. *Prayer and Play in Late Tokugawa Japan: Asakusa Sensōji and Edo Society*. Cambridge, MA: Harvard University Asia Center, 2000.

Hurst, G. Cameron III. "The Development of the Insei: A Problem in Japanese History and Historiography." In *Medieval Japan: Essays in Institutional History*. Edited by John W. Hall and Jeffrey P. Mass. Stanford, CA: Stanford University Press, [1974] 1988.

Ienaga, Saburō. *The Pacific War, 1931–1945*. New York: Pantheon Books, [1968] 1978.

Imamura, Keiji. *Prehistoric Japan: New Perspectives on Insular East Asia*. Honolulu: University of Hawai'i Press, 1996.

Inoue, Shun. "The Invention of the Martial Arts: Kanō Jigorō and Kōdōkan Judo." In *Mirror of Modernity: Invented Traditions of Modern Japan*. Edited by Stephen Vlastos. Berkeley: University of California Press, 1998.

Iriye, Akira. *Across the Pacific: An Inner History of American-East Asian Relations*. New York: Harcourt, Brace, and World, 1967.

———. *China and Japan in the Global Setting*. Cambridge, MA: Harvard University Press, 1992.

Isaacs, Harold R. *The Tragedy of the Chinese Revolution*. Stanford, CA: Stanford University Press, [1938] 1961.

Issenberg, Sasha. *The Sushi Economy: Globalization and the Making of a Modern Delicacy*. New York: Gotham, 2007.

James, Harold. *The End of Globalization: Lessons from the Great Depression*. Cambridge, MA: Harvard University Press, 2001.

Jansen, Marius B. *China in the Tokugawa World*. Cambridge, MA: Harvard University Press, 1992.

———. "Japanese Imperialism: Late Meiji Perspectives." In *The Japanese Colonial Empire, 1895–1945*. Edited by Ramon H. Myers and Mark R. Peattie. Princeton, NJ: Princeton University Press, 1984.

———. *The Making of Modern Japan*. Cambridge, MA: Harvard University Press, 2000.

———. *Sakamoto Ryōma and the Meiji Restoration*. New York: Columbia University Press, [1961] 1994.

Jen, Yu-wen (Jian Youwen). *The Taiping Revolutionary Movement*. New Haven, CT: Yale University Press, 1973.

Jenner, W. J. F. *The Tyranny of History: The Roots of China's Crisis*. Harmondsworth, UK: Penguin Books, 1992.

Jensen, Lionel M. *Manufacturing Confucianism: Chinese Traditions and Universal Civilization.* Durham, NC: Duke University Press, 1997.

Johnson, Chalmers. *MITI and the Japanese Miracle: The Growth of Industrial Policy, 1925–1975.* Stanford, CA: Stanford University Press, 1982.

———. *Peasant Nationalism and Communist Power: The Emergence of Revolutionary China.* Stanford, CA: Stanford University Press, 1962.

Johnson, David, Andrew J. Nathan, and Evelyn S. Rawski, eds. *Popular Culture in Late Imperial China.* Berkeley: University of California Press, 1985.

Johnston, Alastair Iain. *Cultural Realism: Strategic Culture and Grand Strategy in Chinese History.* Princeton, NJ: Princeton University Press, 1995.

Jones, Andrew F. *Like a Knife: Ideology and Genre in Contemporary Chinese Popular Music.* Ithaca, NY: Cornell University East Asia Program, 1992.

———. "The Politics of Popular Music in Post-Tiananmen China." In *China Off Center: Mapping the Margins of the Middle Kingdom.* Edited by Susan D. Blum and Lionel M. Jensen. Honolulu: University of Hawai'i Press, 2002.

Juliano, Annette L., and Judith A. Lerner, eds. *Monks and Merchants: Silk Road Treasures from Northwest China, Gansu and Ningxia, 4th–7th Century.* New York: Harry N. Abrams, 2001.

Kamstra, J. H. *Encounter or Syncretism: The Initial Growth of Japanese Buddhism.* Leiden, Netherlands: E. J. Brill, 1967.

Kataoka, Tetsuya, ed. *Creating Single-party Democracy: Japan's Postwar Political System.* Stanford, CA: Hoover Institution Press, 1992.

Katayama, Kazumichi. "The Japanese as an Asia-Pacific Population." In *Multicultural Japan: Palaeolithic to Postmodern.* Edited by Donald Denoon et al. Cambridge: Cambridge University Press, 1996.

Katz, Richard. *Japanese Phoenix: The Long Road to Economic Revival.* Armonk, NY: M. E. Sharpe, 2003.

Keene, Donald. "The Sino-Japanese War of 1894–95 and Its Cultural Effects in Japan." In *Tradition and Modernization in Japanese Culture.* Edited by Donald H. Shively. Princeton, NJ: Princeton University Press, 1971.

———. *World within Walls: Japanese Literature of the Pre-modern Era, 1600–1867.* New York: Grove Press, 1976.

———. *Yoshimasa and the Silver Pavilion: The Creation of the Soul of Japan.* New York: Columbia University Press, 2003.

Keightley, David N. *Sources of Shang History: The Oracle-Bone Inscriptions of Bronze Age China.* Berkeley: University of California Press, 1978.

Kemenade, Willem Van. *China, Hong Kong, Taiwan, Inc.* Translated by Diane Webb. New York: Vintage Books, 1998.

Kennedy, Paul. *The Rise and Fall of the Great Powers: Economic Change and Military Conflict from 1500 to 2000.* New York: Random House, 1987.

Kieschnick, John. *The Eminent Monk: Buddhist Ideals in Medieval Chinese Hagiography.* Honolulu: University of Hawai'i Press, 1997.

Kihl, Young Whan. *Transforming Korean Politics: Democracy, Reform, and Culture.* Armonk, NY: M. E. Sharpe, 2005.

Kiley, Cornelius J. "Provincial Administration and Land Tenure in Early Heian." In *The Cambridge History of Japan,* vol. 2. *Heian Japan.* Edited by Donald H. Shively and William H. McCullough. Cambridge: Cambridge University Press, 1999.

———. "State and Dynasty in Archaic Yamato." *Journal of Asian Studies* 33, no. 1 (1973).

Kim, Byong-suh. "Modernization and the Explosive Growth and Decline of Korean Protestant Religiosity." In *Christianity in Korea.* Edited by Robert E. Buswell Jr. and Timothy S. Lee. Honolulu: University of Hawai'i Press, 2006.

Kim, Eun Mee. "Globalization of the South Korean Chaebol." In *Korea's Globalization.* Edited by Samuel S. Kim. Cambridge: Cambridge University Press, 2000.

Kim, Jong-myung. "The Tripiṭaka Koreana: Its Computerization and Significance for the Cultural Sciences in a Modern Globalizing World." In *Korea and Globalization: Politics, Economics and Culture*. Edited by James Lewis and Amadu Sesay. London: Routledge-Curzon, 2002.

Kim, Key-Hiuk. *The Last Phase of the East Asian World Order: Korea, Japan, and the Chinese Empire, 1860–1882*. Berkeley: University of California Press, 1980.

Kim, Kichung. *An Introduction to Classical Korean Literature: From Hyangga to P'ansori*. Armonk, NY: M. E. Sharpe, 1996.

Kim, Samuel S. "Korea and Globalization (Segyehwa): A Framework for Analysis." In *Korea's Globalization*. Edited by Samuel S. Kim. Cambridge: Cambridge University Press, 2000.

———. "Korea's Segyehwa Drive: Promise versus Performance." In *Korea's Globalization*. Edited by Samuel S. Kim. Cambridge: Cambridge University Press, 2000.

Kirby, William C. *Germany and Republican China*. Stanford, CA: Stanford University Press, 1984.

———. "The Nationalist Regime and the Chinese Party-State, 1928–1958." In *Historical Perspectives on Contemporary East Asia*. Edited by Merle Goldman and Andrew Gordon. Cambridge, MA: Harvard University Press, 2000.

Kitagawa, Hiroshi, and Bruce T. Tsuchida, trans. *The Tale of the Heike*. Tokyo: University of Tokyo Press, 1975.

Kitagawa, Joseph M. *On Understanding Japanese Religion*. Princeton, NJ: Princeton University Press, 1987.

———, ed. *The Religious Traditions of Asia*. New York: Macmillan, 1987.

Knechtges, David R. "Culling the Weeds and Selecting Prime Blossoms: The Anthology in Early Medieval China." In *Culture and Power in the Reconstitution of the Chinese Realm, 200–600*. Edited by Scott Pearce, Audrey Spiro, and Patricia Ebrey. Cambridge, MA: Harvard University Press, 2001.

Kohli, Atul. "Where Do High-Growth Political Economies Come From? The Japanese Lineage of Korea's 'Developmental State.'" In *The Developmental State*. Edited by Meredith Woo-Cumings. Ithaca, NY: Cornell University Press, 1999.

Konishi, Jin'ichi. *A History of Japanese Literature*, vol. 2. *The Early Middle Ages*. Translated by Aileen Gatten. Princeton, NJ: Princeton University Press, 1986.

Kornicki, Peter. *The Book in Japan: A Cultural History from the Beginnings to the Nineteenth Century*. Leiden, Netherlands: Brill, 1998.

Kosai, Yutaka. "The Postwar Japanese Economy, 1945–1973." In *The Economic Emergence of Modern Japan*. Edited by Kozo Yamamura. Cambridge: Cambridge University Press, 1997.

Krauss, Ellis S. "Politics and the Policymaking Process." In *Democracy in Japan*. Edited by Takeshi Ishida and Ellis S. Krauss. Pittsburgh, PA: University of Pittsburgh Press, 1989.

Kristof, Nicholas D., and Sheryl Wudunn. *China Wakes: The Struggle for the Soul of a Rising Power*. New York: Vintage Books, 1995.

Kuhn, Dieter. *The Age of Confucian Rule: The Song Transformation of China*. Cambridge, MA: Harvard University Press, 2009.

Kuhn, Philip A. *Rebellion and Its Enemies in Late Imperial China: Militarization and Social Structure, 1796–1864*. Cambridge, MA: Harvard University Press, 1970.

———. *Soulstealers: The Chinese Sorcery Scare of 1768*. Cambridge, MA: Harvard University Press, 1990.

Kuroda, Toshio. "Shinto in the History of Japanese Religion." *Journal of Japanese Studies* 7, no. 1 (1981).

Kynge, James. *China Shakes the World: A Titan's Rise and Troubled Future – and the Challenge for America*. Boston: Houghton Mifflin, 2006.

Lach, Donald F. *China in the Eyes of Europe: The Sixteenth Century*. Chicago, IL: University of Chicago Press, 1965.

LaFleur, William R. *The Karma of Words: Buddhism and the Literary Arts in Medieval Japan.* Berkeley: University of California Press, 1983.

Lai, Tse-han, Ramon H. Myers, and Wou Wei. *A Tragic Beginning: The Taiwan Uprising of February 28, 1947.* Stanford, CA: Stanford University Press, 1991.

Lam, Willy Wo-lap. *Chinese Politics in the Hu Jintao Era: New Leaders, New Challenges.* Armonk, NY: M. E. Sharpe, 2006.

Lampton, David M. *The Three Faces of Chinese Power: Might, Money, and Minds.* Berkeley: University of California Press, 2008.

Larner, John. *Marco Polo and the Discovery of the World.* New Haven, CT: Yale University Press, 1999.

Lattimore, Owen. *Inner Asian Frontiers of China.* New York: American Geographical Society, 1940.

Ledyard, Gari. "Galloping Along with the Horseriders: Looking for the Founders of Japan." *Journal of Japanese Studies* 1, no. 2 (1975).

———. "Yin and Yang in the China-Manchuria-Korea Triangle." In *China among Equals: The Middle Kingdom and Its Neighbors, 10th–14th Centuries.* Edited by Morris Rossabi. Berkeley: University of California Press, 1983.

Lee, Don Y. *The History of Early Relations between China and Tibet: From Chiu T'ang-shu, a Documentary Survey.* Bloomington, IN: Eastern Press, 1981.

Lee, Ki-baik. *A New History of Korea.* Translated by Edward W. Wagner. Cambridge, MA: Harvard University Press, 1984.

Lee, Leo Ou-fan. *Shanghai Modern: The Flowering of a New Urban Culture in China, 1930–1945.* Cambridge, MA: Harvard University Press, 1999.

Lee, Peter H., trans. *Lives of Eminent Korean Monks: The Haedong Kosŭng Chŏn.* Cambridge, MA: Harvard University Press, 1969.

———, ed. *Sourcebook of Korean Civilization,* vol. 1. *From Early Times to the Sixteenth Century.* New York: Columbia University Press, 1993.

Lee, Sherman E. *A History of Far Eastern Art.* 5th ed. New York: Prentice Hall, 1994.

Leong, Sow-Theng. *Migration and Ethnicity in Chinese History: Hakkas, Pengmin, and Their Neighbors.* Edited by Tim Wright. Stanford, CA: Stanford University Press, 1997.

Lescot, Patrick. *Before Mao: The Untold Story of Li Lisan and the Creation of Communist China.* Translated by Steven Rendall. New York: Ecco, [1999] 2004.

Levathes, Louise. *When China Ruled the Seas: The Treasure Fleet of the Dragon Throne, 1405–1433.* New York: Oxford University Press, 1994.

Lewin, Bruno. "Japanese and Korean: The Problems and History of a Linguistic Comparison." *Journal of Japanese Studies* 2, no. 2 (1976).

Lewis, Mark Edward. *China between Empires: The Northern and Southern Dynasties.* Cambridge, MA: Harvard University Press, 2009.

———. *The Early Chinese Empires: Qin and Han.* Cambridge, MA: Harvard University Press, 2007.

———. *Writing and Authority in Early China.* Albany: State University of New York Press, 1999.

Lewis, Martin W., and Kären E. Wigen. *The Myth of Continents: A Critique of Metageography.* Berkeley: University of California Press, 1997.

Liang, Heng, and Judith Shapiro. *Son of the Revolution.* New York: Vintage Books, 1984.

Lie, John. *Han Unbound: The Political Economy of South Korea.* Stanford, CA: Stanford University Press, 1998.

Lieberthal, Kenneth. *Governing China: From Revolution through Reform.* New York: W. W. Norton, 1995.

Lipman, Jonathan N. *Familiar Strangers: A History of Muslims in Northwest China.* Seattle: University of Washington Press, 1997.

Liu, Kang. *Globalization and Cultural Trends in China.* Honolulu: University of Hawai'i Press, 2004.

Liu, Lydia H. *The Clash of Empires: The Invention of China in Modern World Making.* Cambridge, MA: Harvard University Press, 2004.

———. *Translingual Practice: Literature, National Culture, and Translated Modernity – China, 1900–1937.* Stanford, CA: Stanford University Press, 1995.

Liu, Shufen. "Jiankang and the Commercial Empire of the Southern Dynasties: Change and Continuity in Medieval Chinese Economic History." In *Culture and Power in the Reconstitution of the Chinese Realm, 200–600.* Edited by Scott Pearce, Audrey Spiro, and Patricia Ebrey. Cambridge, MA: Harvard University Press, 2001.

Liu, Xinru. *Ancient India and Ancient China: Trade and Religious Exchanges* A.D. *1–600.* Delhi: Oxford University Press, 1988.

Livingston, Jon, Joe Moore, and Felicia Oldfather, eds. *The Japan Reader 1: Imperial Japan, 1800–1945.* New York: Pantheon Books, 1973.

Loewe, Michael. "The Campaigns of Han Wu-ti." In *Chinese Ways in Warfare.* Edited by Frank A. Kierman Jr. and John K. Fairbank. Cambridge, MA: Harvard University Press, 1974.

———. "China's Sense of Unity as Seen in the Early Empires." *T'oung Pao* 80, nos. 1–3 (1994).

———. *Everyday Life in Early Imperial China during the Han Period 202* BC–AD *220.* Indianapolis, IN: Hackett, [1968] 2005.

Loewe, Michael, and Edward L. Shaughnessy, eds. *The Cambridge History of Ancient China: From the Origins of Civilization to 221* B.C. Cambridge: Cambridge University Press, 1999.

Mackerras, Colin. *The Uighur Empire According to the T'ang Dynastic Histories: A Study in Sino-Uighur Relations, 744–840.* Columbia: University of South Carolina Press, 1972.

MacMillan, Margaret. *Nixon and Mao: The Week That Changed the World.* New York: Random House, 2007.

Maddison, Angus. *Chinese Economic Performance in the Long Run.* Paris: Organisation for Economic Co-operation and Development, Development Centre, 1998.

Manchester, William. *American Caesar: Douglas MacArthur, 1880–1964.* Boston: Little, Brown, 1978.

March, Andrew L. *The Idea of China: Myth and Theory in Geographical Thought.* New York: Praeger, 1974.

Marks, Robert B. *The Origins of the Modern World: A Global and Ecological Narrative from the Fifteenth to the Twenty-first Century.* 2nd ed. Lanham, MD: Rowman and Littlefield, 2007.

Marshall, Byron K. *Capitalism and Nationalism in Prewar Japan: The Ideology of the Business Elite, 1868–1941.* Stanford, CA: Stanford University Press, 1967.

Maruyama, Masao. *Studies in the Intellectual History of Tokugawa Japan.* Translated by Mikiso Hane. Princeton, NJ: Princeton University Press, 1974.

Mass, Jeffrey P. "The Emergence of the Kamakura Bakufu." In *Medieval Japan: Essays in Institutional History.* Edited by John W. Hall and Jeffrey P. Mass. Stanford, CA: Stanford University Press, 1974.

———. *Yoritomo and the Founding of the First Bakufu: The Origins of Dual Government in Japan.* Stanford, CA: Stanford University Press, 1999.

Mather, Richard B. "The Conflict of Buddhism with Native Chinese Ideologies." *Review of Religion* 20, nos. 1–2 (1955).

———, trans. *Shih-shuo Hsin-yü: A New Account of Tales of the World.* Minneapolis: University of Minnesota Press, 1976.

McClain, James L., and John M. Merriman. "Edo and Paris: Cities and Power." In *Edo and Paris: Urban Life and the State in the Early Modern Era.* Edited by James L. McClain, John M. Merriman, and Ugawa Kaoru. Ithaca, NY: Cornell University Press, 1994.

McCord, Edward A. *The Power of the Gun: The Emergence of Modern Chinese Warlordism.* Berkeley: University of California Press, 1993.

McCord, William. *The Dawn of the Pacific Century: Implication for Three Worlds of Development.* New Brunswick, NJ: Transaction, 1993.

McCormack, Gavan. *Chang Tso-lin in Northeast China, 1911–1928: China, Japan, and the Manchurian Idea.* Stanford, CA: Stanford University Press, 1977.

————. "Kokusaika: Impediments in Japan's Deep Structure." In *Multicultural Japan: Palaeolithic to Postmodern.* Edited by Donald Denoon et al. Cambridge: Cambridge University Press, 1996.

McCullough, Helen Craig. *Brocade by Night: 'Kokin Wakashū' and the Court Style in Japanese Classical Poetry.* Stanford, CA: Stanford University Press, 1985.

McCullough, William H. "The Capital and Its Society." In *The Cambridge History of Japan,* vol. 2. *Heian Japan.* Edited by Donald H. Shively and William H. McCullough. Cambridge: Cambridge University Press, 1999.

————. "The Heian Court, 794–1070." In *The Cambridge History of Japan,* vol. 2. *Heian Japan.* Edited by Donald H. Shively and William H. McCullough. Cambridge: Cambridge University Press, 1999.

————. "Japanese Marriage Institutions in the Heian Period." *Harvard Journal of Asiatic Studies* 27 (1967).

McGray, Douglas. "Japan's Gross National Cool (Globalization at Work)." *Foreign Policy* (May 2002).

McMullen, David. *State and Scholars in T'ang China.* Cambridge: Cambridge University Press, 1988.

McRae, John R. *The Northern School and the Formation of Early Ch'an Buddhism.* Honolulu: University of Hawai'i Press, 1986.

Meisner, Maurice. *Mao's China and After: A History of the People's Republic.* New York: Free Press, [1977] 1986.

Meskill, Johanna Menzel. *A Chinese Pioneer Family: The Lins of Wu-feng, Taiwan, 1729–1895.* Princeton, NJ: Princeton University Press, 1979.

Michael, Franz, in collaboration with Chung-li Chang. *The Taiping Rebellion: History and Documents.* 3 vols. Seattle: University of Washington Press, [1966] 1972.

Millard, A. R. "The Infancy of the Alphabet." *World Archaeology* 17, no. 3 (1986).

Miller, John H. *Modern East Asia: An Introductory History.* Armonk, NY: M. E. Sharpe, 2008.

Miller, Richard J. *Japan's First Bureaucracy: A Study of Eighth-century Government.* East Asia Papers 19. Ithaca, NY: Cornell University, 1979.

Miller, Roy Andrew. *The Japanese Language.* Chicago, IL: University of Chicago Press, 1967.

————. *Japanese and the Other Altaic Languages.* Chicago, IL: University of Chicago Press, 1971.

————. "Yamato and Paekche." *Asian Pacific Quarterly* 26, no. 3 (1994).

Millward, James A. *Eurasian Crossroads: A History of Xinjiang.* New York: Columbia University Press, 2007.

Minear, Richard H. *Victors' Justice: The Tokyo War Crimes Trial.* Princeton, NJ: Princeton University Press, 1971.

Mintz, Sidney W. *Sweetness and Power: The Place of Sugar in Modern History.* New York: Viking, 1985.

Mitchell, Richard H. *Censorship in Imperial Japan.* Princeton, NJ: Princeton University Press, 1983.

Mitter, Rana. *A Bitter Revolution: China's Struggle with the Modern World.* Oxford: Oxford University Press, 2004.

Miyakawa, Hisayuki. "The Confucianization of South China." In *The Confucian Persuasion.* Edited by Arthur F. Wright. Stanford, CA: Stanford University Press, 1960.

Miyazaki, Ichisada. *China's Examination Hell: The Civil Service Examinations of Imperial China.* Translated by Conrad Schirokauer. New Haven, CT: Yale University Press, [1963] 1981.

Moerman, D. Max. "The Archeology of Anxiety: An Underground History of Heian Religion." In *Heian Japan, Centers and Peripheries*. Edited by Mikael Adolphson, Edward Kamens, and Stacie Matsumoto. Honolulu: University of Hawai'i Press, 2007.

Morris, Ivan I. *The Nobility of Failure: Tragic Heroes in the History of Japan*. New York: Holt, Rinehart, and Winston, 1975.

――――. *The World of the Shining Prince: Court Life in Ancient Japan*. Harmondsworth, UK: Penguin Books, [1964] 1985.

Morris-Suzuki, Tessa. "A Descent into the Past: The Frontier in the Construction of Japanese Identity." In *Multicultural Japan: Palaeolithic to Postmodern*. Edited by Donald Denoon et al. Cambridge: Cambridge University Press, 1996.

――――. "The Invention and Reinvention of 'Japanese Culture.'" *Journal of Asian Studies* 54, no. 3 (1995).

Morton, William F. *Tanaka Giichi and Japan's China Policy*. New York: St. Martin's Press, 1980.

Mote, Frederick W. *Imperial China: 900–1800*. Cambridge, MA: Harvard University Press, 1999.

Mungello, David E. *Curious Land: Jesuit Accommodation and the Origins of Sinology*. Honolulu: University of Hawai'i Press, 1985.

――――. *The Great Encounter of China and the West, 1500–1800*. Lanham, MD: Rowman and Littlefield, 1999.

Munsterberg, Hugo. *The Arts of Japan: An Illustrated History*. Rutland, VT: Charles E. Tuttle, 1957.

Murphey, Rhoads. *The Outsiders: The Western Experience in India and China*. Ann Arbor: University of Michigan Press, 1977.

Musgrove, Charles D. "Building a Dream: Constructing a National Capital in Nanjing, 1927–1937." In *Remaking the Chinese City: Modernity and National Identity, 1900–1950*. Edited by Joseph W. Esherick. Honolulu: University of Hawai'i Press, 2000.

Myers, Ramon H., ed. *Two Societies in Opposition: The Republic of China and the People's Republic of China after Forty Years*. Stanford, CA: Hoover Institution Press, 1991.

Najita, Tetsuo. *Hara Kei and the Politics of Compromise, 1905–1915*. Cambridge, MA: Harvard University Press, 1967.

――――. *Visions of Virtue in Tokugawa Japan: The Kaitokudō Merchant Academy of Osaka*. Chicago, IL: University of Chicago Press, 1987.

Nakamura, Kyoko Motomochi, trans. *Miraculous Stories from the Japanese Buddhist Tradition: The Nihon Ryoiki of the Monk Kyōkai*. Cambridge, MA: Harvard University Press, 1973.

Nakamura, Takafusa. "Depression, Recovery, and War, 1920–1945." In *The Economic Emergence of Modern Japan*. Edited by Kozo Yamamura. Cambridge: Cambridge University Press, 1997.

Naoki, Kōjirō. "The Nara State." In *The Cambridge History of Japan*, vol. 1. *Ancient Japan*. Edited by Delmer M. Brown. Cambridge: Cambridge University Press, 1993.

Naquin, Susan, and Evelyn S. Rawski. *Chinese Society in the Eighteenth Century*. New Haven, CT: Yale University Press, 1987.

Nathan, Andrew J., and Robert S. Ross. *The Great Wall and the Empty Fortress: China's Search for Security*. New York: W. W. Norton, 1997.

Nelson, Sarah Milledge. *The Archaeology of Korea*. Cambridge: Cambridge University Press, 1993.

Ng-Quinn, Michael. "National Identity in Premodern China: Formation and Role Enactment." In *China's Quest for National Identity*. Edited by Lowell Dittmer and Samuel S. Kim. Ithaca, NY: Cornell University Press, 1993.

Nish, Ian Hill. *The Anglo-Japanese Alliance: The Diplomacy of Two Island Empires, 1894–1907*. 2nd ed. London: Athlone Press, 1985.

Norman, E. Herbert. *Japan's Emergence as a Modern State: Political and Economic Problems of the Meiji Period*. New York: Institute of Pacific Relations, 1940.

Norman, Jerry, and Tsu-lin Mei. "The Austroasiatics in Ancient South China: Some Lexical Evidence." *Monumenta Serica* 32 (1976).

Oberdorfer, Don. *The Two Koreas: A Contemporary History*. Rev. and updated edition. New York: Basic Books, 2001.

Ogata, Sadako. *Defiance in Manchuria: The Making of Japanese Foreign Policy, 1931–1932*. Berkeley: University of California Press, 1964.

Ogawa, Masashi. "Japanese Popular Music in Hong Kong: Analysis of Global/Local Cultural Relations." In *Globalizing Japan: Ethnography of the Japanese Presence in Asia, Europe, and America*. Edited by Harumi Befu and Sylvie Guichard-Anguis. London: Routledge-Curzon, 2001.

Oh, Young Kyun. "Two Shilla Intellectuals in Tang: Cases of Early Sino-Korean Cultural Connections." *T'ang Studies* 23–24 (2005–2006).

Ohnuki-Tierney, Emiko. "McDonald's in Japan: Changing Manners and Etiquette." In *Golden Arches East: McDonald's in East Asia*. Edited by James L. Watson. Stanford, CA: Stanford University Press, 1997.

Oksenberg, Michel. "Taiwan, Tibet, and Hong Kong in Sino-American Relations." In *Living with China: U.S.-China Relations in the Twenty-first Century*. Edited by Ezra F. Vogel. New York: W. W. Norton, 1997.

Ooms, Herman. *Imperial Politics and Symbolics in Ancient Japan: The Tenmu Dynasty, 650–800*. Honolulu: University of Hawai'i Press, 2009.

———. *Tokugawa Ideology: Early Constructs, 1570–1680*. Princeton, NJ: Princeton University Press, 1985.

Ostler, Nicholas. *Empires of the Word: A Language History of the World*. New York: Harper-Collins, 2005.

Overholt, William H. *The Rise of China: How Economic Reform Is Creating a New Superpower*. New York: W. W. Norton, 1993.

Overmyer, Daniel. *Religions of China: The World as a Living System*. Prospect Heights, IL: Waveland Press, [1986] 1998.

Owen, Stephen. *The Great Age of Chinese Poetry: The High T'ang*. New Haven, CT: Yale University Press, 1981.

———. *The Late Tang: Chinese Poetry of the Mid-ninth Century (827–860)*. Cambridge, MA: Harvard University Asia Center, 2006.

———. *The Poetry of the Early T'ang*. New Haven, CT: Yale University Press, 1977.

Pai, Hyung Il. *Constructing "Korean" Origins: A Critical Review of Archaeology, Historiography, and Racial Myth in Korean State-Formation Theories*. Cambridge, MA: Harvard University Asia Center, 2000.

Palais, James B. *Confucian Statecraft and Korean Institutions: Yu Hyŏngwŏn and the Late Chosŏn Dynasty*. Seattle: University of Washington Press, 1996.

———. "A Search for Korean Uniqueness." *Harvard Journal of Asiatic Studies* 55, no. 2 (1995).

Pan, Yihong. *Son of Heaven and Heavenly Qaghan: Sui-Tang China and Its Neighbors*. Bellingham: Western Washington University, 1997.

Patten, Christopher. *East and West: China, Power, and the Future of Asia*. New York: Times Books, 1998.

Pearson, Richard. *Ancient Japan*. New York: George Braziller, 1992.

Peattie, Mark R. *Ishiwara Kanji and Japan's Confrontation with the West*. Princeton, NJ: Princeton University Press, 1975.

———. "Japanese Attitudes toward Colonialism, 1895–1945." In *The Japanese Colonial Empire, 1895–1945*. Edited by Ramon H. Myers and Mark R. Peattie. Princeton, NJ: Princeton University Press, 1984.

Pempel, T. J. "Prerequisites for Democracy: Political and Social Institutions." In *Democracy in Japan*. Edited by Takeshi Ishida and Ellis S. Krauss. Pittsburgh, PA: University of Pittsburgh Press, 1989.

Pepper, Suzanne. *Civil War in China: The Political Struggle, 1945–1949*. Berkeley: University of California Press, 1978.

Perdue, Peter C. *China Marches West: The Qing Conquest of Central Asia*. Cambridge, MA: Harvard University Press, 2005.

Perry, Elizabeth J. *Rebels and Revolutionaries in North China, 1845–1945*. Stanford, CA: Stanford University Press, 1980.

Petech, Luciano. "Tibetan Relations with Sung China and with the Mongols." In *China among Equals: The Middle Kingdom and Its Neighbors, 10th–14th Centuries*. Edited by Morris Rossabi. Berkeley: University of California Press, 1983.

Peters, Heather A. "Towns and Trade: Cultural Diversity and Chu Daily Life." In *Defining Chu: Image and Reality in Ancient China*. Edited by Constance A. Cook and John S. Major. Honolulu: University of Hawai'i Press, 1999.

Philippi, Donald L., trans. *Kojiki*. Princeton, NJ: Princeton University Press, [712 CE] 1968.

Piggott, Joan R. *The Emergence of Japanese Kingship*. Stanford, CA: Stanford University Press, 1997.

Pines, Yuri. "Beasts or Humans: Pre-imperial Origins of the 'Sino-Barbarian' Dichotomy." In *Mongols, Turks, and Others: Eurasian Nomads and the Sedentary World*. Edited by Reuven Amitai and Michal Biran. Leiden, Netherlands: E. J. Brill, 2005.

———. *Envisioning Eternal Empire: Chinese Political Thought of the Warring States Era*. Honolulu: University of Hawai'i Press, 2009.

Pittau, Joseph. *Political Thought in Early Meiji Japan, 1868–1889*. Cambridge, MA: Harvard University Press, 1967.

Plaks, Andrew H. *The Four Masterworks of the Ming Novel: Ssu ta ch'i shu*. Princeton, NJ: Princeton University Press, 1987.

Pollack, David. *The Fracture of Meaning: Japan's Synthesis of China from the Eighth through the Eighteenth Centuries*. Princeton, NJ: Princeton University Press, 1986.

Pomeranz, Kenneth. *The Great Divergence: China, Europe, and the Making of the Modern World Economy*. Princeton, NJ: Princeton University Press, 2000.

Powers, Martin J. *Art and Political Expression in Early China*. New Haven, CT: Yale University Press, 1991.

Prestowitz, Clyde V., Jr. *Trading Places: How We Allowed Japan to Take the Lead*. New York: Basic Books, 1988.

Prybyla, Jan S. "Economic Developments in the Republic of China." In *Democracy and Development in East Asia: Taiwan, South Korea, and the Philippines*. Edited by Thomas W. Robinson. Washington, DC: AEI Press, 1991.

Puett, Michael J. *To Become a God: Cosmology, Sacrifice, and Self-Divinization in Early China*. Cambridge, MA: Harvard University Press, 2002.

Pulleyblank, Edwin G. *The Background of the Rebellion of An Lu-shan*. London: Oxford University Press, 1955.

———. "The Chinese and Their Neighbors in Prehistoric and Early Historic Times." In *The Origins of Chinese Civilization*. Edited by David N. Keightley. Berkeley: University of California Press, 1983.

Queen, Sarah A. *From Chronicle to Canon: The Hermeneutics of the Spring and Autumn, According to Tung Chung-shu*. Cambridge: Cambridge University Press, 1996.

Rafferty, Kevin. *City on the Rocks: Hong Kong's Uncertain Future*. London: Penguin Books, 1991.

Ramsey, S. Robert. *The Languages of China*. Princeton, NJ: Princeton University Press, 1987.

Rawski, Evelyn S. *The Last Emperors: A Social History of Qing Imperial Institutions*. Berkeley: University of California Press, 1998.

Reichwein, Adolf. *China and Europe: Intellectual and Artistic Contacts in the Eighteenth Century*. Translated by J. C. Powell. New York: Alfred A. Knopf, 1925.

Reischauer, Edwin O. *Ennin's Travels in T'ang China*. New York: Ronald Press, 1955.

_____. *My Life between Japan and America*. New York: Harper and Row, 1986.

Rhie, Marylin Martin. *Early Buddhist Art of China and Central Asia*, vol. 1. *Later Han, Three Kingdoms and Western Chin in China and Bactria to Shan-shan in Central Asia*. Leiden, Netherlands: Brill, 1999.

Rhoads, Edward J. M. "The Assassination of Governor Enming and Its Effect on Manchu-Han Relations in Late Qing China." In *China's Republican Revolution*. Edited by Etō Shinkichi and Harold Z. Schiffrin. Tokyo: University of Tokyo Press, 1994.

_____. *Manchus and Han: Ethnic Relations and Political Power in Late Qing and Early Republican China, 1861–1928*. Seattle: University of Washington Press, 2000.

Robinet, Isabelle. *Taoism: Growth of a Religion*. Translated by Phyllis Brooks. Stanford, CA: Stanford University Press, [1992] 1997.

Robinson, Michael Edson. *Cultural Nationalism in Colonial Korea, 1920–1925*. Seattle: University of Washington Press, 1988.

_____. *Korea's Twentieth-century Odyssey: A Short History*. Honolulu: University of Hawai'i Press, 2007.

Rogers, Michael C. "National Consciousness in Medieval Korea: The Impact of Liao and Chin on Koryŏ." In *China among Equals: The Middle Kingdom and Its Neighbors, 10th–14th Centuries*. Edited by Morris Rossabi. Berkeley: University of California Press, 1983.

Rohlen, Thomas P. "'Spiritual Education' in a Japanese Bank." In *Japanese Culture and Behavior: Selected Readings*. Edited by Takie Sugiyama Lebra and William P. Lebra. Honolulu: University of Hawai'i Press, [1973] 1986.

Ropp, Paul S., ed. *Heritage of China: Contemporary Perspectives on Chinese Civilization*. Berkeley: University of California Press, 1990.

Rosenstone, Robert A. *Mirror in the Shrine: American Encounters with Meiji Japan*. Cambridge, MA: Harvard University Press, 1988.

Rossabi, Morris. *Khubilai Khan: His Life and Times*. Berkeley: University of California Press, 1988.

Rowe, William T. *China's Last Empire: The Great Qing*. Cambridge, MA: Harvard University Press, 2009.

Rozman, Gilbert, ed. *The East Asian Region: Confucian Heritage and its Modern Adaptation*. Princeton, NJ: Princeton University Press, 1991.

Sage, Steven F. *Ancient Sichuan and the Unification of China*. Albany: State University of New York Press, 1992.

Sakamoto, Tarō. *The Six National Histories of Japan*. Translated by John S. Brownlee. Tokyo: University of Tokyo Press, 1991.

Salisbury, Harrison E. *The Long March: The Untold Story*. New York: McGraw-Hill, 1985.

Samuels, Richard J. *"Rich Nation Strong Army": National Security and the Technological Transformation of Japan*. Ithaca, NY: Cornell University Press, 1994.

Sansom, George B. *Japan: A Short Cultural History*. Stanford, CA: Stanford University Press, [1931] 1978.

Sato, Elizabeth. "The Early Development of the Shōen." In *Medieval Japan: Essays in Institutional History*. Edited by John W. Hall and Jeffrey P. Mass. Stanford, CA: Stanford University Press, 1974.

Sawyer, Ralph D. "Military Writings." In *A Military History of China*. Edited by David A. Graff and Robin Higham. Boulder, CO: Westview Press, 2002.

Sawyer, Ralph D., and Mei-chün Sawyer, trans. *The Seven Military Classics of Ancient China*. New York: Basic Books, [1993] 2007.

Schafer, Edward H. *The Golden Peaches of Samarkand: A Study of T'ang Exotics*. Berkeley: University of California Press, 1963.

_____. "The Yeh Chung Chi." *T'oung Pao* 76, nos. 4–5 (1990).

Schell, Orville. *Discos and Democracy: China in the Throes of Reform*. New York: Anchor Books, 1989.

————. *Mandate of Heaven: A New Generation of Entrepreneurs, Dissidents, Bohemians, and Technocrats Lays Claim to China's Future*. New York: Simon and Schuster, 1994.

Schirokauer, Conrad, Miranda Brown, David Lurie, and Suzanne Gay. *A Brief History of Chinese and Japanese Civilization*. 3rd ed. United States: Wadsworth, 2006.

Schmid, Andre. "Rediscovering Manchuria: Sin Ch'aeho and the Politics of Territorial History in Korea." *Journal of Asian Studies* 56, no. 1 (1997).

Schoppa, R. Keith. *Blood Road: The Mystery of Shen Dingyi in Revolutionary China*. Berkeley: University of California Press, 1995.

Schriver, Randall, and Mark Stokes. "Taiwan's Liberation of China." *Current History* 107, no. 710 (2008).

Schurmann, Franz. *Ideology and Organization in Communist China*. 2nd ed. Berkeley: University of California Press, 1968.

Schwartz, Benjamin I. *Chinese Communism and the Rise of Mao*. Cambridge, MA: Harvard University Press, [1951] 1979.

————. *The World of Thought in Ancient China*. Cambridge, MA: Harvard University Press, 1985.

Seeley, Christopher. *A History of Writing in Japan*. Leiden, Netherlands: E. J. Brill, 1991.

Sei Shōnagon. *The Pillow Book of Sei Shōnagon*. Translated by Ivan Morris. Baltimore: Penguin Books, [early 11th century] 1967.

Seidensticker, Edward. *Low City, High City: Tokyo from Edo to the Earthquake*. New York: Alfred A. Knopf, 1983.

————. *Tokyo Rising: The City since the Great Earthquake*. Cambridge, MA: Harvard University Press, 1991.

Sen, Tansen. *Buddhism, Diplomacy, and Trade: The Realignment of Sino-Indian Relations, 600–1400*. Honolulu: University of Hawai'i Press, 2003.

Seth, Michael J. *A Concise History of Korea: From the Neolithic Period through the Nineteenth Century*. Lanham, MD: Rowman and Littlefield, 2006.

Sharf, Robert H. *Coming to Terms with Chinese Buddhism: A Reading of the Treasure Store Treatise*. Honolulu: University of Hawai'i Press, 2002.

Sheridan, James E. *China in Disintegration: The Republican Era in Chinese History, 1912–1949*. New York: Free Press, 1975.

Sherratt, Andrew. "The Trans-Eurasian Exchange: The Prehistory of Chinese Relations with the West." In *Contact and Exchange in the Ancient World*. Edited by Victor H. Mair. Honolulu: University of Hawai'i Press, 2006.

Shiba, Yoshinobu. "Sung Foreign Trade: Its Scope and Organization." In *China among Equals: The Middle Kingdom and Its Neighbors, 10th–14th Centuries*. Edited by Morris Rossabi. Berkeley: University of California Press, 1983.

Shillony, Ben-Ami. *Revolt in Japan: The Young Officers and the February 26, 1936 Incident*. Princeton, NJ: Princeton University Press, 1973.

Shirk, Susan L. *The Political Logic of Economic Reform in China*. Berkeley: University of California Press, 1993.

Shively, Donald H. "Bakufu versus Kabuki." In *Studies in the Institutional History of Early Modern Japan*. Edited by John W. Hall and Marius Jansen. Princeton, NJ: Princeton University Press, [1955] 1968.

————. "The Japanization of the Middle Meiji." In *Tradition and Modernization in Japanese Culture*. Edited by Donald H. Shively. Princeton, NJ: Princeton University Press, 1971.

Skinner, William G., ed. *The City in Late Imperial China*. Stanford, CA: Stanford University Press, 1977.

Smith, Thomas C. *Native Sources of Japanese Industrialization, 1750–1920*. Berkeley: University of California Press, 1988.

————. *Political Change and Industrial Development in Japan: Government Enterprise, 1868–1880*. Stanford, CA: Stanford University Press, 1955.

Smits, Ivo. "The Way of the Literati: Chinese Learning and Literary Practice in Mid-Heian Japan." In *Heian Japan, Centers and Peripheries*. Edited by Mikael Adolphson, Edward Kamens, and Stacie Matsumoto. Honolulu: University of Hawai'i Press, 2007.

Smyth, Alfred P. "The Emergence of English Identity, 700–1000." In *Medieval Europeans: Studies in Ethnic Identity and National Perspectives in Medieval Europe*. Edited by Alfred P. Smyth. New York: St. Martin's Press, 1998.

Snow, Edgar. *Red Star over China*. New York: Grove Press, [1938] 1968.

So, Billy Kee-long. "Legitimizing New Political Order Legally: Legal Reforms in Northern Song China." In *The Legitimation of New Orders: Case Studies in World History*. Edited by Philip Yuen-sang Leung. Hong Kong: Chinese University Press, 2007.

So, Jenny F., and Emma C. Bunker. *Traders and Raiders on China's Northern Frontier*. Seattle, WA: Smithsonian Institution, 1995.

Somers, Robert M. "Time, Space, and Structure in the Consolidation of the T'ang Dynasty (A.D. 617–700)." *Journal of Asian Studies* 45, no. 5 (1986).

Sonoda, Kōyū. "Early Buddha Worship." In *The Cambridge History of Japan*, vol. 1. *Ancient Japan*. Edited by Delmer M. Brown. Cambridge: Cambridge University Press, 1993.

Souyri, Pierre François. *The World Turned Upside Down: Medieval Japanese Society*. Translated by Käthe Roth. New York: Columbia University Press, 2001.

Spector, Ronald H. *Eagle against the Sun: The American War with Japan*. New York: Free Press, 1985.

Spence, Jonathan D. *To Change China: Western Advisers in China 1620–1960*. Boston: Little, Brown, 1969.

_____. *The Gate of Heavenly Peace: The Chinese and Their Revolution, 1895–1980*. New York: Penguin Books, 1981.

_____. *God's Chinese Son: The Taiping Heavenly Kingdom of Hong Xiuquan*. New York: W. W. Norton, 1996.

_____. *Mao Zedong*. New York: Viking, 1999.

_____. *The Memory Palace of Matteo Ricci*. Harmondsworth, UK: Penguin Books, 1983.

_____. *The Search for Modern China*. New York: W. W. Norton, 1990.

Standen, Naomi. *Unbounded Loyalty: Frontier Crossing in Liao China*. Honolulu: University of Hawai'i Press, 2007.

Stanlaw, James. "'For Beautiful Human Life': The Use of English in Japan." In *Re-made in Japan: Everyday Life and Consumer Taste in a Changing Society*. Edited by Joseph J. Tobin. New Haven, CT: Yale University Press, 1992.

Statler, Oliver. *Japanese Inn*. Honolulu: University of Hawai'i Press, [1961] 1982.

Stein, Rolf A. "Religious Taoism and Popular Religion from the Second to Seventh Centuries." In *Facets of Taoism: Essays in Chinese Religion*. Edited by Holmes Welch and Anna Seidel. New Haven, CT: Yale University Press, 1979.

_____. *Tibetan Civilization*. Translated by J. E. Stapleton Driver. Stanford, CA: Stanford University Press, [1962] 1972.

Steinhardt, Nancy Shatzman. "From Koguryŏ to Gansu and Xinjiang: Funerary and Worship Space in North Asia 4th–7th Centuries." In *Han-Tang zhi jian wenhua yishu de hudong yu jiaorong*. Edited by Wu Hong. Beijing: Wenwu chubanshe, 2001.

Storry, Richard. *Japan and the Decline of the West in Asia, 1894–1943*. New York: St. Martin's Press, 1979.

Stross, Randall E. *Bulls in the China Shop and Other Sino-American Business Encounters*. New York: Pantheon Books, 1990.

Suh, Dae-Sook. *Kim Il Sung: The North Korean Leader*. New York: Columbia University Press, 1988.

Swanson, Paul L. *The Foundations of T'ien-T'ai Philosophy: The Flowering of the Two Truths Theory in Chinese Buddhism*. Berkeley, CA: Asian Humanities Press, 1989.

Swope, Kenneth M. *A Dragon's Head and a Serpent's Tail: Ming China and the First Great East Asian War, 1592–1598*. Norman, OK: University of Oklahoma Press, 2009.

Takaki, Ronald T. *Strangers from a Different Shore: A History of Asian Americans*. Rev. edition. Boston: Little, Brown, 1998.

Takeuchi, Rizō. "The Rise of the Warriors." In *The Cambridge History of Japan*, vol. 2. *Heian Japan*. Edited by Donald H. Shively and William H. McCullough. Cambridge: Cambridge University Press, 1999.

Tamura, Enchō. "Japan and the Eastward Permeation of Buddhism." *Acta Asiatica* 47 (1985).

Tanaka, Stefan. *Japan's Orient: Rendering Pasts into History*. Berkeley: University of California Press, 1993.

Taylor, Jay. *The Generalissimo: Chiang Kai-shek and the Struggle for Modern China*. Cambridge, MA: Harvard University Press, 2009.

———. *The Generalissimo's Son: Chiang Ching-kuo and the Revolutions in China and Taiwan*. Cambridge, MA: Harvard University Press, 2000.

Taylor, Keith Weller. "Surface Orientations in Vietnam: Beyond Histories of Nation and Region." *Journal of Asian Studies* 57, no. 4 (1998).

Teiwes, Frederick C., and Warren Sun. *China's Road to Disaster: Mao, Central Politicians, and Provincial Leaders in the Unfolding of the Great Leap Forward, 1955–1959*. Armonk, NY: M. E. Sharpe, 1999.

Teng, Ssu-yu (S. Y.). *The Taiping Rebellion and the Western Powers: A Comprehensive Survey*. Taipei: Rainbow-Bridge, 1972.

Terrill, Ross. *The New Chinese Empire, and What It Means for the United States*. New York: Basic Books, 2003.

Terry, Edith. *How Asia Got Rich: Japan, China, and the Asian Miracle*. Armonk, NY: M. E. Sharpe, 2002.

Thompson, Laurence G. *Chinese Religion: An Introduction*. Fifth ed. Belmont, NY: Wadsworth, 1996.

Thurston, Anne F. *Enemies of the People: The Ordeal of the Intellectuals in China's Great Cultural Revolution*. Cambridge, MA: Harvard University Press, 1988.

Tian, Xiaofei. *Beacon Fire and Shooting Star: The Literary Culture of the Liang (502–557)*. Cambridge, MA: Harvard University Asia Center, 2007.

Tien, Hung-mao. *The Great Transition: Political and Social Change in the Republic of China*. Stanford, CA: Hoover Institution Press, 1989.

Tillman, Hoyt Cleveland, and Stephen H. West, eds. *China under Jurchen Rule: Essays on Chin Intellectual and Cultural History*. Albany: State University of New York Press, 1995.

Tobin, Joseph J. "Introduction: Domesticating the West." In *Re-made in Japan: Everyday Life and Consumer Taste in a Changing Society*. Edited by Joseph J. Tobin. New Haven, CT: Yale University Press, 1992.

Torao, Toshiya. "Nara Economic and Social Institutions." In *The Cambridge History of Japan*, vol. 1. *Ancient Japan*. Edited by Delmer M. Brown. Cambridge: Cambridge University Press, 1993.

Totman, Conrad D. *The Collapse of the Tokugawa Bakufu, 1862–1868*. Honolulu: University Press of Hawaii, 1980.

———. *Early Modern Japan*. Berkeley: University of California Press, 1993.

———. *Tokugawa Ieyasu: Shogun*. San Francisco, CA: Heian International, 1983.

Trauzettel, Rolf. "Sung Patriotism as a First Step toward Chinese Nationalism." In *Crisis and Prosperity in Sung China*. Edited by John Winthrop Haeger. Tucson: University of Arizona Press, 1975.

Trigger, Bruce G. *Understanding Early Civilizations: A Comparative Study*. Cambridge: Cambridge University Press, 2003.

Tsien, Tsuen-Hsuin. *Written on Bamboo and Silk: The Beginnings of Chinese Books and Inscriptions*. Chicago, IL: University of Chicago Press, 1962.

Tsukamoto, Zenryū. *A History of Early Chinese Buddhism: From Its Introduction to the Death of Hui-Yüan*. Translated by Leon Hurvitz. Tokyo: Kodansha, [1979] 1985.

Tsunoda, Ryusaku, Wm. Theodore de Bary, and Donald Keene, eds. *Sources of Japanese Tradition*. Vol. 1. New York: Columbia University Press, [1958] 1964.

Tsurumi, E. Patricia. "Colonial Education in Korea and Taiwan." In *The Japanese Colonial Empire, 1895–1945*. Edited by Ramon H. Myers and Mark R. Peattie. Princeton, NJ: Princeton University Press, 1984.

Tuchman, Barbara W. *Stilwell and the American Experience in China, 1911–1945*. New York: Bantam Books, 1972.

Twitchett, Denis. *The Birth of the Chinese Meritocracy: Bureaucrats and Examinations in T'ang China*. London: China Society, 1976.

Twitchett, Denis, and Michael Loewe, eds. *The Cambridge History of China*, vol. 1. *The Ch'in and Han Empires, 221 B.C.–A.D. 220*. Cambridge: Cambridge University Press, 1986.

Tyler, Patrick. *A Great Wall: Six Presidents and China: An Investigative History*. New York: Century Foundation, 1999.

Unger, Jonathan. "China's Conservative Middle Class." *Far Eastern Economic Review* 169, no 3 (April 2006).

Ury, Marian. "Chinese Learning and Intellectual Life." In *The Cambridge History of Japan*, vol. 2. *Heian Japan*. Edited by Donald H. Shively and William H. McCullough. Cambridge: Cambridge University Press, 1999.

Varley, H. Paul. *Warriors of Japan as Portrayed in the War Tales*. Honolulu: University of Hawai'i Press, 1994.

Vogel, Ezra F. *Japan as Number One: Lessons for America*. Cambridge, MA: Harvard University Press, 1979.

———. *The Four Little Dragons: The Spread of Industrialization in East Asia*. Cambridge, MA: Harvard University Press, 1991.

Wachman, Alan M. *Taiwan: National Identity and Democratization*. Armonk, NY: M. E. Sharpe, 1994.

Wakeman, Frederic, Jr. *The Fall of Imperial China*. New York: Free Press, 1975.

———. *The Great Enterprise: The Manchu Reconstruction of Imperial Order in Seventeenth-century China*. 2 vols. Berkeley: University of California Press, 1985.

———. *Policing Shanghai, 1927–1937*. Berkeley: University of California Press, 1995.

Waley, Arthur. *Three Ways of Thought in Ancient China*. Stanford, CA: Stanford University Press, [1939] 1982.

Waldron, Arthur. *The Great Wall of China: From History to Myth*. Cambridge: Cambridge University Press, 1990.

Walton, Linda A. *Academies and Society in Southern Sung China*. Honolulu: University of Hawai'i Press, 1999.

Wang, Gungwu. *The Nanhai Trade: The Early History of Chinese Trade in the South China Sea*. Singapore: Times Academic Press, [1958] 1998.

Wang, Jing. *High Culture Fever: Politics, Aesthetics, and Ideology in Deng's China*. Berkeley: University of California Press, 1996.

Wang, Peter Chen-main. "A Bastion Created, a Regime Reformed, an Economy Reengineered, 1949–1970." In *Taiwan: A New History*. Edited by Murray A. Rubinstein. Armonk, NY: M. E. Sharpe, 1999.

Wang, Zhenping. *Ambassadors from the Islands of Immortals: China-Japan Relations in the Han-Tang Period*. Honolulu: University of Hawai'i Press, 2005.

Wank, David L. *Commodifying Communism: Business, Trust, and Politics in a Chinese City*. Cambridge: Cambridge University Press, 1999.

Ward-Perkins, Bryan. *The Fall of Rome and the End of Civilization*. Oxford: Oxford University Press, 2005.

Watson, Burton, trans. *Courtier and Commoner in Ancient China: Selections from the History of the Former Han by Pan Ku*. New York: Columbia University Press, 1974.

———. *Early Chinese Literature*. New York: Columbia University Press, 1962.

Watson, James L. "Rites or Beliefs? The Construction of a Unified Culture in Late Imperial China." In *China's Quest for National Identity*. Edited by Lowell Dittmer and Samuel S. Kim. Ithaca, NY: Cornell University Press, 1993.

Watt, James C. Y. "Art and History in China from the Third to the Eighth Century." In *China: Dawn of a Golden Age, 200–750 AD*. Edited by James C. Y. Watt et al. New York: Metropolitan Museum of Art, 2004.

Wechsler, Howard J. *Mirror to the Son of Heaven: Wei Cheng at the Court of T'ang T'ai-tsung*. New Haven, CT: Yale University Press, 1974.

Wei, William. " 'Political Power Grows Out of the Barrel of a Gun': Mao and the Red Army." In *A Military History of China*. Edited by David A. Graff and Robin Higham. Boulder, CO: Westview Press, 2002.

Weinstein, Stanley. "The Beginnings of Esoteric Buddhism in Japan: The Neglected Tendai Tradition." *Journal of Asian Studies* 34, no. 1 (1974).

―――. *Buddhism under the T'ang*. Cambridge: Cambridge University Press, 1987.

Welsh, Frank. *A Borrowed Place: The History of Hong Kong*. New York: Kodansha International, 1993.

Welter, Albert. "A Buddhist Response to the Confucian Revival: Tsan-ning and the Debate over Wen in the Early Sung." In *Buddhism in the Sung*. Edited by Peter N. Gregory and Daniel A. Getz Jr. Honolulu: University of Hawai'i Press, 1999.

West, Philip. "Confronting the West: China as David and Goliath in the Korean War." *Journal of American-East Asian Relations* 2, no. 1 (1993).

Wheatley, Paul. *The Pivot of the Four Quarters: A Preliminary Inquiry into the Origins and Character of the Ancient Chinese City*. Chicago, IL: Aldine, 1971.

Wheatley, Paul, and Thomas See. *From Court to Capital: A Tentative Interpretation of the Origins of the Japanese Urban Tradition*. Chicago, IL: University of Chicago Press, 1978.

White, Donald W. *The American Century: The Rise and Decline of the United States as a World Power*. New Haven, CT: Yale University Press, 1996.

White, Gordon. *Riding the Tiger: The Politics of Economic Reform in Post-Mao China*. Stanford, CA: Stanford University Press, 1993.

White, Theodore H., and Annalee Jacoby. *Thunder Out of China*. New York: William Sloan Associates, [1946] 1961.

Wiens, Herold J. *China's March to the Tropics: A Study of the Cultural and Historical Geography of South China*. Washington, DC: Office of Naval Research, 1952.

Wills, John E., Jr. "The Seventeenth-century Transformation: Taiwan under the Dutch and the Cheng Regime." In *Taiwan: A New History*. Edited by Murray A. Rubinstein. Armonk, NY: M. E. Sharpe, 1999.

Wilson, George M. *Radical Nationalist in Japan: Kita Ikki, 1883–1937*. Cambridge, MA: Harvard University Press, 1969.

Wolf, Margery, and Roxane Witke, eds. *Women in Chinese Society*. Stanford, CA: Stanford University Press, 1975.

Wolff, David. *To the Harbin Station: The Liberal Alternative in Russian Manchuria, 1898–1914*. Stanford, CA: Stanford University Press, 1999.

Woo-Cumings, Meredith. "Introduction: Chalmers Johnson and the Politics of Nationalism and Development." In *The Developmental State*. Edited by Meredith Woo-Cumings. Ithaca, NY: Cornell University Press, 1999.

Woodside, Alexander Barton. *Lost Modernities: China, Vietnam, Korea, and the Hazards of World History*. Cambridge, MA: Harvard University Press, 2006.

―――. *Vietnam and the Chinese Model: A Comparative Study of Nguyên and Ch'ing Civil Government in the First Half of the Nineteenth Century*. Cambridge, MA: Harvard University Press, 1971.

World Bank. *The East Asian Miracle: Economic Growth and Public Policy*. New York: Oxford University Press, 1993.

Wray, William D. "Shipping: From Sail to Steam." In *Japan in Transition: From Tokugawa to Meiji*. Edited by Marius B. Jansen and Gilbert Rozman. Princeton, NJ: Princeton University Press, 1986.

Wright, Arthur F. *Buddhism in Chinese History*. Stanford, CA: Stanford University Press, 1959.

———. *The Sui Dynasty*. New York: Alfred A. Knopf, 1978.

———. "The Sui Dynasty (581–617)." In *The Cambridge History of China*, vol. 3. *Sui and T'ang China, 589–906, Part 1*. Edited by Denis Twitchett. London: Cambridge University Press, 1979.

Wright, Arthur F., and Denis Twitchett, eds. *Perspectives on the T'ang*. New Haven, CT: Yale University Press, 1973.

Wright, David Curtis. *From War to Diplomatic Parity in Eleventh-Century China: Sung's Foreign Relations with Kitan Liao*. Leiden, Netherlands: Brill, 2005.

Wright, Mary Clabaugh, ed. *China in Revolution: The First Phase, 1900–1913*. New Haven, CT: Yale University Press, 1968.

———. *The Last Stand of Chinese Conservatism: The T'ung-Chih Restoration, 1862–1874*. Stanford, CA: Stanford University Press, 1957.

Wu, David Yen-ho. "The Construction of Chinese and Non-Chinese Identities." In *The Living Tree: The Changing Meaning of Being Chinese Today*. Edited by Tu Wei-ming. Stanford, CA: Stanford University Press, 1994.

Xiong, Victor Cunrui. *Emperor Yang of the Sui Dynasty: His Life, Times, and Legacy*. Albany: State University of New York Press, 2006.

Yan, Yunxiang. "McDonald's in Beijing: The Localization of Americana." In *Golden Arches East: McDonald's in East Asia*. Edited by James L. Watson. Stanford, CA: Stanford University Press, 1997.

Yang, Lien-sheng. "Great Families of Eastern Han." In *The Making of China: Main Themes in Premodern Chinese History*. Edited by Chun-shu Chang. Englewood Cliffs, NJ: Prentice Hall, 1975.

Yano, Christine R. *Tears of Longing: Nostalgia and the Nation in Japanese Popular Song*. Cambridge, MA: Harvard University Asia Center, 2002.

Yi, Jeong Duk. "Globalization and Recent Changes to Daily Life in the Republic of Korea." In *Korea and Globalization: Politics, Economics, and Culture*. Edited by James Lewis and Amadu Sesay. London: RoutledgeCurzon, 2002.

Yiengpruksawan, Mimi Hall. *Hiraizumi: Buddhist Art and Regional Politics in Twelfth-century Japan*. Cambridge, MA: Harvard University Asia Center, 1998.

Young, Ernest P. "China in the Early Twentieth Century: Tasks for a New World." In *Historical Perspectives on Contemporary East Asia*. Edited by Merle Goldman and Andrew Gordon. Cambridge, MA: Harvard University Press, 2000.

Young, Kwon Oh. "The Influence of Recent Archaeological Discoveries on the Research of Paekche History." In *Early Korea 1: Reconsidering Early Korean History through Archaeology*. Edited by Mark E. Byington. Seoul: Korea Institute, Harvard University, 2008.

Young, Louise. *Japan's Total Empire: Manchuria and the Culture of Wartime Imperialism*. Berkeley: University of California Press, 1998.

Yü, Ying-shih (Yu Yingshi). *Trade and Expansion in Han China: A Study in the Structure of Sino-Barbarian Economic Relations*. Berkeley: University of California Press, 1967.

Zhang, Liang (pseudonym), compiler. *The Tiananmen Papers*. Edited by Andrew J. Nathan and Perry Link. New York: PublicAffairs, 2001.

Zhao, Ziyang. *Prisoner of the State: The Secret Journal of Zhao Ziyang*. Translated and edited by Bao Pu, Renee Chiang, and Adi Ignatius. New York: Simon and Schuster, 2009.

Zürcher, Erik. *The Buddhist Conquest of China: The Spread and Adaptation of Buddhism in Early Medieval China*. 3rd ed. Leiden, Netherlands: Brill, 2006.

Index